Introduction to
Chemical Dependency Counseling

LIBRARY OF SUBSTANCE ABUSE AND ADDICTION TREATMENT

A Series of Books Edited by
Jerome David Levin, Ph.D.

Substance abuse and addiction are the third most common cause of mortality in the United States. They are among the most prevalent mental illnesses, not only in the United States, but throughout the world. They are also notoriously difficult to treat. Mental health professionals see few patients whose lives or illnesses have not been profoundly affected by their own use or that of their families or peers. Addiction is not peripheral but central to the human condition and research into it is illuminating our understanding of self.

The *Library of Substance Abuse and Addiction Treatment* is dedicated to providing mental health professionals with the tools they need to treat these scourges–tools ranging from scientific knowledge to clinical technique. Non-ideological, it is equally open to behavioral, cognitive, disease model, psychodynamic, and least harm perspectives. An overdetermined disorder affecting millions of people requires multiple viewpoints if it is to be successfully treated. The *Library* provides those multiple perspectives for clinicians, students, and laypeople as articulated by the most insightful workers in the field. Practical, utilitarian, scholarly, and state-of-the-art, these books are addressed to all who wish to deepen their understanding of and increase their clinical efficacy in treating addiction.

Primer for Treating Substance Abusers
Jerome D. Levin

Treatment of Alcoholism and Other Addictions: *A Self-Psychology Approach*
Jerome D. Levin

Recovery from Alcoholism:
Beyond Your Wildest Dreams
Jerome D. Levin

Couple and Family Therapy of Addiction
Jerome D. Levin

The Dynamics and Treatment of Alcoholism: *Essential Papers*
Jerome D. Levin and Ronna Weiss, Editors

Gender and Addictions:
Men and Women in Treatment
S. Lala Ashenberg Straussner and Elizabeth Zelvin, Editors

Psychodynamics of Drug Dependence
Jack D. Blaine and Demetrios A. Julius, Editors

The Hidden Dimension: *Psychodynamics in Compulsive Drug Use*
Leon Wurmser

Substance Abusing High Achievers:
Addiction as an Equal Opportunity Destroyer
Abraham J. Twerski

Creating the Capacity for Attachment:
Treating Addictions and the Alienated Self
Karen B. Walant

Psychotherapy of Cocaine Addiction:
Entering the Interpersonal World of the Cocaine Addict
David Mark and Jeffrey Faude

Drug Dependence: *The Disturbances in Personality Functioning that Create the Need for Drugs*
Henry Krystal and Herbert A. Raskin

Treating Addiction as a Human Process
Edward J. Khantzian

Therapeutic Strategies for Treating Addiction: *From Slavery to Freedom*
Jerome D. Levin

Introduction to Chemical Dependency Counseling
Jerome D. Levin, Joseph Culkin, and Richard S. Perrotto

Managing Addictions:
Cognitive, Emotive, and Behavioral Techniques
F. Michler Bishop

Introduction to
Chemical Dependency Counseling

Jerome D. Levin, Ph.D.
Joseph Culkin, Ph.D.
Richard S. Perrotto, Ph.D.

JASON ARONSON INC.
Northvale, New Jersey
London

MT

This book was set in 10 pt. Palatino by Alpha Graphics of Pittsfield, New Hampshire and printed and bound by Book-mart Press, Inc. of North Bergen, NJ.

Library of Congress Cataloging-in-Publication Data

Levin, Jerome D. (Jerome David)
    Introduction to chemical dependency counseling / Jerome D. Levin, Joseph Culkin, Richard S. Perrotto.
        p.   cm.
    Includes bibliographical references and index.
    ISBN 0-7657-0289-4
    1. Substance abuse—Patients—Counseling of. 2. Dual diagnosis—Patients—Counseling of. I. Culkin, Joseph. II. Perrotto, Richard S. III. Title.
  RC564 .L4823 2000
  616.86′06—dc21   00-038965

Printed in the United State of America on acid-free paper. For information and catalog write to Jason Aronson Inc., 230 Livingston Street, Northvale, NJ 07647-1726, or visit our website: www.aronson.com

12/27/04

Contents

5 Development and Chemical Dependency 77

6 Causes of Chemical Dependency 97

7 Chemical Dependency and Physical Health 121

Preface

Chemical dependency is a serious human problem that causes untold personal suffering, disability, death, and enormous cost to society. During the last quarter century, much scientific effort has been directed toward understanding the nature and causes of drug and alcohol problems and many effective treatments have been developed. Today, individuals who work in the chemical-dependency field can avail themselves of an ever-expanding base of knowledge that they can apply to assessment, diagnosis, and treatment.

The expansion of knowledge and public awareness of the magnitude of the problems brought about by chemical dependency has led to concerted efforts to get more substance-abusing individuals into treatment and to start their treatment earlier than ever. These and other factors have created many opportunities for people who are interested in pursuing careers as chemical-dependency counselors.

About this Textbook

Introduction to Chemical Dependency Counseling is designed to provide students with fundamental knowledge about alcoholism and drug addiction. This is a comprehensive, up-to-date text that covers major topic areas from research, theoretical, and clinical perspectives. Rather than adopting a particular theoretical slant or philosophy, we have endeavored to cover the important scientific and clinical aspects of chemical dependency in a balanced way. Our clinical experience with substance abusers affords us the opportunity to present case vignettes that illustrate important clinical issues.

Our comprehensive, balanced approach makes this book suitable for a variety of student purposes. First, this text can be used by students in preparation for the examination to become a *Certified Alcoholism and Substance Abuse Counselor* (CASAC). Indeed, many of the topics included in the text were drawn from certification exam requirements. Second, this text can stand as a main source for college-level courses in addictions or chemical dependency offered in psychology, social sciences, social work, or health-related programs. Students often take such courses as major or elective requirements. Third, *Introduction to Chemical Dependency Counseling* is suitable for use as the basic text for an introductory course in college-level or freestanding certificate programs in chemical dependency counseling. Last but not least, this text can serve as a reference for professional counselors as well as psychologists, social workers, nurses, clergymen, and others who wish to supplement their knowledge by the acquisition of basic information concerning chemical dependency.

Features of this Text

The pedagogical elements of *Introduction to Chemical Dependency Counseling* were developed to help students understand the basic

principles of chemical dependency and counseling strategies.

1. **Outline.** Each chapter begins with an outline of first- and second-level heads in order to provide just enough information to
   acquaint the reader with the main topics
   of the chapter.
2. **Learning Objectives.** The chapter outline
   is followed by a list of learning objectives
   that focus on the chapter's main topic areas. Each learning objective corresponds
   to topics listed in the chapter outline.
3. **Boldfaced Terms.** The most important
   terms in each chapter appear in boldfaced print and are clearly and succinctly
   explained.
4. **Lists, Tables, and Figures.** Each chapter
   contains bulleted lists, tables, and figures
   to simplify, summarize, illustrate, and
   organize the material and to create visual
   appeal.
5. **Case material.** Important clinical issues
   are illustrated with case material drawn
   from the authors' files.
6. **Summary.** Each chapter contains an end-
   of-chapter summary that highlights major points, numbered to correspond to
   numbered sections of the chapter.
7. **Terms to Remember.** Each chapter summary is followed by an alphabetized list
   of terms assembled from boldfaced terms
   in the chapter.
8. **Suggested Readings.** Each chapter ends
   with a brief list of recommended readings for those students who wish to read
   further.
9. **References.** All source materials cited in
   the text are referenced in the back matter.
10. **Glossary.** All boldfaced terms and their
    definitions are included in a glossary at
    the back of the book.
11. **Index.** Finally, we have included a com-
    bined name and subject index.

INTRODUCTION TO CHEMICAL DEPENDENCY COUNSELING

CHAPTER OUTLINE

LEARNING OBJECTIVES

Upon completing study of this chapter you should be able to:

1. Discuss the scope of activities in the field of chemical dependency counseling.
2. Describe the relationship between chemical dependency counseling and other health professions.
3. Outline the main events in the early movements that preceded modern chemical dependency counseling.
4. Discuss the impact of Alcoholics Anonymous and the Peer-Support Movement on chemical dependency counseling.
5. Indicate the contributions of therapeutic communities to modern chemical dependency counseling.
6. Identify the major steps in professional education and certification in chemical dependency counseling.
7. Outline the principal employment opportunities in the field of chemical dependency counseling.

Susan runs early-recovery groups for adolescent substance abusers at a small community agency in an upscale suburb of New York City. Her clients are between 13 and 20 years of age, mostly boys from well-to-do professional families.

A recovering alcoholic with fourteen years of abstinence, Mike is employed in the alcoholism clinic of a large county hospital in a major urban area. Most of his clients are economically disadvantaged minority males, many of whom also have a history of homelessness and mental illness.

At the private agency where he works, a typical day for Dave consists of conducting intake interviews and making treatment recommendations for new clients who have been referred for evaluation by their employers. In addition Dave spends a great deal of time on the phone with insurance company representatives and health management officers.

Along with thousands of others, the three people mentioned above share a common bond in their work with individuals who suffer from drug and alcohol problems. Of course, there is enormous diversity among the counselors, clients, and job settings in the field of chemical dependency counseling, but at the same time there are also many shared principles, goals, and practices. In this book you will be introduced to a field that we, the authors, find endlessly fascinating, challenging, and engaging. One of the few emotions not engendered by our work in the field is boredom. On the contrary, we are forever being surprised, stimulated, and taken on new journeys as we learn more and more about substance abuse and, indeed, about human nature itself.

In this first chapter you will learn about the scope of chemical dependency counseling, its historical development, and its current status as a health profession.

1–1 THE SCOPE OF CHEMICAL DEPENDENCY COUNSELING

In Roman mythology the god Janus had two faces and could look ahead and back at the same time. Like the mythic Janus, chemical dependency counselors see in two directions at once. In one direction lies the *factual base* on which the field is grounded. This base includes an enormous amount of knowledge about the effects of drugs and the causes of addictions, as well as about many aspects of

human biology and psychology. Looking in the other direction we see the *practical base* of the field, which contains ideas and practices about counseling and therapy drawn from many sources. To become a successful counselor you will need to develop the Janus-like ability to see both ways and use what you see to shape your actions.

What Is Chemical Dependency Counseling?

The term **chemical dependency,** as we use it in this textbook, refers to any type of addiction, that is, a physical and psychological dependency on drugs. When we speak of chemical dependency we explicitly mean addiction to drugs that alter moods, cognitions, and behavior, including alcohol, various "downers" like barbiturates and benzodiazepines, opioids such as heroin, stimulants like cocaine, crack, and amphetamines, and hallucinogens such as mescaline and LSD. There are of course many other drugs such as antibiotics that can affect the mental states (e.g., moods) of those who take them, but the mood-altering qualities such drugs may have are incidental to their main purposes and effects.

Chemical dependency counseling is a mental health specialty that provides therapy for people who are suffering from drug and alcohol addictions and the many complications that attend those addictions. Also known as *substance abuse counselors* and *addictions counselors, chemical dependency counselors* deal not only with chemical addictions but sometimes also with other kinds of addictive behaviors, such as compulsive gambling. However, in general chemical dependency counselors are specialists in dealing with substance abuse.

Basic Assumptions of Chemical Dependency Counseling.
There are a variety of ways in which chemical dependency counselors perform their work. Some counselors are essentially educators. They are involved in educational and prevention programs in the schools, in the media, and in the community. Preventative education, however, is not the primary function of most substance abuse

counselors. On the contrary, they work with people for whom prevention is too late, that is, people who are already chemically dependent. They do this in a variety of work settings, including hospitals, schools and colleges, rehabilitation units, outpatient clinics, and, in so..ıe cases, private offices. They often work with the individual substance abuser, but more often they conduct groups and/or work with families. Usually, chemical dependency counselors assess, diagnose, and treat their clients as part of a treatment team that includes other health professionals.

Chemical dependency counseling is unique in that it is the only profession that treats chemical dependency as a *primary disorder* rather than one secondary to some other condition. Most chemical dependency counselors view the primary disorder of addiction as a disease with a definite etiology (causation), course, progression, and complications. Chemical dependency counselors regard addiction as a unitary phenomenon regardless of the drug that is involved. Whether the addiction is to alcohol, cocaine, heroin, Valium, or some combination of drugs, it is all chemical dependency. That does not mean that we are oblivious to the unique issues in pharmacological, sociocultural, personality, and psychodynamic factors unique to each drug of abuse. As you will learn in later chapters (See Chapters 5 through 10), a great deal is known about the multitude of factors that contribute to addictions. However, we do believe that the commonalities among drug addictions by far outweigh their differences.

Chemical dependency counselors generally hold that abstinence is the sine qua non of recovery and that participation in Twelve step programs such as Alcoholics Anonymous greatly increases the likelihood of recovery. There are counselors who do not believe in that approach and those who view the Twelve step programs as just one among many treatment approaches, but that is atypical. Most people in the field hold to the view that addictions are diseases and should be treated as such, and therefore they strongly encourage their clients to participate in an appropriate Twelve step program. You will learn much more about this approach in Chapters 6 and

11. Although chemical dependency counselors borrow methods from many schools of counseling, they have a specific outlook and set of special techniques that they use in their counseling work. You will learn more about the various schools of counseling and the particular techniques of substance abuse counseling in later chapters.

The Two Sides of Chemical Dependency Counseling. As we mentioned earlier, this field faces in two directions, toward both its factual and its practical bases. As a result, there are two sides of chemical dependency counseling. The *factual side* deals with the incredibly variegated, complex, intriguing, ever-growing web of fact and theory concerning chemical dependency, drawn from disparate disciplines in the social and natural sciences, from medicine and other health fields, and even from the humanities. Chemical dependency counseling both borrows from and contributes to each of these many disciplines, and this makes it a wonderful field for the *generalist*—the person with widespread curiosity and many interests. You do not, however, have to be an expert in any other field to be a chemical dependency counselor, because this field also has a knowledge base uniquely its own.

This broad-ranging knowledge base does add to the interest of the field because it touches on so many different areas of human concern. However, the field also appeals to those with more of a *specialist view* because each of its facets has great depth and is worthy of a lifetime of study. Eventually someone will come along who will be able to see the whole picture—to have what is called a *synoptic vision*—and we will have a general field theory of substance abuse in the same way we have a general field theory of electromagnetism. But that time has not yet come and for now we have both breadth and depth but as yet no final complete vision. Perhaps one of the readers of this text will be the originator of such an all-embracing vision.

The second side of chemical dependency counseling pertains to the work of counseling itself. This *practical side* of the field also draws from and contributes to many disciplines. In particular its treatment strategies and methods are drawn from various models of psychotherapy, as well as from medicine, philosophies of human relations, and the field of group dynamics. The practice of chemical dependency counseling also has its unique approaches to helping people. It has evolved a whole set of techniques specific to working with chemical abusers and their significant others.

Although factual knowledge of addictions is essential for good counseling, mastery of counseling practice itself is just as important. Counseling is both an art and a science. The artistry comes mainly in the creative application of what you know to what you do. Knowledge about addiction alone does not make anyone a good counselor. Consider someone who may speak five languages but who cannot communicate effectively in any of them. Likewise, you might have detailed knowledge of the biology, psychology, and sociology of addiction, but if you cannot use it effectively to help your clients, what good is it? In later chapters you will learn in great detail about the practice of counseling, but only by acquiring experience in the field will you develop into an artful practitioner of what you learn.

Challenges of Chemical Dependency Counseling. Counseling is a rewarding and demanding field that presents both intellectual and emotional challenges for its practitioners. Basically, the field is endlessly fascinating and engaging because it draws on all we have to offer both intellectually and emotionally.

The *intellectual challenges* entail the acquisition of all the knowledge and skills that are required to function as a counselor. Some would-be counselors begin with the simplistic notion that all they need do is be caring enough and all will be well. A big surprise awaits those who minimize the amount of time and energy required to learn about the complex nature of chemical dependency. As you will see when you move on to study subsequent chapters, there is a mountain of information to be mastered to acquire even a preliminary understanding of the symptoms, causes, development, and consequences of substance abuse. Because researchers constantly discover new

facts about chemical dependency, the intellectual challenge never ends. Counselors are always challenged to keep abreast of the field by ongoing study and training.

Although there are many intellectual demands on chemical dependency counselors, those demands are often easier to handle than the *emotional challenges*. What makes counseling so emotionally demanding? Basically, it is because we work with people in great distress who are often in crisis, often do not wish to be helped, and often are enraged with us. For all of our factual knowledge, at bottom our tools are ourselves and our knowledge of ourselves.

Substance abuse counseling has been compared to taking a bone away from a hungry Doberman. Our clients frequently see us as deprivers and deniers. If you cannot handle aggression when it is aimed directly at you, this is not a good field for you. Of course, the client's rage is not personal, and one important thing you must learn is not to take it personally. That's often not easy. In addition, over and above the difficulties of being a frequent target of rage is the emotional stress of witnessing and indeed participating in tragedy. Chemical dependency is a killer, and in the course of your work, you will likely see people die from their substance abuse, both directly and indirectly. You will have all kinds of feelings about that—rage, guilt, helplessness, and perhaps feelings of awe and humility before the process, which is a human life unfolding.

Fortunately, substance abuse counselors not only see tragedies, but are also privileged to see human beings recovering, sometimes in the most spectacular and dramatic ways. These positive results can be a source of great joy and personal satisfaction for the counselor. There is something wonderful, no matter how stressful, about being close to the extremities of human life every day, whether you are feeling the inspiration of seeing human beings transformed and put on the road to growth, or are learning the acceptance of limitation as you watch others go down the spiraling path of self-destruction.

Substance abuse counseling teaches us lessons of humility and the acceptance of limitation. At the same time it induces a satisfaction that is derived from doing what you are able to do to the best of your ability in a field in which the stakes are high. Chemical dependency counseling is intellectually and emotionally challenging primarily because it attempts to find answers to a compelling mystery: Why on earth do people destroy themselves in this manner? That is part of the intellectual challenge, and the feelings engendered in resolving it are part of the emotional challenge.

Generally, two types of people go into substance abuse counseling: (1) nonprofessionals, often people who are in recovery themselves or who come from families that have been impacted by chemical dependency, and (2) mental health professionals who wish to learn more about such an important area of psychopathology. If you belong to the first group you may find the intellectual demands of the field especially challenging. There is much to learn and it does not always fit together smoothly. On the other hand, you have been through a lot of the emotions that chemical dependency elicits and they are no strangers to you. Consequently, for the nonprofessional, mastery of the emotional challenges can often be easier. If you come from the second group, you are probably familiar with at least some of the scientific background needed to practice substance abuse counseling. You may, however, have little preparation for the emotional stress that accompanies working with substance abusers.

In our experience, we have found that both these groups complement each other because they each bring skills and experiences from their backgrounds that facilitate the growth of the other. Regardless of your background, we urge you not to be discouraged by the complexity of the material, nor should you be needlessly anxious about the emotional part of the work. We will take you gently and thoroughly through the learning process to help you master both the intellectual and the emotional challenges.

Chemical Dependency Counseling and Other Health Professions

Earlier in this chapter we emphasized the ways chemical dependency counseling has both drawn from and contributed to many other disciplines. In practical day-to-day terms, counselors in this field have their greatest involvement with other health professionals. Here we examine the relationships of chemical dependency counselors with other counselors, medical professionals, social workers, and psychologists, whose professional responsibilities are summarized in Table 1–1.

Other Counseling Professions. There are many types of **counselors,** health professionals whose efforts are directed at giving advice, guidance, and/or therapy to various populations for specific problems. Given the complexities that obtain in the lives of substance abusers, these individuals are often in need of more than just drug counseling. As the primary provider of services for your chemically dependent clients, you can expect to find yourself interacting with other kinds of counseling professionals.

As the name indicates, *family counselors* work with families who have all sorts of problems that may or may not include substance abuse. The focus of treatment for family counselors is the family, not necessarily the substance abuse. Closely related to the work of family counseling is that of *couples counselors,* who work with couples, not necessarily just married partners, but also gay and lesbian couples and other heterosexual people in committed relationships. Marital and relationship problems are unavoidable among

Table 1–1. Major fields of mental health professionals

Profession	Responsibilities
Counselor	Offer advice, guidance, and therapy for families, couples, and individuals
Psychiatrist	Provide medical treatment and/or psychotherapy for mental illness
Psychologist	Conduct research and provide psychotherapy for psychological disorders
Social worker	Provide psychotherapy and facilitate access to social services

substance abusers, and often need the attention of a specialist. Another reason chemical dependency counselors might refer a client to couples counseling is for sex therapy. Couples counselors are sometimes also experts in treating sexual dysfunction, a not uncommon complication of chemical dependency.

Vocational counselors specialize in helping people with occupational or work-related problems. Testing clients for their vocational interests and ability and organizing job-search plans are two areas in which the vocational counselor can help the chemically dependent client. *Rehabilitation counselors,* who were originally called vocational rehabilitation counselors, are experts at rehabilitating people, that is, returning them to their function in society after they recover from disabling conditions that may be either physical or emotional. For your most severely and chronically addicted clients, rehabilitation counseling can be helpful in getting them started on the road to economic self-sufficiency.

When you interact professionally with other kinds of counselors it is important to keep two points in mind: first, they are the experts in their fields, and second, you are the expert in chemical dependency. For the joint efforts of different types of counselors to help the client, each must respect the expertise of the other. A common mistake novice counselors make is to think that they should be able to help with every problem that the client presents. However,with all the complications in the lives of chemically dependent people, it is easy to get lost in a maze of problems and lose focus on the main agenda, namely, recovery. When your clients need additional work with other counseling issues, you will do well to refer them to a responsible person who is trained to handle those issues, in order not to be distracted from the topic of their addiction.

Medical Professions. Because of the damage that drugs cause to the body, it is mandatory that medical professionals be involved in the treatment of substance abusers. The *medical personnel* involved are most often physicians, but may also be nurses or physicians' assistants. Their job is to address the physical health of the client insofar as that is possible.

Regrettably, some clients have so damaged their bodies that recovery from the medical complications of their substance abuse may be impossible or at best only partial. An important task of chemical dependency counselors is reading medical reports in client case records. As you will learn, various medical complications can profoundly affect the counseling relationship. While it is not expected of you that you be a physician, you do need to be cognizant of the problems your clients are likely to have and the types of treatment for which you should refer them.

A key member of the medical treatment team is the *psychiatrist*. A **psychiatrist** is a medical doctor (M.D.) who specializes in the treatment of mental illness. Psychiatrists often do psychotherapy, but today they also emphasize the prescription of *psychotropic medications*, drugs that lessen emotional symptoms. For your clients who have other mental disorders and for those whose emotional state is severely compromised by subtance abuse, referral to a psychiatrist for medication evaluation is obligatory. Although many psychiatrists are not specially trained in substance abuse, some undergo a two-year fellowship in *addiction medicine* after their psychiatric residence and become certified in that specialty. When possible, it is advisable to refer clients to a psychiatrist who specializes in addictions.

Social Work. The social work profession is in some ways similar to chemical dependency counseling in that while its knowledge base is drawn from many disciplines it also has a body of theory, knowledge, and practice uniquely its own. Most social workers have a Masters of Social Work (M.S.W.) degree, and traditionally, a **social worker** has been a health professional who has either specialized in psychotherapy or in facilitating client access to social services. Many social workers are trained to do both, and some even go on to become substance abuse counselors as well. The line between psychotherapy and counseling is at best a fuzzy one. The most meaningful distinction between the two is that psychotherapy tends to look toward more global changes in functioning and self-image, and to be less symptom-focused than counseling. Counseling traditionally has been characterized by more specific goals. For example, the vocational counselor seeks to help the client choose a job-oriented major in college, while the psychotherapist working with the same client might spend more time looking at the client's identification with various family members and cultural heroes and the role they play in vocational choice. In truth, the line between counseling and psychotherapy is not exactly clear, and just where the boundaries are drawn can vary in different treatment settings and programs.

In addition to their therapeutic and counseling activities, many social workers are skilled in negotiating the often inscrutable maze of social services available in the community. When your clients need housing, financial assistance, family services, and other community supports, social workers are valuable resource people to know.

Psychologists. Psychology is a scientific discipline that studies behavior and mental processes. Some professional **psychologists** have a master's level degree (for example, M.A. or M.S.), but usually they have a doctorate degree, either Doctor of Philosophy (Ph.D.) or Doctor of Psychology (Psy.D.). Ordinarily, psychologists have more background in research and in biological and social sciences than counselors or social workers. Although some psychologists are strictly educators and researchers, many do therapeutic work. The two psychological specialties involved in therapy are *counseling psychology* and *clinical psychology*. Traditionally, counseling psychologists did not deal with severe psychopathology, or mental illness, while clinical psychologists were explicitly trained to do so. Today, however, the boundary between these disciplines has eroded to the extent that the work of both kinds of psychologists is often indistinguishable.

Depending on their training, interests, and beliefs, psychologists can work in many different ways, reflecting all of the major schools of psychotherapy and counseling. In addition, psychologists have unique training in psychological testing and evaluation. Of the many

kinds of testing performed by psychologists the most common are intelligence testing, interest testing, aptitude testing, personality testing, and neuropsychological testing. These test batteries can be extremely helpful to the chemical dependency counselor. In particular, the use of projective personality tests such as the Rorschach—the well-known ink-blot test—can reveal helpful information about clients' vulnerabilities and strengths as well as their defensive style.

To review, chemical dependency counselors can meaningfully interface with many other health professionals. Aside from physicians and other medical personnel, most of our involvement is with other mental health workers, and it is with them that territorial disputes and boundary confusion can make for tension. Fortunately today most health professionals act respectfully toward one another and understand that their first priority is to help the client. Consequently, interdisciplinary cooperation is more the rule than the exception, and each of the professions can find plenty of work to do with the chemically dependent person. Chemical dependency counseling is now an integral part of the mental health professions and indeed its status has grown in recent years. This is so because chemical dependency counseling has carved out a distinct place for itself by developing knowledge of how to treat one of the most prevalent and devastating of mental illnesses.

1–2 HISTORY OF CHEMICAL DEPENDENCY COUNSELING

As far as we know, all human societies have used mood-altering substances. By far the most common of these substances is alcohol, which has been universally used, with the exception only of some tribes living on isolated islands in the South Pacific and certain Native American groups. Not surprisingly, all these drug-using cultures ran into problems with chemical dependency. Sometimes they dealt with them by restricting the use of the drug to a special class of people, generally the priesthood, and by evoking various social sanctions against other use, while at the same time allowing for ritualized bingeing as part of various festivals and festivities, both sacred and secular. From a very early time there must have been people whose job it was to help those who got in trouble with substances, but very little is known about these remote historical ancestors of today's addiction counselors.

A great deal more is certainly known about the more recent history of the field. In this section we will look at some of the early movements and then consider Alcoholics Anonymous and the outgrowth of the peer counseling movement from this first of the Twelve step programs. We will also look briefly at the impact therapeutic communities and employee assistance programs are having on the field today.

Early Figures and Movements

The history of chemical dependency counseling does not follow a straight track with a clear lineage from past to present. Instead, its historical route is more akin to that of modern American society as a whole—a flowing, roiling aggregation of many converging and diverging individuals and ideas.

Benjamin Rush. An important figure in the history of American medicine was the physician Benjamin Rush, who was the Surgeon General of the American Revolutionary Army and one of the first to regard alcoholism as a disease. Rush prescribed a variety of treatments for alcoholism, but at the time he had little immediate impact. It was not until the twentieth century that his work on what he called *inebriety* was rediscovered and that he was seen as a pioneer in alcoholism treatment. Of course by today's standards many of his "treatments," like whipping, would hardly be considered counseling.

The Washingtonians. By the nineteenth century, drunkenness and other forms of chemical dependency were increasingly recognized as problems in American society. The Protestant denominations in the United States often preached abstinence and indeed sometimes advocated prohibition of alcoholic beverages. However, from what we know, these attitudinal changes toward drinking had little ef-

fect on most people's behavior. One of the first groups with any substantive success in dealing with alcoholism was the **Washingtonians**. This group was initiated in Kansas in the 1840s and enjoyed a rapid and indeed spectacular growth, quickly spreading to the eastern United States. The Washingtonians essentially used peer counseling, that is, a method in which people who were in recovery spoke to people who were still addicted and tried to move them toward abstinence. The Washingtonians also established some hospitals, and in fact there is still a hospital in Boston that began as a Washingtonian hospital.

The Washingtonians had group meetings, somewhat like today's Alcoholics Anonymous meetings, and helped a large number of people to achieve sobriety. However, they made mistakes, the most serious of which was to become involved in other causes. The 1840s and '50s were a period of great ferment in American life, and movements such as those for women's suffrage and for abolition of slavery powerfully stirred the hearts of many reformers. The Washingtonians were drawn into these movements and diluted their effectiveness by trying to be too many things for too many people. The involvement of the Washingtonians with other social causes also promoted dissension within the group because not all members were in favor of women's suffrage or of abolition. Ultimately, the group was destroyed by inner divisiveness.

Although it is now difficult to ascertain with any precision it is likely that the success rates of other nonspecialist groups were not particularly high. With the exception of the Washingtonians, who came from the position of peer counseling, most people followed very informal methods. There was no systematic approach or training. Seminaries for training ministers sometimes had courses in *pastoral counseling,* which paid at least passing attention to the treatment of chemical dependency, medical schools taught the medical complications but were therapeutically pessimistic as far as recovery went, and social work schools and psychology departments more or less ignored chemical dependency until very recently. Things changed with the founding of Alcoholics Anonymous in the mid 1930s.

Alcoholics Anonymous and the Twelve Step Movement

By far the best-known self-help organization for alcoholics is **Alcoholics Anonymous** (A.A.), the original Twelve Step program for recovery. From very modest beginnings, Alcoholics Anonymous has grown into an international success story and has inspired the formation of many other Twelve Step associations. In this section you will learn the history of Alcoholics Anonymous and about the impact it has had on the field of chemical dependency counseling.

The Alcoholics Anonymous Story. The creation of A.A. was largely the work of one man, Bill Wilson. Although Wilson is referred to as a co-founder, the other founder being Dr. Bob Smith, it was Wilson who was the driving force behind the movement. Wilson was born in Vermont in the late nineteenth century, the son of an alcoholic who abandoned his family, leaving them in poverty, although they lived on the fringe of the wealthy resort town of Manchester. Wilson's mother later left Bill in the care of her parents while she studied osteopathic medicine in Boston. Wilson had a sense of being an outsider who both aspired to be among and bitterly resented the socialites who showed up in the summer. He carried their golf clubs at the Manchester Country Club, where he later landed a plane blind drunk in the middle of the fairway.

From an early age Wilson found consolation in alcohol. He was studying in a military college when World War I broke out, and served as an officer in that conflict. While in England he had some sort of mystical experience in Winchester Cathedral, but this did not lead to any sustained change in his personality or values. Upon returning from the war, Wilson was caught up in the intoxication, in every possible sense, of America in the 1920s. He married Lois, the daughter of one of the Manchester summer people, a prominent Brooklyn physician whose patients would follow him to Vermont during the summer.

As charming as Bill was, Lois was not to have an easy life with him. After a move to New York, where he worked as a stockbroker, Wilson's alcoholism progressed rapidly. He was in and out of Town's hospital in Manhattan, being detoxed over and over again. Eventually the Depression hit, but by then Wilson was unemployable in any case, and his wife made a meager living for the two of them working at Macy's. By then they were living in Wilson's father-in-law's house in Brooklyn Heights and Wilson was drinking around the clock.

At this low point, his drinking buddy Ebby Thacker, a wealthy alcoholic playboy whose plane they had crashed at the country club, came to visit. Wilson was at first thrilled to have his drinking buddy back— but Thacker wasn't drinking. Instead he told Wilson the story of Roland H., an American businessman who had been treated by the Swiss psychiatrist Carl Jung, a former disciple of Freud. Roland left supposedly cured, but soon returned drunk, and Jung told him that he was hopeless and would either die or be confined to an asylum. Jung's technique of *deepening despair* is still widely used in substance abuse counseling to break down denial. Jung no doubt sincerely believed what he said, and the likely outcome of Roland's continued drinking was exactly what the Swiss psychiatrist predicted. When Roland begged Jung for some ray of hope, Jung told him it could only be provided by a *transvaluation of values*, a phrase borrowed from the philosopher Friedrich Nietzsche. Roland left in despair but soon found the Oxford Movement. The Oxford Group was to play a significant role in Alcoholics Anonymous, and thus in the profession of substance abuse counseling.

Founded in 1908 by Frank Buchman, a YMCA employee, and Dr. Samuel Shoemaker, an Episcopal clergyman, the **Oxford Group** was a self-help movement that emphasized taking stock of oneself, confessing one's defects, and atoning for past wrongs. The Oxford Group had six principles of *spiritual growth*, and Bill Wilson later built upon those principles in formulating the Twelve Steps of Alcoholics Anonymous. In England, the Oxford Movement worked with alcoholics, but that work was not central to its religious purposes. It also worked with people with many different problems and interests. Although Buchman had done a lot of his early work at Pennsylvania State University, the group later became associated with Oxford University in England, and Buchman worked a great deal in Europe. One of Buchman's goals was to convert the higher social classes, who would then act as models to the rest of the community. This approach led to a tendency to talk down to people, which Bill Wilson later found offensive.

After his encounter with Carl Jung, Roland H. joined the Oxford Movement, became sober, and remained sober. He later ran into Ebby Thacker, who was drunk as usual, shared his experience, and urged Thacker to go to an Oxford meeting. He did, and he too got sober. He "ran his story" to the drunken Wilson, who then signed himself back into Town's hospital. Wilson had an intense emotional experience while in the hospital, and later said it was his "hitting bottom," an experience of deep despair, akin to what mystics have called "the dark night of the soul." In the midst of this despair, Wilson had an intense experience of a presence that validated his worth, gave him hope, and affirmed the existence of value in the universe.

Wilson's hitting bottom was an intense *conversion experience*, but he wasn't sure what to make of it and thought he might have had a moment of insanity. He went to the medical director, Dr. William Silkworth, who told Bill that although he did not know what had happened to him, Wilson seemed better than he had been before. Silkworth was to play a major role in both the founding of Alcoholics Anonymous and in the history of the substance abuse counseling profession. Silkworth taught that alcoholism was "an obsession of the mind and a disease of the body." Wilson later incorporated that phrase into the A.A. literature, and it may have been the source of the A.A. notion that alcoholism is a disease.

Transformed by his experience, Wilson left the hospital and never drank again. He joined the Oxford Movement, but from the beginning was dissatisfied with it. He objected that

it seemed to preach and talk down to people rather than speak out of experience peer to peer, soul to soul, tormented alcoholic to tormented alcoholic. Wilson had the insight that peer experience could have a particularly healing quality—particularly for alcoholics, who tend to be so sensitive to criticism and who have had so much experience in being condescended to, despised, and rejected. Wilson felt intuitively that the Oxford way was not the best way, and indeed the group's success rate with alcoholics was not impressive. Additionally, Wilson was by nature a leader and not a follower, more the sort of person who was inclined to found his own group. At one point, Wilson, then employed in the investment business, was on a business trip to Akron, Ohio, where he experienced a strong urge to drink. He realized that his best bet to stay sober was to find another alcoholic to help. Despite his strong ambivalence toward wealth and power, he took advantage of a contact he had and called the Firestones, the wealthiest family in Akron. He told them that he needed a drunk to talk to, and they sure enough knew one, Dr. Robert Smith, an alcoholic physician who was in the midst of a bender. Wilson went to see him, ran his story, and fed Dr. Bob sips of beer to stop his shaking hands as he drove him to the hospital to operate in the morning. Smith never drank again although he had to fight lifelong urges to do so. Out of their shared experience came Alcoholics Anonymous and the Twelve step movement.

Dr. Bob, who lacked Wilson's manic energy and organizational skill, became a worker in the vineyards and helped many of the alcoholics he met on his hospital rounds practice recovery. He always tried to keep Wilson somewhat calm, telling him to "Keep it simple Bill, keep it simple." Today's slogan—KISS, Or "Keep it simple, stupid"—was an outgrowth of Dr. Bob's advice to Wilson. After Wilson returned to New York, he began holding meetings in his home. He used the peer-counseling model for the sharing of experience. This model later became institutionalized in the words of the Alcoholics Anonymous preamble: "A fellowship of men and women who share their experience, strength and hope with each other that they may solve their common problem and help others to recover from alcoholism."

The movement grew slowly at first, with a few groups in Akron and a few in New York, but during this formative period Wilson formulated the *Twelve Steps* of recovery discussed in Chapter 11 (see Table 11–1). He also wrote a book titled *Alcoholics Anonymous*, popularly known today as "the A.A. Big Book." In it, Wilson discussed the steps of the recovery process and presented many "drunkalogs," that is, stories of drinking and recovery. The book has raw emotional power and offers deep insight into the addictive mind. It has now become one of the most influential works of the mid-twentieth century, affecting the lives of millions of people. In 1946 columnist Jack Anderson published a famous article in the nationally popular *Saturday Evening Post* about A.A., and from that point the movement grew rapidly into an international organization with membership numbering in the millions.

From the beginning, A.A. had a strong spiritual slant, although Wilson did not espouse the conventional religion of the Oxford Movement and was ambivalent toward the clergy. Wilson had found a better way to deal with a condition that had long been unsuccessfully treated by clergymen and physicians. In addition to his uneasiness with the religious aspects, Wilson also showed ambivalence toward medical and mental health professionals, sometimes cooperating with them and sometimes criticizing them. Initially, Wilson envisioned having a network of A.A. hospitals similar to those the Washingtonians had established at the peak of their influence. He approached one of the Rockefellers to finance the idea, but was only given a one-time grant of $5,000, which he used to finance the publication of the *Big Book*. When it came to the A.A. movement, Wilson had an uncanny knack for not making mistakes. He took Rockefeller's rebuff and turned it into an A.A. principle of organizational self-sufficiency—basing it on not being involved in anything other than the peer movement it is. Seeking to avoid the mistakes of the Washingtonians, and also to ensure its independence from the health professions, Wilson inserted into the A.A. preamble a principle that is read before every meeting: "A.A. is not allied with any sect, denomination, politics, organization or institution; does not wish to engage in any controversy; neither endorses nor imposes any causes" (Alcoholics Anonymous World Services 1976, 1984).

The Twelve step Movement. Historically, the **Twelve Step movement** has long been dominated by Alcoholics Anonymous, the original and by far the largest and best-known group. The success and popularity of Alcoholics Anonymous gradually led to the formation of many other Twelve step organizations, dedicated to recovery from a variety of addictions. Today the more active Twelve step associations and their target addictions are:

- Narcotics Anonymous (NA): heroin and other narcotics
- Cocaine Anonymous (CA): cocaine and crack
- Overeaters Anonymous (OA): food and compulsive eating
- Pills Anonymous (PA): many non-narcotic drugs, including Valium
- Pot Anonymous (PA): marijuana
- Sexual Compulsives Anonymous (SCA): sex addiction
- Gamblers Anonymous (GA): compulsive gambling

In addition to those Twelve step groups for specific forms of addiction, other spin-off groups have formed for family members of addicted individuals. For example, **Alanon** is a group dedicated to the families and significant others of alcoholics, while a parallel group called **Narcanon** serves families of those addicted to substances other than alcohol.

Despite important differences in their specific addictions, participants in Twelve step programs all share a common agenda, namely, to provide support for one another in the service of recovery. Like Alcoholics Anonymous, all other Twelve step groups are dedicated to the notion of a nonprofessional, peer-support fellowship.

One of the distinctive features of Twelve step organizatons is their use of the **sponsor,** a mentor who shares his or her experience in guiding a newcomer in the steps toward recovery. However, the sponsor's role includes helping him- or herself at least as much as helping the **sponsee.** The sponsor is definitely not a professional counselor, but is nevertheless a powerful resource person for the recovering addict. Any Twelve step veteran will tell you that the right sponsor can make all the difference in the world.

As helpful as sponsors are, it soon became clear that many people need more help than could be offered by a Twelve step sponsor alone. Out of that recognition grew a movement for peer counseling, which we examine in the following section.

The Peer Counseling Movement and Professionalization

The success of Alcoholics Anonymous in helping people achieve sobriety quickly caught the attention of the health professions. Unfortunately, in the first half of the twentieth century professional treatment facilities did not have much to offer in the way of addiction counseling. Historically, the peer counseling movement was a significant bridge to the professionalization of the chemical dependency field.

The Peer Counseling Movement. Recognizing the potential benefits for their patients, some facilities drew on recovering alcoholics as counselors. In this way, the **peer counseling movement,** began as an approach to treatment that employs recovering alcoholics and addicts as substance abuse counselors.

The early peer counselors were *paraprofessionals* rather than true professionals insofar as they had no specialized training or educational credentials. Although their importance was recognized from the beginning, they definitely had a subordinate status in units usually dominated by medical people, and they were usually poorly paid for their work. The first paraprofessional alcoholism counselors worked at the Yale Plan Clinic in Minnesota in 1944. This clinic was the first to include recovering alcoholics who were A.A. members in its alcoholism treatment teams. They

were referred to as *alcoholism workers*. These counselors were highly motivated and they were viewed as uniquely skilled in the art of helping others to recover from alcoholism. But their ability was understood to come from empathy rather than from any particular technical skills. Nevertheless the Minnesota Civil Service Commission recognized their status as paraprofessionals and backed the passage of a state statute legitimizing their role. Expanding on the experience of the Yale Plan, the *Hazelden Rehabilitation Program* was established in Minnesota in 1949 and is still prominent in the field today. From the beginning, the **Hazelden model** of treatment included paraprofessional peer counselors in its treatment teams for alcoholic patients. From that point on, the alcoholism counselor was a standard part of treatment in many other facilities, and it was not long before professionalization of the field followed.

Professionalization of the Field. By the 1970s, chemical dependency counseling had become professionalized. More and more states recognized alcoholism counseling as a profession, the usual qualification being a *Credentialed Alcoholism Counselor* (C.A.C.). State boards began to set educational and experience requirements for C.A.C.s and also produced and administered certification examinations.

With professionalization, the status of workers in the field rose dramatically. By then, A.A. was an international movement with millions of members, and one that had received enormously positive press. The idea of recovery was "in." The recovery movement, of course, continued to be a peer activity, but its success spurred the parallel success of the profession. As time went on, mental health professionals began taking training in substance abuse counseling or alcoholism counseling in order to add a C.A.C. to their other credentials. What had started modestly as a peer counseling activity had become an independent health profession.

Peers or Professionals? Chemical dependency counseling as we know it today evolved gradually from paraprofessional peer counseling. In the early days of chemical dependency counseling, there was a heavy bias in favor of using only recovering people in counseling. There was little professional knowledge involved, and the practice was essentially one of sharing experience; for the most part it was a mentoring rather than a counseling activity. Today, however, practitioners of this discipline may or may not be recovering persons. Although many recovering people get professional training and enter the field of chemical dependency counseling, it is a profession with its own training, rituals, and procedures, its own certification process, and its own requirements for continuing education. It is our experience that whether the counselor is or is not a recovering person has little to do with counseling competence. There are those who are recovering who are able to draw on their own experience in ways that greatly enhance their counseling skills and effectiveness, and there are those who try to impose their own pattern of recovery on clients regardless of whether that model and that path would be helpful to that particular person, in a sort of cookie-cutter manner. Such people are often dogmatic, rigid, and judgmental. In cases like these, being in recovery offers no advantage in counseling work.

> One of the authors (J. L.) directs a program to train chemical dependency counselors. He received a résumé from someone who wanted to become an instructor in that program. When she appeared for an interview the first thing she said was, "I'm a recovering addict." The program director replied, "Having a disease is not a qualification to teach in the University." The candidate did not get the job. Her status as a recovering addict might very well have been an asset to her as a teacher and practitioner of substance abuse counseling, and had she experienced and expressed this fact as a part of a professional identity her self-presentation might have been an advantage in obtaining the job. Unfortunately, however, it was here reified into a kind of magical job qualification, which it is not.

On the other side of the fence, people coming into the chemical dependency profession without personal experience of addiction can lack the ready empathy that being in recovery often brings, and that can result in a tendency to talk down to clients, or to be judgmental. However, many people who enter the field who are not personally affected by the disease make superb counselors. They can draw on their own experience as human beings to understand the compulsions of their clients. In addition, they can have the advantage of greater objectivity, as they are not personally involved in their own recovery. Professional training helps both kinds of counselors draw on the resources they bring to the counseling situation so that their different pathways lead to equally efficacious counseling skills.

As you have learned, peer counseling started it all, and we who are now in the profession owe a deep debt of gratitude to those pioneers who first realized that the health professions were ill equipped to deal with chemical dependency as shown by their poor success with it. These trailblazing counselors had the wisdom and courage to realize that they had something to offer and against considerable opposition had the determination to create a profession.

Employee Assistance Programs

Along with the peer counselors who were working in various treatment facilities, the beginnings of the chemical dependency profession had still another source, which included the various programs instituted by industries and aimed at employees whose performance was impaired by alcohol or other drugs. These **Employee Assistance Programs** (EAPs) were workplace-based programs to which chemically impaired employees were referred for treatment. The intention was to get these workers on the road to recovery, or, failing that, to dismiss them.

One of the first EAPs was set up in the chemical plants run by Dupont in Wilmington, Delaware, in the late 1940s. At first EAPs grew slowly, but by the mid-1960s they were widely distributed, and could be found in industry; unions; smaller businesses: local, state, and federal government; and later in educational institutions. The EAP movement was in part a result of efforts by recovering alcoholics who were A.A. members, who held jobs in various industries, and who suggested such programs to management. Their arguments ultimately convinced management that EAPs were an economically wise thing to do because treating skilled employees is far more practical than dismissing them or, worse yet, ignoring them as their productivity decreases. In a remarkable number of cases, management bought in. Today, EAP counselors almost always have professional credentials and are not necessarily people in recovery. Not uncommonly, they have a mental health degree such as an M.S.W. (Master of Social Work) and certification as an addiction counselor. There is a professional organization for EAP counselors who work in various settings, as well as a professional journal and research literature in this area. For chemical dependency counselors, EAPs are an important source of employment.

Therapeutic Communities

The development of modern chemical dependency counseling has also been influenced by organizations called **therapeutic communities** (TCs), which are residential programs run by and for recovering addicts.

In the late 1950s, a recovering alcoholic named Charles Diederich noticed heroin addicts attending the A.A. meetings that he attended and sometimes led. Diederich became aware that they were marginalized and usually condescended to at these meetings. For A.A. members, a common attitude was that drug addicts were "them" and not "us." Diederich, who was a deeply ambitious and in many ways disturbed man, later left A.A., and in the early 1960s developed a residential treatment facility, which he called *SYNANON* (a word coined by combining "symposium" with "anonymous" with some modifications), for the purpose of treating heroin addicts. Diederich's basic idea was that drug addicts are emotionally immature and cannot function in society. So a prolonged withdrawal from society was necessary and the person needed to be in residential treat-

ment where he would be drug free and be led through a series of steps to a new identity. Originally, Diederich saw the residence as a transitional step leading to a return to the community. Later, he became an advocate of permanent residence in what was essentially a totalitarian community. SYNANON utilized extremely aggressive group encounters, which were led by recovering drug addicts who were either graduates or advanced residents. It also emphasized sharing feelings in a direct and honest manner, adherence to stringent rules, and harsh discipline for rule infractions. Somewhat paradoxically, SYNANON also taught respect and concern for fellow residents and tried to inculcate a strong work ethic. The program used a series of steps from no privileges and little autonomy to working your way up to counselor status with considerable autonomy and many privileges.

The SYNANON program had questionable success, but at that time there were few alternative treatments for drug addicts. Diederich's methods became more extreme as time went on, and he was eventually indicted for putting a rattlesnake in the mailbox of a lawyer who was suing him. By that time Diederich had returned to drinking and that may have had something to do with the demise of SYNANON. But Diederich's model survived and many other therapeutic communities grew out of the SYNANON experience. Daytop Village and Phoenix House, both founded by John Hearst, a graduate of SYNANON, were two of the most successful. Over time TCs became less authoritarian, less dependent on a single charismatic leader, and more open to the use of professionals.

The kinds of drug counselors who came out of the early therapeutic communities were people who had gone through the program and essentially did to others what had been done to them. The approach often entailed a rough initiation, harsh methods, and various humiliation techniques, but also included the transformation from nonfunctional addict to a functional, drug-free person. Later TCs continued to use harshly confrontative methods, but also developed far more global and comprehensive treatment philosophies. The peer counselors who were graduates or advanced members of these various communities continued to play a major role in those organizations. However, over time therapeutic communities increasingly came to employ chemical dependency counselors, not always recovering addicts, and other professionals from psychiatrists to vocational counselors. So here, too, was yet another pool of people in the field moving from peer experience to professional counseling.

1–3 PROFESSIONAL COUNSELING AND CHEMICAL DEPENDENCY

As you have learned, the road to professionalization of chemical dependency counseling was long and sometimes quite bumpy. Ultimately though, it has led to a well-respected health profession with growing educational and occupational opportunities. In the last part of this chapter we will discuss the process of education and certification, as well as employment in this field. Table 1–2 outlines the most common counseling certification categories.

Education and Certification

Earlier in this chapter you read that the first professional certification in our field was the Certified Alcoholism Certificate (C.A.C.). With entry into the field of people from the therapeutic community movement came the recognition that a very large percentage of

Table 1–2. Most common counseling certifications

Title	Description
Certified Alcoholism Counselor (C.A.C.)	First professional certification in chemical-dependency counseling field
Certified Alcoholism and Substance Abuse Counselor (C.A.S.A.C.)	Basic professional credential for drug and alcohol counseling today
Master Addiction Counselor (M.A.C.)	Highest level of certification in National Association of Alcoholism and Drug Abuse Counselors

substance abuse clients were cross-addicted, that is, addicted to multiple substances. Consequently, there was a move to bring alcoholism counseling and substance abuse counseling together in one comprehensive credential, with the intent to make one unified profession out of the several contributing streams. What emerged has the unwieldy name of **Certified Alcoholism and Substance Abuse Counselor** (C.A.S.A.C.), which is today the basic professional credential in the field of chemical dependency counseling.

The development of the C.A.S.A.C. was facilitated in many states by the integration of two bureaucracies, one dealing with alcohol problems and one dealing with drug problems. So now, just as there is a single credential, there is usually one state governmental agency overseeing certification and treatment. The C.A.S.A.C. is now the basic credential that identifies the chemical dependency counselor as a professional. It was designed to meet the credentialing standards developed by the International Certification and Reprprocity Consortium/Drug and other Drug Abuse Incorporated (ICRC-AODA). This organization has succeeded in professionalizing the field internationally. As the requirements for the C.A.S.A.C. set by the ICRC-AODA are accepted by most states in the United States and over thirty foreign countries, there is now wide reprprocity, and after you become credentialed in one state you can easily transfer to another state or indeed to many parts of the world and continue to function as a certified professional.

Obtaining the C.A.S.A.C. requires sitting for a certification exam. In order to sit for the credentialing exam, candidates must possess specific skills, knowledge, and abilities. The eligibility requirements include 350 hours of alcoholism and substance abuse–specific education and 300 hours of supervised practical training. These hours refer to actual clock hours. Each semester credit in a recognized college or university is defined as equivalent of fifteen clock hours. Therefore a three–credit course earns its participants forty-five hours of alcoholism and substance abuse–specific education. The 300-hour internship must be supervised either by a C.A.S.A.C. or other mental health professional. The 350 hours of training must cover a variety of areas, including the knowledge base, counseling techniques, assessment and evaluation, group and family counseling, and ethics. Additionally, there is an experience requirement. For someone without a degree, the requirement is three years' experience in the field; with a bachelor's degree it is two years. With a master's or higher degree it is one year. This experience requirement is not the same as the 300–hour internship. It can be and indeed usually is paid employment. It simply means that one is not eligible to sit for the exam until one has acquired a certain amount of experience in the field. Actually, the experience requirement is defined in terms of clock hours, and these amount to roughly a forty–hour week for a fifty–week year. There is also a basic educational requirement for the C.A.S.A.C., which is either a high school diploma or a high school equivalency diploma (GED), but most counselors have at least some college education, and many have one or more degrees.

The *C.A.S.A.C. examination* is in two parts. The first is a written, multiple-choice exam that tests factual information, knowledge, and its application. The second is an oral examination in which the candidate must present a case and demonstrate knowledge in all of the basic areas of clinical competence in the course of presenting that case.

As professionalization of the field continues, the lack of a college degree will probably become more of a handicap. However, at present chemical dependency counseling is one of the shortest routes into the family of mental health professions. In most states C.A.C.s were grandfathered into C.A.S.A.C. status, but recredentialling is required every two years. In order to be eligible for recredentialling, a C.A.S.A.C. must have forty additional hours of substance abuse–specific education.

In addition to the C.A.S.A.C., advanced credentials are available through the *National Association of Alcoholism and Drug Abuse Counselor* (NAADAC) certification commission. Certification is available at three levels, the highest of which is the *Master Addiction Counselor* (M.A.C.), requiring a master's degree in a related health field as well as pre-existing credentialing as a C.A.S.A.C. While advanced credentials are certainly desirable, they have little impact on one's employment opportunities. It is the C.A.S.A.C. that is recognized as the universal credential in the chemical dependency counseling profession.

Employment Opportunities

Chemical dependency counseling is a profession on the ascent. More and more third-party payers are insisting that those who treat substance abuse have the requisite experience as demonstrated by the possession of a C.A.S.A.C. The C.A.S.A.C. holder with no formal education beyond the high school level might even be eligible to treat patients whom a psychiatrist or psychologist lacking specialized addictions training could not treat. This increases the power and versatility of the C.A.S.A.C. credential. All of this augers well for employment in our field.

Where are chemical dependency counselors employed? By far the largest group of employers at the present time are outpatient treatment programs. Not too long ago most jobs were found in *inpatient rehabilitation units.* However the reluctance of third-party payers to cover inpatient care has greatly reduced the number and scope of such programs, thus reducing the job opportunities in those facilities. However, at the same time *outpatient treatment* has exploded. There are more and more jobs doing counseling, usually as a group leader, but also doing educational work, family work, and individual counseling in these facilities.

Another source of employment is in the schools. Substance abuse counselors are hired at every educational level from elementary schools to universities. Their function is often primarily educational, but they also give advice to staff and administration and provide direct treatment in the form of counseling to students and families. Yet other employment opportunities are found in business, industry, unions, and government, as wells as in Employee Assistance Programs. Those jobs usually pay quite well but usually require one or more degrees as well as the C.A.S.A.C. Methadone maintenance clinics also employ substance abuse counselors and sometimes pay quite well. In some regions chemical dependency counselors are permitted to be in private practice, usually in affiliation with or under supervision by a mental health professional. Those who wish to go into private practice often work for agencies while they obtain professional credentials, like the M.S.W., that qualify them to go into private practice. The criminal justice system also provides many employment opportunities. Most prisons have rehabilitation programs and employ counselors to work in them. Additionally, parole and probation departments often employ counselors for monitoring and for relapse prevention. There are also jobs in various government agencies, in state hospitals, in halfway houses, in therapeutic communities, and in various educational programs.

Entry-level counseling jobs are most often obtained through the contacts students make during their internships. Therefore your internship is not only a learning experience but also an extremely valuable career step in which you can network, make contacts, and indeed start your professional career. Many students in this field are already employed in the field and they are excellent sources of job tips, not only about internships but also about paid employment. Networking definitely pays.

Many counselors love to work with clients and do that throughout their career. Others move into administration and supervision. Some teach or give workshops or do both, and some write books. Chemical dependency counseling is a field with many opportunities, and depending on your talents, skills, and interests, you can find many interesting and gratifying paths to pursue in your professional career.

CHAPTER SUMMARY

1–1

Chemical dependency counseling is a mental health speciality that provides therapy for alcoholism and drug addictions. The field assumes that chemical dependency should be treated as a primary disorder and that addictions are diseases best approached with the Twelve step model of treatment. The two sides of chemical dependency counseling are the factual side, or knowledge about addictions, and the practical side, or the art and practice of counseling. Counseling presents unique intellectual and emotional challenges for those working with chemically dependent clients. In their work with alcoholics and other addicts chemical dependency counselors interact with many other health professionals, including other counselors, medical personnel like psychiatrists, social workers, and psychologists.

1–2

The history of chemical dependency counseling is found in diverse sources. The Washingtonians were an early group movement for promoting self-improvement among alcoholics. The Oxford Group, another self-help recovery group, began in the early 1900s and offered principles that were later integrated into the philosophy of Alcoholics Anonymous. The Alcoholics Anonymous (A.A.) movement was initiated by Bill Wilson as a nonprofessional self-help program for recovering alcoholics. With its Twelve step program, A.A. grew into a widely respected international organization and served as a paradigm for many other Twelve step programs. Growing out of the A.A. movement, peer counseling for alcoholism gained recognition by health care professionals and was a step in the direction of professional chemical dependency counseling. The professionalization of the field has not been without conflict, especially between recovering counselors and others. The modern face of chemical dependency counseling has also been shaped by contributions from Employee Assistance Programs and therapeutic communities.

1–3

The first professional credential in the field was the Certified Alcoholism Counselor certificate (C.A.C.). Today, that credential has been supplanted by the Certified Alcoholism and Substance Abuse Counselor (C.A.S.A.C.) credential. States offer the C.A.S.A.C. credential to individuals who qualify in terms of their educational, and occupational experience, and who successfully pass the C.A.S.A.C. examination. Beyond the C.A.S.A.C. credential are other credentials such as the N.A.A.D.A.C., offered through the National Association of Alcoholism and Drug Abuse Counselor Certification Commission. Job opportunities in chemical dependency counseling include work in outpatient and inpatient facilities, as well as in schools, industry, hospitals, and clinics.

TERMS TO REMEMBER

Alcoholics Anonymous
Certified Alcoholism and Substance Abuse Counselor

chemical dependency counseling
Employee Assistance Programs counselors
Hazelden model
Oxford Group
peer counseling movement
psychiatrist
psychologists
social worker
sponsor
therapeutic communities
Washingtonians

SUGGESTED READING

Alcoholics Anonymous World Services. (1984). *"Pass it on": The story of Bill Wilson and How the A.A. Message Reached the World*. New York: Author.

CHAPTER TWO

Psychoactive Drugs

CHAPTER OUTLINE

Learning Objectives

Upon completing this chapter you should be able to:

1. Describe the electrical and chemical events in neurons.
2. Explain how psychoactive drugs affect neurons and the synapse.
3. Identify the main types of neurotransmitters.
4. Identify the depressant drugs, their main psychoactive effects, and mechanisms of action.
5. Describe the opioids, their main psychoactive effects, and mechanisms of action.
6. Describe the psychoactive effects of stimulants and explain their mechanisms of action.
7. Identify the hallucinogens and discuss their psychoactive effects and mechanisms of action.
8. Discuss the psychoactive effects of the cannabinoids and their mechanisms of action.
9. List the types of inhalants and describe their psychoactive effects.

The use of drugs has been a part of human experience throughout recorded history. People have taken various drugs for medical reasons, to alter their consciousness, and to participate in religious and cultural rituals.

Today, many individuals use drugs for reasons unrelated to their historical purposes, but rather for their psychoactive effects. Whether it is legal or illicit and regardless of the purpose for which it is used, any drug that influences emotions, thoughts, perceptions, motivation, and behavior is called a **psychoactive drug.** These drugs are classified as *depressants, opioids, stimulants, hallucinogens, cannabinoids, and inhalants,* based on their main psychoactive effects.

In this chapter you will learn about the nature and psychoactive effects of many drugs that people commonly abuse and become dependent on. You will develop a basic understanding of the structure and functions of the nervous system and how psychoactive drugs influence the nervous system to produce their psychoactive effects.

2–1 PSYCHOACTIVE DRUGS AND THE NERVOUS SYSTEM

Drugs exert their psychoactive effects primarily by influencing the *nervous system*, comprised of the brain, spinal cord, and peripheral nerves (see Figure 2–1). The nervous system contains hundreds of billions of cells called **neurons,** which are specialized to receive and transmit information. See Figure 2–2. Patterns of electrical and chemical activity in networks of neurons form the physiological

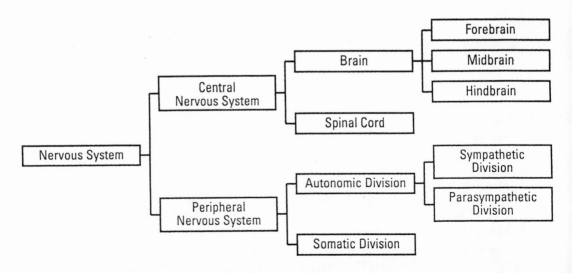

Figure 2–1. Diagram of the Nervous System

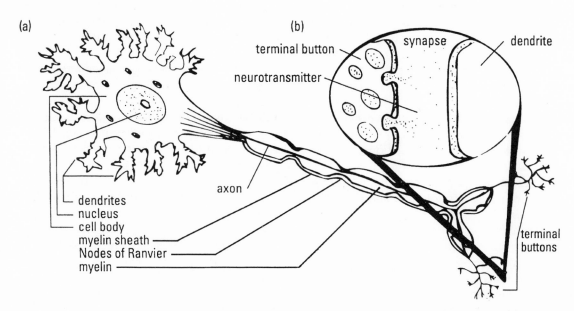

Figure 2–2. A typical neuron and the synapse

foundation of mental events and behavior. Psychoactive drugs exert their effects by altering the normal electrical and chemical activity in neuronal networks.

Electrical and Chemical Events in Neurons

Neurons work by generating tiny electrical currents known as *action potentials,* or neural impulses. When a neuron is stimulated, electrically charged particles called *ions* flow into and out of the neuron. If enough positively charged ions flow into the neuron, it fires an impulse, which travels down its length. The greater the magnitude of the stimulation, the more action potentials are generated.

When a neural impulse reaches the end of the neuron, or the neuron's *terminal buttons,* chemicals called **neurotransmitters** are released into the microscopic, fluid-filled gap between individual neurons called the *synapse.* Neurotransmitters diffuse across the synapse and then attach or bind to specific *receptor sites* on the next neuron (the postsynaptic neuron) the way a key fits into the cylinder of a lock. After a neurotransmitter molecule binds to a postsynaptic receptor site, it influences the neuron to change its electrical

activity. Next, it is immediately released from the receptor site and is either broken down and removed, or reabsorbed into the presynaptic neuron by a process called *reuptake.*

The precise effect of a neurotransmitter on a postsynaptic neuron depends on many factors, including the kind of neurotransmitter and the type and location of the synapse. A neurotransmitter can have an *excitatory effect* on neighboring neurons, meaning that it influences the neurons to fire more rapidly. In many cases, however, a neurotransmitter has an *inhibitory effect,* meaning that it slows the electrical activity of postsynaptic neurons. Thus, a neurotransmitter might serve either an excitatory or inhibitory function depending on whether it increases or decreases the firing rate of other neurons. In a process that is analogous to the way a gas pedal and brakes control the speed of an automobile, excitation and inhibition at synapses, especially in the brain, regulate your thoughts, emotions, and behaviors.

How Psychoactive Drugs Affect Neurons and the Synapse

How do drugs affect neurons and the synapse? Psychoactive drugs work by altering the normal or usual events that occur within neurons and at the synapse. Some drugs have the effect of an **agonist,** meaning that they mimic or increase the effects of a particular neurotransmitter. An **antagonist** is a drug that blocks a neurotransmitter's actions (Hamilton and Timmons 1990, Kalat 1998).

The agonistic or antagonistic effects of a drug can be accomplished in many ways. Some of the mechanisms of action are:

- A drug can influence a presynaptic neuron by modifying ion flow into and out of the neuron.
- A drug can alter neurotransmitter production or the amount of neurotransmitter released into the synapse.
- Drugs with a structure similar to a particular neurotransmitter can attach to a postsynaptic receptor and mimic the neurotransmitter's effects, or attach and then block the neurotransmitter from exerting its effects.
- Some drugs enhance or block reuptake, while others interfere with the process of breaking down a neurotransmitter.

Types of Neurotransmitters

In this section we will identify the different types of neurotransmitters and briefly describe a few of their best-known functions. Later in this chapter you will learn about how drugs affect particular neurotransmitters and thereby alter psychological processes and behavior. As you will see in Chapter 6, several biological explanations of drug addiction are based on drug–neurotransmitter interactions.

More than fifty neurotransmitters have been identified and the actual number is probably hundreds more. Clearly, our understanding of neurotransmitters and how neurotransmitter systems interact is preliminary, at best. Furthermore, each drug produces many psychoactive and physiological effects that probably involve multiple neurotransmitter systems. Bear in mind that it is currently impossible to correlate each drug effect with a particular neurotransmitter. Neurotransmitters, summarized in Table 2–1, are classified as amines, amino acids, and neuropeptides.

Amines. **Amines** include acetylcholine, dopamine, norepinephrine, and serotonin. *Acetylcholine* (Ach) is the principle neurotransmitter found at synapses between neurons and muscle cells. It is responsible for transferring movement commands from the nervous system to muscles. *Dopamine* (DA) controls the beginning and coordination of movements, and plays a major role in arousal, concentration, and our emotional experiences of reward. There is compelling evidence that many drugs produce their pleasurable or rewarding effects by stimulating dopamine transmission in particular brain regions, and these actions are believed to be responsible, in part, for abuse and dependence (see Chapter 6, and Blum et al. 1996, Kalat 1998, Wise 1988).

Norepinephrine (NE) helps in arousal, wakefulness, learning and memory, and in regulating mood. Falling asleep, sensory experiences, and mood are all associated with *serotonin* (5–HT) activity. 5–HT deficits are related to correlated with aggressive behavior and suicide (Linnoila et al. 1983, 1989).

Amino Acids. The best understood *amino acid* neurotransmitter is *gamma-aminobutyric acid* (GABA). As the major inhibitory neurotransmitter in the brain, GABA serves to help the muscles relax and keeps levels of anxi-

Table 2–1. Types of neurotransmitters

Neurotransmitter	Main Functions
Amines	
Acetylcholine (Ach)	Movement and memory
Dopamine (DA)	Movement, arousal, Reward
Norepinephrine (NE)	Arousal, wakefulness, mood, learning, and memory
Serotonin (5–HT)	Sleep, sensory experiences, mood
Amino acids	
Gamma-aminobutyric acid (GABA)	Neural inhibition, relaxation, movement
Glutamate	Neural excitation, movement
Neuropeptides	
Substance-P	Pain sensations
Endorphins	Pain relief, pleasure

ety low. Decreased GABA activity is correlated with muscle tension, convulsions, and anxiety. Some psychoactive drugs work on GABA systems in the brain. *Glutamate* is an excitatory amino acid that functions in movement and arousal and in some aspects of addiction.

Endorphins. *Substance-P* and the *endorphins* are the best-known *neuropeptides*. Substance-P transmits pain sensations from the body to the spinal cord and brain. The endorphins, chemically similar to opioid drugs like heroin and morphine, represent the body's natural painkillers and also are responsible in part for the ability to experience pleasure. Many drugs apparently produce their pleasurable effects by modifying endorphin as well as dopamine activity.

2–2 DEPRESSANTS

Psychoactive drugs that slow the electrical activity of the nervous system, resulting in a tranquilizing effect and sleepiness as well as impairment of higher mental functions, vision, and movement, are called **depressants** (see Table 2–2). These include alcohol as well as sedatives, hypnotics, and tranquilizers (drugs that have anxiolytic, that is, anxiety-reducing effects).

Alcohol

Alcohol is a generic term for a class of molecules that result from the process of fermentation. *Ethyl alcohol*, the kind of alcohol that is typically drunk, is found in beer, wine, liqueurs, and hard liquors.

Psychoactive Effects. Initially, alcohol has a relaxing effect and relieves emotional tension. The person may feel happy, less inhibited, and more confident, especially in social situations. Unfortunately, alcohol produces many negative effects as the person becomes more intoxicated. Reasoning and judgment become impaired, speech may be slurred and garbled, vision is disturbed, and the person has difficulty maintaining balance and motor coordination (American Psychiatric Association 2000).

A prominent consequence of alcohol intoxication is memory loss. Many drunken individuals experience deficits in attention and memory for recent events. With *blackouts,* as such amnesias are commonly called, the now sober person is unable to remember things that were said or done while he was drunk. This neurological dysfunction is the result of depressed electrical activity in regions of the brain, including the *hippocampus* (in the limbic system) and the *frontal lobe* (in the forebrain), two brain areas responsible for the formation of new memories (see Figure 2–3 and 2–4).

Because alcohol depresses parts of the brain in the limbic system and frontal lobe that normally facilitate self-control, emotions, and moral reasoning, it has the apparent paradoxical effect of releasing some people from their inhibitions. The intoxicated individual may exhibit various indiscretions, become boisterous, rowdy, and even violent. Although the precise relationship is not clear, alcohol intoxication is strongly associated with aggression and violent crimes such as assault, homicide, rape, and child abuse (Bushman and Cooper 1990, Ito et al. 1997).

Table 2–2. Psychoactive drugs

Depressants	*Opioids*	*Stimulants*
Alcohol	Morphine	Amphetamines
Barbiturates	Heroin	Cocaine
Benzodiazepines	Methadone	MDMA
	Codeine	
Hallucinogens	*Cannabinoids*	*Inhalants*
LSD	Marijuana	Volatile Solvents
Mescaline	Hashish	Nitrites
PCP		Anesthetic Inhalants

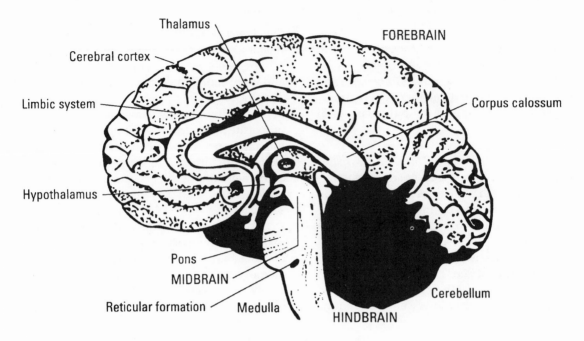

Figure 2–3. A view of the brain—cut in half

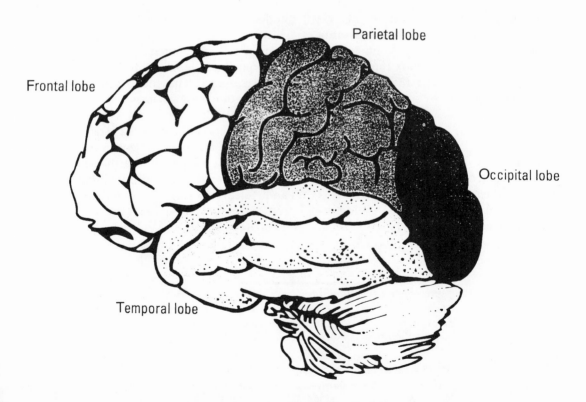

Figure 2–4. Lobes of the Cerebral Cortex

Blood Alcohol Concentration. The intoxicating effects of alcohol mainly depend on *blood alcohol concentration* (BAC), or the percentage of alcohol in the blood. Several factors interact to influence a person's BAC, including the amount of alcohol consumed, body weight, and the rate of alcohol metabolism; that is, how efficiently the body breaks down alcohol molecules. To illustrate, a 160-pound man will have a BAC of 0.04 percent after one hour of consuming two 12-ounce beers or two standard drinks on an empty stomach.

- BAC rises to 0.10 percent after three drinks, and the person shows a loss of motor coordination. The person is considered legally drunk in some states.
- Consumption of seven drinks elevates BAC to 0.20 percent at which point the person becomes confused and speech is slurred.
- At a BAC of 0.40 percent (twelve drinks), the individual is comatose.

Barbiturates and Other Sedative-Hypnotics

Barbiturates are sedative-hypnotic drugs that decrease central nervous system activity. They can calm people, help them fall asleep, and reduce anxiety, and thus are anxiolytic. *Amytal* (amobarbital), *Seconal* (secobarbital), *Fiorinal* (butalbital), *Nembutal* (pentobarbital), and *Luminal* (phenobarbital) are examples of barbiturates. First synthesized in Germany in the late 1880s, barbiturates or "downers" were the first type of tranquilizer. After it was discovered that they were quite habit-forming and that the risk of lethal overdose was high, barbiturates were gradually replaced by tranquilizers that were less dangerous and addictive (Abadinsky 1993). Barbiturates are usually taken orally in pill form, but injectable forms are available.

The psychoactive effects of nonbarbiturate *sedative-hypnotic drugs* are similar to those of barbiturates and alcohol and have abuse potential. *Noctec* (chloral hydrate), *Miltown* (meprobamate), and *Doriden* (Glutethimide) are examples.

Psychoactive Effects. Low doses of barbiturates make a person feel relaxed and light-headed, and impair motor coordination. As the dosage increases, people experience some euphoria, their speech is slurred, their motor coordination gets worse, and then they fall asleep. A transient rush followed by relaxation and sleep may occur at very high doses (American Psychiatric Association 2000, Dupont and Saylor 1991).

Intoxication from high doses of barbiturates can produce stupor, severe amnesia, unsteady gait, and crossing of the eyes (nystagmus). In extreme cases coma and death may occur, especially when barbiturates are taken in combination with alcohol, because these substances enhance each other's effects, a phenomenon called *potentiation*.

Benzodiazepines

The **benzodiazepines** are the most often prescribed anxiolytic (antianxiety) drugs today. This class includes *Valium* (diazepam), *Ativan* (lorazepam), *Xanax* (alprazolam), and *Librium* (chlordiazepoxide), among others. Benzodiazepines are taken most often in pill forms, though preparations are available for injection.

Psychoactive Effects. The effects of the benzodiazepines are similar to alcohol and barbiturates. In low doses, benzodiazepines relax the muscles, make people less fearful and anxious, and help them to fall asleep. In higher doses, they cause drowsiness, difficulties concentrating and thinking, problems in motor coordination, and labored breathing. Though their effects are milder and they certainly are safer than other depressants, they can become addictive and can get a person high, especially if taken together with alcohol. Cross-addiction to alcohol and benzodiazepines is common (American Psychiatric Association 2000, Dupont and Saylor 1991).

One benzodiazepine, *flunitrazepam* or "roofies," is used in Europe for its anxiety-reducing and sleep-inducing effects. In the United States, roofies are dissolved in alcoholic drinks like a "mickey." Unsuspecting women drinkers are then coerced into sexual activities and have little or no memory of being raped.

Mechanisms of Action

Many depressants influence the activity of GABA-containing neurons. Alcohol and barbiturates, for example, directly retard the flow of positively charged ions into the cell and increase the flow of negatively charged ions out. In addition, they have a direct synaptic effect by improving the responsiveness of GABA receptors (Dupont and Saylor 1991, Kalat 1998). As you will see in Chapter 6, alcohol fosters chemical dependency by its effects on other neurotransmitter systems as well.

The ways in which benzodiazepines work on brain neurons are fairly well understood. Studies in the 1970s revealed that many brain neurons have specific benzodiazepine receptors; that is, receptor sites to which benzodiazepines readily attach (Mohler and Okada 1977, Squires and Braestrup 1977). The attachment or binding of benzodiazepines to these receptors modifies their sensitivity, thereby making it easier for GABA molecules to bind. Thus, unlike alcohol and barbiturates, which directly affect ion flow, benzodiazepines do so indirectly. In this way, benzodiazepines reduce anxiety as alcohol and barbiturates do, but without the same risk of overdose, unconsciousness, or death. These findings partly explain why the psychological and behavioral effects are greater when depressants are taken in combination than when any one depressant is taken alone. When this combination effect occurs, we say that the drugs act *synergistically* (Dupont and Saylor 1991).

2–3 OPIOIDS

The **opioids** are narcotic analgesic drugs derived from opium, the sap of poppy plants, *Papaver somniferum*, and related synthetic drugs that have similar effects. When opium is chewed it produces mild euphoria, relaxation, and an increased threshold for pain. Because it affects the brain quickly, smoking opium has a much more powerful effect than chewing it.

The use of opium as a narcotic dates back thousands of years to southeast Asia and Egypt; there are numerous references to it throughout history for its euphoric (pleasure-inducing) and analgesic (painkilling) effects (Thomason and Dilts 1991). Although opium is still taken in its raw form today by some people, most opioids are either direct or synthetic derivatives of opium.

Morphine and Other Prescription Opioids

In the early 1800s scientists were able to extract a psychoactive chemical from the milky substance in opium and called it **morphine,** after Morpheus, the Greek god of dreams. For much of the nineteenth century, morphine was heralded in medicine for its ability to reduce pain, especially in individuals undergoing surgery and for those with severe injuries. Today, morphine holds its place in medicine because of its analgesic properties.

Another analgesic that is similar to morphine and is also found in raw opium is *thebaine*. Many of the opioid analgesics used in modern medicine are derived from morphine and thebaine. *Codeine* is found in raw opium but most of it is converted directly from morphine or thebaine. *Percodan* and *Percocet* (oxydocone) and *Vicoden* (hydrocodone) are other analgesics that are converted from thebaine. Because the psychoactive effects of opioid drugs are roughly similar, we will discuss their effects together in a later section of this chapter (Thomason and Dilts 1991).

Heroin

A slight modification of the morphine molecule results in the opioid compound *diacetylmorphine* or **heroin.** It enters the brain much more quickly than morphine, and it is ultimately converted into morphine there. The speed with which heroin enters the brain makes it about three times more potent than morphine and ten times stronger than raw opium (Holmes 1997, Jaffe 1989a, Thomason and Dilts 1991).

Ironically, heroin was introduced in the 1890s as a nonaddictive, painkilling substitute for morphine that supposedly was just as safe as aspirin. Little did anyone know that heroin was extremely addictive and would become the most widely abused opioid drug.

Heroin, also known as "dope," "junk," and "horse," is available in powdered form and can be sniffed or "snorted" directly into the nostrils. A more dramatic effect is experienced by dissolving the powder and injecting the solution under the skin in a procedure called "skin-popping." The most powerful effects are achieved by shooting heroin directly into a vein, a method called "mainlining." Many users enjoy the effects of shooting "speedballs," a mixture of heroin and cocaine. With the increased potency of heroin on the street today, many individuals, especially urban teenagers and young adults, get high by inhaling the vapors. This is called "chasing the dragon." Others mix it with cocaine and smoke it. At a time when some drug users are concerned about contracting HIV (the virus that causes AIDS) infection from sharing contaminated needles, smoking heroin offers a potent method of getting high without the immediate risk of HIV infection (Jaffe 1997, Thomason and Dilts 1991).

Psychoactive Effects. All opioids have similar psychoactive effects, but each one differs with respect to potency and route of administration, that is, how the drug is taken. Generally, taking an opioid in pill form as would be done with codeine, Vicoden, and Percodan produces a weaker effect than if the drug is smoked or injected.

Because of the quick action and powerful impact, mainlining drugs like morphine and especially heroin is the preferred way to get high. This is done by mixing the dope with water in a spoon, "cooking" it until dissolved, then shooting it into a vein. Immediately after mainlining, heroin hits the brain with full impact, creating a powerful rush that many users describe as just as good or better than an orgasm. During the rush, which can last about a minute or longer, the person feels euphoric and pain-free and may vomit and lapse into a temporary "twilight" state of intense sleepiness or semiconsciousness called "nodding" (Jaffe 1992, Thomason and Dilts 1991).

After the initial rush, the individual goes through a four- to six-hour period of stupor, with feelings of warmth, relaxation, contentment, mild euphoria, loss of motor coordination, and some nodding. Reverie, or drifting

through dream-like experiences, is quite common. Furthermore, the person's needs for food and sex are either greatly diminished or absent. At very high doses, an overdose may occur, with coma, respiratory depression, and death (American Psychiatric Association 2000, Kleber, 1994a). The effects of taking heroin via other routes are similar to mainlining except that they do not occur as quickly, are not as intense, and any rush is not nearly as dramatic.

> Frankie began snorting dope when he worked in the post office while in college. He said it made him "feel nice" and helped him pass the time while sorting mail. Eventually snorting heroin lost its kick, so Frankie started to skin pop, and before long he was mainlining. At the peak of his heroin habit, Frankie would shoot a bag of dope and drift off into reverie with his head tilted and eyes almost shut. Every few minutes he would come to, mumble a few incoherent sentences, then nod back off. Eventually he lost his job and failed out of college. He hardly ate or bothered with anybody. When confronted by friends, all Frankie could say was that the dope felt too good to do anything else.

Methadone

When their opium supply was blocked during World War II, German laboratories synthesized a replacement morphine-like opioid called **methadone**. Today, methadone is used medically as a substitute for heroin.

Psychoactive Effects. The psychological and behavioral effects of methadone are like those of other opioids but, there are important differences due to the usual route of methadone administration and the manner and speed with which it is metabolized (Jaffe 1992, Thomason and Dilts 1991, Substance Abuse and Mental Health Services Administration 1997). Methadone works best when taken orally as a liquid preparation, helping to slow the onset of its effects, which can take more than two hours to peak (Jaffe 1989a, 1992, Thomason and Dilts 1991). Also, it is metabolized more slowly and is longer acting, lasting anywhere from twenty-four to thirty-six hours. Therefore, the typical rush and intense euphoria obtained from heroin are absent. Even though there is a black market for methadone, the abuse potential of methadone is not nearly as great as it is for heroin.

Mechanisms of Action

In the 1970s researchers discovered that opioids attach to specific neuron sites called *opiate receptors,* especially in the limbic system, a collection of brain structures known to regulate aspects of emotionality (Hughs et al. 1975). This finding led to a search for naturally produced chemicals that might attach to opiate receptor sites. Such neuropeptides were eventually found and named *endorphins,* meaning endogenous (produced from within) morphine. Taken collectively, these research findings indicate that opioids are endorphin agonists in addition to their ability to activate dopamine neurons. Actually, several opiate receptors have been subsequently identified, and it appears that most morphine-like opioids mainly activate one site, called the *mu receptor* (Jaffe 1989a).

The analgesic effects of opioids are the result of their ability to block substance-P in the spinal cord. Such an action makes it difficult for pain sensations from the body to be transmitted to the brain.

2–4 STIMULANTS

Drugs that arouse the nervous system, increase energy and alertness, and produce euphoria are called **stimulants.** They include caffeine, nicotine, cocaine, and amphetamines. Though caffeine and nicotine represent significant health hazards, we will turn our attention in this section to *cocaine* and *amphetamines.*

Cocaine

For centuries, some natives of Peru and Bolivia have chewed the leaves of the coca shrub (*Erythroxylon coca*) to energize them and make them less hungry so they could work longer and harder without interruption. The psychoactive ingredient of the coca leaves is **cocaine.** Cocaine was chemically isolated in 1864 and has been used medically as a local anesthetic. Until 1906, its use was legal in the United States and cocaine was often found in many remedies and tonics. In fact, cocaine was initially the "coca" in Coca-Cola. After experimenting with it himself, psychoanalyst Sigmund Freud sometimes recommended cocaine for his patients as a remedy for fatigue and depression (Rosecan and Spitz 1987).

Powdered *cocaine hydrochloride,* often called "blow," "nose candy," or "snow," can be taken directly into the nose by "snorting lines" of cocaine from a smooth surface like a mirror or piece of glass. Using this method, cocaine is absorbed directly into the bloodstream through the nasal tissue. Alternatively, it can be mainlined by injecting the dissolved cocaine directly into a vein, sometimes with heroin (American Psychiatric Association 2000).

Some of the most powerful effects of cocaine are obtained by smoking its vapors in the form of "freebase" or "crack." To smoke it, powdered cocaine must be separated from its base, the hydrochloride molecules. This is accomplished either by using a potentially volatile process of heating cocaine with ether to get freebase, or by heating the cocaine along with a mixture of ammonia, baking soda, and water. The result is an already prepared form of freebase called "crack." The term crack comes from the crackling sounds heard when the "crack rock" is heated. Some users smoke "bazooka," a coca paste that is an intermediate product in the processing of cocaine hydrochloride (Karan et al 1991, National Institute on Drug Abuse 1997a).

Psychoactive Effects. As with any psychoactive drug, the precise effects of taking stimulants largely depend on the route of administration, and, in the case of street drugs like cocaine, the purity of the substance. The rule is that the faster the cocaine hits the brain, the quicker and more intense its effects are. At the same time, quicker action means a shorter duration of the effects. Thus, snorting cocaine produces slower and milder but longer-lasting effects, while injecting and smoking it cause powerful but shorter-lived reactions. (American Psychiatric Association 2000, Gawin 1991, Gold 1997, Karan et al. 1991).

Aside from the strong physiological effects it creates such as blood vessel constriction and dilated pupils, as well as increased heart rate, blood pressure, and body temperature, cocaine has profound psychological and behavioral effects. The fundamental effect of taking cocaine is an intensification of virtually all normal pleasures (Gawin 1991). The individual feels a boost of energy, alertness, elation, exhilaration, and self-confidence. Emotions and sex drive are enhanced. Such effects may last for fifteen to thirty minutes. Some individuals report feeling restless, irritable, and anxious. Shooting or smoking cocaine results in a strong initial rush and more intense symptoms. The effects of smoking cocaine may only last for five to ten minutes and trigger immediate cravings for more of the drug (National Institute on Drug Abuse 1997a).

High doses and/or chronic cocaine use can result in serious emotional and behavioral problems. High doses of cocaine, especially from freebase or crack, often lead to confusion, and to psychotic features such as hallucinations (sensory perceptions without basis in reality), paranoia (pathological suspiciousness), and violent behavior. Many chronic users report little if any pleasure from cocaine use and find themselves deeply depressed without cocaine (American Psychiatric Association 2000, National Institute on Drug Abuse 1997a).

After smoking crack-cocaine daily for almost two years, Larry was referred for treatment because his wife was unable to tolerate his suspiciousness and bizarre behavior. Larry worked nights and his wife worked days. After she left for work, Larry would smoke and lock himself in the bathroom. When his wife returned Larry would peer at her through the keyhole with his knees pressed against the door. At other times he would pile furniture against the front door, believing that undercover cops were trying to break in.

Amphetamines

The **amphetamines** are a type of synthetic stimulant. Like stimulants in general, they arouse the nervous system and increase energy they include *Benzedrine, Dexedrine* (dextroamphetamine), and *Methedrine (methamphetamine).* Although often considered a hallucinogen, *3–4 methylenedioxymethamphetamine* (MDMA or "ecstasy") is derived from amphetamine and will be presented as such here. Amphetamines like Benzedrine and Dexedrine are usually taken as pills, although some amphetamines can be injected or smoked.

Amphetamines or "uppers" are laboratory-synthesized stimulants first introduced in the 1930s to combat asthma and nasal congestion. Soon, they were used as "pep pills" to give people a needed energy boost or to suppress their appetite. Because of their powerful effects on mood and behavior, however, they quickly became frequently abused drugs. Nevertheless, several amphetamines are used medically today in the treatment of obesity and a mental disorder called *attention deficit hyperactivity disorder,* better known as ADHD.

Psychoactive Effects. The effects of amphetamines are similar to cocaine but tend to be longer-lasting. When taken orally, amphetamines lead to increased energy, enhanced concentration, increased sociability, a feeling of well-being, and diminished appetite. Physiologically, they cause increased respiration, blood pressure, and heart rate (American Psychiatric Association 2000, National Institute on Drug Abuse 1997b). These effects might make it easy to understand why amphetamines were routinely given to soldiers during World War II to better withstand the rigors of combat.

Despite the seemingly positive effects of amphetamines, amphetamine intoxication is associated with a host of negative and even dangerous consequences. Short of cardiac arrest and death, extreme intoxication is likely to cause anxiety, tension, confusion, impaired judgment, depression, sadness, social withdrawal, paranoia, anger, and fighting

(American Psychiatric Association 2000, National Institute on Drug Abuse 1997b).

Methamphetamine. The symptoms of amphetamine intoxication are exaggerated and prolonged when using **methamphetamine** (Methedrine), a drug with a very high potential for abuse (Cho 1990). Known on the street as "speed," "meth," and "chalk," methamphetamine has limited medical use; its therapeutic value is clearly outweighed by its abuse potential. Therefore, it is synthesized mainly in illegal laboratories. According to the *Drug Enforcement Administration,* since 1979 methamphetamine has been the most prevalent, illegally produced controlled substance in the United States (National Institute on Drug Abuse 1997c).

Methamphetamine can be snorted or injected intravenously. A particularly potent, pure form called "ice," "crystal," or "glass" consists of clear, chunky crystals that have a low vaporization point and that can readily be smoked like crack. (American Psychiatric Association 2000, National Institute on Drug Abuse, 1997c) Immediately after injection or smoking the drug, the user experiences an intense extremely pleasurable rush or flash that lasts for just a few minutes. The rush is followed by a longer period of elevated mood, increased physical activity, and decreased appetite. Higher doses can result in irritability, insomnia, confusion, tremors, convulsions, anxiety, paranoia, and aggressiveness. Hyperthermia (increased body temperature), convulsions, and the possibility of stroke can cause death (American Psychiatric Association 2000, National Institute on Drug Abuse 1997c).

MDMA. Another amphetamine derivative that has stimulant and hallucinogenic properties is a so-called "designer drug" **3-4 methylenedioxymethamphetamine,** or MDMA. Popularly known as "ecstasy," "Adam," and "X-TC," MDMA is structurally similar to methamphetamine and its use causes similar physical, psychological, and behavioral effects, except that MDMA is more likely than other stimulants to cause hallucinatory, "trip"-like experiences similar to LSD (National Institute on Drug Abuse 1997d).

Mechanisms of Action

There is compelling evidence that stimulants increase the availability of amine neurotransmitters (including dopamine, norepinephrine, and serotonin) in areas of the brain stem and limbic system responsible for experiences of motivation and reward. In other words, drug craving and the pleasurable effects of stimulants are related to the excitation of amine neurotransmitters (Caine and Koob 1993, Caine et al. 1995, Gawin 1991, George and Ritz 1993, Markou et al. 1993, Wise 1988). Stimulants also correspondingly decrease electrical activity in inhibitory neurons (London et al. 1990). Cocaine activates amine neurotransmission by blocking amine reuptake. Amphetamines have an agonistic effect too, insofar as they block reuptake and increase the release of amine neurotransmitters.

Mounting evidence suggests that repeated overstimulation of amine systems by stimulants depletes the neurotransmitter supply. Perhaps this explains why repeated stimulant use often leads to a lack of pleasure from the drug and depression when not using it (Blum et al. 1996, Gawin 1991).

Of great concern are the findings of a number of studies showing that methamphetamine kills dopamine and serotonin neurons. Considering the structural similarity between methamphetamine and MDMA, researchers expect to find that MDMA kills brain cells as well. The destruction of serotonin neurons in particular may account for the aggressive behavior often seen in chronic stimulant users (National Institute on Drug Abuse 1997d).

2–5 HALLUCINOGENS

Naturally occurring, mind-altering substances have long been a part of religious rituals, such as the use of mescaline by Native Americans. Since the 1960s, many individuals have used various drugs of this kind for recreational purposes and to induce spiritual insights and mystical experiences. **Hallucinogens,** as these drugs are called, produce hallucinations and other psychedelic (mind-altering) experiences. Included in this category are drugs such as *LSD, mescaline, psilocybin, STP* (2,5-dimethoxy-4-methylamphetamine), and *DMT* (dimethyltryptamine). Although hallucinations are not necessarily the principal signs of *phencyclidine* (PCP), it has hallucinogenic properties and will be considered here. The focus in this section will be on LSD and PCP.

Lysergic Acid Diethylamide

In 1938 a research chemist, Albert Hoffman, synthesized a new drug, and after taking some he described its effects in the following passage:

> On arriving home, I lay down and sank into a state of drunkenness which was not unpleasant and which was characterized by extreme activity of imagination. As I lay in a dazed condition with my eyes closed ... there surged upon me an uninterrupted stream of fantastic images of extraordinary plasticity and vividness and accompanied by an intense kaleidoscope-like play of colors Hoffman 1971, p. 23

Dr. Hoffman had used **lysergic acid diethylamide** (LSD), a hallucinogen manufactured from *ergot*, a fungus that grows on grains. "Acid," as it is most commonly called, became extremely popular in the 1960s among the "hippy" generation. Though LSD is now not as glorified as in its early days, its use has remained more or less stable since the 1970s (National Institute on Drug Abuse 1997e).

LSD is an illegal drug sold in the streets in tablet, capsule, and occasionally liquid form. It is often added to absorbent blotter paper and divided into squares, each representing one dose or "hit" of "blotter acid." Current doses range from 20 to 80 micrograms compared to the 100 to 200 microgram hits available in the 1960s and early 1970s (National Institute on Drug Abuse 1997e).

Psychoactive Effects. The psychological and behavioral effects of LSD mimic some symptoms of psychotic reactions inasmuch as the individual manifests weird behavior and diminished contact with reality. The dosage,

the user's personality, mood, and expectations, and the surroundings in which the drug is taken can all contribute to LSD's psychotomimetic effects.

Typically, within thirty to ninety minutes the person starts to "trip," and has dramatic sensory experiences in which colors are more vivid, sounds more intense, and objects become distorted. The person begins to see things that do not correspond to external reality. Sensations often "cross over," meaning that the user may feel as if he is hearing colors and seeing sounds. The types of hallucinations and sensory distortions are virtually limitless. Dramatic mood swings, and mystical experiences may occur, while a sense of time and place is often lost (American Psychiatric Association 2000, National Institute on Drug Abuse 1997e).

During a "bad trip," the individual may lose his sense of self, an experience called *depersonalization*, and may also have terrifying thoughts, become fearful of losing control or going insane, or develop paranoid ideas that people are talking about him or out to get him. Some LSD users experience "flashbacks" in which certain aspects of a trip are reexperienced months or year after the drug was last used. Flashbacks are unpredictable; they come on suddenly and may occur at any time. Some LSD users will manifest long-lasting emotional problems that we will discuss in later chapters (American Psychiatric Association 1994).

Phencyclidine

Phencyclidine (PCP) is an illegally manufactured hallucinogen that was introduced in 1959 as an anesthetic in humans, and later used as a tranquilizer in veterinary medicine. Because it rendered people agitated and irrational, its medical use in humans was discontinued in 1965 as it gained some popularity as a street drug. Even though its use has declined over the years, PCP continues to represent a significant health hazard (National Institute on Drug Abuse 1997f).

Phencyclidine is a white crystalline powder that is easily dissolved in water or alcohol and is available in capsules, tablets, or colored powders. It can be snorted, eaten, or smoked by mixing it with mint, parsley, oregano, tobacco, or marijuana (National Institute on Drug Abuse 1997f).

Psychoactive Effects.   The fact that PCP is often called "angel dust," "crystal supergrass," "killer joints." "wack," and "rocket fuel" on the street testifies to the bizarre and unpredictable effects of this dangerous drug. Phencyclidine intoxication causes hallucinations, euphoria, agitation, confusion, slurred speech, numbness, a distorted body image, blurred vision, drooling, impaired motor coordination, and false beliefs (delusions). Many users have feelings of tremendous strength, power, and invincibility, which incline them toward belligerence, rage, and violent behavior. Consequently, hospitalization and/or police involvement is not uncommon (National Institute on Drug Abuse 1997f).

> Henry was arrested for assaulting police officers while under the influence of PCP. After weeks of heavy PCP use, Henry became paranoid, agitated, and violent, believing that co-workers, drug dealers, and the police were plotting to kill him. He put a loaded gun in in the trunk of his car for defense, and for several days he ate, slept, and got high in his car. At times he would drive around to escape from his imagined killers. One day he ran a stop sign at high speed and was eventually stopped by police. Because of the PCP he felt powerful and full of rage. He overcame a number of police officers and several wound up in the hospital before six additional officers subdued him.

Mechanisms of Action

Ample evidence indicates that the chemical structure of LSD resembles that of serotonin, therefore casuing LSD to act as an agonist. Thus, LSD produces some of its hallucinogenic effects by mimicking or enhancing the synaptic effects of serotonin in certain parts of the brain. (Jacobs 1987) Our understanding of the synaptic mechanisms of LSD remains sketchy, however. The surgical removal of serotonin-producing neurons in experimental animals has little effect on LSD's abil-

ity to cause hallucinations. Furthermore, serotonin activity alone cannot explain flashbacks. Long after LSD has been removed from the body, people can have flashbacks for months and even years. Obviously, other neurotransmitters, besides serotonin, and other neural events must act to produce the full range of LSD's hallucinogenic effects (Kalat 1998).

Regarding PCP, most recent research has focused on its effects on NDMA (N-methyl-D-aspartate) receptors. These receptors normally respond to glutamate and other excitatory neurotransmitters. Apparently, PCP produces its behavioral effects by competing with excitatory transmitters (Balster 1995).

2–6   CANNABINOIDS

Drugs whose psychoactive ingredient is *tetrahydrocannabinol* (THC) and that produce mild sedative and hallucinogenic effects are known as **cannabinoids**. Cannabinoids are found naturally in the hemp plant, *Cannabis sativa*, which grows wild in tropical and temperate regions of the world. Hemp is cultivated illegally in many parts of the the world either for personal use or illegal distribution.

Cannabis preparations have been used in Asian medicine for thousands of years for their mild sedative effects. Though arguments rage today about medicinal uses and legalization, cannabinoids such as marijuana and hashish are illicit, widely abused drugs (National Institute on Drug Abuse 1997g, Weiss and Millman 1991).

Marijuana and Hashish

The resin obtained from hemp plants contains more than 80 cannabinoids and over 400 different chemicals, of which THC is the major psychoactive ingredient. Cannabinoids differ mainly with respect to their THC concentration (Weiss and Millman 1991).

The most widely used illicit drug in our society is **marijuana**, a cannabinoid derived from the leaves and flowering tops of the *Cannabis sativa* plant. Known as "pot," "weed," "grass," or "herb," marijuana is relatively low in THC; most of the marijuana used in the

United States has a THC content of between 1 to 10 percent, though more potent varieties are available. Marijuana can be consumed in a drink or mixed in food, but the most common route of administration is smoking (National Institute on Drug Abuse 1997g, Weiss and Millman 1991).

Hashish, or simply "hash," is an extremely potent form of cannabis derived from the resin of the hemp plant. Like marijuana, hashish is usually smoked. Because hashish is mostly derived from the resin itself, it has a very high THC content compared to marijuana. Hashish oil, for example, can have a THC concentration as high as 60 percent (Weiss and Millman 1991).

Psychoactive Effects. The psychological and behavioral effects of cannabinoids largely depend on the THC concentration, but the setting as well as the expectations and personality of the user also play an important role. The user usually starts to feel the effects of marijuana or hashish within minutes after smoking and they can last for several hours. The person generally gets a high feeling, relaxation, and a sense of well-being. Other effects include increased sociability, sedation, lethargy, and giddiness. Visual hallucinations and delusions occur infrequently but sensory distortions are quite common. Enhanced music perception and altered touch, temperature, and pain sensations are a typical part of the marijuana high, as are time distortions, in which minutes may seem like hours or hours like minutes. Furthermore, many users report that boring and repetitive tasks can be performed with great interest and concentration, and activities like cleaning the house or counting units in assembly-line work can be performed with great enthusiasm (American Psychiatric Association 2000, Weiss and Millman 1991).

Cannabinoid intoxication is not fun for all, however. Although some individuals become more sociable, others may become anxious or panic-stricken, depressed, socially withdrawn, and pathologically self-conscious. Impairment of motor coordination and short-term memory as well as an inability to carry out complex mental tasks are just two of the adverse consequences caused by marijuana and hashish intoxication. Many chronic users develop a so-called *amotivational syndrome* marked by apathy, a reduction of goal-directed activities, impaired concentration, and disregard for personal appearance and hygiene (American Psychiatric Association 2000).

> Ralph began smoking pot at age 11 and by 13 he was smoking three to five joints daily. By the time he entered substance abuse treatment at age 22, he had been smoking a dozen joints per day for years. His marijuana smoking prevented him from completing high school because the pot made him uninterested in homework. He also stopped socializing and spent most of his time watching mindless TV programs. Later in his teens, Ralph's parents got him a job as a stock boy in a department store, but he quickly lost it because of his amotivational syndrome.

Mechanisms of Action

The mystery of how THC affects neurons is just starting to be unraveled. In 1988 it was discovered that THC readily binds to certain neurons (Devane et al. 1988). This finding led investigators to reason that the brain must synthesize its own version of THC, much in the same way that the brain produces its own opiatelike compounds. Such a compound was later isolated and called *anandamide* (from *ananda* meaning "bliss" in Sanskrit) (Aceto et al. 1995, Fackelman 1993). How THC and anandamide interact to produce the effects of cannabinoids is not yet understood. One thing is certain, however. THC has a profound effect on neurons in the hippocampus, a structure in the brain's limbic system that is crucial for the formation of new memories. The electrical activity of hippocampal neurons is suppressed by THC, which may account for the memory disturbances seen in marijuana and hashish users (National Institute on Drug Abuse 1997g).

2–7 INHALANTS

Inhalants are a chemically diverse group of volatile drugs that produce short-lived psychoactive effects when they are inhaled (Weiss and Millman 1991). The inhalants encompass a wide range of chemicals readily available in drug paraphernalia stores, hardware stores, factories, supermarkets, restaurant supply houses, and other establishments. A few of these substances, such as amyl nitrite, are obtained by prescription.

Types of Inhalants

There are three types of inhalants:

- *Volatile solvents* include adhesives such as model glue, rubber cement, and polyvinylchloride (PVC) cement; aerosols like hair spray and deodorant; and solvents and gases such as lighter fluid, paint thinner, nail-polish remover, typewriter correction fluid, and dry-cleaner fluid.
- *Nitrites,* called "poppers" or "rush," which include room odorizers like butly and propyl nitrite.
- *Anesthetics;* nitrous oxide or "laughing gas" makes up the major anesthetic inhalants.

Most often, the user inhales the substance from a soaked rag, a paper or plastic bag, or directly from containers or aerosol cans, depending on the substance.

Psychoactive Effects and Mechanisms of Action

Inhalants work almost instantaneously because they are quickly absorbed by the circulatory system in the lungs and sent to the brain and other organs. Their effects usually persist for a few minutes but can sometimes last for nearly an hour because the chemicals are deposited in organs with a high lipid (fat) content. To continue the psychoactive effect, inhalation must be repeated; in some cases the user will inhale the substance hundreds of times a day (Weiss and Millman 1991).

The initial effects of inhalation are a rush followed by a feeling of euphoria, decreased inhibitions, and the feeling of floating, depending on the type and amount of inhalant used. This is often followed by sedation and irritability. Dizziness, impaired coordina-

tion, slurred speech, weakness, belligerence, assaultiveness, apathy, clouded consciousness, impaired judgment, and bizarre perceptual disturbances are common adverse consequences of inhalant intoxication. It is believed that most inhalants have a general depressant effect on neural activity after a brief period of excitation (American Psychiatric Association 2000, National Institute on Drug Abuse 1977h, i, Weiss and Millman 1991).

SUMMARY

2–1

The nervous system consists of billions of neurons. Neurons conduct information via complex electrical and chemical processes. Abused drugs create their psychoactive effects by influencing the activity of neurons, and especially by altering neurotransmitter activity at the synapse. Important neurotransmitters in addiction include dopamine, norepinephrine, serotonin, GABA, glutamate, and the endorphins.

2–2

Psychoactive drugs that slow the electrical activity of the nervous system, resulting in a tranquilizing effect, sleepiness, and impairment of higher mental functions, vision, and movement, are called depressants. They include alcohol and barbiturates as well as other sedative-hypnotics, and anxiolytics. Alcohol's initial effects include relaxation, diminished emotional tension, and increased confidence. Greater intoxication causes impairment of cognitive, sensory, and motor functions and may cause disinhibition. The psychoactive effects of barbiturates and benzodiazepines are similar. Many depressants influence the activity of GABA-containing neurons.

2–3

The opioids are narcotic analgesic drugs derived from opium, and related synthetic drugs that have similar effects. These drugs include morphine, heroin, methadone, codeine, and other prescription drugs. All opioids have similar psychoactive effects, but these vary with respect to the drug's potency and its route of administration, that is, how the drug is taken. Because of the quick action and powerful impact, mainlining of opioids is the preferred way to get high. After the initial rush, the individual goes through a period of stupor, feelings of warmth, relaxation, contentment, mild euphoria, loss of motor coordination, and some nodding and reverie. At very high doses, an overdose may occur, with coma, respiratory depression, and death. Opioids attach to specific neuron sites called opiate receptors, especially in the limbic system.

2–4

Drugs that arouse the nervous system, increase energy and alertness, and produce euphoria are called stimulants. They include caffeine, nicotine, cocaine, and amphetamines. The effects of taking stimulants largely depend on the drug's route of administration and its purity. The fundamental effect of taking stimulants is an intensification of virtually all normal pleasures, and a boost of energy, alertness, elation, exhilaration, and self-confidence. Emotions and sex drive are enhanced. Restlessness, irritability, impaired judgment, anxiety, confusion, psychotic features, violent behavior, depression, paranoia, anger, and fighting often follow high doses or chronic use. MDMA causes similar physical, psychological, and behavioral effects and hallucinatory, "trip"-like experiences similar to LSD.

There is compelling evidence that stimulants increase the availability of amine neurotransmitters, including dopamine, norepinephrine, and serotonin, in areas of the brain stem and limbic system responsible for experiences of motivation and reward. Stimulants also decrease electrical activity in inhibitory neurons.

2–5

Hallucinogens produce hallucinations and other psychedelic (mind-altering) experiences. They include LSD, mescaline, psilocybin, STP, DMT, and PCP. Hallucinogen intoxication mimics psychotic reactions, with weird behavior and diminished contact with reality as well as dramatic sensory experiences. During a "bad trip" the individual may lose his sense of self and may also have terrifying thoughts, experience fear of losing control or going insane, or develop paranoid ideas that people are talking about him or are out to get him. Some LSD users experience flashbacks, in which certain aspects of a trip are reexperienced months or year after the drug was last used. PCP intoxication causes hallucinations, euphoria, agitation, confusion, slurred speech, numbness, a distorted body image, blurred vision, drooling, impaired motor coordination, and false beliefs (delusions). Many users have feelings of tremendous strength, power, and invincibility, which may incline them toward belligerence, rage, and violent behavior. LSD structurally acts as a serotonin agonist. PCP affects NDMA receptors that normally respond to glutamate and other excitatory neurotransmitters. PCP produces its behavioral effects by competing with excitatory transmitters.

2–6

Cannabinoids like marijuana and hashish are derived from the leaves and flowering tops of the *Cannabis sativa* plant. Psychoactive effects include a high feeling, relaxation, and a sense of well-being. Other effects include increased sociability, sedation, lethargy, and giddiness. Visual hallucinations and delusions occur infrequently, but sensory distortions are quite common. Enhanced music perception and altered touch, temperature, and pain sensations are a typical part of the marijuana high, as are time distortions. Some people become anxious or panic-stricken, depressed, socially withdrawn, and pathologically self-conscious. Impaired motor coordination and short-term memory, an inability to carry out complex mental tasks, and amotivational syndrome can occur. THC, the active ingredient of cannabinoids, enhances a naturally occurring brain compound called anandamide.

2–7

Inhalants are a chemically diverse group of volatile drugs that produce short-lived psychoactive effects when they are inhaled. They include volatile solvents, nitrites, and certain anesthetics. The initial effects of inhalation are a rush followed by a feeling of euphoria, decreased inhibitions, and the feeling of floating. This is often followed by sedation and irritability, dizziness, impaired coordination, slurred speech, weakness, belligerence, assaultiveness, apathy, clouded consciousness, impaired judgment, and bizarre perceptual disturbances. It is believed that most inhalants have a general depressant effect on neural activity after a brief period of excitation.

TERMS TO REMEMBER

3–4 methylenedioxymethamphetamine
agonist
alcohol
amphetamines
antagonist
barbiturates
benzodiazepines
cannabinoids
cocaine
depressants
hallucinogens
hashish
heroin
inhalants
lysergic acid diethylamide
marijuana
methadone
methamphetamine
morphine
neuron
neurotransmitters
opioids
psychoactive drug
phencyclidine
stimulants

SUGGESTED READINGS

Hoffman, A. (1971). LSD discoverer disputes "chance" factor in finding. *Psychiatric News* 6:23–26.

National Institute on Drug Abuse (1997b). Common substances of abuse. *NIDA Capsule.* Rockville, MD: National Institute on Drug Abuse.

CHAPTER THREE

The Assessment of Chemical Dependency

Chapter Outline

3–1 THE CLINICAL INTERVIEW
    Underreporting of Drug Use
    Types of Interviews
    Interview Strategies

3–2 SUBSTANCE USE ASSESSMENT INSTRUMENTS
    Screening Instruments
    Structured Interview Schedules
    Assessment of Motivation for Change

3–3 PSYCHOLOGICAL TESTING
    Characteristics of Psychological Tests
    Self-Report Inventories
    Projective Tests
    Intelligence and Neuropsychological Tests

3–4 LABORATORY ANALYSIS
    History and Rationale of Drug Testing
    Drugs Tested and Characteristics of Drug-Testing Methods
    Types of Biological Specimens Analyzed

Learning Objectives

After completing this chapter you should be able to:

1. Specify assessment areas in the clinical interview.
2. Differentiate unstructured and structured interview formats.
3. Discuss fundamental interview strategies.
4. List and describe alcohol/drug screening instruments.
5. Describe structured interview schedules for substance use.
6. Explain the technique of assessment of motivation for change.
7. Define and indicate the purpose of self-report inventories and projective tests.
8. Elucidate the purpose and technique of neuropsychological testing.

9. Differentiate drug screening and drug confirmation methods and describe their relative advantages and disadvantages.
10. Compare and contrast urine, saliva, sweat, and hair testing.

The diagnosis and treatment of any medical disease or psychological disorder requires a comprehensive assessment of the individual's current problems, history, and other factors that can elucidate the nature and severity of the disease. In this respect, chemical dependency is no different. In order for you to be an effective counselor, it is imperative that you conduct a thorough evaluation of the client's drug-taking behavior and the factors that maintain it. Your principal objective is to accurately diagnose substance abuse or dependence and to understand the relationship of these behaviors to other mental and medical disorders. This will help you to plan and implement the most effective treatments (Schottenfield 1994).

In this chapter you will learn about the principles and techniques of chemical dependency assessment. By studying the basics of interviewing, drug-assessment instruments, psychological testing, and drug testing you will be better equipped to carry out your responsibilities as a chemical dependency counselor.

3–1 The Clinical Interview

Most of the information about a client's current and historical drug use comes from self-reports. In this regard, the cornerstone of substance abuse and dependence assessment is the **clinical interview**, in which the client's drug-taking behavior and other aspects of cognitive, emotional, and behavioral functioning are determined by asking probing questions and evaluating the patient's responses. In this section you will examine the components of a clinical interview and the techniques that can be used to elicit relevant information about an individual's drug or alcohol problems.

Underreporting of Drug Use

A significant stumbling block in the assessment of chemical dependency is the client's reluctance to to disclose information concerning drug use. Indeed, the person's drive to minimize or deny the extent of drug use has taken center stage. Consequently, most chemically dependent individuals are evasive, and lie to protect their lifestyle no matter how adverse the consequences may be. Bear in mind that in spite of how prevalent it is, substance abuse is a highly stigmatized behavior in our society.

According to the **social desirability hypothesis,** people are reluctant to disclose illicit drug use because of its negative social image. Even when they do, drug users are more likely to confess to using less stigmatized drugs like marijuana and alcohol than to report the use of more socially unacceptable drugs like heroin or crack. In either case, drug users are inclined to underreport. Validation studies of criminal offenders that compared self-reports to the results of laboratory drug testing (discussed later in this chapter) revealed that actual drug use is more than twice that of claims from self-reports. Non-offenders, too, are reluctant to accurately disclose their drug use, even when confidentiality is guaranteed, for fear of information leaks that could lead to stigmatization and punitive consequences from family, friends, and employers. Furthermore, the client's drug-induced cognitive and emotional state can affect the accuracy of self-reports during an interview (Harrison and Hughes 1997, Schottenfield 1994).

Types of Interviews

In your interviews, you will have to cover a lot of ground in a short period of time in order to derive enough information to plan and carry out effective treatment. Conducting a clinical interview for chemical dependency may seem simple on paper, but we cannot overemphasize that no matter how skilled you may become at interviewing, gathering drug-related information from a client is often an arduous task.

There are two broad types of interviews: *unstructured* and *structured*.

The Unstructured Interview. The **unstructured interview** is a flexible, nonsystematic approach in which clients are free to discuss what is important to them and the counselor does not necessarily cover specific topics or ask predetermined questions. Although this method is valuable in developing counselor–client rapport, it may allow the client to be evasive about drug use.

The Structured Interview. Compared to unstructured methods, the **structured interview** is a systematic method used to gather significant current and historical information concerning drug use and related problems. Although structured interview formats vary, the first step usually involves gathering identifying and demographic information such as name, age, sex, date of birth, marital status, ethnic group, religion, occupation, and education. This is followed by attempts to specify the problems that prompted the person to come in for a consultation.

In your experience as a chemical dependency counselor you will discover that the most effective approach will be a blend of unstructured and structured formats.

Interview Strategies

There is no best way to conduct a drug-use interview. However, a useful interview outline involves investigation of nine broad areas of inquiry (American Psychiatric Association 1995a, b, Pattison 1986). They are:

- The type and quantity of drug and frequency of use
- Intoxication effects
- Tolerance and withdrawal symptoms
- History of attempts to curb or stop use
- Adverse medical consequences
- Related interpersonal/social problems
- Work- and academic-related consequences
- Legal problems
- Psychological disturbances

Keeping in mind the client's defensiveness and impaired cognition and affect, you may find it is not prudent to dive into these areas too quickly. Instead, your goals might be best served if you assume a straightforward, nonjudgmental approach. If you are to gather the information you need, it is not going to be very helpful to launch an interrogation or to moralize about the individual's drinking and drugging; you need to be aware that the interview is not about "them" versus "us." Be guided by the fact that whether the client is self-motivated to get clean or is being coerced to do so by the courts, employers, or family, your job is to derive information that will be used to offer the person a way out of a life of chemical dependency (Senay 1997).

One way to minimize defensiveness and create an atmosphere of helping is to conduct the session in privacy and open the interview by asking the person questions such as "How can I help you?" or "What brings you here today?" Then, give the client some free time to speak his mind without distractions. When you finally begin your questioning, you should initially avoid topics that may provoke defensiveness. Rather than hammer away with questions about drug-taking, you can facilitate the interview process by first taking a life history, in which you can examine the person's strengths and weaknesses as well as successes and failures. When you get around to questions about current and past drug use, it will be a good idea initially to avoid "why" questions. Instead, focus on questions such as:

- Which drugs do you use or have you used?
- How old were you when you began to use drugs?
- How much do you use?
- How often?
- By what method do you take them?
- When, where, and with whom did you use?
- How does it make you feel? Which effects do you like?
- Which effects do you not like?
- Did you ever try to cut back or stop? When? For how long?
- Can you describe the pattern of drug use since you began using?
- How has it changed, if at all? (Senay 1997)

These types of questions are likely to provide useful information without making the individual feel too defensive. This is especially true of individuals who are not seeking help voluntarily, such as those who are mandated into treatment by the criminal justice system or those who been given an ultimatum by their boss or spouse to get clean or else (Schottenfield 1994).

Medical Evaluation. Next, you should inquire about the person's medical condition generally, and specifically as it relates to drug use as well. Unobtrusively observing the individual's overall physical appearance can be be a good preliminary screen of his medical state. You can look for telltale signs of drug use such as skin ulceration, track marks, abscesses, nasal discharge, and pallor. Of course, this cursory evaluation is no substitute for a comprehensive medical examination, but nevertheless your observations should be communicated to the person conducting the medical examination. Medical evaluation should assess the person's overall physical state and should also include laboratory testing for medical conditions related to drug use, as well as screening for infectious diseases such as tuberculosis, HIV infection, and hepatitis (American Psychiatric Association 1995a).

Social and Family Assessment. Chemical dependency brings adverse interpersonal and social consequences. Not only should you examine strained or broken family relationships and friendships, you should also try to determine whether family members or friends have contributed to, that is *enabled*, the person's use. As much as these individuals may want to see the client drug-free, their efforts to protect the client may unwittingly reinforce drug-related behavior. Shame, fear of estrangement, or of serious financial consequences can motivate significant others to cover up, make excuses, lie to employers, give drug money, provide comfortable living arrangements, or simply stick their heads in the sand or ignore the behavior, thereby fostering the very behavior they want to eliminate. Having said this, it is still better for the client to have a support system rather than having no support at all. Therefore, you should assess and point out the strengths of family members during the assessment (American Psychiatric Association 1995a,b).

A more complete picture of the client's drug use, where feasible, can be developed by assessment of the family members, who may be current or past users themselves. It is well-known, for example, that children of alcoholics (COAs) are four to six times more likely to be alcoholic during adulthood than non-COAs (Russell 1990). Influential family factors fall into two categories: *alcohol-specific family influences*, which increase the risk of alcoholism in COAs, and *alcohol nonspecific factors*, which may lead to alcoholism as well as other mental disorders (Ellis et al. 1997; see Table 3–1). In any case, knowledge of these aspects of the family environment can serve to clarify your client's substance-related behavior. Not only do high-risk clients have a biological and/or genetic susceptibility, they are also exposed to family influences characterized by excessive parental drinking, psychopathology, cognitive impairment, and aggression. Even under low levels of environmental stress, they are likely to experience emotional distress and other behavior problems, which can serve to trigger and maintain substance use (Ellis et al. 1997, McGue 1997).

Comorbidity. As you will learn in Chapter 8, many people with substance use disorders are likely to have another mental disorder as well (Kessler et al. 1994). Determining what the time sequences are that link the occurrence of chemical dependency and other mental disorders can help you better understand and manage your client's problems. Chemically dependent individuals with comorbid mental disorders present a special challenge for counselors, not the least of which is to recognize the presence and gravity of these mental disorders. You may need to get specialized clinical training in evaluating mental disorders, if you do not already have it, or have this facet of the assessment conducted by someone who does. To this end, there are several general interview outlines that you can use as a guide (American Psychiatric Association 1995b, MacKinnon and Yudofsky 1986).

Dual-diagnosis clients, as they are sometimes called, are especially difficult, because these individuals are coping with their mental disorders as well as their drug problems.

Table 3–1. Family risk factors affecting the development of psychopathology among children of alcoholics (COAs) compared with children of nonalcoholics

Risk Factor	Research Findings
Alcohol-Specific Family Influences[1]	
• Modeling of drinking behavior	COAs are more familiar with a wider range of alcoholic beverages at a younger age and develop alcohol-use schemas (i.e., experience-based beliefs) earlier.
• Alcohol expectancies	COAs have more positive expectancies regarding the reinforcing value of alcohol (i.e., they are more likely to expect that alcohol will make them feel good).
• Ethnicity and drinking practices	COAs from certain ethnic groups may be at increased risk for alcohol abuse because of the interaction between alcohol expectancies and ethnicity.
Alcohol-Nonspecific Family Influences[1]	
• Parent psychopathology	Certain subgroups of COAs are raised in families in which parents have psychiatric disturbances, such as antisocial personality disorder or depression, in addition to alcohol dependence.
• Socioeconomic status (SES)	COAs are more likely to come from lower SES homes in which the families are exposed to financial stress.
• General family psychopathology	Alcoholic families are characterized by low cohesion (i.e., little closeness among family members) high conflict, and poor problem-solving skills. COAs are more likely to come from broken homes.
• Family aggression/violence	COAs may be more likely to be the targets of physical abuse and to witness family violence.
• Parental cognitive impairment	COAs are more likely to be raised by parents with poorer cognitive abilities and in an environment lacking stimulation.

1. Alcohol-specific family influences selectively predict alcohol abuse and dependence, whereas alcohol-nonspecific family influences predict a variety of psychiatric problems, including alcoholism.
Source: Ellis, Zucker, and Fitzgerald (1997).

Many chemically dependent clients are self-medicators, meaning that they often use drugs to salve their emotional distress. Although stopping their drug use is supposed to make their lives better, it often makes them feel worse because it unmasks the symptoms of their mental disorder. On the other hand, some clients develop mental disorders because of their drug use and the occupational, social, and academic problems that it brings. It is not always easy to determine which came first, as with the proverbial chicken or the egg, but in either case ceasing drug use can lead to very unpleasant feelings.

Tanya was a 35-year-old woman with a long history of depression and chemical dependency. After shooting dope for about nine years, she kicked her habit, and then gradually began to drink. Within a year she was guzzling nearly a quart of cheap vodka most nights after work. As her medical problems mounted and she found it more and more difficult to hold a job, she decided to enter an inpatient rehabilitation program. While withdrawing from alcohol she experienced intense anxiety and panic attacks, and gradually slipped into a deep depression. Indeed, she was released from the rehab clean and sober, but deeply depressed. Once home, Tanya's depression worsened even long after her withdrawal symptoms had disappeared. Trials of antidepressant medication had little effect, and she seriously began to contemplate suicide. Three months after discharge from the rehab, Tanya was admitted to a psychiatric hospital and underwent a course of electroconvulsive therapy (shock treatments). Although she remained depressed, she was improved enough to be discharged, at which point she promptly began to drink heavily again. She reported feeling much less depressed for a while, but then began a recurrent pattern of heavy drinking, rehabilitation, depression, and a resumption of heavy drinking.

Mental Status Examination.   A formal evaluation of an individual's mental state can help to determine the extent to which symptoms of a mental disorder or drug use cause psychological impairment. A semi-structured interview technique to evaluate and record all aspects of mental, emotional, and behavioral functioning is the **mental status examination** (Leon et al. 1989, MacKinnon and Yudofsky 1986). During the exam, the clinician evaluates a range of psychological functions including:

- Appearance: clothing, grooming
- Behavior: facial expressions, posture, movements
- Attitude: cooperative, guarded, hostile
- Mood: sad, depressed, happy
- Perceptual disturbances: hallucinations, illusions
- Thought processes: abstract thinking, calculation
- Thought content: delusions, preoccupations
- Memory: retention of recent and past events
- Knowledge: knowledge of basic facts
- Orientation: awareness of time, place, and person
- Impulse control: ability to control emotions and behavior
- Judgment: ability to make appropriate social decisions
- Insight: awareness and understanding of self

3–2 Substance Use Assessment Instruments

Hundreds of instruments are available to assist counselors in the assessment of chemical dependency (Dennis 1998, National Institute on Alcoholism and Alcohol Abuse, 1995a).

Although most of these tests address alcoholism, they can be easily modified and applied for use in the assessment of problematic behavior with other drugs with just a little ingenuity. Table 3–2 outlines six types of assessment instruments, categorized according to their clinical purpose. They are: diagnosis, assessment of substance use behavior, treatment planning, screening, treatment and process assessment, and outcome evaluation.

Screening Instruments

As you know already, many individuals are in denial about their substance use. Indeed, some people will deny any use at all, whereas others underestimate the severity of their problem. Numerous studies have demonstrated that some problem substance users can benefit from brief interventions if only their problems can be quickly identified (Buchsbaum 1994). Chemical dependency counselors can use **screening instruments**, which are brief, easily administered questionnaires designed to identify problem alcohol or drug users. These assessment devices are invaluable not only in substance abuse programs, but also in primary care settings or in emergency rooms.

Validity.   A critical aspect of a screening instrument is its *validity*, that is, its accuracy. Validity is expressed in terms of sensitivity and specificity. *Sensitivity* refers to the percentage of all clients with a condition, such as alcoholism, who are correctly identified by the instrument. Thus, a sensitivity of 85 percent means that the screening instrument correctly identified 85 percent of people with alcoholism. The percentage of all clients without a condition who are correctly identified as not being alcoholic defines specificity. An instrument with a specificity of 90 percent accurately identifies 90 percent of nonalcoholics. Generally, as sensitivity increases, specificity decreases. You should probably be more concerned with an instrument's sensitivity, because in your work as a chemical dependency counselor it is important to identify all problem substance users, even if you obtain some false alarms (Cherpitel 1997).

Table 3–2. Chemical dependency assessment instruments

Screening	Identifies persons likely to meet diagnostic criteria for substance use disorder and for whom further assessment is warranted
Diagnosis	Provides formal substance use diagnosis or quantifies symptoms central to diagnosis
Substance use behavior	Assesses quantity, frequency, intensity, and pattern of substance use
Treatment planning	Administers instruments to assist the counselor in the development of client-specific treatment plans
Treatment/process assessment	Assists in understanding the process of treatment, including atmosphere, treatment structure, and immediate goals and outcomes of treatment
Outcome evaluation	Is designed to evaluate specific treatment effectiveness

Source: National Institute on Alcohol Abuse and Alcoholism (1995c).

In your counseling work you should be aware of the time frame for which substance use is assessed. Because some instruments are concerned primarily with current use, and others are designed to evaluate lifetime use, your choice of screening instruments should be guided by this consideration.

Types of Screening Instruments. The following is a brief description of some screening tests. The simplest screening device is one called the *Quantity/Frequency Questions*. Developed by the *National Institute on Alcohol Abuse and Alcoholism* (1995a), the **Quantity/ Frequency Questions** consists of three questions that screen for the presence of an alcohol use problem and quickly gauge the amount of alcohol consumed. The three questions are:

1. On average, how many days per week do you drink alcohol?
2. On a typical day when you drink, how many drinks do you have?
3. What is the maximum number of drinks you have had on any given occasion during the past month?

Men who consume more than fourteen drinks per week or more than four drinks per occasion are considered at risk for alcohol-related problems and require further assessment. In like manner, women who have more than seven drinks per week or more than three drinks per occasion are considered to be at risk.

The **CAGE** is a four-question instrument used to identify individuals who currently experience or have ever suffered from alcohol dependence (Ewing 1984). The CAGE asks if the person has ever

- Felt the need to **C**UT down on drinking,
- Been easily **A**NNOYED by others talking about the person's drinking,
- Felt **G**UILTY about drinking, or
- Had an **E**YE-OPENER, that is, taking a drink first thing in the morning to cure a hangover or calm the nerves.

Two or more affirmative responses indicate an alcohol problem and the need for further assessment.

The **Michigan Alcoholism Screening Test** (MAST) is a twenty-five-item screening instrument used in clinical and nonclinical settings (Selzer 1971). The *Brief MAST* (BMAST), a shortened version of the MAST, shows validity and sensitivity similar to the MAST (see Table 3–3; Pokorny et al. 1972). Scores of 6 or higher on the BMAST are indicative of a clinically significant alcohol problem.

The ten-question **Alcohol Use Disorders Identification Test** (AUDIT) is a test designed to identify problem drinkers in primary health-care settings. A score of 8 or more indicates a significant alcohol problem. The **TWEAK** is a relatively new five-item screening instrument consisting of two items from the CAGE, two from the MAST, and one new item (Russell et al. 1994). It assesses alcohol problems by asking clients about their

Table 3–3. The brief MAST

Questions	*Circle Correct Answers*	
1. Do You feel you are a normal drinker?	Yes (0)	No (2)
2. Do friends or relatives think you are a normal drinker?	Yes (0)	No (2)
3. Have you ever attended a meeting of Alcoholics Anonymous (A.A.)?	Yes (5)	No (0)
4. Have you ever lost friends or girlfriends/boyfriends because of drinking?	Yes (2)	No (0)
5. Have you ever gotten into trouble at work because of drinking?	Yes (2)	No (0)
6. Have you ever neglected your obligations, your family, or your work for two or more days in a row because you were drinking?	Yes (2)	No (0)
7. Have you ever had delirium tremens (DTs), severe shaking, heard voices, or seen things that weren't there after heavy drinking?	Yes (2)	No (0)
8. Have you ever gone to anyone for help about your drinking?	Yes (5)	No (0)
9. Have you ever been in a hospital because of drinking?	Yes (5)	No (0)
10. Have you ever been arrested for drunk driving or driving after drinking?	Yes (2)	No (0)

Source: National Institute on Alcoholism and Alcohol Abuse, 1995a.

- **T**OLERANCE to alcohol
- Whether friends or relatives **WORRIED** about the client's drinking in the past year
- **EYE-OPENERS**
- Whether the client ever experienced alcohol-related **AMNESIA**
- If the client ever felt the need to C(**K**)UT down on drinking

- Peer relationships
- Educational status (learning disabilities)
- Vocational status
- Social skills
- Leisure and recreation
- Aggressive behavior/delinquency

Several instruments have been developed for the evaluation of substance abuse/dependence for drugs other than alcohol. The **Drug Abuse Screening Test** (DAST-20) consists of twenty items about drug use and related problems to which the client answers yes or no. Each "yes" response gets a score of 1, and the degree of the drug problem is rated from low to substantial (Skinner 1987).

Assessment of Chemical dependency in Youth.   Screening tools have been developed for adolescents and teenagers as well as adults. (see Table 3–4). One example is the **Problem Oriented Screening Instrument for Teenagers** (POSIT) (Rahdert 1991). The POSIT consists of 139 yes/no items that screen for problems in ten areas of functioning including:

- Substance use/abuse
- Physical health
- Mental health
- Family relationships

In addition to its use in collecting baseline data about substance abuse, the POSIT follow up questionnaire can be used as a change measure. Scoring takes only a few minutes and does not require any special qualifications. The POSIT is useful in a wide variety of settings, including in- and outpatient programs, community service programs, case management systems, schools, and in the juvenile justice system.

Structured Interview Schedules

Screening instruments are useful as quick and easy ways to identify a client's alcohol and drug use. If your goal is to collect diagnostic information and determine addiction severity and related problems, however, you should consider a structured interview schedule, which is a comprehensive questionnaire that uses predetermined questions and standardized numerical scoring methods. Although structured interview schedules offer greater precision in drug assessment, they sacrifice some rapport between counselor and client (Shottenfeld 1994).

Table 3–4. Screening instruments for adolescent alcohol and drug use disorders

Screening Tool	Description
Adolescent Alcohol Involvement Scale	14–item questionnaire that examines current and past alcohol use, drinking context, effects of drinking, and perceptions about drinking
Adolescent Drinking Index	24–item screen that addresses alcohol problems related to psychological, physical, and social functioning as well as impaired control over drinking
Client Substance Index	15–item yes/no questionnaire to identify juveniles in court system who need additional assessment
Drug and Alcohol Problem Quick Screen	30–item questionnaire for use in pediatric settings
Drug Use Screening Inventory	159 true/false questions that evaluate alcohol/drug use and psychosocial functioning
Personal Experience Screening Questionnaire	40–item questionnaire that measures problem severity, alcohol/drug use history, and psychological problems

Source: Martin and Winters (1998).

Form 90 is a group of structured interview schedules designed to provide information about drinking and related variables (Miller 1996). Usually requiring less than forty-five minutes to complete, Form 90 yields a continuous retrospective record of drinking and related variables for a ninety-day period. For statistical purposes, drinking behavior is converted into a standard drink unit called *standard ethanol content* (SEC) which is 0.5 ounce (15 milliliter) of absolute alcohol. A simple way of calculating SEC units is to use the formula:

$$(X \text{ oz}) \times (\% \text{ alcohol}) \times (2) = Y \text{ standard drinks}$$

Using this formula, the interviewer can determine the amount of alcohol consumed for different types of alcoholic beverages. Some examples are:

- Beer — $(48 \text{ oz}) \times (.05) \times (2) = 4.8$ standard drinks
- Wine — $(16 \text{ oz}) \times (.12) \times (2) = 3.8$ standard drinks
- 80 proof spirits — $(6 \text{ oz}) \times (.40) \times (2) = 4.8$ standard drinks
- 86 proof spirits — $(6 \text{ oz}) \times (.43) \times (2) = 5.2$ standard drinks
- 100 proof spirits — $(6 \text{ oz}) \times (.50) \times (2) = 6.0$ standard drinks

Table 3–5 lists some types of statistics that can be derived from a Form 90 interview.

Despite the precision that Form 90 affords, the wide range of detailed information collected increases the risk of measurement errors. Before selecting Form 90, you must consider whether you need the degree of compelexity it presents. Furthermore, adminstration and scoring for this test require considerable training and supervision making use of Form 90 inappropriate for routine clinical use (Miller 1996).

One of the most popular assessment tools in the field of chemical dependency is the **Addiction Severity Index** (ASI), a 155–item semi-structured interview that evaluates alcohol and drug-related problem functioning (McLellan et al. 1980, 1992,). The ASI takes about forty to sixty minutes to complete and provides a severity rating for each of seven problem areas, including *medical, employment, alcohol, drugs, legal, family/social,* and *psychiatric.* Despite the widespread use of the ASI, there is insufficient data on its validity and reliability (consistency of scores). Preliminary studies, however, indicate that the ASI results correspond closely to data from independent patient charts and test data (McDermott et al. 1997).

A version of the ASI is available for the assessment of adolescent substance abuse. The *Teen Addiction Severity Index* (T-ASI) is a 126–item semi-structured interview that provides severity ratings in seven domains: psychoactive substance use, school or em-

Table 3–5. Form 90 statistics

Drinking Behavior

- Total number of SECs consumed
- Total number and percentage of abstinent days and drinking days
- Average number of SECs per drinking day
- Total number and percentage of days in specific consumption categories such as 0.1–2 SECs, 2.1–4.0 SECs, 4.1–6.0 SECs, over 6.0 SECs
- Peak intoxication level for each assessment period, or average intoxication level throughout the assessment period
- Time to events such as first drink or first heavy drinking day
- Longest span of abstinence

Related Variables

- Number of days and types of health-care utilization
- Days of additional treatment received for alcohol/drug problems
- Days of Twelve–Step group attendance and religious attendance
- Days employed or in school
- Lifetime and recent use of drugs other than alcohol
- Days of medication use.

Source: Miller (1996).

ployment status, family functioning, peer and social relationships, legal status, and psychiatric status (Kaminer et al. 1991). As with the ASI, its parent instrument, preliminary data on the validity and reliability of the T-ASI, indicate that it shows promise as an assessment instrument by differentiating between adolescents with and without substance-related disorders (Kaminer et al. 1993).

Although seldom used in practice, structured interview schedules are also available to determine coexisting mental disorders in chemically dependent individuals. Examples include:

- *Schedule for Affective Disorders and Schizophrenia*—SADS (Spitzer and Endicott 1978)
- *Anxiety Disorders Interview Schedule for DSM-IV-TR*—ADIS-IV (DiNardo et al. 1994)
- *Structured Clinical Interview for DSM-IV-TR Axis I and Axis II Disorders*—SCID—I & II (First et al. 1997a,b)

Assessment of Motivation for Change

In addition to instruments designed to evaluate alcohol and drug use and related prob-

lems, chemical dependency experts have endeavored to develop strategies to assess motivation for change. In this section you will examine views on the nature of motivation for change and learn about contemporary methods to assess it.

Historical View of Motivation for Change. Historically, motivation for change has been regarded as an absolute prerequisite for recovery. In this view, lack of motivation presents a significant obstacle to recovery. The popular conception is that motivation is an all-or-none phenomenon akin to *willpower*. You are either motivated or you are not; those who are not are judged to be in *denial* (Clancy 1964, DiCicco et al. 1978). Accordingly, chemically dependent individuals go from unmotivated to motivated by "bottoming out," a point at which the person has endured enough suffering to "want" to change.

Stages of Change. An alternative to the popular "willpower" perspective is the view that one's motivational state varies depending on the interplay of many factors within the person and the social environment (Janis and

Mann 1977). A model has been developed from this approach that contends that people progress through a series of stages as they start and maintain behavior change (DiClemente and Scott 1997, Prochaska and DiClemente 1982, 1986). As shown in Table 3–6, the stages are *precontemplation, contemplation, preparation, action,* and *maintenance*.

The SOCRATES. The **Stages Of Change Readiness and Treatment Eagerness Scale** (SOCRATES) is a nineteen–item assessment instrument that roughly corresponds to the stages-of-change model (Miller and Tonigan 1997). Rather than directly paralleling the five stages of change in the original model, however, SOCRATES yields three factors believed to underlie stages of change: *taking steps, recognition,* and *ambivalence*.

Still in the process of development, the SOCRATES does not evaluate all possible motivational factors, but does a reasonably good job of measuring a person's recognition of drinking problems, his uncertainty about drinking, and his change-related actions. SOCRATES scores can be used to predict compliance with change efforts, to begin discussion of motivation for change with clients, and as a barometer of the effects of therapeutic intervention on the factors that underlie change (Miller and Tonigan 1997).

3–3 Psychological Testing

You learned earlier in this chapter that comprehensive assessment of the chemically dependent person requires an evaluation of co-existing mental disorders as well as alcohol and drug-related problems. **Psychological tests** can assist in these determinations because they are instruments designed to provide insight into mental, emotional, and behavioral functioning.

There are several reasons to include psychological testing in chemical dependency assessment. *First,* test results can provide information about psychological functioning that underlies alcohol/drug abuse. *Second,* abnormal personality characteristics and mental disorders often follow alcohol/drug use. In either case, these factors can pose sig-

Table 3–6. Stages of change

1. *Precontemplation*: A state of unawareness of a problem and any need for change.
2. *Contemplation*: An increase in awareness, which stimulates the individual to weigh the pros and cons of change.
3. *Preparation*: During this stage, the person has already weighed the pros and cons, has leaned toward change, and begins to prepare for it.
4. *Action*: This stage is characterized by the initiation of steps toward change.
5. *Maintenance*: Assuming that the person's actions have successfully led to change, this stage is marked by efforts to prevent relapse or a return to problematic behavior.

nificant impediments to successful treatment of the chemically dependent person. Thus, knowledge of these factors through psychological testing, and their subsequent modification, can improve treatment outcome. *Third,* pressures imposed by a changing health-care delivery environment and local, state, and federal legislation and program-funding formulas have resulted in the call for greater accountability from chemical dependency treatment providers and health-care providers in general (Dennis 1998). More precise assessment can be accomplished by psychological testing, which can provide additional information about psychological functioning that might be difficult to obtain from a typical alcohol- and drug-specific evaluation.

A variety of psychological tests are available to chemical dependency counselors who have the qualifications necessary to administer, score, and interpret them. They are classified as *self-report inventories, projective tests, intelligence tests,* and *neuropsychological tests*. In this section you will learn about the fundamentals of psychological testing and see a sample of specific psychological tests.

Characteristics of Psychological Tests

A psychological test is only as useful as its construction permits it to be. Before any psychological test is used in clinical practice, it undergoes a rigorous process of standardization, and its validity and reliability are determined.

Standardization, Validity, and Reliability. *Standardization* means that test designers have explicitly specified the conditions under which the test is administered and scored. Standardization also means that *norms* have been established, meaning that average or typical scores are used as comparison standards for results from other individuals who take the test.

Validity is a measure of test accuracy. A valid test is one that actually measures what it claims to measure. For example, a test with good *construct validity* is one whose scores accurately reflect a particular theoretical concept or construct, such as self-esteem, impulse control, or psychological defensiveness. Good *predictive validity* is demonstrated by a test whose scores accurately predict some future event, such as the likelihood of alcohol/drug use, criminal activity, or aggression. Be aware that validity is not absolute; tests show different degrees of validity. The use of psychological tests in the arena of chemical dependency assessment, as in any area of clinical practice, should be restricted to those tests with the highest validity.

Consistency of test scores is known as *reliability.* Many psychological characteristics, such as intelligence and personality traits, are believed to be relatively stable over time. Therefore, psychological tests designed to measure these characteristics should demonstrate high *test–retest reliability.* This means that repeated administrations of the same test should yield similar scores.

Limitations of Psychological Tests. Psychological tests do not tell us everything we need to know about abnormal behavior; they are not like blood tests or x-rays that can objectively define illness. Furthermore, data from ethnic and cultural minorities has not yet been adequately incorporated into test construction. Thus, psychological tests should not be used alone in the assessment of chemical dependency. Instead, you should consider them as just one piece of the puzzle.

Self-Report Inventories

Paper-and-pencil questionnaires that ask people to report about aspects of their psycho-logical functioning are known as **self-report inventories**. The most popular is the **Minnesota Multiphasic Personality Inventory** (MMPI) which consists of 550 statements to which the person responds "true" or "false" (Anastasi 1988, Hathaway and McKinley 1940). A restandarized version of the MMPI in current use is the *MMPI-2* (Butcher 1989). Statements that resemble those in the MMPI are shown below.

- There are times when I feel like cursing.
- I should be punished when I do something wrong.
- I am a very nervous person.
- I frequently speak to strangers in stores or buses.
- Sexual matters are repulsive to me.

The subject responds "true" or "false" to each statement depending on whether he believes the statement mainly applies to him and a clinical profile is generated. Table 3–7 provides a description of the MMPI-2 validity and clinical scales. Although the MMPI and MMPI-2 have been used extensively in chemical dependency assessment packages, no specific profile emerges to describe the typical alcoholic or drug addict. Nevertheless, an MMPI profile gives valuable information about many aspects of personality, including emotions, motivations, attitudes, and interpersonal functioning, and permits clinicians to identify personality disorders, family problems, health disturbances, and social maladjustment. Besides its ability to help a clinician gain insight into personality functioning and make diagnoses, the MMPI can be a powerful tool for predicting future behavior and in selecting treatments (Anastasi 1988, Tarter et al. 1991).

Most psychological tests must address the possibility that the individual being tested is responding dishonestly or is too impaired to understand the statements. This is particularly important in chemical dependency assessment, inasmuch as people with alcohol or drug problem are likely not only to withhold information altogether, but also to underreport the magnitude of their problems, or exaggerate them. Not surprisingly, research has

Table 3–7. Description of MMPI clinical scales

Scale Label	High Score Description
Validity Scales	
? Cannot say	Number of questions unanswered; indicates test-taker's uncooperativeness
L Lie	Dishonest responding, suggests person who is trying to look good
F Infrequency	Magnification of symptoms, means tendency to exaggerate
K Subtle defensiveness	Willingness to admit to problems, not willing to divulge information
Clinical Scales	
1. Hs—Hypochondriasis	Bodily complaints, vague physical complaints, whiny, demanding
2. D—Depression	Negative outlook, low self-esteem, depressed mood
3. Hy—Hysteria	Physical symptoms used to escape from responsibilities, dependent, self-centered, dramatic
4. Pd—Psychopathic Deviate	Antisocial style, rebellious, impulsive, alcohol/drug use
5. MF—Masculinity–femininity	Male vs. female personality features. High scores-Males: sensitive, passive, feminine; Females: masculine, rough, unemotional
6. Pa—Paranoia	Mistrust of others: suspicious, sullen, oversensitive, jealous, delusional
7. Pt—Psychasthenia	Tension over obsessive ideas, worried, anxious, tense, phobic, self-doubting
8. Sc—Schizophrenia	Suspicion and alienation, detached, bizarre thoughts, erratic moods
9. Ma—Hypomania	Elevated mood, energetic, agitated, sociable, grandiose
10. Si—Social introversion	Introverted, shy, sensitive, overcontrolled.

Sources: Graham (1990); Greene (1980).

identified three MMPI-2 response styles with alcoholics: *straightforward, defensive,* and *exaggerated.* Furthermore, these response styles remain consistent across different tests and alcohol screening instruments (Isenhart and Silversmith 1997). The special relevance of this finding is that most psychological tests do not have built-in validity checks, and alcohol/drug screening instruments never do. Therefore, it may be advisable to include an MMPI-2 in the assessment of chemical dependency not only because of the clinical information it yields, but also because a determination of response style can be generalized to instruments that do not measure it.

Many other self-report inventories, such as the *Clinical Analysis Questionnaire* (CAQ) (Krug 1980) and the *Millon Clinical Multiaxial Inventory* (MCMI) (Millon 1986), are available to clinicians today, but their popularity and clinical usefulness do not approach that of the MMPI. Self-report questionnaires like the *Symptom Checklist-90* (SCL-90) (Derogatis 1994), and the *Beck Depression Inventory* (BDI) (Beck 1978) are quite popular because they can be completed quickly and are relatively easy to score. The **SCL-90** is particularly useful to chemical dependency counselors because it is a ninety-item self-report inventory which reflects psychological symptom patterns across nine dimensions: *somatization, obsessive-compulsive, interpersonal sensitivity, depression, anxiety, hostility, phobic anxiety, paranoid ideation,* and *psychoticism.* In addition, the SCL-90 yields global measures of symptomatology and psychological distress.

Projective Tests

Instruments that measure aspects of personality functioning by asking subjects to interpret ambiguous stimuli are **projective tests**. The rationale of these tests is based on the *projective hypothesis*, which states that people express attitudes, emotions, and impulses in their interpretation of ambiguous stimuli.

Clinicians who subscribe to the projective hypothesis claim that projective test data are more likely to reveal unconscious processes and that these tests are less susceptible to faking than self-report inventories. Many critics argue that self-report inventories do not evaluate hidden or unconscious aspects of psychological functioning. Therefore, projective tests can be used instead of or as an adjunct to self-report inventories. There are five traditional types of projective tests: *word association tests, sentence completion tests, drawing tests, inkblot tests*, and *picture story tests*.

The Rorschach Inkblot Test.   Perhaps the most popular and best-known projective test is the **Rorschach inkblot test**, which consists of ten cards with a symmetrical inkblot on each card (Rorschach 1942). Five inkblots are black with shades of gray, two have bright red highlights, and the remaining three inkblots are multicolored. Subjects view the cards one at a time and they are asked what each represents. Following the presentation of each card, the examiner inquires about which parts of each inkblot the person responded to and allows the subject an opportunity to elaborate responses (Anastasi 1988).

There are several Rorschach scoring systems and some are standardized, such as the *Comprehensive System* (Exner 1986). The most popular interpretations strategies focus on:

- Location: the part of the blot that the person responded to
- Determinants: Including responses to color, shading, and perceived movement
- Content: includes human and animal figures, inanimate objects, blood, sexual objects, and symbols

For example, responses to "color" suggest emotional expression, and perceiving "human movement" indicates a rich imagination and fantasy life (Anastasi 1988).

The Thematic Apperception Test.   Another type of projective test is the *picture story test*, which has subjects view a picture and then tell a story about it. The **Thematic Apperception**

Test (TAT) is a popular picture story test consisting of nineteen black-and-white sketches and one blank card (Murray 1943). The subject is asked to make up a story that fits each picture and tell the examiner what led up to it, what the characters are doing, thinking, and feeling, and what the final outcome will be. Scoring systems generally involve assessing personality by analyzing the story's content for needs and environmental obstacles to need satisfaction. For example, the subject might state that someone is being criticized or rejected, expressing a need for affiliation (Anastasi 1988).

Intelligence and Neuropsychological Tests

Intelligence, the ability to learn and behave adaptively, is a fundamental aspect of all mental and behavioral functioning. *Intelligence testing*, therefore, is an important focus of psychological testing. However, its application to assessment of chemical dependency is usually within the broader framework of **neuropsychological testing**, procedures to detect and measure brain damage and cognitive disability (Keefe 1995). As you learned in earlier chapters, prolonged alcohol and/or drug use has deleterious effects on brain tissue, placing chemically dependent individuals at increased risk for cognitive disability.

Comprehensive neuropsychological assessment can be accomplished by the use of neuropsychological test batteries such as the *Halstead-Reitan Neuropsychological Test Battery*, which consists of an MMPI; intelligence tests, such as the *Wechsler Scales*; and individual tests of attention; concentration; sensory, motor, and perceptual abilities, and language processing (Reitan and Wolfson 1985). Another battery that affords fuller assessment of neurological dysfunction and more precise identification of behavioral deficits and brain damage localization is the *Luria-Nebraska Neuropsychological Test Battery*. This is a 269–item battery that measures sensory and motor function, as well as speech, reading, writing, arithmetic, and memory (Golden et al. 1985).

Neuropsychological test batteries are excellent tools to use to identify cognitive disability, but the testing procedure is long, arduous, and prohibitively expensive in chemical dependency assessment. In their stead, alternative screening techniques have been developed. The **Neuropsychological Impairment Scale** (NIS) is a fifty-item self-report scale that assesses complaints indicative of brain damage, such as forgetting, bumping into things, and learning difficulties (O'Donnell et al. 1984a,b). Studies show that for alcoholics higher scores on the NIS are associated with poorer performances on neuropsychological tests. However, higher scores are more indicative of anxiety and depression than neurological impairment. Thus, the NIS and other self-report impairment inventories should be used as a supplement to other measures rather than as the exclusive means of identifying neuropsychological impairment. Suspicion or evidence of neurological impairment should prompt you to refer the client to a neuropsychologist for specialized testing (Errico et al. 1997).

3–4 Laboratory Analysis

The accuracy of self-reported alcohol/drug use can be cross-checked by the **drug testing** or laboratory examination of biological specimens for psychoactive substances or their *metabolic by-products*, that is, chemicals that result from the body's breakdown of a drug. In this section you will examine the fundamentals of drug testing, its applications, and its limitations (Cone 1997, Harrision and Hughes 1997).

History and Rationale of Drug Testing

Drug testing is a very recent phenomenon. It originated as part of the pathology services in which hospital laboratories tested biological specimens to determine cause in cases of drug overdose or drug-related deaths, but early methods were rather crude and nonspecific. As alcohol and drug use became a mounting health and social problem, methodologies improved and were more frequently geared toward testing for a wide range of specific drugs (Verebey and Buchan 1997).

With methodological refinements, drug testing became part of chemical dependency assessment and treatment. Increasingly, laboratory analyses were used to monitor abstinence in patients who completed formal rehabilitation programs. Since the 1980s, employee drug testing has become a mainstay in the federal government, the military, and in private-sector jobs. Indeed, many companies post their drug-testing policies conspicuously for all to see in an attempt to discourage would-be applicants who use alcohol and/or drugs. The latest development is in forensic applications, where laboratory results are used in the criminal justice system to help prove culpability or to remove a person from criminal suspicion (Cook et al. 1997, Mieczkowski and Newel 1997, Miller et al. 1997, Verebey and Buchan 1997).

The rationale for drug testing should be fairly obvious to you by now. It can be advantageous for the welfare of the abuser when it leads to treatment, as well as for society insofar as it also allows for the protection of innocent people. Also, drug testing can be a powerful tool to validate information gained from other sources. Remember that a significant obstacle in the assessment of chemical dependency is the client's reluctance to to disclose information concerning drug use. Fear of untoward legal, social, occupational, or academic consequences, along with the client's drug-induced cognitive and emotional state, are major factors that can affect the accuracy of self-reports during an interview and often lead to blatant denial. Although the alcohol and drug use information derived from screening instruments is collected more systematically and is readily quantifiable, it is also subject to self-report bias.

Chemical dependency is not confined only to skid row bums. It can afflict doctors, lawyers, teachers, amateur and professional athletes, bus drivers, jet pilots, bankers, stockbrokers, police officers, firefighters, and others from any walk of life. A moment's reflection should be enough to convince you that even though it brings up difficult issues in civil liberties, testing people in these positions is not only important for the individuals involved but for the welfare of society as a whole (Verebey and Buchan 1997).

Drugs Tested and Characteristics of Drug-Testing Methods

The selection of drugs to be tested for depends on several considerations, including the types of drugs commonly abused, new trends in drug use, and available methods of laboratory analysis. This section considers the types of abused drugs that are tested for and methods of laboratory analysis.

Drugs Tested. The *Substance Abuse and Mental Health Services Administration of the Department of Health and Human Services* (DHHS/SAMHSA) requires the testing of five drugs in order for laboratories to be accredited by their *National Laboratory Certification Program* (Substance Abuse and Mental Health Services administration 1994, 1988). These *Panel I* drugs are amphetamines, cannabinoids, cocaine, opioids, and phencyclidine. *Panel II* consists of drugs that are commonly abused, but for which testing is not required by DHHS/SAMHSA. Panel II drugs are barbiturates, benzodiazepines, propoxyphene (spanish fly), methadone, methaqualone, and ethanol. Some drugs are not routinely tested. These *Panel III* drugs include LSD, fentanyl, psilocybin, MDMA, MDA, and the designer drugs.

Drug Testing Methods. Drug testing is only as useful as its ability to detect the presence of drugs or metabolites of the parent drug in a biological specimen. This aspect of evaluating a drug test's effectiveness is known as *validity* (Gorodetzky 1977). Chemical factors such as *sensitivity*, the smallest amount of detectable drug, and *specificity*, how selective the test is, can influence test results. Dose, time, and route of drug administration, as well as individual differences in metabolism, and rates of absorption and excretion are additional factors that can affect test outcome. Thus, it is recommended that the initial confirmation of test results be corroborated by having greater validity methods, especially in cases of potential litigation (Cone 1997). A variety of drug-testing methods are available for commercial use (see Table 3–8). Because the technical details of these methods are far beyond the purview of this book, the interested reader should consult a current pharmacology textbook for more information.

Drug-testing methods can be broadly categorized as screening methods and confirmation methods. **Screening methods** are commercially available tests that are inexpensive and easy to perform. Methods such as *thin-layer chromatography* and *immunoassays* are employed to eliminate specimens that contain no drugs, or drug levels that fall below the cutoff concentrations. Their drawback is that they sacrifice sensitivity and specificity. **Confirmation methods** include *gas-liquid chromatography* and *gas chromatography-mass spectrometry*. They are considerably more expensive and labor

Table 3–8. Types of drug tests

Thin-layer chromatography (TLC)	Qualitative method of drug detection based on migration and color of spots on TLC; high specificity but poor sensitivity
Immunoassay	Antibodies used to seek out specific drugs in biological fluids; specificity and sensitivity depend on particular type of assay and specific manufacturer
Gas liquid chromatography	Technique that separates molecules by migration; high validity, sensitivity and specificity
Gas chromatography–Mass spectrotometry	Detects molecule fragments or breakage products by electron bombardment of molecules; high validity, sensitivity, and specificity

Sources: Cone (1997).

intensive than screening methods, but they generally yield results with high specificity and sensitivity. The choice of method should depend on the relative advantages or disadvantages of each method, the purpose for which the testing is being conducted, and the type of drug being analyzed (see Table 3–9) (Cone 1997).

Types of Biological Specimens Analyzed

Drug testing can be conducted with urine, saliva, sweat, hair, semen, perspiration, and fecal samples, but the latter three are infrequently used. Just as each laboratory method has advantages and limitations, so too do each of these substances (Cone 1997). The specimen one chooses to analyze should be selected with its relative advantages and limitations in mind (see Table 3–9).

Urine. Urine is produced continuously by the kidneys. After the kidneys reabsorb essential substances, they excrete excess water, waste, and organic and inorganic compounds in the urine. Smoking or intravenously injecting a drug results in instantaneous excretion, but oral administration leads to a delay of several hours. Ordinarily, the highest concentrations of a drug or its metabolites are found in urine samples within about six hours and most of these are excreted within forty-eight hours. Generally, abused drugs are detectable in urine for only two to four days since last use, but the actual time frame varies depending on the type of drug, the dose, frequency of use, test sensitivity, and route of administration. However, there are many exceptions. Long-acting barbiturates and benzodiazepines can be detected for up to thirty days. Chronic use of marijuana or PCP also can extend detection times to thirty days (Cone 1997).

A considerable drawback in urine testing is that many drug users will attempt to escape detection by drinking large amounts of water or herbal teas. To counter this, many laboratories will also test for concentrations of *creatinine*, a protein by-product of muscle metabolism. Because creatinine levels are fairly constant, abnormally low concentrations present a "red flag" suggestive of diluted urine and can justify additional testing. The possibility of urine dilution and other methods of sample contamination make it important that a "chain of custody" be followed and documented, meaning that all samples must be carefully collected and protected to minimize false positives as well as false negatives (Cone 1997).

Table 3–9. Comparison of usefulness of urine, saliva, sweat, and hair as a biological matrix for drug detection

Biological Matrix	Drug Detection Time	Major Advantages	Major Disadvantages	Primary Use
Urine	2–4 days	Mature technology; on-site methods available; established cutoffs	Only detects recent use	Detection of recent drug use
Saliva	12–24 hours	Easily obtainable; samples "free" drug fraction; parent drug presence	Short detection time; oral drug contamination; collection methods influence pH and saliva/plasma ratios; only detects recent use; new technology	Linking positive drug test to behavior and performance impairment
Sweat	1–4 weeks	Cumulative measure of drug use	High potential for environmental contamination; new technology	Detection of recent drug use
Hair	Months	Long-term measure of drug use; similar sample can be recollected	High potential for environmental contamination; new technology	Detection of drug use in recent past (1–6 months)

Source: Cone (1997).

Saliva. Saliva is a glandular secretion consisting of approximately 90 percent water and 10 percent electrolytes, proteins, and hormones. Drugs enter saliva by several methods, the most important being passive diffusion from the blood. Ethanol is an exception. Because ethanol is a small molecule, it enters saliva via a filtration process. In any case, testing saliva offers some advantages over testing urine, inasmuch as it is easy to collect, has a less objectionable nature, and contains a higher concentration of the parent drug.

Despite its apparent advantages, however, drug testing using saliva carries some significant *limitations*. *First*, drugs that are taken orally, snorted, or smoked can contaminate saliva and lead to inaccurate findings. *Second*, the drug-detection time frame with saliva is short compared to urine. Most signs of drugs are gone from saliva within twelve to twenty-four hours. This prevents gathering much information about historical drug use, but does aid in the detection of recent drug use in cases of intoxicated automobile drivers and accident victims, and when testing workers before they engage in hazardous activities (Cone 1997).

Sweat. Sweat is a watery fluid distibuted across the skin surface. Ninety-nine percent of it is water, and most of the remainder is salt. The mechanism of drug entry into sweat is unclear, but passive diffusion from blood is the most likely route. Many psychoactive drugs can be identified in sweat, including amphetamines, cocaine, methadone, methamphetamine, morphine, and PCP. However, sweat analysis is not as popular as other specimen testing because of large individual differences in sweat production and a paucity of suitable sweat-collection methods.

A relatively recent advance in sweat testing is the *sweat patch.* This device consists of an adhesive on a thin, transparent film of surgical dressing, to which an absorbent pad is attached. Sweat that has saturated the pad over several days is then collected and analyzed. Sweat-patch testing for drugs such as cocaine and heroin shows that they can be detected within one hour following use and that their concentrations peak in twenty-four hours (Cone 1977, Cone et al. 1994).

Advantages of the sweat patch include high subject acceptability, low incidence of allergic reactions, and the ability to monitor drug use over several weeks. Furthermore, the patch is tamper-proof. It is designed to be used only once and cannot be removed and then reapplied after a drug-taking episode. On the negative side, there is high intersubject variability in sweat production as well as the possibility of environmental contamination of the patch (Cone 1997, Cone et al. 1994).

Hair. One of the most promising but controversial means of drug testing is hair analysis, which typically involves cutting locks of hair from the scalp. Less frequently, hair is cut from the arm or pubic area. Numerous laboratories offer drug-testing services, and some offer commercial services.

Besides the ease with which a specimen can be obtained, the major advantage of hair testing lies in the fact that the parent drug is often found in higher concentrations in hair than in urine. Furthermore, detection time for many drugs can exceed ninety days. This affords a much broader window of drug use than can be obtained with any other detection method.

Interpretation of the results of hair analysis is problematic, however, for the following reasons (Harrison and Hughes 1997).

- The mechanisms by which drugs enter the hair are unknown.
- The possibility exists that environmental agents or another person's drug-laden sweat could contaminate hair, leading to false positives.
- The relationship between drug dose and concentrations of the drug in hair has not been demonstrated.
- Substantial evidence exists that some drugs, such as cocaine, accumulate more in black hair compared to brown or blonde hair. Such findings may result in ethnic bias.
- There is considerable variability in the degree to which different drugs are absorbed in hair. For example, cocaine readily binds to hair (especially black hair), while marijuana is much less concentrated in hair.

- For opioids and cannabinoids, the results from hair and urine analysis often do not match up.

These problems are not necessarily unresolvable. Despite some shortcomings and cautions related to unresolved issues, hair analysis is being used increasingly in many domains, including private industry, the courts, police departments, and by the FBI. Although the FBI does not routinely employ hair testing, it is used when there is other information to suggest drug use (especially cocaine use) and when the results can remove a person from suspicion of a crime (Miller et al. 1997). Hair analysis has also found its way into schools, as schools attempt to ensure that their students will function in a drug-free environment (Wren 1999).

In conclusion, the accuracy of self-reported alcohol and/or drug use can be cross-checked by drug testing. Despite many limitations and legal issues, drug testing is a promising and useful adjunct in the clinical assessment of substance use.

Summary

3–1

The cornerstone of substance abuse and dependence assessment is the clinical interview. A significant stumbling block in the assessment of chemical dependency is the client's reluctance to to disclose information concerning drug use. The unstructured interview is a flexible, nonsystematic approach in which clients are free to discuss what is important to them and the counselor does not necessarily cover specific topics or ask predetermined questions. The structured interview is a systematic method used to gather significant current and historical information concerning drug use and related problems. The first step involves gathering and identifying demographic information, followed by attempts to specify the problems that prompted the person to come in for a consultation. A useful interview outline involves investigation of nine broad areas of inquiry, including the type

and quantity of drug and frequency of use, intoxication effects, tolerance and withdrawal symptoms, history of attempts to curb or stop use, adverse medical consequences, related interpersonal/social problems, work- or academic-related consequences, legal problems, and psychological disturbances. You should assume a straightforward, nonjudgmental approach by creating an atmosphere of helping. Medical conditions should be evaluated. Social/family evaluation should investigate strained or broken family relationships and friendships, enabling, and drug use in family members. Clients should also be evaluated for psychiatric comorbidity. Mental status examination is a semi-structured interview technique to evaluate and record all aspects of mental, emotional, and behavioral functioning.

3–2

Hundreds of instruments are available to assist counselors in the assessment of chemical dependency. They can assist in diagnosis, assessment of substance use behavior, treatment planning, screening, treatment and process assessment, and outcome evaluation. Screening instruments are brief, easily administered questionnaires designed to identify problem alcohol or drug users. Structured interview schedules, comprehensive questionnaires that use predetermined questions and standardized numerical scoring methods, allow the counselor to collect diagnostic information and determine addiction severity and related problems. The Stages of Change Readiness and Treatment Eagerness Scale (SOCRATES) is used to assess motivation for change and corresponds to the stages of change model.

3–3

Psychological tests are instruments designed to provide insight into mental, emotional, and behavioral functioning that may not be attainable with interviews. Test results can provide information about psychological functioning that underlies alcohol/drug abuse or is a consequence of drug use, and enhance the accountability of chemical dependency treatment providers. Psychological tests include self-report inventories like the MMPI-2, projective tests such as the Rorschach and TAT, intelligence tests, and neuropsychological tests such as the Halstead-Reitan and Luria-Nebraska. Although useful in chemical dependency assessment, psychological tests are limited in their objectivity and are not sensitive enough to racial, ethnic, and cultural factors.

3–4

The accuracy of self-reported alcohol/drug use can be cross-checked by the drug testing or laboratory examination of biological specimens for psychoactive substances or their metabolic by-products. Panel I drugs include amphetamines, cannabinoids, cocaine, opioids, and phencyclidine, and these are routinely tested for. Panel II consists of drugs that are commonly abused, but for which testing is not required by DHHS/SAMHSA. They are barbiturates, benzodiazepines, propoxyphene (spanish fly), methadone, methaqualone, and ethanol. Some drugs are not routinely tested. These Panel III drugs include LSD, fentanyl, psilocybin, MDMA, MDA, and the designer drugs. Drug-screening methods such as thin-layer chromatography and immunoassays are employed to eliminate specimens that contain no drugs or that have drug levels below the cutoff concentrations. Confirmation methods include gas-liquid chromatography and gas chromatography–mass spectrometry, and they yield results with high specificity and sensitivity. The choice of method should depend on the relative advantages or disadvantages of each method, the purpose for which the testing is being conducted, and the type of drug being analyzed. Drug testing can be conducted with urine, saliva, sweat, and hair. The choice of which specimen to analyze should be made with their relative advantages and limitations in mind.

Terms to Remember

Addiction Severity Index
Alcohol Use Disorders Identification Test
CAGE
clinical interview
confirmation methods
Drug Abuse Screening Test
drug testing
Form 90
mental status examination
Michigan Alcoholism Screening Test
Minnesota Multiphasic Personality Inventory
Neuropsychological Impairment Scale
neuropsychological testing
Problem Oriented Screening Instrument for
  Teenagers
projective tests
psychological tests
Quantity/Frequency Questions
Rorschach inkblot test
screening instruments
screening methods
self-report inventories
social desirability hypothesis
Stages of Change Readiness and Treatment
  Eagerness Scale
structured interview
Thematic Apperception Test
TWEAK
unstructured interview

Suggested Readings

Anastasi, A. (1988). *Psychological Testing*, 6th ed. New York: Macmillan.

Cherpitel, C. J. (1997). Brief screening instruments for alcoholism. In *Alcohol Health and Research World* 21:348–351 (NIH Publication No. 98–3466). Washington, DC: US Government Printing Office.

Cone E. J. (1997). New developments in biological measures of drug prevalence. In *The Validity of Self-Reported Drug Use: Improving the Accuracy of Survey Estimates*, ed. L. Harrison and A. Hughes, pp. 108–130. National Institute on Drug Abuse (NIDA Research Monograph 167). Rockville, MD: National Institutes of Health.

DiClemente, C. C., and Scott, C. W. (1997). Stages of change: interactions with treatment compliance and involvement. In *Beyond the Therapeutic Alliance: Keeping the Drug-Dependent Individual in Treatment* (National Institute on Drug Abuse Monograph 165). Rockville, MD: National Institute on Drug Abuse.

Wren, C. S. (1999). Hair testing by schools intensifies drug debate. *New York Times*, June 14, p. A16.

Diagnosis and Types of Chemical Dependency

Chapter Outline

Learning Objectives

After completing this chapter you should be able to:

1. Cite major findings from the National Household Survey on Drug Abuse.
2. Distinguish between substance abuse and substance dependence using *DSM-IV-TR* criteria.
3. Present prevalence data regarding substance abuse and substance dependence based on the NCS survey and the National Household Survey on Drug Abuse.
4. Describe withdrawal syndromes.
5. Outline the course of substance abuse.
6. Describe the course of substance dependence.
7. Explain Jellinek's and Blane's typologies of alcoholism and discuss their relevance to

chemical dependency assessment and treatment.

8. Distinguish between the typologies of Cloninger, Zucker, and Babor.
9. Present an integrative view of typologies.

One purpose of chemical dependency assessment is to organize relevant information into a psychiatric diagnosis. Notwithstanding criticisms of diagnostic classification systems, diagnosis permits the counselor to make predictions about future behavior and to consider treatment options that might otherwise be difficult to ascertain. Aside from formal diagnoses, the organization of drug-relevant information can also be used to determine patterns of alcohol and/or drug use that integrate information about symptom picture, cause, course, and outcome.

In this chapter we turn our attention to the diagnosis and patterns of chemical dependency. You will learn about the prevalence of drug use, the classification and prevalence of drug-related problems, and the types of abnormal behavioral patterns exhibited by people who abuse drugs.

4–1 The Scope of Psychoactive Drug Use

In this section you will learn about the scope of psychoactive drug use. The kinds of drugs people use and the prevalence rates for different drugs will be examined.

Epidemiology of Psychoactive Drug Use

The morning mug of coffee, the cigarette break, and the "Pepsi" pick-me-up are just a few examples of drug use in everyday life. As hazardous to health as nicotine and caffeine are, more to the point of this textbook are the use of alcohol and illicit drugs, along with the nonmedical use of prescription drugs. The widespread use of psychoactive drugs is a fact of life in American society today and, for many, a significant source of impairment in everyday functioning.

One way to measure psychoactive drug use is to conduct epidemiological studies; **epidemiology** is the study of the distribution of disorders in the general population. Applied

originally to specific medical conditions, epidemiology is now also used to ascertain estimates of drug use and drug-related problems. Be aware that epidemiology tells nothing about causes, but only informs us about prevalence—about how many use or are affected by these substances.

One important epidemiological statistic is the **prevalence rate** or the percentage of a population or group that has a particular disorder. Applied to the subject of drug use, *prevalence* refers to the percentage of the U.S. population that has ever used a psychoactive drug. Epidemiological studies estimate prevalence rates by carefully surveying subjects about their drug use, but, as you learned in Chapter 3, individuals are reluctant to admit to using drugs. This means that prevalence rates are estimates of drug use rather than exact indications. In addition, epidemiological studies on drug use typically exclude data from military personnel, homeless people, and others who are institutionalized in jails and hospitals. Prevalence studies, therefore, probably underestimate the scope of the problem. Despite their shortcomings, however, numerous prevalence studies reveal that the use of alcohol and other drugs is alarmingly high.

The National Household Survey

The most comprehensive survey of drug use in the United States is the *National Household Survey on Drug Abuse* (NHS), which annually studies alcohol and drug use in U.S. household residents 12 years of age and older (Substance Abuse and Mental Health Services Administration 1999). The NHS offers a wealth of information about drug and alcohol use, some of which is summarized below.

- An estimated 13.6 million Americans were current users of illicit drugs in 1998 and 113 million were current users of alcohol, meaning that they had used an illicit drug at least once in the past thirty days (see Figures 4–1, 4–2).
- Marijuana is the most commonly used illicit drug (see Figure 4–3).
- Regarding age, males between the ages of 18

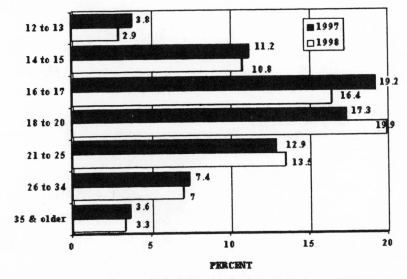

Figure 4–1. Past month use of any illicit drug by age, 1997–1998
Source: Substance Abuse and Mental Health Services Administration (1999).

and 20 years of age show the highest rates of current illicit drug use (see Figure 4–4).
- Alcohol use is also highest among 18- to 20-year-old males.
- The rate of current illicit drug use is slightly higher among blacks (8.2 percent) than it is for whites (6.1 percent) and Hispanics (6.1 percent).
- Whites have the highest rates of alcohol use whereas alcohol use is more moderate in blacks than in other racial/ethnic groups.

- Males have higher rates of both illicit drug use and alcohol use than do females.

The Monitoring the Future Study

Another angle on drug-use prevalence is to study drug use in teenagers. A major ongoing study called the *Monitoring the Future Study* (MFS) is being conducted by the University of Michigan's Institute for Social Research (Johnston et al. 1999). In this project, thousands

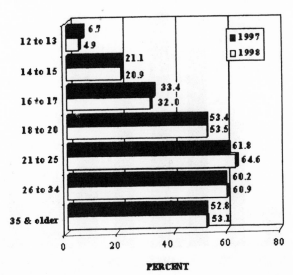

Figure 4–2. Past month use of alcohol by age, 1997–1998
Source: Substance Abuse and Mental Health Services Administration (1999).

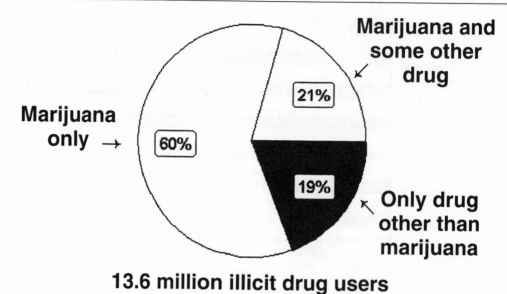

13.6 million illicit drug users

Figure 4–3. Types of drugs used by past month illicit drug users, 1998
Source: Substance Abuse and Mental Health Services Administration (1999).

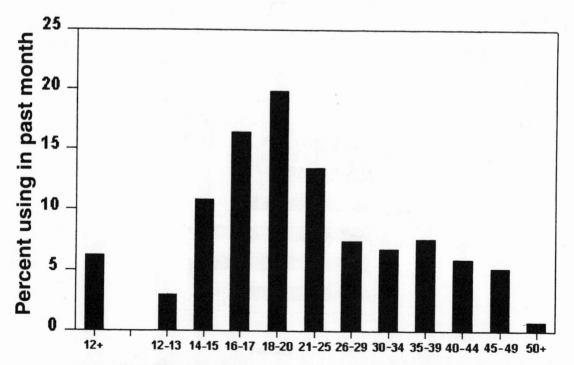

Figure 4–4. Past month use of any illicit drug by age, 1998
Source: Substance Abuse and Mental Health Services Administration (1999).

of eighth grade and high school students are being surveyed about their drug use. As the statistics in Figure 4–5 indicate, illicit drug use peaked in 1996 and 1997 and has decreased slightly since then. The use of marijuana, amphetamines, hallucinogens, tranquilizers, and heroin has remained more or less constant since the peak, but the use of MDMA (ecstasy) increased among tenth and twelfth graders. Most of the slight decline in illicit drug use among was accounted for by a decline in the use of inhalants, methamphetamine, and crack. An alarming statistic from the MFS is that heavy drinking among teenagers has risen slightly since the early 1990s (see Figure 4–6).

4–2 The Diagnosis of Substance-Related Disorders

The mere fact that an individual has used a drug or alcohol does not really give an indication of pathological drug use. Indeed, many individuals experiment with drugs and never develop significant problems. At what point does an individual cross the line from drug use into abuse and addiction? In this section you will learn about the diagnosis of substance abuse and dependence.

Substance-Related Disorders and the **DSM-IV-TR**

Many systems have been proposed to classify abnormal behavior, and even today there is no lack of alternative models (Wulfert and Greenway 1996). The most widely used classification system for mental disorders, including drug and alcohol problems, is the *Diagnostic and Statistical Manual of Mental Disorders—Fourth Edition,* or *DSM-IV-TR* (American Psychiatric Association 2000). Because it is likely that your role as a chemical dependency counselor will require some familiarity with the *DSM-IV-TR,* we will present some of its main features as they pertain to drug and alcohol problems.

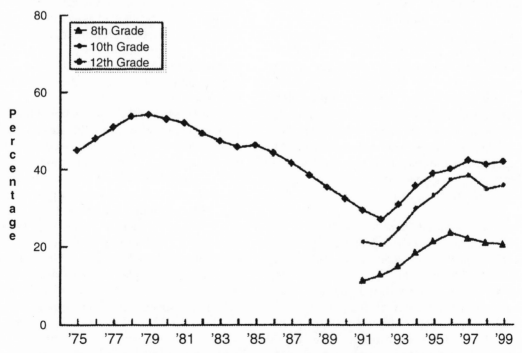

Figure 4–5. Trends in annual prevalence of an illicit drug use index for eighth, tenth, and twelfth graders
Source: National Institute on Drug Abuse (1999b).

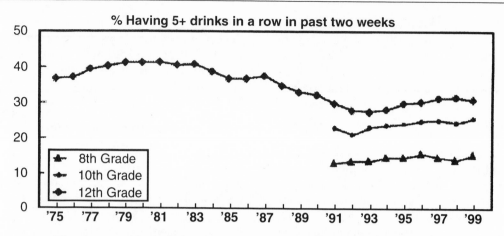

Figure 4–6. Alcohol: Trends in two-week prevalence of heavy drinking
Source: National Institute on Drug Abuse (1999b).

The DSM-IV-TR. Drug-related problems are classified in the *DSM-IV-TR* as mental disorders because they are characterized by abnormalities in behavior, mental processes, and emotions. If you look at the DSM-IV-TR definition of a mental disorder you can see why drug-related problems are classified as such. To paraphrase the *DSM-IV-TR*, a **mental disorder** is a clinically significant pattern of behaviors, thoughts, and emotions in an individual that is associated with distress or impairment or an elevated risk of suffering, death, disability, or loss of freedom (American Psychiatric Association 2000, p. xxi).

Another important point about the *DSM-IV-TR* is that it classifies mental disorders according to categories of abnormal behaviors regardless of causes. Although causes may be important in understanding chemical dependency and in treatment planning, they are irrelevant in making a diagnosis.

Substance-Related Disorders. Most people refer to alcohol and drug problems by using blanket terms like "alcoholism" and "drug addiction." Your experience as a chemical dependency counselor will tell you, however, that there are a variety of drug and alcohol problems and that they differ in many respects. Consider the following example. One person with an alcohol problem exhibits a steady pattern of occasional, heavy weekend drinking broken by weeks of abstinence. With this pattern, the individual is only dysfunctional during the binges. On the other hand, another person's alcohol problem may involve daily heavy drinking and significant everyday impairment. In either case you would probably say that both people are alcoholic.

Behavioral observations using the *DSM-IV-TR*, however, would likely lead to another conclusion. The weekend binger would probably be categorized as an *alcohol abuser*; the daily drinker would be viewed as *alcohol dependent*. Apart from their being too broad, the terms alcoholic and drug addict are disparaging and characterize the person rather than the pathological behaviors such as the *DSM-IV-TR* describes.

The *DSM-IV-TR* classifies behaviors, not people, by providing guidelines for diagnoses based on discernible differences in behavior. Significant drug problems are categorized as **substance-related disorders**, marked by abnormal behaviors related to drug-taking, the side effects of a medication, or to toxin (poison) exposure (American Psychiatric Association 2000). There are two main categories of substance-related disorders: *substance use disorders*, which include substance abuse and dependence, and *substance-induced disorders*, which are specific psychiatric reactions directly caused by taking a drug. In the next sections we will focus on the diagnostic criteria for abuse and dependence and one type of substance-induced disorder called substance withdrawal.

Substance Abuse

Although there are some peculiarities of symptoms characteristic of persons using each drug, the diagnostic criteria for substance abuse are the same, regardless of which drug is abused. Often a single individual will meet the diagnostic criteria for more than one substance.

The Diagnosis of Substance Abuse. The main feature of **substance abuse** is a maladaptive or abnormal pattern of substance use marked by significant negative consequences related to the repeated use of the substance (American Psychiatric Association 2000). In other words, substance abuse involves the harmful effects of taking a particular drug. Specifically, the drug user must demonstrate one or more of the following behaviors or impairments during a twelve-month period, and must have never met the criteria for substance dependence for that drug, to receive a substance abuse diagnosis.

1. Recurrent substance use leads to a failure to fulfill major role obligations. For example, the individual might often miss work or perform poorly, or often be absent, suspended from, or expelled from school. More evidence of abuse would show in the person's failure to attend to household responsibilities or in the neglect of children.
2. There is evidence of recurrent substance use in situations in which it would be physically hazardous to use drugs. Driving a motor vehicle or operating equipment like a bulldozer or factory machinery while intoxicated are examples of such dangerous behaviors.
3. Substance abuse is often marked by recurrent legal problems, like being arrested for disorderly conduct or driving while intoxicated. With illicit drugs, legal problems may extend to possession, sale, or manufacture of the substance.
4. The person continues to use the drug in spite of repeated or persistent problems either caused or worsened by using the drug. Drug-related arguments and fistfights are just a couple of examples.

Roger was a 37-year-old salesman who was mandated to treatment because of a DWI. Historically, he would have a couple of drinks at weddings or other social gatherings, but his drinking never caused any problems or impairment. However, a work promotion afforded him the opportunity to entertain clients at luncheons and dinners where he began to drink wine more heavily at least once a week. He also had "a few brews" after Sunday softball or football games that he played in. When he came home intoxicated he would talk nastily to his wife, drink more at dinner, then just crash in front of the TV. Roger's wife told him many times that she did not like his behavior while he was intoxicated, but he just shrugged her off. Even his 9-year-old son thought that Roger drank too much, but his pleas fell on deaf ears. As far as Roger was concerned he went to work every day and brought home the paycheck, so his family "had nothing to bitch about." Although Roger never drank alone, never became stone drunk, and occasionally lasted a couple of weeks without a drink, his drinking created many family problems. He refused to fix things around the house and was unable to attend to other family matters while intoxicated. Furthermore, he repeatedly drove a car while legally intoxicated, culminating in a DWI arrest.

The Prevalence of Substance Abuse Disorders. Many studies have estimated the prevalence of substance abuse disorders in the United States. (Helzer et al. 1991, Institute of Medicine 1990, Regier et al. 1993) Two caveats are worth mentioning. *First*, it is difficult to arrive at accurate figures due to differences in survey methods, statistical analyses, and characteristics of samples across studies. Consequently, most studies have probably underestimated substance abuse in America. *Second*, most prevalence studies of drug abuse do not generally provide prevalence data for each individual drug.

A major survey of Americans aged 15 to 54, based on an earlier version of the *DSM*, the *DSM-III-R*, will give you an idea of the scope of the problem of substance-related disorders (American Psychiatric Association 1987). Known as the *National Comorbidity Survey* (NCS), this study surveyed more than 8,000

Americans using structured psychiatric interviews (Kessler et al. 1994). It reveals high rates of substance abuse and indicates that the chances of getting a diagnosis of alcohol abuse in one's lifetime are more than 9 percent, and 4 percent for drug abuse (see Table 4–1). Whether alcohol abusers and drug abusers are separate groups is not clear from this study. Clinical experience informs us that it is likely that many of the same people abuse both drugs and alcohol.

Substance Dependence

Some individuals exhibit a more disruptive and severe type of substance use disorder. In cases in which mental, behavioral, and physiological symptoms indicate that the individual continues to use a drug despite significant substance-related problems, the diagnosis is *substance dependence*.

The Diagnosis of Substance Dependence. Commonly called *alcoholism* or *drug addiction*, **substance dependence** is marked by at least three symptoms indicative of tolerance and withdrawal or compulsive drug use (American Psychiatric Association 2000). Drug **tolerance** is defined either by the need for increased amounts of the drug to get the same psychoactive effects, or when the user derives markedly lesser effects from taking the same amount of the drug. For instance, with tolerance a heroin addict must inject two bags of heroin to get the same effects that were previously derived from doing a single bag of equal quality. *Cross-tolerance* may also be evident, insofar as tolerance develops to several drugs in the same class. For example, tolerance to heroin will result in some degree of

tolerance to all opioid drugs. *Withdrawal* means unpleasant, substance-specific symptoms that occur after the effects of the drug wear off.

Tolerance and withdrawal, the classic signs of alcoholism and drug addiction, indicate physiological dependence, and many individuals mistakenly believe that they are necessary to prove substance dependence. According to the *DSM-IV-TR*, however, these signs are neither necessary or sufficient. Compulsive substance use can also define dependence, even in the absence of physiological signs, especially with drugs such as marijuana or LSD that do not produce clear-cut signs of tolerance or withdrawal symptoms. In many cases, the individual will demonstrate both tolerance and withdrawal and a compulsive pattern of drug use. Signs of *compulsive use* include:

1. Taking the drug in larger amounts or over a longer period of time than the user intended. For example, a person goes to a party and vows to have just one drink, but winds up having a dozen.
2. The user displays a persistent desire to cut down on drug use or has made repeated, unsuccessful attempts to control drug use.
3. Increasingly more time and effort is spent to obtain the drug or recover from its effects. Traveling long distances to get drugs, visiting many doctors for prescriptions, scheming up new ways to get money, or spending days in bed after a cocaine binge are a few examples.
4. Important social, occupational, or recreational activities are reduced or given up because of drug use. Missing work, failing to attend family functions, and giving up

Table 4–1. Lifetime and twelve-month prevalence of substance use disorders

| | Percentage of Subjects | | | | | |
| | Male | | Female | | Total | |
	Life	12–mo.	Life	12–mo.	Life	12–mo.
Alcohol abuse	12.5	3.4	6.4	1.6	9.4	2.5
Alcohol dependence	20.1	10.7	8.2	3.7	14.1	7.2
Drug abuse	5.4	1.3	3.5	0.3	4.4	0.8
Drug dependence	9.2	3.8	5.9	1.9	7.5	2.8
Any substance abuse/dependence	35.4	16.1	17.9	6.6	26.6	11.3

Source: Kessler et al. (1994).

recreational activities are common among people who are drug dependent.

5. The person continues to use the drug despite knowledge that drug use either creates or worsens his physical and/or psychological health. For example, an individual with alcohol dependence will continue to drink in spite of liver disease, or a cocaine-dependent individual may continue to do cocaine knowing that his depression is caused by continued use.

Renee was a 41-year-old secretary with a long history of drinking problems. She typically had a few cocktails at lunch, then after each workday she immediately bought a bottle of vodka and proceeded to consume it until she passed out. On the weekends she would lie in bed and start drinking shortly after awakening. At first, her drinking caused little interference in daily functioning, but gradually she was finding it difficult to get up for work, and frequently called in sick. She also experienced blackouts, often forgetting entire weekends. Furthermore, on those rare days when she did not drink during lunch, Renee started getting the shakes by 2:00 or 3:00 P.M. and sometimes left work early so she could drink. Renee had realized for a long time that she was dependent on alcohol, but repeated attempts to quit failed. Finally, she feared that she would soon die if she did not stop drinking so she voluntarily entered an alcohol rehabilitation program. During her detoxification, Renee had delirium tremens for days. She shook, became disoriented, and hallucinated that bugs were crawling all over her.

Polysubstance dependence. If the individual repeatedly uses three or more substances during a twelve month period and is dependent on the group of drugs, but not on a single substance, the diagnosis of *polysubstance dependence* is made. For example, an individual may compulsively use cocaine, alcohol, and marijuana either together or successively, yet not meet dependence criteria for any one of the drugs (American Psychiatric Association 2000). Clearly, the *DSM-IV-TR* diagnosis of polysubstance dependence differs somewhat from popular conceptions, which suggest that the individual is addicted to several drugs

simultaneously. Notwithstanding diagnostic hairsplitting, polysubstance dependence represents a challenge to chemical dependency counselors.

The Prevalence of Substance Dependence. According to the *National Comorbidity Survey* (NCS) cited earlier in this section, the lifetime prevalence is about 14 percent for alcohol dependence and over 7 percent for the other substances considered as a group (Kessler et al. 1994).

Consistent with the NCS and other epidemiological studies of abuse and dependence, the NCS demonstrates that males are at greater risk than females for a substance-dependence disorder; the male to female ratio in the NCS is approximately 1.5:1. The NCS shows that prevalence declines with age for both males and females (Kessler et al. 1994).

Race is another demographic variable that has been investigated extensively in epidemiological research. Most research, including the NCS study, shows a higher prevalence of substance abuse and dependence in young whites compared to blacks, but the data for Hispanics are conflicting. The National Household Survey indicates that whites are more likely than Hispanics to have ever used drugs, but prevalence studies suggest a higher risk of substance dependence in Hispanics (Regier et al 1993). In contrast, the NCS study found that Hispanics and whites have a roughly equal risk of developing substance abuse and dependence (Kessler et al. 1994).

Finally, a curious relationship seems to exist between substance dependence and socioeconomic status. After ranking subjects as having either a high, medium, or low amount of education, the NCS study found that, for unknown reasons, individuals in the middle education group had the highest prevalence of substance dependence (Kessler et al. 1994).

Using *DSM-IV-TR* criteria, the *National Household Survey on Drug Abuse* estimates that in the United States nearly 10 million people are dependent on alcohol, and that more than 4 million are dependent on illicit drugs. Nearly 1 million of the drug-dependent individuals are kids aged 12 to 17 who are dependent on marijuana (see Figure 4–7, Substance

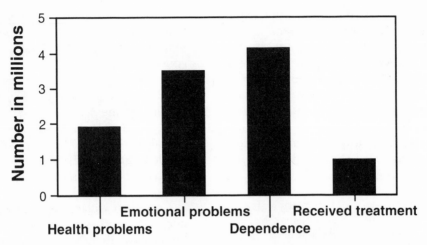

Figure 4–7. Past year health and emotional problems, dependence, and
treatment for illicit drug use, 1997–1998
Source: Substance Abuse and Mental Health Services Administration (1999).

Abuse and Mental Health Services Administration 1999).

In conclusion, common sense and clinical experience inform us that substance dependence is an equal opportunity disorder; there is no immunization against it. Although we do not intend to caution that everyone is subject to an equal risk, any male or female, regardless of age, race, or socioeconomic status theoretically could develop serious drug problems. Despite numerous exceptions, epidemiological research indicates that young, white, middle-class males are at above-average risk.

Substance Withdrawal

The key feature of **substance withdrawal** is an unpleasant substance-specific behavioral change, with physiological and mental symptoms, due to stopping or reducing heavy and prolonged drug use (American Psychiatric Association 2000). A rule of thumb in predicting withdrawal symptoms is to figure that whatever effects a drug has when it is taken, the opposite will occur during withdrawal. This *opponent process* is an integral part of the addictive process, leading the user to indulge repeatedly in order to avoid the discomfort of withdrawal (Solomon 1977). Understanding and managing withdrawal is an important element in chemical dependency treatment programs as you will see in later chapters.

To repeat a point made earlier, drugs vary with respect to whether and to what degree they produce tolerance and withdrawal symptoms. Many people mistakenly believe that if quitting a drug does not produce identifiable withdrawal symptoms, it must not be addictive. There is little doubt that cutting back or stopping the use of opioids and depressants can result in extremely unpleasant, even dangerous symptoms of withdrawal, and therefore these drugs are unquestionably addictive. However, the nature and intensity of withdrawal from drugs such as cocaine and marijuana is not as clear and is the subject of continuing investigation. In this section we will highlight some of the major withdrawal symptoms of alcohol, heroin, cocaine, and marijuana.

Alcohol Withdrawal. Alcohol withdrawal symptoms occur within a variable time frame, and many people do not suffer the full range of symptoms. Indeed, fewer than 5 percent of those withdrawing from alcohol develop dramatic symptoms (American Psychiatric Association 2000). In any event, the many nutritional and metabolic disturbances during alcohol withdrawal are caused when the constant exposure of the central nervous system to alcohol is interrupted (Saitz 1998).

Within four to twelve hours after drinking, the person may experience sweats, hand tremors, insomnia, nausea and vomiting, agitation, anxiety, and headaches. Symptoms usually persist for a few days, and then their severity wanes. Some people experience mild anxiety, restlessness, distractibility, depression, insomnia, and some physical problems for as long as three to six months after drinking. Some people experience fleeting auditory, tactile, or visual illusions, and approximately 3 percent of individuals are beset by full-blown epileptic seizures. The frightening hallucinations and profound disorientation found in *delirium tremens* or "DTs" are likely the result of medical complications (American Psychiatric Association 1994, Gallant 1994, Goodwin 1989, Satel et al. 1993).

Characteristics that confer a risk of more severe alcohol withdrawal symptoms (Saitz 1998) include:

- More severe alcohol dependence prior to withdrawal
- Higher levels of alcohol intake
- Longer duration of alcoholism
- Abnormal liver function
- Prior detoxification
- Past experiences of seizures or DTs
- Intense cravings for alcohol
- Older age
- Use of another drug in addition to alcohol
- More severe withdrawal symptom at the outset of treatment.

Sedative Withdrawal. Not surprisingly, the symptoms of withdrawal from sedative, hypnotic, and anxiolytic drugs are similar to those of alcohol. However, the time frame tends to be more variable, depending on how long it takes for the drug to be metabolized and cleared from the body, that is, its *half-life.* Drugs with a half-life of less than ten hours, such as Ativan, generally produce withdrawal symptoms within four to six hours, which peak on the second day and then improve within a few days thereafter. Withdrawal symptoms from drugs with longer half-lives, like Valium, is delayed for several days before building and then lessening over a period of several weeks (American Psychiatric Association 2000).

Opioid Withdrawal. The symptoms of opioid withdrawal are anxiety, restlessness, yawning, muscle aches especially in the legs and back, abdominal cramps, nausea, diarrhea, vomiting, dilated pupils, tearing, runny nose, and fever. During this time there is intense drug craving, which often prompts the person to get high to relieve the distress (American Psychiatric Association 1994, Kleber 1994).

The rule for opioid withdrawal is that the slower the onset of its effects and the longer the drug works, the less intense but longer-lasting the withdrawal symptoms will be (Kleber 1994). Heroin withdrawal, for example, begins six to twenty-four hours after the last dose, peaks in a couple of days, and then mostly resolves within a week. Some less-intense withdrawal symptoms may linger for weeks. With methadone, on the other hand, symptoms may take several days to appear with no substantial improvement for ten to twelve days (Kleber 1994b), and withdrawal may continue at a lower level of intensity for much longer (American Psychiatric Association 2000).

Cocaine Withdrawal. Until quite recently, the conventional wisdom was that abstaining from cocaine and other stimulants did not result in withdrawal symptoms. Therefore stimulants, especially cocaine, were not considered to be physically addictive but only psychologically addictive. In other words, it was believed that people only experienced psychological craving for the drug but that there was no physiological need.

Research in the 1980s, however, began to dispel that notion. Now there is a wealth of animal and human data showing that the use of cocaine and other stimulants produces neurophysiological disturbances that outlast drug use. Unlike the withdrawal symptoms that occur with alcohol and heroin, these disturbances primarily result in psychological instead of physiological signs (Gawin 1991, Gawin and Kleber 1986, Gawin et al. 1994).

A distinct, three-stage **cocaine abstinence syndrome** is characterized by *crash, withdrawal,* and *extinction phases* (American Psychiatric Association 1994, Gawin 1991, Gawin and Kleber 1986, Gawin et al. 1994).

1. Phase 1: Crash. Prolonged cocaine binges lead to acute tolerance and a reduction in euphoria and increased anxiety, fatigue, depression, irritability, and paranoia. To escape from the throes of overstimulation and depression, the individual resorts to alcohol or sedatives to induce sleep. Whether induced or not, sleep eventually overcomes the crashing individual and he may sleep for days with brief waking periods and overeating. The period of excessive sleep is followed by a markedly improved mood with little, if any, craving for cocaine. This is very different from alcohol and heroin withdrawal in which craving is immediate, intense, and likely to lead to drug use to relieve the unpleasant withdrawal symptoms.

2. Phase 2: Withdrawal. Following the crash there is period of a few hours to several days in which the person vividly remembers the crash and realizes how drugs are ruining his or her life. Such memories and realizations are gradually replaced by irritability, anxiety, a lack of motivation, inertia, and an inability to experience pleasure. Comparing the current displeasure to memories of getting high can stimulate craving and make a return to drug use very attractive.

3. Phase 3: Extinction. Months or even years of on-and-off stimulant craving follow withdrawal in response to both negative and positive emotions as well as people, places, or things. Almost any stimulus can trigger craving and relapse if it was previously conditioned to drug use. Getting into an argument with a spouse or friend, seeing a drug buddy, hearing a particular song, having money, or seeing a pipe or single-edged razor blade are just a few examples of stimulus situations that can trigger cravings.

Marijuana Withdrawal. The possible existence of a marijuana withdrawal syndrome has been even more controversial than for cocaine. People who use marijuana frequently do not appear to build a tolerance to it and there is no compelling evidence of clinically significant withdrawal symptoms, although many exhibit compulsive use. Whatever symptoms do appear are comprised chiefly of mild distress or anxiety with no apparent physiological impairment.

Recent animal studies have shown that drugs that block THC at the synapse result in rapid and intense withdrawal symptoms including "wet shakes," facial rubbing, ear twitching, and chewing and licking movements (Aceto et al. 1995, National Institute on Drug Abuse 1997; Tsou et al. 1995). These findings, of course, do not prove that marijuana withdrawal occurs in humans, but do rejuvenate interest in continued exploration of the matter.

4–3 The Course of Substance Abuse and Dependence

Predicting the sequence of events in the life of a substance abuser or dependent person is important in treatment planning. The sequence of events, known as the *course*, varies considerably with the type of substance, its route of administration, and many other personal and environmental factors. Nonetheless, a few generalizations can be made.

General Trends

At any age, episodes of substance abuse tend to be sporadic and brief and usually will not induce the user to seek help unless he is coerced. Impairment in meeting everyday responsibilities, although evident to some, is usually not severe (American Psychiatric Association 1994, 1995a, Dupont 1984). Indeed, many individuals carry on a long-term pattern of drug abuse without becoming dependent. These "chippers" seem to be able to use when they want to and quit when they wish. Although they remain at risk for drug dependence and are not without their problems, they seem to defy the assumption that there is an inevitable progression from drug abuse to dependence (Clayton 1992).

No single path to substance dependence has been identified. With many drugs, substance dependence can occur at any age, but for alcohol, it is usually diagnosed when people are in their twenties, or later, especially in men (American Psychiatric Association

1994, 1995a, Ellickson et al. 1992, Goodwin 1989, National Institute on Drug Abuse 1997k). We usually witness long episodes of daily, heavy use, especially with drugs that produce strong tolerance and withdrawal. Dependence is marked by severe impairment followed by periods of abstinence that can last for months or longer. Some individuals may abstain from drugs for a while in reaction to legal action, medical problems, or marital, group, or job pressure (Leino et al. 1995). However, the abstinence period is often succeeded by a relapse and a return to pathological drug use. Most people relapse during the first couple of years and especially during the first twelve months of abstinence (American Psychiatric Association 1994, 1995a).

Therapeutic intervention can favorably alter the course of substance dependence. Research has shown that regardless of its type, intensity, and duration, treatment is associated with an increased likelihood of reducing or eliminating drug use (McLellan et al. 1983). The majority of people treated for substance dependence eventually are able to stop compulsive drug use and either abstain or have brief episodes of drug use (American Psychiatric Association 2000).

Ninety percent of people who are drug-free after two years are likely to be drug-free after ten, and more than 90 percent of those will be abstinent after twenty years. About 20 percent, however, exhibit a pattern of chronic relapse over ten to twenty years (American Psychiatric Association 1994, Brecht et al. 1987, Vaillant 1973, 1988).

The Course of Alcohol and Drug Dependence

You learned earlier in this chapter that the rates of alcohol abuse and dependence are higher than for any other drug. Considering this fact, the course of alcohol dependence has been investigated more frequently than for any other drug.

The results of a study of 636 alcohol-dependent male inpatients, summarized in Table 4–2, reveal a typical trend in the progression of alcohol-related problems that is consistent with clinical experience and previous research (Mulford 1977, Pokorny et al. 1981). Heavy drinking begins years earlier, escalates further in the individual's late twenties, and is followed in his early thirties by significant impairment in most or all areas of everyday functioning. A loss of control over drinking, worsening of social and occupational problems, and physical deterioration are evident by the person's late thirties (Schuckit et al. 1993).

Another study (Vaillant 1996) beginning in 1940 followed 268 former Harvard undergraduates and 456 nondelinquent inner-city adolescents using questionnaires and physical examinations. By age 60, 18 percent of the college alcohol abusers had died, 11 percent were controlled drinkers, and 59 percent continued to abuse alcohol. Likewise, 28 percent of the inner-city alcohol abusers had died, 30 percent were abstinent, 11 percent were controlled drinkers, and 28 percent were still alcohol abusers. For both groups, remaining abstinent for five years was a good predictor of stable abstinence. However, attempts to control drinking usually failed for both groups.

The specific course of drug dependence varies because of differences in the types of drugs and routes of administration. Most of the research in this area has looked at the course of narcotics like heroin. These studies demonstrate a pattern of drug abuse escalating to dependence, then treatment, abstinence, and relapse (Simpson et al. 1986, Vaillant 1973). During the course of drug dependence, users are likely to have extensive involvement with the criminal justice system; to use other drugs such as alcohol, cocaine, and marijuana; and to have a high mortality rate.

In one representative study, heroin addicts in a compulsory treatment program were followed for twenty-four years (Hser et al. 1993). Although the average age upon admission to the program was 25, at follow-up nearly 28 percent of these people had died by their late forties. Forty-one percent of those interviewed tested positive for opioids at follow-up and more than 15 percent were not tested

Table 4–2. Sequence of Alcohol-Related Life Events in Alcohol-Dependent Men

Event	% Patients	Average age of onset	Average number of times
Demoted	17	26.8	2.0
Drank—12 hours straight	74	27.7	64.7
Drank before noon	96	29.7	85.0
Drunk—arrested	41	30.4	6.7
Jailed	62	30.6	6.4
Withdrawal symptoms	91	30.6	——
Blackouts	82	31.2	46.7
Car accident	49	32.0	1.9
Morning shakes	76	32.8	62.5
Driving arrest	72	33.3	3.1
No control over drinking	86	34.3	49.8
Divorced/separated	61	34.5	2.1
Fired from job	43	34.6	3.6
Vomited blood	17	35.1	8.0
Hallucinations	13	36.7	16.9
Convulsions	5	40.0	3.6
Hospitalized	24	40.8	3.1
Health problem	37	41.7	2.5
Hepatitis/pancreatitis	26	41.9	3.3

Source: Adapted from: Schuckit et al. (1993).

because they either refused to give urine specimens or were incarcerated. More than 7 percent (probably an underestimate) remained opioid-dependent and frequently abused cocaine and marijuana, too. Compared to active users, heroin addicts who were abstinent after twenty-four years reported less criminal involvement but more drinking.

4–4 Types of Alcoholism

Chemical dependency is often viewed as a single category in psychiatric classifications. There is abundant clinical and scientific evidence, however, that substance-dependent individuals display a varying array of clinical characteristics. For example, two alcohol-dependent men may present with differences in drinking patterns, causes, developmental features, degrees of impairment, and outcome. Recognizing this, clinicians and researchers have searched for unique types of chemical dependency, particularly with regard to alcoholism.

In this section you will learn about the more prominent types of alcohol dependency. Understanding these types will help you to make predictions and more successfully treat people who are dependent on alcohol.

Early Views of Alcoholism Types

This section presents a few early views of types of alcoholism. Although their validity has not been demonstrated scientifically, you will see that many of the behaviors and issues displayed by these types must be considered in the treatment of chemically dependent individuals (Levin 1995).

Jellinek's Model. One of the most influential early views of alcoholism types belongs to Jellinek (1946, 1960), who developed a typology based on drinking patterns reported by *Alcoholics Anonymous* (A.A.) members. He identified five types of alcoholism: alpha, beta, gamma, delta, and epsilon. *Gamma and delta alcoholism* are most relevant to the treatment of chemical dependency because they are types that most clearly meet the *DSM-IV-TR* criteria for alcohol dependence.

Jellinek described **gamma alcoholism** as a chronic, progressive disease characterized by a high psychological vulnerability to dependence, loss of control over drinking, emotional and psychological impairment, and tolerance and withdrawal symptoms. Gamma alcoholism is the most prevalent type. According to Jellinek, all members of A.A. as well as people seen in alcoholism clinics and detoxification units fit the gamma type.

The loss of control over drinking is an especially relevant feature in chemical dependency counseling. Many alcoholics mistakenly think that they can drink safely, believing that they can just have a drink or two and stop there. This is rarely a possibility. According to A.A. (1976), "one drink is too many, but a thousand is not enough." Part of your job as a chemical dependency counselor will be to identify those individuals who fit the gamma type and help them to understand the riskiness of having just one drink.

In contrast to the gamma type, **delta alcoholism** is marked by physical dependence and few symptoms. Individuals with this type typically do not lose control, do not get drunk, violent, or pass out, but nevertheless cannot stop drinking without experiencing withdrawal symptoms.

Blane's Dependency Types. Psychologist Howard Blane (1968) proposed a typology of alcoholism based on his clinical experience with alcoholic men. Blane maintains that alcoholic types can be differentiated by the ways in which they manage their dependency needs. The *dependent type* is not only dependent on alcohol but also displays an unhealthy dependence on others for money and other forms of support. The prognosis for this type is poor. People who handle their dependency needs by denying that they need anybody are known as *counterdependent types.* These are the alcoholics who are likely to trash the bar and show other evidence of what they view as their independence. Like the dependent type, this type has a poor prognosis. Finally, the *dependent-counterdependent* type actively struggles with dependency needs. Because people who fit this type are in the most emotional pain, they are the most likely to benefit from treatment. Even though Blane's typology has not received scientific support and is out of fashion, dependency needs certainly are expressed in alcoholic behavior and must be considered in the treatment of many alcoholics (Levin 1987).

Primary and Secondary Alcoholism. Winokur and associates (1971) distinguish between primary and secondary alcoholism. *Primary alcoholism* is a type that is not preceded by a major mental disorder, such as depression. By contrast, *secondary alcoholism* follows and is presumably influenced by depression. This type is most common in women.

Winokur also drew another important distinction, which is the one between primary alcoholism and alcoholism secondary to *sociopathy*, an antisocial behavior pattern. In this view, primary alcoholics might engage in antisocial behavior while intoxicated but they are not sociopaths. Sociopaths, on the other hand, may be heavy drinkers without necessarily being alcoholic.

Although they have some clinical usefulness, the views of Jellinek, Blane, and Winokur are one-dimensional. More recent scientifically based typologies attempt to arrive at types by combining information about risk factors, development, clinical characteristics, course, and outcome.

The Type 1–Type 2 Model

Psychiatrist Robert Cloninger's (Cloninger 1987, Cloninger et al. 1981, 1988) typology based on adoption studies distinguishes two types of alcoholism: *Type 1* and *Type 2.* This model weaves presumed causes, clinical features, underlying neurophysiology, course, and outcome to explain variations in alcohol dependence (Bohn and Meyer 1994).

Type 1 Alcoholism. A type of alcoholism that affects men and women almost equally, has an onset after age 25, and is shaped in part by the the childhood family environment is known as **Type 1 alcoholism**. Type 1 alcoholics have the ability to abstain from drinking temporarily and possess personality traits that incline them to avoid harm and to depend on external rewards. Their tendency toward *harm avoidance*, a temperament trait, often inhibits them from heavy drinking for fear of losing control, injury, or becoming violent. However, Type 1 people turn to external rewards, like alcohol, in order to combat negative emotional states, such as depression. In other words, Type 1 alcoholics are *self-medicators.* Compared to Type 2 alcoholics, Type 1 alcoholics generally have a better response to treatment.

Type 2 Alcoholism. **Type 2 alcoholism** is a heritable form of this condition that begins before age 25, primarily affects men, and is marked by heavy drinking and an inability to abstain. The tendency to drink is strongly determined by father-to-son genetic transmission, having little to do with environmental factors. Type 2 alcoholics often have alcoholic fathers and brothers, and all are likely to have a history of antisocial acts like fighting and intoxication-related arrests. Type 2s typically suffer numerous medical and social problems because of their drinking.

Presumably because of their peculiar physiology, Type 2 alcoholics drink for pleasure and are bound to engage in heavy-drinking episodes. They are not motivated by a fear of harm and so they have little concern that drinking might be risky. Overall, the outcome for Type 2 alcoholics is poor.

> When Billy was referred for alcoholism treatment at age 33, he had already been drinking heavily for many years. He vividly recalled that when he was 12 years old, his parents had house parties where plenty of liquor was available. Billy remembered often having a couple of friends over to sneak some hard liquor. He told his counselor with a gleam in his eyes that "the first time I took a drink I knew it was for me." He loved the way alcohol made him feel, and even back then he realized that he could drink a lot more than any of his friends without getting too intoxicated. Further assessment revealed that Billy's father was clearly alcoholic and one of his brothers also had both drug and alcohol problems. All three got into bar fights, abused their wives, and had numerous scrapes with the law. As Billy entered his teen and adult years, he abused many drugs, but alcohol remained his favorite. Billy was eventually killed in a motorcycle accident while drunk.

A Biopsychosocial Model

Psychologist Robert Zucker's (Zucker 1987, 1994, Zucker et al. 1993, 1994, 1995a, 1996a) **biopsychosocial model** of alcoholism is a ty-

pology based on the interplay of biological, psychological, and social variables. The model proposes four types of alcoholism: *antisocial alcoholism, developmentally limited alcoholism, negative affect alcoholism,* and *primary alcoholism* (Bohn and Meyer 1994).

A type of alcoholism with an early onset, severe persistent alcohol-related problems, and antisocial behavior is known as **antisocial alcoholism**. It is found mostly in men, is associated with fighting and other antisocial behavior, and is believed to have a strong hereditary basis as indicated by a family history of alcoholism. The outcome for individuals with antisocial alcoholism is poor.

Adolescent alcohol problems that are associated with socially deviant behaviors and affiliation with a deviant peer group are called **developmentally limited alcoholism**. This type affects both men and women and develops from an accumulation of drinking and delinquent behavior. However, aggression is less prominent in this type compared to antisocial alcoholism, and environmental factors are more influential than hereditary variables in shaping the person's behavior. Characterized by heavy drinking during times of increased independence in early adulthood, developmentally limited alcoholism is usually preceded by a period of better adjustment when compared to antisocial alcoholism. Eventually, it disappears as the adolescent makes the transition into adulthood.

In **negative affect alcoholism**, there is a later onset than for the other types, and it is preceded by negative emotional states, such as depression, where drinking takes place against a backdrop of depression in the family. This type is more prevalent in women who use alcohol to enhance relationships and lift their mood.

Finally, **primary alcoholism** is a type of this condition in which problem drinking comes before and is independent of other mental disorders. Any mental disorders result from problem drinking and the stress that results from it. Often, someone who is already drinking may consume more when drinking disrupts the marriage or causes occupational problems. This is generally a milder form of alcoholism than the other types.

Recently, Zucker (Zucker et al. 1996b) has refined his model by identifying two main types of male alcoholism: *antisocial alcoholism* (AAS) and *non-antisocial alcoholism* (NAAS). In this scheme, the two are distinguished from each other by age of onset, severity of symptoms, life-position status (socioeconomic status, education, work), associated psychopathology, and family history of alcoholism. In general, AAS has an earlier onset with more severe symptoms, and involves a lower life-position status, worse psychopathology, and a family history of alcoholism.

The Type A–Type B Model

Psychologist Thomas Babor and associates (Babor et al. 1992) have proposed a typology of alcoholism based on measures of vulnerability to alcoholism, as well as its severity. Their research defines two types: *Type A* and *Type B* (Litt et al. 1992)

Type A alcoholism is a less severe form characterized by later onset, less severe dependence, fewer childhood risk factors, and better overall functioning. Found mostly in men, **Type B alcoholism** is a more severe form marked by childhood problems, a family history of alcoholism, more severe dependence on alcohol, poorer overall functioning, and other substance abuse.

As you might suspect, Type A and Type B alcoholism are further distinguished from each other by their outcome. Babor's (Babor et al. 1992) research shows that 45 percent of Type A alcoholics are likely to relapse within one year, compared to 64 percent of Type B alcoholics. Not only do the two types differ with respect to relapse probability, they also differ with regard to how quickly they relapse and the amount of alcohol consumed during a "slip." Type B individuals return to drinking sooner than do Type As, and when they do, they drink more heavily (Litt et al. 1992).

Although still in its preliminary stages, research on Type A/Type B distinctions indicates that the typology fits cocaine abusers as well. In one study (Ball et al. 1995), 399 inpatient, outpatient, and non-treatment-seeking male and female cocaine abusers were systematically assessed. Babor's model fit the data well for white men and less so for African Americans and women. Type B abusers were more likely than their Type A counterparts to display an earlier onset, more childhood problems, a family history of alcohol abuse, antisocial behaviors, more psychopathology and overall impairment, and more severe drug and alcohol abuse.

Alcoholism Types: An Integration

In studying the types of alcoholism just discussed, you must certainly have noticed parallels in the models. There is much scientific and clinical support for typing alcoholism along the dimensions of antisocial personality traits, age of onset, gender, family history of alcoholism, and outcome (Hesselbrock et al. 1992, Kranzler and Anton 1994, von Knorring et al. 1985a,b, 1987, Yates and Miller 1993). In this regard, as shown in Table 4–3, there are similarities between Cloninger's Type 1, Zucker's non-antisocial alcoholism, and Babor's Type A. Likewise, there are resemblances between Type 2, antisocial alcoholism, and Type B alcoholism.

In conclusion, much still needs to be learned about typing chemically dependent individuals. Nevertheless, the current state of the art has much to offer in helping you in your work as a chemical dependency counselor.

Table 4–3. Dimensions of Alcoholism Types

Type 1, NAAS, Type A	Type 2, AAS, Type B
Less antisocial behavior	Antisocial personality
Onset after age 25	Onset before age 25
Affects men and women	Affects mainly males
Weak family history	Familial alcoholism
Good outcome	Poor outcome

Terms to Remember

antisocial alcoholism
biopsychosocial model
cocaine abstinence syndrome
delta alcoholism
developmentally limited alcoholism
Diagnostic and Statistical Manual of Mental Disorders—Fourth Edition

epidemiology
gamma alcoholism
mental disorder
negative affect alcoholism
prevalence rate
primary alcoholism
substance abuse
substance dependence
substance-related disorders
tolerance
Type A alcoholism
Type B alcoholism
Type 1 alcoholism
Type 2 alcoholism
withdrawal

Summary

4–1

One way to measure psychoactive drug use is to conduct epidemiological studies; epidemiology is the study of the distribution of disorders in the general population. These studies provide prevalence rates, or the percentage of a population or group that has a particular disorder. The most comprehensive survey of drug use in the United States is the National Household Survey on Drug Abuse. It shows high rates of alcohol and marijuana use. The Monitoring the Future Study shows stable drug and alcohol use among 12- to 17-year-olds.

4–2

The most widely used classification system for mental disorders, including drug and alcohol problems, is the *Diagnostic and Statistical Manual of Mental Disorders—Fourth Edition (DSM-IV-TR)*. Drug-related problems are classified in the *DSM-IV-TR* as mental disorders because they are characterized by abnormalities in behavior, mental processes, and emotions. Significant drug problems are categorized as substance-related disorders, marked by abnormal behaviors related to drug-taking, the side effects of a medication, or to toxin exposure. The main feature of sub-

stance abuse is a maladaptive or abnormal pattern of substance use marked by significant negative consequences related to the repeated use of substances. The NCS study reveals high rates of substance abuse and indicates that the chances of getting a diagnosis of alcohol abuse in one's lifetime is more than 9 percent, and 4 percent for drug abuse. Commonly called alcoholism or drug addiction, substance dependence is marked by at least three symptoms indicative of tolerance and withdrawal or compulsive drug use. The NCS study estimates a lifetime prevalence of about 14 percent for alcohol dependence and over 7 percent for the other substances. Substance withdrawal is an unpleasant substance-specific behavioral change, with physiological and mental symptoms, due to stopping or reducing heavy and prolonged drug use. A general rule in estimating its impact is to figure that whatever effects a drug has when it is taken, the opposite will occur during withdrawal. This opponent process is an integral part of the addictive process, leading the user to indulge repeatedly to avoid the discomfort of withdrawal.

4–3

Episodes of substance abuse tend to be sporadic and brief and usually will not induce the user to seek help unless the person is coerced. Impairment in meeting everyday responsibilities, although evident to some, is usually not severe. No single path to substance dependence has been identified. With many drugs, substance dependence can occur at any age, but it is usually diagnosed when individuals are in their twenties, or later for alcohol, especially in men. We usually witness long episodes of daily, heavy use, especially with drugs that produce strong tolerance and withdrawal. Dependence is marked by severe impairment followed by periods of abstinence that can last for months or longer. Some individuals may abstain from drugs for awhile in reaction to legal action, medical problems, or marital, group, or job pressure. However, the abstinence period is often succeeded by a relapse and a return to pathological drug use.

Most people relapse during the first couple of years and especially during the first twelve months of abstinence (American Psychiatric Association 2000, 1995a). Therapeutic intervention can favorably alter the course of substance dependence.

4–4

Jellinek identified five types of alcoholism. Gamma and delta alcoholism are most relevant to chemical dependency. Jellinek described gamma alcoholism as a chronic progressive disease characterized by a high psychological vulnerability to dependence, loss of control over drinking, emotional and psychological impairment, and tolerance and withdrawal symptoms. Delta alcoholism is marked by physical dependence and few symptoms. Blane proposed a typology based on ways in which alcoholics manage their dependency needs. Winokur and associates distinguish between primary and secondary alcoholism. Primary alcoholism is a type that is not preceded by a major mental disorder, such as depression. By contrast, secondary alcoholism follows and is presumably influenced by depression. Cloninger's typology based on adoption studies distinguishes two types of alcoholism: Type 1 and Type 2. Type 1 affects men and women almost equally, has an onset after age 25, and is shaped in part by the the childhood family environment. Type 1 alcoholics are self-medicators. Type 2 alcoholism is a heritable form that begins before age 25, affects men primarily, and is marked by heavy drinking and an inability to abstain. Zucker's biopsychosocial model of alcoholism is a typology based on the interplay of biological, psychological, and social variables. The model proposes four types of alcoholism: antisocial alcoholism, developmentally limited alcoholism, negative-affect alcoholism, and primary alcoholism. Babor proposed a typology of alcoholism based on measures of vulnerability to alcoholism as well as its severity. Type A alcoholism is a less severe form characterized by later onset, less severe dependence, fewer childhood risk factors, and better overall functioning. Found mostly in men, Type B alcoholism is a more severe form marked by childhood problems, a family history of alcoholism, more severe dependence on alcohol, poorer overall functioning, and other substance abuse.

Suggested Readings

Dupont, R. L. (1984). *Getting Tough on Gateway Drugs: A Guide for the Family.* Washington, DC: American Psychiatric Press.

Jellinek, E. M. (1946). *Phases in the Drinking History of Alcoholics.* New Haven, CT: Hillhouse.

Levin, J. D. (1987). *Treatment of Alcoholism and Other Addictions: A Self-Psychology Approach.* Northvale, NJ: Jason Aronson.

——— (1995). *Introduction to Alcoholism Counseling: A Bio-Psycho-Social Approach,* 2nd ed. Washington, DC: Taylor & Francis.

CHAPTER FIVE

Development and Chemical Dependency

Chapter Outline

5-1 PRINCIPLES OF HUMAN DEVELOPMENT
    The Developmental Perspective
    Developmental Models and Chemical Dependency

5-2 DEVELOPMENTAL RESEARCH
    Retrospective Research
    The Longitudinal Method
    Vulnerability, Risk, and Protection

5-3 DRUG USE ACROSS THE LIFESPAN
    Childhood
    Adolescence
    Adulthood

Learning Objectives

Upon completing study of this chapter you should be able to:

1. Discuss the assumptions of the developmental perspective.
2. Describe the developmental phases in addiction.
3. Characterize the biopsychosocial model of chemical dependency.
4. Discuss the features of longitudinal research.
5. Outline the methods and limitations of retrospective research.
6. Identify the main risk factors and protective factors in the development of chemical dependency.
7. Discuss patterns of substance use and vulnerability in childhood.
8. Use the major theories to explain the transition from drug use to abuse in adolescents.
9. Describe developmental changes in drug use in adulthood.

In the previous chapter you learned that chemical dependency is the most extreme end of the drug-use spectrum and that patterns of drug use vary dramatically between individuals and in the same individual over time. Like other behavioral and psychological problems, chemical dependency is an outcome of the complex forces of human development that act on individuals over the course of the life span. In this chapter you will examine chemical dependency through the lens of developmental psychology and learn about the principles and research studies that pertain to drug use, abuse, and dependence.

5–1 Principles of Human Development

Developmental psychology is a rich and fascinating field that seeks to explain the nature and causes of individual change over the life span. In recent years this field has been integrated with the study of abnormal behavior in order to understand the developmental course of psychological and behavioral problems, including substance use disorders. In this section we explore ways in which ideas about development are used to illuminate how chemical dependency evolves and how best to treat it.

The Developmental Perspective

Take a minute and try to define the concept of *development.* Like most people you might define it with words such as "change," "progress," "stages," and "growth." In fact all of those words are important in our understanding of development. The **developmental perspective** is a point of view that examines the patterns and causes of change in individuals across the life span, and this perspective can be applied to both normal and abnormal behavior (Wenar 1994). The main assumptions behind the developmental perspective are discussed in the following sections.

Quantitative and Qualitative Change. Development entails both quantitative and qualitative changes. Time is a critical dimension in development. Over time the patterns of change in behavior may be defined both in terms of *quantity*—the level or amount of some variables, and *quality*—the kinds or types of variables (Wicks-Nelson and Israel 1997).

Quantitative change in development is found when specific behaviors, traits, and other characteristics vary over time in terms of *how much* is present, that is, their frequency or intensity.

An example of quantitative change would occur when a person increases the frequency of drug taking, as when alcoholics engage in more and more episodes of heavy drinking over time. A change in the intensity, dosage, or potency of drug use also shows quantitative change, such as when an alcohol abuser switches from beer to stronger beverages like whiskey and vodka. You may recall from Chapter 3 that such quantitative changes in drug taking were mentioned as signs of physical tolerance, a key element of addiction.

When an individual shows distinctively different kinds of behavior or traits over time, *qualitative change* is present. This phenomenon is illustrated by a person who begins experimenting with marijuana in mid-adolescence and later switches to several other hard drugs before establishing dependence on cocaine in young adulthood. Qualitative changes also occur in regard to traits associated with drug use; for instance, emotional conditions like depression and anxiety may be caused by long-term use.

Developmental Paths. Considering the obvious individual differences among people, it should not surprise you to learn that human development follows many pathways. A **developmental path** is defined by a progression of behaviors, events, and circumstances that evolves over time, as well as the influences on that progression. People can follow different paths from similar starting points, and in addition, people may arrive at similar conditions along different paths (Loeber 1991).

With regard to chemical dependency, we can say for certain that although two patients may have the same condition, for example alcoholism, they have not developed their conditions in exactly the same fashion. Just because two people have similar behavior does not mean that they have followed the same developmental path. Alcoholics, for instance, come from all walks of life, family backgrounds, faiths, and social classes. In addition, the paths to dependence on different drugs are not necessarily the same, as indicated in Figure 5–1. Despite some general similarities among chemically dependent people, their lives tend to follow relatively

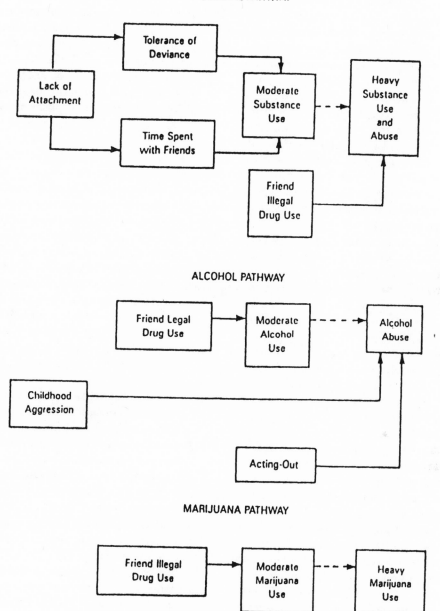

Figure 5–1. Developmental pathways to chemical dependency
Source: Brook et al. (1992).

unique *paths* determined by the drugs that they use and numerous factors that pertain in their lives. Because of the great variability in developmental paths to chemical dependency, it is important to avoid overgeneralizing about how chemically dependent individuals got that way (Woody et al. 1992, Zucker 1994)

Multidimensional, Overdetermined, Interactional Development. The process of change in human development can be best described as multidimensional, overdetermined, and interactional.

To say development is a *multidimensional process* means that change proceeds along many dimensions or aspects of behavior simultaneously. Just consider how many different ways you have changed since you were a child: your personality, emotions, social behavior, cognitive skills, and other psychological characteristics are certainly different now than when you were very young. Many theories of development have focused on one or another dimension of change, but a comprehensive developmental perspective considers all dimensions and their relationships with one another. Later in this chapter we will examine in more detail how the development of chemical dependency involves many aspects of psychological change at different stages of life (Newcomb 1992).

Because so many influences determine the course of development it is described as an *overdetermined process.* Rarely is a single developmental influence responsible for a complex human behavior or condition. Many factors play a role in the evolution of drug and alcohol problems. Biology, personality, emotions, family, and social environment all contribute. Although theorists and researchers disagree about the importance of different factors, all agree that no single factor can be identified as "the cause" of those problems (Wicks-Nelson and Israel 1997).

The many dimensions of development and the many influences on development are entwined with one another in a very complex manner. When development is assumed to be an *interactional process,* what is meant is that the dimensions and influences assert mutual effects on one another. In other words, the different aspects of development are not independent of one another, but rather they interact with one another. A common type of interaction, for example, is the interplay between personality traits and environmental factors. Alcoholism and other dependencies develop not simply from personality alone or the environment alone, but instead from the many interactions over time between personality traits and environmental influences (Sadava 1987).

Developmental Continuity. Development involves functional relationships between earlier and later events. "The child is father to the man" is an old saying that conveys a basic fact of development. Many behaviors, traits, and experiences that occur at earlier stages or ages of development are linked with behaviors, traits, and experiences later in life. Explaining the manner in which earlier and later development are linked is a challenge that has generated many debates and theories, but the *functional relationship* between earlier and later events can be described in three basic terms: continuity, predisposition, and consequence, (Lerner et al. 1994, Wenar 1994, Wicks-Nelson and Israel 1997).

Developmental continuity means that later events are a continuation or extension of developmentally earlier events. For instance, the aggressive behavior of a prealcoholic boy may continue into adolescence as the teenage alcoholic's extreme antisocial activity, such as theft and fighting. Continuity does not necessarily mean that the same exact behavior or trait is retained over time. You should realize that many traits and behaviors, like aggression, can be expressed in different forms at different times.

The link between earlier and later events may also result from a *predisposition* that is stable and influences events across time. The predisposing condition may involve persistent biological, psychological, and/or environmental variables. For instance, temperament problems that originate early in life have been identified as predisposing influences in alcoholism and its accompanying antisocial behavior (Tarter and Vanyukov 1994).

Finally, the developmental link between earlier and later variables may be due to the *causal impact* of earlier variables on later ones. In other words, later events are the *consequence* of earlier events. However, the later event may not be the direct consequence, but rather an indirect result of some earlier event. The impact of earlier events on later ones is often mediated by a cascade of intervening events. For example, in Figure 5–1 the general pathway shows a relationship between early "lack of attachment" and later "moderate substance use." The relationship, however, is an indirect one that is mediated by the factors of "tolerance of deviance" and "time spent with friends" (Brook et al. 1992).

It is important to realize that for complicated conditions like chemical dependency it is difficult to clearly disentangle all the contributing developmental issues. Attempts to clarify the course of development involve an interplay between conceptual models and empirical studies of development.

Developmental Models and Chemical Dependency

To understand complex phenomena, scientists devise *models* that represent the important features of those phenomena. A **developmental model** is a representation of a developmental sequence over time and the relationships among variables that play a role in the sequence. Based on what you have learned so far in this chapter, you might rightly expect that no one developmental model of chemical dependency can successfully describe every case. However, the general features of a successful model can be identified. In this section we describe those features and discuss an example of a well-respected developmental model of alcoholism.

Phases and Context of Development. In order to successfully describe the changes in and influences on behavior over time, a developmental model must characterize the *phases of change* as well as the *context* in which change occurs.

The paths to alcoholism and drug addictions are indeed diverse, but the typical phases in the evolution of chemical dependency can be identified. The **developmental phases** of chemical dependency are initiation, escalation, and addiction. These phases are defined by the transitions between conditions of nonuse, use, abuse, and dependence. As shown in Figure 5–2, the *initiation phase* involves the transition between a condition of drug nonuse to use; the *escalation phase* refers to the transition from drug use to drug abuse; and the *addiction phase* indicates transition from drug abuse to dependence (Clayton 1992, Marlatt et al. 1988).

Although these developmental phases have general relevance, a few qualifications are in order. First, the phases are not linked to specific ages or stages. Certainly most cases of chemical dependency develop from adoles-

cence through young adulthood, but not all do. The phases may occur at many points in the life span from childhood to late adulthood. Also, this model does not specify the length of time required to develop chemical dependency. The spectrum of drug involvement from nonuse to dependency is very broad. Some people move rapidly to dependency while others show very gradual movement over long periods of time. How long it takes to become addicted depends on many things, not the least of which is the type of drug. Alcohol addiction, for example, is generally much slower to develop than cocaine addiction. Finally, no assumption is made that these transitions are inevitable. Obviously, not all drug users become drug abusers, and not all drug abusers become chemically dependent. However, people who are chemically dependent have progressed through these phases, and so it is a useful sequence to apply in understanding their development (Newcomb 1992).

As mentioned earlier, development results from many factors. The **developmental context** includes any variable that influences development across the life span (Wicks-Nelson and Israel 1997). A model of chemical dependency must describe this array of influences and the mechanisms by which they affect development. We can describe the context of development in terms of two major classes of variables: the individual domain and the environmental domain.

Phase 1: Initiation
Transition from nonuse to
drug use

⇓

Phase 2: Escalation
Transition from drug use to
drug abuse

⇓

Phase 3: Addiction
Transition from drug abuse
to drug dependency

Figure 5–2. Developmental phases of chemical dependency

The *individual domain* includes variables that characterize the individual, in particular psychological and biological influences. The *biological variables* are genetic predispositions, neurological factors, biochemical events, and other bodily processes that exert an impact on development. Personality traits, emotional states, cognitive processes, and other mental or behavioral events are *psychological variables.*

Variables outside the individual are the *environmental domain,* encompassing the physical environment and social environment. Geographical location, climate, environmental pollutants, and physical hazards are elements of the *physical environment.* Clearly, for chemical dependency models, the *social environment* is more influential. The family environment entails not just family members, but the relationships among family members and between the family and the world. In addition sociocultural factors such as peer groups, social institutions (such as schools and the legal system), cultural norms and traditions, and historical trends play important roles.

A Biopsychosocial Model of Alcoholism. An useful example of a developmental model is found in psychologist Robert Zucker's model of alcoholism (Zucker 1987, 1994). Zucker describes his work as a **biopsychosocial model** because it characterizes the development of alcoholism in terms of the interplay between biological, psychological, and social variables over the life span. This model makes four important assumptions about how alcoholism develops.

1. People vary along a *continuum of risk* or vulnerability to alcoholism. Individual risk at any age or stage is best described probabilistically, that is, in terms of the likelihood of alcoholism;
2. What determines an individual's overall risk is his *risk load,* or the combination of alcoholism-promoting influences from the biological, psychological, peer, familial, and sociocultural domains. At any age or stage, alcoholism risk is defined by multiple, interacting influences;

3. The *domains of influence* have different importance for alcoholism development at different ages or stages; and
4. Some *influences* on alcoholism development are specific to alcoholism, but other nonspecific influences affect other conditions as well.

Zucker's model is flexible enough to allow for the description of four different kinds of alcoholism that are distinguished by their developmental paths: antisocial alcoholism, developmentally limited alcoholism, negative-affect alcoholism, and primary alcoholism.

- *Antisocial alcoholism* is a type with early onset of alcohol abuse and severe, persistent alcohol-related problems, as well as significant antisocial behavior. The developmental background is marked by a family history of alcoholism indicating a genetic predisposition, and an individual history of aggressive and antisocial behavior during childhood.
- *Developmentally limited alcoholism* is a predominantly adolescent-stage problem associated with other socially deviant behaviors and affiliation with a deviant peer group. This type of alcoholism is usually preceded by a period of better adjustment compared with antisocial alcoholism, and it tends to disappear as the adolescent makes a successful transition into young adulthood.
- *Negative affect alcoholism* is a later-onset type that is typically preceded developmentally by negative emotional states such as depression rather than by antisocial behavior. The symptoms of this type are somewhat less severe and it is more prevalent in women than are the other types.
- *Primary alcoholism* is a pattern in which alcoholism-specific influences are dominant and that is not clearly linked with developmentally earlier disturbances. This type is a cumulative result of problem drinking and the stresses that result from drinking, such as occupational troubles and marital disruption, and is generally a milder form of alcoholism than the other types.

Like other contemporary developmental models of chemical dependency, the biopsychosocial model is based on the results of empirical studies; thus, its success depends on how well it organizes and explains the facts accumulated by those studies. In the next section you will learn about the methods and findings of developmental research on chemical dependency.

5–2 Developmental Research

Questions about development are best answered through systematic research that examines the changes in people's lives over time. Ultimately, developmental research will determine which models of chemical dependency are most accurate. To date, numerous investigations have been conducted on the ways in which alcoholism and drug addictions evolve in the human life span, but many questions still remain unanswered. In this section you will learn about three kinds of developmental research: (1) retrospective research, (2) the longitudinal method, and (3) research on vulnerability, risk, and protection.

Retrospective Research

In working with clients, counselors often inquire about their personal histories, family backgrounds, and significant experiences in order to try to piece together an account of their life stories. Developmental researchers, too, do something similar, albeit in a more controlled and objective manner. In **retrospective research**, development is studied by collecting information about the past from people's recollections and reports. The term retrospective refers to a looking back at events that have already occurred. By pooling retrospective information from many individuals, researchers hope to piece together a general picture of development.

One example of retrospective research in the substance abuse field is found in the *National Household Survey on Drug Abuse*, a large survey of more than twenty-five thousand Americans from ages 12 through adulthood (National Clearinghouse for Drug and Alcohol Information 1998). Among other questions, survey participants were asked to report the age at which they first used specific drugs in order for researchers to estimate year-to-year trends in the initiation of use for different drugs. First use of marijuana, for example, was reported by 2.1 million people in 1997, while only 1.4 million new users were identified in 1991. The study concluded that the increased incidence was accounted for mainly by new users in the 12- to 17-year-old age group.

As valuable as retrospective data is, there are several potential problems with this type of research. If you have ever tried to recall specific facts about your behavior several years or longer ago, you know that it is not always easy. Memory can be unreliable, vague, and fickle. Any finding from a retrospective study, therefore, is potentially limited by inaccuracies in the recollections of its participants. In addition, reports are subject to bias because of the participants' reluctance to admit to drug use, especially the use of illegal drugs. Because of such methodological limitations, the findings of retrospective research should be interpreted with caution.

The Longitudinal Method

The **longitudinal method** is a research strategy that monitors or tracks individual development over a long period of time. Investigations with this method are sometimes called *follow-up studies* because the participants are "followed" over time; that is, they are evaluated periodically over the course of the study's duration. Unlike retrospective research, the longitudinal method does not rely on participants' recollections. The advantage of this method is quite simple: the researcher can gain a perspective on the sequence and impact of variables on the individual's behavior over long time intervals. By evaluating the relationship of variables in an extended time sequence, researchers are able to draw conclusions about the relative strength of many influences on development (Lerner et al. 1994).

Many good longitudinal studies have been conducted on various issues in drug use, abuse, and dependence. To illustrate two approaches to this method we will discuss the investigations of Shedler and Block (1990) and the Michigan State University/University of Michigan Longitudinal Study (Fitzgerald et al. 1995, Zucker 1994).

The Shedler and Block Study. In this study an attempt was made to evaluate the links between personality and social behaviors in childhood and later adolescent drug use patterns by following the study's participants from preschool age to age 18. Based on their patterns of drug use at age 18, the participants were placed in three groups: (1) "abstainers," who showed no drug use, (2) "experimenters," who had tried marijuana on a few occasions and had tried at least one other drug, and (3) "frequent users," who had used marijuana once or more per week and had also used other drugs.

The three groups were assessed in terms of their adjustment at age 18 and were found to differ in several important respects. Unsurprisingly, frequent users were maladjusted, exhibiting unhappiness, social alienation, hostile and antisocial attitudes, and poor self-control. Unexpectedly, the abstainers were found to have some adjustment problems also; they tended to be tense and emotionally restricted (uptight) as well as having social anxieties. Of the three groups, the experimenters seemed to be the most well-adjusted, sociable, and stable in terms of self-control. For the abstainer and frequent-user groups, characteristics at age 18 were associated with similar characteristics at age 7. Furthermore, the abstainer and frequent-use groups both contained participants whose childhoods were marked by a poor relationship with their mothers, many of whom were described as cold and unresponsive.

The researchers concluded that some experimental use of drugs like marijuana may be a normative event that is part of the adolescent transition for relatively well-adjusted youths. Frequent users and drug abusers have less healthy backgrounds and traits that predict their inclination toward maladaptive drug taking. This study (Shedler and Block 1990) supports the idea that the developmen-

tal paths for drug nonuse (abstainers), drug use (experimenters), and drug abuse (frequent users) are distinctive.

The Michigan Longitudinal Study. Begun in 1982, this project assessed the developmental progress of a sample of boys whose fathers are alcoholic (Zucker 1987, Zucker et al. 1994). Many studies have demonstrated that paternal alcoholism dramatically increases the likelihood of alcoholism among the male children. Thus, sons of alcoholics are considered a **high-risk group,** with abnormally high risk for chemical dependency. The researchers intend to monitor this high-risk group from the ages of 3 to 5 years forward to age 21 in order to evaluate the impact of numerous influences on alcoholism development.

An important feature of this study is the use of a *comparison group* of boys of similar ages and social-familial characteristics, but whose fathers are not alcohol or drug abusers. When the high-risk and comparison groups are compared, the data show that dissimilarities exist as early as the preschool period. High-risk boys are found to have more behavioral difficulties (e.g., impulsiveness and aggressiveness), cognitive deficits (e.g., inattention), and problems in the home environment (e.g., results of inadequate parental skills) than their age peers in the comparison group (Jansen et al. 1995, Zucker et al. 1996a).

In conjunction with the results of other longitudinal research this study has provided support for Zucker's classification of alcoholism in terms of developmental paths. In addition, the findings from this study have promoted interest in early intervention for high-risk children in the hope of reducing their risk for drug and alcohol problems (Nye et al. 1995).

Limitations of Longitudinal Research. Despite the significant findings it can provide in developmental studies of chemical dependency, the longitudinal method is not perfect. In interpreting the results of such research you should bear in mind some of its limitations.

The relationships between earlier and later variables are assessed in terms of statistical associations called *correlations*. Although correlations suggest cause-and-effect links between variables, they never absolutely prove cause-and-effect. For instance, in the Shedler and Block (1990) study, the correlation between impulsiveness at age 7 and drug abuse at age 18 does not prove that the early impulsiveness causes later drug-taking problems. Neither does the timidity of children at age 7 necessarily cause their later abstention from drug use.

In addition, longitudinal studies are sometimes hampered by the loss of participants as time goes by. This problem of participant *attrition* is especially serious for very long-term studies because of the difficulty in maintaining contact with participants, as well as the waning of participants' motivation over long periods of time. The loss of participants means a loss of data, and that interferes with the ability to draw conclusions about the meaning of a study's results.

Last, the longitudinal method is limited by some problems that are common to many research strategies. In particular, *sampling*—the selection of participants—is itself a potential source of trouble. What you will find in your study depends on whom you study. If a sample is too small or unrepresentative of the population at large, then the results are likely to be biased or distorted.

Vulnerability, Risk, and Protection

As you have seen, a major goal of developmental studies is to assess an individual's potential for chemical dependency and to identify variables that influence that potential. **Vulnerability** is a condition that refers to an individual's susceptibility to drug involvement based on the balance between variables that increase *risk* and those that provide *protection*. Investigations reveal that vulnerability is no simple matter, but rather a product of many developmental variables, in particular risk and protective factors.

Risk Factors. Any variable that increases the likelihood of a developmental event or behavior is a **risk factor** for that event or behavior. In Table 5–1 we summarize the most commonly found risk factors for chemical dependency in the three developmental phases. Please note that risk factors of earlier phases may continue to exert influence on later phases. In other words, there can be considerable developmental continuity between earlier and later risk factors.

The general individual profile of *initiation-phase risk* is an active, impulsive person who has trouble controlling emotions and is something of a thrill seeker. Children at high risk for drug use often have behavioral and emotional disturbances, such as anxiety, depression, aggression, and antisocial behavior. In the environmental domain the easy availability of drugs and alcohol is an important risk factor. Children whose parents, siblings, and peers use substances have much greater access to and more opportunities to begin using drugs and alcohol. In addition, the initiation risk increases when the individual has difficulty in school and lives in a distressed family environment in which conflict is prevalent.

The level of *escalation-phase risk* depends mainly on three conditions: (1) the drugs serve to satisfy important psychological and social needs for the user, (2) the motivation for avoiding drugs is weak, and (3) the opportunities for regular drug use are reliable (Kaplan and Johnson 1992). Escalation to drug abuse is also strongly predicted by the age at which the person begins to use drugs. Generally, the earlier in life the initiation phase begins, the higher the risk for escalation and ultimate dependency. Frequent use of several drugs, especially if they are used in high dosages, further increases potential for escalation to substance abuse. Substance abusers are more apt to have been socially maladjusted and alienated than most people, and many also have a history of delinquent behavior. Although family problems are risk factors for escalation, a more important factor is the peer group, especially during adolescence, the prime *age of risk*. When peers abuse drugs and exhibit socially deviant behaviors, the risk of developing abuse increases dramatically.

Transition from abuse to addiction is affected by the presence of biological or genetic predispositions, especially for people with a family history of alcoholism. *Addiction-phase risk* also depends on the presence of serious

Table 5–1. Risk factors for chemical dependency development

| Phase | Risk Factor Domains | |
	Individual	Environmental
Initiation	Poor impulse control	Drug availability
	Poor self-regulation	Parent drug use
	Sensation seeking	Peer drug use
	Aggressiveness	Family discord
	Unconventionality	School problems
	Overactivity	
Escalation	Early first use of substances	Peer drug abuse
	Frequency and·intensity	Deviant peer group
	of substance abuse	Parental drug abuse
	Emotional problems	Family discord
	Delinquency	Poor attachment relationships
	Social maladjustment	School failure
Addiction	Biological/genetic predisposition	Multiple stressors
	Psychopathology	Poverty
	Euphoria-seeking	Unemployment
	Poor coping skills	Relationship failure
	Self-destructiveness	

psychological disorders like depression and antisocial personality. Poor coping skills and self-destructiveness also contribute to dependence. Although environmental risk factors for chemical dependency are less potent than they are for substance abuse, multiple stressors such as poverty and unemployment do make a difference. In the transition from abuse to dependency it is worth remembering that many of the risk factors are also the accumulated consequences of abusing drugs. For example, the impoverished, unemployed alcohol abuser may be poor and out of work as a result of drinking, and those stressors serve to increase risk for alcohol dependency.

Clearly, assessment of individual risk requires attention to many aspects of the person's biological, psychological, family, and social milieu. To conclude our discussion of risk factors for chemical dependency, let's consider these general *principles of risk.*

1. Risk factors come from both individual and environmental domains. No single factor is always present for all chemically dependent people, and risk factors tend to converge and interact with one another over time.
2. Risk factors have different impacts at different periods of development. The im-portance of any risk factor depends on the individual's age, stage, or phase of development.
3. Risk factors have a cumulative impact over time. The presence of multiple risk factors leads to a snowballing of vulnerability (Brook et al. 1992, Clayton 1992, Glantz and Pickens 1992, Hawkins et al. 1992, Marlatt et al. 1988, Newcomb 1995, Zucker 1994).

Protective Factors. In the matter of developmental vulnerability to chemical dependency, risk is only one side of the coin. The other side is *protection*. Protection, however, does not mean simply the absence of risk, but rather the presence of positive, health-promoting influences that act to reduce overall vulnerability. Such influences are called **protective factors**, that is, variables that reduce the likelihood of drug involvement. The major protective factors for chemical dependency are shown in Table 5–2 (Clayton 1992, Hawkins et al. 1992, Kandel and Davies 1992, Newcomb 1995).

In the individual domain, personal coping skills and problem-solving ability are paramount protective factors. Those traits are labeled *resilience* by Rutter (1987), who considers them significant buffers against a variety of adjustment problems as well as drug involve-

Table 5–2. Protective factors for chemical dependency development:

Protective Factors and Domains	
Individual	*Environmental*
Adaptability	Family religiosity
Academic committment	Family stability
Proactive assertiveness	Family support
Religiosity	Social norms against drugs
Resilience	Social role incompatibility
Self-efficacy	Social support systems

ment. Additionally, vulnerability is reduced by the characteristics of self-assertiveness and self-efficacy, or belief in one's competence to act with success. For children and adolescents dedication to school and to academic success are also valuable, as is a sense of personal religious conviction or religiosity.

Environmental protective factors mainly include family characteristics. A stable family structure, an emotionally supportive family, and the family's commitment to a religious belief system add to protection. The presence of reliable social support systems in the community and consistent antidrug norms in the social environment also matter. When the individual's social role demands are incompatible with drug use, protection is enhanced; for example, a student-athlete whose participation in a team sport is inconsistent with drug use is less likely to use drugs.

By definition, protective factors lessen vulnerability to chemical dependency. But how do they accomplish that? In general, two mechanisms of protection are at work.

1. Protective factors offset or compensate for the impact of risk factors, providing a *buffer* against risk. For example, a high-risk adolescent may benefit from the protective value of special attention and support from teachers and guidance personnel.
2. Protective factors promote health-enhancing experiences and events. For example, a high-risk child who develops a strong dedication to school will open up other opportunities such as social success and positive peer group attachments that enhance overall protection (Brook et al. 1990, Newcomb 1995).

Like risk factors, protective factors also have a cumulative impact on vulnerability. The individual's vulnerability is determined by the unique constellation of risk and protective factors that pertains at any given time, but protective factors, like risk factors, have different impacts at different ages or stages. In the next section of this chapter you will learn more about the issues that affect development of drug use, abuse, and dependence at different periods of the life span.

5–3 Drug Use Across the Life Span

Like most people you probably think of drugs as a major concern for adolescents and young adults. If so you are correct, but only partially. Although the peak period of drug use is in the late teens and twenties, people at many stages of life use and abuse drugs. In this section we will explore the developmental issues that pertain to drug involvement in childhood, adolescence, and adulthood.

Childhood

To many, even the thought of children using drugs seems ridiculous and improbable. Yet drugs are commonplace in our society and even young children have an awareness of, and often even have experiences with drugs. Through exposure to drug use in their families and in the media, children learn from an early age about different kinds of drugs, the settings in which drugs are used, and ways of using drugs (Noll et al. 1990).

Drug Use by Children. Do you recall being allowed a sip of wine from your parent's glass at dinnertime? Such instances of *guided experimentation* are quite prevalent in our culture, and in these episodes many young children are provided their first psychoactive drug-taking experiences. However, guided use is not as great a concern as the independent use of drugs by children, because of the potential such independent use has for setting a foundation for later abuse. In general, the earlier a child starts to use drugs, especially illicit drugs, the more likely he or she is to develop a number of serious psychosocial problems, including drug and alcohol problems. Independent intentional drug use by preadolescent children is assumed to be quite uncommon, especially in children younger than 9 years, but there is little systematic evidence about drug use by very young children. Clinical and legal reports of illicit drug use before age 9 typically show a child who is emotionally disturbed and whose family is quite dysfunctional (Newcomb and Bentler 1989).

The American Drug and Alcohol Survey (ADAS) is an important source of data about the reported use of psychoactive substances in preadolescents, and is based on surveys of about 25,000 elementary-school children nationwide. Table 5–3 summarizes the findings of the 1995 ADAS for grades four to six.

During the mid-1990s, cigarette and inhalant use among sixth graders increased, but no significant change has been noted in use of those substances for fourth and fifth graders. In addition, no major change occurred in use of alcohol and marijuana in 4th- to 6th-grade students (Edwards 1996). Of special concern is the prevalence of inhalant use in preadolescents. Inhalants are more problematic than even marijuana, probably because of their easy availability and low cost. By the eighth

Table 5–3. Drug use in elementary school children, 1995

	Percentage Reporting Use		
	Grade 4	*Grade 5*	*Grade 6*
Alcohol	2	3	5
Cigarettes	10	15	26
Inhalants	6	7	12
Marijuana	1	2	3

Source: Adapted from Edwards (1996).

grade, marijuana surpasses inhalants in popularity, and inhalant use declines from eighth grade through high school. However, inhalants are associated with many severe problems. Children who use inhalants often use other drugs too, and are more likely to be from a background with multiple risk factors such as poverty and poor parental supervision (Beauvais 1992).

Studies of children at high risk for delinquency reveal that the early onset of drug use in preadolescents is linked with other behavioral and social disturbances. For instance, an investigation (Inciardi and Pottieger 1991) of young adolescents who were involved in selling crack/cocaine found that in their preteen years most of these children had used alcohol and marijuana, and had engaged in other criminal and antisocial activities. In general, a preadolescent start to illicit drug use predicts more severe delinquent behaviors and substance abuse problems in adolesence. Although drug use and delinquency reinforce each other, drug use has more impact on stimulating delinquent behavior than delinquency has on drug use (Huizinga et al. 1994).

Childhood Vulnerability. Earlier in this chapter you learned about some general risk and protective factors associated with drug involvement. Here, we will emphasize the factors that are most pertinent to preadolescents. Although there is a significant amount of drug use among preadolescents, diagnoses of substance-related disorders are very uncommon. Identification of chemical dependency in this group is unlikely owing to the youth of its members. Preteen drug users typically have not had enough time or drug experiences to develop dependence.

The major influences on vulnerability in preadolescents appear to be individual temperament traits and the social environment, especially the family. **Temperament** refers to basic emotional and behavioral response tendencies that are strongly driven by heredity. The temperament traits that most influence drug use are *high activity level, high emotionality, low sociability, low attention capacity,* and *low soothability.* In other words, a child who is extremely active and restless (activity level), who has strong moods or feelings (emotionality), who is socially isolated and introverted (sociability), who is easily distracted (attention capacity), and who is hard to calm down (soothability) is at risk (Tarter and Vanyukov 1994).

Temperament traits emerge early in life and establish a foundation for later personality, as well as emotional and social characteristics. However, temperament alone is not the whole story. Rather, a child's temperament interacts with the social environment to shape the child's psychological state. An infant with a *difficult temperament*, who is hyperactive, cranky, and emotionally overresponsive, may provoke negative reactions from the parents, resulting in a disturbed parent–child relationship. Later, in elementary school years, the child with poor social skills and poor emotional control is likely to be unpopular with age peers and become somewhat isolated from normative peer supports (e.g., school clubs). By late-childhood the high-risk child often begins to form links with other socially deviant peers (Brook et al. 1995, Glantz 1992, Lynskey and Fergusson 1995).

The family environment is of special importance for the status of the child's vulnerability. When a child is raised in a family with inadequate support and supervision and weak emotional attachments between the child and parents, risk is greatly enhanced. Drug availability also plays a role in drug use. Here too, the family is instrumental in increasing or lessening vulnerability. When parents and older siblings use drugs, those drugs are likely to be accessible to the child in the home. In addition, drug-using parents and siblings convey information to the child about the acceptability of drug consumption, thus promoting a drug-tolerant attitude in the child. Studies of high-risk children demonstrate that as early as preschool age they form alcohol-relevant beliefs and perceptions by observing alcohol use in family members, and those cognitive schemas may set a basis for their later vulnerability (Newcomb 1995, Zucker et al. 1995b).

Adolescence

The teenage years are a critical developmental time in many respects, as social, sexual, cognitive, and physical changes occur rapidly and dramatically at that time. Just as adolescence carries potential for healthy growth, it also contains many potential hazards. In regard to drug involvement, adolescence is a crucial period for two reasons: (1) most initiation to drug use occurs in adolescence, and (2) most escalation to more serious drug abuse and dependency problems begins in adolescence.

Drug Use by Adolescents. Beginning in early adolescence and continuing through the late teenage years, overall use of drugs tends to increase, and the late teenage years are a peak age of risk for escalation to substance abuse. Evidence of the extent of adolescent drug-use is provided by the *Monitoring The Future Study* (Monitoring the Future 1999), a nationwide drug-use survey of American adolescents in the eighth, tenth, and twelfth grades. Table 5–4 summarizes the findings of the 1999 version of that survey.

In 1998–99, alcohol use was reported by 43.5 percent of eighth graders, 63.7 percent of tenth graders, and 73.8 percent of twelfth graders. In addition "any illicit drug" use was reported by 20.5 percent of eighth graders, 35.9 percent of tenth graders, and 42.1 percent

Table 5–4. Monitoring The Future study, 1998–99

	Percentage Reporting Past-Year Use		
	8th Grade	*10th Grade*	*12th Grade*
Any alcohol use	43.5	63.7	73.8
Any illicit drug	20.5	35.9	42.1
Marijuana/hashish	16.5	32.1	37.8
Any illicit drug other than marijuana	10.5	16.7	20.7

Source: Monitoring The Future (1999).

of twelfth graders. Marijuana was by far the most common illicit drug reported. Although these figures indicate a slight drop from the previous year for eighth graders, small increases in reported use were found for both tenth and twelfth graders. Following a period of declining illicit drug use in the 1980s, an upsurge of drug use in adolescents was seen in the 1990s began to level off around 1997. Most of the increase seems to be accounted for by marijuana use, but some increases in use of cocaine, stimulants, and hallucinogens also occurred.

As you see in Table 5–4, the increase in alcohol and illicit drug use by teens is most apparent between eighth and tenth grade, or the early adolescent years from approximately ages 12 to 15. The use of marijuana by teens is especially noteworthy because marijuana is considered a **gateway drug**, that is, a drug that introduces youths to illicit substance use, and that can promote subsequent use of other illicit drugs. In fact, teens who are regular marijuana users do typically use other drugs as well, especially alcohol, hallucinogens, and cocaine (Johnston et al. 1995a, Kandel 1982, National Clearinghouse for Alcohol and Drug Information 1996a).

Other indicators of the potential for development of substance abuse in adolescence are findings showing that daily use of alcohol is reported by 1 percent of eighth graders, 1.9 percent of tenth graders, and 3.4 percent of twelfth graders. Surprisingly, even higher levels of daily marijuana use are reported: 1.4 percent by eighth graders, 3.8 percent by tenth graders, and 6 percent of twelfth graders (Monitoring The Future 1999). Additionally, in recent years high school students report that they are getting more intoxicated on various drugs, including marijuana, stimulants, and hallucinogens (National Clearinghouse for Alcohol and Drug Information 1996a, Substance Abuse and Mental Health Services Administration 1996b).

Precise information on the prevalence of substance use disorders in adolescents is rare. Disagreements about the diagnosis of those disorders in teens emphasize the fact that more attention to age-relevant symptoms is needed before exact data will be available

(Bukstein and Kaminer 1994). However, some evidence (Lewinsohn et al. 1993) shows rather high rates of substance use disorders among American adolescents for the following substances: alcohol 6 percent, cannabis 6.5 percent, amphetamines 2 percent, and cocaine 0.5 percent. These figures are consistent with adult data, in that these disorders are generally more prevalent among boys, with the exception of amphetamine-use disorders, which are twice as common in girls. A recent nationwide survey of drug abuse, the National Household Survey of Drug Abuse, (National Clearinghouse for Alcohol and Drug Information 1998) reported that approximately 915,000 youths age 12 to 17 were alcohol dependent, and that an estimated 1.1 million youths were dependent on an illicit drug, mostly on marijuana.

Although no single developmental pattern applies to every adolescent, researchers have identified a common sequence of escalation that many follow: (1) beer and wine, (2) cigarettes and liquor, (3) marijuana, (4) problem drinking, and (5) other illicit drugs. This progression is certainly not absolute or inevitable, but the vast majority of teens who end up abusing illicit drugs have followed a similar sequence. The **gateway theory** of drug abuse proposes that the early use of cigarettes, alcohol, and marijuana (the *gateway drugs*) increases the likelihood of youths progressing to even harder substances (Kandel 1982, Kandel and Yamaguchi 1993). In recent years inhalants seem to have overtaken marijuana as a gateway drug, particularly for younger and economically disadvantaged teens. Inhalant abuse at a young age is a strong predictor of later, multiple drug abuse (Edwards 1996). The progression to substance abuse is not guaranteed, by any means, and in fact most gateway drug users will not become substance abusers. They do, however, have greater risk for developing more serious drug problems than youths who never use any drugs.

A compelling feature of teenage substance abuse is its association with other serious academic, social, and psychological disturbances. According to **problem-behavior theory**, drug use by adolescents is only one dimension of a general pattern of *deviance proneness* that is expressed in many areas of psychosocial functioning (Jessor 1987, Jessor et al. 1991). Support for this theory comes from many sources. Studies of adolescent delinquency find that delinquent youths have abnormally high rates of drug and alcohol use and that their delinquent behaviors are often substance-related. For adolescent girls, substance abuse is connected with pregnancy, and the rates of childbearing in this group are especially high for girls with emotional disturbances and substance abuse (Substance Abuse and Mental Health Services Administration, 1995a). Academic difficulties, too, are part of the problem-behavior package: school failure, dropping out, and learning disabilities further complicate the picture for teenage substance abusers (Fox and Forbing 1991, Kaminer 1991).

Vulnerability in Adolescence.   A glance at Table 5–4 will reveal that drug use by adolescents is relatively commonplace. By their senior year of high school, most American teens will have used alcohol, and a large minority will have tried one or more illicit drugs, especially marijuana. Such widespread drug use has led some researchers to describe drug use as a *normative behavior* for the adolescent. In this view, the adolescent attempts to make the transition into an independent adult role by testing adult behaviors, including drug use (Jessor 1987, Shedler and Block 1990).

More than a dozen theories have been proposed to explain why adolescents begin to experiment with drugs, but no single theory has completely succeeded in describing all the variables that move a nonuser to initiate use (Petraitis et al. 1995). Most theories agree that the initiation of drug use by teens depends mainly on influences from the social environment. Certainly, peer use is important, but peer use alone is not as potent as a combination of peer use with a strong peer orientation on the part of the adolescent. Additional impetus is provided by parental and sibling drug use. Cross-cultural studies find that adolescents' drug use is shaped both by the degree of acceptance of drugs in the culture, and by the adolescents' identification with cultural

values and traditions (Oetting and Beauvais 1991). Given the saturation of modern American society with drugs and alcohol, the level of our teens' drug usage should be no surprise.

Although some drug use may be considered a normative process for the adolescent, drug abuse and dependency are not. Problems in the family and drug abuse and antisocial behavior by peers appear to be the main environmental risk factors for the development of substance use disorders. High-risk teens come from families in which their emotional needs are neglected and little parental supervision is offered, and in which parents and siblings abuse substances. Paternal alcoholism is a major risk factor for both drug-use initiation and escalation, and is linked with family stress and negative emotional states in the adolescent (Chassin et al. 1996, Duncan et al. 1996). Often as a reaction to difficulties in their family environment, adolescents affiliate with other unconventional, antiauthority peers. Participation in deviant peer groups in turn increases the likelihood that drug involvement and other delinquent activities will occur and that school commitment and achievement will decline.

Escalation to drug abuse in teens is also associated with intraindividual characteristics. Psychological disorders such as depression and eating disorders are common problems that provoke substance abuse in adolescents. In addition, the transition from use to abuse is more likely in teens who have deficient social and academic skills, poor self-control, and low self-esteem (Wills et al. 1996). Teens who are integrated into antisocial, deviant peer systems may develop a **negative identity**, a self-concept organized around rejection of social norms, including those norms prohibiting drug use (Wenar 1994).

What prevents so many teenage drug users from progressing to drug abuse and dependency? The major protective factors for teens are family variables. The presence of both biological parents in the family has a strong protective effect, as does the degree of emotional support that parents provide for their adolescent child. In addition, the family's sanctions against drug use act as a deterrent, especially for a teen who has close, positive relationships with family members. According to the **social developmental model**, healthy adolescent development depends on the presence of prosocial adults, environmental norms against drug use, a sense of bonding to the teen's school, and a desire for academic achievement (O'Donnell et al. 1995).

In addition to the family's sanctions, peer disapproval of drug use has a protective role. Recent studies find a general decline in adolescents' disapproval of drug use, particularly for marijuana, and this change in attitude may partly explain the rise in use of marijuana and other drugs in the past few years (National Clearinghouse for Alcohol and Drug Information 1996a). However, even when peers use drugs, protection against drug involvement is provided by the teenager's own self-acceptance; that is, teens who accept themselves and have adequate self-esteem are better able to resist peer pressure to use drugs (Newcomb 1995).

Adolescent drug abuse has serious implications for the individual abuser as well as for society. Adolescence is a period of transition to adulthood in which the teen is acquiring the traits and skills need to function as an adult. Drug abuse interrupts adolescents' maturation in many ways that jeopardize their later adjustment. For instance, the disruption of academic achievement leads to occupational distress and economic difficulties, which in turn often reinforce the drug abuser's rejection of and alienation from mainstream society. In addition, the adolescent with a drug problem has considerable difficulty in establishing healthy relationships with the majority of people who do not have those problems, such as teachers and bosses. Usually drug abuse and dependency in adolescence set a very poor foundation for the teen's transition into adulthood (Kaminer 1991, Kandel 1984).

Adulthood

Exactly when adolescence ends and adulthood begins is a point open to question. Chronological age is sometimes a poor measure of entry into adulthood; some 20-year-olds are less adult than many 17-year-olds. Because researchers usually label the 18- to 25-year

range as young adulthood, our discussion of drug use in adults begins with that group. Compared with childhood and adolescence, adulthood is obviously a more extended developmental period, so in this section we examine drug involvement in three groups: young adults, middle-aged adults, and the elderly. The findings of the recent *National Household Survey on Drug Abuse* (1999) indicate a gradual drop-off of reported use for all major drugs during adulthood, as indicated in Table 5–5.

Drug Use in Adults. The state of affairs during young adulthood is somewhat paradoxical. Beginning in the early twenties, substance use tends to decline, yet young adulthood is the prime time for substance use disorders. The decline is especially significant for use of illicit drugs like marijuana, cocaine, and hallucinogens. Although alcohol use slows with age, nearly two-thirds of adults drink alcohol to some degree. The drop-off in substance use on entry into adulthood is probably associated with the individual's assumption of adult roles and responsibilities as well as changing social norms about acceptable behavior in adulthood. However, while it is true that most substance users curtail their drug taking in young adulthood, the more seriously drug-involved individuals are consolidating their substance use problems and developing numerous associated difficulties during this period. For them, young adulthood often in-

Table 5–5. Drug use in adults, 1998

Percentage Reporting Use in the Past Year		
	Ages	
	18–25	*26–34*	*35+*
Any illicit drug	27.4	12.7	5.5
Any illicit drug but marijuana	13.4	6.1	2.4
Alcohol	74.2	74.5	64.6
Cocaine	4.7	2.7	0.9
Hallucinogens	7.2	1.1	0.2
Heroin	0.4	0.1	0.0
Inhalants	3.2	0.5	0.2
Marijuana/hashish	24.1	9.7	4.1

Source: National Clearinghouse for Alcohol and Drug Information (1998).

volves progression to multiple drug abuse and substance dependence.

Despite the overall reduction of drug use during adulthood, the peak period for development of substance dependence is from an individual's early twenties to mid-thirties. According to the American Psychiatric Association (1994), the approximate prevalence rates of substance use disorders (substance abuse and substance dependence) in adults are as follows: alcohol 19 percent, amphetamines 2 percent, cannabis 4 percent, cocaine less than 0.5 percent, hallucinogens less than 0.5 percent, nicotine 20 percent, opioids less than 1 percent, and sedatives/hypnotics/anxiolytics 1 percent. In general, about one in five adults will develop a substance use disorder during their lifetime. During young adulthood, it is estimated that about 15 percent of alcohol users, 25 percent of marijuana users, and 37 percent of cocaine users are dependent on those substances. In addition, there are high rates of *dual dependence* in this age group; for example, about two-thirds of cocaine-dependent individuals are also dependent on alcohol (Clayton 1992, Newcomb 1992).

By middle age, the prevalence of illicit drug addictions has decreased dramatically. The **maturing-out hypothesis** explains the low rate of chemical dependency in middle-aged adults as a result of positive maturational changes that lead to a cessation of drug use (Winick 1962). While some addicts may mature their way out of chemical dependency, others stop for different reasons, including poor health and legal problems. Drug-related death is also a significant problem among adults; adults 35 to 54 years old account for more than half of drug-related deaths (Substance Abuse and Mental Health Services Administration 1995a). While illicit-drug dependence typically tapers off in adulthood, alcohol dependency usually reaches its peak in the 40 to 50 year period and declines thereafter. Most cases of alcohol dependency are apparent by the mid-forties, but some adults show a *late-onset alcoholism* that may not begin until they are in their fifties or later. Compared with alcohol dependency that starts in young adulthood, late-onset alcoholism is associated with fewer health problems and psychological

disorders and is often triggered by age-related stress (Abrams and Alexopoulos 1991). Although many chemically dependent people improve in adulthood, others maintain and extend their dependency over many years. As an example, consider that since 1990 the number of drug-related incidents requiring emergency room treatment has risen steadily for cocaine, heroin, and marijuana in both young adults 18 to 34 years old, and in adults 35 to 54 years old (Substance Abuse and Mental Health Services Administration 1995b).

Attention to drug use in older adults is a relatively recent phenomenon, but one that promises to expand as the baby boom generation ages. The two drug problems most noted in older populations are alcoholism and prescription drug abuse. The complications of drug and alcohol use for individuals in this age group are more serious than for younger individuals due to age-related changes in bodily functioning. For example, alcohol is metabolized more slowly in the elderly, thus increasing its toxicity as well as its impact on the nervous and cardiovascular systems. Besides alcohol, prescription drugs are also prone to abuse in the elderly, who receive a large percentage of all prescriptions written. For instance, nearly one-third of all daily benzodiazepine users are elderly (Abrams and Alexopoulos 1991)

Vulnerability in Adulthood. Compared with younger drug users, adults are less influenced by forces in the social environment and more affected by individual characteristics. Among adult psychological variables, adult antisocial personality is a leading risk factor for addictions, especially in men. Emotional problems, too, strongly affect drug and alcohol use in adults, but the relationship of emotional conditions and substance use is not altogether clear. For example, in older adult women an increase in alcohol consumption is associated with a decrease in feelings of depression, but for older men increased feelings of depression are linked with a decrease in alcohol use (Schutte et al. 1995). However, for chemically dependent adults mood disorders are prominent associated disturbances, particularly for women (Turnbull and Gomberg 1988).

Biological vulnerability to dependence may be partly genetic and partly the consequence of long-term substance abuse. The **pharmacological model** of chemical dependency attributes most of the vulnerability to dependence to the abuser's *drug consumption*. According to that model, the main risk factors for dependence are the amount, frequency, and types of drugs consumed, as well as the psychological and biological consequences of drug abuse (Newcomb 1992). Adults with a long, rich history of substance use and abuse are likely to accumulate increasing degrees of biological vulnerability from their lifelong consumption.

Environmental influences also matter in adult vulnerability. Marital status and employment are two major elements in adulthood. Generally, marriage acts as a protective factor, whereas divorce and separation increase risk of drug use. Higher rates of drug problems tend to occur in single, separated, and divorced adults, especially males. In addition, job status affects drug use. Unemployment increases risk for several reasons: it imposes financial stress on the unemployed individual, damages the person's self-concept, and alienates the person from mainstream society. Some caution is in order in interpreting the associations between these factors and chemical dependency because such problems as marital discord and joblessness may be as much a result of drug involvement as a cause (Flewelling et al. 1992).

Employment does not necessarily always protect against drug problems. In fact some kinds of employment seem to increase the risk. Data on drug and alcohol use by people employed in various job categories shows that people in traditional blue-collar occupations, especially construction workers, have relatively high rates of alcohol and illicit drug use, while the white-collar occupations have relatively low rates (Hoffman et al. 1996). Nevertheless, some higher-status occupations provide more opportunities to obtain and use drugs than others. For example, physicians, dentists, and nurses have easier access to a variety of controlled substances, and consequently have high rates of abuse for certain drugs. Interpreting these findings is difficult because so many variables are associated with different occupations, including education, socioeconomic status, gender, and job stress.

The relation between socioeconomic status (SES) and vulnerability to drug involvement is puzzling. In general, SES is only modestly correlated with overall drug involvement. However, low SES (poverty) is strongly linked with illicit-drug problems and heavy alcohol use, but whether by itself it is more a cause than an effect is still open to debate. In considering this association it is important also to note that as a group poor people have higher-than-average rates of abstention from drugs (Flewelling et al. 1992).

Chapter Summary

5–1

The developmental perspective examines patterns of change across the life span. It assumes that development involves both quantitative and qualitative changes; follows many paths; is a multidimensional, overdetermined, and interactional process; and entails functional relationships between earlier and later events. Developmental models represent sequences of development over time. In terms of chemical dependency, the phases of development are initiation, escalation, and addiction. The developmental context of chemical dependency includes variables in both the individual and environmental domains. Zucker's biopsychosocial model of alcoholism is an example of a developmental model.

5–2

Developmental research includes retrospective studies, the longitudinal method, and research on vulnerability, risk, and protection. The retrospective method looks back on development by using the participants' recollections about past events; it is limited by memory inaccuracies and reporting biases. The longitudinal method follows up on development by monitoring participants over time, as in the Shedler and Block study and the Michigan Longitudinal Study. Longitudinal studies are limited by the inability of correlations to prove causation, by the attrition of participants, and by sampling bias. Vulnerability is susceptibility to drug involvement, based on a balance between risk and protection. Risk studies examine risk factors for drug use and abuse. Protective factors lessen the likelihood of drug use and abuse.

5–3

Childhood drug use often begins by guided experimentation. The American Drug and Alcohol Survey reveals the extent of drug use in elementary school. Childhood vulnerability to drug use is based on temperament and aspects of the family environment. Adolescence is a high-risk period for drug use and abuse. The Monitoring The Future study shows the prevalence of drug use in American teenagers. The transition from drug use to abuse and dependence in adolescence is addressed by several theories, including the gateway theory, the problem-behavior theory, and the social developmental model. Major risk factors for teens include use of gateway drugs, negative identity, peer deviance, and family discord. Young adulthood is a period of significant drug use and abuse. Throughout middle adulthood, drug use declines through a maturing-out process, although many adults exhibit abuse and dependency problems. Risk for drug abuse in adults involves pharmacological effects of drugs, psychopathology, and psychosocial stressors.

Terms to Remember

biopsychosocial model
developmental context
developmental model
developmental path
developmental perspective
developmental phases
gateway drug
gateway theory
high-risk group
longitudinal method
maturing-out hypothesis
negative identity
pharmacological model
problem-behavior theory
protective factors
risk factor
social developmental model
temperament
vulnerability

Suggested Readings

Glantz, M., and Pickens, R., eds. (1992). Vulnerability to drug abuse: introduction and overview. In *Vulnerability to Drug Abuse*, pp. 1–14. Washington, DC: American Psychological Association.

Rahdert, E., and Czechowicz, D. (1995). *Adolescent Drug Abuse: Clinical Assessment and Therapeutic Interventions* (NIDA Research Monograph 156). Rockville, MD: National Institute on Drug Abuse.

Causes of Chemical Dependency

Chapter Outline

6–1   BIOLOGY OF CHEMICAL DEPENDENCY
    The Disease Model of Chemical Dependency
    Hereditary Influences
    Neurophysiology of Addiction

6–2   PERSONALITY AND CHEMICAL DEPENDENCY
    Psychodynamic Views
    Personality Traits

6–3   LEARNING AND CHEMICAL DEPENDENCY
    Classical Conditioning
    Operant Conditioning

6–4   COGNITIVE INFLUENCES ON CHEMICAL DEPENDENCY
    Social Learning and Social Cognitive Theory
    Expectancy Theory

6–5   MOTIVATION AND EMOTION
    Tension and Stress Reduction

6–6   SOCIOCULTURAL INFLUENCES
    The Family
    Social Factors

Learning Objectives

Upon completing study of this chapter you should be able to:

1. Discuss the modern disease model of chemical dependency.
2. Describe the evidence for hereditary predispositions to chemical dependency.
3. Outline the principal neurophysiological mechanisms involved in addictions.
4. Characterize the psychodynamic view of personality in addictions.
5. Discuss the research on personality traits and addiction.
6. Identify and explain the role of classical and operant conditioning principles in chemical dependency.
7. Describe the main concepts of social learning and social cognitive theories as they pertain to chemical dependency.
8. Discuss the expectancy theory of substance abuse.
9. Compare and contrast the tension reduction, stress-response dampening, and self-medication theories of drug use.
10. Outline the significant family variables that influence chemical dependency.
11. Discuss the role of social factors in chemical dependency.

How many times have you wondered what causes chemical dependency? Although the question seems straightforward enough, you will see that it is phrased in a deceptively simple way. In previous chapters you learned that drug involvement is a terrifically complicated phenomenon involving many different drugs, patterns of use, and developmental variables. So perhaps you will not be surprised to learn in this chapter that there is no easy answer to the question about the causes of chemical dependency. Nor is it easy to learn about those many causes. You will have to work hard to master this chapter with its terminology from different realms of discourse. One fact is certain: there is no single cause. As you will see in this chapter, chemical dependency results from the convergence of many influences, both from within the individual, and from the environment.

6–1 Biology of Chemical Dependency

In Chapter 2 you learned about the complex effects of psychoactive drugs on the brain and body. Given the impact these substances have on so many biological processes, it should not be surprising to learn that the development of drug dependencies entails sophisticated biological mechanisms. In this section you will examine the modern disease model of addictions, as well as the roles heredity and neurophysiology play in the causation of addictions.

The Disease Model of Chemical Dependency

The **disease model** refers to the belief that alcoholism and other drug addictions are biologically based illnesses. In the United States, the Alcoholics Anonymous movement became synonymous with the disease model, and by the 1950s medical professionals started to describe alcoholism as a disease. The history of the disease model, however, is marked by considerable disagreement about the meaning of terms like "disease," "alcoholism," and "addiction." In this section you will learn about the evolution of the disease concept and its current status.

Starting in the 1930s, Alcoholic Anonymous promoted a view that alcoholism is an illness of body, mind, and spirit. Today, the "whole person" disease is a central tenet of A.A. and other Twleve step programs, which argue that alcohol and drug addictions are incurable, but that recovery is possible through lifelong abstinence (A.A. World Services 1976). E. M. Jellinek (1960) popularized the disease concept of alcoholism, and his work influenced its adoption by American medicine. As you learned in Chapter 3, Jellinek defined alcoholism as a disease of physical dependence and tolerance for alcohol as well as a loss of control over drinking leading to a progressive deterioration. However, Jellinek recognized that only the most extreme type of alcoholics, so-called *gamma alcoholics*, fit the disease concept.

Following Jellinek's work, many health, medical, and psychiatric professionals adopted the view that drug and alcohol addictions are illnesses rooted in biological mechanisms. In 1976 the National Council on Alcoholism adopted a definition of alcoholism as a "chronic, progressive, and potentially fatal disease" characterized by tolerance, physical dependence, and/or pathologic organ changes (National Council on Alcoholism 1976). Today, in the *DSM-IV-TR* system physical dependence and tolerance are still considered important diagnostic features for substance dependence (American Psychiatric Association 2000).

Many challenges have been raised to the early disease model. Critics object that calling alcoholism and other addictions diseases is misleading because they lack distinctive physical causes and often do not follow the progressive course described in the classic concept of disease. Its opponents assert that the disease model overlooks psychological and environmental factors, thereby limiting the understanding and treatment of addictions to a medical approach. Furthermore, some interpret the disease model to mean that alcoholics and other addicts cannot be held responsible for their drinking and drugging, thus providing them with an excuse to continue (Jaffe and Meyer 1995, McCrady 1994, Peele 1989).

The modern disease model recognizes that alcohol and other drug addictions cannot be narrowly viewed like other medical illnesses. Instead they are considered *biopsychosocial diseases* with many interacting influences expressed in diverse ways over the lifespan (Devor 1994, DuPont 1997, Jaffee and Meyer 1995, Royce and Strachley 1996). Later in this chapter you will learn about the many biological influences on chemical dependency. Although no single biological cause accounts for all addictions, there is no doubt that they are affected by hereditary and neurophysiological processes. However, there is also no doubt that nonbiological influences play an important role, and they, too, are examined carefully in later sections of this chapter.

Hereditary Influences

The idea that addictions to alcohol and other drugs result from inherited predispositions is not new. Early in its history the Alcoholics Anonymous movement proposed that an in-

herited "allergy" to alcohol was to blame for alcoholism. In more recent years, however, studies of the hereditary basis of drug and alcohol problems have produced a more detailed understanding of the role of genetic factors.

Behavioral Genetics. The search for hereditary influences on chemical dependency involves the research methods of *behavioral genetics*. Three study methods in particular—family, twin, and adoption studies—are useful in evaluating **heritability**, the degree of hereditary impact on a condition, trait, or behavior.

Family studies look at the prevalence of drug abuse in biological relatives of individuals with chemical dependency. These studies find evidence of alcoholism's heritability in the above-average rates of alcohol abuse among alcoholics' *first-degree relatives*, namely their parents, siblings, and children (Cook and Gurling 1991). The preponderance of alcohol problems in certain families has led to the concept of **familial alcoholism**, indicated by a prominent family history of drinking problems, early onset of alcohol abuse, and severe dependence (Goodwin and Warnock 1991). Of all relatives, the sons of male alcoholics have the greatest likelihood of developing alcoholism (Schuckit and Smith 1996). Other evidence shows clusters of heritable psychological problems among children of alcoholics, suggesting that there may be more than one kind of familial alcoholism (Finn et al. 1997). Few family studies of addictions other than alcoholism have been conducted. However, some investigators have found evidence of heritability for opiate and cocaine dependence. For example, siblings of narcotics addicts have above-average rates of opioid and alcohol abuse, and cocaine and alcohol abuse is prevalent among first-degree relatives of cocaine addicts (Rounsaville et al. 1991).

Family studies provide some support for hereditary factors in alcohol and drug problems, but they leave many questions unanswered because they do not separate the impact of heredity and environment. Higher rates of chemical dependency in relatives of addicted persons may reflect a shared environment as well as shared genes.

Another behavioral genetics method, the *twin study,* is more successful in separating genetic and environmental factors. Identical or *monozygotic twins* are genetically the same, having grown from a single fertilized egg, but fraternal or *dizygotic twins* develop from two independently fertilized eggs and so share only 50 percent of their genes. Comparisons of monozygotic and dizygotic twins reveal the separate contributions of heredity more clearly than a family study can. Twin studies of alcoholism find that identical-twin pairs are much more likely to both have alcoholism than is the case with fraternal twin pairs (Cook and Gurling 1991). The strongest evidence comes from studies of male twins with early-onset alcoholism (McGue et al. 1992). However, alcoholism heritability is also shown in studies of female twins (Kendler et al. 1992). Some twin data suggest that different genetic factors might account for gender differences in alcoholism (Pickens et al. 1991) Twin studies of other drugs are rare, but some support has been found for heritability of abuse and dependence in drugs besides alcohol (Breslau et al. 1993, Pickens et al. 1991).

The most convincing evidence of heritability is given by *adoption studies,* which examine alcohol and drug use by the adopted-away, biological children of chemically dependent parents. For such adopted children, genetic factors and environmental factors are independent. Adoption studies find that the biological children of alcoholics have significantly higher-than-average rates of alcohol and other drug problems even when raised by nonalcoholic adoptive parents (Cadoret et al. 1986, Cadoret et al. 1995, Searles 1988). Furthermore, a large Swedish adoption study found evidence for genetic distinctiveness of Type 1 and 2 alcoholism, as described in Chapter 3 (Sigvardsson et al. 1996).

Behavioral genetics research provides compelling support for the hereditary roots of chemical dependency, but caution is needed in interpreting these findings. Alcoholism and other drug addictions are assumed to be the products of *gene–environment interactions,* not simply the result of genetic factors alone.

Studies showing support for genetic factors do not indicate that the genes are fully in control, however. For example, about 20 to 30 percent of children of alcoholics develop alcohol problems, but the majority do not (Goodwin and Warnock 1991). Environment also counts. Consider, for instance, that the risk of alcoholism in adopted-away children of alcoholics is even higher when the adoptive parents are psychologically disturbed (Cadoret et al. 1995). Further complicating the interpretation of genetic and environmental factors is the finding that in addition to their greater risk for substance abuse, the relatives of addicts also have above-average rates of psychological disturbances such as depression, aggression, and antisocial personality. The occurrence of so many problems in families with chemical dependency suggests a possible shared inheritance of a cluster of associated problems (Cadoret et al. 1995, Kendler et al. 1993, Miller et al. 1989, Rounsaville et al. 1991, Sigvardsson et al. 1996).

Genetic Mechanisms. Despite offering support for the heritability of chemical dependency, behavioral genetics studies do not reveal the genetic mechanisms behind the problem. The search for genetic mechanisms requires more sophisticated biological and chemical methods to identify the locations of specific genes linked with addictions.

Addiction researchers try to track genetic mechanisms by identifying **biological markers**, genetic physical characteristics linked with addiction. *Linkage studies* demonstrate one thing for certain: no single gene is to blame for chemical dependency. Like other complex disorders, addictions seem to result from the combined effects of many genes. Linkage evidence further suggests that some genetic predispositions are specific to chemical dependency, while some affect both chemical dependency and other disorders as well (Devor 1994, Uhl 1995).

One particular area of genetic research has generated considerable excitement. Studies have found a link between alcoholism and a gene that affects a neuronal receptor site for the neurotransmitter dopamine, an essential ingredient in the brain's reward system (Blum et al. 1996). This same gene, called the *D2 receptor gene,* has also been linked to increased risk for cocaine dependence and for other types of substance abuse (Devor 1994, Noble et al. 1993). As important as these findings are, they are limited by the fact that many alcoholics and other addicts do not have that gene and many nonalcoholic and nonaddicted people do have it (Gelernter et al. 1993). You will learn more about the role of the dopamine system in addictions later in this chapter.

Another biological marker linked to alcohol problems is an enzyme, *ALDH (aldehyde dehydrogenase)*, that aids in the liver's metabolism of alcohol. An unusual version of the gene that controls production of ALDH has been found in a large minority (30 to 50 percent) of Japanese, Korean, and Chinese people. This form of the gene inhibits breakdown of alcohol and results in greater sensitivity to alcohol's intoxicating effects (Devor 1994, Newlin 1989). A recent study of Japanese adults indicates that this gene might act as a protective factor, reducing the risk of alcoholism by discouraging alcohol consumption (Higuchi et al. 1995). However, psychological factors can override genetics, as evidenced by many Japanese businessmen who participate in a heavy-drinking male culture.

Neurophysiology of Addiction

Neurophysiology refers to the functioning of the nervous system. In regard to chemical dependency, the main neurophysiological factors are the brain's neurotransmitter systems and the inborn vulnerabilities of the nervous system in addiction-prone people. While genetic factors partly account for the neurophysiology of addiction, many other influences also count, including hormones, diet, experiences, and of course, the use of psychoactive drugs.

Neurotransmitters and Chemical Dependency. In Chapter 2 you learned about the impact of psychoactive drugs on the neurotransmitter systems of the brain. The way in which persistent drug use affects those systems contributes strongly to the development of chemical dependency. Ongoing drug consumption changes the nervous system gradually in such a manner as to set up the physical basis for

addiction. Different neurotransmitters mediate the impact of different drugs, but two distinctive systems, the *dopamine and serotonin systems*, are most instrumental in addiction (George and Ritz 1993).

The dopamine (DA) systems of the brain are responsible for the rewarding or reinforcing effects of many addictive drugs, including alcohol, cocaine, and the opioids. Addictive drugs interact in various ways with the dopamine neurons and induce the experience of reinforcement or pleasure. Cocaine, for example, directly stimulates dopamine system activity by increasing the availability of dopamine messages. In contrast, opioids have an indirect effect; they inhibit neurons that slow the DA system, thus enhancing dopamine activity (Blum et al. 1996, DuPont 1997, Ellinwood and King 1995, George and Ritz 1993, Wise and Rompre 1989). Figure 6–1 shows a diagram of the main structures of the *dopamine reward system.*

One puzzling fact about chemical dependency is that most people who use addictive drugs do not become addicted to them. A possible reason is that addiction-prone individuals have abnormal dopamine systems that make them more vulnerable to the reinforcing effects of drugs. Researchers hypothesize that a **reward-deficiency syndrome** is a hereditary predisposition to dopamine underactivity, leading to greater risk for addiction. According to this hypothesis, a defective dopamine receptor gene causes underarousal of the dopamine reward system, thus making some people deficient in the experience of reinforcement or pleasure. Such addiction-prone individuals might overcome the dopamine deficiency by using drugs. The gene in question has been linked with alcoholism, cocaine addiction, and polysubstance abuse, as well as antisocial behavior and eating disorders (Blum et al. 1996).

Not only do addicts experience reward from drug use, but they also cannot resist their drug-taking urges. This lack of control invites the initiation of a pattern of compulsive drug consumption that is linked to the neurotransmitter *serotonin*. Oddly, the compulsive drive to use a drug is somewhat independent of the drug's reinforcing qualities. The major

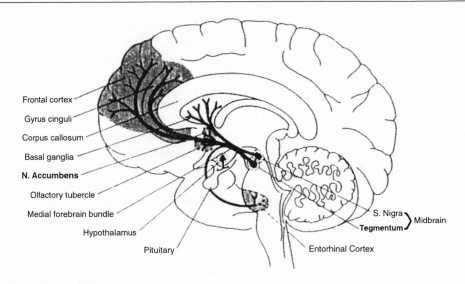

Frontal cortex
Gyrus cinguli
Corpus callosum
Basal ganglia
N. Accumbens
Olfactory tubercle
Medial forebrain bundle
Hypothalamus
Pituitary

S. Nigra ⎫
Tegmentum ⎬ Midbrain
⎭
Entorhinal Cortex

Figure 6–1. Diagram of the brain's dopamine system
Source: Cohen and Servan-Schreiber (1993).

addictive drugs increase activity in the brain's serotonin systems that in turn sustain the user's appetite for drug consumption (George and Ritz 1993, Kranzler and Anton 1994, Satel et al. 1995). According to the **serotonin deficiency hypothesis,** a hereditary deficit in the serotonin system predisposes individuals to alcoholism and is also linked with antisocial behavior, aggression, and depression (Fils-Aime et al. 1996, Kranzler and Anton 1994).

You learned in Chapter 2 that opioids like heroin stimulate the endorphin neurotransmitters, which regulate pain and pleasure. Endorphin arousal is certainly a factor in opioid addiction, but also appears to play a role in other addictions. Alcohol, for example, also increases endorphin arousal. Some evidence points to reduced levels of endorphin activity and sensitivity in alcoholics and in high-risk sons of alcoholics (Gianoulakis et al. 1996, Kranzler and Anton 1994). It is therefore believed that an *endorphin deficiency* contributes to the vulnerability to alcoholism and opioid addiction (Ellinwood and King 1995).

The Brain's Adaptation to Drug Abuse. Chronic consumption of addictive drugs alters the balance among neurotransmitter systems and changes the responses of neurons to the drugs.

Like other bodily systems, the nervous syste[m] functions to maintain its equilibrium, a[nd] when psychoactive drugs disrupt the equili[b]rium the nervous system responds to corre[ct] the disruption. Chronic use of drugs induc[es] the brain to exhibit **compensatory adap[]-tions,** that is, changes in the structures a[nd] functions of neurons that compensate for t[he] effects of drugs on them. These adaptatio[ns] in turn change the nervous system such th[at] further drug use is motivated (Hyman a[nd] Nestler 1996).

You might think of these adaptations as t[he] brain's tugging back in a tug-of-war with t[he] drugs. The more the user floods his brain w[ith] the drugs, the more the brain tugs back to [re]store its equilibrium, and in turn the more t[he] user will consume. Two major kinds of co[m]pensatory adaptations are: down-regulati[on] and up-regulation.

1. *Down-regulation.* After a drug stimula[tes] some neurotransmitter system, the brain co[m]pensates by reducing arousal of that syste[m.] Down-regulation causes subsequent drug u[se] to have less impact and is central to the ph[e]nomenon of drug tolerance in addicts. Hero[in,] for instance, causes dopamine arousal, wh[ich] induces down-regulation (slowing) of dopa[m]ine neurons (Ellinwood and King 1995, Hym[an] and Nestler 1996).

2. *Up-regulation.* After a drug inhibits a neurotransmitter system, the brain compensates by increasing arousal of that system. Alcohol, for example, inhibits neurons that use *glutamate*, the major excitatory chemical of the brain. The adaptive response to alcohol is *up-regulation* of glutamate neurons, causing an unusually high excitation of that system. In alcoholics, the chronic overarousal of glutamate neurons can cause permanent damage to regions of the brain that regulate learning and memory (Tsai et al. 1995).

High-Risk Research. A promising approach to studying the neurophysiology of addictions uses individuals with a family history of chemical dependency. As you learned in an earlier section of this chapter, such individuals have unusually high risk for developing addictions. *High-risk research* examines the differences between high-risk individuals and people with no family history of addictions in the hope of identifying possible markers of vulnerability.

An important technique used in high-risk research on alcoholism is the **alcohol challenge**, in which subjects are given a controlled dose of alcohol and their responses are measured. Typically, high-risk subjects show more subdued physical effects to the alcohol challenge, indicating a higher *metabolic tolerance* for alcohol. In addition to their greater tolerance for alcohol, high-risk subjects have more rapid initial *sensitization* to alcohol, that is, they feel the intoxicating effects faster after a drink than others do (Newlin and Thomson 1990).

Both genetic and biochemical factors shape the distinctive effects of alcohol on high-risk subjects (Gianoulakis et al. 1996, Pihl et al. 1990, Schuckit and Smith 1996). Their elevated sensitization and tolerance establish a physical basis for their vulnerability to alcoholism. In fact, longitudinal studies of high-risk males find that a lowered response to the alcohol challenge is a strong predictor of later alcohol dependence (Schuckit and Smith 1996, Volavka et al. 1996).

Along with findings from the alcohol challenge, other methods also confirm the presence of *neuropsychological deficits* in high-risk individuals. The most popular of these methods measures a neuronal reaction called the *P300 wave*, an electrical response to visual or sound stimuli. Nonalcoholic sons of alcoholics have smaller-than-average P300 wave patterns, and this deficiency appears to be inherited (Noble et al. 1994, Polich et al. 1994). Other signs of brain dysfunction in high-risk subjects are their cognitive impairments in memory, learning, attention, information integration, and verbal skills. The signs suggest a deficiency in the frontal lobe that controls the brain's *executive functions* (Azar 1996, Harden and Pihl 1995). The combination of brain dysfunction and cognitive impairment limits these subjects' ability to learn coping skills, and increases their vulnerability to developing alcoholism (Finn et al. 1994, Harden and Pihl 1995). In conclusion, it is important to realize that while no single pattern of neuropsychological abnormalities is always found in high-risk individuals, they do tend to show more of those dysfunctions than the average person does (Tarter et al. 1990, 1993).

6–2 Personality and Chemical Dependency

Chemical dependency has often been blamed on defects in the personality or character of the addicted individual. Historically, for example, many believed that alcoholism reflected a moral defect. Although today we no longer take such a judgmental view, addictions are seen as results of maladaptive personality processes or traits. Here we explore two very different approaches to the study of the personality–addiction relationship: the psychodynamic view and the trait view.

Psychodynamic Views

Starting with Freud's psychoanalytic theory, the **psychodynamic view** of personality has characterized abnormal behavior, including chemical dependency, as a product of powerful unconscious drives and emotions and the defenses raised against them. The capacity for managing psychic conflict and coping with the world depends on personality structures which, if inadequate, make the person vulnerable to psychopathology. Another aspect of the psychodynamic view is that it applies a developmental perspective, recognizing that the roots of addictions lie in events that occur during the childhood years.

Psychoanalytic Personality Theory. Traditional psychoanalytic theory focuses on the role of personality processes in the dynamics of addictions and proposes several hypotheses about the influence of personality structures on drug and alcohol use (Frances et al. 1994).

In this view, the *ego* is the personality structure that regulates drives and emotions and mediates between the individual and the external world. Basic *ego functions* include reasoning, perception, memory, and the defenses, which are strategies to subdue psychological conflict and stress. A precondition for chemical dependency is the ego's failure to regulate emotions and drives. This failure leads to a profound inability for self-care. Drugs and alcohol serve as an artificial, chemical substitutes for the ego's self-regulation abilities. Opiate addicts, for example, rely on those drugs to substitute for their failed anxiety-reducing defenses, and the sedative effect of heroin bolsters their defenses of repression and denial (Chien et al. 1964).

Another personality structure, the *superego*, also contributes to the predisposition to chemical dependency. The superego controls the moral, evaluative functions of personality, that is, the superego judges right and wrong. Disturbances in superego self-evaluations produce strong feelings of guilt and shame that motivate self-punishing, self-destructive behavior such as drugging and drinking. Addicts exhibit characteristics indicative of superego-involved conflicts, including self-esteem disruption and problems with the expression of power and love (Khantzian 1995, Wurmser 1974).

Developmental Issues. Classical psychoanalytic theory attributed alcoholism to the unconscious urge to compensate for unsatisfied needs from the earliest stage of development, the *oral stage*. In this view, an infant whose oral needs for food and love are inadequately met will be compelled to seek oral gratification through means such as excessive drinking. The notion that alcoholism represents a **developmental fixation**, or unresolved developmental problem, is a key to traditional Freudian theory (Menninger 1938). As you have already seen in Chapter 3, oral dependency is a major psychodynamic theme in alcoholism and has been linked to different types of alcoholism (Blum 1966).

Developmentally, personality defects that predispose to chemical dependency are thought to originate in family disturbances. Inconsistent nurturing and a lack of parental responsiveness to the child's needs set the stage for the shortcomings in personality. During the early years of life inadequate care and protectiveness by the parents creates conflicts in the child that then have adverse effects on personality development. *Object relations theory*, a modern psychodynamic view of development, believes that inconsistencies in the parents' feelings and actions toward the child lead to inconsistent elements of self-concept in the child, setting a foundation for later emotional distress and vulnerability to substance abuse (Volkan 1994).

Personality Traits

Outside the psychodynamic tradition, personality researchers have looked for a connection between specific traits and the risk for chemical dependency. However, because a unified theory is lacking in these trait studies, many independent investigations have been conducted with different methods of trait testing and evaluation. In the interest of simplifying a complex and confusing area of research, we will restrict our discussion to studies on the addictive personality and temperament.

Is There an Addictive Personality? Most people assume the answer to this question is "yes, of course." In fact, the belief in an **addictive personality** as constituting a presumed common core of traits for alcoholic and other drug-addicted individuals has become deeply embedded in conventional wisdom about chemical dependency. A powerful historical impetus to the acceptance of this idea was the Alcoholics Anonymous notion that character defects contribute to problem drinking. Efforts to pin down the addictive personality usually involved studies of actively alcoholic and drug-addicted individuals. Such studies number in the hundreds, and they have produced a bewildering array of findings about the traits of chemically dependent individuals. The problem with those studies is that there is no way to know whether the traits identified are the causes or the consequences of the addiction, or perhaps just characteristics associated with addiction (Lavelle et al. 1993, Marlatt et al. 1988).

Consider an example of this dilemma posed by a study of opioid abusers (Brooner et al. 1994). Compared with average individuals, opioid abusers have higher levels of traits like neuroticism and excitement-seeking and lower levels of traits such as conscientiousness, warmth, and agreeableness. However, simply identifying trait differences between the drug-abusing group and others does not mean that those traits are responsible for the drug abuse. Isn't it possible that being an opioid abuser might cause the traits or be linked with other behaviors that are responsible for the traits? For instance, the high neuroticism (defined by anxiety, hostility, depression) might be a consequence of the opioid user's lifestyle, in which pursuit and possession of illegal drugs is central.

No single trait or set of traits has been found to consistently define "the" addictive personality (Lang 1983). Given the many types of alcoholism and other addictions, perhaps the failure to find a single addictive personality profile is unsurprising. This failure, however, does not mean that personality traits are irrelevant to chemical dependency. Today researchers recognize that different kinds of individuals are susceptible to alcoholism and other drug addictions, and that no one trait or set of traits will account for all cases. Besides, personality traits alone can never fully explain any behavior. Instead, the interaction of traits with other influences, such as environmental variables, must be taken into account. From the perspective of the chemical dependency counselor, it is necessary to distinguish between the *pre-addictive*

personality—the personality style that inclines someone to addiction—and the *clinical addictive personality* that is present in the addicted client with whom you are working. Even if the traits of the clinical addictive personality are caused by the addiction, counselors and clients must work together to deal with them.

One alternative to traditional trait studies is to examine the links between personality traits and chemical dependency with *longitudinal research* (see Chapter 4). With this method researchers evaluate which personality traits contribute to drug and alcohol problems by testing personality in subjects *before* they develop substance use disorders. In addition, longitudinal studies allow for a comparison of the impact of personality traits and other variables, as well as an analysis of the interactions between traits and other influences. Traits that are commonly found to predict the likelihood of substance abuse and dependence include antisocial behavior, impulsiveness, hyperactivity, nonconformity, aggressiveness, low ego-strength, rebelliousness, and low self-esteem (Cox 1987, Donovan 1986, Hawkins et al. 1992, Marlatt et al. 1988, Vaillant and Milofsky 1982). It is important to note that these traits do not always precede substance use disorders, nor do they necessarily predict only those problems. Like the more traditional trait studies, longitudinal research has not found consistent evidence for a single addictive personality profile.

Temperament and Chemical Dependency.

You may recall from Chapter 4 that childhood temperament is a risk factor for developing substance abuse. Temperament is an innate foundation for personality and social behavior, and several dimensions of temperament have been linked with chemical dependency, especially with alcoholism.

An important approach is found in Cloninger's **temperament model**, which proposes four dimensions of temperament as strongly heritable, emotion-based skills and habits, as shown in Table 6–1 (Cloninger et al. 1993, Svrakic et al. 1996). An attractive feature of Cloninger's model is its integration of temperament with research on genetics, neurophysiology, and chemical dependency. In

Table 6–1. Cloninger's temperament model

Temperament Dimension	Low Level	High Level
Harm avoidance	daring	fearful
	energetic	fatigable
	optimistic	pessimistic
	outgoing	shy
Novelty seeking	reserved	exploratory
	deliberate	impulsive
	thrifty	extravagant
	stoical	irritable
Reward dependence	detached	sentimental
	aloof	open
	cold	warm
	independent	appreciative
Persistence	lazy	industrious
	spoiled	determined
	underachiever	enthusiastic
	pragmatist	perfectionistic

Source: Based on Svrakic et al. (1996).

Chapter 3 you learned about Cloninger's Type 1/Type 2 distinction in alcoholism and its association with genetic predispositions and symptom patterns. Different combinations of temperament and associated traits appear to be responsible for the two types of alcoholism. High harm-avoidance and low novelty-seeking apply to Type 1, while Type 2 is linked with low harm-avoidance, low reward-dependence, and high novelty-seeking (Cloninger et al. 1988).

Along with Cloninger and his colleagues, other researchers have examined the relationships of temperament traits with chemical dependency. One of the most commonly studied variables is *sensation-seeking*, a predisposition to impulsive, thrill-seeking behavior and immediate need gratification (Zuckerman 1987). The sensation-seeking concept is very similar to Cloninger's dimensions, appearing to be a combination of low harm-avoidance and high novelty-seeking, and like those temperament patterns sensation-seeking is also a heritable characteristic (Kosten et al. 1994). Both alcoholism and cocaine addiction are associated with high levels of sensation-seeking, and this trait also contributes to polysubstance abuse. Substance abusers with a high level of sensation-seeking tend to develop problems at a younger age and go on to more severe dependence (Ball et al. 1994, Wood et al. 1995).

Beyond its role in chemical dependency, sensation-seeking affects other behaviors that are correlated with drug and alcohol use. In general, people with a high level of sensation-seeking are risk takers who thrive on behavior that is dangerous and exhilarating, such as gambling, drag racing, bungee jumping, stealing, and of course, extreme drinking and drugging. A prime motive for these high-risk takers is the thrill of living on the edge, achieving maximum stimulation, and defying danger to prove that they are in control. Such "edgework" provides the person with a sense of mastery and accomplishment (Lyng 1990).

6–3 Learning and Chemical Dependency

Understanding the causation of chemical dependency can also be approached from the learning perspective. The school of psychology known as *behaviorism* has long emphasized the importance of learning experiences in the development of both normal and abnormal behavior. The **behavioral view** of chemical dependency argues that learning mechanisms determine the acquisition of habits that promote excessive drugging and drinking. In other words, addictions are learned habits. The two learning mechanisms behind the development of addictions are classical conditioning and operant conditioning.

Classical Conditioning

Classical Conditioning Principles. In the early 1900s the Russian physiologist Ivan Pavlov identified a simple learning procedure while observing the behavior of his laboratory dogs. Pavlov noticed that when a tone stimulus was paired repeatedly with a food stimulus that alone triggered salivation, the tone stimulus alone also came to trigger salivation, as shown in Figure 6–2. This phenomenon is known as **classical conditioning**, a form of *association learning* in which a reflexive response is associated with a new stimulus by pairing the new stimulus with a stimulus that naturally triggers the reflex. In the language of classical conditioning, the tone is the *conditioned stimulus*, and the food is the *unconditioned stimulus*. Salivation is called the *unconditioned response* when it is elicited by the food, but is labeled the *conditioned response* when elicited by the tone.

Classical Conditioning and Drug Use. What can salivating dogs possibly have to do with drug-abusing humans? Like food, psychoactive drugs are powerful unconditioned stimuli that provoke many automatic unconditioned responses, especially physiological and emotional reactions. People, places, and things present at the time of drug use act as conditioned stimuli, and can trigger drug-related reactions. Stimuli associated with drug use serve as signals or cues to elicit automatic responses, such as feelings of craving. In this view, craving is an anticipatory drug response provoked by a conditioned drug stimulus. For instance, the sight of a drinking buddy can arouse a desire to "have a few beers" in the alcoholic. This phenomenon of *conditioned craving* is one of the reasons that counselors advise their clients to strictly avoid the people, places, and things associated with drug use. Besides conditioned craving, classical conditioning can also create learned withdrawal responses. Cues associated with withdrawal reactions can in the future trigger feelings of withdrawal, and in turn those *conditioned withdrawal responses* can motivate renewed drug use. Thus, classical conditioning responses can contribute to both the acquisition of chemical dependency and to the maintenance of drug-taking habits (Robbins 1995).

Another aspect of addiction that is affected by classical conditioning is tolerance. Animal research shows that drug tolerance is not wholly due to physical mechanisms, but is also shaped by learned associations between drug stimuli and drug responses. As you learned earlier in this chapter, the brain's self-regulatory mechanisms use compensatory reactions to restore the equilibrium that is disrupted by drug use. Consequently, repeated drug use acts as a conditioned stimulus for those compensatory responses, in turn resulting in decreased responsiveness to the drug, or tolerance. This *conditioned tolerance effect* is present in both addicts and in addiction-prone individuals, such as sons of alcoholics (Ramsey and Woods 1997).

Operant Conditioning

The kind of learning described as classical conditioning is limited to associations between stimuli and reflexive reactions. Most of our learned behavior, however, is not simply

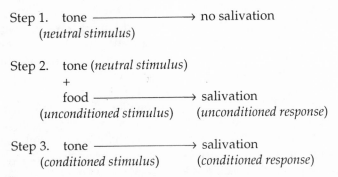

Figure 6–2. Classical conditioning

reflexive, but involves complex actions that we perform to control and interact with our environment. Such actions are called *operant behavior*. The famous behaviorist B. F. Skinner (1974) advocated a theory of operant behavior centered on **operant conditioning**, a type of learning by which behavior is shaped through the influence of reinforcement and punishment.

Operant Conditioning Principles. The most important concepts of operant conditioning are *reinforcement* and *punishment*. Reinforcement means that a stimulus, called a reinforcer, is used to strengthen a behavior. *Positive reinforcement*, or reward, involves the giving of a stimulus following a behavior to strengthen that behavior. In contrast, *negative reinforcement* means the removal of a stimulus (usually an unpleasant one) following a behavior to strengthen the behavior. Not to be confused with negative reinforcement, *punishment* is a procedure that employs stimuli as consequences to weaken or eliminate behavior.

In addition to their impact on behavior, both reinforcers and punishers create associations between stimulus cues in the environment and the behaviors that are performed. A reinforced action is thus associated with environmental cues present at the time of reinforcement, so that in the future those cues can prompt the behavior in anticipation of further reinforcement. The impact of reinforcing and punishing consequences on behavior and on the association of stimulus cues with behavior depends on several variables.

- *Timing*: Immediate consequences are more effective than delayed consequences.
- *Potency*: Intense consequences are more effective than weak consequences.
- *Context*: The effectiveness of consequences depends on the availability of other consequences in the learning environment.

Operant Conditioning and Drug Use. You learned earlier in this chapter that addictive drugs have powerful effects on the brain's reward centers. Consequently, drug use is strengthened by physiologically based positive reinforcement. The principles of timing and potency are clearly relevant to drug-taking behavior. The more intense the reinforcer and the more quickly it follows the behavior, the more reinforcing it is. Drugs that rapidly produce powerful pleasurable effects are especially likely to motivate durable drug-taking habits. Reinforcers that contribute to drug use also come from the environment as well as from within the individual. As studies of adolescent drug abusers demonstrate, social reinforcement in the form of attention from and interaction with peers is a leading factor in drug abuse. The context principle also applies to drug consumption. The reinforcement value of drugs will be highest for someone who has access to few other available reinforcers.

In addition to receiving positive reinforcement through physiological, emotional, and social means, drugs often reduce or remove unpleasant, aversive feelings and sensations, and, drug consumption is thus also affected by negative reinforcement. The relief of pain, fear, sadness, anger, and other aversive states is an important function of drug use. This is known as *escape behavior*, and is highly resistant to extinction, the weakening of the behavior after reinforcement stops. For the chemically dependent person, the habit of drug consumption is maintained by the simultaneous action of both positive and negative reinforcement, and each time the drug is used the strength of the habit grows (Robbins 1995, Wise 1988).

Many people have wondered why alcoholics and other drug addicts persist in their habits despite the long-term punishing consequences of their behavior. An examination of the many severe problems that chemical dependency causes might suggest that operant conditioning is wrong. Although it is true that chronic drug abuse ultimately causes serious distress and suffering, those long-term punishments are less influential than the short-term reinforcement that drugs provide. Remember the principle of timing? It applies to punishment, too, and in the case of addictions one thing is clear: immediate reinforcement always beats delayed punishment.

As you might guess, many variables affect the impact of both reinforcers and punishers on behavior. According to the **behavioral theory of choice**, both the preference for a drug and the motivation to abuse the drug-of-choice depend on two types of variables: constraints against drug use, and availability of other reinforcers. What constrains someone from drug use? Lack of access to the drug, the anticipation of punishment following drug use, and the presence of competing non-drug behaviors are very important. In addition to antidrug constraints, access to other reinforcing behaviors matters. As the context principle states, people who derive strong reinforcement from other behaviors, hobbies, and exercise are less vulnerable to the seductions of drugs. In sum, the person who has easy access to drugs, who expects little or no punishment for drug use, who has no alternative motives competing with drug use, and who has few other reinforcing behaviors is most likely to say "yes" to drugs (Vuchinich and Tucker 1988).

Classical and Operant Conditioning Interaction. As you have just seen, classical and operant conditioning involve different mechanisms of learning. However, both kinds of learning are instrumental in the acquisition and maintenance of drug-taking habits. The **conditioned incentive model** offers an integrated explanation of chemical dependency in terms of the combined influence of classical and operant conditioning mechanisms (Stewart et al. 1984).

In this model, classical conditioning gives drug-related cues the power to elicit drug-associated reactions, such as craving and withdrawal. Those reactions have a *priming effect* on drug use because they prompt drug consumption in anticipation of the reinforcing consequences. In other words, cue-triggered drug cravings or withdrawal reactions serve as cues to motivate the person to use the drug of choice. Operant conditioning then strengthens the association between those conditioned cues and drug use by virtue of the drug's reinforcing effects. Over time, the entire system of learned associations between drug cues, drug-related reactions, and reinforcers is consolidated into a powerful addiction habit.

6–4 Cognitive Influences on Chemical Dependency

Since the 1970s, a cognitive revolution in psychology has significantly altered the way we explain behavior. *Cognitions*, meaning thoughts, perceptions, and beliefs, are now considered a central part of learning, motivation, and personality. As a result of the cognitive revolution, our ideas about chemical dependency now require a careful consideration of the role played by cognitive processes.

Social Learning and Social Cognitive Theory

Psychologist Albert Bandura is the central figure in both social learning and social cognitive theory. His earlier work on learning processes is the focus of social learning theory, while his more recent interests in personality and motivation are emphasized in social cognitive theory.

Social Learning Theory. **Social learning theory** is a view of learning that emphasizes the role played by cognitive processes that occur in the context of *socialization* and considers the relationship of person and environment as one of ongoing interaction (Bandura 1977a). Originally developed to explain social behavior, social learning theory has been extended to many topics in psychology, including the addictions.

The major mechanism of social learning is **modeling**, a type of learning by which behaviors are internalized and imitated through observing a model, someone who performs the behavior. Modeling has also been called *observational learning* or *imitation learning* (Bandura and Walters 1963). Modeling involves not just overt behavioral change, but also subjective cognitive change as well. Observed actions and their consequences are stored in memory and associated with motivational and emotional processes. For example, a young boy who who observes his father's behavior learns to act similarly, to want to imitate his father, and to feel good about imitating his father. For children in particular, the *identification* with a model, such as a parent, is a significant part of the motivation to imitate.

The principles of social learning theory apply directly to the development of substance-related problems. In Chapter 4 you learned how influential the behavior of drug-using parents and peers is on the initiation and escalation of substance use among adolescents. The role of modeling is apparent in many instances, especially among high-risk children who are exposed to the drinking and drugging of their parents. Children who are raised in an substance-saturated environment learn early in life to use alcohol and other drugs as a normal part of everyday life. Family studies showing above-average rates of alcohol and other drug use in children of alcoholics may be interpreted as evidence not only for genetic influences, but also as evidence of the effect of modeling (Abrams and Niaura 1987).

Through the selective interaction with drug-using peers, adolescents learn to develop positive attitudes about drugs and behaviors associated with drug consumption. Learning how, what, where, and when to use alcohol and other drugs occurs in a social context, that is, among peers who are engaging in drug use. Besides peers and family, other social models can provide information about drug-taking behavior. For example, even very young children who watch TV are witness to many instances of drinking and drugging. Television is a force to reckon with in the socialization of children into substance use (Akers 1992).

Social Cognitive Theory. Since the 1970s, Bandura has extended and modified social learning theory to focus more on the role of cognitive variables within the individual. **Social cognitive theory** is a view that explains personality, motivation, and behavior in terms of active, self-regulating processes that shape individual interactions with the environment (Bandura 1986). A fundamental assumption of social cognitive theory is that people are capable of *self-regulation*. The well-adjusted person adapts to the world by applying self-regulation in the pursuit of personal goals. The poorly adjusted individual, by contrast, exhibits many failures of self-regulation. The success or failure of personal adjustment depends on the person's use of *cognitive coping abilities* such as planning, self-reflection, and symbolizing experience in memory.

A key concept of social cognitive theory is **self-efficacy**, which refers to your expectations about your capability to perform a behavior. If you anticipate success in performing some action, you are said to have *positive self-efficacy*; if you expect to fail, however, your belief indicates *negative self-efficacy*. Self-efficacy expectations are important cognitive elements of personality, and are reflected in the individual's general self-esteem and self-concept. Typically, positive self-efficacy predicts better overall adjustment, and negative self-efficacy is linked with many psychological disturbances (Maddux 1995).

Problems in self-regulation and self-efficacy are relevant to several aspects of drug use, abuse, and dependence. As longitudinal studies show, individuals who have poor self-regulatory skills (for example, antisocial, impulsive teenagers), are at high risk for early initiation of drug and alcohol use. Deficits in managing emotional distress also indicate self-regulation failure and are risk factors for substance abuse. In alcoholics, a critical self-regulation process is *drinking restraint*, the cognitive control over drinking. The alcoholic who tells himself "I'll stay an hour and have two drinks," but who ends up closing out the bar shows his failure to set limits on drinking and to control his behavior to satisfy those limits. Restraint failure is a factor in binge-drinking episodes and in relapses during recovery, especially when the loss of restraint is followed by self-blame and emotional distress (Collins 1993, Marlatt 1985). The role of these cognitive factors in relapse and recovery will be explored more fully in Chapter 14.

The role of self-efficacy in substance abuse is complicated. Expectations about coping capabilities influence drug-taking behavior in several ways. *First*, people who believe that using drugs will improve their behavior are more likely to use drugs. For example, an adolescent who thinks drinking makes her a better conversationalist will want to drink in preparation for a party. *Second*, someone with negative self-efficacy expectations regarding their coping skills will be inclined to use drugs to help with coping. For example, an anxiety-prone adult who doubts his own ability to cope with stress may rely on alcohol to get through a rough day. *Third*, for the chemically dependent person, self-efficacy beliefs are often inseparable from expectations about drug effects. The addict who thinks, "I can't function unless I'm high" reveals the destructive link between his drug consumption and self-efficacy (DiClemente et al. 1995).

Expectancy Theory

Social cognitive theory examines one type of expectation in its concept of self-efficacy. In addition to these self-efficacy expectations, other kinds of expectations also influence the use and abuse of psychoactive substances.

Expectancy Theory. What you think about the possible effects of drugs is a factor in deciding whether you will use them. **Expectancy theory** is a perspective that attributes the motivation for drug use mainly to expectations about the consequences of drugs and drug intoxication. Such expectations are called *outcome expectancies*. So if you believe that you are funnier and sexier when drunk, you have a positive outcome expectancy about alcohol. Generally, people who have strong positive expectancies regarding drugs are more inclined to use them than people with negative drug expectancies. Alcoholics not only have much more positive drinking expectations than others do, but they also have more specific expectations that connect alcohol use with particular areas of behavior, for example, a belief that drinking makes your job tolerable (Goldman et al. 1987, Marlatt et al. 1988, Sher et al. 1996).

Studies of drug expectancies reveal many kinds of beliefs that are linked with drug use (Brown 1993, Goldman et al. 1987). Several common expectancies are:

- Drugs relieve tension and stress;
- Drugs "lubricate" social activities;
- Drugs enhance power, pleasure, and sexual performance;
- Drugs transform experience in a positive way.

The motivational impact of expectancies is due to the emotions associated with beliefs about drug-related situations, intoxication, and drug consequences (Brown 1993, Smith et al. 1995, Stacy et al. 1991). Consider the following example.

> Tim thinks that when he gets high, social interactions are more exciting (situation expectancy), he is more charming and seductive (intoxication expectancy), and that people like him a lot better (consequences expectancy).

Tim is a likely candidate for getting high regularly because his drug expectancies are colored with positive emotions. Personal drug experiences shape drug expectancies, and in turn drug expectancies shape drug experiences. The feedback loop connecting drug use and expectancies is crucial in the progression of chemical dependency. The more positive drug experiences you have, the more positive expectancies you will have, and the more reason you will have for continued drug use (Sher et al. 1996).

In recovery, too, drug expectancies are critical. Relapses are less common in recovering patients when they have strong negative drug expectancies (Jones and McMahon 1994). Conversely, relapse potential increases with the persistence of positive expectancies. Unfortunately, positive expectancies are very durable cognitive structures that persist long after abstinence begins (Brown 1993, Goldman et al. 1991).

Expectancy–Behavior Relationship. Many studies support the expectancy–behavior relationship in regard to drug use. Nevertheless, many people who have positive drug expectancies do not become substance abusers. To explain these individual differences requires a consideration of some variables that mediate the link between drug expectancies and drug activity.

Situational factors make a big difference. Recall Tim from earlier in this section. He wouldn't think of getting high at work. Despite his positive expectancies he discriminates between work-appropriate behavior and drug-related behavior. At a party, however, Tim's drug expectancies are much more prominent and more likely to prompt drug consumption. Clearly, drug expectancies differ according to situations, and people tend to act upon situationally relevant expectancies (Brown 1993).

Culturally based beliefs, too, shape drug experiences; for example, in cultures where there is no expectation that violence is linked with drunkenness, it typically is not. In addition, in cultures that impose harsh sanctions against intoxication the expectation of punishment for drinking and drugging can mitigate against the pleasure of those experiences.

Personality also determines the impact of expectancies on behavior. As you read earlier, positive self-efficacy is a protective factor against drug use. Individuals who expect that they have the ability to cope well and enjoy life are not likely to abuse drugs even if they think that drugs have some positive effects. For some people, however, the knowledge that drugs have negative impact can motivate their drug use. In such "self-handicapping" people, drug use provides an excuse for failure and personal limitations (Berglas 1987).

Because drug expectancies are influenced by personal experiences of drug intoxication, physiological variables that affect intoxication will also mediate the expectancy–behavior relationship. Biological research tells us that some people are physiologically more sensitive to the effects of drugs. They might, therefore, be more prone to develop positive drug expectancies. Evidence from sons of alcoholics supports this idea, showing that high-risk males tend to have more positive alcohol expectancies than the average person (Sher et al. 1996).

6–5 Motivation and Emotion

So far you have read about theories that emphasize the impact of biology, personality, learning, and thinking on drug use. Although several earlier explanations involved ideas about drug-taking motives and emotional fac-

tors, here we direct your attention to a few models that focus on more specific motives and emotions that prompt drug consumption.

Tension and Stress Reduction

What could be more commonsensical than the notion that alcohol relieves emotional tension or distress? As you read in the previous section, one of the most prevalent beliefs about alcohol and other drugs is that they reduce unpleasant arousal almost as if they were magic potions. In this section we analyze two views of drug-use motivation that present similar ideas: the tension-reduction theory, and the stress-response dampening theory.

Tension-Reduction Theory. In the 1950s some animal and human studies demonstrated that alcohol lessened the tendency to escape from or avoid aversive stimuli and conflict situations, and found that when subjects are in such situations they are more likely to perform tasks to get alcohol. From such observations was born the classic **tension-reduction theory**, a view that people are motivated to drink alcohol because it reduces or alleviates feelings of tension. According to this theory, the *drive to reduce tension* is the primary force behind drinking, and the *relief of tension* is the main reinforcer of drinking (Conger 1956).

One of the most valuable features of this theory was its ability to generate research on the effects of alcohol. There is no doubt that alcohol can lessen your feelings of tension. Some other drugs too, have tension-reducing consequences, especially opioids and sedatives. However, for several reasons this theory has failed as a general explanation of alcohol and other drug use. First, there are different signs of tension, including physical, emotional, and behavioral indicators, and these different aspects of tension do not necessarily always lessen in response to alcohol consumption. Second, alcohol consumption sometimes increases tension as well as creating behavior whose consequences lead to an increase in tension. Last, drinking is not simply motivated by a drive to reduce tension. Many people who are not tense drink anyway, and besides people often drink to increase positive feelings as much as they do to reduce negative tension (Cappell and Greeley 1987).

What then is the connection between tension and drinking? They apparently have no simple relationship, but instead the links between them are mediated by a number of variables (Stritzke et al. 1996). In sum, the answer to the tension–drinking question is that it all depends on other influences, including the setting, the drinker's personality, alcohol expectancies, and motives that compete with the tension-reduction drive.

Stress-Response Dampening Theory. In light of the shortcomings of classic tension-reduction theory, researchers sought to modify their thinking about the tension–alcohol relationship. **Stress-response dampening (SRD) theory** is a view that assumes the motive for alcohol use is to dampen or lessen the intensity of the stress response. The theory maintains that stress results from a person's *cognitive appraisals*, or judgments of threatening or challenging stimulus events. In this regard SRD theory is related to other cognitive perspectives on drug involvement, such as expectancy theory. An individual's stress response is measured mainly in terms of the physiological and emotional arousal triggered by stressful stimuli (Sher 1987).

Although studies of alcohol's influence on unstressed subjects yield inconsistent results, the effects of alcohol on the stressed individual are more supportive of SRD theory. Generally, alcohol reduces signs of cardiovascular arousal, for example heart rate, and lessens muscle tension. For alcoholics and high-risk children of alcoholics, the stress-dampening effects of alcohol are somewhat more pronounced than for the average person (Finn and Pihl 1987). Besides its relevance to alcohol, SRD theory also speaks to the use and abuse of other drugs. Several studies demonstrate that substance use is predicted by stress, and that escalation to drug abuse is prompted by stress (Chassin et al. 1993, Wagner 1993, Wills et al. 1996).

Unlike tension-reduction theory, SRD theory acknowledges the mediating influence of many variables on the stress–alcohol/drug relationship. Emphasis is given to cognitive processes that have an impact on both the effects of alcohol and on the stress response. That is, your expectancies about the stress-reducing or pleasure-enhancing effects of drugs can dampen your stress response (Sher et al. 1996). Alcohol and other drugs often lessen your level of self-awareness or self-consciousness, which in turn also lowers the intensity of your arousal (Berglas 1987). For people who have a negative self-image (like many addicts), reduced self-awareness can be highly reinforcing. In addition, intoxication diminishes your attention and perception capacity so that you might not notice or clearly interpret the meaning of stressful stimuli, and consequently react less to them (Sayette 1993; Steele and Josephs 1990). Finally, your self-efficacy or confidence in your ability to cope with stress makes a difference. The use of alcohol to dampen stress is most likely in those who lack other adequate coping skills (Chassin et al. 1993).

The Self-Medication Hypothesis. Earlier in this chapter you learned that the psychodynamic view assumes that the psychological predispositions for drug and alcohol addiction are set early in life through the influence of developmental events on personality. Those predispositions alone do not necessarily produce addictions unless the person finds that the effects of drugs and alcohol provide significant relief from psychological distress. An extension of the psychodynamic view is the **self-medication hypothesis**, which states that drug and alcohol abuse are motivated by the desire to alleviate emotional pain and suffering. Psychological vulnerability to addiction results from severe emotional distress and personality deficiencies that limit coping abilities. Such vulnerable individuals are most prone to attempt to treat or "medicate" themselves with drugs. You can easily imagine how self-medication is self-defeating in the long run, because drugs will not correct the underlying psychological problems responsible for the distress. Ultimately, the self-medicating alcoholic or drug addict just aggravates those problems and creates new ones requiring even further medication. (Khantzian 1985, 1995).

Although Freud did not propose the self-medication hypothesis himself, he did notice through his personal experimentation with cocaine in the 1890s that it was an antidote for his feelings of depression and helplessness. As the self-medication hypothesis recognizes, the choice of a drug is not random. Instead, drug preference is guided by the nature of the person's emotional state, which is a product of childhood developmental history. For example, a person who is full of rage and aggressive urges would be inclined to abuse heroin for its sedative value. By contrast, someone who is prone to depression might prefer stimulants such as cocaine for their energizing, antidepressant effects.

Support for the self-medication hypothesis is found in many areas. For instance, the prevalence of psychological disturbances in people with substance use disorders is much higher than in the general population (Regier et al. 1990). Substance abuse is strongly predicted by the presence of several mental disorders, including anxiety disorders, depression, personality disorders, post-traumatic stress disorder, and schizophrenia (Jeste et al. 1996, Kushner et al. 1990, Liu et al. 1996, Stewart 1996). In addition, developmental studies show that emotional distress is a potent risk factor for chemical dependency in adolescents and young adults (Chassin et al. 1993, Hawkins et al. 1992).

6–6 Sociocultural Influences

Previously in this chapter and in Chapter 4 you have encountered theories and research that suggest the role of sociocultural influences on drug involvement and the development of chemical dependency. The sociocultural context in which drugs and drug use exist has considerable impact on the likelihood of an individual becoming an abuser or addict. Here we will consider the contributions of three aspects of the social environment: family, peers, and ethnicity.

The Family

As you may remember from Chapter 4, the results of developmental studies show that the family setting is a key element in whether a child or adolescent begins using drugs, and in whether drug use progresses to abuse and dependence. Certainly the experiences in the family set a foundation for either healthy or deviant behavior. Below we discuss family risk factors for chemical dependency, and some theories that seek to explain how family variables assert their influence.

Vulnerability and the Family. The family environment significantly affects vulnerability to drug involvement. Research on children and adolescents consistently finds that the main risk and protective factors are directly or indirectly tied up with family characteristics and conditions. The main *family risk factors* are listed below.

- Parental drug abuse, especially paternal alcoholism
- Sibling drug abuse, especially by older siblings
- Family mental health problems, especially maternal depression
- Family antisocial behavior
- Family conflict and discord
- Poor supervision of child behavior
- Alienation and isolation of the family from social support networks

Besides the contributions it may make to risk, the family is also the source of the most powerful protection against drug involvement. In particular, the emotional support and guidance provided by parents, along with family sanctions against drug use, lessen the likelihood of serious drug problems in children and adolescents (Newcomb 1995, Zucker et al. 1995a).

Why is the family so important? This question may sound very naive, but it is a critical one. Clearly, family life entails powerful forces for our individual development. You have already learned about the hereditary contributions of the family to addiction-proneness, but genetic influences also operate within the rich and complex psychological environment defined by the family. For most of us, the family is our primary developmental framework during childhood, and its impact on the life paths we follow is hard to overstate. As you have already learned, many psychological theories of chemical dependency make reference to family issues. In the next section we will look at several key areas of family functioning.

Family Relationships.   For most children, the family is the primary agent of socialization, the process by which individuals are taught social behavior, attitudes, and values. In earlier sections of this chapter you read about some examples of the way failed socialization contributes to drug involvement. In psychodynamic theory, for instance, an assumption is made that the personality defects responsible for addiction-proneness are due to early disruptions in the parent–child relationship. Social learning theory, too, attributes the inclination to drug and alcohol use to modeling influences in the family, such as, parental drinking. Despite some basic differences, many theories agree on the central role played by family relationships in the development of drug problems.

The impact of family relationships is highlighted by **attachment theory,** a view that attributes social, emotional, and personality development to the quality of the parent–child relationship. Originally focused on the mother–infant bond, attachment theory has been extended beyond infancy to include the parent–child relationship in childhood and adolescence (Bowlby 1988). This theory assumes that early attachment relationships serve as frameworks for children to construct internal *mental models* of their social world and of themselves. In this way, the quality of early attachment determines later social behavior and personality traits. When early attachment is disrupted by separation, loss, abuse, or neglect, the course of development is jeopardized. Many later problems have been linked with early *attachment disorganization,* including aggression, delinquency, depression, and drug abuse (Carlson and Sroufe 1995, Main 1996, Nurco and Lerner 1996).

Recent work on adolescents finds that attachment disturbances in adolescents contribute to substance abuse. This link is most prominent in teens who have a *dismissive attachment style,* meaning that they deny or downplay the importance of family attachments and positive feelings associated with attachments while freely expressing hostility toward attachment figures. Dismissive teens are not only at risk for substance abuse, but also for emotional distress, poor social relationships, and antisocial behavior (Rosenstein et al. 1996). In addition, adolescent attachment problems also increase the chance of hard-drug abuse and antisocial behavior in young adulthood (Allen et al. 1996).

Parenting Behavior.   Family socialization has also been examined from the perspective of the ways parents discipline their children. Differences in *parenting styles* are reflected in the methods of child management used by parents to regulate and respond to their children's behavior (Baumrind 1987). Inconsistent discipline and the reliance on hostile and/or punitive control is associated with various behavior problems in children and adolescents. For example, a study of polydrug-dependent teenaged girls found that their parents alternated between supporting the daughters' efforts at independence and strongly condemning those efforts. These mixed messages produced high levels of family conflict and hostility for which the daughters usually were blamed (Humes and Humphrey 1994).

In general, parents of substance-abusing adolescents have been found to use less-effective methods of discipline than other parents (Tarter et al. 1993). Often the failure of other child-management methods results in abusive physical punishment, and physically abused children are at higher risk for later substance use disorders (Malinowsky-Rummel and Hansen 1993). Although parenting deficits are associated with substance abuse, no specific parenting variable is exclusively linked with drug and alcohol problems in children and adolescents. Instead, certain parenting practices establish an overall negative emotional tone for parent–child interactions and increase the level of risk for many problems (Jacob et al. 1991). While parents' behaviors surely are predictive of their children's problems, keep in mind that the child's behavior and traits also affect the parent's disciplinary practices. For example, children with a difficult temperament are more likely to provoke negative, punishing reactions from their parents. Thus, you need to recognize that parent–child relations are a two-way street, and that the outcome of these relations is a product of interactions of both parties (Blackson et al. 1994).

Social Factors

You probably know at least one person who developed a drug problem despite being raised in a good family environment. The family is surely an influential social agent, but it is not the only one. The use and abuse of psychoactive drugs is also determined by social groups and influences outside the family. Of the extrafamilial factors in chemical dependency, peers and ethnicity are the most prominent.

Peer Influence. Developmental studies show time and again that adolescents are most likely to use and abuse drugs when their peers are drug involved. The relationship of peers to drug use is not simply a matter of the adolescent buckling under peer pressure. People choose their peers because they are like-minded individuals. **Peer cluster theory** proposes a view of peer influence that characterizes peer groups as the social framework in which many deviant behaviors, including substance abuse, can emerge. The *deviant peer cluster* is a group whose social bonds and behaviors are based on shared unconventional attitudes and traits, as well as common antagonisms to family and mainstream society. Within the peer cluster are mutually reinforcing relationships that maintain the behavior patterns of cluster members (Oetting and Beauvais 1986, Oetting et al. 1994).

What causes an adolescent to gravitate to a deviant peer group? Most often disturbances in the family set the stage for the adolescent to focus outside the family. When teenagers feel devalued by their families, they will seek support and validation for their worth elsewhere, as in unconventional or antisocial networks of peers. Weak emotional bonds, inadequate parental suppor and supervision, and dysfunctional family behavior enhance the adolescent's detach ment from normal social controls (Kaplar 1996). While the impact of peers is signifi cant, it is also important to recognize that the behavior of parents affects the child's choice of peers. When parents are disconnected from healthy, supportive social networks the child's opportunities for establishing re lations with healthy peers is limited, and so the inclination to affiliate with deviant peer increases (Kandel 1996).

Ethnicity

Culture is an inescapable force in everyday life Different cultural traditions and values are embodied by various ethnic and racial groups and those cultural forces assert themselves ir both subtle and dramatic forms that can affec the risk of drug involvement. Drug use anc abuse are not distributed evenly among ethni groups—in fact, there are big differences be tween groups both in the United States anc internationally that demonstrate the impact o ethnic factors in drug involvement.

Group Differences in Drug Involvement. Worldwide, alcoholism is apparently mor prevalent in groups with a cultural traditior of wine making, such as in France, and ir countries like the United States, where alco hol is easily available. By contrast, alcoho dependency is rare in Islamic nations where religion and legal sanctions discourage alco hol use. In the United States, alcoholism is more common in Native Americans than ir most other ethnic groups, but American Jew: and Asian Americans have very low alcohol ism rates (Helzer 1987).

While most illicit drug use in the United States is accounted for by non-Hispanic white Americans, some minority groups are distin guished by disproportionately high rates o illicit drug use. For example, narcotic anc crack/cocaine addiction rates are elevatec among African-American males in economi cally disadvantaged inner cities. Among His panic Americans, men have above-average rates of cocaine abuse, but women have a very low prevalence of substance abuse (National Institute on Drug Abuse 1995, Substance Abuse and Mental Health Services Administration 1996).

Why Does Ethnicity Matter? A person's ethnicity is tied in with many variables that influence the likelihood of drug involvement and dependence. Ethnicity is linked with our genes, family environment, religion, values, and socioeconomic class, all of which are vital matters.

Earlier in the chapter you learned about a genetic trait in many Asian people that may act as a protective factor against alcoholism—perhaps the low rates of alcoholism among Chinese and Japanese individuals reflect a genetic intolerance of alcohol. On the other hand, whether specific genetic mechanisms account for the increased vulnerability to alcoholism of certain other ethnic groups is not yet known.

Beyond genetic factors, numerous social variables that are correlated with ethnicity contribute to drug and alcohol use. The level of *cultural tolerance* for drugs is reflected in attitudes about drugs and drug use. Despite noisy antidrug rhetoric, cultural tolerance for drugs is relatively high in the United States compared with other nations, as for example Saudi Arabia. Within American society considerable variation in attitudes toward drugs is found among differing racial, ethnic, and religious groups. Mormons, for instance, prohibit alcohol use on religious grounds, while Mexican-American men see their drinking as a normal part of social behavior (Zucker et al. 1995a).

Cultural tolerance affects the availability of drugs, and drug availability increases the potential for abuse. Recent debates about cigarette advertisements aimed at youth (e.g., the Joe Camel campaign) highlight society's concern about prompting children to try easily available gateway drugs. However, the existing ambivalence in this country about drugs and drug control has led to uncertainty about how to limit drug use and how to punish those who break the rules. Generally, in cultures with strong antidrug sanctions, chemical dependency is relatively uncommon.

In the United States, ethnicity is often confounded with socioeconomic status (SES). Typically, individuals in ethnic minorities are more likely to be economically disadvantaged than the white majority. Any elevation in chemical dependency among African Americans, Hispanic Americans, and Native Americans might, therefore, reflect SES as much as any ethnicity-specific influences (Lillie-Blanton and Arria 1995). The **social stress hypothesis** attributes psychological disturbances to the impact of a stressful social environment. Membership in a disadvantaged group imposes considerable social stress on the individual, and thus increases the risk for chemical dependency and other disorders associated with stress (Bruce et al. 1991, Lex 1985).

Chapter Summary

6–1

The disease model of addictions views chemical dependency as a biologically based physical illness. The modern disease model describes addictions as biopsychosocial diseases with a multitude of causes and a variety of forms. Behavioral genetics studies using the family, twin, and adoption methods give evidence of the heritability of chemical dependency, especially male alcoholism. Genes that influence the brain's dopamine receptors and the liver's metabolism are suspected of contributing to addiction proneness. The dopamine reward system regulates the reinforcing impact of addictive drugs, and addiction-prone people are thought to have a dopamine reward-deficiency syndrome. Serotonin deficiency is also linked with alcoholism. Persistent drug abuse causes the brain to employ compensatory adaptations such as down-regulation and up-regulation to restore equilibrium. Research with the alcohol challenge shows greater metabolic tolerance for alcohol in high-risk subjects. High-risk individuals also exhibit abnormal neuropsychological features in terms of the P300 wave and executive function deficits.

6–2

Traditional psychodynamic personality theory views addictions as the consequence of developmental failures of ego functions such as the defense mechanisms and superego conflicts. Developmental fixations such as an oral fixation are also thought to contribute to alcoholism. Psychodynamic object relations theory attributes addictions to family disturbances that adversely affect personality development. Trait studies find little support for the notion of a specific addictive personality profile. Traits associated with addictions might be causes, consequences, or correlates of the addiction. Longitudinal research finds some personality predictors of addiction proneness. Temperament research also suggests links between certain temperament dimensions and alcoholism.

6–3

Classical conditioning principles apply to the learning of associations between drug-related stimuli and craving, withdrawal, and tolerance responses. The operant conditioning principle of reinforcement is central to the development of addiction habits and their maintenance. Positive reinforcement comes both from the biological impact of substances on the brain and from the social reinforcements for substance use. Negative reinforcement affects the escape behavior of addicts. According to the conditioned incentive model, classical and operant conditioning both influence addiction development.

6–4

Social learning theory emphasizes the role of modeling, or observational learning, in the development of chemical dependency. In social cognitive theory, interactions between the person and the environment are emphasized, and the role of self-regulation failure

in addiction is considered central. Negative self-efficacy expectations, too, contribute to drug use and general maladjustment. According to expectancy theory, expectations about drug use outcomes motivate persistent use, but the link between expectancies and behavior is mediated by situations, culture, and personality.

6–5

Tension-reduction theory explains alcohol abuse in terms of the relief of tension that follows drinking. According to stress-response dampening theory, alcohol use lessens the individual's physiological response to stressful events. The self-medication hypothesis states that drug abuse is motivated by the need to relieve emotional pain and suffering.

6–6

Sociocultural factors in chemical dependency include the family, peers, and ethnicity. Many family risk factors can contribute to a child's vulnerability to substance abuse because of their impact on the child's development. Problems in attachment relationships and parenting behavior are particularly significant factors in substance abuse. According to peer cluster theory, the deviant peer group is the main socialization agent for teen drug abuse. Ethnic differences in rates and types of chemical dependency might represent distinctive genetic, family, and/or socioeconomic variables linked with ethnicity.

Terms to Remember

addictive personality
alcohol challenge
attachment theory
behavioral theory of choice
behavioral view
biological markers
classical conditioning
compensatory adaptations
conditioned incentive model
developmental fixation

disease model
expectancy theory
familial alcoholism
heritability
modeling
operant conditioning
peer cluster theory
psychodynamic view
reward-deficiency syndrome
self-efficacy
self-medication hypothesis
serotonin deficiency hypothesis
social cognitive theory
social learning theory
social stress hypothesis

stress-response dampening theory
temperament model
tension-reduction theory

Suggested Reading

Blane, H. T., and Leonard, K. E., eds. (1987). *Psychological Theories of Drinking and Alcoholism*. New York: Guilford.

DuPont, R. L. (1997). *The Selfish Brain: Learning from Addiction*. Washington, DC: American Psychiatric Press.

Jellinek, E. M. (1960). *The Disease Concept of Alcoholism*. New Haven, CT: College and University Press.

Chemical Dependency and Physical Health

Chapter Outline

Learning Objectives

After completing this chapter you should be able to:

1. Outline the general health risks associated with substance use.
2. Describe the effects of alcohol on the cardiovascular system.
2. Describe the effects of cocaine on the cardiovascular system.
3. Indicate and describe the effects of alcohol and cocaine on the nervous system.
4. List and describe the effects of drugs and alcohol on the liver, gastrointestinal system, and pancreas.
5. Explain the relationships between drug use and HIV infection.
6. Describe how drug use is related to the surge in tuberculosis cases.
7. Explain the mechanisms of prenatal exposure to drugs.
8. Describe the effects of alcohol on the developing fetus.

Consider these facts:

- About 44 percent of all deaths caused by cirrhosis in North America are alcohol-related.
- The incidence of cocaine-related strokes has reached epidemic proportions since 1985.
- The physical complications of chemical dependency cost Americans billions of dollars annually.
- Thirty to 40 percent of inner-city intravenous drug users test positive for HIV.

These facts inform you that drugs not only have psychoactive effects, but that they also have serious physical consequences. Substance-dependent people are at risk for many potentially disabling and deadly medical problems (American Psychiatric Association 1995a, Majewska 1996, National Institute on Alcoholism and Alcohol Abuse 1990). In this chapter you will examine some of the most common medical disorders that are associated with pathological drug use.

7–1 General Health Risks

The physical effects of drugs, chaotic and disorganized lifestyles, and lack of access to health care place chemically dependent people at great risk for medical problems, disability, and death. Cocaine, heroin, and other drugs all cause significant medical problems, but because of alcohol's potent physical effects and the high prevalence of alcohol-use disorders, the majority of drug-related medical conditions are caused by alcohol (American Psychiatric Association 1995a).

Drugs impair physical functioning directly and indirectly. Direct influences include the acute effects of intoxication and overdose, the physical symptoms of withdrawal, and the complications of chronic heavy use. Physical problems also occur indirectly by way of behaviors associated with drug use. Snorting, smoking, and injecting drugs, and other unsafe behaviors like having unprotected sex, create their own complications in addition to the psychoactive effects of these drugs.

By whatever the means, drugs affect virtually every organ system. Indeed, chemical dependency is associated with a host of neurological, cardiovascular, hepatic (liver), gastrointestinal, and immune system problems. Sadly, many pregnant women are substance dependent, too. Drug use is not only unhealthy for the expectant mother but it can also cause irreparable damage to the developing fetus because many drugs cross the placenta and invade the fetus' circulatory system. From a public-health perspective, the most important medical consequences of substance dependency are tuberculosis and AIDS because they are communicable diseases.

Complications Due to Route of Administration

The first point to consider about the physical effects of drugs are the hazards posed by the methods used to take the drugs. Snorting, inhaling, smoking, or injecting a drug all carry their own risks, in addition to the problems caused by the drug's effects on organs.

Most medical problems due to snorting are associated with the use of stimulants. Breathing in amphetamines or cocaine causes irritation of the soft nasal tissue. The greater damage, however, is attributable to these stimulants' effects on blood vessels. Stimulants reduce the size of blood vessels and with chronic use can severely limit blood flow. Impaired blood flow prevents tissue repair and so cells die. Repeated snorting, as is done in a cocaine binge, can cause holes in the *septum* or dividing tissue between the nostrils (Smith and Seymour 1995). Inhalants also cause soft-tissue damage.

Medical complications due to smoking principally involve lung or pulmonary problems. Smoke from virtually any material irritates the trachea (windpipe) and lungs, and increases the risk of respiratory ailments such as *bronchitis, emphysema,* and *cancer* (Smith and Seymour 1995). Lung damage from smoking marijuana and crack is not uncommon.

Injecting drugs probably causes the greatest range of physical problems. In addition to transmitting AIDS, and causing liver, and other infections, injection causes skin, muscle, and blood vessel damage. Damage can result from repeatedly injecting into the same site, from failure to clean the area or the needle, or from impurities in the drug. The most common type of damage is needle marks, called "tracks," or scars caused by unsterile injection equipment or impurities. Carbon deposited on a needle when the person is trying to sterilize the needle by heating it with a match will cause tattoo-like skin discolorations and possibly an **abscess**, or area of infection and inflammation characterized by redness, stinging, itching, swelling, and pus formation. Abscesses, like most skin problems in drug users, are caused by unsterile injection equipment (Smith and Seymour 1995).

Overdose and Withdrawal

As you learned in Chapter 2, all psychoactive drugs produce intoxication and some lead to withdrawal symptoms that can range from extremely uncomfortable to life-threatening.

Overdose. Despite its general physical symptoms, intoxication usually does not lead to a significant medical hazard unless the person takes more of a drug than the body can handle. An **overdose** refers to the severe intoxicating or physical effects of taking too much of a drug or one that is too potent. The physical consequences of overdose depend on the type of drug, its route of administration, and the quantity and purity of the drug, as well as the user's tolerance level. Because many psychoactive drugs are synthesized in clandestine laboratories and sold illicitly, there is considerable variability in drug quality and purity; moreover these drugs are often diluted with potentially toxic substances. These factors make drug overdose a distinct possibility in recreational users and even in substance-dependent individuals. Worse yet, polysubstance use is the norm. In this pattern, most users take different drugs either successively or in combination, making the possibility of overdose resemble a game of Russian roulette.

One way of indirectly gauging the physical consequences of drug overdose is to examine statistics on drug-related hospital emergency room (ER) admissions and mortality rates. Data from twenty U.S. cities show that overdose is a common reason for ER admission for all classes of psychoactive drugs, and that cocaine and heroin are the most frequently involved (National Institute on Drug Abuse 1996a). Indeed, cocaine and heroin overdoses account for the majority of drug-related deaths, and the rates are increasing. Emergency room admissions and overdose-related deaths from other stimulants, especially methamphetamine, depressants, and other opioids, are fairly common, too. Drug combinations account for a sizable percentage of overdose and deaths. In Seattle, for example, 30 percent of all drug deaths in 1995 were due to injecting "speedballs" (heroin–cocaine combinations). Furthermore, about 25 percent of depressant-induced deaths involved depressants, usually Valium, taken together with alcohol. Compared to other drugs, ER admission and overdose mortality rates from LSD and PCP are low, but they are increasing in most areas of the country. When deaths do occur from hallucinogens they usually come from suicide or reckless behavior instead of direct medical complications (National Institute on Drug Abuse 1996a).

Withdrawal.   Substance withdrawal involves both physiological and psychological symptoms (see Chapter 2). From a medical standpoint, however, it is much more likely to cause temporary misery than permanent medical problems or death. The physical symptoms of withdrawal eventually resolve or go away even without treatment, but life-threatening complications do occur, especially with alcohol and other depressants. It was not that long ago that the mortality rate for people experiencing severe alcohol withdrawal was 20 percent, but improved diagnosis and medical treatment has now lowered that number to 1 percent (Ciraulo and Shader 1991). However withdrawal from sedatives and tranquilizers will cause dysregulated body temperature and heart function that is sometimes fatal (Jaffe 1989b). Withdrawal from depressants is also associated with uncontrollable movements or seizures.

7–2 Cardiovascular Disorders

One way that drugs imperil users is by damaging the **cardiovascular system**, which includes the heart and the blood vessels that transport blood. Reduced pumping capacity, abnormal beating rhythms, clogged and damaged arteries, high blood pressure, heart muscle damage, and heart attacks are the user's ultimate fate. Although most psychoactive drugs have cardiovascular effects, alcohol and cocaine use are prominent causes of cardiovascular disease.

The Heart and Cardiovascular Function

Many of the most serious medical consequences of drug use involve the cardiovascular system. To better appreciate how drugs affect it we will present a brief description of cardiovascular function.

Veins return used, deoxygenated blood to the heart by way of the right atrium (see Figure 7–1). Blood from the heart itself is also drained into the right atrium. From there, the right ventricle is filled, which then pumps the blood into the lungs where it is oxygenated; it is then returned to the heart via the left atrium and then to the left ventricle, from which oxygenated blood is pumped through the aorta into all the arteries of the body.

The heart works electrically, too. Heart rate is controlled by nerves in the *autonomic nervous system* that regulate a pacemaker area in the right atrium. In considering how drugs affect the heart, we must thus consider the heart's ability to fill with blood, its pumping capacity, and its electrical conduction. Blood vessels within the heart itself and throughout the body must be clear and open enough to transport blood and return it to the heart.

Alcohol and the Cardiovascular System

Alcohol is known to directly affect the heart muscle as well as blood vessels. It is important to understand that although alcohol's long-term cardiovascular effects are well known, a person does not necessarily have to drink heavily for years to suffer cardiovascular problems. Drinking too much on a single occasion can be life-threatening, even in people without preexisting cardiovascular disease. Alcohol's effects on people who have heart disease obviously are much more dangerous.

Acute Effects.   Alcohol causes many biochemical changes in heart-muscle tissue. Less than six ounces of alcohol can lead to weakened heart-muscle contractions and result in less blood being pumped each time the heart beats (Jaffe 1995a). Reduced pumping capacity is compensated for partially because, although alcohol is a depressant, the heart beats faster when the person is intoxicated. This happens because alcohol slows down messages from the autonomic nerves that ordinarily regulate heart rate. In any event, an overdose can cause heart failure, in which the heart stops beating altogether (National Institute on Alcohol Abuse and Alcoholism 1990).

The combination of impaired heart muscle contractibility and neural inhibition often leads to a **cardiac arrhythmia**, the abnormal beating rhythm of the heart caused by electrical conduction problems (Zakhari 1997). The

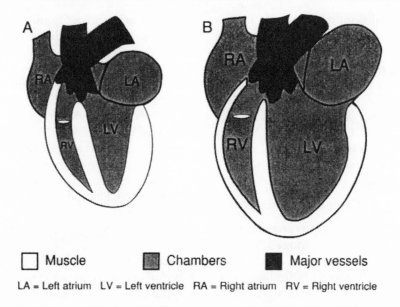

Figure 7–1. Schematic illustration of a normal heart (A) and a heart in dilated cardiomyopathy (B). Both hearts are shown in their state at the end of contraction (i.e., at end-systole).
Source: Zakhari (1997).

most common alcohol-related arrhythmia is *atrial fibrillation*, in which the atria beat fast and irregularly (Jaffe 1995a, National Institute on Alcohol Abuse and Alcoholism 1990, Zakhari 1997). Sometimes called the *holiday heart syndrome*, atrial fibrillation can occur during intoxication, but is most often seen after a heavy drinking binge, suggesting that it may be a sign of mild alcohol withdrawal. Fortunately, atrial fibrillation is not usually fatal, though the risk of death is greater for drinkers who already have underlying heart disease (Jaffe 1995a).

Effects of Chronic Use. Beyond the short-term dangers of intoxication and overdose, chronic drinking gradually damages the heart, arteries, and veins. This happens because certain chemicals alter heart and circulatory function to raise blood pressure each time the person drinks. Repeated alcohol use eventually causes chronic **hypertension**, or high blood pressure. Indeed, studies show that up to 24 percent of cases of unexplained hypertension can ultimately be linked to excessive drinking (Klatsky 1987). The alcohol–hypertension connection is strongest in white

men over age 55 who consume more than three drinks a day (Klatsky 1987). In addition, long-term drinking impairs heart muscle metabolism. Eventually, heart muscle is replaced by fat and fiber, and the heart loses its ability to contract, becomes enlarged, and the person experiences heart failure. This condition is called **alcoholic cardiomyopathy** (see Figure 7–1). Statistics indicate that 20 to 50 percent of all cases of cardiomyopathy in Western countries are due to heavy alcohol consumption (Zakhari 1997).

Alcohol constricts the arteries that feed the heart muscle, and in so doing increases the risk of spasm and chest pain from insufficient oxygen, an experience called *angina pectoris*. This is especially likely in individuals who already have **coronary artery disease** (CAD), a narrowing of the coronary arteries due to a buildup of plaque (National Institute on Alcohol Abuse and Alcoholism 1990).

Research on the effects of alcohol on coronary arteries has had conflicting outcomes. Although some studies have linked CAD to prolonged drinking, much research actually indicates that alcohol actually has a beneficial effect on coronary arteries. Low to moderate daily doses of alcohol may actually have a protective effect on the heart and reduce the likelihood of coronary artery damage by increasing HDL, the "good cholesterol," and by reducing blood clotting. (Criqui 1986, National Institute on Alcohol Abuse and Alcoholism 1990, Shaper et al. 1987, Stampfer et al. 1988, Zakhari 1997). Of course, the numerous adverse physical effects of alcohol clearly outweigh its benefits.

Cocaine and the Cardiovascular System

The picture of cocaine's effects on the cardiovascular system is bleak. Indeed, cardiac problems are the most frequent and hazardous medical complications of stimulant overdose (Jaffe 1995a, Majewska 1996). Cocaine affects the heart in three important ways. *First*, it anesthetizes heart muscle, which slows heart rate and results in the heart's failure to adequately pump blood (Jaffe 1995a, Karch 1993, Polkis et al. 1987, Volkow et al. 1996). *Second*, cocaine stimulates the adrenal glands to produce adrenaline and noradrenaline, chemicals that accelerate heart rate, increase blood pressure, and constrict arteries (Karch 1993, Majewska 1996). *Third*, cocaine produces physiological changes in blood chemistry that result in a risk of *thrombosis* or abnormal blood clotting (Siegel et al. 1999).

Acute Effects. The most common cause of death from cocaine overdose is from cardiac arrhythmias. Moderate doses of cocaine can trigger abnormally fast heart rate, or *tachycardia*; massive doses will cause *bradycardia*, or slowing. In either case, heart attack is a distinct possibility from cocaine toxicity.

Heart attacks can be caused by cocaine's anesthetic effects on the heart, too. When muscle cells are anesthetized, they fail to conduct electricity and the heart abruptly stops beating. Imaging studies of heart function during intoxication and autopsies of people who died of cocaine overdose show significant accumulations of cocaine in the heart itself (Karch 1993, Majewska 1996, Volkow et al. 1996).

Complications from Chronic Use. Numerou studies show that cardiovascular disease fo lows the repeated long-term use of cocaine ar other stimulants. Chronic use of cocaine is a sociated with CAD and plaque deposits in th *aorta*, the main vessel through which oxyge ated blood is pumped from the heart. Even patients without arterial narrowing, the lon term risk of heart attack is increased, becau repeated cocaine use is associated with bloc clotting, arterial spasm, and arterial dama (Jaffe 1995a, Siegel et al. 1999).

7–3 Neurological Disorders

Because psychoactive drugs produce the behavioral and psychological effects by mo fying the activity of the nervous system, yo should not be surprised that drug use caus neurological complications. These invol direct toxic effects on neurons and blood ve sels as well as indirect effects from wit drawal, nutritional deficiencies, head injuri and disturbances of the liver and other inte nal organs, especially from alcohol (Berna 1994).

Alcohol and Neurological Damage

It is well known that heavy, prolonged drin ing causes neurological dysfunction and ps chiatric symptoms due to damage to the bra and peripheral nerves (see Figure 7–2).

Cerebral Atrophy. Brain-imaging studies alcoholics show evidence of general **cerebr atrophy,** defined by decreased brain weigl increases in the spaces between brain regio (sulci), and enlarged ventricles (fluid-fill chambers). Furthermore, 50 to 70 percent detoxified alcoholics with brain damage e hibit impaired performance on neuropsych logical tests of attention, problem solvin perception, memory, and motor coordin tion (Oscar-Berman et al. 1997). Alcohol direct effects on the brain result in sleep a normalities, personality changes, and abnc mal emotional expression; on the positi side, alcohol abstinence is related to some ir provement in brain abnormalities and cogi

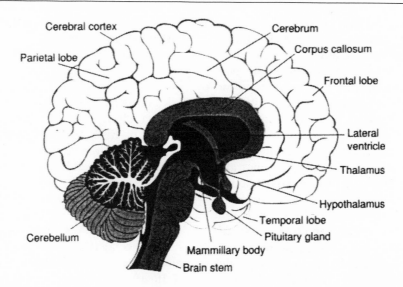

Figure 7–2. Schematic of a lengthwise cross-section through the human brain. Brain structures that most frequently have been implicated in alcohol-related neurological disorders include parts of the diencephalon (i.e., the mammillary bodies of the hypothalamus and the dorsomedial nucleus within the thalamus), the cerebral cortex, and several central neurotransmitter (i.e., nerve cell communication) systems.
Source: Oscar-Berman et al. (1997).

tive function (Freund and Ballinger 1988, Jaffe 1995a, National Institute on Alcohol Abuse and Alcoholism 1990, Oscar-Berman et al. 1997, Pfefferbaum et al. 1988).

Korsakoff's Psychosis. Long-term drinking can result in a severe memory disorder called **Korsakoff's psychosis** in which the individual forgets incidents of daily life shortly after they occur. The condition is caused by extreme thiamine deficiency, and the individual affected by it has difficulty retaining new information for more than a few minutes. Although remote memory is largely intact, there are gaps that force the person to confabulate or make up stories (Lechtenberg 1982, Oscar-Berman et al. 1997).

Alcohol can also damage the nerves that connect to the spinal cord. Prolonged, heavy drinking is associated with *alcoholic peripheral neuropathy*, or simply the destruction of nerves. Because these peripheral nerves project to all the muscles as well as internal organs, when they are damaged many medical and behavior problems can result.

Cocaine and Neurological Damage

Although cardiac and psychiatric complications are the most common medical emergencies in cocaine overdose, neurological disorders are frequent and severe. Neurological symptoms, including headache and movement abnormalities, may account for 20 to 40 percent of patient complaints (Brody et al. 1990, Rich and Singer 1991). Two of the most serious neurological complications of cocaine overdose, however, are *stroke* and *seizures*.

Stroke. A **stroke** is an intracranial hemorrhage or ruptured blood vessel in the brain. The mechanisms by which cocaine causes a stroke are not fully understood, but it appears that cocaine increases nervous system activity, leading to hypertension, tachycardia, and vasoconstriction (narrowing of blood vessels).

Hypertension can cause stroke by bursting an *aneurysm* (a thinned, expanded section of blood vessel) or some otherwise malformed blood vessel in the brain. Intracranial bleeding from *ischemia*, or reduced blood flow and oxygen supply, can also occur and is especially likely from a crack overdose (Daras 1996).

What is particularly frightening is that cocaine-induced neurovascular complications can occur in young adults who have no history of neurological symptoms and in whom traditional stroke risk factors are absent (Daras et al. 1994, Levine et al. 1990). Although cocaine can cause a stroke by itself in otherwise healthy people, the risk escalates when cocaine and alcohol are combined (Perez-Reyes and Jeffcoat 1992).

Seizures. In addition to its potentially lethal effects on blood vessels in the brain, cocaine causes disorganized electrical brain activity, called an epileptic seizure, in a small percentage of users (Daras 1996). Although there are several types of seizures, cocaine overdose will usually cause a *generalized seizure* marked by a loss of consciousness followed by extreme muscle stiffness (tonic phase), then uncontrollable thrashing and jerking of the limbs and trunk (clonic phase). Lasting for one to two minutes, the clonic phase of the seizure may also be accompanied by tongue biting as well as difficulty holding urine or feces. Following the seizure, the person experiences headache, fatigue, confusion, and total amnesia for the event (Berg et al. 1987, Lechtenberg 1982). Generalized seizures are not uncommon during alcohol withdrawal, too (Oscar-Berman et al. 1997).

7–4 Liver, Gastrointestinal, and Pancreatic Disorders

The liver and gastrointestinal tract are responsible for drug metabolism and digestion. Although most drugs are inactivated by the liver, they rarely cause liver damage directly; alcohol is an important exception. Alcoholic liver disease is one of the most serious medical complications of drinking because alcohol not only causes liver problems, but also leads to a number of gastrointestinal and pancreatic disturbances.

Liver Diseases

Located in the upper right section of the abdomen, the liver is the largest organ in the body. The liver serves many life-sustaining functions. It filters circulating blood, removes toxic substances, stores vitamins, helps in digestion, controls the concentration of body fluids, and regulates blood-clotting, to name just a few of its most important functions (National Institute on Alcohol Abuse and Alcoholism 1993a). It is also the primary site where alcohol is deactivated into harmless chemicals (Jaffe 1995a, National Institute on Alcohol Abuse and Alcoholism 1993a, 1995d).

Although the precise nature of the causal relationship remains to be determined, it is clear that excessive drinking is strongly associated with the risk of liver diseases that include *fatty liver, alcoholic hepatitis,* and *cirrhosis.* Not all heavy drinkers develop serious liver ailments, however. It appears that genetic vulnerability, gender, and many dietary factors modify the risk for liver diseases (Maher 1997).

Fatty Liver. One relatively benign consequence of prolonged heavy drinking is a fatty liver, characterized by excess fat in the liver. At least 90 percent of heavy drinkers have a fatty liver and most do not even feel ill. Fatty liver alone poses no major health risk and it is reversible with abstinence (Jaffe 1995a, National Institute on Alcohol Abuse and Alcoholism 1993a, 1995).

Alcoholic Hepatitis. A more serious type of liver disease occurs in nearly 50 percent of alcoholics. This condition, called alcoholic hepatitis, is an inflammation of the liver identified by fever, jaundice (yellowing of the body), and abdominal pain. Examination of liver tissue reveals inflammation and scarring. People with this condition vary with respect to how sick they really are. Some feel well and only laboratory tests reveal the disease, but most patients with alcoholic hepatitis manifest moderate degrees of illness. Like fatty liver, alcoholic hepatitis is potentially reversible with abstinence (Jaffe 1995a, Maher 1997, National Institute on Alcohol Abuse and Alcoholism 1993a, 1995).

Apart from the conditions resulting from the direct effects of drinking, other liver diseases are commonly seen in people who use drugs. *Viral hepatitis* is a name given to liver disease caused by viruses. Unlike alcoholic hepatitis, which is drug-induced, forms of viral hepatitis are transmitted by blood contact. Contaminated needles and syringes, blood-to-blood contact during sexual intercourse, and mother-to-fetus infection are the most likely modes of transmission in drug users (Jaffe 1995a).

One type of viral hepatitis is *hepatitis B,* whose signs range from mild flu-like symptoms to fever, jaundice, coma, and death. *Hepatitis C,* a severe and often incurable condition, is identified by the presence of an antibody similar to HIV, the virus that causes AIDS. Intravenous drug users are the major source of hepatitis C transmission. Chronic hepatitis, cirrhosis, and liver cancer are all associated with hepatitis C infection (Jaffe 1995a).

Alcoholic Cirrhosis. Chronic drinking and hepatitis lead to end-stage liver disease in about 15 to 30 percent of alcoholics. Called **alcoholic cirrhosis**, this disease is marked by dead liver cells and scar tissue that chokes off blood vessels and impairs liver function. Cirrhosis is irreversible and potentially fatal. Although the incidence of cirrhosis has steadily declined since 1976, it is still one of the ten leading causes of death in the United States, and nearly half of the cases are attributable to drinking (Maher 1997). Historically, it was thought that cirrhosis was the end of a progression from fatty liver to hepatitis to cirrhosis. However, many individuals develop alcoholic cirrhosis without ever having fatty liver or hepatitis.

Gastrointestinal Disorders

The *gastrointestinal (GI) system* consists of the mouth, esophagus, stomach, and intestines, the structures necessary for food intake, di-

gestion, and elimination (see Figure 7–3). In this section you will examine how alcohol damages health by impairing gastrointestinal functioning.

Gastrointestinal Complications. If you have ever taken a drink of alcohol you must have noticed that it irritates the lining of your mouth and burns going down. The mouth, esophagus, and stomach take the brunt of alcohol's damaging effects because they are exposed to the highest concentrations of alcohol. Furthermore, a significant amount of alcohol is metabolized in the stomach. Alcohol slows the rate at which the stomach empties its contents into the intestines, but once it arrives, alcohol causes poor digestion and impairs the intestines' ability to

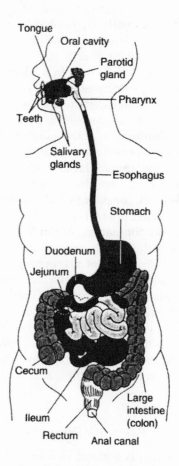

Figure 7–3. Schematic representation of the human gastrointestinal tract. The small intestine comprises the duodenum, the ileum, and the jejunum.
Source: Bode and Bode (1997).

absorb nutrients (Bode and Bode 1997, National Institute on Alcohol Abuse and Alcoholism 1990).

GI Ulcers and Cancer.   Regular drinking will aggravate an existing **peptic ulcer** or open sore in the stomach. Alcohol does not seem to cause ulcers (cigarettes do) but it does interfere with healing. Considering that many heavy drinkers also smoke, the risk of peptic ulcers is high in alcoholics (Sullivan 1995).

Alcohol consumption is associated with cancer, too. **Cancer** refers to a group of diseases characterized by the presence of abnormal cells that grow out of control, and the formation of masses called tumors that destroy normal tissue. Two to 4 percent of all cancers are thought to be caused either directly or indirectly by excessive drinking (National Institute on Alcohol Abuse and Alcoholism 1993b). Specifically, repeated inflammation of the GI tract from alcohol is associated with an increased risk of cancer of the mouth, esophagus, pharynx, and larynx. Stomach irritation can lead to chronic *gastritis,* an inflammation of the stomach that can progress to stomach cancer. Surely, the risk of cancer in the upper GI tract is elevated with drinking. To get an idea of how strong the association is, consider that alcoholics bear a higher risk of upper GI cancer than people in the general population. About 50 percent of cancers of the mouth, larynx, and pharynx, and about 75 percent of all esophageal cancers in the United States are linked to chronic, excessive alcohol use (Blot 1992, Franceschi et al. 1990, Klygis and Barch 1992, Stinson and DeBakey 1992). Furthermore, the risk increases as the amount of alcohol consumed rises, and lessens during abstinence (National Institute on Alcohol Abuse and Alcoholism 1993b).

Pancreatic Disorders

The *pancreas* is a gland that lies across the posterior wall of the abdomen. When you think of the pancreas you probably think about its role in the secretion of *insulin,* a hormone important in sugar metabolism. As you probably know, the failure of the pancreas to synthesize sufficient amounts of insulin is the cause of *diabetes.* You may not know, however, that the pancreas synthesizes enzymes that are discharged into the intestine to aid in digestion. Heavy drinking is one of the two leading causes of **pancreatitis,** a condition manifested by severe abdominal pain, nausea, vomiting, fever, and tachycardia. Some alcoholics suffer *acute pancreatitis* and do well after a few days of standard treatment. Others, however, experience additional complications, and about 5 percent of all alcoholics with acute pancreatitis die (National Institute on Alcohol Abuse and Alcoholism 1990).

Five to ten years of heavy drinking increases the risk of *chronic pancreatitis,* and more than 75 percent of people with this condition have a long history of heavy drinking. The symptoms are like those of acute pancreatitis, except that abdominal pain is so severe that surgical removal of the pancreas is sometimes necessary. By the time the person has the first attack of abdominal pain, permanent pancreas damage has already occurred. Within three to four years of the initial attack, pancreatic hormone deficiencies are evident resulting in reduced flow of enzymes to the intestines, poor absorption of nutrients, and malnutrition. And as if this were not bad enough, sugar metabolism is disrupted as well (Apte et al. 1997).

7–5 Immune System Disorders

Cardiac arrhythmias, stroke, pancreatitis, and cirrhosis are examples of diseases caused directly by excessive drug use. Unfortunately substance-dependent individuals are also prone to to infectious diseases because of suppressed immune function and risky behaviors. In this section you will study the relationship between drug use and infectious diseases such as AIDS and tuberculosis.

The Immune System

The **immune system** is a series of structures and bodily mechanisms that identify and eliminate foreign substances. The immune system protects you against microorganisms like viruses and bacteria. Among the most important elements of the immune system are *leukocytes*, or white blood cells, which are produced in the bone marrow and then migrate to the spleen, thymus gland, and lymph nodes. When your immune system is in good working order leukocytes and other immune cells are able to identify microorganisms, attach to them, and inactivate them (Kalat 1992, Szabo 1997).

Chronic stress (and some microorganisms) can suppress immune function. Drugs suppress immune activity, too. Indeed, alcohol consumption decreases the overall number of white blood cells and generally suppresses many immune responses. Consequently, alcoholics are susceptible to cancers, bacterial lung infections, and other infections as well (National Institute on Alcohol Abuse and Alcoholism 1992, Szabo 1997). There is evidence that even occasional drinking can suppress immunity by rendering white blood cells more vulnerable to HIV (Bagasra et al. 1989).

Immunosuppression is also caused by cocaine and opioids. Cocaine directly suppresses immune-cell activity as well as the release of hormones involved in preserving immunity. Cocaine addicts are likely to maintain poor eating habits as well, thereby furthering immunosuppression. Opioids affect immunity by their direct actions on immune cells. There is compelling evidence of the existence of opioid receptors on human immune cells, which probably allows opioid drugs to modulate immune-cell activity (Watson 1995).

AIDS and HIV Infection

One dreaded problem related to drug use is **acquired immune deficiency syndrome** (AIDS), an incurable disorder caused by the human immunodeficiency virus (HIV). The virus destroys the immune system and renders the individual susceptible to deadly infections. HIV is transmitted through blood and other body fluids and may lay dormant for many years without the person showing clinical signs of AIDS. Eventually, lung infections, brain degeneration, and skin cancers rarely seen in people with a strong immune system begin to devastate the body.

In the United States, more than 540,000 cases of AIDS have been reported to the *Centers for Disease Control and Prevention (CDC)* in Atlanta. Male cases outnumber female cases by about five to one, and many hundreds of thousands more people are HIV-infected but do not yet have AIDS symptoms. Sadly, 50 percent of those who have tested positive for HIV (HIV+ or HIV-positive) are expected to develop full-blown AIDS within ten years, and 90 percent will probably have symptoms within twenty years after initial infection (Chin and Lwanga 1992). All told, the CDC reports that nearly 350,000 people have already died from AIDS complications (Centers for Disease Control and Prevention 1997c). The outlook for people with AIDS seems to be improving, but it remains pretty grim. Early estimates were that about 85 percent of people with AIDS would die within five years of diagnosis; however, improvements in diagnosis and advances in treatment have allowed many individuals to live much longer (Rothenberger et al. 1987). In fact, for the first time since AIDS was identified in the early 1980s, 1996 was the first year in which the death rate dropped (Centers for Disease Control and Prevention 1997c).

Drug Use and AIDS

What does drug use have to do with HIV/AIDS? Drug use is related to HIV infection and AIDS in at least two ways. *First*, psychoactive drugs suppresses immunity, as you already learned. You cannot get AIDS, however, unless you are exposed to the HIV virus, leading to the *second* point, which is that although AIDS is caused by a virus, it is transmitted by behavior. Drugs are dangerous not only because of their direct physical and psychological effects and because they suppress immunity, but also because many behaviors associated with drug use are conducive to the transmission of HIV. Injection drug use and unprotected sex are the most likely causes of HIV transmission in substance-dependent individuals.

HIV Transmission and Drug Use. It is well known that the greatest risk for HIV infection has been and continues to be found in sexually active homosexual or bisexual men who engage in unprotected sex. As shown in Table 7–1, however, injecting drug-users (IDUs) comprise the second largest percentage of AIDS cases. Also, whereas the risk of AIDS in homosexual men has declined steadily since 1985, AIDS prevalence among IDUs has remained more or less steady in the last few years at around 26 percent of all AIDS cases.

There are several ways by which HIV is transmitted through intravenous drug use. Sharing HIV-contaminated needles, syringes, and other drug equipment such as cookers, cotton, and mixing containers is common practice among intravenous drug users (IDUs). Furthermore, several studies indicate that HIV can survive in ordinary tap water for extended periods of time and that many IDUs clean their equipment or "works" in the same container of water that was used to prepare for shooting (Koester et al. 1990).

The risk of HIV/AIDS varies with the injection method, too. "Booting" is a way of injecting drugs that involves drawing blood from the vein into a drug-filled syringe, then injecting the solution back into the vein. Many IDUs think this procedure strengthens the drug's effect, but true or not, booting certainly increases the odds of HIV contamination because traces of blood are left in the syringe (Stephens and Alemagno 1994).

The use of "shooting galleries" poses a very high risk of HIV/AIDS contamination. Many of them offer a fairly private place to get high and some will rent or sell syringes and other injection equipment to users. In this scenario, blood residue is visible on many needles and even some of those without signs of blood may still be contaminated. One study of 255 men and women in three South Florida shooting galleries showed that 10 percent of apparently clean needle–syringe combinations were HIV contaminated (Chitwood et al. 1990).

Finally, the risk of HIV/AIDS also depends on the type of drug injected. Due to cocaine's short duration of action, it must be injected often for the user to stay high. Compared to heroin users, cocaine IDUs inject more often and are more likely to share needles, thereby increasing the risk of HIV/AIDS (Stephens and Alemagno 1994).

Sexual Behavior and AIDS

The second way in which drug use is associated with increased risk of HIV/AIDS is through unprotected sex. The problems caused by using contaminated injection equipment are compounded by the fact that the majority of IDUs are sexually active heterosexual males. Indeed, heterosexual transmission of HIV/AIDS is on the rise, and much of the increase is attributable to intravenous drug use (Centers for Disease Control 1997d). The picture becomes even more tangled when you consider that unprotected sex among IDUs also increases the risk of other sexually transmitted diseases such as *chlamydia, gonorrhea,* and *syphilis,* which in turn, weaken the immune system and facilitate HIV transmission (Centers for Disease Control 1997b).

Research shows that white IDU males are likely to have IDU female sex partners; African Americans are more likely to have non-IDU female sex partners. Whether white or black, male IDUs report a very low use of condoms, making it easy for HIV to be spread to their sexual partners (Ross et al. 1992, Stephens and Alemagno 1994). Many personal and cultural factors undoubtedly contribute to an unwillingness to use condoms even in the face of HIV/AIDS. One factor that has received much attention is the use of drugs itself. Although research is in its preliminary stages and firm conclusions cannot be drawn yet, it appears that drugs and alcohol increase the risk of HIV/AIDS by stimulating sexual desire, decreasing inhibitions, and interfering with good judgment (Leigh and Stall 1993). In other words, intoxicated people stupidly wind up having unprotected sex with the wrong people.

More evidence that use of injected drugs is not the only way for drug use to increase the risk of HIV/AIDS comes from studies of heterosexual non-IDUs who get AIDS by having sex with HIV-positive women. Although male-to-female HIV transmission is more common, at least in the United States, female-to male infection is not only possible but readily occurs.

Many heterosexual men frequent drug-addicted, HIV-positive prostitutes. In one

Table 7-1. AIDS cases by age group, exposure category, and sex, reported through June 1999, United States

Adult/adolescent exposure category	Males July 1998–June 1999 No.	(%)	Males Cumulative total No.	(%)	Females July 1998–June 1999 No.	(%)	Females Cumulative total No.	(%)	Totals July 1998–June 1999 No.	(%)	Totals Cumulative total No.	(%)
Men who have sex with men	15,999	(45)	334,073	(57)	—		—		15,999	(34)	334,073	(48)
Injecting drug use	7,493	(21)	130,727	(22)	3,043	(28)	48,501	(42)	10,536	(23)	179,228	(26)
Men who have sex with men and inject drugs	1,940	(5)	45,266	(8)	—		—		1,940	(4)	45,266	(6)
Hemophilia/coagulation disorder	150	(0)	4,741	(1)	21	(0)	269	(0)	171	(0)	5,010	(1)
Heterosexual contact:	2,754	(8)	24,984	(4)	4,296	(40)	45,597	(40)	7,051	(15)	70,582	(10)
Sex with injecting drug user	604		8,370		1,208		18,895		1,812		27,265	
Sex with bisexual male	—		—		200		3,263		200		3,263	
Sex with person with hemophilia	7		49		27		396		34		445	
Sex with transfusion recipient with HIV infection	20		382		18		569		38		951	
Sex with HIV-infected person, risk not specified	2,123		16,183		2,843		22,474		4,967		38,658	
Receipt of blood transfusion, blood components, or tissue	146	(0)	4,811	(1)	120	(1)	3,619	(3)	266	(1)	8,430	(1)
Other/risk not reported or identified	7,436	(21)	43,522	(7)	3,361	(31)	16,635	(15)	10,798	(23)	60,159	(9)
Adult/adolescent subtotal	35,918	(100)	588,124	(100)	10,841	(100)	114,621	(100)	46,761	(100)	702,748	(100)

Source: Centers for Disease Control and Prevention (1999).

study of New York City women hospitalized for pelvic inflammation, for example, 56 percent reported crack use and 20 percent were HIV infected (Inciardi 1994). The picture of female-to-male transmission is even more frightening in cases of heterosexual non-IDU men who barter crack for sex. In a typical "crack house" a man gives crack to a female addict in exchange for sexual favors. A major problem with crack house sex is that condoms are scarce. In addition, crack use makes it difficult for men to maintain an erection and delays orgasm in both men and women. Therefore, the prolonged and vigorous intercourse necessary for orgasm results in much penile and vaginal bleeding. The risk of HIV infection in crack house sex is increased by oral sex, too. Genital ulcers, lesions on the lips and tongue, and abrasions on the penis and vagina make blood-to-blood contact certain.

If this were not gruesome enough, crack house women typically have multiple partners often in rapid fire succession. The woman often has leftover blood and semen in her vagina from previous partners that mix with semen and blood from her current sexual partner. If the man contracted HIV during this type of sex, it would be difficult indeed to determine whether he caught it from the woman's blood and vaginal secretions, from the other men's blood or semen, or from some combination thereof. Frequent sex during menses only adds to the the likelihood of HIV infection (Inciardi 1994). In conclusion, het-erosexual transmission of HIV among drug users can be from male-to-female, female-to-male, and male-to-male.

The picture of intravenous drug use, unprotected sex, and HIV infection is magnified among the homeless population, where it is compounded by the fact that these people are often mentally ill and usually beyond the reach of health education, health care, and social services. One study (Susser et al. 1996) assessed drug use and sexual behavior among 218 homeless men in a New York City shelter. Fifty (23 percent) had injected drugs, and the vast majority regularly engaged in behaviors associated with HIV transmission. Of these fifty subjects, 66 percent shared needles and 64 percent used shooting galleries. By contrast, only 22 percent had ever used bleach to clean needles and only 2 percent had ever participated in a needle-exchange program. In the prior six months, 48 percent had had unprotected sex with women and 10 percent with men.

In conclusion, drug use is related to HIV/AIDS primarily through injection behavior and risky sexual behavior. The main thrust of these findings, as shown in Table 7–2, is typified in a study sample of South Florida IDUs.

Drug Use, HIV/AIDS, and Tuberculosis

Drug use not only increases the odds of HIV infection, it is associated with susceptibility to other infections as well. From a public health standpoint, the fairly recent rise in *tuberculo-*

Table 7–2. Percentage of drug users engaged in HIV/AIDS risk behaviors in last twelve months

Injection behavior	Cocaine Only	Cocaine/Opiates
Injected daily	41.1	61.3
Booted	67.9	83.4
Shared cooker	51.8	75.9
Shared works	58.9	75.4
Shared works at shooting gallery	16.1	28.6
Sexual Behavior		
Sexually active	91.1	91.0
IDU-sexual partner(s)	53.6	50.8
Other sexual partner(s)	57.1	64.9
Never use condom	76.8	69.8
Use condom at least 50% of time	10.7	10.2

Source: Adapted from Chitwood et al. (1990).

sis cases is troubling because it is associated with HIV/AIDS and it is a contagious disease.

Tuberculosis (TB) is a disease of the lungs caused by bacteria called *Myobacterium tuberculosis*. The incidence rates of TB, once the leading cause of death in the United States, had declined greatly since the 1940s in response to effective antibiotic treatments. Since the emergence of AIDS in 1981, however, TB prevalence rates have risen steadily (Centers for Disease Control and Prevention 1997d).

Tuberculosis is spread by coughing and sneezing. Most people who breathe contaminated air become infected but do not become sick, have no symptoms, and cannot spread the disease because they have a healthy immune system that is capable of fighting off the bacteria and preventing them from its flourishing. People with an immune system that is compromised, however, cannot combat the TB bacteria and develop active *tuberculosis disease*, manifested by cough, chest pain, coughing up blood or phlegm, fatigue, weight loss, fever, chills, and night sweats (Centers for Disease Control and Prevention 1997d).

Both the time frame for the recent rise in TB cases and the places where most TB cases are concentrated point to a connection between TB, HIV/AIDS, and drug use. Tuberculosis was uncommon until AIDS cases began to escalate around 1985. Today, it is especially concentrated in inner-city areas of high IV drug use and high HIV/AIDS prevalence, and in other places where IDUs and AIDS cases flourish, such as homeless shelters, prisons, and jails (Friedland 1991).

That TB rates are correlated with IDU and HIV/AIDS suggests but does not prove a causal relationship. However, it is well known that the risk of active TB is elevated in those with suppressed immunity, and we already know that drug use and HIV infection have that effect. Furthermore, although HIV-positive and HIV-negative IDUs have about the same rate of TB infection, HIV-positive subjects have a twenty times greater chance of having active TB disease (Friedland 1991). These findings lend strong support to the idea that IDU and HIV/AIDS contribute to the risk of TB disease.

7–6 Prenatal Exposure to Drugs

It should be clear to you by now that drug addiction is associated with a variety of medical problems; no organ is spared the adverse effects of drugs. Although the majority of chemically dependent individuals are male, drug abuse and addiction in women are not uncommon, and many women persist in their drug use during pregnancy.

Prenatal exposure to drugs is a major public health concern because it affects the lives of hundreds of thousands of babies born to drug-dependent mothers each year. Apart from suffering, the cost of intensive medical treatments for drug-exposed infants is enormous; the cost of treating just one damaged infant could easily exceed $100,000 (Kilbey and Asghar 1991). And that doesn't include the financial burden to the foster-care system, where many infants born to substance-dependent mothers wind up, and the enduring medical and psychological difficulties that often persist through childhood and well into adulthood.

An accurate assessment of the long-term consequences of prenatal exposure to drugs is difficult because of the many confounding factors that go along with substance dependence. Poor nutrition, sexually transmitted diseases, poor or nonexistent prenatal care, and polysubstance use make it difficult to disentangle the web of factors that can affect the fetus. Furthermore, the usual methodological problems and the use of biased samples can also lead to inaccurate conclusions about drug effects (Zuckerman 1991).

Mechanisms of Prenatal Exposure

Drugs have direct and indirect effects on the developing fetus. Direct fetal exposure to drugs occurs by way of the *placenta*, a temporary organ that carries nourishment to the fetus from the mother's circulatory system and rids the fetus of waste. Drugs can affect the fetus by direct transfer through the placenta, or by modifying placental function to restrict the flow of oxygen and nutrients. For example, cocaine not only passes through the placenta but it also constricts placental blood vessels (Szeto 1991). All drugs pass through the placenta with relative ease although they differ with respect to the rate and extent of transfer. Ethanol, opioids, and cocaine pass very rapidly and reach peak levels within a few minutes. By contrast, after tetrahydrocannabinol (THC) passes through the placenta, its concentrations in the fetus do not peak for one to two hours (Gabriel et al. 1998, Szeto 1991).

After a drug passes through the placenta, it enters the fetus's bloodstream, and then circulates to every part of the body, including the brain. Drugs affect fetal organs in much the same way that they influence those of adults. Because fetal organs are immature, however, they are especially sensitive to the damaging effects of drugs. Besides their direct effects, drugs also alter the normal physiology of the mother, resulting in numerous hormonal disturbances that ultimately produce adverse effects on the fetus (Gabriel et al. 1998).

Alcohol

The fetus is most vulnerable to alcohol's effects during the first trimester, that is, in the first three months of pregnancy. The mother's drinking is associated with various fetal problems, including spontaneous abortion, growth retardation, and mild nervous system dysfunctions that may lead later to attentional difficulties and hyperactivity in the youngster (Nace and Isbell 1991).

Heavy drinking is likely to cause neurological complications. **Fetal alcohol syndrome** (FAS), caused by prenatal exposure to alcohol, is identified by prenatal and postnatal growth retardation, cranial/facial defects, central nervous system dysfunctions, and organ malformations. In addition to their physical disabilities and odd-looking facial defects, FAS children suffer lasting intellectual impairment, hyperactivity, speech disabilities, and anxiety. The enduring cognitive deficits are quite striking, as shown by the high proportion of these children who require special education for learning disabilities (National Institute on Alcohol Abuse and Alcoholism 1990). A few studies have suggested that many of the so-called unique clinical features of FAS may not in fact be so. For example, certain antiepileptic drugs and metabolic diseases can

produce physical complications indistinguishable from those of FAS (Zuckerman 1991). These finding do not negate the fact that heavy drinking causes birth defects, but simply indicate that the defects might be caused by different factors.

Although the prevalence of FAS is far less than 1 percent of the general population, it represents a major public health problem that costs more than a third of a billion dollars a year. Alcohol-related neurological problems, including FAS, are among the leading causes of mental retardation in the Western world (National Institute on Alcohol Abuse and Alcoholism 1990).

Cocaine and Opioids

Like alcohol, cocaine and the opioids readily cross the placenta and influence the developing fetus. Cocaine produces tachycardia and hypertension in the fetus as well as having direct toxic effects on heart muscle. Such effects are associated with arrhythmias, heart malformations, abnormal breathing patterns, and impaired physical growth and development (Scalzo and Burge 1995). Because of cocaine's cardiac effects and its direct effects on brain tissue, the mother's exposure to cocaine is also associated with fetal strokes. Several studies have documented intracranial hemorrhages in newborns (Schreiber 1995).

Cocaine stimulates dopamine, norepinephrine, and serotonin neurotransmitter systems in the fetal brain. In addition, the mother's cocaine use induces hypertension, tachycardia, and reduced oxygen supply in the fetus, and consequently causes impaired brain development. Either by its toxic effects on neurons, its vascular effects, or both, cocaine is related to reduced cranial size, increased electrical abnormalities, and brain structural damage in some newborns (Kosofsky 1991).

Even without clear-cut physical signs of brain damage, behavioral and cognitive dysfunctions in infancy and childhood suggest the occurrence of cocaine-induced brain injuries during the fetal period. Difficulties in orientation to stimuli, alertness, delayed language acquisition, and pervasive cognitive problems have been reported. Although some children display persistent problems for many years after birth, the majority of babies exposed to cocaine during the fetal period show normal brain physiology and neurological test results within the first year. Early claims that "cocaine babies" who were born addicted were doomed to a lifetime of psychiatric and neurological problems have not been consistently supported by careful scientific research (Chasnoff et al. 1985, Kosofsky 1991).

Finally, there is a correlation between maternal substance abuse and respiratory problems in infancy. The data suggest a strong relationship between maternal opioid use and *sudden infant death syndrome* (SIDS), in which the infant suddenly stops breathing and dies, and it has been hypothesized that opioids depress respiratory areas of the brain (Olsen and Murphy 1995).

Summary

7–1

Chemically dependent people are at great risk for medical problems, disability, and death. Direct influences include the acute effects of intoxication and overdose, the physical symptoms of withdrawal, and the complications of chronic heavy use. Physical problems also occur indirectly by way of behaviors associated with drug use. Chemical dependency is associated with a host of neurological, cardiovascular, hepatic (liver), gastrointestinal, and immune system problems.

7–2

One way that drugs imperil users is by damaging the cardiovascular system by causing reduced pumping capacity, abnormal beating rhythms, clogged and damaged arteries, high blood pressure and heart muscle damage; heart attacks are the user's ultimate fate. Alcohol causes cardiac arrhythmias, hypertension, angina pectoris, and coronary artery disease. Cardiac problems are the most frequent and hazardous medical complications of stimulant overdose. Cocaine anesthetizes heart muscle, and stimulates the adrenal glands to produce adrenaline and noradrenaline, resulting in accelerated heart rate, increased blood pressure, and constricted arteries; it also produces physiological changes in blood chemistry that result in a risk of thrombosis.

7–3

Brain-imaging studies of alcoholics show evidence of general cerebral atrophy and enlarged ventricles that lead to impaired performance on neuropsychological tests of attention, problem solving, perception, memory, and motor coordination, as well as sleep abnormalities, personality changes, and abnormal emotional expression. Long-term drinking can result in a severe memory disorder called Korsakoff's psychosis and peripheral neuropathy. Neurological disorders from cocaine use include headache, movement abnormalities, stroke, and seizures.

7–4

Excessive drinking is strongly associated with the risk of liver diseases that include fatty liver, alcoholic hepatitis, and cirrhosis. Regular drinking will aggravate an existing peptic ulcer and cause cancer. Heavy drinking increases the risk of chronic pancreatitis.

7–5

Drugs and alcohol suppress immune activity and increase the risk of HIV infection and AIDS. Drug use is related to HIV infection and AIDS insofar as psychoactive drugs suppresses immunity, as well as by drug-related behavior such as IV drug use and unprotected sex. Drug use is associated with susceptibility to other infections as well, like tuberculosis.

7–6

Prenatal exposure to drugs is a major public health concern that affects the lives of hundreds of thousands of babies born to drug-dependent mothers each year. Drugs have direct and indirect effects on the developing fetus. Direct fetal exposure to drugs occurs by way of the placenta. All drugs pass through the placenta with relative ease, and then enter the fetus' bloodstream to circulate to every part of the body, including the brain. Besides these direct effects, drugs alter the normal physiology of the mother, resulting in numerous hormonal disturbances that ultimately produce adverse effects on the fetus. The mother's drinking is associated with fetal problems that include spontaneous abortion, growth retardation, and mild nervous system dysfunctions that may lead later to attentional difficulties and hyperactivity in the youngster. Cocaine produces tachycardia and hypertension in the fetus as well as having direct toxic effects on heart muscle. Such effects are associated with arrhythmias, heart malformations, abnormal breathing patterns, and impaired physical growth and development. Due to cocaine's cardiac effects and its direct effects on brain tissue, fetal exposure to cocaine is also associated with strokes.

Terms to Remember

abscess
acquired immune deficiency syndrome

alcoholic cardiomyopathy
alcoholic cirrhosis
alcoholic hepatitis
cancer
cardiac arrhythmia
cardiovascular system
cerebral atrophy
epileptic seizure
fetal alcohol syndrome
hypertension
immune system
Korsakoff's psychosis
overdose
pancreatitis
peptic ulcer
stroke
tuberculosis

Suggested Readings

Alcohol's Effect on Organ Function. (1997). National Institute on Alcohol Abuse and Alcoholism, vol. 21:1. Washington, DC: US Government Printing Office.
Jaffe, J. H. (1995a). *Encyclopedia of Drugs and Alcohol*, vol. 1. New York: Simon & Schuster Macmillan.

Chemical Dependency and Mental Health

Chapter Outline

Learning Objectives

Upon completing study of this chapter you should be able to:

1. Discuss the meaning of mental health in terms of adjustment and coping, subjective well-being, and the spectrum-of-functioning concept.
2. Identify mental disorders that are comorbid with substance-use disorders, and define substance-induced mental disorders.
3. Describe the types of delirium induced by substance use.
4. Define substance-induced dementia and amnesia.
5. Discuss substance-induced anxiety disorders and their relationship with substance use.
6. Discuss substance-induced mood disorders and their relationship with substance use.
7. Discuss substance-induced psychotic disorders and their relationship with substance use.
8. Discuss substance-induced personality disorders and their relationship with substance use.
9. Discuss substance-induced eating disorders and their relationship with substance use.
10. Discuss substance-induced impulse-control disorders and their relationship with substance use.

Experienced counselors know that chemically dependent patients are prone to many forms of psychological disturbance. Addictions often develop along with other mental disorders and in your counseling work you will find that it can be very hard to tease apart the nuances of psychological distress that accompany substance-use disorders. For some clients psychological problems precede the addiction, while for some the addiction is directly or indirectly responsible for other mental symptoms. Chemical dependency counselors must be attentive to the mental-health issues that are associated with drug and alcohol disorders in order to understand and treat the client effectively. Our objective in this chapter is to introduce you to the important and often puzzling relationship between chemical dependency and mental health.

8–1 What Is Mental Health?

Before discussing various psychological problems that are linked with chemical dependency we should examine some of the ways that *mental health* can be defined and evaluated. You undoubtedly know some people who seem mentally healthy and others whose mental health is impaired. But exactly what do you mean when you characterize someone as mentally "healthy" or "unhealthy"? When they are compared with our thinking about physical health, our concepts of mental health often reflect contrasting theoretical assumptions and sociocultural norms. In this section we address the concept of mental-health and the ways in which mental health problems can be associated with chemical dependency.

Concepts of Mental Health

Most of this chapter is devoted to a description of mental disorders that are associated with chemical dependency. When we talk about mental disorders, however, we assume certain notions about the meaning of mental health. After all, to say someone has a mental disorder implies that there is a deviation from mental health. Let's consider three concepts of mental health that set a foundation for our later examination of mental disorders.

Mental Health and Adjustment.   The mentally healthy person is a well-adjusted individual. By **adjustment** is meant a condition in which the person demonstrates successful coping with the circumstances of everyday life. To paraphrase Sigmund Freud, the well-adjusted person is someone who is successful in love and work. By contrast, the poorly adjusted individual is one who struggles to cope with the demands of work, school, social relationships, family, and other aspects of daily living.

Psychological adjustment requires good *coping skills*. Well-adjusted individuals have three kinds of coping skills that they apply in everyday life (Lazarus and Folkman 1984):

- *Problem-focused coping* refers to skills that are used to change situations or circumstances. For instance, self-assertiveness and good communication are problem-focused coping skills that enable a person to interact successfully with other people.
- *Emotion-focused coping* involves skills that regulate emotional responses. An example of emotion-focused coping is temper control, a skill needed to maintain good social relationships.
- *Perception-focused coping* means skills that allow effective perceiving or thinking about circumstances. Evaluating the importance of events, for example, is a kind of perception-focused coping. The person who can put things in perspective by clearly evaluating what is and what isn't important has a coping advantage.

As you already know, chemically dependent people ordinarily lack adequate coping skills, and for many this fact has been instrumental in the development of their addiction as well as in the psychological complications of the addiction. In later chapters you will learn about how counselors can help their clients improve their coping skills, and thus help their overall psychological adjustment.

Mental Health and Subjective Well-Being. How are you feeling? Your answer indicates your **subjective well-being,** or self-perception of psychological health. Subjective well-being is mainly a reflection of our emotional states. People who are happy, contented, and satisfied emotionally report higher levels of well-being than those who are depressed, frustrated, anxious, and angry. Emotional health, however, is not the sole meaning of well-being; it also pertains to the way we view our own personalities and social circumstances. Your self-image and self-esteem are personality features that relate to well-being. If you have a positive self-image and high self-esteem, your well-being is enhanced. Evaluations of our social relationships also affect subjective well-being; satisfying friendships, family

bonds, and romantic relationships matter a great deal.

Naturally, psychological adjustment and well-being go hand in hand. Well-adjusted people tend to feel good about themselves, and people who feel good about themselves tend to cope well. These two concepts of mental health, however, do not always correlate. Someone may have adequate coping skills, but still feel badly about himself. Conversely, some people feel good about themselves despite their lack of successful coping skills. Self-perceptions are prone to distortion, and, more than most, chemically dependent people tend to rely on defenses like denial to maintain a false sense of well-being. In fact you will find that many of your clients sustain an *illusory well-being* that only promotes their addictions.

A Spectrum of Functioning. Mental health is not an all-or-nothing characteristic, that is, something you either have or you do not have. Instead it is a condition with many degrees or levels. A helpful way to think about mental health is in terms of a *spectrum of functioning*, anchored on one end by people with extremely good mental health and on the other by people with very poor mental health.

At the low-functioning end of the spectrum are people who may be diagnosed with mental disorders. Following the *DSM-IV*, we define a *mental disorder* as a clinically significant pattern of symptoms (a *syndrome*) associated with distress, functional impairment, or risk of harm (American Psychiatric Association 2000). In addition to individuals with clearly diagnosable mental disorders, many people also show *subclinical conditions:* their symptoms and impairments indicate poor functioning, but are not severe enough to warrant a diagnosis.

Any judgment that someone has a mental disorder reflects our opinions about what is normal and what is abnormal. However, these concepts are open to different interpretations, and there is no absolute agreement about which is best. Generally, the term *abnormality* has four different meanings: (1) the person has violated some social norm or convention, (2) the person's behavior is statistically unusual or uncommon, (3) the person experiences significant emotional distress, and (4) the person's behavior is maladaptive or in-effective. Consequently, although the con-cept of a mental disorder assumes abnormal-ity, it does not specify which of these meanings is intended.

The mental-health spectrum concept helps us to characterize individual differences among people in terms of degrees of function-ing, allowing for the possibility that an individual's level of mental health may move up or down the spectrum at different times. An example of this concept of mental health is found in the *DSM-IV*'s **global assessment of functioning (GAF)**, a dimension of diag-nosis based on the individual's overall level of psychological, social, and occupational functioning. The individual is rated on the GAF scale from 1 (lowest functioning) to 100 (superior functioning), based on his or her current status (American Psychiatric Associa-tion 2000). For instance, an unemployed, de-pressed alcoholic man who was recently ar-rested for assaulting his wife would be assessed with a GAF around 45, indicating se-rious symptoms and functional impairment.

Drug Use and Mental Disorders

In your work as a counselor you will often be confronted with patients who have a number of serious mental-health problems in addition to their substance-use disorders. Chemically dependent individuals have significantly above-average rates of other mental disor-ders. Exactly how those mental disorders re-late to chemical dependency is not always clear. What is clear, though, is that you, as the counselor, will be responsible for trying to understand the relationship between your clients' addictions and these other disorders. In this section we discuss the main issues that pertain to the link between drug use and mental disorders.

Comorbidity and the Primary/Secondary Disorder Distinction

When two or more distinctive disorders occur simultaneously, **comorbidity** is said to exist between those disorders, and the person is referred to as a *dual-diagnosis patient*. Experts estimate that more than 50 percent of people with substance-use disorders also have one or more comorbid mental disorders (Anthony 1995). As you can see in Figure 8–1, a large national study (Regier et al. 1993) in the United States found that one-third of people seeking help for drug addictions—about 5 million patients—have a comorbid mental disorder. Chemically dependent clients who meet the criteria for both a substance-use disorder and one or more other severe mental disorders are often labeled as dual-diagnosis or "MICA" (mentally ill chemical abuser) patients.

The exact extent of comorbidity with substance-use disorders is unknown because of differences in the way mental disorders and drug problems have been assessed. In addition, comorbidity depends on several variables, such as the age and gender of the abuser, the severity of abuse, and the type of sub-stance abused. Some researchers believe that comorbidity is routinely overestimated be-cause of the overlap in symptoms of certain disorders, but all agree that the mental health of chemically dependent people is much shakier than the average person's (Kadden et al. 1995). Complicating the matter even further is the fact that people with mental disorders are more likely to also have substance-use disor-ders. It is estimated that nearly 40 percent of people in treatment for mental disorders also have a drug or alcohol problem (Regier et al. 1993). Thus, comorbidity can mean that a per-son with a mental disorder also has a substance disorder and that a person with a substance disorder also has a mental disorder.

What difference does it make which type of comorbidity is present? Actually, the dif-ference can be crucial in understanding the patient's dilemma and counseling needs. The **primary/secondary disorder distinction** characterizes comorbidity in terms of the or-der of onset of the symptoms: *primary disor-ders* occur first, and *secondary disorders* occur second. You should be cautious in interpret-ing cause-and-effect links between primary and secondary disorders. Just because they come first, primary disorders are not neces-sarily the causes of secondary disorders. Simi-larly, the disorders may be causally indepen-

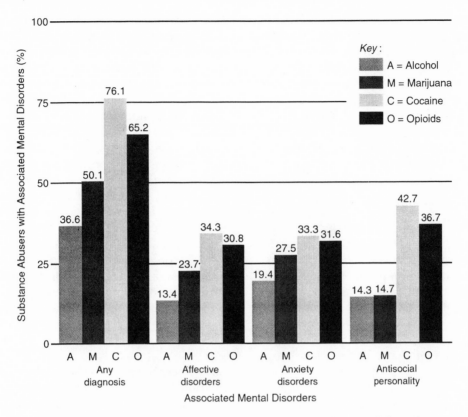

Figure 8–1. Substance use disorders and comorbid mental disorders
Source: Based on Regier et al. (1990).

dent problems, but that does not mean they are unrelated. In fact, comorbid substance disorders and mental disorders have a strong mutual impact on one another. As an example of the primary/secondary distinction, consider that the occurrence of primary depression in alcoholics is no greater than in the population at large, but that secondary depression, that is, depression that begins after the alcoholism, is found in about 40 percent of alcoholics (Cook and Winokur 1995). Interestingly, secondary depression remits quickly after abstinence is achieved. To accurately appreciate your patient's status, you need to know whether the substance disorder or mental disorder is primary or secondary.

Substance-Induced Mental Disorders. In addition to comorbid substance and mental disorders, there are individuals whose mental disturbances are the consequence of their substance abuse or dependency. A **substance-**

induced mental disorder is the direct result of substance use, develops in the context of substance intoxication or withdrawal, and may persist even after the substance is no longer present in the user's system. *Post-cocaine anxiety syndrome,* for example, is a clinically significant example of a substance-induced condition that sometimes persists long after drug use ceases. With substance-induced mental disorders, the substance disorder is always primary and the mental disorder secondary.

How can you tell if your client's mental disorder is substance-induced or an independent comorbid condition? A few guidelines are worth keeping in mind to make the evaluation. *First,* the substance-induced mental disorder must always follow, and never precede, the onset of the substance disorder. *Second,* the substance-induced mental disorder will usually not persist more than about four weeks after the last intoxication or the end of withdrawal. Although the four-week rule of thumb is a useful guide, some substance-induced conditions last long after cessation of intoxication and withdrawal; such conditions are known as *persisting disorders*. *Third*, the substance-induced mental disorder often has unusual or atypical features when compared with similar primary mental disorders; for instance, it may begin at a much later age than is expected for a primary disorder. (American Psychiatric Association 2000)

8–2 Cognitive and Perceptual Disorders

Disturbances in cognition and perception are prominent effects of many psychoactive drugs. For some substance abusers, the degree to which thinking and perceiving are affected during intoxication or withdrawal warrants a diagnosis of substance-induced disorder. In this section you will learn about three cognitive disorders, *delirium, dementia*, and *amnesia*, and one perceptual disorder, *flashbacks*.

Delirium

A severe disruption of consciousness accompanied by cognitive or perceptual disturbances is called **delirium**. In delirium, consciousness is clouded in such a way that the person's awareness of the world is reduced, and the ability to pay attention and focus is impaired. In addition, cognitive deficits in memory and language occur, and speech is often confused and rambling. *Disorientation* is also part of delirium. In their disoriented state, delirious patients have trouble identifying time and place; for instance, the person cannot tell you if it is morning or evening, and may not even know where he or she is. Various perceptual disturbances also may occur, such as misinterpreting events or experiencing *illusions*, such as misperceiving a loud noise to be a pistol shot. In extreme delirium, outright hallucinations can occur.

Substance Intoxication Delirium. A *substance intoxication delirium* is a condition in which delirium symptoms usually develop within a short period of time after drug consumption. However, different drugs and routes of administration have different time-

tables. For example, smoking crack/cocaine can induce delirium within minutes, whereas alcohol may be drunk in high doses for a few days before delirium begins. Once begun, the symptoms of delirium tend to fluctuate in severity during the course of the disorder. Symptoms usually stop within hours of the end of intoxication, but can sometimes last a few days.

Intoxication delirium can result from many drugs, including alcohol and other depressants, stimulants, cannabis, hallucinogens, and opioids. Although the general symptoms of delirium are common to all drugs, some drug-specific features of delirium can be identified. For instance, *stimulant delirium* is sometimes accompanied by extreme anxiety and even paranoid features, while belligerence, violence, and feelings of unreality are more typical of *PCP delirium* (American Psychiatric Association 1994, Daghestani and Schnoll 1994, Gawin et al. 1994).

Substance Withdrawal Delirium. When delirium symptoms emerge either during the withdrawal period or shortly thereafter, a *substance withdrawal delirium* is diagnosed. The duration of this delirium depends on the substance involved. Longer-lasting substances, such as certain barbiturates, cause more prolonged withdrawal delirium for two or more weeks, but drugs with a briefer half-life, such as cocaine, induce much shorter delirium, in some cases lasting for just several hours.

The best known type of withdrawal delirium is the *alcohol withdrawal delirium*, also called *delirium tremens*, or the DTs. Although observed in a minority of extreme alcoholics undergoing withdrawal, the DTs are very severe and lead to death in 10 to 15 percent of untreated cases, usually from heart failure. In this state, the alcoholic is emotionally agitated, out of touch with reality, frightened, disoriented, and often hallucinating. It is no wonder that one slang name for delirium tremens is the "horrors." In addition to these delirium symptoms the person often exhibits involuntary tremors, or "the shakes." On the average the DTs will last about forty-eight to seventy-two hours before the symptoms disappear (Nace and Isbell 1991).

Dementia and Amnesia

Cognitive disturbances involving memory abilities are shared features of the disorders called *dementia* and *amnesia*. The *DSM-IV* refers to these conditions as "persisting" disorders because their symptoms last beyond the usual intoxication or withdrawal period of the substance involved. In both disorders the symptoms are serious enough to cause significant social or occupational impairment and a decline from a previously higher level of functioning.

Dementia. The condition called **dementia** is defined by multiple cognitive deficits manifest in memory and in language, motor, sensory, and higher-order executive functions. *Substance-induced persisting dementia* is the direct result of substance use. The memory disturbances include problems in learning new information and recalling facts already learned. As a result the person is extremely forgetful and absentminded. The loss of personal belongings and even getting lost are common signs of dementia. Apart from such memory deficits, dementia also entails language difficulties, or *aphasia*, shown in the person's inability to name common objects, to speak comprehensibly, and to understand others' communications. In more severe cases of dementia, sensory and motor symptoms interfere with the ability to perform often very simple behaviors, such as getting dressed or cooking a meal. Some patients even fail to recognize everyday objects, although their vision is normal. Higher-order executive functions such as decision-making, planning, and abstract thinking are impaired, too, resulting in considerable disorganization in everyday life.

Symptoms of dementia may last for many years, and for some people remain a permanent condition. Dementias have been reported most commonly for alcohol, sedative/hypnotics, benzodiazepines, and inhalants. However, the most prevalent and best understood of these dementias is *alcohol dementia*, or in common parlance "wet brain." Alcohol dementia is the second most common type of dementia, next to the dementia of Alzheimer's disease. An estimated 9 percent of chronic alcoholics develop dementia as a result of the toxic impact of long-term alcohol abuse on the brain (Nace and Isbell 1991).

In addition to the many cases of diagnosable dementia, many chronically substance-dependent individuals have *subclinical cognitive impairments* that are milder, but lasting versions of dementia symptoms. More than half of chronic alcoholics develop such cognitive impairment, and many inhalant and PCP abusers also experience long-term disruptions of memory and general intellectual functioning due to the cumulative effect of those substances on the brain (Carlen and McAndrews 1995, Daghestani and Schnoll 1994, Gallant 1994, Weiss and Millman 1991).

Amnesia. A substantial memory impairment that interferes with the ability to learn new information and recall learned information is **amnesia**. When the amnesia is a direct consequence of substance use, the condition is called *substance-induced persisting amnestic disorder* (American Psychiatric Association 2000). In contrast to dementia, the symptoms of amnestic disorder are limited to memory functions. Amnesia for previously learned information, for example, facts, names, and addresses, is *retrograde amnesia*. The inability to learn new information and create new memories is called *anterograde amnesia*. These symptoms cause dramatic confusion and emotional distress. Sometimes the amnestic person will invent stories and "facts" to fill in the gaps in their past; this invention of imaginary memories is called *confabulation*.

The best documented form of amnestic disorder is *Wernicke-Korsakoff syndrome*, an extremely disabling outcome of chronic alcoholism characterized by amnesias and other cognitive and motor impairments. As you learned in Chapter 7, this syndrome is linked with thiamine deficiency and brain damage. Wernicke-Korsakoff syndrome generally appears in alcoholics over 40 years of age who have been drinking heavily for many years. For most the damage is permanent, and although recovery of some memory functions after abstinence is possible, the majority show minimal improvement (American Psychiatric

Association 1994, Carlen and McAndrews 1995, Nace and Isbell 1991).

Flashbacks

The recurrence of perceptual disturbances that were part of hallucinogen use after the intoxication period ends is called a **flashback**, or as the *DSM-IV* prefers to call the condition, *hallucinogen persisting perception disorder*. Flashbacks may involve several kinds of perceptual distortions, such as seeing designs or geometrical hallucinations, seeing false movement or colors, the appearance of halos around objects, as well as "trailers," light images that follow in the trail of a moving object. In addition to the visual symptoms, some people experience emotional and somatic features as well, such as fear responses. Although flashbacks cause emotional distress or impairment, the person recognizes that they are distortions due to drug use rather than real events. (American Psychiatric Association 1994, Weiss and Millman 1991)

Flashbacks are associated with use of powerful hallucinogens like LSD, but only a minority of hallucinogen users ever experience flashbacks. The flashback may appear unpredictably, or may be triggered by stress, illness, and fatigue. Generally, a state of emotional stress and hyperarousal is present at the onset of the symptoms. Another less-common reason for the onset of symptoms is pot smoking. Marijuana can trigger flashbacks in users with a previous history of hallucinogen use. The symptoms of this disorder do not have any obvious relationship with forms of brain damage, and they usually disappear within a few months after the person stops hallucinogen use. However, for some individuals the flashbacks can persist up to several years (Ungeleider and Pechnick 1994).

8–3 Anxiety Disorders

Feelings of anxiety, apprehension, and fear are present in everyone from time to time. Some individuals, however, experience them so frequently and intensely that their everyday functioning is jeopardized. When significant social and occupational impairments occur as a result of anxiety symptoms, the person is said to have an **anxiety disorder**. In fact, the anxiety disorders are the most common type of mental disorder, and they are characterized by many symptoms besides just emotional distress, as summarized in Table 8–1.

Types of Anxiety Disorders

Depending on the person's combination of symptoms, different anxiety disorders will be diagnosed. An important aspect of the anxiety disorders is that there is a great deal of overlap among them. In other words, people with one anxiety disorder often have symptoms of another comorbid anxiety disorder as well. The anxiety disorders that often occur comorbidly with substance use disorders are generalized anxiety disorder, phobias, panic disorder, and posttraumatic stress disorder.

Generalized Anxiety Disorder. A person whose anxieties and worries about a variety of events and activities are excessive and hard to control has **generalized anxiety disorder** (GAD). Individuals with GAD tend to be very restless, irritable, and tense most of the time. Their concentration is impaired to the extent that they may "go blank" for a few moments, and they typically have problems sleeping. Because their worries are not connected with a specific issue, but instead are spread around to many concerns, they are described as having *free-floating anxiety*.

Table 8.1. Symptoms of anxiety

Emotion	Cognition	Behavior	Physiology
apprehension	confusion	avoidance	dizziness
fear	distraction	irritability	faintness
nervousness	hyperalertness	nervous habits	headache
uneasiness	memory problems	restlessness	palpitations
worry	preoccupation	shakiness	sweating

In addition, people with GAD express *anticipatory anxiety*, that is, worry about future feared events out of proportion to the anticipated event; for instance, fear of going shopping because there may be no convenient parking space. GAD is apparently more common in women than men; about two-thirds of cases are females (American Psychiatric Association 2000).

Phobias. An excessive fear accompanied by a strong tendency to avoid or escape from the feared stimulus is a **phobia**. The fears of the phobic person are often quite irrational or exaggerated. Strong fears alone do not make a phobia, but the combination of fear and avoidance or escape behavior that disrupts everyday life does. Phobias are apparently rather common, affecting about 10 percent of people at some point during their life span.

Different kinds of fears define different types of phobias. A *specific (simple) phobia* involves persistent, excessive fear directed at a specific object or situation, such as acrophobia, a fear of heights. People with specific phobias usually realize that their fears are unreasonable, but still feel very frightened in the presence of the phobic stimulus.

When people fear social situations in which they might be embarrassed or in which their performance might be negatively evaluated by others, a *social phobia* is present. Social phobics are usually very inhibited or shy about interacting with unfamiliar people or placing themselves in unfamiliar social surroundings.

A complex fear problem is *agoraphobia*, in which the person is afraid of being in situations from which escape is difficult, or in which help, if needed, will be unavailable. Agoraphobics typically have multiple fears, including traveling, being alone, and shopping, and their fears can literally trap them in a lifestyle of isolation and avoidance. These individuals tend to dramatically restrict their activity to a "safety zone," such as their own home or neighborhood. As you will see below, agoraphobia often accompanies another anxiety disorder, called panic disorder. (American Psychiatric Association 2000)

Panic Disorder. The symptoms of **panic disorder** are recurring and unexpected episodes of very intense and threatening anxiety known as *panic attacks*. A panic attack is usually a brief period of intense fear in which numerous unpleasant experiences converge on the individual, including palpitations, sweating, trembling, choking, nausea, chest pain, dizziness, shortness of breath, and a feeling of losing control of one's mind. Although panic attacks can occur in other anxiety disorders (e.g., phobias), they are the central feature of panic disorders and often cause the person to worry in advance about the when, where, and why of the next attack.

Panic disorders often precede and cause agoraphobia. For some panic sufferers, the restriction of behavior associated with panic attacks gradually becomes agoraphobia. The person with unpredictable panic attacks may defend against the possibility of future attacks by strictly avoiding any situations in which an attack might occur. Whether or not panic disorder is linked with agoraphobia, it is much more common in women than men (American Psychiatric Association 2000).

Posttraumatic Stress Disorder. An anxiety disorder whose symptoms are provoked by exposure to an extreme traumatic event is **posttraumatic stress disorder** (PTSD). The initial traumas are experiences in which the person is seriously injured, threatened with injury, or witnesses another being injured. During the traumatic event, the person is overwhelmed by fear and helplessness. Traumatic stressors are events that go way beyond the usual everyday kind of stress and include experiences of victimization (e.g., rape, assault), kidnapping, natural disasters, and serious accidents.

Following the trauma, people with PTSD exhibit several characteristic symptoms that are the direct result of their experience and last at least one month. Reexperiencing the trauma is a symptom in which the person replays the event in his or her own mind. Recurrent thoughts, memories, and nightmares about the event are common, and in some flashbacks to the event occur. In addition, PTSD patients will strongly avoid anything, anyone, and anyplace associated with their trauma. They may also experience a numbing, in which they become emotionally dulled and detached, as well as persistent anxiety symptoms such as irritability and poor concentration (American Psychiatric Association 2000).

Substance Use and Anxiety Disorders

The connections between substance use and anxiety disorders are rather complex. You have learned in earlier chapters that anxiety disorders sometimes affect the development and course of chemical dependency. In this section we will discuss two further aspects of their relationship by examining the substance-induced anxiety disorders and the comorbidity of anxiety and substance disorders.

Substance-Induced Anxiety Disorder. When prominent anxiety symptoms, such as panic attack, occur as a direct consequence of substance intoxication or withdrawal, the diagnosis of **substance-induced anxiety disorder** is made. As in other substance-induced disorders, the anxiety symptoms do not represent a primary disorder that began before the substance use. This disorder has been identified in connection with many different drugs, including depressants, stimulants, inhalants, and hallucinogens.

The exact symptoms of substance-induced anxiety disorder vary according to which drug is involved and whether the condition results from intoxication or withdrawal. Cocaine and marijuana intoxication, for example, are likely to induce symptoms of panic (Mirin and Weiss 1991, Weiss and Millman 1991). Panic is also an element in hallucinogen-induced anxiety reactions, or bad trips, but other symptoms too are provoked, including confusion and a diminished sense of self (Ungeleider and Pechnick 1994). By contrast, withdrawal from alcohol and benzodiazepines is apt to provoke strong, generalized anxiety. While it is true that most symptoms diminish within a few weeks after the end of withdrawal, after stopping some drugs, such as alcohol and benzodiazepines, more *protracted withdrawal syndromes* can follow that

may last several months or longer, durir which time the anxiety and other symptom continue (Gallant 1994, Smith and Wessc 1994). Because these anxiety symptoms ca trigger relapse, it is important for counselo to warn their clients that they might occur ar inform them that the symptoms will dissipa over time if no further substance use occur

Comorbid Anxiety and Substance Disorder

A high degree of comorbidity exists betwee the anxiety disorders and chemical depen dence. Alcoholics are particularly prone t these problems, and 25 to 45 percent of alcc holics develop an anxiety disorder during the lifetime (Brown and Barlow 1992). Findings the National Comorbidity Study (Magee et a 1996) show that agoraphobia is present in ove one-fifth of alcoholics and in 17 percent of othe drug addicts, and social and simple (specifi phobias occur in nearly one-quarter of alcoho ics and 15 percent of other drug addicts. Ger eralized anxiety disorder, too, is commor Overall, nearly one in ten substance abuser exhibit comorbid GAD symptoms, but the ra of GAD in alcoholics is over 20 percer (Schuckit and Hesselbrock 1994, Westermeye et al. 1995). Studies (Liskow et al. 1995, Thevc et al. 1993) also indicate that PTSD is signif cantly comorbid with both alcoholism and cc caine dependence.

The nature of comorbidity between anxiet disorders and substance disorders has nc been fully unraveled. Anxiety symptoms drug effects, and personal characteristics a determine the individual's condition. For ex ample, one investigation (Thevos et al. 1993 that compared alcoholism and cocaine dependence found that PTSD is more com mon among cocaine-dependent men than al coholic men, but that panic disorder is mor common among alcoholics of both sexes thar in cocaine-dependent men and women. Othe evidence (Brady et al. 1993) suggests tha social phobias and PTSD are more prevalen in alcoholic women than in alcoholic men.

At present there is simply not sufficien information to clearly explain all the pattern of comorbidity. Many people with anxiety disorders appear to self-medicate with alco hol, benzodiazepines, and other depressants. Agoraphobics and social phobics are most inclined to develop substance problems in this manner. By contrast, panic symptoms and generalized anxiety are often a consequence of substance abuse (Kushner et al. 1990). Furthermore, anxiety disorders affect the course of chemical dependency. A follow-up study of alcoholics one year after the end of treatment showed that those who remained abstinent had far fewer anxiety problems than those with high levels of anxiety symptoms (Schuckit and Hesselbrock 1994).

8–4 Mood Disorders

Persistent and disabling disturbances in a person's general emotional state, or mood, are the central features of the **mood disorders**. Second in prevalence only to anxiety disorders, mood disorders are thought to affect upwards of one person in five during their lifetimes. Among chemically dependent individuals, however, the likelihood of mood disorders is even greater. Mood disorders include several kinds of disturbances that vary in terms of their symptoms, severity, and course. In this section you will learn about the mood disorders that are most closely linked with drug and alcohol problems.

Types of Mood Disorders

The main types of mood disorders are defined by the presence of depressive and manic symptom patterns. The *depressive disorders* contain only symptoms of depression, and the *bipolar disorder* has symptoms of both mania and depression.

Depressive Disorders. Symptoms of depressed mood define the two main *depressive disorders*: major depressive disorder and dysthymic disorder. The core of both is a persistent emotional malaise, but other symptoms are also experienced. **Major depressive disorder,** or simply *major depression*, is a condition that features one or more *major depressive episodes* characterized by a period of significantly depressed mood or the loss of interest

or pleasure in everyday activities. In addition, major depressive episodes are marked by

- Somatic symptoms: fatigue, loss of energy, weight loss
- Cognitive symptoms: poor concentration, feelings of worthlessness, guilt, suicidal ideas
- Behavioral symptoms: agitation, slowness, sleep disturbances

The depressive symptoms persist for at least a couple of weeks and produce a significant amount of interference with everyday behavior; work, school, and family life are seriously affected. At least half of the cases involve more than one episode, and for many people multiple episodes will occur over the span of many years. Some episodes last only a few weeks, but as many as 40 percent continue for at least one year. This disorder is twice as common among women as men and is associated with increased risk for suicide in both sexes.

Another type of depressive disorder is the **dysthymic disorder,** which is marked by a depressed mood on most days for most of the day and lasts for at least two years in adults or one year in children and adolescents. People with this disorder chronically feel "blue." Besides the depressed mood, dysthymic disorder also displays many features similar to major depression, including appetite and sleep disturbances, hopelessness, low self-esteem, fatigue, and concentration problems. Like major depression, dysthymic disorder is more prevalent in women.

Bipolar Disorder. Commonly called manic-depression, **bipolar disorder** is characterized by a combination of major depressive episodes and manic episodes. While the depressive features of bipolar disorder are much like those in the depressive disorders, the manic episode is specific to this disorder. The core of a *manic episode* (mania) is a period of extremely elevated, expansive, or irritable mood. The person may be terrifically cheery, euphoric, and enthusiastic about things in general, but will also show great irritability when frustrated or contradicted. In addition to the manic mood disturbance, several other symptoms indicate a manic episode:

- Inflated self-esteem or grandiosity
- Increased activity level, agitation, sleeplessness
- Extreme talkativeness, racing mind, distractibility
- Involvement in many pleasurable, but potentially risky behaviors (including drug and/or alcohol binges)

A manic episode can last from a few days to several months and usually occurs just before or after a major depressive episode. Although most manic and depressive episodes are separate, in some cases manic and depressive symptoms occur together in a *mixed episode*. Most bipolar disorders are chronic conditions with many recurring episodes over a long period of time. Compared with depressive disorders, bipolar disorder is relatively rare, affecting about 1 percent of the population, with equal male and female prevalence.

Substance Use and Mood Disorders

From what you have learned previously about the impact of many psychoactive drugs on moods and emotions, you can probably anticipate that a strong link exists between substance use and mood disorders. Depression in particular has been identified as a potent risk factor in the development of alcohol and other drug problems. What follows is an examination of the impact of substances on mood and the comorbidity of these disorders.

Substance-Induced Mood Disorder. Most drugs have some influence on your mood state. When substance use causes an intense and persistent mood disturbance, depressed or manic or both, the condition is diagnosed as **substance-induced mood disorder**. The nature of the disorder depends on the person, the drug in question and whether symptoms occur during intoxication or withdrawal.

Depressed mood may result from intoxication with CNS depressants like alcohol and barbiturates, as well as from benzodiazepines

and inhalants. Intoxication-induced manic symptoms, however, are most likely when stimulant drugs are taken. High doses of cocaine, for example, can create a condition that mimics a manic episode. You may recall from the discussion of withdrawal in Chapter 4 that the symptoms of withdrawal are often the opposite of intoxication symptoms. With that in mind you will not be surprised to learn that withdrawal-induced depression is prominent for stimulants like cocaine and the amphetamines (Karan et al. 1991). In fact, depression is a defining part of the early phase of the *cocaine abstinence syndrome* (Gawin 1991). By contrast, CNS depressants, like barbiturates, may induce mania-like symptoms during withdrawal.

A relationship between chronic marijuana abuse and depression-like symptoms has been the subject of investigation. In some longtime heavy pot smokers a persistent state of lethargy, dullness, and apathy develops. This condition has been labeled *amotivational syndrome* to suggest the lack of motivation and energy in the individual. Whether this syndrome reflects a mild mood disturbance, a socially conditioned lifestyle, or a variation of cannabis dependence is still unclear (Millman and Beeder 1994, Weiss and Millman 1991).

Comorbid Mood and Substance Disorders. Unusually high rates of depression have been found in individuals with addictions to several major drugs, including alcohol, cocaine and heroin. Estimates of comorbidity vary widely, depending on the diagnostic criteria employed and the subjects who are studied, but the evidence indicates that depression accompanies substance use disorders in 25 to 45 percent of alcohol cases, 35 to 50 percent of cocaine cases, and more than 50 percent of opioid cases (Brown et al. 1995, Johnson et al. 1995b, Karan et al. 1991, Liskow et al. 1991, Mirin and Weiss 1991, Regier et al. 1990, Senay 1994, Thomson and Dilts 1991).

The link between depression and chemical dependency may be partly controlled by genetic factors. Research shows increased rates of substance-use disorders in biological relatives of people with depression, and increased depression in relatives of chemically dependent

dent people, especially alcoholics. These findings suggest that a common genetic vulnerability may give a push to both kinds of disorders in family members. (American Psychiatric Association 2000)

Gender also plays a part in the comorbidity of depression and chemical dependency, especially in alcoholism. Compared with the general population, male alcoholics are more likely to also be depressed than the average male. Female alcoholics, however, despite higher rates of depression than male alcoholics, are not more likely than nonalcoholic women to be depressed. In addition, depression in male substance abusers tends to follow the onset of alcoholism, whereas it typically precedes substance abuse in women. Self-medication for depression seems more characteristic in depressed women than men. (Brady et al. 1993).

As compelling as the link between depression and substance disorders is, the relationship of bipolar disorder to drug and alcohol problems is even more powerful. In most cases bipolar disorder is the primary disorder and substance disorders are secondary, but in some people who are genetically vulnerable to bipolar disorder substance abuse can trigger the symptoms. A study (Mirin et al. 1988) of opioid, cocaine, and depressant addicts undertaken in Massachusetts found that fully 10 percent of the sample had bipolar disorder, a figure ten times the rate in the general population.

Men with bipolar disorder are especially prone to develop alcoholism. As a group they have three to six times the prevalence of alcoholism found in other males (Brown et al. 1995, Winokur et al. 1995). One large study (Winokur et al. 1995) of bipolar men found that 46 percent had a history of alcoholism. Furthermore, the combination of bipolar disorder and alcoholism was associated with much more severe symptoms and a heightened risk of violence. The extreme alcohol abuse in this group was more closely linked with the men's manic episodes than with depression.

Why might bipolar disorder be such a risk for substance problems? You might remember from Chapters 5 and 6 that personality traits of impulsiveness, emotionality, and hyperactivity contribute to addiction-proneness. Those traits closely resemble the unstable personality features of bipolar individuals in the manic phase, and in fact they often precede the onset of bipolar disorder. In addition, genetic predispositions to both bipolar disorder and alcoholism aggregate in certain families, so that their comorbidity may indicate a shared vulnerability (Winokur et al. 1995).

Suicide. In an average year about thirty thousand Americans kill themselves, and a quarter million or more try to kill themselves by various means (Davison and Neale 1994). Of all the reasons for suicide, the hopelessness and pain of depression are by far the most common. Next to depression, however, substance abuse is the second biggest factor. It is estimated that one-third to one-half of all suicide attempts occur in people with substance-use disorders (Secretary of Health and Human Services 1990). One recent study (Beautrais et al. 1996) found that among those who attempted suicide nearly one-third had alcohol problems and one in ten had other drug problems. To put these findings in clearer perspective, consider that suicide attempts are five times more likely in people with alcohol problems, and greater than fifty times more likely in people with other drug disorders.

Substance abuse not only increases the risk of suicide attempts, but also of completing the act. Approximately 15 percent of individuals with substance disorders die by suicide, a rate three to four times greater than the national average (Mirin and Weiss 1991). A thirty-year longitudinal investigation (Berglund 1984) of more than 1,300 alcoholics found that 16 percent of the deaths in the sample were due to suicide. The link between suicide and alcoholism is not just an American phenomenon, but has also been noted in other countries. A large Finnish study (Henriksson et al. 1993) concluded that nearly half of the suicides in that country in a one-year period involved substance-dependent people, and that alcoholism was present in 43 percent of suicides.

One of the most distinctive differences between depressed alcoholic men and non-depressed alcoholic men is their heightened *suicidality*, as indicated by self-damaging actions and low self-esteem (Cornelius et al. 1995). Alcoholism not only increases the potential for suicide, but also affects the method of suicide. More impulsive acts, including more violent forms of self-destruction, are associated with alcohol. For example, suicide by gunshot is about five times more likely when alcohol is used than in other cases (Secretary of Health and Human Services 1990).

The connection between substance disorders and suicide is apparently very strong, but that link is influenced by many factors. Gender is a major risk factor for suicide. Whether chemically dependent or not, men are much more likely to kill themselves than women, but women are more likely to attempt suicide than men. Mental health also matters, and in addition to depression serious personality disorders contribute to suicide risk. The combination of substance disorders, mental health problems, and male gender is an especially risky one for suicide potential (Beautrais et al. 1996).

8–5 Psychotic Disorders

By nearly any standard, the conditions that are labeled psychotic are the most severe and disabling mental disorders. A **psychotic disorder**, or *psychosis*, is broadly defined as a condition that dramatically disrupts judgments and perceptions about reality; more narrowly defined, it is a disorder with delusions, hallucinations, and profound mental disorganization (American Psychiatric Association 2000). In this section you will learn about the nature of psychotic disorders and their connection to chemical dependency.

Schizophrenia

The best-known and most thoroughly studied psychotic disorder is *schizophrenia*, and because of the abundance of available research our discussion will highlight this disorder.

Symptoms of Schizophrenia. Arguably the most serious mental disorder, **schizophrenia** is a psychotic condition characterized by sig-

nificant disturbances in thinking, perception, emotion, and behavior, resulting in extreme functional impairments in many areas of life. Many myths and misconceptions about this disorder have developed through the years, and you may be aware of some. One of the most common is that schizophrenics have a "split personality." Although they certainly do not have split personalities, they experience many other serious symptoms, major types of which are listed below.

- Delusions: false, improbable, absurd, unrealistic beliefs
- Hallucinations: false or distorted perceptions; hearing and seeing things with no basis in fact
- Mental disorganization: incoherent speech, irrationality, disorganized behavior
- Catatonic behavior: immobility, unresponsiveness, stupor
- Negative symptoms: flat affect, lack of initiative, impoverished thinking

Delusions and hallucinations are especially characteristic of schizophrenia. They are known as the *positive symptoms*, indicating that they reflect an excess or distortion of normal functions. By contrast the *negative symptoms* reflect the absence of normal abilities; for instance, the lack of normal emotional responses is called "flat affect." The symptoms must be present continuously for six months for the diagnosis of schizophrenia to be made. Typically, schizophrenia begins in young adulthood and lasts for many years, with recurrent episodes and periods of remission. Slightly less than 1 percent of the population has schizophrenia, and both sexes are equally affected. Several types of schizophrenia can be distinguished according to their symptoms, and they are described below.

Types of Schizophrenia. *Paranoid schizophrenia* is marked typically by delusions and hallucinations focused on the themes of persecution, grandeur, or both. People with the persecutory theme believe someone is persecuting or threatening them, and they often hallucinate voices talking to, cursing, and commanding them. A theme of grandeur in paranoid schizophrenia is expressed by delusions of power, greatness, and special status; for example, the person may think that he is a special emissary from God to save the world from annihilation.

In *disorganized schizophrenia* the main symptoms are disorganized behavior and speech, and emotional disturbances such as flat or inappropriate affect. Such individuals express themselves in rambling, incoherent statements and tend to have erratic, unpredictable emotional reactions or little emotion at all. Their behavior generally appears purposeless or silly to an observer, and they often exhibit significant mental disorientation.

A third type, *catatonic schizophrenia*, is dominated by a lack of movement and responsiveness. In their stupor, catatonics are silent, withdrawn, and mostly oblivious to the world. Although the negative symptoms are most prominent in this type, excessive agitation and excitability may also appear. When the patient emerges from a stupor he or she tends to be confused and tense. Catatonic negativism is shown by the person's lack of cooperation and refusal to respond.

Along with the three main types of schizophrenia mentioned above, two other types can be identified. When a person's symptoms indicate a mixture of features that do not fit any one major type, the diagnosis given is *undifferentiated schizophrenia*. The diagnosis of *residual schizophrenia* is given to a patient whose main psychotic symptoms have lessened substantially after an active episode, but who still has residual, or leftover, negative symptoms.

Substance Use and Psychotic Disorders

Psychotic disorders are conditions at the extreme low end of the mental-health spectrum. In some cases psychotic symptoms are the product of extreme drug abuse, but in others they actually promote substance abuse. In the following section you will learn about both of these possibilities as you examine substance-induced psychotic disorders and comorbid substance use and psychotic disorders.

Substance-Induced Psychotic Disorder.
When drug use directly triggers hallucinations

or delusions, but the person does not realize those symptoms are drug-induced, a diagnosis of **substance-induced psychotic disorder** is in order. Unlike the person whose hallucinations or delusions are created by drugs like LSD, the individual with substance-induced psychotic disorder lacks insight into the link between the drug and the symptoms. This diagnosis is not made if the person has a primary psychotic disorder such as schizophrenia, or if the symptoms persist more than one month after intoxication or withdrawal (American Psychiatric Association 2000).

Quite a few substances can provoke this psychotic condition, either during intoxication or withdrawal, but most cases involve stimulants and hallucinogens. *Stimulant-induced psychotic disorder* due to cocaine or amphetamine intoxication resembles paranoid schizophrenia insofar as delusions of persecution are common. In addition to visual hallucinations, tactile or touch hallucinations also appear; for example, patients may say they feel bugs crawling on or under their skin (Flaum and Schultz 1996, Gawin et al. 1994).

Potent hallucinogens like LSD and PCP can trigger *hallucinogen-induced psychotic disorder*. While most hallucinogen users recognize that the drugs are responsible for their hallucinations, some forget that they have taken the drug and find the hallucinations terrifying and inexplicable. With LSD and similar hallucinogens, the psychotic condition has paranoid features (Ungeleider and Pechnick 1994). By contrast, *PCP-induced psychosis* is marked by hostility and agitation. Three stages of this psychosis have been described: (1) violent agitation, (2) mixed restlessness and unpredictability, and (3) resolution of the main psychotic symptoms with residual sensory distortions (Daghestani and Schnoll 1994, Weiss and Millman 1991). Although it is rare, cannabis-induced psychosis does occur, but is thought to be most prevalent in users with a vulnerability to psychotic disorders. In all likelihood, when marijuana smoking induces a psychotic disorder, it does so as the result of a *kindling phenomenon*: the drug kindles or starts a psychotic process to which the person was already predisposed (Millman and Beeder 1994).

Comorbid Substance Use and Psychotic Disorders. Primary psychotic disorders are associated with a very high prevalence of drug and alcohol problems. Between one-third and one-half of schizophrenics also have diagnosable substance-use disorders. Alcohol is the most common drug of abuse among psychotic patients, but stimulants and marijuana also are popular (Jeste et al. 1996, Kwapil 1996, Mueser et al. 1992). Not only is alcoholism more common among schizophrenics than in the general population, but schizophrenia appears to be more prevalent in alcoholics. In a study (Liskow et al. 1995) of male alcoholics seeking treatment at a Veterans Administration clinic, researchers found that 7 percent were schizophrenic. Findings of that kind strongly suggest that chemical dependency counselors will be working with addicted schizophrenic patients from time to time. In Chapter 16, you will learn more about the special counseling needs of the severely mentally-ill client, and the methods used to address those needs.

The adverse influences of drugs and alcohol on psychotic patients are clear and powerful, as evidenced by increased relapse of psychotic episodes, more hospitalizations, heightened suicide risk, and various cognitive and neurological deficits. Why then do schizophrenics rely so much on drugs and alcohol? In some ways, their reasons are the same as those of any other chemically dependent person, but self-medication is the biggest reason. The psychological distress of schizophrenia is hard to overestimate, and drugs help to ease some of that distress. Alcohol and marijuana sedate the individual against anxiety, paranoia, and other forms of psychological turmoil. Stimulants, too, serve a purpose by offsetting the negative symptoms, energizing the person, and increasing positive affect (Linszen et al. 1994, Mueser et al. 1992, Serper et al. 1995)

Some longitudinal evidence suggests that the comorbidity of schizophrenia and substance dependence may be a result of interacting developmental influences between drug consumption and a biological vulnerability to psychosis. *Psychosis-prone individuals* tend to have a family history of psychotic disorders, and they exhibit the psychological traits of magical thinking and perceptual aberration. In adulthood those people have significantly elevated rates of substance-use disorders, especially if the psychosis-prone traits accompany the trait of impulsive nonconformity (Kwapil 1996).

8–6 Personality Disorders

Personality is a major part of the psychological framework in which healthy and unhealthy behavior occurs. In earlier chapters you learned that certain personality traits contribute significantly to the development and course of chemical dependence. Individuals with seriously disturbed personalities show strong inclinations toward many mental disorders, including substance-use disorders. Clinical experience and research both show that drug and alcohol problems are linked with **personality disorders**, which are enduring and maladaptive patterns of traits that produce significant impairment (American Psychiatric Association 2000).

Despite the fact that their traits are responsible for numerous difficulties in everyday life, personality disordered individuals often lack awareness that there is something wrong, and tend to perceive their traits as "just the way I am" rather than as symptoms of a serious disorder. Counselors often find that their personality disordered clients are their toughest cases because these clients do not recognize that they need to change fundamental aspects of themselves.

Types of Personality Disorder

Everyday experience tells us that personality comes in many flavors, and the same is true of abnormal personality. The *DSM-IV* identifies ten specific types of personality disorder that are organized into three groups or *clusters* based on general trait similarities. *Cluster A* includes people whose personality traits are perceived as odd or eccentric; *Cluster B* disorders have dramatic, emotional, or erratic qualities; and *Cluster C* contains disorders marked by anxiety and fear. Although many personality disorders may influence substance use, a thorough discussion of all those types is beyond the scope of this section. Our intention here is to describe the five types that are most strongly associated with chemical dependency: antisocial personality disorder, borderline personality disorder, narcissistic personality disorder, paranoid personality disorder, and avoidant personality disorder.

Antisocial Personality Disorder (ASPD). One of the most severe of all personality disorders is the **antisocial personality disorder,** which is defined by a pervasive disregard for and violation of the rights of other people. ASPD is a Cluster B disorder that has also been called *psychopathy* and *sociopathy*, and you will sometimes hear people with ASPD referred to as psychopaths or sociopaths. The pattern of antisocial behavior begins in childhood or adolescence and persists into the adult years, and has several pathological characteristics.

- Nonconformity to social norms
- Violations of the law
- Deceitfulness, lying, conning
- Impulsiveness, lack of foresight
- Aggressiveness, fighting, irritability
- Irresponsibility, recklessness
- Disregard for own or others' safety
- Lack of remorse and guilt

Although they may appear superficially charming, psychopaths typically lack empathy for anyone, and they tend to be callous, egocentric, and manipulative in dealing with others. As you can imagine, this personality disorder makes for a lifestyle with significant interpersonal conflict. A person with ASPD is incapable of sustaining healthy relationships and often becomes entangled with the legal system for various crimes. ASPD is much more prevalent in men than women; an estimated 3 percent of men are affected.

Borderline Personality Disorder (BPD). The most compelling feature of the **borderline personality disorder** is persistent instability in relationships, self-image, and emotions. The relationships of persons with BPD are marked by frantic efforts to avoid abandon-

ment and extremes of feeling that fluctuate between passionate attachment and intense hatred. Their behavior is impulsive, reckless, and self-damaging, and they commit suicidal and self-mutilating acts. The borderline's emotional instability displays itself as moodiness, feelings of emptiness, intense anger, and occasional feelings of paranoia.

The interpersonal difficulties of persons with borderline personality present a constant dilemma for them. Others perceive them to be fickle, unpredictable, and erratic. Their intensity is threatening, especially when it involves their highly volatile anger. Inconsistencies in self-image lead to many failures in work and personal matters. Borderline individuals cannot seem to make up their minds about who they are or who they want to be. In addition, BPD increases the risk for mood disorders, and a depressed borderline personality is strongly inclined to self-destructive behavior.

Along with antisocial personality disorder, borderline personality disorder is a member of Cluster B. It occurs in about 2 percent of the general population, but about three-quarters of cases are female. In most people BPD symptoms stabilize somewhat during middle adulthood, allowing for improvements in overall social functioning.

Narcissistic Personality Disorder (NPD). Another Cluster B disorder, **narcissistic personality disorder**, is defined by a pattern of grandiosity, need for admiration, and a lack of empathy for others. Aptly named for the mythic youth Narcissus, who fell in love with his own reflection, NPD is marked by the individual's exaggerated feelings of importance, talent, and beauty. The general prevalence of NPD is about 1 percent, and most of these are men.

People with NPD believe themselves to be very special and thus deserving of admiration and attention. Because they feel entitled to special treatment they are unreasonably demanding and arrogant in their dealings with people. The narcissistic person is the center of his universe and lacks empathy for or interest in anyone else. Consequently, a self-centered, unempathic narcissist is quite willing to exploit others for his own gain. On the surface, narcissistic personalities present themselves as confident and self-assured, but their self-esteem is vulnerable and emotionally they bruise easily. Their inability to tolerate criticism and humiliation interferes with both social interactions and occupational functioning. Predictably, many narcissistic personalities suffer from depression (American Psychiatric Association 2000).

Paranoid Personality Disorder (PPD). **Paranoid personality disorder** is a Cluster A disorder defined by the core traits of persistent suspiciousness and distrust of others. People with PPD believe, without sufficient reason, that others are untrustworthy, deceptive, and manipulative. The paranoid personality automatically assumes that people are that way, and so behaves in a guarded, defensive manner around others. For instance, the paranoid individual will never confide a secret to you for fear that you will use it against him. People with PPD seem petty and vengeful. They cannot forgive a slight to themselves and carry many grudges against those whom they imagine have insulted them. Given their belief that people are untrustworthy, it is not surprising that they misperceive others' actions and remarks as personal attacks or threats.

You probably recall the term paranoid from the earlier section of this chapter on paranoid schizophrenia. Like paranoid schizophrenics, people with PPD exhibit unusually high levels of fear and anxiety about others. However, the degree of impairment in PPD pales in comparison with paranoid schizophrenia, and PPD is certainly not a psychotic condition. Nevertheless, behavioral genetics studies suggest a hereditary link between the two disorders. Although PPD occurs in only about one to two percent of the general population, it is somewhat more prevalent in biological relatives of people with schizophrenia (Baron et al. 1985).

Avoidant Personality Disorder (APD). A Cluster C disorder, **avoidant personality disorder** is dominated by social inhibitions, feelings of inadequacy, and extreme sensitivity to the negative evaluations of others. As with other Cluster C disorders, people with APD are driven by fear and anxiety. Affected individuals avoid activities and situations out of fear of disapproval or criticism, and they are very tentative about interacting with unfamiliar people. Shy and easily embarrassed, they see themselves as inferior or inadequate and expect that others also will view them in that way. In regard to their social lives, avoidant personalities are very limited in their activities due to their reluctance to take chances and meet new people.

Equally common in both men and women, APD affects less than 1 people of the population. Typically, this personality disorder evolves from childhood shyness and anxiety, and in adults it is associated with social phobias and depression (American Psychiatric Association 2000).

Substance Use and Personality Disorders

Personality disorders develop gradually from traits that first appear during childhood. Consequently, when personality and substance use disorders occur together, the personality disorders are almost always the primary ones. In fact, the *DSM-IV* does not even recognize a diagnosis for personality disorders induced by substance use. That does not mean substance abuse has no impact on personality, but rather that the effects of drugs and alcohol on personality generally are exacerbations of preexisting traits.

Comorbid Substance Use and Personality Disorders. The comorbid link between chemical dependency and personality disorders is greater than with any other type of mental disorder. In general, cocaine addicts have the highest level of comorbid personality disorder. Two recent studies clearly illustrate this phenomenon. The first study, (Marlowe et al. 1995), of mostly black, inner-city men with cocaine addictions, identified one or more personality disorders in nearly three-quarters of the subjects, and over one-third of those addicts had more than a single personality disorder. Most subjects had Cluster B disorders, including ASPD (23 percent), BPD (22 percent), and NPD (17 percent). A second study, (Barber et al. 1996) part of the

National Institute on Drug Abuse Collaborative Cocaine Treatment Study, found that nearly half of cocaine addicts in treatment have comorbid personality disorders. Thirty percent involve the Cluster B disorders of ASPD (19 percent) and BPD (11 percent), and significant numbers of PPD (10 percent) and APD (9 percent) were also identified. The severity of pathology was greatest in addicts with both borderline and antisocial traits.

Alcoholics and opioid addicts, too, have been found to have an abnormally high prevalence of personality disorders. Research (Morgenstern et al. 1997) on alcoholism reveals that nearly 60 percent of chronic alcoholics have a personality disorder, and half have more than just one. The same study found equal rates (22 percent) of ASPD and BPD, but ASPD was twice as common among males versus females and BPD twice as common in females versus males. In addition, high rates of PPD (20 percent) and APD (18 percent) were found and occurrence of both disorders was approximately equal in both sexes. The majority of heroin addicts also have comorbid antisocial personality disorder, and many other opioid abusers exhibit features of paranoid personality disorder (Thomson and Dilts 1991).

Personality Disorders and Addictions: Why the Link? You have seen already that personality disorders are a diverse collection of social, emotional, and cognitive problems. Any attempt to understand their link with substance addictions requires an appreciation of the complexity of personality. Although we cannot provide a comprehensive explanation of personality disorders here, we are able to point out several reasons that they correspond with substance disorders.

Cluster B disorders, especially the antisocial and borderline personalities, are generally the most common in chemically dependent individuals (Oldham et al. 1995). ASPD is linked with alcoholism, heroin and cocaine addictions, and polysubstance dependence. Borderline personalities are often alcoholic, cocaine addicted, and benzodiazepine-dependent (American Psychiatric Association 1994, Brooner et al. 1992, Mirin and Weiss

1991, O'Boyle 1993). Some common features of ASPD and BPD suggest that the vulnerability to substance abuse in these individuals is partly due to a fundamental deficit in the inhibition of behavior. The impulsivity, recklessness, and erratic behavior of these people shows that they cannot adequately regulate themselves. The failure of needed inhibition may be a result of neurocognitive dysfunctions associated with these personality disorders (Hemphill et al. 1994, Judd and Ruff 1993, Morgenstern et al. 1997, Sher and Trull 1991).

Other commonalities for people with these personality disorders that may also affect their risk of substance abuse are developmental problems due to maltreatment. Rates of reported physical and sexual abuse during childhood are unusually high among both ASPD and BPD patients. Early maltreatment not only jeopardizes personality development, but also acts as a risk factor for many psychological disturbances, including substance-use disorders (American Psychiatric Association 1994, Brady et al. 1995).

For many types of personality disorders, high rates of other mental disorders are also present. Anxiety disorders and mood disorders are especially common among personality-disordered individuals. Along with the emotional and interpersonal distress that results from their maladaptive personalities, they suffer the consequences of additional psychological disorders. Mood disorders are common in BPD and NPD, and anxiety symptoms often accompany APD and PPD. In light of the complex sources of emotional distress for these persons, it is reasonable to consider the role of self-medication in regard to their substance abuse. As the self-medication hypothesis predicts, the choice of drug is guided by the personality disturbance. Narcissistic personalities can use cocaine to bolster their feeling of potency and ward off self-doubt. Paranoids by contrast prefer alcohol and opioids to sedate them against their constant anxiety (Halikas et al. 1994, Johnson et al. 1995b, Khantzian 1995, Stein et al. 1993a).

Finally, the possibility of hereditary predispositions underlying both personality disorders and chemical dependency has been put forth. Behavioral genetics studies often show increased vulnerability for both conditions among close biological relatives. The genetic association is particularly close for ASPD and alcoholism, but family members of borderline personalities also have increased vulnerability to substance-use disorders (American Psychiatric Association 1994, Mirin and Weiss 1991).

8–7 Impulse Control and Eating Disorders

Two key features of substance-use disorders are the person's difficulty in controlling the urge or impulse to drink and drug, and the resulting compulsive use of substances. Impulse-control failures and compulsive behavior patterns are found not only in alcohol- and drug-abusing individuals, but are part of other disorders as well. In this section you will learn about two kinds of disorders in which those features are present and to which drug and alcohol problems are related.

Impulse Control Disorders

We all have impulses to do things that we shouldn't from time to time, but most of us can control those impulses when they are inappropriate or potentially dangerous. People with **impulse-control disorders**, however, are unable to resist the impulse or temptation to do things that are harmful to themselves or others. Their impulses cause a buildup of tension until they perform the action, and afterward they feel pleasure from relief of the tension. Several different kinds of impulse control disorders have been identified, each of which involves distinctive impulses such as stealing (*kleptomania*) and fire-setting (*pyromania*), but here we will focus on *pathological gambling*, because of its strong link with substance-use disorders.

Pathological Gambling. Gambling is a very widespread and popular activity in the United States and many other countries. Millions of recreational gamblers enjoy the excitement of wagering and the hope of winning. Most people who gamble would never con-

sider using up their life savings or borrowing enormous sums of money they can never repay to keep "in the game," but *the pathological gambler* won't hesitate. Found in 1 to 3 percent of the population, **pathological gambling** is an impulse control disorder in which the persistent and maladaptive habit of gambling dominates the person's life and leads to disastrous results.

In pathological gambling the individual is so preoccupied with gambling that other dimensions of life are seriously neglected. Family, friends, and work are a distant second to the pursuit of "action." Many resort to deceptive and illegal activities to acquire the money needed to continue gambling and to pay their gambling debts. No matter how much is lost, the pathological gambler wants to keep "chasing" the losses. Like other compulsive behaviors, pathological gambling relieves tension, and if it is thwarted the person becomes distressed and agitated.

Over time, pathological gamblers, most of whom are men, find themselves drawn into a lifestyle increasingly organized around betting and finding money. As they fall deeper into debt their gambling escalates in a desperate attempt to break even and get ahead. As you can imagine, this lifestyle promotes both significant psychological distress and physical health problems, such as high blood pressure. Depression is extremely common among these gamblers, and many will ultimately attempt suicide (American Psychiatric Association 2000).

Substance Use and Pathological Gambling. A high degree of comorbidity exists between pathological gambling and substance use disorders (Murray 1993). About 25 percent of cases also exhibit one or more substance-use disorders, particularly involving alcohol and cocaine. In one study (Blume and Lesieur 1987) of treatment-seeking cocaine-dependent patients, 30 percent had gambling problems and nearly half of those were pathological gamblers. Gambling has been called "addiction without a drug" because its symptoms often resemble those found in drug addicts. Features common to both include a loss of control, progressive escalation of self-damaging behaviors, and compulsive involvement in pursuing the desired goal. Like drug addicts, pathological gamblers love the high feeling in what they do, and when they cannot gamble they experience a kind of withdrawal malaise. In addition, like other addicts, these gamblers lie, cheat, and manipulate to maintain their habit (American Psychiatric Association 1994, Blume and Lesieur 1987, Rosenthal 1992).

It is unlikely that substance abuse causes pathological gambling or vice versa. Instead, the association between these two disorders is probably due to similarities in the individual's personality and biochemistry that predispose to both conditions. Two personality traits shared by substance-dependent people and pathological gamblers are impulsivity and sensation-seeking (Ciarrocchi et al. 1991, Roy et al. 1988b). You probably recall the similar link between these traits found in antisocial personality disorder and alcoholism, as discussed in earlier chapters, so you may expect that an association also exists between ASPD and pathological gambling—and it does. Another comorbid condition characteristic of pathological gamblers is mood disorders, especially depression. The thrill of gambling may act to offset feelings of depression, and the comorbid link between gambling and substance abuse may reflect the impact of primary depression on both disorders. However, depression may also be a result of the gambler's stressful lifestyle rather than its cause (Nevid et al. 1997, Roy et al. 1988b).

In addition to the psychological predispositions that contribute to gambling and substance abuse, certain biochemical factors are also involved. Impulse-control deficits have been connected to inadequate activity in the brain systems that use the neurotransmitter serotonin. Generally, serotonin works to inhibit behavior, and a lack of serotonin promotes impulsivity and behavior disinhibition. As we discussed in Chapter 6, serotonin deficiency has been associated with chemical dependency. Evidence of low serotonin levels has also been found in pathological gamblers, suggesting a possible biochemical connection of these disorders (Holmes 1997, Stein et al. 1993a).

Eating Disorders

A severe disturbance in eating behavior is the defining feature of *eating disorders*. Problems in appetite regulation and food consumption can appear at any age, but the most severe eating disorders usually begin in adolescence and young adulthood. The vast majority—about 90 percent—of cases are young women. The eating disorder known as *bulimia nervosa* is most often connected with substance-use disorders and so that condition is our focus in this section.

Bulimia Nervosa. Many people overeat at certain times. You have probably stuffed yourself on special occasions like Thanksgiving dinner or at a wedding reception. People with **bulimia nervosa**, however, frequently exhibit extreme episodes of overeating, or *bingeing*, during which they lose control over their eating and consume an enormous amount in a brief period, after which they seek to compensate, or *purge* themselves, by various means including vomiting, laxative use, and fasting. Bulimia nervosa is often called the *binge–purge syndrome*, and the most common means of purging is self-induced vomiting. Typically, the bulimic will put her finger or some other object down her throat in order to gag and vomit up the food eaten in her binge.

Episodes of bulimia nervosa generally occur during or after dieting, and many bulimics have a history of weight-control problems and *dieting–bulimia cycles*. The bulimic individual often responds to her failure to keep to a diet by going overboard and bingeing on "forbidden foods" like high-calorie sweets, cookies, ice cream and the like. Bulimics have abnormally high rates of depressive disorders; these sometimes begin prior to the eating disorder but more often follow the onset of bingeing. Feelings of depression can act as a trigger for a bulimic episode, and the guilt and anxiety over bingeing trigger the purge.

Substance Use and Bulimia Nervosa. As many as one in three bulimics has a comorbid substance-use disorder, especially involving alcohol or stimulants. Alcohol can act as a sedative for the emotional distress of the bulimic, and stimulants can also ease the individual's depression. Although bulimics' stimulant use ordinarily starts with pills taken to help their dieting, it can quickly turn into a pattern of abuse (American Psychiatric Association 2000).

An interesting link between bulimia nervosa and substance-use disorders is suggested by genetic and biochemical investigations. Family studies identify heightened risk for both alcoholism and depression among close biological relatives of bulimics. These findings hint that a shared hereditary vulnerability to those conditions may contribute to the comorbidity of bulimia and substance dependence (Kendler et al. 1991). Other family research also suggests a possible hereditary link between bulimia and personality disorders, especially borderline personality disorder, a condition also known to be comorbid with drug and alcohol problems (American Psychiatric Association 2000). As many as 75 percent of substance-abusing bulimics have borderline personality disorder (Sansone et al. 1994).

Bulimia nervosa is also related to serotonin deficiency in the brain, in a way similar to what has been found for pathological gambling. Abnormally low levels of serotonin are correlated with the frequency of binges among bulimics. As with substance abuse and impulse-control problems, bulimia also may represent a failure of the brain's impulse-inhibition mechanisms due to inadequate serotonin activity (Holmes 1997, Jimerson et al. 1992).

Addiction concepts have been extended to bulimics, as they have to pathological gamblers, because bulimics show loss of control over the impulse to eat and a pattern of compulsive, self-damaging behavior. The *lack of restraint* that is noted in chemically dependent individuals is also present in the bulimic. In fact there is a curious parallel between the bulimic's loss of dietary restraint and subsequent bingeing and the alcoholic's loss of drinking restraint. However, despite some similar behavioral features of bulimia and drug addictions, the addiction concept has only limited relevance for many bulimics.

Unlike drug addicts, bulimics do not use substances that cause enduring changes in the brain's structure and function (Barlow and Durand 1995, Wilson 1991).

Chapter Summary

8–1

Mental health is conceptualized in terms of individual adjustment, subjective well-being, and the spectrum-of-functioning notion. Adjustment is determined by the presence of problem-focused, emotion-focused, and perception-focused coping. Subjective well-being is a function of emotional states, such as self-esteem. The spectrum of mental health functioning extends from good health to extreme mental disorder. Substance-use disorders and other mental disorders commonly have comorbidity. Substance-induced mental disorders are the direct result of substance use.

8–2

Cognitive and perceptual disorders linked with substance use include delirium, dementia, amnesia, and flashbacks. Substance-induced delirium is a disruption of consciousness with cognitive and perceptual symptoms linked with intoxication and/or withdrawal. Dementia is a condition of multiple cognitive deficits, and can be substance-induced. Amnesia, a memory impairment, can be caused by substance use, as in the Wernicke-Korsakoff syndrome in alcoholism. Flashbacks, or hallucinogen-persisting perception disorder, are recurrent perceptual disturbances that remain after hallucinogen use.

8–3

Feelings of anxiety, apprehension, and fear are key features of anxiety disorders. The several types of anxiety disorders include generalized anxiety disorder, phobias, panic disorder, and posttraumatic stress disorder. Substance-induced anxiety disorder is marked by significant anxiety symptoms directly due to substance use, and is especially common among alcoholics and benzodiazepine abusers.

8–4

Mood disorders are disturbances in a person's general emotional state. They include depressive disorders, such as major depressive disorder, dysthymic disorder, and bipolar, or manic-depressive, disorder. The most common substance-induced mood disorder is major depressive disorder, which is strongly comorbid with alcoholism and other addictions, especially cocaine and opioid addiction. Comorbid depression and alcoholism are more prevalent among females than males. Bipolar males have high rates of alcoholism. The combination of depression and substance abuse is a strong predictor of suicide risk.

8–5

Psychotic disorders entail dramatic disruptions of judgment, perception, and mental organization. The best-known psychotic disorder is schizophrenia, which comes in several types: paranoid, catatonic, disorganized, undifferentiated, and residual. Schizophrenia-like symptoms are present in substance-induced psychotic disorder as a direct result of substance use, especially with stimulants and hallucinogens. Extremely high levels of substance abuse are found among individuals with primary psychotic disorders.

8–6

Personality disorders are enduring maladaptive traits that produce significant impairment. The *DSM-IV* identifies three groups or clusters, labeled Clusters A, B, and C. Of the many personality disorders, those having the greatest association with substance-use disorders are the antisocial (psychopathic), borderline, narcissistic, paranoid, and avoidant personality disorders. There is greater comorbidity of substance-use disorders with personality disorders than with any other kind of mental disorder. Personality disorders establish a psychological vulnerability to substance use

and abuse and sometimes have a shared genetic basis with substance-use disorders, especially alcoholism.

8–7

People with impulse-control disorders are unable to resist impulses to do self-harmful actions. Pathological gambling is an impulse-control disorder that is highly comorbid with substance abuse, particularly alcohol and cocaine abuse, and also shares some psychological features with drug addictions, such as loss of control and compulsiveness. Eating disorders, like bulimia nervosa (the binge–purge syndrome) are highly comorbid with alcoholism and diet-pill (stimulant) abuse. The link between bulimia and substance-use disorders entails putative biological and psychological vulnerabilities.

Terms to Remember

adjustment
amnesia
antisocial personality disorder
anxiety disorder
avoidant personality disorder
bipolar disorder
borderline personality disorder
bulimia nervosa
comorbidity
delirium
dementia
dysthymic disorder
flashback
generalized anxiety disorder
global assessment of functioning
impulse-control disorders
major depressive disorder
mood disorders
narcissistic personality disorder
panic disorder
paranoid personality disorder
pathological gambling
personality disorders
phobia
posttraumatic stress disorder
primary/secondary disorder distinction

psychotic disorder
schizophrenia
subjective well-being
substance-induced anxiety disorder
substance-induced mental disorder
substance-induced mood disorder
substance-induced psychotic disorder

Suggested Reading

American Psychiatric Association. (1994). *Diagnostic and Statistical Manual of Mental Disorders*, 4th ed. Text Revision. Washington, DC: Author.

Nevid, J. S., Rathus, S. A., and Greene, B. (2000). *Abnormal Psychology in a Changing World*, 4th ed. Upper Saddle River, NJ: Prentice-Hall.

CHAPTER NINE

Chemical Dependency and the Family

Chapter Outline

Learning Objectives

Upon completing study of this chapter you should be able to:

1. Distinguish the several meanings of the notion that addiction is a family disease.

2. Discuss the concept of homeostasis as it applies to families.

3. Identify and detail three versions of the addicted family.

4. Characterize the rationale and methods of strategic family therapy.

5. Characterize the rationale and methods of structural family therapy.
6. Characterize the rationale and methods of experiential family therapy.
7. Characterize the rationale and methods of intergenerational systems family therapy.
8. Characterize the rationale and methods of behavioral family therapy.
9. Characterize the rationale and methods of psychodynamic family therapy.
10. Distinguish among the different family therapy approaches in the case of the Baker family.

In earlier chapters much of what you learned about chemical dependency concerned the impact of substances on many levels of individual functioning, including the molecular, behavioral, affective level and cognitive levels. As important as the individual-focused examination of chemical dependency is, it is nevertheless not the only possible way of looking at substance abuse. Substance abusers are members of families, belong to social classes, have ethnic, religious, and racial identities; they are also influenced by their cultures, and are members of society. All of these relationships and identifications influence every aspect of their lives, including their substance abuse, and their substance abuse impacts their families, social classes, ethnic, religious and social groups, cultures, and societies. We call such *reciprocal relationships* where each party affects the other dialectical or recursive. The term dialectical is borrowed from philosophy, the term recursive from mathematics. A group of entities such as family members who have *recursive relations* with one another are said to constitute a system.

Although all of these complex social interactions are important, the most profound impact is that of the family on the user and of the user on the family. For most people, including chemically dependent individuals, the family is their primary social framework. Consequently, an understanding of the role of family life in addictions and their treatment is essential for the counselor. In this chapter we explore the notion that addiction is a family disease, and we examine both the effect of

substance abuse on the family and the effect of the family on substance abuse. In addition we will describe how the major schools of family therapy can be adapted for use in substance abuse counseling, and provide an extended case illustration of the approaches these schools take with a troubled family.

9–1   Substance Abuse as a Family Disease

Substance abuse is often said to be a family disease, but exactly what does that mean? On the surface that seems absurd. Surely substance abuse is about a particular person and his or her use of substances; moreover, as you have learned, we can explain a great deal about substance abuse without bringing in the family. So perhaps it is not a family disease but a person disease. The person disease view is of course true, yet it is also untrue. The paradoxical nature of addiction is analogous to a similar paradox in physics. When physicists explain light, they sometimes regard it as a particle and sometimes as a wave. According their *principle of complementarity*, light is both particle and wave depending on how you observe and measure it. Similarly, in studying addictions it is sometimes most useful to look at things from the perspective of the user and sometimes most helpful to look at things from the perspective of the family. The family perspective will enrich your understanding and give you a new way of seeing things.

To return to the original question: In what sense is addiction a family disease? To begin with, it runs in families—of this there is no doubt. The empirical evidence is overwhelming in support of **familial aggregation**, or the clustering in families of drug and alcohol problems. In Chapter 6 you learned that the vulnerability to addiction is partly genetic, so perhaps addiction runs in families because the predisposition is shared by family members. However, addiction perhaps also runs in families because it is learned through modeling and the transmission of family attitudes and values. Another possibility is that addiction runs in families because of defensive *identification with the aggressor*, that is, the children in addicted families cannot cope with their parents' dysfunction and the resultant pain in any other way than becoming like the substance-abusing parents. In other words, "if you can't beat them, join them." Yet another possible reason for familial aggregation might be that growing up in an addicted family is so painful and leaves such emotional scars that substances come to be used as anesthetics and self-medication. Or perhaps all of these play a role in the familial confluence of substance abuse. Whichever one or more of these mechanisms is involved, the fact remains that if the parents are substance abusers, the odds are high that at least one of the children will also be. In the case of familial alcoholism the evidence is highly robust and consistent (Bleuler 1955, Goodwin 1988), and for other drugs of abuse both clinical experience and research evidence strongly suggest that addiction runs in families.

The second meaning of addiction as a family disease takes the focus off of the identified patient and looks at addiction as a symptom of *systemic family dysfunction*. In this sense addiction reflects the general maladaptive relationships and interactions among family members. The addict may be seen as a scapegoat, as a deviant necessary to strengthen family cohesiveness, delineate family boundaries, and clarify mainstream values; as a target and focus of family aggression; as necessary to the stability of the family; or as a distraction and defense against facing other conflicts. From this point of view it is the family that "owns" the addiction; that is, although one or more specific family members may be addicted, the addiction itself is considered a property of the family system as a whole. An important clinical implication of this view is that the family "needs" the addiction because of the purpose or purposes it serves in the family.

The third sense in which addiction is a family disease is perhaps the most apparent and least controversial of its meanings. Few in the recovery, professional, or scientific communities doubt that the presence of an addicted family member has profound effects on all other family members. In this sense the addiction of one family member "infects" all the others. This does not imply that everyone else

in the family is infected in the sense that they, too, become addicts. However, the emotional, spiritual, and behavioral disturbances of the addicted person do have a profound impact on the psychological condition of other family members. These effects are particularly pronounced when the addict is a parent and the family member is a child. Hence rehabilitation programs typically emphasize family counseling. The vast and growing popular and professional literature on *Adult Children of Alcoholics* (ACOAs), as well as the ACOA and *codependency* movements, attest to the wide acceptance of this meaning of the family as the seat of addiction.

Homeostasis

Homeostasis is a term used to describe the family's tendency to maintain stability or equilibrium. Families tend to function in a conservative manner, that is, they seek to preserve the *status quo*. The concept of homeostasis is borrowed from the famous physiologist, Walter Cannon (1932), who coined the term to explain the way the body maintains optimal levels of such biological necessities as glucose, oxygen, steady temperature, and respiration. According to the principle of homeostasis, any change in the system will be resisted, and mechanisms will be invoked to restore the system to its optimal level. For example, following a meal your blood sugar rises, signaling your liver to convert the excess into glycogen and to store it until needed. If your blood sugar later falls too low, the liver is signaled to convert glycogen back into blood sugar.

Families are also believed to operate according to the principle of homeostasis. Families resist change by enacting mechanisms to maintain the status quo and to restore it when it is disrupted. There is inertia in the family—it "works" to keep everything running on in a straight line. We particularly see this in substance abuse, at times when a family member gets "straight" (which has long been the stated wish of the other family members) and all hell breaks loose. Put simply, human beings and their relatives do not change gladly. So the family has a strong *homeostatic tendency* that requires an equally strong countervailing force to overcome it.

> The principle of homeostasis as extrapolated to the family is illustrated by the story of the man who goes to the psychiatrist, desperate for help for his son who believes that he is a chicken. The psychiatrist listens to the father's story and tells him, "Delusions like your son's are common but fortunately we psychiatrists can cure them rather easily. Talk it over with your son and call back for an appointment and I am sure I can help him relinquish his belief that he is a chicken." A month passes and there is no call from the father, so the psychiatrist calls him and says, "I was expecting to hear from you. I wonder why you haven't called?" "Well, doctor," says the father, "I haven't called because the family talked it over and we decided we need the eggs."

There are many families with substance-abusing members who decide that they need the eggs. Homeostasis is to family dynamics and therapy what resistance is to individual dynamics and therapy. Homeostatic forces are not the only forces at work in families. If that were the case, change would not be possible, at least not without leaving the family, and indeed this sometimes happens. But most families do find ways to accommodate and even initiate change. Therefore, some family theorists hypothesize that there are innate, growth-promoting mechanisms as well as inertial ones in family systems. Counselors need to be equally aware of homeostasis and of the evolutionary forces in the families they work with.

General Systems Theory

General systems theory is a conceptualization in which the whole is seen as something greater than the sum of its parts; those parts only being fully comprehensible, totally understood, when they are seen as part of an interactional system (Bertalanffy 1968). Each part, or subset of the totality, is determinative of and determined by the sum total of its interactions with all the other subsets of the system. As you have already learned, systems work to preserve their homeostasis or equilibrium. In a system, the *levels of organization* are hierarchical. In the body, for example, the levels of organization ranging from lower to higher are atoms, molecules, cells, tissues, organs, and organ systems. Lower levels are understandable in relation to their context, that is, in relation to the higher levels in which they are embedded. In sum, within a system everything is related to everything else, and relationships among system parts are reciprocal, interactive, and recursive. Yet this hierarchy cannot exist apart from the larger physical environment, the energy and gravitational pull of the sun, and the influence of moon and stars, ad infinitum.

Bertalanffy's (1968) understanding of the embeddedness of biological systems rightly makes him the founding father of contemporary ecological theory and indeed the spiritual father of the ecological movement. Bertalanffy's biological model was undoubtedly influenced by **ethology**, the scientific study of animal behavior. Early German ethologists spoke of the *Umwelt*, literally translated as the "around world," or "surround." The notion is that no animal exists nor can be understood apart from his or her surround. The surround is everything from the immediate natural environment with its physical ecology, climate, and plants and animals, to the universe. The surround, however, in one of its meanings, is also subjective—it is the animal's experience of its physical and biological situation. Thus a rabbit's surround in the more subjective sense may be primarily grass, its burrow, and predators, while the fox's surround—in exactly the same physical and biological situation—may be primarily rabbits, jumpable fences, and vixens. Thus the surround is both the surround for the organizer, based on its values, and the totality of the situation in which the animal exists.

The human surround in a family system is constituted by other family members, existing both as members' conscious awareness of relationships in that family, and as the subtotal of all the unconscious transactions that occur in that family. Of course the human surround consists of more than the family, encompassing also social class, economic structure, political entities, and all of nature. The degree of awareness of this indeed infinite concatenation of interrelated complexities varies enormously both across and within persons; that is, different people have different levels of awareness of their environments and their interactive relationship to them, while even the same person's level of insight will change with maturation, education and experience. For addicted clients, counseling fosters the awareness of this human surround.

The Addicted Family

The addicted family has been described in many varied and indeed contradictory ways. Some descriptions of addicted families have an empirical or research basis, while others are more intuitive, having been inspired by clinical work. In this section we explore the major views on addicted families from researchers and clinicians.

Roles in the Addicted Family. A **role** is a socially defined pattern of behavior that serves one or more specific functions within a social system. Members of all families play certain roles, and those roles are significant for the family's ability to maintain itself. In addicted families, too, the members play roles that are functional within the family system, but which at the same time can maintain the addiction. Virginia Satir (1972) and Sharon Wegschieder-Cruse (1985) have described a set of roles played by children in addicted families: the Hero or parentified child, the Lost Child, the Mascot, the Scapegoat, and the Rebel.

The Hero learns early in life that the addicted Mom, Dad, or both are incompetent and so he or she takes over. In the process, the Hero is deprived of a childhood. Heroes grow up to be angry controllers who know that somehow they have been deeply cheated. They tend to be perfectionistic high achievers. *The Lost Child* suffers emotional and sometimes physical neglect, and grows up feeling lost, unloved, and directionless. He or she may also have learned all too well how to get lost, to hide, and may have terrible difficulty integrating into any group. *The Mascot*, sometimes called the Clown, has learned how to cheer up the addicted and/or depressed grownups as well as him- or herself. The Mascot may or may not consciously feel the despair beneath this manic defense. *The Scapegoat* is the kid who gets the beatings, or physical and/or emotional abuse, and often grows up rageful and looking for somebody else, who usually turns out to be a spouse or child, to beat in turn. There is also *The Rebel*, who is probably the healthiest if the rebellion stops short of overt criminality. The Rebel is most likely to be the addict of the following generation.

There is a whole library of books on these roles and, in counseling we certainly see people who enact them, yet these roles lack consistent empirical support. Studies of children of alcoholics (COAs) find them to be at high risk for a variety of emotional and behavioral problems (National Clearinghouse for Alcohol and Drug Information 1999b). However, most COAs do not fit neatly into one specific role, and many manifest behaviors of more than one role. We sometimes tell patients or families about the roles that clinicians have described in addictive families and suggest that one or more of them fit the patient or are being enacted by the family. This provides cognitive structure, reduces anxiety, and makes sense of what is experienced as chaos. There is, however, also a danger in using this shortcut, cookie-cutter set of categories in that they may close down process and exploration in both individual and family. Like all abstractions, these COA roles oversimplify and like all abstractions, they help organize experience. To learn that you are or were the Scapegoat may be helpful, but not nearly as helpful as feeling your "scapegoatedness" in all of its nuances and intricacies.

Peter Steinglass: Families with Alcoholism. Clinician and researcher Peter Steinglass (1994) sees the addicted family as a problem-solving organism adapting to an illness, and at times using that illness to solve impasses in the family life-cycle. Steinglass makes a distinction between *alcoholic (addictive) families*, in which the family is organized by the alcoholism and members' reaction to it, and *families with alcoholism*, which have a sick member whose illness causes distortions, but does not dominate family life. The former type is of course more problem-ridden than the latter, but Steinglass does not stress pathology; his stance as researcher and clinician is empathic and nonjudgmental. His interest is in how both types of families manage to perform the life tasks that even the most addicted, disorganized, enmeshed or unrelated family must perform.

Steinglass's research concludes that alcoholic families are far more stable (in fact, all too stable), less chaotic, and less violent and abusive than has often been reported in the clinical and popular literature (Steinglass et al. 1987). In short, alcoholic families are not necessarily sociopathic, and in fact most are not. Steinglass points out that addiction occurs in cycles—no one drinks or drugs all the time—so that the family dynamic is biphasic. His families adjusted to this alternation of sobriety and drunkenness. In effect, the COAs have two mothers (or fathers), one drunk, one sober—a reality that reinforces the psychological defense of splitting, that is, of seeing a parent as two people. For COAs, splitting can be adaptive, allowing the child to feel loved in spite of the unloving behavior of the intoxicated parent. Among Steinglass's families, drunken parents rarely engaged in the more extreme behavior described in some literature, but were more of an embarrassment when they acted "like assholes." Certainly this is damaging to a child, but not in the same way as being raped or beaten. One wonders how much Steinglass's research data on alcoholic families was skewed by his families' denial, disavowal, repression, and defensive idealization of their lifestyles. The clinician simply has a different database than the researcher, and this partly accounts for the disparate pictures they paint.

Steinglass is particularly interested in the effects of alcoholism in or of the family on daily routines, family rituals, and problem-solving family episodes and techniques throughout the family life-cycle. Those families that were able to maintain their daily routines and rituals and who had a family identity broader than or different from that of

addictive family suffered the least from the invasive effects of the drinking. Steven Wolin and Leonard Bennett (1984), two of Steinglass's collaborators, believe that the preservation of family rituals and their protection from contamination by the effects of drunkenness is the key variable distinguishing "healthy" and "unhealthy" alcoholic families. This is interesting in light of the overwhelming clinical evidence that in the memories of COAs holidays and vacations were hellish and dreaded. Possibly Wolin and Bennett are right and the COAs whose families preserved their rituals intact do not come for treatment.

The familial transmission of alcoholism is a life-cycle phenomenon, the key phase of which is the establishment of the new family. If the COA forming this new family can establish rituals in which alcohol is peripheral or absent, then the generational transmission is likely to come to an end. This outcome is most likely if the routines and rituals of the COAs' families of origin are relatively uncontaminated by the familial alcoholism. Having a strong identity as a new family also reduces generational transmission. Another way of understanding this is that the COAs of the less-enmeshed families have the best chance of establishing nonalcoholic families of their own.

Steinglass (1994) emphasizes the need for the clinician to see the family as it is, with its strengths and weaknesses, and not to discredit it under the broad label of "dysfunctional family." For individuation of the family to be possible, it is particularly vital that the counselor be cognizant of both the life-cycle stage and the addictive-family stage the family is struggling through or stuck in. Yes, there is a stultifying stuckness in addictive families, but they too change as they must, and perhaps even grow.

In line with the aims of all family therapies, Steinglass attempts to enable that growth through a combination of insight and direction. Therapy is conceptualized as a four-stage process: (1) diagnosing alcoholism and labeling it a family problem; (2) removing alcohol from the family system; (3) helping the family pass through the emotional desert, that is, the emptiness and confusion and loss of alcoholic problem-solving techniques in early sobriety; and (4) facing the struggle between *family restabilization*, which perpetuates the routines, rituals, and problem-solving techniques of the family in a context of sobriety, and *family reorganization*, the psychologically healthy reconstruction of the family. Steinglass finds that family reorganization is by far the most common outcome of sobriety, and that the inertia inherent in these families can make for a highly stable sobriety.

John Bradshaw: Treatment of Shame Based Behavior.

John Bradshaw (1988a,b), a charismatic former theologian, is a recovering alcoholic who has had tremendous impact on the community of recovering persons. He writes for the general public, and his popular books and seminars have had wide influence. A systems theorist who draws on much of the work we have already discussed, his basic position is that addiction is a family disease that perpetuates itself through *poisonous pedagogy*. In such families the children's spirit must be broken for them to be under social control; this reduces them to objects, and the breaking process manifests itself as physical, sexual, and emotional abuse, resulting in shame and its repression. He calls this condition **toxic shame**—shame that comes from having been abused as a child or from growing up in an addictive home, particularly when it is anesthetized, denied, repressed, or acted-out shame. Bradshaw is primarily speaking to and about those alcoholics whose parents were alcoholic. In contrast to Steinglass's addictive family, Bradshaw describes a more disturbed and indeed pathological system in which violence and abuse are endemic. He claims, for example, that around 50 percent of adult COAs have been sexually abused.

Bradshaw's treatment recommendations are a synthesis of the psychodynamic methods involving recovery of repressed memories and dream work, and cognitive-behavioral strategies such as cognitive restructuring and self-efficacy training (See Chapter 11 on counseling techniques). He stresses work with the *inner child*, the part of adult personality that embodies the vulnerable and victimized self from childhood. In many ways still the theologian, Bradshaw sees addictions of any type as the equivalent of original sin and recovery as a kind of spiritual and emotional redemption. The Bradshaw model of an addictive family is characterized by violence, rage, incest, and abuse of all kinds. Strongly influenced by Alice Miller (1981) and her notions of the cataclysmic consequences of the ways humans have treated their children, Bradshaw sees the "family sin" of addiction as rooted in pathological child-rearing practices. All addictions act as "mood changers," ways of not feeling genuinely. What the addict does not want to feel is shame, pain, guilt, rejection, loss, grief, mourning, mortality, separateness, and aloneness. Bradshaw puts great emphasis on the addict's need for *individuation*, or becoming an individual. Healthy relating is only possible for those who are whole and complete in themselves, and therefore capable of affiliating out of love rather than out of need.

9–2 Major Family Therapy Approaches

Both clinical experience and research point to the necessity of including family work in counseling chemically dependent clients. *Family therapy*, however, is not a single unitary approach to treatment. Instead several important schools of family therapy offer different models of how to intervene in disturbed families. Although these family-therapy approaches did not evolve specifically through work with addicted and/or alcoholic families, they all contain useful methods that can be adapted for that purpose.

The major theories of family dynamics and systems of family therapy you will learn about in this chapter are: strategic family therapy, structural family therapy, experiential family therapy, intergenerational systems therapy, behavioral family therapy, and psychodynamic family therapy. Table 9–1 summarizes the major features of these schools.

Strategic Family Therapy

You will probably not be surprised to learn that **strategic family therapy** is an approach defined by strategies, especially involving

Table 9–1. Major schools of family therapy

School	Characteristics
Strategic	Uses communication strategies to change unhealthy homeostasis
Structural	Changes maladaptive family structures like boundaries, roles, and triangles
Experiential	Focuses on immediate here-and-now emotional processes in session
Intergenerational	Emphasizes transmission and recurrence of unhealthy family patterns from generation to generation
Behavioral	Teaches family members to interact more effectively
Psychodynamic	Seeks family insight into unconscious and developmental roots of symptoms

communications and instructions, by which the therapist self-consciously seeks to bring about systemic family change. Such strategies are by their very nature improvised ad hoc—designed to fit a particular situation—and in that sense they are spontaneous and creative. They also tend to be manipulative and gimmicky. The whole emphasis is on what the family does and how it does it, rather than on why.

Strategic family therapy grew out of Gregory Bateson's work on families with schizophrenia (Bateson et al. 1956). In his view, the families of schizophrenics drove these individuals mad without the least awareness that they were doing so by using a communication pattern called the *double bind*. In a double bind, there is no way for the recipient of the communication to win, and no way to be right. It is a damned-if-you-do, damned-if-you-don't trap. The *double-bind theory* asserts that the only way out of the damned-if-you-do, damned-if-you-don't family environment is to go mad. Another way out is to drink or drug.

We all communicate double binds on occasion, but what makes the schizophrenic family different is the pervasiveness and persistence of this mode of interaction. Bateson gives the example of the mother of a schizophrenic child. The child was a patient, and doing rather well in the hospital, when the mother visited. As she walked into her son's room, the mother said, "Aren't you going to embrace your mother?" But when the patient embraced her, she said, "Stop smothering

me." The *patient* immediately began acting crazy. It is essential to the double bind that it not be commented upon; that is, there is an unspoken rule that specifies there is to be no communication about communication. In our example, if the "crazy" son could say, "Mother, you are telling me to get close and pushing me away at the same time," he would not have had to go crazy. However, he can't, either because he lacks the insight into the double bind in which he is trapped, or because the rules of the family prohibit such an utterance. These possibilities are not mutually exclusive. The lack of insight and the prohibition against communication reinforce each other. The counselor who does have insight into the double-bind situation can comment on it, thereby breaking the double-bind impasse. Such an interpretation is not usually well received and is often not heeded, illustrating the inertia of the system and its tendency to resist change in order to maintain its homeostasis. Families with addiction demonstrate lots of double-binding behavior and counselors need to comment on it.

Strategic family therapy is largely the creation of Jay Haley (1976, 1984, 1990) who started by analyzing the communication patterns of disturbed families. Pathology was seen as garbled communication, and the task of the therapist was to improve communication by making the covert overt, clarifying, disturbing double binds by commenting on them, pointing out various language games people play, and so on. Improving communication is certainly work fit for the gods. Yet it has become a cliché. We haven't seen a couple in years in which at least the wife, and often both partners, didn't say, "We are having trouble communicating." Sometimes that is true, maybe even often, and the couple does not exist whose communication cannot be improved, but very often communication isn't really the problem. "Communication" has become another place to hide, another defense. The real problem isn't lack of communication; it is what the communication is about, a content one or both of the partners doesn't wish to hear. A very effective, albeit painful, intervention is to point out that the problem isn't lack of communication but the content of the communication.

Watzlawick (1978) developed a technique or strategy involving the **therapeutic double bind** that takes the form of prescribing the symptom. Bateson (1971), in his paper on addiction, alludes to A.A. members telling a recalcitrant drinker to "go out and tie one on." If the drinker follows that "prescription," John Barleycorn himself may convince the drinker the game is not worth the gamble, and if he doesn't follow the prescription he gets a chance to try sobriety. Ideally, the therapeutic double bind sets up a win–win situation. In following the therapists suggestion, such as "I want you to become more anxious," the anxious person may increase his anxiety only to discover that he can control his anxiety— or he may refuse, similarly learning that he can control his anxiety, thereby changing if he does and changing if he doesn't. Strategists use the unconscious, rather than trying to understand it.

Playing with fire like anxiety is an inherently risky business, but the therapeutic double bind has its uses. Great caution, however, is needed in gauging when and with whom to use this *paradoxical method*. The chance that the method will backfire and cause more harm must be carefully considered beforehand. For an addict, the approach of prescribing the symptom can lead to a binge of substance abuse with unpredictable consequences. Before counselors utilize this technique they would do well to weigh the risks against possible gains and to evaluate the ethics of their intervention.

Another strategic family therapy technique is *reframing*, also called relabeling, which usually means putting a positive spin on a symptom or symptomatic behavior. To the pot-smoking college student who angrily says to his furious mother, "You really don't want me to stop or you wouldn't have given me that bottle of whiskey for Christmas," the therapist might say, "They were trying to save you money so you could put it toward tuition." Absurd as they sound to clients, reframing comments can be highly effective, especially when they reveal a truth about the function of the symptoms for the client or family. The counselor might remark, "Your drug use is your way of asserting your identity," thus reframing the symptom and interpreting its adaptive meaning.

Haley's central insight is that all relationships, including the one between counselor and client, are power relationships. Whether by language, gestures, body postures, or behavior, people establish relationships with elements of dominance and control. Of course people can control through weakness and no one is more attuned to the power of *passive aggression* than Haley. Recognizing the immediate effects of the ubiquity of power in human relations, Haley stresses the absolute necessity of the counselor taking control. According to Haley, all therapy is directive, and there is always an enormous power differential between therapist and patient. Whether it is acknowledged or not, the therapist controls the patient; that is exactly the way it should be, except that in therapy the control should be overt and self-conscious. Haley's analysis of symptoms also centers on control. The purpose of a symptom is to control others. Further, the symptom may serve as a control device or power advantage for other members of the family. In his view, a symptom cannot be understood as an intrapsychic or biochemical event, but only as an interpersonal one.

The implications of this view for drug-addiction treatment are clear. Drug abuse, like any symptom, must have some interpersonal significance—for example, to ensure that the person is taken care of by the other family members. Haley would not offer interpretations, as might a dynamic therapist, but would instead urge the family members to continue to caretake, on the assumption that they will resist him and cease caretaking, which will deny the drugger his or her payoff and presumably put an end to the symptom. Haley takes an extreme (and highly questionable) position that the patient cannot get well unless the family does. Because the function of the symptom is to control the family, there would be absolutely no reason to change if the family continued to let itself be controlled. Conversely, if the family were threatened by the patient changing (and thus jeopardizing its homeostasis), they would undermine the patient to make sure no change occurred. From a systems viewpoint, Haley is right, but people do flee systems, and they change in spite of environmental resistance to that change. If they could not and did not, there would be no hope for the many addicts who live in dysfunctional families. Although Haley overstates his case, it is true that it is extraordinarily difficult to change when everyone around you is fighting that change—even as they loudly advocate it. If the patient is a child or otherwise totally dependent, the situation may indeed be hopeless unless the system can be broken up. For Haley, family counseling is the only way to go, since change is only possible if everyone in the system changes.

To summarize, strategic therapy is marked by several features:

- It establishes the therapist's control.
- It is highly directive.
- It believes that the whole system needs to be changed.
- It devises strategies to bring about the required change.
- It relies heavily on reframing, paradoxical interventions, and prescribing the symptom.
- It views symptoms as having covert, interpersonal purposes that are under the control of the patient.

Structural Family Therapy

Structural family therapy is an approach that seeks to elucidate and change the structure of the family system. *Family structure* refers to the family's recurrent patterns of interaction, hierarchies, boundaries, and coalitions. Like strategic family therapists, structural family therapists agree that no individual change is possible unless the family is modified.

The creator of structural family therapy is Salvador Minuchin (1992), an Argentine psychiatrist, who formulated his methods in his work with highly recalcitrant minority children and families from impoverished inner-city neighborhoods. With these children, Minuchin (Minuchin et al. 1967) found that individual therapy was ultimately ineffective because the family structure quickly undid whatever gains were made.

Minuchin (1992) tells us that, "The therapeutic process will be that of changing family members' psychosocial position vis-à-vis each other" (p. 6). So the therapist is going to actively assert control in order to change the role relations within the system. The family structure is seen as the sum total of the customary interactions within the system. They are relatively enduring, but in health not invariant or inflexible. Within that structure are coalitions, or subsystems—spousal, parental, sibling, and individual. In health, the subsystems are hierarchical and stand in reciprocal, complementary relationship to one another. For example, one cannot be a father without a child.

In structural family therapy, great attention is paid to **boundaries**, the behavioral and emotional divisions among family members. If boundaries between subsystems are too rigid, the result is *disengagement*, as in a family characterized by lack of cohesion, support, and warmth. At the opposite pole is the *enmeshed family*, which is characterized by all-too-permeable, diffuse boundaries, intrusions, and lack of differentiation. A healthy, nurturing environment both meets the needs of its members for affiliation and bonding, and provides the matrix out of which differentiation and individuation occur. As Minuchin (1992) puts it, "Dependency and autonomy are complementary, not conflicting, characteristics of the human condition" (p. 2). Paradoxically, the disengaged family disables the development of autonomy no less than the enmeshed one. Addicted families tend to be either highly enmeshed or disengaged.

Minuchin sees family pathology as a rigidity, a quality that sets in if the stress is too great for the resources of the system. Thus pathology is seen as a response to overload. Healthy families are basically open; they have conservation mechanisms that guarantee stability and on-goingness, but they are also flexible and responsive to internal and external change. The inherent homeostatic mechanisms do not ossify. But when the resources of the system are depleted and overloaded, as by the stress of alcoholism, a defensive rigidity sets in and the homeostatic mechanisms go into overdrive.

In trying to understand the family structure, Minuchin pays particular attention to alignments and coalitions. Is the son in alignment with the mother? Do the children form a coalition against the parents? Clearly, part of Minuchin's concern with coalitions is in clarifying and making overt the power relationships in the family. For Minuchin as for Haley, power is primordial and ineluctable. Far from seeing power as a malignant force, Minuchin sees the origin of much pathology as flowing from weakness and lack of power, particularly on the part of parents. In his work, Minuchin creates *structural maps* that make immediately clear the relations in the family—its hierarchies and subsystems; its clear, diffuse, or rigid boundaries; its affiliations, conflicts, coalitions, enmeshments, and detouring. Later in this chapter you will see an example of a structural map to illustrate structures in the Baker family case.

What do structural family therapists do? The structuralist is active, directive, and provocative. He or she challenges frozen dysfunctional patterns, and insists that parents exercise parental authority (use their power), and that subsystems be differentiated. One form of that challenge is a reframing, not in terms of putting a positive twist on the symptom, but rather in terms of redefining the symptom itself as belonging to a system. The identified patient ceases to be the patient and the family structure is put on the couch. This in itself radically changes structure. There is no attempt at insight; action precedes understanding, but insight may follow the change. The switch is from an individual to a systems

viewpoint: change relationship patterns and the cure is here.

All this is very well; just get the parents to be parents, engage but do not enmesh, establish clear boundaries, and everyone will be fine. Maybe, but how? Minuchin tells us the counselor must be a commanding presence. He gets to be that commanding presence by joining the family. He does this by adopting or accommodating to the family's style, imitating their speech patterns, pace, and idiosyncrasies. The therapist must be a superb actor. Having joined the family, the therapist can now participate in and take a control stance toward the family interactional pattern; that is, toward its structure. But the therapist is not a family member, so he or she simultaneously is in and out of the family and, as an "out," can command. Minuchin does such things as making enmeshed members literally move away from each other by changing chairs, and by taking sides, often with the weak against the strong. This is sometimes called *unbalancing*. The *chair game*, in which the family relationships are seen to be expressed in their physical deportment, has been generalized into an important family-counseling technique called a *family sculpture*. In a family sculpture the family is asked to represent their relationships by the placement of their bodies by one or more members of the family.

To sum up, the structural family therapist reframes the problem as a systemic one, "joins" the family, takes control, challenges pathological structure, uses directives to establish clear boundaries and hierarchical subsystems, and uses enactments to bring the problems into the treatment room. All of this is done with humor, warmth, and authority.

Experiential Family Therapy

In the approach called **experiential family therapy,** the experience that the family has with the counselor enables change. Change comes from the immediate here-and-now counseling experience, not from the counselor's manipulation or communication strategies. Change is not a result of counseling; it is instead what happens during the counseling.

There is something quintessentially American about experiential family therapy. It is pragmatic, skeptical of theory, and action-oriented. Its principal advocate is Carl Whitaker, who proposes two key technical means to deal with the resistance inherent in any family system (Whitaker and Bumberry 1988). The first is the *struggle for structure*, the second, the *struggle for initiative*. In the struggle for structure, the therapist establishes control. Whitaker (Whitaker and Bumberry 1988) insists that all members of the family attend the first session, and he refuses to deal with them if the family won't play by his rules. In the struggle for structure, Whitaker defines himself as parent, not peer. He also reframes the problem as a systemic and interpersonal one, not an individual one. He does this not by teaching, because, as Whitaker says, "Nothing worth knowing can be taught," but by doing (p. 85). The family, having learned that the therapist is a parent who imposes the structure, naturally looks to the therapist for answers which occasions the struggle for initiative. The therapist must firmly place the ball in the family's court. To do so, he or she vigorously leaps from the pedestal of authority, saying such things as, "I'm lucky if I can muddle through my own life let alone live yours," making it clear that he has no "reality" answers. His function is to enable growth, not to tell anyone how to live. Whitaker uses all sorts of confrontations, humor, and absurdity to win the battle for initiative. There is a paradox here. The therapist is demanding that the patient—the family—be free and responsible. Merely saying "I order you to be free" somehow doesn't work, but returning the ball does. Another kind of reframing goes on here, as the problem is redefined during the struggle for initiative from symptom removal to growth. The therapist has no particular interest in symptom removal.

This approach raises real questions for the substance abuse counselor who does think that he or she knows a better way of living, namely sobriety. Perhaps there is no way out of this dilemma, and substance abuse counseling is incompatible with experiential therapy. As part of his insistence on spontaneity and aliveness, Whitaker also abhors history-taking, calling it voyeuristic "pornography." No psycho-socials for him. For Whitaker, there is also no diagnosis.

The political struggle is over once the family accepts responsibility, and we are in the middle of the "journey of family therapy [which] begins with a blind date and ends with the empty nest" (p. 53). Blind dates engender anxiety, and Whitaker makes it clear that anxiety is the motivating force for change. Accordingly, he does nothing to reduce the anxiety level; on the contrary, he makes moves to heighten it.

Whitaker also relishes his own toughness, comparing therapy to surgery. Like the surgeon, he feels it is his business to cut away diseased tissue, not to avoid bloodletting. Perhaps related to toughness is Whitaker's use of the bataca (pillow bat), which he encourages the family members to use on each other. This more direct variant on pounding the pillow both brings suppressed (or repressed) anger and aggression to the surface and demonstrates (gives individuals the experience of) that anger need not destroy its object.

The middle phase of experiential family therapy is characterized as symbolic therapy, which deals with unconscious process. "Just as water flows through pipes under our streets, impulses flow through our unconscious. . . . We all have these emotional infrastructures that ensure the flow of our impulse life" (p. 75). The themes of loneliness, rage, sexuality, and death are universal; they are particularized among other ways in family rituals. Whitaker does not interpret the unconscious; rather, he surfaces these connections, largely through the use of his own associations. Since the themes are universal, the therapist's articulation of his thoughts and feelings frees up the family to reveal its infrastructure. Whitaker also uses confrontation and reductio ad absurdum techniques. "My husband always runs away from me" is answered by, "Why don't you shoot him?" "How could I?" His answer, "With a gun, or you might use a bow and arrow." Before long the wife's murderous rage surfaces, having been tapped by Whitaker's literalism. Whitaker's whole technique has been calle a "theater of the absurd." Particular emphasis is put on death and loss.

Whitaker advocates starting with the father; since he believes that gender differences are biological and that men are less in contact with feelings, symbols, and impulses, he goes after Dad first and hard. Whitaker emphasizes the intergenerational transmission of patterns, shared symbols, and rituals. He believes that at least three generations are germaine to the current family functioning, and he includes grandparents, if he possibly can, saying such things as, "We are stuck and need help. Would your parents (the grandparents) come and help us?"

Experiential family therapy, would appear to have limited application to the treatment of substance abuse or the actively addicted family. Its indifference to symptom removal and diagnosis, and its focus on the symbolic representation and enactment of unconscious impulses seem too removed from substance abuse therapy in which the therapist takes a strong stand for sobriety. Whitaker, however, would disagree. He says, "Alcoholics drink because they're afraid of being afraid" (p. 86). If that is the case, then experiential therapy, with its push toward experiencing the anxiety intrinsic to being fully alive and aware, would seem to be just the thing. The problem is that if the counselor ignores the substance-induced regression that comes from addiction, the experiential approach may become irrelevant. Experiential family therapy appears to be much more suited for work with families who are somewhat advanced in recovery rather than actively addicted families.

Intergenerational Systems Family Therapy

The creation of psychiatrist Murray Bowen (1978a,b), **intergenerational systems family therapy** is an approach whose cornerstone is differentiation of the family system. In systems terms, **differentiation** refers to the articulation and organization of separate parts. All development entails differentiation. In the embryo, for example, undifferentiated cells differentiate into layers which in turn differentiate into even more specialized cells that ultimately become integrated tissues and organ systems. In Bowen's approach, differentiation involves not only change in the family as a system, but also change in the individual members as independent selves.

Because development involves both differentiation and integration, the loss of differentiation, or *de-differentiation*, is always pathological. In families it is manifested in a lack of differentiation of the individual self from the *undifferentiated family ego mass*. Bowen often speaks of the client being stuck in the family ego mass. There are feelings of being ensnarled, of stickiness and entrapment—images of flies caught by flypaper or entangled in spider webs come to mind. Bowen would be an apt candidate for spiritual grandfather of the codependency movement, because to be codependent is to be undifferentiated.

For Bowen, differentiation is not only interpersonal, or between people, but also intrapersonal, or within the realm of individual thought and feeling. Intrapersonal differentiation entails being able to separate your thoughts from your feelings. The failure to do so is a mark of being ensnarled in the family ego mass. Bowen has developed a scale to estimate the degree of differentiation, and he maintains that a relatively undifferentiated family can function well under conditions of low stress, but falls into dysfunction as stress escalates.

Another of Bowen's key concepts is *triangulation*. Bowen sees the family and indeed all human relations as systems of interlocking interpersonal triangles. *Triangles* are essentially defenses against twoness, against pairing. Relationships are intrinsically stressful; conflict between people is inevitable, and people flee from the tension of dyadic relationships, of I–thou relating, of two-person intimacy, to triangular relationships. One or both members of the pair suck in another person to deflect, to support, to ally, to defend, and to dilute. Triangles, inevitable as they are, are the great danger. For Bowen, if the therapist becomes triangulated into the system, all is lost. The primary task of the therapist is to remain untriangulated so he or she can coach the patient on de-triangulation. The only way the therapist can avoid triangulation is to have worked through differentiation from his or her family of origin. The therapist is a calm, uninvolved, objective teacher explaining the triangulation process in the family and helping develop strategies for de-triangulation.

Substance abusers are triangulators par excellence, and the addictive family is one of triangular entanglements, so Bowen's analysis of triangulation is directly applicable to the treatment of addicted families. If Bowen's fear of being drawn in to the family's patterns seems excessive, it is a real danger for the substance abuse family counselor, who needs to be aware of the contending forces trying to enlist him or her as an ally in the family struggle. This gets tricky when there is an active user. There joining the triangle against the user is sometimes necessary. Bowen would not agree. He has written on alcoholism (1974) and sees the alcoholic as the least differentiated member of the family system. He sees the cure as a process that enables differentiation rather than focusing on the symptom—for example, the drinking.

The dysfunctional family's overall lack of differentiation is projected onto the symptomatic family member. The real problem is family fusion, for in the fused family members either have no-selves or pseudo-selves, never real selves. There is often a pattern of overadequate–underadequate role assignment, the underadequate person being presented as the problem in what is clearly a relationship problem. This has direct relevance to substance abuse treatment. Bowen (1974) presents the alcoholic as the overadequate partner who is in reality undifferentiated or defending against that undifferentiation by overcompensation. Alcohol enables the fusion that the overadequacy denies. This is a variation on the **dependency-conflict theory** of addiction, which states that *counterdependent* people, who are phobic about intimacy and deny their need for it, covertly meet their dependency needs through the use of substances, particularly alcohol. This dynamic is usually a male pattern, but need not be. The drinker/drugger maintains that he needs no one and is totally independent, while in reality being totally dependent. Returning to Bowen's view, as the addiction progresses,

the roles reverse, and the drinker becomes underadequate. The possibilities between these two extremes are legion, and Bowen's point is that it isn't the drinking, it's the fusion and its by-products that need to be addressed.

People tend to select spouses on the same level of differentiation (or undifferentiation) as themselves. Undifferentiated parents in turn project—that is, unconsciously attribute—their undifferentiation onto and triangulate with their offspring; and there is usually a favorite target who becomes the most fused family member. This sets up a *multigenerational transmission process* in which the less differentiated marry the undifferentiated who produce at least one even less-differentiated child, who marries in the same way. With each generation the level of family differentiation decreases, not via genetic means, but by relational means. The relevance of this process to substance abuse is significant. Counselors frequently see families in which a parent (usually the father) is a functional alcoholic, or as one of our patients put it, "I want to be a successful alcoholic like my father," while one or more of the children are dysfunctional drinkers or druggers who are unable to make it in the world.

Also applicable to substance abuse is Bowen's concept of the *emotional cutoff*. This is like moving to northern Alaska and exchanging Christmas cards with the family in lieu of true differentiation. It is a defensive movement that is bound to fail (although it may be better than total submergence in the fused family), since the substance abuser's fused family remains in his head awaiting projection and reenactment. We also see this in addicts who fuse with their substance of choice instead of with their families. Twelve step groups speak of this as *isolation*, a character flaw of the addicted.

When a recovering person returns to his addicted family, the entire family may move from the fusion implicit in addiction and the games played around it to sobriety and greater differentiation. However, more often than not, that is not the outcome, and the recovering person's hurt, disappointment, and rage may endanger his or her recovery. Bowen would say that the recovering addict lacked the calm and ability to differentiate between thought and feeling characteristic of the true self and needed more therapy before attempting further differentiation through differentiation of the family. This seems rather utopian, but helping recovering people recognize and avoid enmeshment and triangulation in their still-addicted families is highly therapeutic. Some degree of emotional cutoff may be adaptive and indeed necessary to continued recovery.

Intergenerational family systems therapy is interested in genealogy. Therapists enjoin patients to trace their families with a **genogram**, or family history chart. All Bowen's patients, be they individuals, couples, or families, prepare genograms as part of the evaluation process. The genogram is a pictorial representation of multigeneration family structures going back at least three generations. Bowen has a system of symbols for birth, death, divorce, and so forth, but the therapist can use any symbols that highlight and vivify relational patterns. The genogram is of particular relevance to substance abuse treatment, where the family's intergenerational pattern of use and abuse needs to be made manifest. This technique is illustrated later in the Baker family case.

Behavioral Family Therapy

Behavioral family therapy works on extinguishing the effects of maladaptive past learning, changing present contingencies and reward patterns, and challenging the attitudinal components of dysfunction. Although most often used in individual therapy, these techniques can be adopted to couple and family work with chemically dependent clients (O'Farrell 1993).

Behavioral family therapy has many incarnations, but these days is strongly cognitively oriented. Counselors who use this approach take an active role as teachers or coaches, and utilize a variety of techniques to help family members acquire more effective coping and interpersonal skills. As an illustration, behavioral family therapy uses homework assignment. For example, spouses may be directed to say something positive to each other every day. Another common method is *contingency contracts* in which rewards are given to family members (especially children) for their performance of desired behaviors, such as doing homework.

Behavior therapy encourages self-monitoring, the keeping of diaries, and training in problem-solving. The behavioral approach to family problems is most often used with families with recalcitrant teenagers. Generally speaking, the behavior therapist focuses on the individual patient, seeing the patient's problems as the cause of the difficulties in the family. This is the direct opposite of the systems approach, although behavioral family therapists recognize that the family members may be unwittingly reinforcing the aberrant behavior.

Two behavioral approaches that can be extremely helpful with recovering families are *parental skills training* and *conjoint sex therapy*. There are several varieties of parental skills training, but all are essentially educational and all seek to help reduce family conflict. Parenting sober is very different from parenting while drug-involved. Consequently, concrete, didactic training, advice, and guidance can substantially reduce anxiety and conflict in the recovering parent and his or her family. By learning better parenting skills the client's growth as a responsible, emotionally available father or mother is fostered. When one member of a couple is addicted, sexual problems in the relationship are predictably common. In conjoint sex therapy, treatment focuses on improving the relational and sexual skills of both parties through structured exercises. While certainly no cure for chemical dependency, this approach can benefit the couple as they struggle to maintain recovery. Further exploration of behavior therapy techniques will be found in Chapter 11.

Psychodynamic Family Therapy

Psychodynamic family therapy is an approach that aims at insight into the family's behavioral patterns and interactions, and their unconscious reenactments, projections, and identifications. Using some methods of other approaches, psychodynamic family therapy works in a *nondirective way* through which the therapist helps family members increase self-awareness, particularly awareness of their unconscious processes. Here you will examine some classical ideas from the pioneers of this approach as well as well as two important contemporary models.

Sigmund Freud.   Almost all of Freud's work is about individual psychology, yet he was very well aware of the effects people have on one another, especially people in families. Freud (1921) concluded that men in groups undergo regression and de-individuation. Building on the work of LeBon (1895) on the psychology of crowds, McDougall's (1920) theory of the highly organized group, and Trotter's (1916) theory of a herd instinct, Freud developed his own theory of *group psychology*, which also applies to the group called a family. He concluded that groups work because all of the members feel equally loved by the leader, and this equality reduces sibling rivalry and makes for feelings of solidarity. Being equally loved by the "father figure" is essential to group cohesion. The children in families with addiction rarely feel loved as much as the parent loves his or her substance, and the conditions for group cohesion are absent. The success of Twelve step groups may have much to do with either inducing feelings of being equally loved by the program and by one's Higher Power.

The implications for family dynamics of Freud's group psychology are fairly obvious. Leaderless families will be more primitive, more emotional, less rational, and more erratic and unstable than those with a strong leader. Paradoxically, the strongly led group, provided that the leader (parent) loves the followers (children) equally, will be more democratic, or at least more egalitarian within the sibling system than one with diffuse leadership. Further, group cohesion is only possible through the relinquishing of self-love. The family will share an *ego-ideal*, which is an identification with the parent(s), and this shared ego-ideal facilitates their mutual identification. The conversion of the sexual into the affectionate is a necessary condition of group solidarity, so whatever else incest and sexual abuse—both common in addicted families—may do, it makes family solidarity and cohesion impossible.

Wilfred Bion.   One of the most clinically useful as well as conceptually powerful analyses of group behavior was made by Wilfred Bion (1961), an English psychiatrist and analyst. Bion saw that every group operated on two levels simultaneously: at a realistic task or work level, and on an unconscious or basic assumption level. There is a clear parallel here to the distinction between the conscious and unconscious processes in individuals. Every group is a work or task group, including the family. Every group simultaneously pursues its basic assumptions—its unconscious aggressive, sexual, and dependence needs. Aggression is expressed by fight-or-flight fantasies and action, and dependency needs by dependent fantasies and behavior, while sexual needs are met by pairing. The unconscious fantasy of both the group and the couple doing the pairing is that they will conceive the Savior or Messiah. It is only because the group believes that the pair will conceive the Messiah that it tolerates pairing. David Scharff (1992) has added a fourth basic assumption: fusion-fission—the need to fuse (merge) and the need to isolate (fragment).

Families are very usefully viewed as simultaneously pursuing tasks—raising children, mourning losses, earning money—and pursuing the unconscious basic assumptions of fight-flight, dependency, pairing, and fusion-fission. The basic assumption may contribute to the work of the group or it may undermine it, but in either case it is a mostly unconscious process. Addicted families tend to do poorly as task groups and to be driven, more than most, by their unconscious basic assumptions.

Nathan Ackerman.   Ackerman's (1994) major theoretical contribution has been to understand psychopathology as being simultaneously intrapsychic (within the mind) and systemic (familial). Ackerman characterizes family dysfunction as arising from roles and enactments becoming fixed, rigid, and dead. The family then deals with the unresolved conflict manifested in the stalemate by scapegoating, the scapegoat most usually being the identified patient.

What makes Ackerman a psychodynamic family therapist is his emphasis on the unconscious nature of the unresolved conflict. In disturbed families the central conflict is between the parents, who use *scapegoating* as both a diversion and a defense. **Scapegoating** means that the parents displace their distress and conflict on another family member, that is, they find a convenient victim and dump their burdens on him. This is an extremely common dynamic when the identified patient is an adolescent or young adult substance abuser. On a conscious level, the parents are passionately and genuinely invested in halting the adolescent's substance abuse; yet on an unconscious level they need the adolescent to continue to use and to be a problem so he or she can be available for scapegoating, and so the parents don't have to look at the disturbance in their own relationship. Inevitably the scapegoat is only too willing to continue in that role, and the drug use remains unabated. Ackerman would see this as a case of interlocking pathology.

Ackerman, like the other founding fathers of family therapy, is a charismatic person. Anything but neutral, he takes sides and works to unbalance, particularly with the scapegoat. Ackerman openly commented on his feelings. In part this is modeling—for example, modeling openness about sex, dependence, aggression, and anxiety. Ackerman's aims are to always increase the self-awareness of both repressed and projected aspects of self, including the enactment of interacting psychopathologies. He sees the counselor as a catalyst of change, and views all technique as being subordinate to the catalytic role. There is a great deal of value in Ackerman's approach, particularly in his understanding of the concept of mutually interlocking psychopathologies, that readily lends itself to work with addicted and recovering families.

Object Relations Family Therapy.   Another psychodynamic approach is called **object relations family therapy**, an approach that relies heavily on transference interpretation (Scharff and Scharff 1991). Therapists following this approach interpret the projections that the family members make onto the therapist, and also use their own feelings as a source of insight as to what is going on in the family. Object relations family therapy sees family interaction as a projection of and enactment of the internal worlds of the family members. Those internal worlds are assumed to be mental representations of early relationships. The processes of intergenerational internalization and projection cast much light on the pathology we see in alcoholic and substance abusing families. For example, the adult alcoholic whose father was alcoholic might see in his own son elements of himself that were repudiated by his father, and in turn repudiate his son for the same reason.

By interpreting the attitudes and interactions of family members in terms of each individual's early interpersonal experiences insight is gained. In addition, object relations family therapy also incorporates the interpretation of dreams and drawings, as well as play.

9–3 Family Counseling Illustrated: The Baker Family

Up to this point in the chapter, you have learned about the many varied ideas and practices of the major schools of family therapy. To illustrate these ideas in the context of an actual case, in this section we will take a look at how different therapists might work with the same family, the Bakers. We invite you to come along on an imaginative journey in which several family therapists work with the Bakers.

Meeting the Baker Family: Initial Session

We see the Bakers in an opening session, greatly distressed by the behavior of their older son who has recently returned home from a therapeutic community (TC) and resumed daily marijuana smoking. Tom is 16; his younger brother, Sam, is 12. The parents are fortyish. They are neatly albeit informally dressed, the boys in age-appropriate jeans and T-shirts, Father in hard-pressed work pants and a short-sleeve shirt, Mother in a bright, not-quite-loud cotton dress and heels;

she wears slightly too much makeup. Rob is a muscular, powerful-looking man. Harriet is plump, not quite fat. The family enters the consulting room in single file, Mother first, followed by Father, Tom and Sam. Tom is sullen, and stares at the floor. Sam seems distracted and not quite there. The substance abuse counselor wonders if Sam is the "lost child" in this family. Mother enters purposefully, almost marching, and proceeds to the most distant chair, followed by her husband, to whom she says, "I want the kids to sit next to me; you sit at the end." Tom raises his eyes from the floor and looks at her hatefully but sits next to her. Sammy and Father make up the rear, taking the remaining seats just as they were told to do. Mom is the one who contacted the therapist, telling of Tom's return to drugs, and about her anger and despair, and her fear (possibly her wish) that Daddy will "beat the shit out of him."

Mother (pointing at Father): He was circumcised at age 26 for me. (Laughs.) But that's not why we're here. I've been in love with Rob from the beginning, but I wouldn't have married him unless he had a *bris*. We did, and we've had a great time ever since. I'm in electronic parts and I make a helluva lot of money. I barely got out of high school, and I never expected to make so much money, but I turned out to be one helluva saleswoman. Rob's in the best construction union in the city, and he makes out like a bandit. Sam is a doll. He gets great grades, he's going to be Bar Mitzvah, and things are great—except for that fucking kid. Two months out of New Start and he's back at it. ("Fucking kid" seems discordant, and is said without visible anger in the same animated, pressured voice she's been using all along.)

Father (angrily): I'm going to break his fucking neck if he doesn't stop. (His biceps harden as he says this, and he looks like he's about to get up and do it.)

Mother: We're not putting up with this shit anymore.

Tom (mutters): Fuck you! (Father starts to go for him, thinks better of it, and sits back down.)

Strategic therapist (more to Mother, but to the entire family): You don't communicate directly. Tom's right here, but you talk about him instead of to him.

Father: Talking to him is like talking to the wall. What he needs is the strap, and he's not too big for it either.

Strategic therapist: You're still talking about him, not to him.

Father: If I talk to him, he's not going to like what I say. I want that fucking kid to go to college. I didn't go, and he's going to go even if I have to kill him.

Structural therapist: Mr. Baker, I want you to sit next to your wife. Tom and Sam, you sit down at this end.

Strategic therapist: I won't tolerate threats in the session. I want you to speak emotionally but civilly to one another. No threats.

Sam: (Giggles.)

Mother (starts giggling too) (to Sam): Come sit next to me.

Structural therapist: No, I want you to sit next to your husband.

Intergenerational therapist: Let's back off and find out a little more about your family. (To the parents.) I'd like to know more about your families of origin. I'd like all of you to help me draw a genogram—a picture of the relationships in your family.

Structural therapist (to Mother, referring to her opening remark): What did you do with the tip? The rabbi gets the salary; the *Mohel* (ritual circumciser) gets the tip. (Mom puts her arm around Sam and seems to be flirting with him.)

Psychodynamic therapist (to Father): How does it feel to have your wife tell us that you were circumcised for her?

Tom (trembling with fear but defiant): Daddy's a monk because Mom made him cut off a piece of his dick. (He runs out of the room.)

Father (Looking at Tom): He's a real asshole. (Shouts.) Tom, come back in here! (Tom peeks in, realizes his father isn't really mad at him, and goes back to his place.)

Mother (to Tom): You should only be as much of a man as your father.

Father: (Beams.)

Behavioral therapist (Unconsciously moves his hand to his crotch.)

Psychodynamic therapist (Thinks to himself: *Mom reminds me of Judy, the lady I treated last year who couldn't understand why giving an enema to her 16-year-old son wasn't a good idea. My association to the enema-giving mother makes me wonder if this isn't an anal family characterized by "messy" acting out. They need to "get their shit together." Is all their anger anal sadism and anal explosiveness? Should I say that and speak directly to their unconscious? That would be a metaphor this family can understand.*) (Speaking): You're here to get your shit together, but you can't seem to do it even here.

Mother (starts to cry): We can't get our shit together. This just goes on and on—counselors, getting thrown out of school, talking to him, beating him, the T.C. Now he's smoking again. I can't stand it. I can't stand it. He's got everything. I was poor. My father was a shoemaker. Rob had it real rough. He ran in gangs, drank like a fish, went to reform school. I loved him from the first time I saw him, but I wouldn't go to bed with him unless he married me. Rob's a man, not like my father—or that damned kid. My father's a wimp. Never made much of a living and was pussy-whipped all his life. My kids love him, but they've known Grandma wears the pants almost since they were born. (To therapist): Yeah, that's the way we talk. We let it all hang out in my family. (All of the therapists wonder, is Rob pussy-whipped too, in spite of his super masculinity and Mom's denial?)

Structural therapist: (Mentally notes, "My" rather than "our" family.)

Mother: My ignorant parents said they would sit *shivah* (go through the mourning ceremony) if I married Rob. He was 25; tough as nails, and was he handsome! My mother said the tattoos made her sick. I love them. Anyway, Rob converted and we got married, and now my folks love him. Tom has had it good from the beginning. Everyone adored him. My parents really changed after he was born and accepted Rob. Rob stopped drinking—once in a while he has a beer, but he doesn't even like that anymore.

Tom (mumbling): Yeah, Dad doesn't drink, so how can he understand why I smoke? Some macho! The only reason he doesn't drink is because my mom doesn't let him. (Starts to say, "He is a pussy," but looks at his dad and gets scared, so pussy doesn't quite sound.)

Mother: Then Rob got in the construction union. His family never did shit for him. His dad was a drunk; it killed him—shot his liver, and his mom's a doormat. She's got rosary beads up her ass. Always praying; never did a thing for the kids. Rob's lucky he's in the union; never graduated high school. He's done real good. Nobody works

as hard as my Rob. The rest of his family is a total loss. All of his brothers drink and fight and are just horrible. We stay away from them. I'm really proud of Rob.

Intergenerational, psychodynamic, strategic, and structural therapists concur, thinking: (She regards him as a child—her child. What does that say to the kids? Can they be kids too? On one hand she presents father as both castrated and pussy-whipped like her father, and on the other hand, as a 'real' man. The boys must have a very split image of their father and major difficulties in male identification. There is also an historical split between Dad, the delinquent drunk, and Dad, the heroic success overcoming his background to become the hardworking provider. Sam, the good boy, identifies with the hardworking father; Tom, the bad boy, with the delinquent father.)

Mother: Once the kids were in school, I got a job in the office of a defense industry plant. After a few years, they realized I had the gift of gab. (All of the therapists think, *"Yep, to the point where no one can get in a word edgewise"*). They gave me a crack at sales. Boy, am I good at it! A woman too—the only one. So now we have plenty of money, a lovely home, two dogs and a cat—they always had all the toys in the world and a great life. Sam appreciates it—I don't know what went wrong with Tom. He was a good kid. When he wasn't, Rob would take the strap to his bare backside and he would straighten out quick. My dad used a razor strap on my brothers when my mother told him to. I think that's good for boys. But now when they get into it, Rob punches him in the head sometimes—and I hate that. Someone's going to get hurt, and that's one reason I called you. You tell Rob to keep his hands to himself. Anyway, Tom's always had it real good. My mother still spoils him rotten. All we ever asked of him was a little respect and good grades. Sam's an honor student.

Father (with rage and in a loud voice): And Tom flunks damn near everything. You'd think he was a real dumb kid but he ain't—just a fuckoff.

Tom (muttering, still looking at the floor): You can't even read.

Father: Like hell I can't.

Mother: Well, not too good, dear.

Father: (Blushes.)

Mother: The only thing we want from our kids is that they go to college. We never had a chance to go, and that's really important to us. They can study anything they want, do whatever they want, as long as they graduate. That's not much to ask. (Cries.)

Sam: (Giggles.)

Mother: Zero point zero averages don't graduate. The trouble started around eighth grade. Tom never did too good in school, but he got through; then all of a sudden, he started cutting classes and Rob spanked him good and hard, but that didn't work, and his grades went to Fs. Then he found the grass.

Father: It was his scumbag friends.

Mother: Rob's right—his friends get worse every year. Nobody but the scumbags wants anything to do with him. Anyway, we tried counseling; he was in special class. Rob wouldn't go after a while. We yelled, we hit, we begged, we bribed, we told him we'd do anything for him if he just stopped getting stoned. Nothing helped. The school sucks too. They kept putting him into the next highest grade, even though he hadn't learned anything. Then he was even more lost. You don't know how many times I've said, "Tom, please tell me what's really bothering you," and all he says is, "Leave me alone." And I just wanted to slap him. Sometimes I did, other times I cried. Finally the guidance counselor said he should go to New Life. That was last year, after he got caught shoplifting. He fought us like hell, but Rob said it was jail or the T.C. So he went. It was like a miracle. When we got to visit him, or went to their family days, he was a different kid. There was one family session when he and Rob were crying and hugged each other, and told each other how much they loved each other, and then cried some more. Tom even told us that he knew how much he hurt us and felt really rotten about it.

Tom: I must have been out of my mind.

Mother (ignores him): It was wonderful. No chip on his shoulder, no sullen, miserable attitude. He went through their whole program—eighteen months to reentry. Now he's home and back in school, and the same rotten kid.

Father: And his scumbag friends are back.

Mother: We knew he was smoking before we found it. It's his attitude. As soon as he smokes . . .

Father (interrupting): He starts acting like an asshole. We even let him bring his girl to his room, and he fucks his brains out. What other parents would let him do that?

Structuralist, Intergenerationalist, Psychodynamic and Addictions Therapists all wonder: What kind of mixed message is being given here. It is also interesting to hear that Tom has a girl. All the counselors want to hear more about her. Is Tommy more together than we think?)

Mother: You have to help us. I'm going to pull my hair out of my head.

Experiential therapist: You have the resources to help yourselves.

Mother: No, we don't. That's why we're here. What should we do?

Asking Questions and Sorting Issues

Clearly the Bakers are troubled. On the surface, there is only one problem—drug use by the identified patient. However, a great deal more is going on that needs to be addressed. How can we understand the material presented by the Bakers? How would therapists from the various schools understand it? What would they do with it? On one level, the system is unbalanced, or skewed by a domineering, perhaps castrating mother, and it is not unreasonable to think that her interaction with the family and their reaction to it may be a big piece of the action. Is Tom's drug use a maladaptive way of coping with Mother, of avoiding her, of rebelling, of expressing rage at her? As the strategic therapist points out, the family members all too often talk about rather than to each other. Therapists of whatever school can't miss the lack of generational boundaries in this family. The parents' sex life is all over the room, with Dad being simultaneously presented as a pussy-whipped castrati and as a hypermasculine stud. In either case, he seems to be defined by Mother. What sort of anxiety does this blatant and exhibitionistic sexuality stir up in the boys? To grow to manhood must simultaneously mean that one will be castrated and that one cannot possibly compete with a father with whom Mother is "madly in love" (or is she?), and who is not so implicitly presented as a great lover. Better remain a helpless child, albeit a counterdependent, pseudo-autonomous one, by staying stoned, than be either castrated or inadequate.

The lack (or blurring) of generational boundaries is clear, and the lines are in need of repair. Perhaps the reason this family is stuck, or unable to move to the next stage of its life cycle, is that the very absence of boundaries makes progression appear much too dangerous. Does the family need Tom to stay stoned so they can stay stuck? What about Dad's rage and his physicality with his children? After all, one of Mother's reasons for making the appointment is her fear that "Dad will beat the shit out of him." What is Father so angry about? His wife's demeaning him? Her apparent dominance? His failure to be able to control his son? His envy of his son's freedom to act out after his renunciation of such freedom in exchange for carrying family responsibility? Or is this historical anger? We know that his childhood was painful and deprived. What is his anger a defense against? Pain? Hurt? What sort of pain or hurt? Ancient wounds? Something about his marriage? The implicit rejection of his love in his son's disobedience? His renunciation of his youthful wildness? Pain experienced in the reformatory?

Let's look at Father from Tom's side. Father was a drunk. Being a pothead is thus both an identification ("I get high like Dad did"), and a disidentification ("Dad never used grass"). He can be like Father and feel close to him in what is perhaps the only way he can feel that closeness, and simultaneously feel safely removed from him. It may be that one of the most powerful factors keeping Tom stoned is his semiconscious belief that he, like Father, can safely live a drug-dominated, acting-out adolescence and easily and painlessly emerge from it in his early twenties. That is a dubious proposition, at best—counselors frequently see a generational cycle in which the children, usually of alcoholic fathers who are still functioning, go rapidly downhill as either their drug use or drinking progresses to dysfunction. A related aspect of Tom's magical thinking is that he believes he does not need to get clean yet, perhaps a denial of the fact that he cannot get clean ("I can stop whenever I want, but I don't want to just yet"). Tom believes that he does not have to get clean and graduate from high school because Daddy can always get him into the union where he can "make out like a bandit."

What about Sam, the "good boy"? Given the amount of attention Tom gets from this family, it will be remarkable if Sam is not tempted to go in the same direction. "Good boy" is, to say the least, not the easiest of roles. He did indeed seem lost in the session. His occasional use of humor would be consistent with his being in the mascot role. For all this seeming isolation, one wonders about the sexualized teasing by Mother. What is that like for a pubescent boy? Again we have an example of the boundary problem in this family. What is Sam's role in the family's dynamics? Is he ever allowed to be bad? Does he occupy all the good space, leaving no good space for Tom? Does the family put Tom in a kind of double bind overtly enjoining him to be good while covertly telling him that his role is to be the bad boy? Perhaps Dad needs him to enact the self that he has relinquished.

Is Tom the least differentiated of the family members, or paradoxically, is it Sam, the good boy? Have Mom and Dad projected their undifferentiation from their respective families onto Tom? They don't come across as undifferentiated, yet it is possible. The parents are people who struggled mightily to emerge from the pathology of their families of origin, and they have in some ways admirably succeeded, yet they may be unconsciously recreating some of the undifferentiation in their own families. Does some of Dad's rage at Tom come from him "seeing" his alcoholic father recreated in his drug-addicted son? Another aspect of the *intergenerational drama* has to do with the significant amount of exclusively male alcoholism in Father's family, reminiscent of Cloninger's (1983) male-limited alcoholism, which has a heavy genetic loading. Although the heritability of other chemical addictions is inferential, one wonders how much such genetic loading predisposes Tom to addiction. Clearly he does not "smoke well." He is not a kid partying; he is an addict.

What are the *existential issues* here? What does Tom's addiction help him and his family avoid—separation, tension in the marriage, aging, the decline of the maternal grandparents who have become parents to both Harriet and Rob? Suspicion that their material success isn't enough and that something—something in the realm of meaning or values—is missing? Struggling to care for a sick (addicted) kid gives meaning and purpose to one's life. Would Tom's cure leave this family at sea and directionless?

Finally, what basic assumptions are being played out in this family? On the conscious level, this session is a task group working to help Tom get clean; at an unconscious level, there is a dependence of all on all, and of all on the whole, that is mostly unacknowledged or denied; fight-and-flight are all over the place. Coalitions—pairs and triangles—are also there. The main pairs, Mother and Father, Sam and Mother, and Tom and Mother, are also parts of fiery triangles. Familial fusion and fission, and the defenses against them are readily apparent. All families work on both task and basic assumptions levels, but in this family, the basic assumptions overwhelm the tasks.

Strategic Approach with the Bakers

The strategic therapist would immediately search for strategies for engaging and changing this family. The strategist would be concerned with taking control of the therapeutic situation. Mother's dominance is seen to effectively blunt communication in the Baker family. So the first strategy will focus on containing Mother and corresponding bringing out the other family members. The second problem is the behavior of the identified patient. Whatever function his addiction serves for the other family members, Tom's drug use is unquestionably problematic. It requires immediate attention and a strategy must be devised for dealing with it. Antecedent, to the work, though not entirely distinct from containing Mother and sobering Tom, is the strategic therapist's need to take control. The implication of power for therapeutic technique is that the first task of the therapist's is to gain control of the session and of the treatment. Concretely, this means activity and directiveness on the part of the therapist.

Mother's control is perhaps not only the easiest to see, but the easiest to deal with. She is up-front, the boss, making the appointment, presenting the problem, literally putting the family members in their places. Dad's style is physical intimidation. However much Mom

appears to be boss, Dad may very well have the final say: "One reason I called is I was afraid that Dad would beat the shit out of Tom." Dad has his own strategies for dominance and control, and the therapist must settle his hash also. One wonders if Haley would duke it out with him. Tom is perhaps the most interesting power broker. As the "perp," or perpetrator, as they say in police circles, or here the identified patient, Tom is at the center of things. That in itself gives him enormous power. In a very real sense, he, not Mother, controls the Baker family. This is secondary gain, and may very well be powerfully maintaining Tom's addiction. Getting the family's focus off of Tom may be curative, although he presumably would fight such a loss of control by escalating his acting out. The family needs to be told that the tail is wagging the dog, and Tom needs to know that he is getting off on the attention his drug use brings him. In strategic therapy we don't ask why, only what and how.

> *Strategist:* Nobody in this family talks to anyone else. You talk about each other, but not to each other.
> *Mother:* Talking to him is useless.
> *Strategist:* I want you to pretend that he doesn't exist. (This is a paradoxical intervention.)
> *Tom:* She never listens to me.
> *Father:* Why should she? Your brain has turned to shit and you don't make sense.

Note that they are now talking to each other, and that the therapist has taken control of the session. What about a double bind? Are the Bakers telling Tom that if he continues to smoke, he is hateful and bad, yet also telling him that if he quits the family will suffer in some catastrophic way? There is certainly a subtext here, and some family needs are being met by Tom's continuing use—Mother's for power, Father's to stay angry and perhaps vicariously act out, Sam's to continue as good boy and favorite, and there is perhaps some avoidance of latent conflict between the parents as well. Yet this family sincerely wants Tom to stop and this is not a classic double-bind situation. So the therapist in this case isn't going to go after the double bind. What he will do is to formulate a plan—a strategy—to effectuate change and to take control by using directives, perhaps even paradoxical directions.

> *Strategist*: I want you all to totally control Tom. Tell him how to run his life down to the last detail. Tell him when he's going to shit, when to get up, when to eat and what to eat, what programs to watch, what music to play. (This is a form of prescribing the symptom; the hoped-for result is for the family to realize that they can't control Tom. As they let go, he will cease to have a reason to rebel and insofar as his addiction is driven by rebellion, will smoke less or not at all.)
>
> (to Sam): I want you to do everything you're told, to clean the house, to help Tom in any way you can, to help Dad and Mom. I want you to be so good that your brother will learn how he should act. I want you to study more and work harder at your Bar Mitzvah lessons. (Presumably, our good boy Sam will be unable to stand such an overdose of goodness and will rebel. In his rebellion, he will gain some freedom for himself, shake up the family system, relinquish his form of control—good boys are rewarded and loved and parents jump through hoops for them—and occupy some of the bad boy-space now exclusively occupied by Tom, perhaps driving him out of it.)
>
> (to Tom): I want you to smoke as much pot as you can. Light up a joint when you get out of bed. Have one with breakfast. Stay stoned all day and all night and make sure you have a joint before you go to bed.

Presumably having permission to get high will take some of the kick out of it for Tom. No more rebellion. If he follows the instruction, he will be too stoned to get any pleasure out of it, and may voluntarily give it up, or he may rebel and be oppositional by not smoking—so if he follows the instruction he may get clean, and if he does not, he may get clean. The strategist has now taken control. He is enacting his power in his paradoxical directives. He has a strategy. He may have laid the ground for his interventions by asking the family what they were prepared to do to solve the problem. If they say they will do anything, he has set them up, and the Bakers are desperate enough to probably agree that they will

do anything to get Tom clean. If the strategy works, things are certainly going to escalate in the Baker family. Things may become hellish, but the status quo—the homeostasis that is also hellish—will be disturbed.

All in all, it is not a bad strategy, but what about prescribing around-the-clock pot smoking for Tom? This has some support in the A.A. statement that "John Barleycorn is the best convincer," and the not infrequent injunction to resistant members to "go out and tie one on." Nevertheless, we have doubts. Tom's level of psychopathology is an unknown. He may be a kid who could be driven into a psychotic break by saturation cannabis intake. It is risky. But Tom has had a lot of treatment and nothing has worked. Desperate situations sometimes call for desperate responses, and a case can be made for the strategist's paradoxical directives to the Bakers, including the one to Tom to smoke pot around the clock.

Structural Approach with the Bakers

The structural family therapist is also interested in power and control, both between therapist and family and within the family itself. Generally speaking, the structuralist will work to strengthen the parents.

> *Structuralist* (early on, when Mom has described Dad's circumcision; mostly to Mom but directed at all): What happened to the tip? Do you still have it?

This intervention does several things. As we saw earlier, when all the therapists were speaking together, it elicited some rebellion and humor on the part of Sam. More importantly, it takes power away from Mother, essentially neutralizing her. From the structuralist's viewpoint, this is an enmeshed family. Differentiation is difficult, and one reason Tom may hold onto his addiction is to differentiate himself from the enmeshment going on, in spite of the strong identification with Father in Tom's addiction. One way to demonstrate the enmeshment is to construct a structural map (see Figure 9–1 and Figure 9–2). The usefulness of the structural map is clear. The aloofness shown by Sam, the lack of hierarchy,

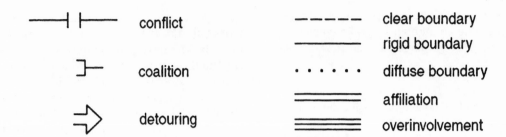

Figure 9–1. Minuchin's symbol system

and the weakness and confusion of the parental alliance are very clear in the map. The
structuralist moves to strengthen the parents
in their alliance and to help them "control" the
"bad boy."

> *Structuralist* (to parents): You have to stop
> Tom's drug use immediately.
>   *Mom and Dad:* We'd love to but we can't.
>   *Structuralist:* You support him, don't you?
>   *Mom:* Of course.
>   Structuralist: You'll support him into the
> grave. Tell him he can't live in *your* home if
> he smokes and that you won't give him a
> cent until he stops, except for treatment.

Here the structuralist is teaching "tough
love." Note "*your* home," which simultaneously points to a source of parental power
and speaks to parental alliance—they own
their home together and have the power to
decide who will live in it.

> *Mother:* We can't just throw him out.
>   *Father:* Why not?

> *Mother:* People will say we're monsters.
>   *Structuralist:* That's a cop-out.
>   *Tom:* You can shove your house up
> your ass.
>   *Structuralist:* If they do, you sure won't be
> able to live in it.
>   *Tom* (to Structuralist): Fuck you.
>   *Structuralist* (to parents): Are you serious
> about wanting Tom to get clean? If you are,
> you have to be tough. Tell him he's out, and
> you won't do a thing for him if he uses.
>   *Mother:* Right now?
>   *Structuralist:* You bet.
>   *Father* (to Mother): Harriet, let's do it.
>   *Mother* (looking shook): Okay.
>   *Structuralist:* Tell him.
>   *Father:* You're out of here if you use any
> more of that shit.
>   *Structuralist:* Mother?
>   *Mother:* I agree.
>   *Structuralist* (to Mother): Tell Tom, "Dad
> and I have decided no drugs in our house.
> And no users either."
>   *Mother* (weeping): Tom, the therapist is
> right. Dad and I won't let you live with us if
> you keep smoking.

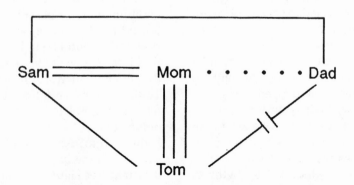

Figure 9–2. Structural map of the Baker family

Structuralist (raising the ante): And you have to arrange urine monitoring. I'll tell you how.

Tom: A piss test too?

Structuralist: If you're taking piss tests, you can't get pissed.

Tom (to Structuralist): Asshole. (But his bravado is crumbling. He is clearly upset.)

Structuralist (to Sam): Tell Tom you won't have anything to do with him if he uses.

Sam (gloating and joyful): I won't give you shit if you get stoned.

Structuralist (to Sam): You're really getting off on this, but that's not important now. The important thing is to get Tom clean. (To Tom): You have no place to go, kid.

Tom: (Cries.)

Structuralist (to Tom): We will do anything to help you stop. Perhaps you can't stop—if you need detoxification you can have it; if you need medication, that can be arranged; if you need to go back into the T.C. or to a rehab, that's okay too; or you can keep coming here.

Here the structuralist is using a little paradox—"Perhaps you can't stop"—although that may be true, and he is being supportive. Structuralists often support or ally with the identified patient to unbalance the system. Another structuralist approach that would do that might be:

Structuralist No. 2: "Being high must be great. What's it like?" or, "Your parents are really up your ass."

In both these interventions, the structuralist is tracking, joining the family, unbalancing, and forming an alliance with Tom all at once. Our first structuralist indirectly joined with Father in his question about the foreskin. A more direct approach would have been:

Structuralist (to Father, interrupting Mother): You don't get to say much, do you?

Or the first structural intervention could have been addressed to the lost child, Sam, the good boy.

Structuralist (to Sam): Do your parents ever pay any attention to you?

This also unbalances the family, disrupts their obsession with Tom, and shakes the homeostasis, making change at least possible. It may also serve to help the family member in the most long-term danger. Reframing is another typically structural intervention. If it were the case, the structuralist might say, "Tom stays stoned to keep the family together. If he gets clean, you two (indicating the parents) are going to have to talk to each other and deal with your problems. Tom is afraid you won't be able to do that and will divorce." Another reframing would be, "Tom uses because he thinks that's what everyone expects him to do—and he doesn't know how to fill any other role." This makes Tom less the bad child, cuts down on the recrimination, and makes Tom's use a system problem. It isn't used here because the structuralist chooses to address the crisis, but that does not preclude its later use.

Our structuralist has done a good job. He has played to the strengths of the family, successfully joined them, made good use of tracking, clarified and strengthened boundaries, and given the family a means of dealing with their crisis. Tom is probably going to get clean.

Experiential Approach with the Bakers

Unlike most other family therapists, an experientialist would wade right in, joining and engaging in the political battle.

Experientialist: Shit, I can't even control my own kids, how the hell do you think I'm going to control yours? Half the time, I can't even control myself.

Father: I can kick his ass the fuck out of the house.

Experientialist (Thinks: *I won that political battle. Dad's taking responsibility.*) (To Dad): That's not a bad idea.

Mom: We can't do that.

Experientialist (Thinks: *I should have known that was too easy.*) (To Mom): Well, if you don't want to exile the kid to Siberia, you could try to make things more peaceful at home.

Mom: How?

Experientialist: You could build him a greenhouse to grow pot in.

Father: You're nuts.

Experientialist: Dad, you could design it, and all of you could build it. It would bring the family together. You could all work on it. Mom could order the best seeds, Tijuana Gold. And Sam, you could water them every day. Dad, you could run in the electric power and pipe, and Tom, you could hoe. And it should have air conditioning and a state of the art stereo system.

Mother: We couldn't do that; we'd go to jail.

Experientialist: That's good. Tom's heading for jail, so that would help you understand him.

Tom: Assholes. He thinks you're helping me use by letting me live in the house, so he's making fun of you.

Experientialist (to Tom): Who, me?

Sam: I think we should build a tower on the greenhouse for Tom to hang himself from.

Experientialist: Maybe your parents could hang themselves too.

Mother (starts crying): I really do wish I was dead. I am so ashamed. I am so scared. I know Tom's going to die if he keeps this up and I can't live through that.

Experientialist (to Tom): What kind of funeral do you want? Shall we throw grass seeds on the grave?

Tom: Let me out of here. He's nuts.

Experientialist: Or maybe you'd like to go to Mom's funeral if they let you out of jail to attend.

Tom: Oh fuck.

Father (to therapist): He ain't no tough guy. I've been on the street and in the can. I know what it's like. It sucks, it really sucks.

Mother: Stop! I don't want to hear about it. Oh . . . Oh. Tom, you can't live in our house if you get high. You're out.

Experientialist: What would become of the greenhouse?

Tom: I can't stop. I feel like shit when I don't smoke. (Pauses.) Just don't make me go back to that school and I'll try.

Father: Trying is bullshit. You can stop.

Mom (sobbing): Tom, just stay clean and I won't ask anything else.

Tom: Yeah, okay.

Mother: (Embraces Tom. He pulls away, then returns the embrace.)

Sam: Oh, shit.

Mother: (pulls Sam into the embrace.)

Father: Maybe it'll work this time.

Experientialist (to Dad, wiping away a tear): Maybe. (Looking at Mother and the boys.) I feel left out. How 'bout you and I hugging? (They do.)

Here our experiential therapist tries some theater of the absurd. Sensing that the family is enabling Tom in one way or another, he makes that enabling transparently clear, and that clarity shakes the family, moving them to remove their destructive support. The experientialist also intuits some of the subterranean themes in the Baker family: their fears (and perhaps wishes) that Tom would die, Dad's acquaintance with the night, Sam's hostility to Tom, and the desperate need of all four for love. A great deal of this surfaces in response to the experientialist's absurdity. This openness could be therapeutically exploited and expanded in a variety of ways, perhaps by probing for the parents' fears of death, which may be motivating their ambivalent enabling. For Tom to really move toward adulthood underscores their own passage through time and the life cycle. There is some mourning work to be done before they can let Tom go.

Intergenerational Systems Approach with the Bakers

The genogram is integral to the intergenerational approach, and the systemic therapist would make construction of the genogram one of his or her first therapeutic tasks; examples are illustrated in Figures 9–3 and 9–4.

Intergenerationalist: Did anyone in your family of origin drink heavily? Who? Have there been any deaths associated with drinking or drugging? Divorces?

Dad: My Dad's liver went and it killed him. My brothers are heading in the same direction.

The intergenerational therapist needs to forge a therapeutic alliance. The construction of a genogram with the family builds this alliance. The therapist is the expert, engaged in a cooperative venture with the family, the construction of the genogram. It is a tool that can be used to demonstrate the dim odds of Tom becoming an occasional pot smoker. It is an artifact that is hard to dispute, and it serves

☐ — male   ◯ — female

Ages are placed in box or circle, for example

40 for father and (40) for mother in the Baker case.

Names appear above box/circle. For example:

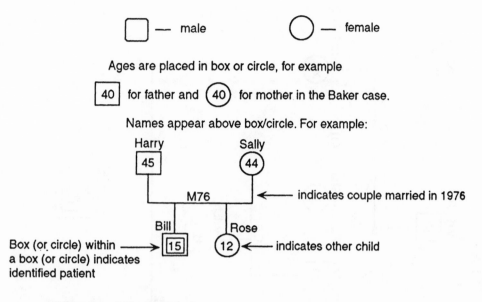

indicates couple married in 1976

Box (or circle) within a box (or circle) indicates identified patient

indicates other child

Other conventional symbols:

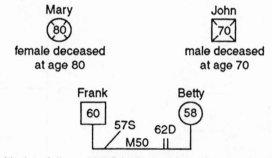

Mary — female deceased at age 80

John — male deceased at age 70

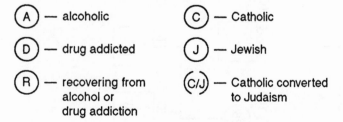

Slant line with date followed by S indicates date of separation. Parallel lines perpendicular to marriage line with date followed by D indicates date of divorce.

We will add symbols for substance abuse and religion.

(A) — alcoholic   (C) — Catholic

(D) — drug addicted   (J) — Jewish

(R) — recovering from   (C/J) — Catholic converted
      alcohol or   to Judaism
      drug addiction

Figure 9–3. Genogram symbols

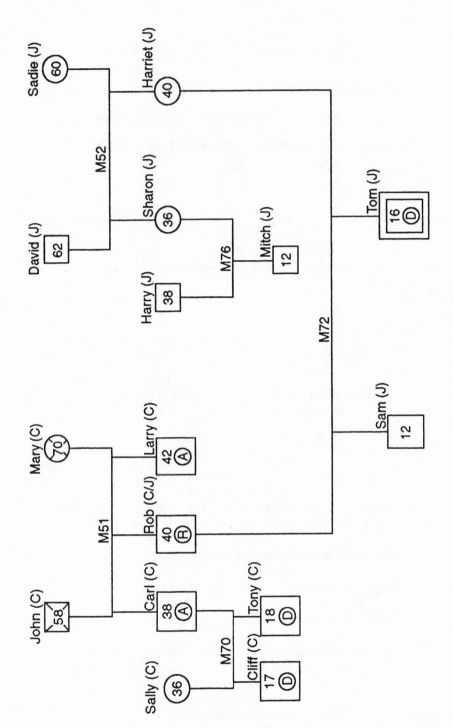

Figure 9–4. The Baker family genogram

as a form of dispassionate evidence. In the case of the Bakers, the information necessary for the construction of the genogram was easily elicited. This is by no means always the case. Family secrets are not easily divulged. This is particularly true of substance-abusing families, as recognized by the Twelve step slogan, "You are as sick as your secrets." It isn't so much the content as the secretiveness itself that sometimes literally drives people crazy. Families that lie, distort, deceive, and withhold often make the construction of a meaningful genogram difficult. Substance abuse in significant others, spousal abuse, child abuse—physical and sexual—and suicide are not readily shared. However, you don't have to be an intergenerationalist to love genograms; therapists of many schools find them useful. This is particularly true for substance abuse counselors who are rightfully interested in addiction in the family.

Our systemic intergenerationalist works in the dispassionate manner of a researcher in eliciting the information needed to construct the genogram. Further, he or she works individually; that enables the therapist to question each family member separately rather than eliciting a "familial" response; the intention is to encourage individuation, or, to use Bowen's word, *differentiation*, to in a way sculpt individuals out of the "family mass." The intergenerationalist's goal in this first session is evaluation.

> *Intergenerationalist:* Mr. Baker, can we analyze the drinking in your family? If we do, we can clearly see that all of the men have trouble with alcohol. Your son's drugging is entirely consistent with your family history.
> *Mother* (humorously, to husband): I knew the problem was on your side.
> (To therapist): Okay, it runs on Dad's side. How does that help us?
> *Intergenerationalist* (refusing to be triangulated): Mrs. Baker, I'm talking to Mr. Baker about his family.
> *Mother* (to Tom): You see, you just can't get high; you have the addiction gene from Dad.
> *Intergenerationalist:* Mrs. Baker, you're bringing Tom into it because you don't want to deal with my saying to you that I was talking to your husband. First you broke up

my dialogue with your husband, and now you're bringing in your son It's hard for you to stay with or tolerate two-person relationships. You either become the third person or you bring one in.

Here the intergenerationalist interrupts the elucidation and elaboration of the intergenerational analysis to comment on and indeed arrest attempts at triangulation in the here-and-now of the family session. He sees triangulation rather than castration by Mrs. Baker. In her own undifferentiation, she has trouble allowing the differentiation of others. From this point of view, although her aggression appears to be in the service of separation, it is actually driven by the need for fusion, which is seen as central to the family dynamic. Tom is a clear case of emotional cutoff, resulting in a false self or a pseudo self-sufficiency. He is neither fused nor differentiated, and uses drugs to do both: he fuses with the drug and simultaneously isolates himself from his family.

> *Intergenerationalist* (to Tom): When you get high, you feel independent. Then you're able to get some distance from your family. But just when you're feeling like yourself, you lose yourself in the fog of your high.

More typical of the Bowen approach would be to see Tom's drug problem as a correlate of his parents' relative undifferentiation and their projection of undifferentiation onto him. So a Bowenian therapist might say:

> *Intergenerationalist:* In our session today, I've been able to see some patterns both in your immediate family and in your extended family. I'd like to coach you in ways to change some of those patterns, the ones that are making it difficult for Tom to grow up. The best way I can do that is by meeting with Tom's parents. Mr. and Mrs. Baker, would you be willing to meet with me without the children?
> *Mr. Baker:* If you're trying to put it on us, you're crazy, Doc.
> *Intergenerationalist:* Not at all. I always suggest meetings with the parents to help them help their children become independent.
> *Tom:* If you want to cook up some scheme for my folks to run my life, go ahead. It ain't gonna work.

Intergenerationalist: My meeting with your parents scares you so you butt in.

Tom: Fuck you.

Mr. Baker: Let's do it.

Mrs. Baker: What the hell, okay.

And the arrangement is made. The intergenerationalist will coach the parents in differentiating themselves from their families of origin, thereby reducing or eliminating their need to triangulate Tom and to project undifferentiation onto him. Sam, who may actually be the less differentiated child, although not caught up in emotional cutoff, would also benefit from this strategy. An alternative intergenerational strategy would be to coach Tom individually, focusing not on his drug use but on his lack of differentiation. Yet another intergenerational strategy would be to continue to work with the genogram, not to increase the Bakers' awareness of the neurochemical genetic, but of the larger intergenerational transmission patterns that are culminating in Tom's addiction.

Behavioral Approach with the Bakers

In behavioral family therapy the therapist would focus on Tom's problem behavior as the target for change. The *identified patient* is indeed the patient, although the family may be unwittingly reinforcing the objectionable behavior. So our behaviorist's work will be with the whole family and yet will focus on Tom. The therapist will attempt to elicit drug signals, teach coping skills, and suggest ways the family can help Tom achieve abstinence. Constructing contingency schedules and other learning opportunities for the family is the essence of this approach. The therapist's role is that of a teacher.

Behaviorist: There's an awful lot of anger directed at Tom. It's hard to stay clean when everyone is putting you down. I wonder if you would agree to say something positive to Tom three times each day until our next session.

Dad: I've heard that positive reinforcement shit before. He never does anything right, so what could we reinforce?

Mom: He's not that bad.

Sam: (Giggles.)

Behaviorist: Mr. Baker, I'm not asking you to reinforce behavior, just to say something positive. For example, "Thank you, Tom, for coming to therapy tonight." Or, "You look spiffy today."

Sam: Spiffy?

Mom (to Dad): You're too quick to hit. Why not try this? Do it for me.

Dad: Well, he's handsome when he doesn't look strung out. That's not surprising since he looks like me. I'll tell him that.

Behaviorist: Sam, what about you?

Sam: Yeah?

Behaviorist: (hands out forms). There are three spaces in each of two columns on these forms. I want you to write down your positive comments to Tom and we'll discuss them next week.

(To Tom): Tom, I need you to do something too. I want you to tell your parents and your brother that you appreciate their saying positive things. Just check it off each time you do that on this form. (Hands form to him.)

Tom: What if I don't feel it?

Behaviorist: Say it anyway.

Tom: That's like the N.A. (Narcotics Anonymous) slogan, "Bring the body and the mind will follow."

Behaviorist: Exactly. Will you do it?

Tom: Okay.

Notice how the behaviorist cools the situation by being rational, calm, and reasonable, and how he ignores a lot of the emotion coming from the Bakers. He elicits cooperation by asking little, and his minimalist approach may open a door allowing broader change. He goes on to deal with drug signals.

Behaviorist (to Tom): You don't want to get high all the time, do you?

Sam: Yes, he does.

Tom: Shut up, creep. No, not all the time.

Behaviorist: So something must happen to make you want to smoke. We call that something a "trigger"; N.A. talks about "places, people, and things" that make people want to use drugs. I want you to notice when you want to get high and write it down on this chart. For now, I am not asking you to stop getting high, only to record each urge, each usage, and what set you off. It's kind of like a scientific experiment—are you game?

Tom: I don't have to stop using?

Behaviorist: Not this week.

Dad (to therapist): Are you sure you know what you're doing?

Behaviorist (to Dad): I'm sure.

Sam: Why don't you give me some pot and those forms, and I'll do the experiment too.

Behaviorist: Now Tom, I've got one more chart for you. This one is to record how you feel after you use, if you do.

Mom: He'll be so busy writing it all down, he won't even get a chance to light it.

Behaviorist: So Mr. and Mrs. Baker, you have to agree to let this run—not to yell at Tom if he smokes this week.

Mom and Dad: Okay.

Behaviorist: Now Sam, I do have a chart for you. I want you to record Tom's behavior and moods before and after he smokes, just like you see them, if he does smoke grass. All you have to do is put a check mark next to the word that describes them best. See, column one, date and time, column two, before, column three, after.

Sam: Most of the time he gets high out of the house.

Behaviorist: But I'll bet you know when he does.

Sam: Yeah.

Behaviorist: Then record as much as you see.

Sam: I love this.

Behaviorist: I think we have a deal. I call it a contract, and I want everyone to sign it. Mr. Baker, you agree to say three positive things to Tom each day, record them, and not interfere with Tom's use or non-use this week. Sign here. Mrs. Baker, the same for you. (They sign.) And Sam, you're going to try and say one positive thing to Tom each day, record it, and if you see him high, check what you see. Okay? (Sam signs.) And Tom, your contract stipulates that you thank Sam and your parents for the positive things they say to you, and that you record your urges and usage just as I explained.

Tom: I'll sign.

Behaviorist: Great. I think we're on the right track. I'll see you all the same time next week.

Well, our behaviorist has laid it all out. Next week he can go on to contingency contracting—rewards for abstinence and sanctions for use, and start to teach coping behaviors, self-efficacy skills, and alternate behavior to Tom, along with teaching the family ways of helping Tom cope as well as going over their homework, both for its intrinsic value and as a way of building a "we-ness" in solving Tom's problem without undermining Tom's responsibility for his own behavior. Our behaviorist will also use Tom's self-observations and Sam's observations as feedback loops to bring triggers that are presently automatic and out of awareness into consciousness and awareness. After that, the next step is to work on alternate responses to those triggers. Notice that the family craziness is ignored, and that the behaviorist focuses almost entirely on the identified patient's problems and the family's response to them. This elicits cooperation and lowers resistance by turning the whole thing into a kind of game.

Psychodynamic Approach with the Bakers

The psychodynamic approach to the Bakers is here represented by an *object relations therapist*. In general, psychodynamic therapists are not too active in an opening session, since interpretation requires knowledge of the family's dynamics and the acquisition of this knowledge takes time. Having said this, it is important to remember that the opposite of activity is not passivity; rather, it is receptivity and therapeutically tactful interpretation. Typically, the dynamic family therapist provides drawing materials, and if there are younger children, play materials. Our object relations therapist has done so, and Sam has been doodling during session, as shown in Figure 9–5 and 9–6.

Object Relations Therapist: Would you share your drawings with us, Sam? (Sam blushes but hands over the drawings. The therapist passes them around.) Any thoughts about Sam's drawings?

Mom: I'm all teeth. Twice.

Dad (to Sam): You got Tom right with that smirk and that joint hanging out of his mouth.

Tom: You sure can't draw.

Fascinated by Sam's representation of his mother as a semihuman devouring beast, the

Figure 9–5. Sam's drawing (part one)

object relations therapist played a hunch that Tom was so afraid of his castrating, devouring Mother that he needed to get high in order to have sex.

Object Relations Therapist: Sam's drawing makes me anxious, and my anxiety must be mild compared to yours. Your whole family lives in a condition of high anxiety. Tom, I don't quite know why, but when I realized how anxious everyone is, I thought, "Tom smokes to control his anxiety," and I wondered if you were so anxious that you had to get high to have sex. Have you ever had intercourse straight?

Tom (blushes beet red): No, I never got laid unless I was high. It makes it better. (Angrily.) You ought to try it, Doc.

Object Relations Therapist: That's kind of sad, Tom, that you can't even enjoy your own body without getting high. Really sad.

Mother: The doctor is right. It really is sad that you can't get laid without getting high.

Father: He can't do anything without getting high!

Object Relations Therapist (to Father): Do you realize you're attacking Tom when he's just made himself vulnerable? No wonder he closes down emotionally.

Tom: He's like that. That's why Sam drew him with his fist cocked.

Object Relations Therapist (Thinks: *Mother's all sexual aggression. Dad's aggression aggression. If I were Tom, I'd be stoned all the time too.*) (to Dad): Mr. Baker, any more thoughts about this drawing?

Father: I always said my wife had a big mouth. But it bothers me that Sam sees me as all fist. I got a heart too, you know. Hey, Doc—What's the kid so anxious about? Like I told you, he's got it made except for the grass.

Mom: Sam, you drew yourself like a baby. You're kind of lost too.

Sam: Who'd want to grow up in this family?

Object Relations Therapist: I don't understand that. Do you mean it feels better to be a baby?

Sam: Naw, I just meant I don't want to be like him (sticks his tongue out at Tom).

Mom

Also Mom

Figure 9–6. Sam's drawing (part two)

Object Relations Therapist: Tom, what's it like to have a dad with such big fists?

Tom: Scary, man, scary. He's violent.

Father: Don't scapegoat me, you asshole.

Object Relations Therapist: You need to be angry at each other.

Mom: Yeah, they're always fighting.

Object Relations Therapist: (to Father): I think you see a part of yourself you don't like in Tom, and that infuriates you.

Father: Yeah, he's the asshole I used to be. I don't like to think about what a punk total-loss kid I was.

Tom: Dad, I'm not you. I don't know how to be you. You make money. People respect you. You can go to a party and nurse a beer all night.

Object Relations Therapist: (to Father): That punk kid's still a part of you. You must have had it pretty rough. Can you feel any compassion for him?

Father: No, he's just a loser.

Object Relations Therapist: Seeing him in Tom infuriates you.

Father: I get it. You want me to lay off him.

Object Relations Therapist: I wonder if you also see something of your drunken father in Tom and then you really hate him.

Father (looks shook, even shattered. His hands shake): Christ, you're right. I'm afraid of Tom when he's stoned out of his mind, and I ain't afraid of anything. I don't like admitting that.

Object Relations Therapist: So you're afraid of each other.

Tom: I'm not afraid. (Hesitates.) Shit, yes I am.

Object Relations Therapist: (to Tom): I think you're sitting on so much rage you're afraid you're going to explode, so you tranquilize your rage with pot, run away from it, or put it on your dad. The way you do that is to provoke him until he is in a rage, which isn't too hard to do. And then your rage, which you can't handle, is in him and not you, and you can run away from it. You can't run away from the rage inside, but if you put it on him or in him, it's outside you and you can deal with it. Besides having Dad foaming gives you a reason to get high and you want to do that for other reasons, including the fact that you're hooked. So each of you puts a part of yourself into the other because it's easier than having the rage inside for Tom and the hurt, confused, wild child within for Dad. Mr. Baker, in a funny way, except it isn't funny, you need Tom to stay a stoned, hurt, lost kid— although I know that another part of you really and sincerely wants him to get clean—to protect you from feeling the sorrow and pain inside you.

Tom: Dad, I need you. I know you love me, but I can't get close to you. You're too strong.

Object Relations Therapist: And frightening.

Tom: (Weeps).

Mother: (Rises to comfort him.)

Object Relations Therapist: (gently): No, Mother, this is men's stuff. Don't get between them. You're afraid to let your husband be emotional, to be a wimp like your father—you need him to be "strong," so you rush in and Tom and Dad never make contact.

Mother (sits on her hands): You're right. That's why I love Rob, he's so masculine. I'm the boss, but that doesn't make him a wimp. (Father and Tom talk to each other intensely but not audibly.)

Father (embraces Tom): So you have to stop. I don't want you to die like my Dad.

Substance Abuse Approach with the Bakers

The substance abuse counselor would incorporate elements of all of the schools in his or her treatment, yet would keep the focus on the substance abuse. Tom and his family have had a great deal of treatment that doesn't give our substance abuse counselor his usual scope. Such typical interventions as exposition of the disease model of addiction, explanation of and referral to Twelve step program meetings, making the family aware of their enabling, and giving the family mem-

bers an opportunity to express and work through their feelings of shame, rage, and guilt enlisted by and directed toward the substance abuser have been repeatedly made. That doesn't mean that all of that doesn't need to be done again. Given the power of resistance and denial, and the need for working through, reiteration is certainly in order, yet this family is not a "virgin" to therapy and none of this has worked before. As with all of our therapists, the substance abuse therapist listens very carefully, and he asks some characteristic questions.

Substance abuse therapist: I need to know a lot more about Tom's treatment and your treatment as a family as well. (The Bakers detail the therapists, the programs, the experiences they have had.)

Substance abuse therapist: Did anything help?

Dad: Only the T.C., but it didn't last.

Substance abuse therapist: Tom?

Tom: I hated the T.C. They shaved my head and made me wear stupid signs.

Substance abuse therapist: They used shame as a therapeutic tool.

Tom: Well I didn't feel shame. I felt rage.

Substance abuse therapist: And you started smoking again to get back at them.

Tom: You're damn right.

Substance abuse therapist: That's pretty stupid, isn't it?

Tom: Yeah. I know that.

Substance abuse therapist: And to get back at your parents for putting you there.

Tom: Yeah.

Substance abuse therapist (to all): Do you know addiction is a disease?

Bakers: Yeah.

Substance abuse therapist: Tell me what you know.

Bakers (Demonstrate a good collective and individual understanding of the disease concept of addiction.)

Substance abuse therapist: Tom, if you really believe addiction is a disease, then you know that you've lost control and that if you continue to smoke, you're going to go down the tubes.

Tom: Yeah, I know.

Substance abuse therapist: Your smoking is like getting back at somebody by giving yourself cancer.

The substance abuse therapist is concentrating on the identified patient, yet he involves the family. They are seen as part of the solution, not part of the problem. For the moment, their pain and rage is ignored or acknowledged but not dealt with. They will have ample opportunity to deal with their issues after Tom gets clean; right now, those issues are put aside. Enlisting them as helpers raises their self-esteem and generally strengthens them.

The substance abuse therapist takes Tom through his experience in the T.C. in considerable detail and elicits information that it was not altogether a negative experience for Tom. In particular, Tom pleasurably bonded with some of his fellow T.C. patients. It also became clear that Tom found the rigid structure of the T.C. helpful, however much he hated the therapeutic methods it used. This argues that firmness would be helpful for him.

Substance abuse therapist: I want to hear from all of you and from Tom himself just how he got into drugs and what his relationship to drugs has been over the years.

The taking of a painstakingly detailed drug history, bolstered by many questions from the substance abuse therapist, constitutes both a cooperative effort between the family and therapist and a vital source of information. It differs from the detailed history-taking of the genogram drawing by the intergenerationalist in that it concentrates on Tom's drug history. As Tom's drug history unfolded, it became clear that Tom was enacting a dismally familiar story. He was the marginal kid, always the outsider, academically pushed by his upwardly mobile parents, yet with scant academic skills and limited potential. The therapist wondered about learning disability and attention deficit disorder, problems commonly linked with substance abuse, and the possibility of remediating or treating them.

In finding pot, Tom also found acceptance, even leadership, and an easy escape from self-esteem–deflating activities all at once at age 3. It was love at first sight. Within a year, Tom was trapped—incorrigibly identified with what he and his parents call the scumbag crowd, hopelessly behind in school, and completely scorned by the college-bound crowd. There was no way back. The rest followed as night follows day: three years of progressive decline, rageful arguments at home, trouble in school, eventuating in round-the-clock pot smoking, Tom's collapse, and his entry into the T.C. For all his hatred of it, the T.C. had possibly saved Tom's life. Tom's re-entry into school, with which he could not cope socially or academically, left him with no place to go except back to the scumbag crowd, and he quickly relapsed.

Equipped with this detailed history of Tom's drug use and treatment and remembering Tom's pleading not to have to go back to school early in the session, the substance abuse therapist made a dramatic, early move, intervening in a directive way with the Bakers. Further, sensing Tom's unconscious belief that he, like his Father, could recover, join the union and live happily ever after whenever he wanted to, so he didn't need to stop smoking pot, the substance abuse therapist wove a firm repudiation of this belief into his interventions.

Substance abuse therapist: Tom, I'll make a deal with you. You want to drop out of school but you can't without your parents' permission. I'll help you get that permission . . .

Mother and Father: Over my dead body.

Substance abuse therapist: . . . If you agree to get a job, to go to meetings (meaning Twelve step meetings), and to stop smoking grass.

Sam: He's too dumb for school anyway. I get *A*'s.

Tom (to Sam): Shut up.

Substance abuse therapist: Will you do it?

Tom (Remains silent.)

Substance abuse therapist: You think you can do anything you want, stay stoned right around the clock, then get clean when you're ready, and your old man will get you a job in the union and you'll be just fine. I think your family believes that at some level too, though they don't know it. It isn't true. The longer you smoke, the sicker you'll get, and there may be no turning back. Or you'll have to much catch-up to do so that you'll be overwhelmed and really screwed. Each day you smoke, you get sicker. How about a deal? I'll help you get your Father's permission. We can work together in therapy and you'll be out of an impossible situation.

Tom (screams): Okay! Okay! Just get them to agree.

Mother and Father: No!

Substance abuse therapist (to parents): I know it breaks your heart to have Tom drop out of school, but you *have* to let him. He just *can't* do it. He's too far behind academically. The straight kids won't accept him and he has no place to go except back to the scumbags, and that means being stoned. I know how much you love Tom, and I know you'll do this for him. He can get a high school equivalency (G.E.D.) at night when he's in stable recovery. I'll get him into the GED. program when he's ready.

Mother: (Cries.)

Father: Okay, but he's got to get a job.

Mother: I can get him a job in the warehouse where I work.

Tom: I'll take it.

Notice how strongly our substance abuse counselor speaks—"you *have* to let him"— and how much responsibility he takes for Tom's life. The counselor may be wrong, and dropping out could be a disaster for Tom, but the substance abuse counselor senses that the present situation is hopeless, and there is nothing to lose by taking such a bold step. It is highly doubtful that Tom would be allowed to continue in school for very long in any case. Notice also how direct he is with Tom, and simultaneously how unashamedly manipulative he is in forging an alliance with Tom. He is similarly manipulative with the parents, appealing to both their love and their guilt. All he needs now is closure.

Substance abuse therapist: I'll see Tom individually for two weeks and then we will have another family session. Okay, Tom? (Tom nods.) And we will keep that format— two sessions with Tom and then a family session. Tom has absolute confidentiality unless his life is in danger so he can be free to say anything here. I try to respect everyone else's confidentiality, but since we will be meeting as a family, it is less of an issue and Tom is the primary patient. I'll see you next week, Tom.

As therapy proceeds, the substance abuse-therapist will engage the Bakers to give them an opportunity to express their feelings about Tom's addiction and to give them some support. The substance abuse therapist will probably be especially supportive of Sam, who as a lost child needs bringing out, but for now, Tom is the primary patient and the family's role ancillary to his recovery.

For the substance abuse counselor, each of the therapeutic approaches—strategic, structural, intergenerational, experiential, behavioral, psychodynamic—has its place in working with addicted families.

Chapter Summary

9–1

The notion that addiction is a family disease has several meanings: first, addiction is familial insofar as it can be transmitted genetically and psychosocially from parent to child; second, addiction can be a reflection of a highly dysfunctional family system; last, addiction in one family member causes serious problems in all other members. Families with addiction act according to the principle of homeostasis, which serves to maintain the status quo or equilibrium in the family. According to general systems theory, families are defined by ongoing reciprocal and recursive interactions by virtue of which members are both cause and effect of one another's actions. Addicted families are often marked by members' roles, such as Hero, Lost Child, and Scapegoat Steinglass views the alcoholic (addicted) family as trying to adapt to events in the family life cycle. Bradshaw considers addiction to be a shame-based condition traceable to severe dysfunction in the family system.

9–2

Strategic family therapy emphasizes the use of communication as an intervention to correct unhealthy homeostasis in the family system. In structural family therapy the therapist directs change in the system by altering the dysfunctional family structures, such as boundaries, triangles, and roles. The emphasis of experiential family therapy is on the family's immersion in the immediate here-and-now emotional process during sessions. Intergenerational systems therapy frames current family problems in terms of a lack of differentiation due to patterns transmitted across several generations. In behavioral family, therapy the identified patient is the focus of change and family members are taught better coping skills. Insight is the primary objective of psychodynamic family therapy, in which families are helped to be more aware of the unconscious and developmental origins of their problems.

9–3

The Baker family is the focus of treatment by family therapists from each school. The strategic therapist helps them understand how their maladaptive patterns of communicating contribute to their son's drug problem. The structural therapist attacks the drug problem by unbalancing and reorganizing the family's power structure and role system. The experiential therapist enables the Bakers to get in touch with and express the powerful emotional themes that bind them to each other and to their son's addiction. By examining the family's history and development over a couple of generations, the intergenerational systems therapist demonstrates to the Bakers how they are repeating pathological patterns all over again. The behavioral family therapist teaches the Bakers how to reinforce positive behaviors in one another and to maintain desirable changes that occur. The psychodynamic therapist helps the family understand how the parents' relationship to each other

and to their children is affected by their relationships to their own parents. Drawing on ideas from all the approaches, the substance abuse counselor targets change in the son's drug use and helps the family devise a feasible plan to start him on the path to recovery.

Terms To Remember

behavioral family therapy
boundaries
dependency-conflict theory
differentiation
ethology
experiential family therapy
familial aggregation
general systems theory
genogram
homeostasis
intergenerational systems family therapy
object relations family therapy
psychodynamic family therapy
role
scapegoating
strategic family therapy
structural family therapy
therapeutic double-bind
toxic shame

RECOMMENDED READING

Ackerman, N. (1994). *The Psychodynamics of Family Life: Diagnosis and Treatment of Family Relationships*. Northvale, NJ: Jason Aronson.

Bradshaw, J. (1988b). *Healing the Shame That Binds You*. Deerfield Beach, FL: Health Communications.

Whitaker, C. A. and Bumberry, W. M. (1988). *Dancing with the Family: A Symbolic-Experiential Approach*. New York: Brunner/Mazel.

CHAPTER TEN

Chemical Dependency and Society

Chapter Outline

Learning Objectives

Upon completing study of this chapter you should be able to:

1. Outline the main events in the social history of drugs from the ancient world through the twentienth century.

2. Discuss the cultural purposes of drug use.

3. Describe the major sociological theories of drug use.

4. Explain the methods used to estimate the economic impact of chemical dependency.

5. Characterize the relationships among drug use, aggression, and violence.

6. Discuss the links between chemical dependency and crime.
7. Identify the main elements in American society's legal, political, and educational responses to chemical dependency.
8. Describe the response to chemical dependency by the health professions.

In previous chapters you learned about the development and causation of chemical dependency from the perspective of the chemically dependent individual, upon whom many influences converge. As you have already seen, some of those influences on individuals are sociocultural forces. In this chapter we take a different look at chemical dependency and society by examining drug use within a broader perspective focused not on the individual but on society and culture. In the sections that follow you will learn about the social history of drug use, the links between drugs and culture, and the costs of drugs to society, as well as society's response to the drug problem.

10–1 Social History of Drugs

Public opinion polls often find that people consider drug abuse one of the leading issues of the day. Although alcohol, marijuana, and many other drugs have been used for thousands of years, the perception that drug use is a societal problem is a relatively modern one. Today's concern about "the drug problem" is an outcome of numerous sociohistorical events and attitudes that have evolved over many years.

Throughout most of recorded human history drugs were used in the framework of clearly defined social activities for spiritual, medicinal, and communal purposes. The average person lived and died in the context of close-knit kinship and social groups with deep traditions and shared values. In the aftermath of the sixteenth- and seventeenth-century European age of discovery and with the onset of the Industrial Revolution in the Eighteenth century, traditional societies gave way to our more familiar modern world with its modern ills, including the drug problem. In this section we present a brief historical summary of drug use and its place in society from ancient to modern times.

The Ancient World

Exactly when and how people first began to use drugs remains a mystery, but anthropological and archeological evidence indicates that some forms of drug use were familiar to cultures in many parts of the world from ancient times. Although we cannot know for certain why prehistoric men and women used psychoactive drugs, they probably did first through accidental means and later by intentional design.

Alcoholic beverage production was under way at least five thousand years ago when the process of controlled fermentation was mastered. Except for groups of native people in North America and the Pacific islands, the inhabitants of most regions of the world had some kind of alcoholic beverage. In ancient societies as different as the Egypt of the pharaohs and Aztec Mexico, alcohol was associated with religious and spiritual rituals and was often offered as a gift to the gods. In ancient societies where drugs were imbued with religious ritual significance, the production and use of drugs was limited by strong social traditions and laws. As long ago as 2000 B.C., the legal code of the Babylonian king Hammurabi restricted the making and selling of wine and beer (Jaffe 1995b).

The Aztecs of pre-Columbian Mexico present a good example of the religious use of alcohol and the imposition of strict social controls to regulate it. The Aztecs used a potent alcoholic drink called *pulque* which they employed ritually in conjunction with a dozen annual religious ceremonies. In Aztec culture, however, pulque drinking was restricted by a rigid social code, and the penalty for pulque drunkenness was death. The *Codex Mendoza*, a sixteenth-century Aztec manuscript, described the rules of pulque misuse: "According to the laws and customs of the lords of Mexico, they forbade drunkenness except to those of seventy years of age, man or woman, if such people had children and grandchildren . . . [A younger person] who drank excessively died for it (Anawalt 1997, p. 24).

Although we cannot know for sure how successful the Aztecs' social controls against drinking were, the harshness of the punishment for drunkenness suggests that perhaps there was a problem that required severe measures. You might wonder how well their social controls worked if they needed to implement such a draconian punishment as the death penalty.

In addition to alcoholic beverages, other drugs also have a long history, and virtually every ancient culture seems to have employed one or more psychoactive substances. In addition to the place these substances had in religious rituals, many ancient people relied on alcoholic beverages as dietary supplements. Alcohol and other drugs served as medicines as well as sources of commercial wealth and influence. In the Middle East and Africa, cannabis and stimulants like caffeine and *qat* were widely used. Native North Americans used tobacco and some hallucinogenic drugs, such as peyote, and South American peoples long knew of the stimulant properties of coca leaves. Historical records from Asian countries such as India and China show that cannabis and opium were popular for medicinal and ritual purposes (Way 1982).

In the ancient world the use of alcohol and other drugs was closely associated with and colored by cultural and religious symbolism and limited by traditions. The altered state of consciousness produced by drugs was revered as a means of making contact with the spiritual world, and many drugs were perceived as gifts to mankind from the gods. Like other sacred actions, drug use was subject to communal customs that were widely respected and followed by members of the group. However, with the gradual encroachment of the modern world most aspects of life in traditional societies changed, including patterns of drug use (Westermeyer 1991).

The Early Modern World

The emergence of what we call the modern world was a gradual process extending over a long stretch of time. Although it implies a somewhat culturally biased view of history, the notion of the modern world originated in Europe. From antiquity through the Middle Ages, the rhythms and practices of life were dominated by long-standing religious and cultural traditions. Little is known for certain about the extent of drug and alcohol use among the average people, most of whom were peasant farmers.

By the fifteenth century, several events in European civilization began to converge and to promote a dramatic alteration of daily life. This transition from the Middle Ages was marked by the Renaissance in the arts, medicine, and science; the Protestant Reformation; and the European age of exploration and colonization. These historical events brought about conditions in which the use of alcohol and drugs and the perception of their use changed significantly (Jaffe 1995b).

In Western countries the clearest illustration of the impact of modernization is seen in regard to the use of alcohol. Increasing urbanization concentrated many impoverished people in large cities, where they were cut off from their traditional social supports and customs. The use of alcohol grew separate from the traditional religious and cultural festivals, as well as from the former social controls, such as community censure for drunkenness. Although distillation of alcohol had been known for centuries, technological advances at this time permitted the relatively inexpensive production of distilled spirits whose intoxicating effects were more potent than beer and wine. A clear example of the combined impact of urban poverty and cheap distilled spirits is found in the "gin epidemics" of sixteenth-century London, during which thousands of poor city dwellers lapsed into chronic alcohol abuse that provoked wide public outcry against the evils of spirits. Curiously, despite the obvious peril of gin and whisky, most people at the time considered beer and wine to be healthful beverages (DuPont 1997).

With the spread of European colonialism, alcohol and other drugs like tobacco and opium became important commodities for trade. As a result of their profitability, drugs and alcohol were more significant in international commerce than ever before. Internationalization of the drug trade and the spread of technology for drug manufacture and consumption altered patterns of drug use in many parts of the world. For example, opium had been introduced to China by Arab traders in the seventh century, but for nearly a thousand years it was taken orally mainly for medicinal purposes; only in the seventeenth century did pipe smoking of opium begin. This method of drug consumption was adopted by Europeans from Native North Americans who smoked tobacco. Eventually pipe smoking was transported to the Orient by Dutch and Portuguese traders. In China, the growing popularity of opium smoking created a social problem large enough to justify several Imperial Edicts banning opium sales (Way 1982).

Eighteenth- and Nineteenth-Century America

During the colonial period of American history the European population was predominantly rural, and included mostly Protestants of English and Scottish stock. Except within the Puritan colonies of New England, the general attitude toward alcoholic beverages was tolerant. Despite the Puritans' official position against alcohol, Puritan men did often drink to excess despite the standard punishment of whipping. In the late 1700s alcohol was much more widely used than today, with the per capita consumption about three times the current level. People of all ages, even children, consumed alcoholic beverages, especially beer, which was considered a healthful beverage. That alcohol abuse was a problem in eighteenth-century America is suggested by the efforts of Benjamin Rush, the famous Revolutionary War patriot and physician, who sought to curb drunkenness in the colonial army.

By the early 1800s changes in the social, scientific, and political arenas ushered in the Industrial Revolution, and the transition from a predominantly rural, agricultural way of life to an urban, commercial, technological society was under way. These societal changes were accompanied by dramatic revisions of many traditional norms, including those that pertained to the use of drugs and alcohol (Musto 1996). A contribution to the growing

anti-alcohol sentiment of that era was made by New England Protestant clergy who perceived some decline in their social role and looked to temperance as a cause that might bolster their influence.

The nineteenth century marked a time of immense demographic shifts and corresponding changes in social attitudes and perceptions. By the 1840s the social climate in the United States had begun to turn toward an anti-immigrant position. The growing influx of Irish Catholics and non-English-speaking Europeans, especially Germans, provoked a negative response in many native-born citizens. The appearance of the American Temperance Society in 1826 was partly a reaction against the perceived threat posed by alcohol-consuming immigrant males, many of whom concentrated in urban areas, and was also motivated by a religious conviction that drunkenness was a morally depraved condition. The success of the pre-Civil War temperance forces is shown by the fact that thirteen states and territories enacted alcohol prohibition laws by 1855. However, many of those laws were revoked during the Civil War because of the government's need for tax revenues from alcohol sales.

In the years following the Civil War, the temperance movement was reborn as the Women's Christian Temperance Movement (WCTU), an organization dedicated to the abolishment of saloons, which were viewed as symbols of social and moral decay. Alcohol consumption in the United States continued to decline from its peak in the early 1800s, and by the 1880s some states had again instituted prohibition laws. Curiously at this time the use of other drugs was on the rise. Morphine and cocaine in particular grew in popularity, especially among the middle class. Easy availability of those drugs and the introduction of hypodermic needles for intravenous injections increased their use. By the late 1800s **morphinism**, an addiction to morphine, became a prevalent problem, particularly among American women, many of whom were given morphine for medical purposes. Morphine was also prescribed by physicians as a cure for alcoholism and cocaine addiction. Ironically, in the late nineteenth century the general perception of alcohol was more negative than that of cocaine and morphine, and less social stigma was attached to being a "morphinist" than to being a drunkard. One telling sign of the acceptability of those drugs was that the original formula for Coca-Cola contained cocaine, while the drink was touted as a cure for hangovers (Jaffe 1989b).

The Twentieth Century

In the United States public opinion on drugs shifted toward a negative view in the early 1900s. The passage of the Harrison Narcotics Act of 1914, which codified antidrug sentiment into law, severely restricted the sale and use of opiates and cocaine. In the aftermath of this law, use of morphine, opium, and cocaine was criminalized, and users were no longer supplied the drugs by physicians. As the legal penalties and social stigma associated with these drugs increased, their use grew more limited except among people on the fringes of mainstream society.

The culmination of the temperance movement in the United States was the 1920 enactment of *Prohibition*, in the form of the 18th Amendment to the Constitution, which prohibited the manufacture, sale, and transportation of intoxicating beverages. Although the law applied no penalty for the use of alcohol, the Prohibition era saw a sharp decline in alcohol consumption as well as in alcohol-related health problems such as liver disease and hospital admissions. However, public and political dissatisfaction with Prohibition ultimately led to its repeal in 1933. After the repeal of Prohibition alcohol consumption slowly increased, although use of illicit drugs in the population at large was apparently quite rare except among certain hard-core users in inner cities (Jaffe 1995b).

The 1960s changed the general pattern of drug consumption with an explosion of drug use in young, middle-class Americans. The "discovery" of marijuana, cocaine, and heroin by American youth, as well as the introduction of newer drugs such as LSD, made for an unprecedented epidemic of drug abuse. Alcohol consumption per capita also increased to its highest level in a century. The adverse consequences of the anything-goes, "sex, drugs, and rock-and-roll" philosophy of the '60s youth culture spawned a strong social backlash that by the 1980s had created the contemporary antidrug movement. Since the late 1970s, both drug and alcohol use have declined, marking another temperance era in American history.

The history of social attitudes toward drug and alcohol use in this country appears to have a cyclical pattern. Periods of temperance and restriction lead to declining use, followed by a rise in use and acceptance, and then a renewal of temperance attitudes (Musto 1996). To this point, studies of American youth show increases in use of marijuana and illicit drugs from the mid-1980s to the mid-1990s as well as less negative attitudes toward drug use (National Clearinghouse for Alcohol and Drug Information 1996a). In the late 1990s, however, drug use among teens has leveled out, and for some drugs has even declined. This change might signal that the pendulum has begun to swing away from the intemperance position and back toward temperance.

10–2   The Sociocultural Context of Drug Use

Because drug use and abuse occur within a complex sociocultural framework, an appreciation of that context is essential for understanding chemically dependent people. In addition, knowledge of sociocultural issues regarding drugs is important for your own self-awareness. Like other chemical dependency counselors you, too, are a participant in your culture, and so to some degree your actions are shaped, explicitly or implicitly, by the prevailing attitudes of that culture.

In this section we examine the cultural purposes of drug use, the cultural context of drug problems, and the leading sociological perspectives on drug abuse.

Drugs and Culture

As you have seen, patterns and perceptions of drug use have varied dramatically over time in different parts of the world. In any era, however, the significance of drug use is shaped by the culture in which it occurs. Here we will consider some of the cultural purposes of drug use and the conditions in which drug problems can emerge.

Cultural Purposes of Drug Use. To some degree the use of psychoactive substances has existed since the earliest known human societies. Patterns of drug use and other culture-relevant behaviors have evolved together throughout human history, during which time drugs have acquired several important functions, as summarized in Table 10–1. For the individual, the meaning and purpose of drug use is shaped by culturally defined ideas. Cultural differences in the patterns and consequences of drug use are partly accounted for by **pharmacodynamics**, which include the influences of cultural traditions, taboos, expectations, and attitudes about drug use on the effects of drugs (Westermeyer 1991). Consider the following question: What differences would occur in the experiences of two people under the influence of the hallucinogenic drug mescaline if one is a 17-year-old American high school student at a wild party and the other is a shaman (holy man) of the Native American Church at a healing ritual for a fellow tribesman? The actions of these two individuals would certainly reflect the attitudes and beliefs about the drug's purpose as determined by their respective cultural traditions.

The *ceremonial function* of drug use describes its most general and ancient purpose in all cultures. Consuming drugs as part of spiritual or secular activities is probably the original culturally determined form of psychoactive substance use. The marking of transitional events such as births, deaths, marriages, promotions, and graduations often implies drug use. In contemporary American culture alcohol is the most obvious example of a ceremonial drug. For example, what wedding would be complete without the toast of the couple by the best man?

As you already know, beer and wine have long been important foodstuffs in Western history. In countries with wine-producing cultures such as France and Italy, alcoholic beverages are traditionally common mealtime drinks. The *dietary function* of drugs, however, is not limited to alcoholic beverages and Western culture. For example, in Southeast Asia cannabis is sometimes used as a spice to enhance the taste of food.

The *medicinal function* of psychoactive drugs is readily apparent in most parts of the world, past and present. Many of the substances that we consider part of the drug problem can be used for legitimate medical reasons. For example, think about the alcohol in most cough syrups, or the codeine in pain killers. Even cocaine has a role in medicine: because of its anesthetic effect it can be helpful when used in eye surgery. The current debate in the United States over allowing AIDS patients to use marijuana for pain relief indicates a cultural conflict about what is and is not appropriate medical practice.

When people use drugs in the course of socializing with friends and family, their *recreational function* is apparent. Alcohol use in particular has come to be linked with leisure-time social interactions, such as the "happy hour" in your local bar. Advertisers are fond of emphasizing the recreational use of alcoholic beverages, as you can see in TV spots for "Miller Time" and other beers. In American society, the initiation of youths into drug consumption typically occurs in the context of recreation.

Table 10–1. Cultural purposes of alcohol use

Purpose	Example
Ceremonial	The "toast" to bride and groom at a marriage
Dietary	Wine as part of a meal
Medicinal	Alcohol as cough suppressant
Recreational	"Happy Hour" cocktails with friends
Religious	Offering of wine at Catholic Mass

Source: Based on Westermeyer (1991).

Drugs have served a purpose in religious rituals for thousands of years perhaps because the altered state of consciousness created by drugs induces a feeling of contact with another, spiritual dimension. The *religious function* of drugs is manifest today in many parts of the world and in many religions. Wine, for example, has a special symbolic place in the Catholic mass and in the Jewish Sabbath and the Passover seder. Other drugs, too, are central to some religious traditions. The Native American Church of the Southwestern United States uses the hallucinogen mescaline as a sacred substance for promoting spiritual growth and healing (Kiyaani 1997).

Cultural Context of Drug Problems. Inasmuch as the purpose and meaning of drug use is understood in a cultural context, the existence of drug problems and the perception of them as problems also are conditioned by cultural factors.

Periods of cultural turmoil are times during which drug problems are likely to emerge. Two clear examples of this phenomenon are found in the period of the European Industrial Revolution, when large numbers of rural people were transplanted to the cities, and in the 1960s counterculture revolution in the United States. In times of transition from a prior cultural system, the supports and controls that formerly regulated drug consumption are weakened. Tragic examples of the impact of such cultural breakdown are found among people from traditional cultures who are uprooted by modernization. The high rate of alcoholism among Native North Americans is a powerful illustration of this phenomenon. The lack of social support and control is also a factor that contributes to the high rates of illicit drug use in impoverished inner-city groups for whom mainstream middle-class culture is quite alien (DuPont 1997, Westermeyer 1991).

The existence of a drug problem in a culture is also dependent on how members of the culture have been educated with regard to drug use. Attitudes toward drugs and intoxication are learned as part of the socialization process. In cultures such as Italy that sanction moderate alcohol use but condemn drunkenness, alcoholism is not a serious problem. Obviously, in cultures whose value system prohibits drug use altogether, children learn to avoid drugs. For example, in Moslem cultures alcohol is forbidden, and rates of alcoholism are exceedingly low. In the United States, socialization about drugs and alcohol is riddled with mixed messages: children are instructed to "just say no," but at the same time media images glamorize drug and alcohol use by celebrities, athletes, and musicians.

The impact of drug socialization is shown by the **acculturation effect**, an increase in drug and alcohol use in ethnic groups following immigration to the United States. For example, second-generation Hispanic and Asian Americans have significantly higher alcohol use than their parents, suggesting that they have been socialized into the American way of drinking (National Institute on Alcohol Abuse and Alcoholism 1994).

Sociological Perspective on Drug Problems

In this section we consider drug problems from a *sociological perspective*, which views substance abuse and dependency as *socially situated phenomena*, that is, behaviors that can only be interpreted within the framework of societal norms (Orcutt 1996).

Drugs and Social Deviance. Whereas psychology and psychiatry consider drug abuse and dependency to be forms of mental disorder, the sociological perspective views them as expressions of *social deviance*, behavior that violates the rules or norms of society. Like other types of social deviance such as crime, drug abuse and dependency are considered problematic because of the social circumstances within which the behaviors occur (Weber 1995).

According to **labeling theory**, deviance is not a trait inherent in behavior, but rather a social status conferred upon individuals because of their unacceptable behavior. Deviance is a label assigned to those who break the rules set down by society. As a consequence of being labeled deviant, the person's behavior is channeled in directions consistent with the label, both because of the expectations of other people, and because of the impact of the label on the person's self-image. So for example, a teenager who is diagnosed (labeled) an addict may be influenced to continue his drug-taking to satisfy the demands of his social status, others' beliefs about him, and his own image of who he is (Kendall 1996).

Although labeling theory addresses the manner in which society responds to deviance and the way society's response may affect the person labeled as deviant, it does not explain why the person has violated societal rules or norms in the first place. By contrast, **social strain theory** explains the onset of deviation in terms of inadequate opportunities to achieve socially approved goals. *Social strain* occurs when the individual is confronted by circumstances that inhibit the pursuit of socially approved goals or when the means to achieve those goals are unavailable (Kendall 1996).

Social alienation, an estrangement from societal norms and values, is one product of social strain. The socially alienated person may seek achievement in ways that are not available through legitimate channels. If deviant opportunities are the only ones available, they are likely to be chosen. For example, impoverished inner-city youths from dysfunctional families often lack the psychological resources necessary to achieve economic self-sufficiency by normal means such as a job, and thus are at risk for seizing illicit opportunities such as gang-related drug sales. Alienation and deviance have a reciprocal association: social alienation leads to deviance, which in turn leads to a more marginalized social status, which ultimately causes more alienation (Weber 1995).

Drugs and Social Constructs.   A central assumption of the sociological perspective is that our thinking about drugs and drug users reflects *social constructs*, concepts that are shaped by societal norms, attitudes, and policies. Like other social constructs, drug-related concepts, such as addiction and disease, are subject to revision over time as society and its norms change (Peele 1989).

As recently as the late 1800s in the United States the concept of addiction was popularly understood as a voluntary habit, rather than an uncontrollable biological condition as it is conceived of today. Even the concept of disease itself was not as thoroughly a medical notion as we know it today. Early disease models of alcoholism, for example, conveyed a moral message: the drunkard was morally or spiritually unfit, as much as physically ill. During the twentieth century, a marriage of medical opinion, public policy, and social science has emerged and has given a new spin to some old ideas. As you have already learned in Chapter 6, the disease model of addiction is the dominant construct in the field of chemical dependency today. This modern view has medicalized chemical dependency and its treatment, as well as removing some of the social stigma attached to chemically dependent individuals (Jaffe and Meyer 1995).

During the same period that the modern disease model of addiction emerged, public policy toward chemically dependent people has increasingly criminalized their behavior. Whereas in the last century drunkards were viewed as morally depraved sinners in need of reform, today's addicts are seen as sick deviants in need of treatment, legal punishment, or both (Gusfield 1996). Inconsistencies in our social constructs for chemically dependent individuals have created more than a little confusion in our society's efforts to effectively address the problem. Because they are criminals, they need punishment, and because they are ill, they need treatment. As you will learn in later sections of this chapter, society's response to the drug problem has elements of both approaches.

10–3 Economic Impact of Chemical Dependency on Society

In earlier chapters you learned that pathological drug use causes many negative psychological and physical effects. Rarely is the user the only one who suffers, however. Family, friends, and society at large also feel the impact of chemical dependency. In this section we turn our attention to the adverse economic affects of chemical dependency on society.

Chemically dependent individuals pay a heavy price for their drug use, measured in pain and suffering, disability, and death. What about the burden to society? When drug use results in traffic accidents, property damage, lost wages, and law-enforcement efforts, society pays, too. Understanding and calculating the cost of chemical dependency is important, not only from the point of view of personal suffering, but also from a prevention and treatment standpoint. Estimates of societal cost help to shape political and social policy and determine the allocation of limited federal funds to agencies engaged in the war on drugs (Humphreys and Rappaport 1993, Pincus and Fine 1992). Effective prevention and treatment policies and programs can go a long way in improving the quality of life for many, as well as offsetting the staggering monetary costs to society (Crits-Christoph and Siqueland 1996, McCrady and Langenbucher 1996). It has been estimated that California alone would save $1.5 billion per year, mostly in reduced crime, by providing effective treatment for its 150,000 drug abusers (Gerstein et al. 1994).

Of course it is impossible to determine precisely the societal cost of chemical dependency. Because even experts disagree on what to measure and how to measure it, we can only estimate its cost. Nevertheless, the two cost-assessment methods that have been most often used are the *cost-of illness* and the *external social cost* approaches.

The Cost-of-Illness Method

The **cost-of-illness** (COI) approach measures the cost to society in terms of expenditures for drug and alcohol-related problems and the loss or diversion of productivity due to drug use. The rationale is that pathological drug use reduces productivity because it leads to psychological and physical health problems that eventually make it difficult for the person to work and attend to children and other home-related responsibilities. Drug abuse treatment, medical care, and law-enforcement costs also figure into the formula (Cook 1995, National Institute on Drug Abuse 1991).

The most comprehensive study using the COI approach was conducted in 1985 and refigured for 1990 (Rice et al. 1990, 1991). The study estimated the total cost of alcoholism and drug abuse to be nearly $100 billion and $67 billion respectively in 1990. For alcoholism, where most of the research has been focused, nearly 75 percent of the cost comes from the adverse effects of drinking on health. Thirty-nine percent comes mainly from the treatment of alcohol-related medical problems, alcoholism treatment, and lost income and productivity due to functional impairment. Another 34 percent is attributable to premature deaths. The remaining costs are accounted for by traffic accidents, crime, and so-called special costs, such as those related to the treatment of babies with fetal alcohol syndrome. Medical treatment and premature deaths deserve special consideration because of their large economic impact.

Medical treatment. Medical treatment for alcoholism consists of direct alcoholism treatment and treatment for the various secondary medical disorders caused by drinking that you learned about in Chapter 7. Alcoholics are among the highest-cost users of medical care in the country; their medical costs make up 15 percent of the national health-care budget, with the bulk of the outlay spent on medical consequences of drinking rather than on alcoholism treatment (McCrady and Langenbucher 1996, Rice et al. 1990, 1991). When you consider drug and alcohol dependence together, more than 3 million people make a total of 56 million mental health and addiction-related visits a year to outpatient facilities. Another 437,000 people utilize inpatient services (Manderscheid et al. 1993, Narrow et al. 1993).

Premature Deaths. Drinking and death are strongly associated. Alcoholism reduces life expectancy by an average of twenty-eight years and causes more than 100,000 deaths annually in the United States (McCrady and Langenbucher 1996, National Clearinghouse for Alcohol and Drug Information 1996b), and see Table 10–2. The social price tag of alcoholism due to premature deaths was estimated at nearly $34 billion in 1990, but that figure is undoubtedly an underestimate because it is

Table 10–2. Deaths Due To Alcohol

Cause	Percent
Drunken driving	24
12 ailments caused wholly by alcohol (includes cirrhosis, alcoholism)	18
Cancers	17
Alcohol-related homicide	11
Alcohol-related suicide	8
Stroke	9

Source: National Clearinghouse for Alcohol and Drug Information (1996b).

impossible to place a dollar value on human life and future earnings lost (National Institute on Drug Abuse 1991). Although the total number of deaths per year has remained fairly stable, the alcohol-related mortality rate has declined slightly since the early 1980s and parallels a decline in alcohol consumption (National Clearinghouse for Alcohol and Drug Information 1996b).

Apparently, the social cost of drinking is especially hard-felt in Alaska, California, Nevada, Arizona, New Mexico, and many counties of the plains and mountain states, where mortality rates are especially high. High rates in these regions are believed to be attributable, in part, to heavy drinking among Native Americans. High mortality rates for the South Atlantic states are due largely to heavy drinking among both whites and blacks.

The External Social Cost Model

Although it is the method used by the federal government, the COI approach has been criticized because it is based on drug-related expenditures and lost productivity. Alternatively, many economists prefer the **external social cost** model (ESC), in which the cost to society is equal to the economic harm that substance dependence imposes on people other than the user. The question posed here is whether drug addicts and alcoholics pay their own way. There is no doubt that drinking and drugging have many adverse effects on the user, but they do not necessarily impact on society.

Suppose somebody gets fired for repeatedly missing work because of drugs. In this case, the cost may only be *internal* inasmuch as the drug user experiences an expected consequence of drug use and may be the only one harmed. He or she is the one that suffers guilt, embarrassment, and lost income. The lost productivity would be figured into the COI model, but not in the ESC framework unless the person's drug use could be demonstrated to have a harmful effect on others. Getting into a car crash may be another matter, however. When a drunk driver crashes, other innocent people may be harmed. The physical, emotional, and economic damage done to others is an *external* cost and therefore, a cost to society in the ESC model.

Traffic Fatalities. Using external harm as the ESC measuring stick, the cost of alcoholism is about $30 billion per year, a figure that is considerably less than the COI estimate (Cook 1995, Manning 1991). Nearly half of the external cost of alcoholism is accounted for by traffic fatalities. The external cost is apparent when you consider that about one-third of alcohol-related deaths involve innocent people; that is, individuals who were not intoxicated at the time of the accident. In such cases, not only does the drunk driver suffer a loss of productivity, but the ESC model presumes that the innocent peoples' lives are valuable; they enjoyed life, and then they were harmed and had their lives involuntarily taken from them.

Lost Earnings. Another $6.5 billion is lost due to lost earnings. Heavy drinkers contribute less to society because their earnings are reduced owing to their illness, disability, early retirement, and death. Alcoholics impose an additional financial burden on society insofar as illness-related early retirement means that they contribute less to the Social Security system they collect from while they are alive. In some ways, however, society reaps some economic benefits in that, when a drinker dies, society no longer must kick in for that person's pension benefits and medical expenses. Overall, however, the external harm to society is certainly greater than such minor economic benefits. The remaining $7 plus billion in social cost comes mainly from the burden of prosecuting alcohol-related crimes, and the insurance costs of property damage caused by drunk drivers.

Educational Attainment

Although educational achievement is not figured in either the COI or ESC frameworks, it is not hard to imagine how it could have a financial impact not only on the individual, but on the family and society. Generally, educational failure has an overall negative effect on role functioning, financial security, and quality of life (Wolfarth et al. 1993).

Data from the National Comorbidity Survey (NCS) study (Kessler et al. 1995) indicate that drug use is associated with reduced educational attainment. In studies that compare people without drug problems or any other mental disorder, to people who have a drug-related diagnosis that diagnosis has been shown to be a strong predictor of failure to complete high school, enter college, and complete college. The relationship between educational attainment and drug use is strongest for high-school dropouts. Indeed, the odds of a drug user failing out of high school are more than two to one. Furthermore, roughly 23 percent of high school dropouts born between 1966 and 1975 had psychiatric disorders and most involved substance use disorders. Although the NCS study does not prove that drug use causes educational failure, it is likely to be true in most cases.

10–4 Aggression, Crime, and Chemical Dependency

The general public belief that there is an association among substance use, aggression, violence, and crime dates back thousands of years and persists today. Professionals are split in their beliefs on this question, however. Although some claim that there is no relationship at all, the preponderance of scientific evidence, indicates that drug and alcohol abuse is a strong predictor of aggression, violence, and crime (Monohan 1992, Moss and Tarter 1993). Indeed, one large-scale study showed that, when compared to people with no diagnosis, individuals with alcohol-ism and drug abuse are twelve to sixteen times more likely to commit acts of violence (Swanson and Holzer 1991).

Aggression, Violence, and Drugs

Despite compelling evidence linking chemical dependency, aggression, and violence, the precise relationship is complex. **Aggression** refers to a behavior that directs intentional harm at another person; sometimes aggressive behavior turns to *violence*.

The most prevalent view among laypersons and many professionals alike is that drugs, most notably alcohol, directly cause aggression and violence by their actions on the brain. The conventional wisdom is that alcohol causes aggression and violence through **behavioral disinhibition**, a condition in which an individual shows impulsiveness, impaired judgment, and emotional unpredictability; in other words, a major loss of inhibition (Moss and Tarter 1993).

The argument that drugs directly lead to violence has been extended to the use of amphetamines, cocaine, opioids, hallucinogens (especially PCP-phencyclidine), and cannabinoids, too. If not by a simple process of behavioral disinhibition alone, as with alcohol, other drugs are believed to cause aggression and violence by creating psychotic states marked by suspiciousness, hallucinations, agitation, and impaired judgment. Nowhere is the belief in a direct causal relationship between drugs and violence more apparent than in the derivation of the word hashish. You may have heard that the word *hashish* is believed to be derived from *hashashin* after a tenth-century Persian religious sect, the *Assassins*, who held power by assassinating rival leaders while under the influence of hashish (Moss and Tarter 1993).

Despite its intuitive appeal, the behavioral disinhibition explanation of drug-induced violence does not fit observations. Matters are much more complex. A more reasonable explanation is that drugs do not directly cause violence, but instead modify the judgment and self-control that might otherwise contribute to a lessening of violent behavior. Experts agree that drug use is related to violence by a complex interaction of the pharmacological effects and dosage of the drug, a predisposition comprised of psychological and biological characteristics of the individual, and the specific situation in which the drug is used.

Pharmacological Effects.   Drugs like alcohol *do* produce disinhibition, but that alone is not sufficient to cause aggressive behavior. If alcohol's direct effects on the brain were sufficient to cause disinhibition and violence then the same amount of alcohol in different drinks should produce the same disinhibition effect. That does not happen. One study (Taylor and Gammons 1975) showed that despite equivalent concentrations of alcohol, vodka produced more aggression than did bourbon. Other researchers have observed that male liquor drinkers are more aggressive than male beer drinkers, while just the reverse is true for females, despite equivalent blood alcohol levels (Murdoch et al. 1988, Pihl et al. 1984).

Psychological and Biological Characteristics.   *Predisposition* is important because it apparently lays a foundation for drug-elicited aggression and violence. Behavioral characteristics like hyperactivity, a motivational tendency toward aggression, and antisocial personality disorder involve poor regulation of aggressive impulses and seem to create a predisposition to both drug abuse and drug-induced violence. A history of childhood aggression is a particularly strong predictor of both violence and substance abuse. Boys whose fathers are drug abusers (more so than alcohol abusers) are quite prone to violence and other antisocial behaviors. For boys who eventually become substance abusers themselves, violent behavior often precedes drug use. Such findings strongly suggest that those who are most likely to behave violently while intoxicated are the ones with an aggressive temperament. Aggression and violence occur when that temperament combines with the disinhibiting effects of alcohol (Gabel and Schindledecker 1993, Moss and Tarter 1993).

Emotional factors, too, are influential in drug-elicited aggressive and violent behavior

during intoxication. Because many subjective effects of intoxication are shaped by one's preintoxicated emotional state, those who are typically anxious, agitated, unhappy, unfriendly, and easily angered are most at risk to act out. Finally, low serotonin levels, as you discovered in Chapter 6, are associated with aggression, depression, suicide, and aggressive behavior. For some, low serotonin may be part of a biological predisposition to a host of problems, including drug-elicited violence (Moss and Tarter 1993, Moss et al. 1990, Roy et al. 1988a).

Besides the pharmacological effects of alcohol or a specific drug, and the psychological and biological features of the user, the situation is also important in determining the chances for aggressive or violent behavior. One situational factor known to instigate violence is provocation by another person. In general, higher doses of alcohol and more intense and frequent provocations are associated with an increased likelihood of aggressive or violent behavior (Moss and Tarter 1993).

Chemical Dependency and Crime

There is solid evidence that drug use is correlated with crime. Consider the following facts:

- Drug users are more likely than nonusers to commit crimes and have criminal records.
- Individuals with criminal records are much more likely than those without criminal records to be drug users.
- The number of crimes committed by drug users increases with the frequency of drug use (Bureau of Justice Statistics 1992).

Drugs and crime are related in three ways. *First*, many individuals commit crimes by violating laws that prohibit or regulate the possession, use, sale, or manufacture of illicit drugs. *Second*, drug-related crimes are committed as a consequence of the drugs' psychoactive effects. Examples include rape, assault, stealing, and the violence often observed against competing drug dealers. More than 50 percent of arrestees in custody test positive for drugs, indicating recent use, and nearly a third of jail inmates are intoxicated at the time of their offense. *Third*, drug use and crime often are part of a deviant lifestyle in which drug users expose themselves to situations that encourage crime. The risk of criminal activity is increased because drug users often associate with other criminals and learn criminal skills from them (Bureau of Justice Statistics 1992).

Drug-related crimes often are perpetrated against other drug users, dealers, or both to protect or broaden drug markets, threaten competitors, and exact retribution against sellers or buyers suspected of cheating (Bureau of Justice Statistics 1992). Prostitution, assaults (including homicide), and robberies are common among drug users and dealers, and retaliations against drug dealers for deceitful drug transactions are everyday events within illegal drug networks. Indeed, nearly 80 percent of assailants in drug-related homicides know their victims. Forty-eight percent of all murders in the United States are drug-related, and the majority of them are associated with illegal drug distribution (Drug Enforcement Administration 1997b). Today, drug traffickers form sophisticated gangs; these are ruthless and violent people who will not stop short of shooting or otherwise eliminating anyone, including innocent people, who get in their way (Drug Enforcement Administration 1997a).

Drug deals, executions, and drive-by shootings turn neighborhoods into war zones. As these activities attract more crime to the area, nonusing citizens are victimized as well and some may get entangled in the illicit drug world. Apart from drug-related gang crime, many drug users resort to crime to support their drug use by way of burglaries, robberies, stolen vehicles, and theft of and other property (Bureau of Justice Statistics 1992).

10–5 Societal Response to Chemical Dependency

Society has enacted a multifaceted approach to the problem of chemical dependency. In this section you will learn about legal and political responses to the situation, and the roles of education and of the health professions in prevention and treatment.

Legal and Political Responses

One large part of the legal and political attempt to fight chemical dependency has centered on development of legislative policies and related strategies and other tactics to control the drug problem.

Prohibition. One important policy is **prohibition**, the legislated ban on the distribution, possession, and use of specified drugs, and the application of criminal penalties to violators (Bureau of Justice Statistics 1992). Federal and state laws make it possible to exact stiff penalties for illicit drug trafficking. Depending on the type of drug, the quantity involved, and the number of prior convictions, drug traffickers can be slapped with hefty jail sentences as well as heavy fines. For example, the first offense of selling one kilogram or more of a heroin mixture could bring a prison sentence of ten years to life and a fine of up to $4 million. Within the domain of prohibition, user accountability laws are designed to punish minor drug offenders with civil fines up to $10,000 without giving the offender a criminal record for possession of small amounts of drugs (Drug Enforcement Administration 1997b). Although the intent of such penalties is a good one, namely the discouragement of drug use, the unintended result is often that people who commit even relatively minor offenses can be financially devastated.

Regulation. Prescription drugs are subject to **regulation**, or the legal control over the distribution, possession, and use of specified drugs (Bureau of Justice Statistics 1992). One form of regulation is the placement of both legal and illicit substances into categories, known as Schedules I through V, based on their medical use, abuse potential, and safety or dependence liability. *Schedule I* includes drugs without currently accepted medical use and that have a high potential for abuse and/or dependence, while drugs in *Schedule V* are relatively safe when used under medical supervision and present a low abuse/dependence potential. Table 10–3 describes the five schedules.

The federal drug schedules, despite their legal significance and even some degree of practical value, group these substances together in a puzzling and potentially misleading fashion. Marijuana, for instance, is a Schedule I drug along with heroin, although they are hardly equal in terms of abuse/dependency potential. In addition, the Schedule III drugs, such as barbiturates, presumably have lower abuse/dependency potential than the Schedule I drugs, but in fact marijuana (Schedule I) does not even come close to the addictiveness of the barbiturates (Schedule III).

In addition to authorizing the tactic of apprehending and punishing drug offenders, legal and political policies utilize many other strategies to stem the drug problem. Educating the public about the adverse consequences of drug use and the treatment of chemical dependency is a policy aimed at reducing demand. At the same time, diplomatic, law enforcement, and military resources focus on supply reduction by influencing foreign countries to control drug production and export, and by maintaining surveillance of smuggling routes and supervising border control (Bureau of Justice Statistics 1992).

Drug Testing and Other Tactics. Testing people for the presence of drugs in the body is another tactic to control drug use (see Chapter 3). Although most people think of drug testing as a way of gathering evidence to punish someone, it can also deter drug use, lead to treatment for the user, and protect the public from the damaging effects of drug use.

Drug testing is commonly authorized for criminal offenders, as a measure to reduce criminal behavior. The use of drug testing for criminal justice employees, such as police officers and prison guards, is also a common way of fostering public trust in the integrity and professionalism of these individuals. Drug testing is also the rule within branches of state and federal governments and in regulated industries such as defense contracting, nuclear energy, and transportation. Although workers in private businesses are seldom tested, most states authorize drug testing, especially in applicants, for those whose jobs pose safety risks or where there is a reasonable suspicion that drug use is affecting job performance (Bureau of Justice Statistics 1992).

Federal and state legislative policy is strongly focused on controlling alcohol-related problems. Alcohol taxes, raising the minimum drinking age, lowering the allowed blood-alcohol limits in motorists, driver's license revocation laws, placing of warning labels on alcoholic beverages, and limits on advertising have had a measurable effect on alcohol consumption and other alcohol-related problems (National Institute on Alcohol Abuse and Alcoholism 1996a).

Educational Responses

As you have learned in earlier chapters, drug use often begins during the teenage years or earlier, then may escalate in later years. Mindful of this fact, strategies have been developed to educate people, especially our youth, about the consequences of chemical dependency. To this end, public health agencies, schools, and law enforcement have teamed together in the prevention effort.

Prevention refers to educational efforts that inform potential drug abusers about the risks associated with drug use with the goals

Table 10–3. Federal Drug Scheduling

Schedule	Drug
I	Heroin, LSD, marijuana, methaqualone
II	Morphine, PCP, cocaine, methadone, methamphetamine
III	Anabolic steroids, codeine, barbiturates
IV	Darvon, Valium, Xanax
V	Cough medicines with codeine

Source: Drug Enforcement Administration (1997b).

of limiting the number of new drug users and discouraging casual users from continued use. *Primary prevention* seeks to prevent or at least delay the onset of drug use. Preventing casual users from escalating their drug use is known as *secondary prevention* (Bureau of Justice Statistics 1992). In both cases, prevention strategies hope to educate people about the harmful effects of drugs, teach adolescents to resist peer pressure, correct youths' misperceptions about drugs, address associated problems such as teen pregnancy, school underachievement, and family problems, and mobilize community support for prevention activities.

Schools are a prime focus of drug-education classes because school-age people are especially vulnerable to begin drug use. The fact that youths spend a great deal of their time in school also makes them accessible to drug-prevention messages. Understandably, law-enforcement agencies are heavily involved in prevention activities especially in conjunction with schools. In the *Drug Abuse Resistance Education program* (DARE), for example, police officers run a seventeen-week course in the schools. Through lectures, exercises, audiovisual material, and role playing, students learn to "say no" to drugs and develop a positive attitude about law enforcement. Millions of students receive DARE training each year.

The Federal Bureau of Investigation and the Drug Enforcement Administration also sponsor prevention programs in alliance with local law-enforcement agencies, schools, community groups, and sports organizations. Government agencies sponsor and develop videos, music, coloring books, comic books, posters, and a wealth of educational pamphlets with an antidrug message. Private sector foundations, corporations, and the mass media also make a significant contribution to the antidrug effort. Certainly, most of you have seen a prominent sports figure warn against the use of drugs on TV.

Does prevention work? Numerous studies reveal that prevention efforts have led to a decline in drug use in the last decade or so (National Clearinghouse for Alcohol and Drug Information 1997). Unfortunately, certain segments of the population apparently do not benefit. Prevention efforts typically focus on the general population, but the majority of people who receive prevention education are probably not at risk for a significant drug problem anyway (Tarter 1992). The most effective prevention strategies must target those who are most at risk, and this requires early intervention. Single-factor approaches like boosting self-esteem and educating people to "just say no" are bound to be ineffective because, as you have already learned, the nature and causes of chemical dependency are complex and not well understood (Office for Substance Abuse Prevention 1990, Tarter 1992).

Health Profession Responses

Psychologists, psychiatrists, and other health professionals have made major contributions to the war on drugs. Their research has shed considerable light on the psychosocial and biological causes of chemical dependency, and as a result many effective prevention programs have been devised.

Perhaps the most significant contributions in this area are found in the development of treatments. Although there is certainly no cure for chemical dependency, important treatment advances have been made. Detoxification, drug counseling and education, psychotherapy, pharmacotherapy, vocational services, and relapse prevention are just some of the treatment tools used by health professionals (Bureau of Justice Statistics 1992).

The problem of chemical dependency also has motivated health professionals to specialize in the area of addictions and to offer certification for those who are qualified. *The American Academy of Addiction Psychiatry* and the *American Psychological Association Division of Psychopharmacology and Substance Abuse* are examples of health profession specialties. The American Psychological Association also offers a *Certificate of Proficiency in the Treatment of Alcohol and Other Substance Use Disorders*. Finally, the federal government has established agencies to provide research funding for health professionals who study and treat chemical dependency. These include the *National Institute of Mental Health*, the *National Institute on Drug Abuse*, the

National Institute on Alcoholism and Alcohol Abuse, and the *Substance Abuse and Mental Health Services Administration*.

Chapter Summary

10–1

The social history of drugs informs us of the role of changing attitudes toward drugs and drug users over time. Most ancient cultures have left indications of their ceremonial use of drugs, most commonly in religious rituals, and the social controls for use. The modernization of Western civilization disrupted traditional societies and led to increased drug and alcohol use along with urbanization and colonialism. In the United States, the Industrial Revolution of the eighteenth and nineteenth centuries was a period in which norms of alcohol use changed, population demographics changed, and eventually a temperance movement arose. In the early twentieth century the federal government enacted laws to control the use of narcotics, and in 1920 the era of Prohibition was marked by criminalization of alcohol manufacture and distribution. American society has exhibited a cyclical pattern in its attitudes for and against drug use.

10–2

Cultural traditions and attitudes influence the patterns of drug use and the effects of drugs on users. Several cultural purposes of drug use have been identified, including the ceremonial, dietary, medicinal, recreational, and the religious. Periods of cultural turmoil and change are times when drug-use problems are likely to arise. Drug use is influenced by culturally sanctioned attitudes that are taught in the process of socialization. The sociological perspective on drug problems views them as expressions of social deviance. Labeling theory sees deviance as a label assigned to those who violate societal norms. According to social-strain theory, social deviation results when people have few opportunities to pursue socially approved goals. Concepts like

addiction are social constructs that are shaped by societal norms and policies.

10–3

Chemical dependency exacts a high price from society in terms of costs of treatment, accidents, lost productivity, and law enforcement. The cost-of-illness approach measures the cost of chemical dependency at about $100 billion annually in terms of expenditures for drug problems and loss of productivity due to drug use. The external social cost model of measurement estimates the costs of chemical dependency as the amount of economic harm that it causes, including such consequences as traffic fatalities and lost earnings. The cost of chemical dependency can also be evaluated in terms of loss in educational attainment and its consequent financial harm.

10–4

Drug and alcohol abuse is a strong predictor of aggression, violence, and crime, but the links among these variables are complex. Drugs can increase aggression by behavioral disinhibition, that is, loss of inhibition, but drug use alone is not necessarily the direct cause of aggression. Drugs interact with individual biological variables and psychological characteristics to increase aggression risk. Drug use is strongly correlated with crime because illicit drug use is a crime, crimes are committed under the influence of drugs, and drug users have deviant lifestyles that encourage crime.

10–5

Society has exhibited a multifaceted response to chemical dependency. The legal and political response to drug abuse entails the prohibition, or legal ban, of drugs, as well as regulation and legal control over drug use, both of which are supported by legal penalties for violations. Drug testing is another tactic for controlling drug use. Educational interventions emphasize the importance of prevention as a method of drug control, and the schools are a major focus of educational efforts. The response of the health professions to chemical dependency involves mainly research to understand the causes of drug abuse and the best treatments for drug abusers, as well as efforts to educate professionals to specialize in treatment of chemical dependency.

pharmacodynamics
prevention
prohibition
regulation
social strain theory

Terms to Remember

acculturation effect
aggression
behavioral disinhibition
cost-of-illness
external social cost
labeling theory
morphinism

Suggested Reading

Levin, J. (1990). *Alcoholism: A Bio-Psycho-Social Approach*. New York: Hemisphere.

Rice, D. P., Kelman, S., Miller, L. S., and Dunmeyer, S. (1990). *The Economic Costs of Alcohol and Drug Abuse and Mental Illness: 1985*. Rockville, MD: National Institute on Drug Abuse.

Weber, L. R. (1995). *The Analysis of Social Problems*. Boston: Allyn & Bacon.

Principles of Chemical Dependency Counseling

Chapter Outline

In the preceding chapters you learned about psychoactive drugs and the nature, types, causes, and consequences of chemical dependency. The remainder of this textbook focuses on the many issues that pertain to counseling the chemically dependent patient. In this chapter you will begin to examine the fundamental principles of counseling alcoholic and drug-addicted individuals. The assumptions of the disease model of chemical dependency and its implications for treatment are discussed. Next, the role of chemical dependency counselors is examined, as well as their basic tasks and responsibilities.

11–1   The Disease Model in Chemical Dependency Counseling

Conceptual models serve a valuable purpose in the treatment of physical and psychological disorders by helping to describe and explain the features of disorders and to point to methods of treatment. As you learned in Chapter 6, the complex causes of chemical dependency have been addressed from many theoretical points of view, and although each theory has certain merits, the planning and implementation of chemical dependency treatment is best served by the disease model. The *disease model* describes chemical dependency as a chronic, progressive, and incurable illness with periods of *abatement, remission,* and *relapse.* As you will see, this model helps to characterize many experiences and behaviors of drug and alcohol addicts as they struggle with their habitual substance use.

The disease model is most useful in drug and alcohol counseling because it provides both the counselor and patient with a framework for understanding the course of the problem, as well as providing prescriptions for counselors and patients to follow. In addition, the disease model allows counselors and patients to anticipate what can happen if treatment prescriptions are not followed or if patients do not respond well to prescribed treatments. Of course, like every model, the disease model is not a one-size-fits-all proposition, and you will find many clients who abuse substances yet are not physically addicted to them. For such clients the disease model is not as directly applicable, although it does still offer helpful treatment guidelines (DuPont 1997, Jellinek 1960).

The Course of Chemical Dependency

The sequence and patterns of change in an illness over time is known as the *course* of the illness, and for chemical dependency the course is *chronic and progressive.* By so characterizing it, we mean that it typically persists over a long period of time, and for many addicts involves increasing loss of control.

Chemical Dependency Is Chronic. A *chronic disease* is a condition that persists for a long period of time, usually lasting over many years. Calling chemical dependency a chronic disease does not necessarily mean that patients will use drugs or alcohol every day, day after day, year after year for the rest of their lives. However, chemically dependent people commonly do use drugs and alcohol for long periods of time, and they do remain at high risk for substance-related problems for many years. Even if they manage to stop for a time they are at serious risk for later relapse. Most evidence indicates that alcoholics and drug addicts can

never safely use alcohol or drugs again if they want to remain well.

To say that chemical dependency is a chronic disease might suggest that it is incurable. Does that mean no one improves and recovery is impossible? Of course not. If that were the case, there would be no reason to write about (or read about) treatment. Chemically dependent people can improve, and recovery is certainly possible, albeit difficult and demanding. **Recovery** means maintaining a drug- and alcohol-free lifestyle, and developing a repertoire of coping skills that promote ongoing abstinence. Remember that recovery is a process, a long and trying process, not a discrete event. Successful recovery requires that clients become actively engaged in changing not only their substance consumption, but also correcting other patterns of behavior, emotion, and thought, as well as acquiring insight into the workings of their own minds.

Recovering clients remain especially vulnerable to the damaging effects of drugs and alcohol for their entire lives and are never again able to use those substances without severely jeopardizing themselves. Alcoholics cannot drink again, and addicts cannot use drugs or alcohol again without running into trouble. For the patient who is serious about recovery there is no such thing as "just one" drink or pipeful without the extreme danger of renewing the dependency. While a complete cure is not possible, chemically dependent patients can be taught to manage their disease so the problem is kept in check as their recovery progresses.

Chemical Dependency Is Progressive. In earlier chapters you have learned about the numerous symptoms and consequences of chemical dependency. Because these symptoms and consequences tend to become compounded over time, chemical dependency is considered a *progressive disease,* one in which there is an increasing loss of control over substance use. As a result of these compounding effects, chemically dependent patients tend to experience an accelerating *downward spiral* of severe problems. If untreated, chemical dependency can be fatal. Alcoholics and drug addicts have a high risk of premature death due to the influences of substance abuse and its consequences. Besides the harm done to physical health, chemical dependency also leads to accelerated psychological and social deterioration. Marital and family disruption are unavoidable for the chemically dependent person. Likewise, trouble in the workplace is expected owing to absenteeism, intoxication, and poor job performance, and such occupational distress inevitably causes financial difficulties (DuPont 1997, Levin 1995, National Institute on Drug Abuse 1990).

> In his mid-forties, but looking much older, Frankie was referred for outpatient drug counseling by his union's health-care office after he showed up positive for codeine on a drug test at work. He had been a laborer for a major urban transportation authority for more than twenty years. Frankie was also substance dependent, and had been since his late teens. At different times during the course of his addiction career he had developed dependencies on alcohol, heroin, methadone, Valium, Demerol, and most recently codeine. A three-time veteran of drug rehabs, Frankie was facing the very real prospect of losing his job despite his considerable seniority. His desperation to hold his job was based not only on financial considerations, but also on the fact that he did not have much else in his life. His two marriages had failed because of his drinking and drugging, and his three children, finding him an embarrassment, were alienated from him.

The disease model anticipates that chemically dependent people like Frankie will experience ongoing, increasing deterioration as the physical, psychological, and social effects of their addiction multiply and interact with one another. You will likely find that, as in Frankie's case, many of your clients have been in one kind of treatment or another before, but that despite prior treatment their addictions have regained control over their lives. However, as with other chronic, progressive diseases, chemical dependency does not always follow the same pattern in every client. Certainly you will find countless variations in

the symptoms, complications, behaviors, and lifestyles of chemically dependent individuals.

Phases in Chemical Dependency Treatment

In the course of chemical dependency treatment three common phases appear: abatement, remission, and relapse. In this section you will examine the features of those phases and their implications for counseling work.

Abatement. The phase of **abatement** is a period when alcoholics or drug addicts stop using their substances or significantly reduce their level of substance use. If they completely stop using substances for a significant time, they are said to show **abstinence**. In an effort to avoid or limit the negative social, physical, and psychological consequences of their substance abuse, many chemically dependent people attempt to cut back on using, or manipulate their pattern of use. For example, if a man drinks after work during the week he may be often late for work due to hangovers, and to avoid getting in trouble he will try to drink less, use less potent alcohol (for example, switch to beer from vodka), or confine his drinking to the weekend. Abatement may succeed for a while, but in most cases the person's substance use will resume at its previous level unless help is sought.

Patients at the beginning of treatment typically are in this abatement phase, either through their own voluntary efforts to regulate drug and alcohol use or through coercion by others. For the new patient, abatement is accompanied by mixed feelings and reactions. Some are pleased and proud of their efforts at self-control, others are angry and resentful, and still others show diverse emotional reactions such as anxiety, elation, and depression. New patients in abatement are quite vulnerable to resuming their drugging and drinking and thus need dependable support from and monitoring by the counselor. For many, the brief glow of abatement is too short-lived and is followed by a sharp realization that overcoming chemical dependency will be hard work over a long period. The main challenge to the counselor in this phase is to engage the patient in treatment, establish a sound working relationship, and support efforts to become abstinent.

> With a history of multiple rehabs behind him Frankie could readily "talk the talk" of recovery. He knew just what he was supposed to say to the counselor to look like a good patient and get a good report for his employer. However, after a few sessions it was clear that his heart was not in it. He complained about feeling too pressured to stop using the codeine that he had been prescribed for back pain due to a workplace injury, and tried to sell the idea that he was only taking the pills for pain control, not because of addiction. Additionally he balked at the weekly drug-testing requirement and mandatory attendance at Twelve step meetings. Like many people who are coerced into treatment Frankie felt resentful and he showed his ire by being late, canceling sessions, and not paying his fee regularly. Frankie's counselor intervened by supporting his abatement of codeine use, encouraging him to become engaged in the treatment opportunities at the agency, and helping him examine his feelings of helplessness and depression over the turn of events in his life.

Remission. The arrest of the disease process and disappearance of its symptoms is known as **remission**. In chemical dependency, remission means that the patient has exhibited intentional abstinence from alcohol and drug use for a significant period. However, abstinence alone does not indicate remission. As you learned in Chapter 4, drug and alcohol abuse are not the only symptoms of substance use disorders. True remission requires significant change in the patient's state such that the negative psychological, social, and biological consequences of substance abuse are lessened.

Spontaneous remission is the arrest of a disease without formal treatment. Longitudinal studies of alcoholics show that spontaneous remission is commonplace, yet many authorities believe that such remissions are usually temporary. A typical example of spontaneous remission would be the alcoholic who forces himself to stop drinking because of an overwhelming and dangerous accumulation of health problems. *Full, sustained remission* is a thorough arrest of the symptoms of dependency for at least twelve months (American Psychiatric Association 2000). Such normalization of the person's condition usually depends on a successful engagement in a treatment program and is a good sign that the recovery process has been initiated.

In this phase counselors need to encourage the patient's continued efforts toward recovery and to help put the patient's remission experience in a proper perspective. Remission is not recovery, but a step in the direction of recovery. Maintaining remission is more difficult than simply avoiding drugs or alcohol, and it demands considerable psychological change from the patient. Although patients may abstain from drug and alcohol use, their old behavior patterns may linger. As an example consider the *"dry drunk" syndrome* in the following case:

> The Jeffries family sought counseling after the oldest of their four teenage daughters attempted suicide by swallowing a bottle of aspirin. Although it was not a very serious suicidal effort, it was sufficient to alert her mother to the need for help. Despite his initial reluctance, Mr. Jeffries agreed to participate in family sessions. With two plus years of abstinence behind him, Mr. Jeffries felt good about his recovery from alcoholism. He had had a serious drinking problem for many years, following his military service, but finally felt confident that his drinking days were over. Mrs. Jeffries agreed that he had stopped drinking, and she was very supportive of his abstinence, but she was disappointed that abstinence had not improved his personality. His wife and daughters all agreed that Mr. Jeffries was just as self-centered as ever; his wife complained that he was "addicted" to his recovery and cared more about his "program" than about their family. The girls concurred that despite liking him better since he got sober their father tended to ignore them except to give commands. They called him "the dictator" because of his way of laying down the law and his unwillingness to listen to their point of view. His typical way of handling family problems was to scream and threaten anyone in sight. The rigidity, self-centeredness, and

antagonistic interpersonal style that were elements of Jeffries-the-alcoholic were also still in evidence in Jeffries-the-dry-drunk.

As Mr. Jeffries' case suggests, abstinence by itself does not guarantee successful recovery. Patients like Mr. Jeffries accomplish little beyond simply avoiding alcohol and remain at high risk for resuming their addictions because they have not improved their ability to cope with life and deal with people on a day-to-day basis. Unfortunately for Mr. Jeffries and many other dry drunks, the anger, rage, and low tolerance for frustration can lead back to drinking.

Relapse. For many clients, the progress they make initially is only temporary, and they find themselves slipping back into substance use. **Relapse** is the resumption of substance use following a significant period of abstinence. In the disease model, relapse is a process involving changes in the person's attitudes, thought patterns, feelings, and behavior, resulting in a return to drugs and alcohol. Although relapse is very common among chemical dependency patients, it is preventable.

Because the disease model assumes that chemical dependency is chronic and progressive, counselors must put maximum effort into the prevention of relapse once a patient achieves abstinence. The counselor must help the patient to identify signs of impending relapse and symptoms of actual relapse, as well as help the patient learn to prevent subsequent relapses. An important part of good counseling is to alert patients to their vulnerability to relapse and to teach them how to foresee and avoid the circumstances that promote relapse. You will learn more about relapse prevention methods in Chapter 14.

After nearly eight months in treatment Frankie had made good progress. He stopped using codeine, got hooked up with a Narcotics Anonymous (N.A.) sponsor whom he respected, and settled into the weekly routines of group, program, and individual sessions. His depression was also under control in part due to antidepressant medication. Things at work were okay again, too,

and he felt that they were not constantly looking over his shoulder anymore. In short, he was feeling pretty good about himself and had even gone on a few dates with a woman he met at his N.A. group. In this state where his life was moving ahead in a positive direction, he started thinking about getting high and he admitted that he had gotten close to calling one of the doctors who would write him prescriptions for codeine. In response to these relapse alarm bells his counselor focused their sessions on relapse-prevention skills, and with the counselor's encouragement Frankie also started to address his feelings with his group and sponsor.

11–2 The Professional Counselor's Role and Tasks

You learned in Chapter 1 that modern chemical dependency counseling emerged from the peer support movements of Alcoholics Anonymous and other Twelve step programs, as well as the therapeutic community movement. As the success and popularity of these movements grew, many recovering addicts and alcoholics developed the methods and roles that serve as the foundation for modern chemical dependency counseling. Eventually, alcoholism counseling and substance abuse counseling emerged, and in recent years those professions have shown signs of greater collaboration. Because of the unique history of their field, chemical dependency counselors find themselves in a profession that is still seeking to define itself and its relationship with other health-care professions. In this section you will explore the main elements in the professional role of chemical dependency counselors.

Who Is the Chemical dependency Counselor?

Like other professions, chemical dependency counseling draws many kinds of individuals with diverse backgrounds, personalities, and talents. The identity of the chemical dependency counselor is based mainly on the ideas applied in the relationship with patients, and on the status of the profession.

A Framework for Chemical dependency Counseling. Alcoholics Anonymous (A.A.) and other peer support programs established the historical foundation for chemical dependency counseling. As you learned in Chapter 1, A.A. promoted a pathway to recovery based on the famous Twelve Steps, as shown in Table 11–1. The **Twelve step model** of counseling emphasizes the disease concept of addictions, the need for abstinence, and of course following the *Twelve step program* (Alcoholics Anonymous 1976, Alcoholics Anonymous World Services 1984). Although this model was initially intended for alcoholism, it has been widely applied to other drug addictions as well as to addictive behaviors in general, such as gambling and overeating. Today, most treatment programs for alcoholics and drug addicts incorporate the Twelve step model as a guideline for recovery. Consequently, most counselors integrate their individual therapeutic work with clients with the clients' work in their own Twelve step program (Bean-Bayog 1991, Doyle-Pita 1994). Of course counselors must always keep in mind that Twelve step participation will not always be necessary for every client's recovery, nor will Twelve step participation necessarily guarantee a client's recovery. Nevertheless, counselors do well to recommend that clients try a Twelve step program at the outset of treatment.

Before the development of a *disease model* of chemical dependency there was no organized and comprehensive theory that professionals could use to treat addiction that was based on principles of recovery rather than causation. Alcoholism counselors influenced by the A.A. outlook on alcoholism as a disease were among the first professionals to employ the disease model as a framework for treatment. Earlier in this chapter you learned how central the disease model is to the work of the counselor today. A significant factor in the development of modern chemical dependency counseling was the marriage of the disease model with the Twelve step model. As you will learn in more detail in later chapters by using the principles of these models as guides both the counselor and patient are able to focus on the four *primary demands of treatment:* (1) producing abstinence, (2) preventing relapse, (3) addressing the consequences of addiction, and (4) creating a chemical-free lifestyle for recovery.

Professionalization of Chemical Dependency Counseling. For many years the fields of alcohol and drug counseling were the domains of peer counselors. Alcoholics helping alco-

Table 11–1. The Twelve Steps of Alcoholics Anonymous

1. We admitted that we were powerless over alcohol . . . that our lives had become unmanageable.
2. Came to believe that a Power greater than ourselves could restore us to sanity.
3. Made a decision to turn our will and our lives over to the care of God *as we understood Him.*
4. Made a searching and fearless moral inventory of ourselves.
5. Admitted to God, to ourselves and to another human being the exact nature of our wrongs.
6. Were entirely ready to have God remove all these defects of character.
7. Humbly asked Him to remove our shortcomings.
8. Made a list of all persons we had harmed, and became willing to make amends to them all.
9. Made direct amends to such people wherever possible, except when to do so would injure them or others.
10. Continue to take personal inventory, and when we were wrong promptly admitted it.
11. Sought through prayer and meditation to improve our conscious contact with God, *as we understood Him*, praying only for knowledge of His will for us and the power to carry that out.
12. Having had a spiritual awakening as the result of these steps, we tried to carry this message to alcoholics, and to practice these principles in all our affairs.

Source: Alcoholics Anonymous World Services (1952). The Twelve Steps are reprinted with permission of Alcoholics Anonymous World Services, Inc. (A.A.W.S.). Permission to reprint the Twelve Steps does not mean that A.A.W.S. has reviewed or approved the contents of this publication, or that A.A.W.S. necessarily agrees with the views expressed herein. A.A. is a program of recovery from alcoholism *only*-use of the Twelve Steps in connection with programs and activities which are patterned after A.A., but which address other problems, or in any other non-A.A. context, does not imply otherwise.

holics and addicts helping addicts were the main themes. While peer support in Twelve step programs continues as an important part of recovery, the field has become increasingly professionalized. The fact that you are reading this book indicates a central factor in the professionalization of chemical dependency counseling, namely specialized education. Where peer counselors' expertise depended on their personal experiences with addiction and recovery, the professional counselor's expertise depends on more specific knowledge based on formal training.

Unlike earlier peer counselors, chemical dependency counselors are trained experts in the area of addictions and addiction treatment. In the counselor–client relationship, the counselor's role is defined by his or her professional expertise, which is directed at furthering the client's recovery. As it is in other helping professions, the success of chemical dependency counselors is influenced strongly by the confidence and trust placed in them by the client. By acquiring specialized knowledge and skills relevant to addictions, counselors are legitimately able to present themselves to clients as competent specialists who understand the client's condition and how best to combat it. Clients who trust in the expertise of their counselor are more open to therapeutic intervention and more hopeful about the prospects of change.

The professionalization of the field has not evolved without conflict and dissent. The peer counseling movement has had enough success to convince many people that only an addict can help another addict. Certainly, recovering peer alcoholics and drug addicts have the advantage of personal experience with addiction and recovery that they can share with others. The bonds of shared experiences can mold a close counseling relationship. Clients tend to feel admiration and respect for addicts who have achieved some measure of recovery and may be inspired to try to imitate their success. However, the achievement of personal recovery is no guarantee of success as a peer counselor. For some peer counselors, the lack of professional education and the emotional closeness to their clients' problems can lead to unfortunate misjudgments that are not in the clients' best interest. Good intentions and personal experience alone are no substitute for counseling skills, and chemical dependency counseling requires a considerable array of skills that an untrained peer counselor may lack.

Basic Tasks of Chemical Dependency Counselors

Chemical dependency counselors are required to perform a variety of tasks to facilitate the recovery of their clients. As an addictions expert you will take the initiative in defining the course of treatment and recovery for your clients. Most treatment programs employ counselors as part of an interdisciplinary team, along with psychologists, psychiatrists, social workers, physicians, and other health professionals. Because counselors often have the most frequent contact and therapeutic involvement with clients, they occupy a critical position on the treatment team. However, they must also recognize the limits of their training and learn to rely on the expertise of other professionals in a comprehensive treatment program. The main tasks that fall to the counselor are promoting client abstinence, educating the client about chemical dependency and recovery, and facilitating successful recovery.

Promote Client Abstinence. The first goal of counseling is to establish the emphasis on the abstinence that begins the recovery process and starts to arrest the progression of the disease. To achieve this goal the counselor must assess the patient's ability and willingness to confront the addiction. This confrontation demands that patients recognize that they have an addiction and acknowledge the need for abstinence. Through the counselor's careful assessment of the patient's substance use, behavior and events related to substance use, and belief systems about substance use, clients come to recognize and understand their own chemical dependency. Demonstrating to patients the connections between negative experiences in their lives and their drinking and drugging is one way that the counselor helps to foster insight in the patient. Early in treatment, the counselor works with the client toward creating an **alliance-for-abstinence** in which the counseling relationship is focused on successfully maintaining abstinence. Decades of experience in working with alcoholics and drug addicts have convinced most chemical dependency professionals that the long-term goal of treatment for addicted individuals should be lifelong abstinence, albeit "one day at a time." Encouraging addicted individuals to cut down or to have "normal" substance use is not a widely accepted notion, and in fact many consider such advice as a prescription for failure. The way to successfully arrest the progress of addictions is to abstain completely (Alcoholics Anonymous 1976, Alterman et al. 1991, Jellinek 1960, O'Connor 1978).

Individual counseling is rarely the only treatment provided to the patient. A comprehensive program will also include group therapy, family counseling, and peer support groups such as Alcoholics Anonymous and Narcotics Anonymous. The counselor uses the one-on-one contacts in individual sessions to focus on the specific experiences and behaviors of the client as they pertain to the client's own unique circumstances and recovery needs. In therapy groups the counselor encourages a group of clients to share openly with and learn from one another for the benefit of all group members. The inspiration, confrontation, and support from other therapy group members can enhance the changes begun in individual sessions when the counselor integrates group experiences into individual sessions. In addition to individual and group sessions, family counseling is an important element in treatment. Because the family has played a major role during the course of the addiction and will be critical to recovery, the counselor must address the many issues, conflicts, and relationships among family members. The counselor also encourages and supports the client's attendance at Twelve step meetings. For most clients, involvement in Twelve step programs will continue after formal counseling has concluded. It is important for the counselor to help the client assimilate into a peer support community during treatment in order to continue benefitting from the resources of that community when treatment ends.

Educate the Client. Another basic task for the chemical dependency counselor is to educate. In their **didactic role**, counselors educate clients about drugs and alcohol, the nature of chemical dependency, the disease process, and the path to recovery. To this end your work as a counselor will also make you a teacher whose job is to help patients learn the skills and knowledge needed for successful recovery. Oddly, many alcoholic and drug-addicted individuals are quite naive and uninformed about alcohol and drugs and have little understanding about the nature of chemical dependency. The skilled counselor combines therapeutic and educational activities by taking advantage of opportunities to inform and instruct patients in regard to their own personal experiences and behaviors. For example, in early recovery an alcoholic patient may complain of many physical discomforts that were never a problem while he was drinking, and the counselor can take the opportunity to give some information about the sedative and pain-suppressing effect of alcohol.

Along with teaching about drugs and alcohol, counselors will also educate patients about themselves. As is true with many people who have serious psychological disorders, chemically dependent people often have limited insight into the workings of their own minds. Absorption in drugs and alcohol prevents a person from looking at himself, and for many patients a major function of substance abuse is just that: to avoid thinking about themselves. You will find that many patients learn about themselves only through difficult and painful self-confrontations. As a teacher your task is to help the patient learn in a way that is most beneficial to recovery. For the counselor-as-teacher a few simple *educational principles* are worth following:

1. Start simply and move slowly to complicated problems.
2. Proceed at a pace that the client can tolerate.
3. Help the client learn to learn by himself.
4. Support, praise, and encourage progress in learning.
5. Be respectful of efforts and tolerant of mistakes.

As a teacher you are in a position of providing a powerful *role model* for patients. Consequently, your actions and attitudes have a strong impact on your patients and provide a set of guidelines for them. Modeling healthy, appropriate, and responsible behavior is especially important when working with patients who have few positive role models in their lives. Being a role model does not mean pretending to be Mr. or Ms. Perfect, but rather presenting a realistic (even if somewhat flawed) picture of how to act. Counselors need to manage their own behavior with an awareness of how their behavior may be perceived by and influence the patient. With that need in mind you must conduct yourself in a way that promotes the patient's health (Powell Davids 1993).

Facilitate Client Recovery. The process of recovery from chemical dependency is lengthy, painful, and demanding. During the course of treatment the counselor's task is to enable the patient to develop the confidence and competence to continue along the road to recovery after treatment ends. Achieving abstinence is an important step, but just a first step, and many recovering addicts and alcoholics will tell you that it was the easy part. What can the counselor do to increase the chances that recovery will persist? Three actions that the counselor can take to meet this goal are:

1. Carefully monitor the client's progress,
2. Teach specific recovery skills, and
3. Work on relapse prevention.

The counselor monitors a patient's progress continuously throughout treatment. Assessment is an ongoing task that requires careful attention to the patient's behavior, emotional state, social functioning, and of course, substance use. Because the likelihood of relapse is so great, counselors need to remain alert to any signs of active drug and alcohol use as well as potential dangers to abstinence in the patient's everyday behavior and circumstances. Sudden, uncharacteristic, and extreme changes in how the person feels and what the person does may be warning signs. Whether consciously or unconsciously intended, many patients will give off signals that they are close to trouble or in trouble, and the counselor should be vigilant enough to take notice. Progress is also indicated by the patient's faithful attendance at and involvement in group, family, and peer activities, so a counselor is expected to maintain communication with other professionals involved in treating his or her patients.

Urine monitoring is a significant part of keeping track of patient progress. Urine testing today is sophisticated enough to give a dependable reading of drug and alcohol use by detecting the presence of drug by-products in a patient's urine. Not only is it essential to know whether your patient is using his or her drug of choice, but you also need to *monitor any drug use*, including prescribed medications. As you learned in Chapter 3, cross-tolerance is a big problem with many drugs, and people who abuse a variety of drugs are vulnerable to becoming addicted to several different substances. What if your alcoholic patient becomes addicted to a tranquilizer prescribed by her family doctor for anxiety? Without proper urine testing you might never know about the tranquilizer and the jeopardy in which it puts her (Cohen 1981).

To facilitate recovery also means to help patients acquire the skills needed for successful coping with everyday life. Unfortunately many people think that all they have to do is stop drinking and drugging and everything will turn out just right. Such magical thinking usually leads to disappointment, because alcoholics and drug addicts have depended so much on their substances they have not learned other ways to deal with life. **Recovery skills** are coping and self-management strategies that promote continued abstinence and long-term recovery. Dealing with emotional turmoil, handling family conflicts, interacting with bosses and coworkers, engaging in recreation, and other normal activities are difficult for recovering patients, who may have never done any of those things without being intoxicated. Successful recovery demands a reorganization of the person's lifestyle, and the counselor is a key figure in directing the patient to that goal.

Perhaps the most critical area of lifestyle reorganization is *relapse prevention*. Relapse is all too common in recovering patients, and thus they must be prepared to anticipate and cope with the many threats to abstinence (Marlatt and Barrett 1994). In Chapter 14 you will read in more detail about specific techniques employed in relapse prevention, but for now consider a few basic principles that clients should learn to reduce the risk of relapse:

- *Avoid all psychoactive drugs.* The use of any drugs, even many medications prescribed for physical problems, can trigger relapse. Clients should inform their physicians about their condition, and when medications are needed the least risky option should be requested. For instance, the alcoholic patient can request a non-narcotic painkiller when painkillers are needed. Of course, when drugs—even addictive drugs—are medically necessary they can be used in an appropriate and closely monitored fashion. The important goal is for clients to avoid unnecessary use of addictive drugs, not to make them suffer needlessly.

- *Avoid people who use psychoactive drugs.* Many chemically dependent individuals have developed their closest social relationships with other drug and alcohol users. The mere presence of other people who are actively using substances can influence the behavior of the client in a way that causes relapse. Whether they mean to or not, drug-using acquaintances can motivate the client's renewed use.

- *Avoid places associated with psychoactive drugs.* You wouldn't advise a hay fever patient to picnic in a field full of ragweed would you? For similar reasons, chemically dependent individuals should avoid situations in which they are in danger. Bars, clubs, parties, and other circumstances in which drinking and drugging are prevalent should be avoided if possible, and when necessary approached only with the greatest caution and advance preparation.

- *Avoid things associated with psychoactive drugs.* Drinking and drugging are behaviors that are easily conditioned to many stimuli.

Syringes, razor blades, rolled-up bills, pipes, and other things linked with drug use may trigger more cravings and drugging. For the alcoholic, seeing a sign for a favorite pub or picking up a paycheck may stimulate the urge to drink. Avoiding such loaded stimuli reduces relapse potential.

> Steve, an alcoholic, was about four months out of rehab and five months abstinent when he presented what felt like a crisis to his counselor. He was invited to his niece's wedding and although he greatly wanted to go, he was afraid that there would be too much temptation to drink. Despite having done well so far, Steve was still in early recovery and his confidence was minimal. Luckily, he and his counselor had a couple of months before the wedding to prepare Steve with some skills and to plan ahead. They did some troubleshooting about the wedding reception where plenty to drink and plenty of drinkers were sure to be found. They focused on simple practical details and actions: who to sit with, who to stay away from, when to arrive, when to leave, and so on. Initially, Steve seemed to grow more confident that he could handle it, but as the weeks went by and the date got closer his resolve weakened and he became very anxious. Both his counselor and A.A. sponsor advised Steve to reconsider attending the wedding reception if he was so uncertain about his sobriety. Members of his early-recovery group also suspected that he might just be looking for trouble. After much soul-searching Steve decided that he just wasn't ready yet for such a big step. His counselor supported his decision and reinforced Steve for his honesty.

11–3 The Counselor's Responsibilities

In the previous section you learned about the professional counselor's identity and the basic tasks performed in the counseling relationship. Although the counseling relationship is a dynamic and mutual connection between individuals, it is not a relationship of equals. As a counselor you are the more influential member of that relationship. Patients seek your help and advice in turning their lives around and overcoming their addictions as well as in changing the many areas in their lives that have suffered from their substance use. The position in which chemical dependency counselors find themselves is one that carries important responsibilities.

The section that follows addresses three major areas of responsibility that you will confront in your role as a chemical dependency counselor: therapeutic responsibilities, ethical responsibilities, and professional development.

Therapeutic Responsibilities

Like other counselors, chemical dependency counselors are obliged to act in the service of their clients. But how can you know what the client's therapeutic needs are? As discussed earlier in this chapter, the goal of long-term recovery must be your guiding principle. Counselors are obliged to evaluate each client as an individual with unique traits, strengths, and weaknesses in determining how to meet those needs. Each client will present unique characteristics and problems that will have to be approached with respect for the person's own character and individuality. A successful counselor will develop an approach that is flexible enough to accommodate the many kinds of clients who will be encountered.

Despite the differences in style and approach that counselors take with different clients, some common characteristics of effective counselors can be identified (Kottler and Brown 1992). Counselor skills can be categorized in a variety of ways. *Instrumental skills*, for example, are those that facilitate the client's efforts toward achieving recovery. Goal-setting, confrontation, and reinforcing are three kinds of instrumental skills. In contrast, skills such as active listening, empathy, reassurance, and communication are important *interpersonal skills* that help create and maintain a therapeutic relationship. In addition, good counselors need to acquire *self-management skills* like self-awareness and self-regulation of their own emotions.

Your counseling skills, however, will only help your clients if you apply them with an appreciation of your broader responsibilities as a health professional. Skills alone are mean-ingless unless used in a responsible manner. This section examines four fundamental therapeutic responsibilities: (1) placing the client's needs first; (2) being yourself, (3) giving emotional support, and (4) maintaining a therapeutic attitude.

Placing the client's needs first. This point may seem obvious, but it is essential to keep your focus on this fundamental principle. Counselors who forget that the work they do is for the client, not themselves, do more harm than good. A counselor's need for success, control, praise, and self-esteem will interfere with the therapeutic work if those needs are foremost in the counseling relationship. The good counselor, therefore, develops self-understanding and self-control in order to act in the service of the client's needs rather than his or her own needs.

A basic respect for the client as a person is fundamental to placing the client's needs first. Respecting your clients does not mean accepting their behavior regardless of its nature. You will find that some of your clients have behaved in ways that you find personally repulsive or morally unacceptable. Keep in mind that many addicts have lifestyles that the so-called average person could barely imagine. Despite their behavior and lifestyle, your clients deserve and need to perceive that you respect them as individuals. The famous humanistic psychologist Carl Rogers (1961) described this respectful attitude with "no strings attached" as **unconditional positive regard,** and he considered it a necessary element in successful counseling. With chemically dependent clients maintaining positive regard is especially important as they often have little respect for themselves, often seeing themselves as unworthy of others' respect. If the client perceives the counselor's respect, he or she may begin to act with self-respect.

Being yourself. As a counselor your main tool is yourself, and you must learn to use it wisely. Your intelligence, talents, humor, judgment, intuition, and other personal qualities are your equipment. Rogers (1961) insisted that counselors should strive for **genuineness** in the therapeutic relationship by presenting themselves in a straightforward, honest manner. Being yourself does not mean completely divulging every detail of your personal life, thoughts, and deepest secrets. Self-disclosure is therapeutic if pertinent to the client's needs at the moment, but inappropriate self-disclosure can be confusing and threatening to the client. For self-disclosure to be therapeutic it should serve a function, such as expressing empathy (for example, by conveying a similar experience from your own past) or giving instruction (for example, telling how you once learned an important lesson from a big mistake). Excessive, poorly timed, and egocentric self-disclosure by the counselor can damage the therapeutic relationship. When the counselor uses self-disclosure merely to lecture, brag, or impress the client, the counselor is placing his or her needs before those of the client (Lawson, et al. 1984).

Giving emotional support. For counseling to promote the client's growth, the emotional atmosphere of the client–counselor relationship should be safe. **Empathy**, the understanding of another person's emotional state, is a primary therapeutic responsibility. Having empathy does not mean that you "share the pain," but rather that you are able to comprehend how the client feels and relate to his feelings from your own personal experiences. Many chemically dependent people experience profoundly distressing emotional states, such as depression, shame, anxiety, rage, and guilt. Inexperienced counselors often feel overwhelmed by their clients' intense emotions and try to avoid or downplay them. Nevertheless, those feelings must be acknowledged and the client's expression of them encouraged for therapeutic gains.

Providing emotional support does not mean encouraging the acting out of all feelings. For example, a client who is enraged at her sexually abusive father and feels that she could kill him should obviously not be directed to do so, but should be helped to learn a healthier and more realistic way of managing that emotion. The counselor is responsible for helping the client to develop control over potentially destructive expressions of emotion. Empathizing with a potent feeling is therapeutically sound,

but the counselor should help the client recognize the difference between acknowledging the feeling and acting on it, particularly when such action is self-defeating.

Maintaining a Therapeutic Attitude. To sustain an effective counseling relationship, the counselor must maintain an attitude that fosters the client's continued involvement and effort. Being a client is hard work, and many are discouraged to the point of quitting before they are ready. The counselor must help keep the client engaged in treatment and motivated to change by expressing a **therapeutic attitude** of compassionate neutrality, optimism, confidence, and realism.

Compassionate neutrality is an essential ingredient of the therapeutic attitude. You must retain a neutral or objective position, but at the same time keep your emotional sensitivity to the client. Neutrality does not mean that you feel indifference or apathy about the client; if you are indifferent to your client's condition you should seek another line of work. Compassionate neutrality means that you avoid imposing your personal values and judgments on the client, maintain an objectivity about the client, and keep your client's needs separate from your own needs (Perez 1985). As you read earlier in this section, your responsibility is to the client's needs, not your own.

The counselor's attitude about the counseling process also matters. A blend of optimism, confidence, and realism is important. The counselor who conveys a sense of hope to the client is likely to instill hope in the client. People in chemical dependency treatment often have a long history of failure, not just in regard to substance use, but also in other areas of their lives. As a consequence, they learn not to expect much of themselves and others. If your clients perceive that you expect them to fail, they are likely to do just that. In contrast, your expectation that they can succeed if they put forth the effort can help induce some much-needed hope.

A therapeutic attitude also includes the counselor's confidence in his or her own ability. Psychologist Albert Bandura (1982) contends that an individual's achievement depends on *self-efficacy*, the belief that your abilities will allow you to act competently. The counselor who acts with confidence conveys a sense of competence to the client, and a client who has faith in the ability of the counselor will respond better to treatment by that counselor. Many new counselors find it hard to act confidently because their experience is still too limited. Be aware that a counselor's lack of confidence can be contagious and can infect the client. Many longtime addicts are experts at detecting others' weaknesses and taking advantage. For the diffident novice counselor, supervision by a more seasoned counselor is of enormous value. Of course, true confidence comes only from experience with success.

Finally, counselors should keep a realistic attitude toward their clients and the counseling process. Chemically dependent individuals have serious problems that do not change overnight and often change will occur only after considerable struggles, sacrifices, and setbacks. In conveying a therapeutic attitude to clients you need to paint a picture of what they can expect in order to counter some exaggerated and unrealistic notions. Many drug- and alcohol-addicted clients are inclined to magical thinking and extend it to counseling thinking "This should take a couple weeks." "A few sessions is all I really need" and similar comments are not unusual from new patients in a hurry to "get it over with." People who expect a magical cure are sure to be disappointed. The counselor's responsibility is to convey a realistic perspective about experience and the duration of the recovery process.

Ethical Responsibilities

Counseling is a profession that involves many ethical questions, dilemmas, and obligations (Bissell and Royce 1994). Here we will introduce you to the basic ethical responsibilities of chemical dependency counselors, and later in this book (Chapter 16) you will examine in more detail the specific ethical and legal concerns that pertain to the field.

Safeguard the Client's Well-being. The most basic ethical responsibility in counseling is to safeguard the well-being of your clients, in-cluding both their physical and psychological well-being. Your clients are in a vulnerable state during counseling and need you to act in a manner that provides them with some protection against themselves and their drinking and drugging. Decisions you make and actions you take, even if they seem trivial, may have unforeseen effects on the client's welfare. In addition, things you don't do may jeopardize the client's welfare. Counselors rarely mean to neglect their clients, but may nevertheless be negligent. Not noticing changes in client behavior that may indicate an impending relapse, ignoring a client's "joking" about using drugs, skipping a weekly drug test because it is inconvenient, and many other instances of negligence that seem small may lead to serious problems.

No counselor can completely safeguard a client, nor is it reasonable for a counselor to try to protect a client against any and every hazard that life presents. However, in the context of counseling activity you will have the obligation to be attentive to the impact of what you do and what you don't do on the client's well-being.

Protect Client Confidentiality. Trust is essential to successful counseling. Clients reveal very personal and private information to their counselors and it is expected that the counselor will protect the *confidentiality* of those revelations. The ability to create a therapeutic relationship with your client depends on earning the client's trust and protecting that trust. However, even confidentiality has its limits. Some circumstances require that confidentiality be broken or temporarily suspended. What are some of those exceptions? Court orders, probation and parole requirements, reports of criminal activity (e.g., child abuse), and medical emergencies (e.g., suicide attempts) are common reasons that confidential records or conversations with your clients may have to be shared with a third party. Today, however, the most common reason is to satisfy the need for information by insurance companies and managed-care organizations.

As you will learn in Chapter 16, there are many legal limits to confidentiality. Not only do you need to be aware of those legal requirements, but you must also inform your clients about them. For example, the most common limit on confidentiality involves supervision. During supervision meetings you will be discussing your work with your clients, and in so doing revealing to your supervisor what they have shared with you. You must make your clients aware that supervision is an important part of their counseling and inform them that for their treatment to be effective you will be discussing their case with one or more supervisors.

Act within Limits of Professional Competence. Like other health professionals, chemical dependency counselors are obliged to receive specialized training in their chosen field and are required to limit their activities to only those areas in which they have *professional competence*, as defined by their education and certification. You would not expect your dentist to set a broken leg, would you? Similarly, your work as a counselor must be restricted to your area of specialization. In most cases chemical dependency counselors will work as part of an interdisciplinary team along with other health providers. Each team member serves an important function, and the team will function best when everyone attends to his or her own area of competence.

Sometimes counselors are asked to perform activities that they are not well-qualified to perform. For example, your client may ask you for legal advice in regard to a technicality in a probation matter. Counselors are well-advised to refer their clients to proper legal experts in such situations. Although you may be tempted to play the know-it-all with your clients, your ethical responsibility is to do only what you are trained to do.

Professional Development

Learning is a lifelong process in all professions. Research constantly revises our understanding of chemical dependency and successful counseling strategies. To remain an effective counselor you must remain current in your knowledge of the field, and that ap-

plies not only to book knowledge, but your practical knowledge as well.

Learn from Your Clients. New counselors often perceive and worry about a separation of theoretical ("book") knowledge and real-life experience with clients. Of course the theories and research discussed in books are more remote, impersonal, and abstract than the immediate, personal, and concrete realities found in counseling sessions. An important task for counselors is to bridge the gap between books and everyday life by learning from your clients about the individual and specific events that pertain to them. Some counselors make the mistake of being blinded by book knowledge to the extent that they are unable to appreciate the individuality of the client. From time to time you might run across a "textbook case," but more often you will find that your client's unique characteristics and circumstances do not fit neatly into any one theory or generalization.

While it is important to have a good foundation of knowledge about the general principles of chemical dependency, it is just as important to approach your counseling work with a flexible and adaptable attitude and a respect for the uniqueness of each client. There is an old saying: "If your only tool is a hammer, you treat everything like a nail." In counseling, your ideas are your tools, and just as no one idea fits all clients, no single strategy works for everyone. Your responsibility includes learning to adjust your counseling activity to your client's personality, ethnicity, social background, emotional state, and other unique characteristics.

Learn from Your Supervisor. Along with the counselor–client relationship, the counselor-supervisor relationship is crucial in your professional development. Inasmuch as counselors may be teachers and role models for clients, supervisors act as teachers and role models for counselors. Ideally, your supervisor will serve as a mentor and guide to help you acquire the professional skills to best serve your clients. Naturally, even the best supervisor cannot make a difference unless the counselor is receptive to learning. To benefit from your supervision you should bear in mind these two points: nobody knows everything, and everybody makes mistakes.

Some inexperienced counselors, and even some experienced ones are reluctant to admit that they don't understand their clients and don't know exactly what to do with them. The fear of being judged ignorant can be a big obstacle in supervision if it prevents you from asking for direction and advice when you are stuck. In taking advantage of your supervision it helps to remember that your primary task is to help the client. We all know that people make mistakes, and yet many counselors hesitate to admit their mistakes in supervision. No counselor has ever had an error-free career, including your supervisor, and neither will you. The purpose of supervision is to examine those mistakes and learn from them so you will not repeat them with other clients.

Learn from Continuing Education. In a complex, growing field such as the treatment of chemical dependency there is always something new to learn. For most health professions continuing education is a requirement for maintaining one's license to practice. Whether through ongoing formal training, refresher courses, or keeping up with the latest journals and studies, there are many opportunities for the counselor who seeks to remain up to date. Many organizations, schools, and agencies offer classes on chemical dependency for professionals in the field, and it is the personal responsibility of the counselor to take advantage of those resources.

Chapter Summary

11–1

The disease model describes chemical dependency as a chronic, progressive illness, that is, one whose course persists and steadily worsens over a long period of time, resulting in numerous adverse physical and psychosocial consequences. Based on this model, counseling addresses the needs of patients in three phases of chemical-dependence treatment:

abatement, remission, and relapse. Abatement is a temporary stoppage or reduction of substance use; remission is the arrest of the disease process and disappearance of symptoms; and relapse is a resumption of substance use following a period of abstinence.

11–2

The professional chemical dependency counselor relies on the Twelve step model of counseling that combines the disease model with the Twelve step programs originated in Alcoholics Anonymous. Chemical dependency counseling is a profession based on specialized training and education in the field of addictions. The primary tasks performed by professional counselors are to promote client abstinence through individual, group, and family counseling; to educate clients about the nature and consequences of drugs and alcohol; and to facilitate client recovery by monitoring behavior and progress and teaching recovery skills such as lifestyle management skills and relapse-prevention skills.

11–3

The major responsibilities of chemical dependency counselors pertain to therapy, ethics, and professional development. Therapeutic responsibilities include placing the needs of clients first, presenting yourself in a genuine manner, providing emotional support and empathy, and maintaining a therapeutic attitude. Safeguarding the client's well-being, protecting client confidentiality, and acting within the limits of professional competence are the main ethical responsibilities of counselors. The counselor's responsibility for professional development requires a continued learning both from clients and supervision, as well as active pursuit of continuing education.

Terms To Remember

abatement
abstinence
alliance-for-abstinence
empathy

genuineness
recovery
recovery skills
remission
Twelve step model
therapeutic attitude
unconditional positive regard

Suggested Reading

Alcoholics Anonymous World Services. (1952). *Twelve Steps and Twelve Traditions.* New York: Alcoholics Anonymous World Services.

Doyle-Pita, D. (1994). *Addictions Counseling: A Practical Guide to Counseling People with Chemical and Other Addictions.* New York: Crossroad.

CHAPTER TWELVE

Planning, Selecting, and Implementing Treatment

Chapter Outline

Learning Objectives

After completing this chapter you should be able to:

1. Explain the general principles of effective treatment.
2. Distinguish between the different typers of treatment settings and explain the factors that determine choice of setting.
3. Describe the general principles and methods of detoxification.
4. Explain the rationale of pharmacotherapy for chemical dependency.
5. Discuss the four categories of drugs used in pharmacotherapy.
6. Explain the philosophy and practice of self-help groups.
7. Differentiate individual, group, and family therapies and present evidence for their effectiveness.
8. Outline the fundamental principles and practice of treatments to enhance motivation.
9. Describe the rationale and practice of cognitive-behavioral coping skills therapy.
10. Discuss Twelve step facilitation therapy in the context of Alcoholics Anonymous.

The many manifestations and the variety of factors that contribute to its causation and maintenance make the treatment of chemical dependency a difficult but rewarding task. In this chapter you will examine crucial factors to consider in planning, selecting, and implementing a treatment program for your clients. You will learn how to establish therapeutic goals and the types of treatment settings available. Next, you will be informed about the variety of treatment modalities. A fundamental knowledge of these alternative approaches will assist you in selecting and implementing the most effective treatment program for your clients.

12–1 Treatment Goals and General Principles of Treatment

The necessary first step in the treatment of chemical dependency is to conduct a com-

prehensive assessment (see Chapter 3). Information gained from assessment can be used to establish treatment goals. As you will learn later in this chapter, the chosen goals will determine the treatments you select to achieve them.

Treatment Goals and Planning Treatment

When we talk about establishing treatment goals for chemical dependency your first reaction might be to ask, "Why spend so much time and effort establishing goals when everyone knows that there is only one goal: to help the client become abstinent?" As you will learn, however, things are rarely this simple.

During the early days of the substance abuse treatment conducted at the U.S. Public Health Service Hospital in Lexington, Kentucky, the only goal of treatment was abstinence and the sole measure of treatment success was whether the person relapsed after treatment. Of course, most patients engaged in some subsequent substance use and so treatment was generally considered to be a failure. This conclusion was based on a mistaken, simplistic assumption that chemical dependency is an all-or-nothing phenomenon.

Many years of clinical practice and research inform us that chemical dependency is difficult to conquer. The nature of the beast is such that addiction is characterized by compulsive and at times uncontrollable drug craving, seeking, and use that persists in spite of extremely negative consequences. Furthermore, addiction is a chronic, biopsychosocially determined condition marked by a high risk of relapse even after long periods of abstinence. Although it is axiomatic that addiction treatment should strive toward abstinence, this cannot be accomplished by trying to pull a rabbit out of a hat. Many clients are either unmotivated or unable to reach abstinence, especially in the early stages of treatment. The harsh reality is that many chemically dependent individuals *never* achieve abstinence, and those who do attain it only after many years of treatment marked by periods of relapse (American Psychiatric Association 1995a, National Institute on Drug Abuse 1999a, Substance Abuse and Mental Health Services Administration 1997

Another unfounded assumption of early addiction treatment programs was that abstinence would somehow magically relieve addicted individuals of most of their other life-role problems. Whereas this assumption may be borne out for some, the typical addicted client finds that abstinence is just the dawn of a long, laborious journey to reconstruct a life left in shambles by pathological drug abuse. Abstinence also means facing life's many problems and the psychiatric disturbances that preceded the onset of addiction, without the crutch of mind-altering drugs. Indeed, recovery is not an end goal as much as it is a lifelong struggle that is never completed. The moment that the recovering client believes the addiction is conquered, he runs the risk of falling prey to it once again (American Psychiatric Association 1995a, National Institute on Drug Abuse 1999a).

The foregoing should impress upon you that planning treatment for chemical dependency requires the establishment of multiple goals as well as abstinence. As outlined in Table 12–1, these goals involve many spheres of functioning, including modifying drug-related behaviors as well as seeking improvements in medical and physical health, psychosocial functioning, employment stability, and reduced criminal justice involvement (Schuckit 1994, Substance Abuse and Mental Health Services Administration 1997).

General Principles of Effective Treatment

A prerequisite to planning treatment is to consider the numerous problems that must be addressed. It is always better, if possible,

Table 12–1. Addiction treatment outcome measures

Substance use	*Abstinence and sobriety* Reduced substance consumption Fewer days or periods intoxicated Substitution of illicit drug with an authorized medication
Medical and physical health	Basic food and shelter needs met Improved overall health Fewer medical problems Reduced use of health-care services Reduced use by spouse and family of health services Reduced high-risk sexual behavior Reduced use of needles or shared needles
Psychosocial functioning	Creating an substance-free life style Improved quality of interpersonal relationships Reduced family dysfunction, abuse, and neglect Improved psychological functioning Treatment of emotional problems Treatment of psychiatric disorders Improved parenting
Employment stability	Increased likelihood in obtaining work Increased job retention Improved job performance Increased number of days worked Reduced accidents and absenteeism
Criminal justice involvement	Reduced involvement with criminal justice system Reduced DUI or DWI arrests Reduced involvement in illegal activities Reduced violent behavior
Relapse prevention	Reduced likelihood of using substances again Prepare for the possibility of relapse Minimize the adverse effects of relapse

Source: Substance Abuse and Mental Health Services Administration (1997).

to understand what you will be getting into rather than to fly by the seat of your pants.

Attempts to modify pathological substance use have flourished since the dawn of civilization. As you learned in earlier chapters, the treatment of chemical dependency has occupied the minds of clinicians, clergymen, and ordinary people alike throughout the twentieth century, too. In the last quarter century we have witnessed intensive scientific research and clinical progress that have significantly advanced our knowledge about the effectiveness of different treatments for chemical dependency. Although a panacea certainly has proven elusive, experts in the field of addiction treatment are now able to demonstrate that addiction can be effectively treated and that these therapies are as effective as treatments for other chronic medical conditions. We are also able to identify the relative effectiveness of different treatments. Of course, treatment does not necessarily mean cure. Just as it is possible to treat (but not cure) diabetes with insulin, it is also possible to treat chemical dependency with a variety of approaches that you will explore in the remainder of this chapter.

For the purposes of planning, it is worth belaboring the point that the best treatment consists of a combination of therapies and other services designed to meet the needs of individual clients. Thus, comprehensive addiction treatment should consider factors such as age, race, culture, sexual orientation, gender, pregnancy, parenting, housing, employment, and physical and sexual abuse (National Institute on Drug Abuse 1999a). Figure 12–1 illustrates the components of a comprehensive chemical dependency treatment program.

With regard to the matter of which treatments work best, addiction experts are now able to delineate a set of fundamental principles that characterize effective chemical dependency treatment. The thirteen principles are:

1. No single treatment is appropriate for all individuals.
2. Treatment should be made readily available.
3. Effective treatment attends to multiple needs.
4. Treatment must be flexible.
5. Clients should remain in treatment for a

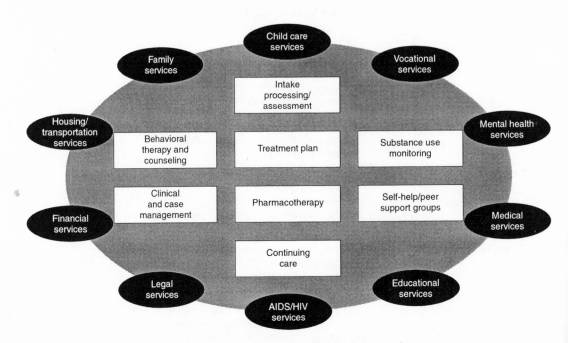

Figure 12–1. Components of a comprehensive chemical dependency treatment program
Source: National Institute on Drug Abuse (1999a).

considerable period of time for it to be effective.

6. Individual and/or group counseling and other behavior therapies are critical components of effective treatment.

7. Medications are an important element of treatment for many patients.

8. Addicted or drug-abusing individuals with comorbid mental disorders should have both disorders treated in an integrated way.

9. Medical detoxification is only the first stage of treatment.

10. Treatment does not need to be voluntary to be effective.

11. Possible drug use during treatment must be monitored continuously.

12. Treatment programs should provide assessment for HIV/AIDS, hepatitis B and C, tuberculosis, and other infectious diseases.

13. Recovery from addiction is a long-term process.

You should keep these principles in mind because they constitute guidelines that chemical dependency counselors can use to plan treatments that correspond to the achievement of multiple treatment goals (National Institute on Drug Abuse 1999a).

Motivation: Treatment Compliance and Involvement

Many chemically dependent individuals are able to change their lives without the assistance of professional treatment. As a counselor, you will not be concerned with these individuals. Your interest is in those people whose efforts to change have failed, so that they now seek assistance, either voluntarily or by coercion. Hundreds of studies have clearly shown that people can change with the help of professional treatment, but typical clinical outcome studies do not help us understand *how* people change (DeRubeis and Crits-Christoph 1998, Lambert and Bergin 1994). It is quite clear that *motivation* to change is a key element in treatment and recovery (DiClemente et al. 1999). Thus, a key facet of treatment planning often will be the creation of an atmosphere that fosters increased client motivation.

What is the relationship between motivation and treatment outcome? To answer this question, we will briefly review our earlier discussion of the *stages-of-change model*, based on the notion that one's motivation to change depends on the interplay of many factors within the person and the social environment (see Chapter 3). Within this framework, people progress through a series of changes stages labeled *precontemplation, contemplation, preparation, action,* and *maintenance*. Individuals with substance problems who participate in treatment vary significantly in their levels of motivation to change. They are not necessarily at the action stage during which people modify their behavior, experiences, or environment to overcome their problems. A common error in chemical dependency treatment, unfortunately, is to ignore this fact and to implement treatments that might be beneficial to those who are highly motivated and at the action stage. This means that a particular therapeutic intervention may be effective with some clients, but ineffective and even detrimental to others. From the stages-of-change perspective, many substance-dependent people do not benefit from treatment because the type of treatment they receive does not match their motivational level (DiClemente et al. 1999, DiClemente and Scott 1997, Prochaska et al. 1992).

Motivation is positively correlated with treatment compliance and treatment involvement; higher motivation increases the likelihood of both. **Treatment compliance** is defined as actions on the part of the client to follow the instructions and requirements of treatment. Attending therapy sessions, Alcoholics Anonymous meetings, or getting regular drug screens are indicators of compliance. In this sense, treatment compliance is a restrictive set of events and a weak predictor of treatment success because many people comply by going through the motions of their program without much committment; they are not necessarily motivated to change. The naked truth is that many chemically dependent clients are pressured into treatment and are not ready to change. Low levels of motivation are usually construed as denial, resistance to treatment, defensiveness, not really wanting to get clean, or just symptoms of the disease.

Treatment involvement goes beyond compliance in that the person is engaged in the treatment process, subscribes to the treatment rationale, and has formulated goals consistent with the treatment philosophy. As such, treatment involvement consists of higher levels of motivation and is a better prognostic indicator of change. Compared to unmotivated clients, highly motivated alcoholics and addicts are not only more likely to be involved in treatment, they also are likely to complete it and maintain abstinence after treatment (DiClemente et al. 1999, DiClemente and Scott 1997).

Sources of Motivation. Broadly speaking, there are two sources of motivation: intrinsic and extrinsic. *Intrinsic motivation* refers to an internally generated drive toward change, such as feeling a sense of accomplishment or knowing that the person is doing the right thing. *Extrinsic motivation*, in contrast, involves external incentives or pressures. For example, an alcoholic may be motivated stop drinking to reap financial reward (incentive) or to avoid having his driver's license revoked or losing a job (pressure) (Deci and Ryan 1987).

Intrinsic motivation is associated with increased treatment involvement and retention and improved long-term outcome. Indeed, more severe alcohol problems are usually associated with high levels of intrinsic motivation for treatment presumably because high levels of distress influence the alcoholic to seek treatment. Thus, the popular notion that the alcoholic must "hit bottom" in order to get sober is supported by clinical research (Ryan et al. 1995).

Relying solely on external incentives and pressures (extrinsic motivation) to promote long-term abstinence is less effective than appealing to an individual's sense of personal responsibility (intrinsic motivation). Nevertheless, extrinsic motivation can help to promote short-term abstinence. Consistent with the advice to take one day at a time, sources of extrinsic motivation may help chemically dependent individuals buy some time during which they ultimately may develop the intrinsic motivation necessary to progress through the stages of change (DiClemente et al. 1999).

12–2   Treatment Settings

A fundamental decision to be made in the treatment planning for chemically dependent clients is the choice of treatment setting. In this section you will examine the different types of treatment settings available and the factors to weigh in making a decision.

Factors That Determine the Choice of Setting

Clients with substance abuse and dependence problems can receive treatment in a variety of settings. Making a decision among the alternatives requires careful consideration of several important factors. On the simplest level of determination, clients can be treated in an *inpatient* facility or on an *outpatient* basis. Remember that somebody must pay for the treatment. Whether you are dealing with a so-called self-pay client or someone insured by private insurance, Medicare, or Medicaid, cost is an unfortunate but inescapable factor in determining choice of setting. Bear in mind that in the age of managed care, treatment decisions are influenced, unfortunately, by managed-care, protocols and insurance fee schedules as much as by clinical necessity. Because inpatient programs are significantly more expensive than outpatient programs you may be involved in selecting outpatient treatment for a client who you think might show greater improvement in an inpatient program.

Beyond these financial and insurance considerations, your selection of an inpatient or outpatient setting depends on a variety of client variables and other factors not involving the client. Some important factors include the client's clinical status, availability of treatment capacities, restrictiveness of the therapeutic environment regarding access to substances and potential for other high-risk behaviors, hours of operation, the overall milieu, and the treatment philosophy (American Psychiatric Association 1995a).

Clients should receive treatment in the *least restrictive environment* that is likely to be safe and effective. In any case, clients should be moved from one level of care to another based on the counselor's assessment of their readiness and ability to benefit from a less intensive level of care (American Psychiatric Association 1995a). Specifically, variables that must be examined in making a decision for treatment setting include the client's

- Capacity and motivation to cooperate with treatment;
- Capacity to care for himself or herself;
- Need for structure, support, and supervision to ensure safety and continuing engagement in treatment away from environments and activities that might lead to a resumption of substance use;
- Need for treatments to deal with comorbid medical or psychiatric conditions; and
- Need for specific treatments or an intensity of treatment that might be provided only in a particular setting.

Types of Treatment Settings

A continuum of treatment settings is available to people suffering from chemical dependency, ranging from most to least restrictive. These include *inpatient hospitalization, residential treatment, intensive outpatient treatment*, and *outpatient treatment* (see Table 12–2). The vast majority of chemically dependent individuals are treated in outpatient programs (Fuller and Hiller-Sturmhoffel 1999, Substance Abuse and Mental Health Services Administration 1997).

Inpatient Hospitalization. The term **inpatient hospitalization treatment** (or inpatient rehabilitation) means the provision of medical and often psychological services within a hospital or similarly licensed facility that is designed to treat chemical dependency. This level of care includes twenty-four-hour observation, monitoring, and treatment by a team of physicians, nurses, psychologists, social workers, and other professionals and paraprofessionals with expertise in addiction treatment. These inpatient units may be locked and very restrictive, or permit visitors, telephone calls, and mail contact under monitoring and supervision.

Inpatient treatments include detoxification (considered in a later section of this chapter), medical and psychiatric crisis management, individual and group therapy, education, and psychosocial rehabilitation. Inpatient hospitalization also introduces patients to self-help groups and affords opportunities for posthospital care that emphasize relapse prevention. Such treatment may be provided in a general medical hospital, psychiatric hospital, or freestanding rehabilitation facility. Some of these programs specialize in the treatment of dual-diagnosis patients, that is, patients with chemical dependency and comorbid mental disorders. Inpatient rehabilitation was usually a twenty-eight-day program, but insurance company regulations generally permit only much shorter stays today (American Psychiatric Association 1995a, Fuller and Hiller-Sturmhoffel 1999, Substance Abuse and Mental Health Services Administration 1997, Weiss 1994).

Considering the great expense of inpatient programs, much thought must go into

Table 12–2. Treatment settings

Inpatient hospitalization	Provides medical and psychological services within a hospital or similarly licensed facility.
Residential treatment	Provides treatment programs with 24-hour care and support for people who live on the premises of the program for extended periods of time.
Intensive outpatient treatment	Involves 9 to 70 hours of addiction services weekly in an outpatient setting.
Outpatient treatment	Involves nonresidential chemical dependency treatments for individuals who are able to function in the context of their usual living arrangements.

deciding which clients are best suited to the inpatient hospitalization model. Patients who fit one or more of the following categories should be considered candidates for inpatient rehabilitation:

- Occurrence of drug overdoses that cannot be safely treated on an outpatient basis
- Presence of medically dangerous withdrawal symptoms
- A documented history of receiving no benefit from outpatient treatment or other less-structured, less-intensive treatments
- Presence of coexisting mental disorders and dangerousness to themselves or others

Residential Treatment. A common sequel to inpatient rehabilitation is **residential treatment**, which means treatment programs that provide twenty-four-hour care and support for people who live on the premises of the program for extended periods of time. This type of treatment setting is recommended for individuals who do not meet the criteria for hospitalization or who have already completed an inpatient hospitalization program. It is judged that they cannot function well in outpatient treatment because their lives have become dominated by chemical dependency and they lack the motivation and substance-free social supports to remain abstinent in the community.

One form of residential treatment is the *therapeutic community* (TC), which refers to a variety of short- and more often long-term, highly structured, intensive programs designed to change the lifestyle of chemically dependent individuals. The TC is designed for addicted patients whose psychosocial adjustments to conventional family, social, and occupational responsibilites were severely damaged before addiction, worsened by addiction, and often involved criminal behavior. Considering that many involved in the TC experience were socially disadvantaged even before their addiction, the goal for them is *habilitation* rather than *rehabilitation*. In other words, the lives of individuals residing in the TC had been unproductive before their drug use and addiction has made their lives truly unmanageable. They need many months and

more likely years to make the massive changes necessary to lead productive, substance-free lives (DeLeon 1994, Substance Abuse and Mental Health Services Administration 1997).

SYNANON was the first TC, established in Santa Monica, California, in 1958 primarily for recovering alcoholics and heroin addicts. Individuals who are severely impaired from years of abusing many drugs are typical TC residents today. In any event, the TC philosophy consists of four fundamental views.

1. Drug abuse is viewed as a disorder of the whole person affecting most areas of functioning.
2. The TC distinguishes individuals according to their dimensions of psychological dysfunction and social deficits instead of patterns of drug use.
3. The goal of recovery is to habilitate or rehabilitate the whole person in terms of core changes in lifestyle and personal identity.
4. The TC assumes an unambiguous morality and set of values. It adheres to the notion that there is a "right" way to live.

The TC stresses honesty, alcohol and drug abstinence, self-reliance, and personal responsibility. Residents receive occupational training, education, and behavior modification, and participate in reality-oriented, peer encounter sessions that focus on problems in daily living. To assist in the therapeutic process, TC residents are segregated from the surrounding community and live under strict hierarchies, with newcomers assigned to the most menial social status and chores and the fewest privileges. Progression up the ladder requires that the individual assume increasingly more responsibility for his or her behavior and remain substance-free. With higher status come more privileges, such as leaving the premises, attending school, and getting a job. Many TC graduates ascend to staff counselor positions (DeLeon 1994, Substance Abuse and Mental Health Services Administration 1997).

Another form of residential treatment is the **halfway house**, which is a transitional living facility that provides a supportive environment and rehabilitive services for clients who have completed inpatient or residential treatment but who are not fully prepared to reenter the community. Some halfway houses are staffed by professionals and provide treatment modalities similar to TCs. Others provide little or no formal professional treatment. Instead, they offer peer support, Twelve step program participation, and encouragement to seek employment. Less-structured halfway houses are often called *sober houses*. Usually, residents of halfway houses are people with few of the social and environmental supports necessary to remain clean and sober (American Psychiatric Association 1995a, Fuller and Hiller-Sturmhoffel 1999, Substance Abuse and Mental Health Services Administration 1997).

Intensive Outpatient Treatment. An alternative to inpatient hospitalization and residential treatment is **intensive outpatient treatment**, which involves nine to seventy hours of treatment weekly in an outpatient setting. Intensive outpatient treatment programs offer a wide range of addiction services, including group and individual counseling, withdrawal management, family involvement, and relapse-prevention training. Some programs provide psychotropic medication.

For some clients who have completed inpatient treatment, intensive outpatient treatment provides for continued addiction treatment as they make the transition to a productive substance-free life. Unlike the halfway house, however, the clients in intensive outpatient treatment live at home and travel to the program site each day. Intensive outpatient treatment programs affiliated with hospitals are called *partial hospital programs* and usually require the client to attend the program during the day as if he or she were going to work. For people in need of intense outpatient treatment and who hold jobs during the day, evening programs are available three to five nights per week (American Psychiatric Association 1995a, Fuller and Hiller-Sturmhoffel 1999, Substance Abuse and Mental Health Services Administration 1997).

Outpatient Treatment. Nonresidential chemical dependency treatment for individuals who are able to function in the context of their usual living arrangements is called **outpatient treatment**. In this setting, clients attend regularly scheduled treatment sessions that usually total fewer than nine hours per week. Outpatient treatment usually involves individual and/or group therapy, and involvement in self-help groups. Medication management and medical treatment can be arranged if necessary (American Psychiatric Association 1995a, Fuller and Hiller-Sturmhoffel 1999, Substance Abuse and Mental Health Services Administration 1997).

Treatment Setting and Effectiveness

The conventional wisdom is that inpatient treatment is more effective than any form of outpatient treatment because it is very structured, intensive, and is likely to involve the most treatment components. Scientific proof for this belief has been difficult to find, however. Most of the research suggests that the majority of addicted patients show meaningful improvement in most areas of functioning regardless of the specific setting. The services provided may be more important than the setting in which the treatments are offered (McLellan et al. 1997, 1994).

These findings must be interpreted with great caution for the following reasons. *First*, the bulk of the research in this area focuses on alcoholism. Much less is known about treatment outcome involving people addicted to other substances. *Second*, studies comparing treatment effectiveness in one setting versus another generally measure global treatment effectiveness for generic or average addiction patients. Few studies consider differences in patient-specific variables such as addiction severity, drugs of abuse, and comorbid mental and/or medical disorders. Those studies that do tend to confirm the idea that outpatient treatment is appropriate for clients with sufficient social resources who do not have coexisting medical and psychiatric conditions. Conversely, inpatient treatment should be reserved for clients who lack social resources and who suffer from comorbid conditions. Regardless of research findings, rising health-care costs make outpatient treatment the most popular alternative (American Psychiatric Association 1995a, Finney et al. 1996, Fuller and Hiller-Sturmhoffel 1999, Guydish et al. 1998, Simpson et al. 1999, Substance Abuse and Mental Health Services Administration 1997).

12–3   Detoxification

Abuse of psychoactive substances creates a toxic state and a variety of medical as well as psychological problems. Reaching the goal of long-term abstinence requires that the chemically dependent individual first be taken off the drug in a medically safe manner. After this is accomplished, therapy can proceed with the application of psychological and medical treatments. In this section you will learn about the principles and practice of detoxification.

General Principles

An initial step in the treatment of alcoholism and addiction is **detoxification** (commonly called "detox"), a process by which a chemically dependent individual is taken off the substance either abruptly or gradually (Kleber 1994). Detoxification is an important beginning or prelude to treatment for any type of substance abuse problem, and an absolute imperative and a matter of life or death for clients who demonstrate tolerance and withdrawal symptoms. People who are dependent on alcohol, opioids, and benzodiazepines, or barbiturates and other sedatives, are especially at risk to experience severe (and in some cases life-threatening) reactions to withdrawal. The simultaneous abuse of multiple drugs, like alcohol and Valium, heroin and cocaine, or alcohol and cocaine, may produce significant withdrawal to one or all of the substances in the combination (American Psychiatric Association 1995a, National Institute on Drug Abuse 1999b).

The precise mechanics of detoxification and the time frame required for it largely depend on the type of drug(s) abused, the severity of the addiction, and the aggressiveness of the treatment protocol. In any case, detoxi-

cation should be accomplished safely, as quickly as possible, and with a minimum of patient discomfort.

The first step in the detoxification process is to conduct a thorough interview that details drug history, addiction treatment history, psychosocial functioning, and medical history. A comprehensive medical examination with laboratory testing is always indicated to determine which drugs are present and to evaluate the person's overall medical status. Although counselors are sometimes involved in decisions about detoxification, the ultimate decision should be made by medically trained personnel (Kleber 1994b).

Currently, detoxification for alcoholism begins with the **Clinical Institute Withdrawal Assessment for Alcohol** (CIWA-Ar), a questionnaire that evaluates the presence and severity of various withdrawal symptoms. Symptoms assessed by the CIWA-Ar include nausea and vomiting, tremors, sweating, agitation, sensory disturbances, headaches, and disorientation. The higher the score on the CIWA-Ar, the greater the risk that the patient will experience serious withdrawal symptoms (Foy et al. 1988, Sullivan et al. 1989).

Medications for Detoxification

Although drug abuse education and counseling is one of its important components, the major thrust of detoxification treatment for severely addicted individuals is the use of medications to relieve the symptoms of withdrawal. Realistically, many addicts are unable to focus on getting their life together while they are in the throes of severe withdrawal symptoms. Nevertheless, they are in crisis and may be receptive to educational and counseling interventions.

The effectiveness of benzodiazepines, such as diazepam (Valium) and chlordiazepoxide (Librium), is well-documented in alcohol detoxification. For patients who experience moderate to severe withdrawal symptoms according to the CIWA-Ar, low dosages of these drugs minimize withdrawal symptoms and are especially helpful in reducing the risk of seizures. *Anticonvulsant drugs* may be combined with benzodiazepines for patients who show a history of seizure disorders unrelated to alcoholism. Patients with mild withdrawal symptoms generally do not require medication. Typically, detoxification from alcohol lasts for six to nine days, but insurance constraints may reduce the time allowed for treatment (Fuller and Hiller-Sturmhofel 1999, Hayashida 1998).

Withdrawal from opioid drugs is extremely unpleasant, as you learned in Chapter 2. Despite the severity of symptoms, however, opioid withdrawal is usually not life-threatening. For those unable or unwilling to kick cold turkey, the physician can taper the dosage of the opioid drug and introduce *clonidine*, an antihypertensive agent that eases the discomfort associated with withdrawal. Some addiction experts prefer methadone substitution and withdrawal. In distinction to methadone maintenance therapy, to be discussed later in this section, the former involves replacing an opioid with another longer-acting synthetic narcotic, methadone, then gradually withdrawing the user from it. Using this approach, short-term detoxification lasts up to 30 days; up to 180 days are allowed under Food and Drug Administration guidelines for long-term detoxification. Many patients, however, are unable to withdraw successfuly from methadone due to a fear called "detoxification phobia" and end up in methadone maintenance therapy (Kleber 1994b, Milby et al 1994).

Because abrupt withdrawal from benzodiazepines and other sedative drugs can lead to serious medical complications and death, in order to be handled safely, detoxification involves gradually reducing the dosage of the abused drug. In cases of benzodiazepine withdrawal, some experts recommend replacing the abused drug with a long-acting barbiturate such as phenobarbital, and then gradually tapering the phenobarbital until withdrawal symptoms are minimal. For individuals dependent on both benzodiazepines and alcohol, the method is to substitute a long-acting benzodiazepine, such as chlordiazepoxide (Librium, and then taper the dosage over a period of one to two weeks (Kleber 1994b).

Outpatient and Inpatient Detoxification

Detoxification can be accomplished in either outpatient or inpatient settings. With outpatient detoxification, the patient travels to a hospital or other facility daily except weekends. Following a drug use and psychosocial assessment, physical examination, and laboratory testing, the detoxification procedure usually lasts one to two hours on the first day. Typically, detox sessions last for fifteen to thirty minutes thereafter until the process is complete usually in three to fourteen days. If combined with participation in a hospital day program, sessions can last for several hours per day. Inpatient detoxification requires that the individual be admitted to a hospital where the detox procedure is carried out over a five- to fourteen day period.

Outpatient and inpatient detoxification each have their advantages and disadvantages. Patients involved in outpatient detoxification can continue to function and maintain employment as well as social and family connections. Outpatient detox is also much less expensive and time consuming. A major concern, however, is that the very social contacts that could be advantageous can increase the risk of relapse by behaving in a way that facilitates substance use. Outpatients are also more likely than inpatients to miss appointments or drop out altogether (Hayashida 1998).

Inpatient detoxification is clearly the rule for people whose substance withdrawal may be medically dangerous or life-threatening. It is also indicated for clients who are suicidal or homicidal or for those whose social and family life or jobs are extremely disruptive. The main disadvantage to inpatient detoxification is its cost.

There are few well-controlled studies that compare the long-term outcome of outpatient versus inpatient detoxification. The few available studies do not prove that one is superior to the other, whether the outcome measure is one's score on the *Addiction Severity Index*, the likelihood of enrolling in subsequent long-term treatment, or abstinence six months later. Regardless of setting, one-third to one-half of patients who enter detoxification relapse within six months. Apparently, detoxification treatment outome is more strongly associated with patient characteristics than with setting. Not surprisingly, clients with a high incidence or severity of psychiatric symptoms, a history of alcohol-related seizures, current unemployment, and intoxication at the initial visit stand a poor chance of successfully completing detoxification (Hayashida 1998, Hayashida et al. 1989).

12–4   Pharmacotherapy

The therapeutic use of drugs to alter brain chemistry, called **pharmacotherapy**, is one of the most controversial aspects of treatment for chemical dependency. In many programs the use of drugs to treat drug problems is considered ridiculous, dangerous, and strictly forbidden. "You can't treat a drug problem with a drug" is a phrase you will soon hear if you have not heard it already. Indeed, many people believe that the only reasonable approach to recovery is to undergo detoxification and achieve and maintain abstinence by way of psychological therapies and/or Twelve step programs. This attitude is unfortunate and is driven by ideology, not by treatment considerations.

Rationale for Pharmacotherapy

The nondrug treatment approach certainly is preferred, but this strategy does not work for all clients, and especially those with psychiatric comorbidity. Denial or lack of motivation may be an accurate explanation for the treatment failures of some alcoholics and drug addicts in drug-free therapies, but other factors may be potent, too. During the last quarter-century, as you have learned, researchers have begun to elucidate the neurochemical mechanisms by which alcohol and drugs produce their psychoactive effects. Furthermore, research in this area has revealed that chronic use of psychoactive substances produces lasting changes in those neurochemical mechanisms. From this perspective it makes sense that drugs can aid in treatment if they modify the addiction's underlying pathological neurochemical mechanisms, without producing psychoactive effects themselves. In this section we will discuss the use of medications for alcoholism and addiction after detoxification. Even though some of the drugs used in post-detoxification pharmacotherapy are also used to manage withdrawal symptoms during detoxification, the use of medications after detox serves an entirely different purpose (O'Brien 1997).

One way to classify drugs used in post-detoxification treatment is according to their therapeutic purposes. They are: (1) drugs *to decrease the reinforcing effects of abused substances*, (2) *drugs to discourage the use of substances*, (3) *agonist substitution drugs*, and (4) *medications to treat comorbid psychiatric conditions*. Currently, pharmacotherapy is instituted primarily for alcoholism and opioid addiction. Although many drugs are used to treat other forms of addiction, especially addiction to cocaine, their effectiveness has not been unequivocally demonstrated (Tai et al. 1997).

Drugs to Decrease the Reinforcing Effects of Abused Substances

This category of drugs includes substances that diminish or block the euphoric effects of an abused drug without producing any prominent pleasurable effects themselves. The most commonly used drug in this category is **naltrexone**, an opioid antagonist that blocks opioid receptors in the brain (see Chapter 2). The rationale for its use is that because it blocks the euphoric effects of an abused substance, the perceived bond between having the abused drug and getting its pleasurable effects is broken or weakened. Put simply, individuals who adhere to a naltrexone treatment regimen find it difficult to get high from abused drugs, and their drug craving subsequently fades out or extinguishes (American Psychiatric Association 1995a, O'Brien, 1997, Substance Abuse and Mental Health Services Administration 1997).

Naltrexone was originally developed in the 1980s to treat opioid (particularly heroin) addiction. The initiation of naltrexone treatment requires a drug-free interval of at least five to seven days for heroin and ten to fourteen days for methadone. This treatment op tion is most effective for clients who are highly motivated, involved in a meaningful relationship with a nonaddicted partner, or with those attending school and living with nonaddicted, fairly well-adjusted family members. Unfortunatley, naltrexone is underused in heroin addiction treatment because few street addicts show any interest in it, drug-addiction treatment programs rarely encourage it, and few physicians are trained in its proper use. Compliance is poor, particularly for clients who do not fit the profile just described (O'Brien 1997, Substance Abuse and Mental Health Services Administration 1997).

In 1994 the Food and Drug Administration approved the use of naltrexone as an adjunct in the treatment of alcoholism. This treatment makes sense from a physiological perspective because alcohol produces its reinforcing effects partly by its action on opioid receptors in the brain. Several large-scale studies have shown that participants who received naltrexone combined with psychosocial treatments experienced reduced euphoric effects from alcohol, diminished craving, and lower relapse rates when compared to subjects who did not receive naltrexone treatment. Furthermore, most patients are able to take naltrexone without serious side effects (Croop et al. 1997, Johnson and Ait Daoud 1999, O'Malley et al. 1992, Volpicelli et al. 1992).

Naltrexone certainly is the principal drug used to reduce the reinforcing effects of psychoactive drugs, especially opioids and alcohol. Expanding knowledge of the brain mechanisms by which drugs produce their pleasurable effects will inevitably lead to newer, more effective drugs to treat chemical dependency. Currently, clinical trials are underway to test the effectiveness and safety of another opioid antagonist, *nalmefene*. Like naltrexone, nalmefene blocks opioid receptors and has no abuse potential. It has several distinct advantages, however, that make its therapeutic use more promising. *First*, nalmefene's antagonistic actions last longer. *Second*, whereas natrexone attaches preferentially to one type of opioid receptor, nalmefene binds to several types known to mediate the reinforcing effects of alcohol. *Third*, it produces fewer side effects, a factor

that may result in higher treatment retention rates (Mason et al. 1999).

Some evidence suggests that actions of the excitatory neurotransmitter glutamate may also contribute to some of alcohol's effects, especially intoxication, cognitive impairment, and some withdrawal symptoms (see Chapters 2 and 6). *Acamprosate* is an experimental drug that can reduce the intensity of alcohol craving by blocking glutamate receptors (Swift 1999). Perhaps the most promising of the experimental drugs in the treatment of early- but not late-onset alcoholics is a serotonin antagonist called *ondansetron*. It has been proposed that ondansetron produces its reinforcement-reducing effects by restoring normal levels of the neurotransmitter serotonin, which in turn increases the inhibitory effects on dopamine neurons involved in reinforcement (Johnson and Ait-Daoud 1999).

Drugs That Discourage the Use of Abused Substances

In contrast to antagonists, drugs in this category discourage the use of abused substances by inducing illness only when the substance is used while the therapeutic drug is in the person's system. The only drug approved for such use in the United States is **Antabuse** (disulfiram), which inhibits the activity of an enzyme that breaks down alcohol. An individual who consumes alcohol after pretreatment with Antabuse, even days before, will experience many unpleasant and potentially dangerous symptoms; (in some rare circumstances these can be lethal). Thus, Antabuse curbs impulsive alcohol consumption. Many proponents consider compliance with an Antabuse regimen to be a symbol of the client's commitment to treatment. Treatment with Antabuse should not be considered a sole treatment for alcoholism, but rather an adjunct to a comprehensive biopsychosocially oriented treatment program (American Psychiatric Association 1995a, Substance Abuse and Mental Health Services Administration 1997).

A therapeutic procedure in which the individual associates the abused drug with unpleasant consequences is called *aversion therapy*. With this approach a noxious stimulus is repeatedly paired with a dose of the abused drug until the drug itself produces unpleasant effects. Although aversion therapy is a type of behavior therapy rather than a medical treatment, we discuss it here because the noxious stimulus is a specific drug such as *succinylcholine*, which depresses respiration, or *emetine*, which induces vomiting, or can be an electrical shock. This type of drug treatment is often confused with Antabuse treatment. Although both Antabuse and emetine are used to discourage substance use, the former is introduced in the hope that the person will never drink alcohol while on Antabuse. By contrast, emetine is given, along with alcohol, to foster a conditioned emotional response to the psychoactive drug (American Psychiatric Association 1995a, Substance Abuse and Mental Health Services Administration 1997).

Agonist Substitution Drugs

Another form of medication treatment is to replace an abused drug with one from the same class, but which, if properly prescribed and administered, does not produce the same euphoria and cravings. These drugs are called *agonists* because they influence some of the same brain receptors as the abused drug.

The drug most commonly used as an agonist in the treatment of chemical dependency is *methadone* (see Chapter 2). In distinction to the use of methadone for heroin detoxification, **methadone maintenance treatment** is an outpatient clinic program in which a medically safe, long-acting medication of known purity, potency, and dosage is substituted for heroin, combined with biopsychosocial treatment services. Properly prescribed, methadone does not produce the rush and subsequent craving the way heroin does because it is taken orally and works gradually. It does not block heroin, as naltrexone does, but rather produces cross-tolerance. Thus, methadone suppresses narcotic withdrawal for twenty-four to thirty-six hours and does not usually interfere with everyday activities. A methadone maintenance patient who gets high and cannot function on the drug is overmedicated or is

"double-dipping" (Senay 1994, Substance Abuse and Mental Health Services Administration 1997).

The rationale for methadone maintenance treatment is clear. As a group, heroin addicts are poorly motivated to achieve abstinence. The majority relapse even after detoxification and intensive long-term treatment. Furthermore, heroin use is associated with numerous medical complications, like HIV infection, work impairment, and criminal behaviors. For many, substituting methadone relieves them of the burden and danger of injecting heroin two or three times a day and affords them an opportunity to become productive citizens.

More than three decades of outcome research show that methadone maintenance treatment is far more effective than any other treatment approach for heroin addiction. Although the methadone maintenance patient is not abstinent in the strict sense, roughly one-third give up illicit drugs, reduce their criminal activity, hold jobs, maintain relationships, and show overall improvement in many other areas of functioning. Another third waver between good and bad functioning, and the remaining third never abandon their drug-dominated lifestyle (O'Brien 1997, Senay 1994, Substance Abuse and Mental Health Services Administration 1997).

Recent research suggests that one possible reason why so many methadone maintenance patients continue to use heroin and other psychoactive drugs is that they may be undermedicated. Many clinics do not adjust methadone doses to meet individual needs. Instead, one clinic might adminsister fixed does of 25 mg to all patients while another may prescribe 60 mg. Federal regulations set a ceiling of 100 mg per day (except in special circumstances), but until recently no studies have evaluated the effectiveness of dosages from 80 mg to 100 mg. One study compared differences between moderate (40 mg to 50 mg) versus high doses (80 mg to 100 mg) of methadone with respect to self-reported heroin use and objective presence of heroin metabolites in urine. As shown in Figure 12–2, the high-dose group reported using heroin less frequently than the moderate-dose group and their self-reports were corraborated by urine analysis.

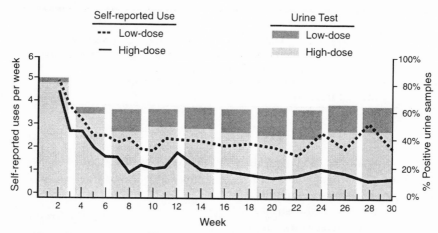

Figure 12–2. Patients receiving high-dose methadone treatment used drugs less often than those receiving moderate-dose treatment
Source: National Institute on Drug Abuse (1999b).

These findings provide preliminary evidence that better outcomes can be achieved at doses higher than 50 mg per day (National Institute on Drug Abuse 1999a).

Methadone is the most predominant agonist used in the treatment of heroin addiction, but another agonist is available in some clinics. This drug, **levo-alpha-acetyl-methadol** (LAAM), is similar to methadone but has a longer half-life, which permits dosing three times per week instead of the daily dosing required with methadone. Furthermore, LAAM's more gradual effects make it less subject to abuse than methadone (O'Brien 1997, Substance Abuse and Mental Health Services Administration 1997).

An experimental drug expected to receive Food and Drug Administration (FDA) approval is *buprenorphine*, a mixed agonist-antagonist that has effects similar to both methadone and LAAM (an agonist) as well as naltrexone (an antagonist). This means that buprenorphine blocks opioid withdrawal and cravings and also decreases the euphoric and reinforcing effects of opioids. Once the FDA approves buprenorphine, clinicians will have a third pharmacological choice in the battle against heroin addiction (Ling et al. 1996, O'Brien 1997, National Institute on Drug Abuse 1999a, Strain et al. 1994, Substance Abuse and Mental Health Services Administration 1997).

Medications to Treat Comorbid Mental Disorders

Thus far we have discussed the use of specific medications to modify the neurochemistry directly associated with chemical dependency. These drugs, however, do not moderate the influences of coexisting mental disorders. Chemically dependent clients with comorbid mental disorders often fall between the cracks of service delivery systems and end up in a setting in which either their addiction or their mental disorders are undetected or mismanaged. As you learned earlier in this chapter, a fundamental principle of treatment is to have both types of disorders treated equally. Pharmacotherapy for dual-diagnosis patients is especially challenging because research with this population has been limited and some of the psychotropic drugs used in psychiatry are themselves drugs of abuse. Thus, the prescribing physician must exercise great caution.

Notwithstanding these limitations, pharmacotherapy for comorbid mental disorders involves the use of five types of medications, which are prescribed to reduce specific types of psychiatric symptoms (see Table 12–3). Considering that mental disorders often have high comorbidity themselves, some clients may receive drugs from more than one class. Generally *antipsychotics* are prescribed to reduce the

Table 12–3. Drugs to Treat Comorbid Mental Disorders

Drug Type	Trade Names
Antipsychotics	Thorazine, Haldol, Prolixin, Risperidol, Zyprexa, Navane
Antidepressants	Prozac, Paxil, Zoloft, Elavil, Tofranil, Wellbutrin, Serzone, Remeron
Mood Stabilizers	Lithium, Tegretol, Depakote, Neurontin
Anxiolytics	Valium, Xanax, Librium, Ativan, Buspar
Psychostimulants	Ritalin, ADDERAL

hallucinations, delusions, and agitation found in psychotic conditions like schizophrenia. Symptoms of depression require the use of *antidepressants*. The restlessness, euphoria, and inflated self-esteem seen in mania are treated with *mood stabilizers*, and symptoms of fear, worry, tension, and apprehension characteristic of anxiety disorders are moderated by *anxiolytics* (usually benzodiazepines). Finally, some clients with *attention-deficit hyperactivity disorder* (ADHD) can benefit from *psychostimulants*, which are amphetamines or amphetamine-like compounds.

Generally, antipsychotics, antidepressants, and mood stabilizers do not have high abuse potential because increased doses produce unpleasant side effects. Benzodiazepines and psychostimulants do carry the risk of abuse, so they must be prescribed cautiously. The biggest risk with any of the psychotropic drug is that clients may combine them with their drugs of abuse.

12–5   Self-Help Groups and Psychosocial Treatments

Despite impressive progress in our understanding of the neurochemical bases of chemical dependency and recent advances in pharmacotherapy, the mainstays of chemical dependency treatment remain involvement in self-help groups and the psychosocial approaches. Despite the fact that pharmacotherapy can alleviate some of the physiological underpinnings of chemical dependency, it cannot attend directly to the myriad of psychological, social, and spiritual concomitants of addiction. In this section you will examine the basic principles and practices of self-help groups, learn about the techniques of psychosocial treatment approaches, and re-

view scientific data on comparative treatment effectiveness.

Self-Help Groups

Peer-led groups that provide mutual support and guidance to deal with chemical dependency are known as **self-help groups**. They can be viewed as a grassroots response to a perceived need for services and support.

Alcoholics Anonymous.   The prototypical self-help group in the realm of chemical dependency is *Alcoholics Anonymous* (A.A.). A.A. has provided a *model* for the proliferation of other similar groups, including *Narcotics Anonymous* and *Cocaine Anonymous*, as well as such offspring as *Al-Anon*, *Alateen*, and *Adult Children of Alcoholics*. A.A. and similar self-help groups do not view themselves as treatment groups, but rather as lay self-help fellowships whose members are connected by their common addiction. Indeed, the only professionals to be found in the rooms of A.A. are other recovering alcoholics. Unquestionably, A.A. is the most widely accessed resource for alcoholics (Galanter et al. 1991, Humphreys 1999).

Officially, A.A. makes no commitment to any particular causal model of addiction. Instead, fellowship members subscribe to the belief that alcoholism is a chronic, progressive illness characterized by inevitable loss of control over drinking and denial that will eventually lead to jail, mental institutions, or death if not arrested through total, lifelong abstinence. A popular A.A. saying is that "one drink is too many and a thousand are not enough." Recovery means spiritual growth that comes from working through the Twelve steps (see Chapter 11). In a nutshell, A.A.

members admit that they are powerless over alcohol, that their lives have become unmanageable, and that they must surrender to God or a "higher power" who will help them gain control over drinking. "Working the steps" also means changing one's personal context from isolation to social, personal, and spiritual relationships. The individual must strive to break his self-absorption and move toward self-examination and personal change, improvement of self-esteem, resolution of guilt, and learn to work with other alcoholics (Bean-Bayog 1991).

Does A.A. work? Despite claims by members that A.A. is not only effective, but the only means to recovery, few studies have been able to prove it until recently. A boom of outcome research in the early 1990s has now demonstrated the benefits of A.A. participation, and has led to the development of therapies crafted to encourage Twelve step involvement (McGrady and Miller 1993).

A.A. and related Twelve step programs are not for everyone, however. Many A.A. members find it difficult to subscribe to A.A.'s dogmatic philosophy. Moreover, others find that A.A. is not enough to remedy the variety of problems preceding or accompanying alcoholism. To be sure, the authors have encountered many clients who have diligently attempted to work the steps, and even though these people have been able to stay clean and sober for many years, they continue to be dogged by personal and interpersonal problems. Indiscriminate prescriptions to attend A.A. meetings may have deleterious effects on some alcoholics and their relatives (Emrick 1994). For example:

> Kevin, who had been clean and sober for twelve years, continued to attend A.A. meetings at least twice a week and often stayed awake until all hours of the night communicating with other alcoholics in Twelve Step–oriented Internet chat rooms and through e-mail. While Kevin invested much time and effort on his sobriety, his marriage was steadily crumbling and his relationship with his four children was strained. His wife repeatedly pleaded with him to work on the marital and family problems and eventually coaxed him into

weekly couples counseling with her. Kevin's time spent in the chat rooms and online became a main theme in couples counseling, and as the therapy proceeded it became increasingly clear that he was unwilling to budge from his Twelve step contacts. In the eyes of his wife, Kevin was as addicted to the Twelve step mentality as he ever was to drugs and alcohol.

The Minnesota Model. The **Minnesota model** is characterized by the use of the Twelve step philosophy of A.A. as the foundation for therapeutic change. The treatment goal is total abstinence from substances and an improved quality of life. Sometimes known as the *Hazelden model* after its origins in the Hazelden private residential facility in Minnesota, the Minnesota model represents a common residential treatment approach for alcoholism and drug abuse that is practiced throughout the United States (Stinchfield and Owen 1998).

Founded on the Twelve step philosophy, the Minnesota treatment model consists of group therapy, individual therapy, lectures and group discussions, homework assignments, and attendance at community self-help groups. Treatment services are provided by a multidisciplinary team headed by a chemical dependency counselor along with a nurse, psychologist, chaplain, recreational therapist, and consulting physican. Treatment goals are objective and tailored to individual needs.

Few studies have addressed the efficacy of the Minnesota model. Those that do generally indicate that about 50 percent of program completers remain abstinent at one year follow-up, and another 35 percent demonstrate significantly reduced substance use (Stinchfield and Owen 1998).

Individual, Group, and Family Therapies

For many years the primary psychosocial treatment for chemical dependency was **psychotherapy**, which describes a spectrum of psychological treatments that aim to change problematic thoughts, feelings, and behaviors that play a causal role in abnormal behaviors. With regard to chemical dependency, the focus of psychotherapy is to discover and remediate the cognitive, emotional, and behavioral factors that promote pathological drug use (Woody et al. 1994).

Individual Psychotherapy. The most common psychotherapy format is *individual psychotherapy*, which involves any form of one-on-one verbal interaction between the client and a therapist or counselor. The assumptions, techniques, and processes of individual psychotherapy vary depending on the theoretical orientation from which the psychotherapy is derived. You will learn more about individual psychotherapy counseling techniques in Chapter 13.

Individual psychotherapy is best for patients who are verbal or who are reluctant to disclose personal information to group members. Individual psychotherapy can also be advantageous because it facilitates a controlled, dependent relationship with the therapist that allows the therapist to influence the patient to change problem behaviors. Influencing patients requires considerable clinical skill on the part of the therapist because evoking a dependency that is too strong can thwart individual growth (Woody et al. 1994).

Group Therapy. Many experts in the field of addiction treatment prefer and recommend *group therapy* because it offers clients the opportunity to identify with others with similar problems, learn more about their own and others' thoughts and feelings, and begin to communicate needs and feelings more adaptively. Ideally, the dynamic interaction of group members exerts its healing power by providing a sense of belonging and support, as well as the education necessary for individuals to conquer their addiction. Although not conceptualized as therapy, per se, Twelve step programs are essentially a form of group therapy. On the negative side, the sometimes confrontational approach of group therapy drives some people away (American Psychiatric Association 1995a, Golden et al. 1994).

Family Therapy. As you learned in Chapter 9, a variety of family problems and dysfunctional structures are often either at the root of chemical dependency or a consequence of it. Recognition of this situation has led to the development and application of *family therapy* in the solution of chemical dependency. Whatever the underlying theoretical model, family therapy strives to modify dysfunctional family structure and dynamics in the service of encouraging family support for abstinence (American Psychiatric Association 1995a, Steinglass 1994).

Family therapy is recommended in cases where it is clear the family contributes either to the causation or maintenance of the individual's substance problems (see Chapter 9). Substance-abusing adolescents also seem to benefit from family therapy more than they do from individual or peer-group treatments (Crits-Christoph and Siqueland 1996).

An Evaluation of Individual, Group, and Family Therapies

Large-scale clinical outcome studies consistently prove that psychosocial treatments provide substantial benefit for people with chemical dependency (Crits-Christoph and Siqueland 1996). The critical issue for you as a chemical dependency counselor is to figure out which type of therapy format to select for your clients. The reality is that whether a client receives individual, group, or family therapy is often determined by variables beyond your control. Factors such as insurance constraints, staffing, and the fundamental treatment philosophy of the setting in which you ply your trade usually will rule the decision.

For cases in which you are given some decision-making latitude, you should consider the general principles of chemical dependency treatment outlined earlier in this chapter. Especially noteworthy is the fact that no single specific treatment or treatment format is effective for all clients. Whereas many studies have demonstrated the effectiveness of individual, group, and family therapies, you must evaluate the unique characteristics of each individual client to determine which format might work best. You would do well to weigh the many advantages and disadvantages of each approach in the context of each client's clinical picture (American Psychiatric

Association 1995a, Crits-Christoph and Siqueland 1996, Golden et al. 1994, Steinglass 1994, Woody et al. 1994).

Your choice of treatment should also take into consideration that both the intensity and content of treatment matter, and that a combination of approaches may be necessary to ensure change. For example, a study of 487 cocaine-dependent individuals indicated that patients who received a combination of individual and group drug counseling showed the greatest improvement on Addiction Severity Index scores (National Institute on Drug Abuse Collaborative Cocaine Treatment Study Group 1999).

12–6 Manual-Guided and Other Treatment Modalities

Recognition of the difficulties inherent in treating alcoholism and drug addiction has led to much research geared toward the discovery of specific treatments. One important result has been the development of **manual-guided treatments**, which apply specific structured treatment techniques in a time-limited fashion. Another trend in recent years has been to compare the effectiveness of specific treatments with subpopulations of chemically dependent individuals. You should consider these approaches in your planning because they provide you with additional options to add to your armamentarium of treatments.

Treatments to Enhance Motivation

As certainly as the sun rises each day, you will encounter difficult clients who are not amenable to treatment. Traditional approaches to the treatment of unmotivated clients use aggressive, confrontational stategies to counteract denial. Just as a football coach may increase the motivation of some players by getting in their face, so too does confrontation get the motivational juices flowing in some alcoholics and drug addicts. Not everyone responds favorably to confrontation, however. In some individuals it may not only fail to enhance motivation, but also actually act to foster denial. Considering the heterogeneity of the chemically dependent population, it may be advisable to use tactics that are motivation-generating and less confrontational (Miller 1985, Miller and Rollnick 1991, Miller et al. 1993).

Brief Motivational Therapy. Heeding the word from research on motivation and treatment outcome, you will be a more successful counselor if you utilize techniques that enhace patients' intrinsic motivation. One approach is called **brief motivational therapy** (BMT), which uses straightforward advice and information about the adverse effects of alcohol abuse in order to motivate patients to reduce or stop their harmful behavior. This type of therapy usually consists of one to four sessions lasting approximately ten to sixty minutes each. During the sessions, treatment providers advise clients about the risks of excessive drinking and provide feedback about their substance abuse in the hope that new information may motivate reduced consumption, if not cessation. For example, the client may be informed about a variety of health risks that he or she was previously unaware of. This approach refrains from confrontation in the hope of minimizing defensiveness (DiClemente et al. 1999, Substance Abuse and Mental Health Services Administration 1997).

At first glance you may think that BMT would be about as effective in treating alcoholics as trying to slay an elephant with a pea shooter. However, research shows that it reduces consumption in some alcohol abusers. These individuals are not usually self-referred because they generally do not believe they have a significant drinking problem. Presumably, the increased awareness of the problem might be enough to motivate change in some of these clients. Research (Wilk et al. 1997) indicates that BMT is beneficial for heavy drinkers as well. Compared to control subjects, those who receive BMT are almost twice as likely to reduce drinking within the following year.

Motivational Enhancement Therapy. A more structured approach to increasing motivation is **motivational enhancement therapy** (MET), a systematic intervention that applies the principles of motivational psychology to mobilize rapid, internally motivated change. MET begins with extensive motivation interviewing lasting seven to eight hours, and with a breath test at the initial interview and before each treatment session to ensure sobriety. This is followed by four treatment sessions spaced over a twelve-week period. Session 1 consists of providing feedback to the client about the initial interview, problems associated with drinking, the amount of alcohol consumed and resulting symptoms, and building motivation for change. Session 2 continues motivation enhancement and working toward a stronger commitment to change. These sessions are followed by two follow-through sessions at weeks 6 and 12, at which points the therapist continues to monitor and encourage progess (Miller et al. 1999).

Unlike other forms of therapy, MET does not strive to guide and train the client through recovery. Instead, it employs motivational strategies to mobilize the client's own change resources. Thus MET assumes that the responsibility and capability for change rests within the client. Rather than have the client depend on therapy sessions to improve, MET attempts to create a set of conditions that will enhance the client's own motivation. Underlying this approach is a therapist attitude marked by the expression of empathy, development of a sense of discrepancy in the client (a perceived difference between where the client is and where he wants to be), avoidance of argumentation, rolling with the resistance, and introducing the support of self-efficacy (Miller et al. 1999).

This particular therapeutic attitude is consistent with the findings of extensive clinical outcome research that reveals a common core of elements that motivate change. The active ingredients for change in alcoholics can be summarized by the acronym FRAMES:

- *Feedback* of personal risk and impairment;
- Emphasis on personal *Responsibility* for change;
- Clear *Advice* to change;
- A *Menu* of alternative change options;
- Therapist *Empathy*; and
- Facilitation of client *Self-Efficacy* or optimism.

In conclusion, motivation-based approaches to the treatment of alcoholism can improve drinking outcomes, and such approaches are becoming more common in many types of treatment programs. Much needs to be learned about how to increase patient motivation, however. Moreover, whether motivational treatment approaches can be successfully applied to dual-diagnosis patients and to chemically dependent individuals other than alcoholics is a potentially fertile area for future research.

Cognitive-Behavioral Coping Skills Therapy

Motivation to change drinking and drugging undoubtedly is a critical ingredient in the process of recovery, but it may not be sufficient given that many chemically dependent clients lack the tools necessary to effectively resist substance abuse and to cope with their numerous problems. Clinicians have developed specific treatment strategies and programs to help clients develop the necessary tools.

Cognitive-behavioral coping skills therapy (CBST) refers to a family of related treatments for alcoholism and other substance-related disorders that aim to improve the cognitive and behavioral skills necessary to change problem behaviors. Because CBST is conducted on an outpatient basis, clients' daily lives can be described in treatment sessions and used as a foundation for problem-solving exercises, role playing, and homework assignments. Clients are expected to be actively involved in treatment and assume responsibility for learning the self-control skills necessary to stem future substance use. You will learn more about relapse prevention in Chapter 14 (Longabaugh and Morgenstern 1999, National Institute on Alcohol Abuse and Alcoholism 1995b).

CBST is scheduled as a twelve-session intervention that covers eight core topics as follows:

- Session 1: Introduction to coping skills training
- Session 2: Coping with cravings and urges to drink
- Session 3: Managing thoughts about alcohol and drinking

- Session 4: Problem solving
- Session 5: Drink-refusal skills
- Session 6: Planning for emergencies and coping with a lapse
- Session 7: Seemingly irrelevant decisions
- Session 8: Final session; termination

After the first seven core sessions have been completed, the therapist will move on to one or more elective topics.

Despite the cookbook appearance of CBST, general rules for conducting psychotherapy still apply, including the establishment of rapport, setting limits, and the expression of empathy (National Institute on Alcohol Abuse and Alcoholism 1995b).

Outcome research on CBST indicates that it is an effective treatment for alcoholism, although its effectiveness does not seem to differ significantly from other treatments when used as a stand-alone treatment. However, CBST can improve the outcome for alcohol-dependent individuals when integrated into a more comprehensive therapeutic regimen (Longabaugh and Morgenstern 1999).

Twelve step Faciliation Therapy

Another treatment approach for chemical dependency is **Twelve step facilitation therapy** (TSFT), a brief, structured, outpatient treatment to encourage affiliation and involvement in Alcoholics Anonymous. Although originally designed for alcoholism, TSFT has also been used in the treatment of drug abuse and dependence.

Twelve step facilitation therapy has two major goals, which relate to issues addressed in the first three of the Twelve Steps: acceptance and surrender. These two goals are reflected in a series of specific cognitive, emotional, behavioral, social, and spiritual objectives that are congruent with the A.A. view of alcoholism. For example, clients must understand how their thinking reflects denial (cognitive), how negative emotional states like anger can lead to drinking (emotional), the need to get active in A.A. (behavioral), the need to find a sponsor and participate in A.A. social activities (social), and the need to acknowledge character defects and experience

hope (spiritual). Like CBST, the facilitation program consists of twelve sessions (National Institute on Alcohol Abuse and Alcoholism 1995c).

The results of clinical outcome studies of TSFT are generally positive. In a study of clients in twenty-six Los Angeles treatment centers, the addition of Twelve step participation increased the likelihood of abstinence at the six-month follow-up point (see Figure 12–3). Twelve step participation can serve as a useful and inexpensive aftercare resource to help patients maintain abstinence. Also, preliminary studies indicate that when there is Twelve step participation before and during treatment people are likely to stay in treatment longer and to maintain abstinence longer after treatment ends (National Institute on Drug Abuse 1999c).

Matching Treatments to Patient Needs

The repeated observation that no single treatment is effective for all individuals has spurred addiction researchers to look toward better patient–treatment matching to maximize positive outcome. According to the **matching hypothesis**, improved results can be attained if treatment is tailored to individual patient needs and characteristics rather than treating all patients with the same diagnosis in the same way. In other words, whereas different treatments do not appear to be effective when applied to a diverse group of alcoholics, specific treatments may be effective when applied to specific subgroups of the population (National Institute on Alcohol Abuse and Alcoholism 1996b).

Project MATCH. To test the matching hypothesis, the *National Institute on Alcohol Abuse and Alcoholism* initiated a five-year study in 1989. Called *Project MATCH* (Project MATCH Research Group 1997), the objective of this ambitious study was to determine if subgroups of alcoholics would respond differentially to three treatments: (1) *motivational enhancement therapy,* (2) *cognitive-behavioral coping skills therapy,* and (3) *Twelve step facilitation therapy.*

Project MATCH consisted of 1,726 subjects (76 percent male) recruited from both outpa-

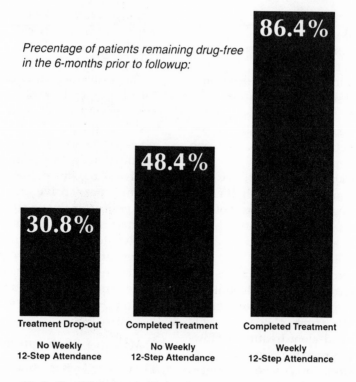

*Precentage of patients remaining drug-free
in the 6-months prior to followup:*

30.8%

48.4%

86.4%

Treatment Drop-out | Completed Treatment | Completed Treatment

No Weekly
12-Step Attendance | No Weekly
12-Step Attendance | Weekly
12-Step Attendance

Figure 12–3. Participation in drug abuse treatment and Twelve step
program improves treatment outcomes
Source: National Institute on Drug Abuse (1999b).

tient settings and aftercare settings following inpatient hospitalization or day programs. Overall, Project MATCH participants showed significant and sustained improvement in the percentage of abstinent days, drinking consequences, employment days, liver function, and psychological symptoms at one-year follow-up. There was little difference in outcomes by treatment type except that patients who received outpatient TSFT were slightly more likely to remain abstinent in the year following treatment and at the three-year follow-up. One robust match was found between TSFT and low psychiatric severity. Clients treated with TSFT who were low in psychiatric severity had more abstinent days compared to other treatments. Clients with high psychiatric severity did not fare well no matter which treatment they received (Humphreys 1999).

The failure of Project MATCH to discover dramatic outcome differences among the three psychosocial treatments may indicate that all of them are high-quality, well-delivered treat-

ments. Rather than view the study as a failure, treatment providers and clients might feel confident that such effective therapies are available. Furthermore, Project MATCH does not speak to matching patient types to different treatment settings, therapists, or psychotherapies other than those studied, nor does it cover pharmacological treatments. In the view of some experts, the logical next step is to test psychosocial treatments in conjunction with promising pharmacological treatments for alcoholism (National Institute on Alcohol Abuse and Alcoholism 1996b).

Other Methods of Matching. Aside from matching patients to specific manual-guided treatments, another way to match is by providing treatments for specific target problems within the broader context of chemical dependency. One study of this type evaluated target problems using the Addiction Severity Index (see Chapter 3). Next, patients received either standard treatment or focused services in the areas of employment, family relations, or psychiatric problems, depending on their needs. As shown in Table 12–4, matched patients stayed in treatment longer, were more likely to complete treatment, and showed better six-month outcomes than patients who received standard treatment. Much more research is needed to determine precise patient variables and treatment interactions, although logistical and financial circumstances are likely to hamper attempts at this type of treatment matching. The results are encouraging, nonetheless, and should be considered where feasible in chemical dependency treatment (McLellan et al. 1997, National Institute on Drug Abuse 1996b).

Summary

12–1

Planning treatment for chemical dependency requires the establishment of multiple goals, beginning with abstinence and including improvements in mental and physical health, psychosocial functioning, employment stability, and reduced criminal justice involvement. The best treatment consists of a combination of therapies and other services designed to meet the needs of individual clients. Motivation is positively correlated with treatment compliance and treatment involvement; higher motivation increases the likelihood of both. Sources of motivation are intrinsic and extrinsic. Therapy should focus on building intrinsic motivation.

12–2

Clients can be treated in an inpatient facility or on an outpatient basis. The choice requires a consideration of the client's clinical status, availability of treatment facilities, restrictiveness of the therapeutic environment regarding access to substances and potential for other high-risk behaviors, hours of operation, the overall milieu, and treatment philosophy. Clients should receive treatment in the least restrictive environment that is likely to be safe and effective, and should be moved from one level of care to another based on the counselor's assessment of their readiness and ability to benefit from a less intensive level of care. Treatment settings include inpatient hospitalization, residential treatment, intensive outpatient treatment, and outpatient treatment. The vast majority of chemically dependent individuals are treated in outpatient programs. Most of the research suggests that a major percentage of addicted patients show meaningful improvement in most areas of functioning regardless of the specific setting, and that the services provided may be

Table 12–4. Changes in Addiction Severity Index variables

Problems	Standard Treatment Patients		Matched Services Patients	
	On Entering Treatment	Six Months After Discharge	On Entering Treatment	Six Months After Discharge
Problems not targeted				
Days of alcohol use	12	2	15	1
Days of alcohol intoxication	11	2	13	1
Days of opiate use	3	1	1	1
Days of cocaine use	4	1	5	1
Days of medical problems	4	5	3	3
Targeted problems				
Days worked	16	14	14	17
Employment income	$1,318	$1,072	$1,042	$1,435
Days of family problems	4	4	3	1
Days of psychological problems	10	7	11	4

Variables reflect the 30 days prior to treatment admission and 6-month follow-up.

Source: National Institute on Drug Abuse (1999b).

more important than the setting in which the treatments are offered.

12–3

Reaching the goal of long-term abstinence requires that the chemically dependent individual first be taken off the drug in a medically safe manner. An initial step in the treatment of alcoholism and addiction is detoxification. Following assessment, the major thrust of detoxification treatment for severely addicted individuals is the use of medications to relieve the symptoms of withdrawal. Detoxification can be accomplished in either outpatient or inpatient settings. Both have their advantages and disadvantages. There are few well-controlled studies that compare the long-term outcome of outpatient versus inpatient detoxification, and those that are available do not show that one method is superior to the other.

12–4

The therapeutic use of drugs to alter brain chemistry is called pharmacotherapy. Although this use of drugs is controversial, the rationale for it is that they can aid in treatment if they modify the pathological neurochemical mechanisms underlying the addiction without producing psychoactive effects themselves. The drugs used are categorized according to their therapeutic purposes. They are: (1) drugs to decrease the reinforcing effects of abused substances, (2) drugs to discourage the use of substances, (3) agonist substitution drugs, and (4) medications to treat comorbid psychiatric conditions. Currently, pharmacotherapy is instituted primarily for alcoholism and opioid addiction.

12–5

Peer-led groups that provide mutual support and guidance to deal with chemical dependency are known as self-help groups. The prototypical self-help group in the realm of chemical dependency is Alcoholics Anonymous (A.A.). A.A. makes no commitment to any particular causal model of addiction. Instead, fellowship members subscribe to the belief that alcoholism is a chronic, progressive illness characterized by denial and inevitable loss of control over drinking and that will eventually lead to ruin. Working the steps means changing one's personal context from isolation to social, personal, and spiritual relationships. The individual must strive to break his self-absorption and move toward self-examination and personal change, improvement of self-esteem, resolution of guilt, and work with other alcoholics. Outcome research in the early 1990s has demonstrated the benefits of A.A. participation, leading to the development of therapies crafted to encourage Twelve step involvement. A.A. and related Twelve step programs are not for everyone. The Minnesota model is characterized by the use of the Twelve step philosophy of A.A. as the foundation for therapeutic change. The treatment goal is total abstinence from substances and improved quality of life. The Minnesota model represents a common residential-treatment approach for alcoholism and drug abuse that is practiced throughout the United States. About 50 percent of program completers remain abstinent at one year follow-up, and another 35 percent demonstrate significantly reduced substance use. Individual psychotherapy involves any form of one-on-one verbal interaction between the client and the therapist or counselor. Group therapy offers clients the opportunity to identify with others with similar problems, learn more about their own and others' thoughts and feelings, and to communicate needs and feelings more adaptively. The dynamic interaction of group members exerts its healing power by providing a sense of belonging and support, as well as the education necessary for individuals to conquer their addiction. Family therapy strives to modify dysfunctional family structures and dynamics in the service of encouraging family support for abstinence. Large-scale clinical outcome studies consistently prove that psychosocial treatments provide substantial benefit for people with chemical dependency.

12–6

Manual-guided treatments apply specific, structured treatment techniques in a time-limited fashion. Brief motivational therapy uses straightforward advice and information about the adverse effects of alcohol abuse in order to motivate patients to reduce or stop their harmful behavior. Motivational enhancement therapy is a systematic intervention that applies the principles of motivational psychology. Cognitive-behavioral coping skills therapy refers to a family of related treatments for alcoholism and other substance-related disorders that aims to improve the cognitive and behavioral skills necessary to change problem behaviors. Twelve step facilitation therapy is a brief, structured, outpatient treatment to encourage affiliation with and involvement in Alcoholics Anonymous. According to the matching hypothesis, improved results can be attained if treatment is tailored to individual patient needs and characteristics rather than treating everyone with the same diagnosis in the same way. Project MATCH attempted to determine if subgroups of alcoholics would respond differentially to three treatments: motivational enhancement therapy, cognitive-behavioral coping skills therapy and Twelve step facilitation therapy. Results showed little difference in outcomes by treatment type except that patients who recieved outpatient TSFT were more slightly likely to remain abstinent in the year following treatment and at the three-year follow-up. Another robust match was found between TSFT and low psychiatric severity. Clients treated with TSFT who were low in psychiatric severity had more abstinent days compared to other treatments. Clients with high psychiatric severity did not fare well no matter which treatment they received.

Terms To Remember

antabuse
brief motivational therapy
Clinical Institute Withdrawal Assessment for Alcohol
cognitive-behavioral coping skills therapy
detoxification
halfway house
inpatient hospitalization treatment
intensive outpatient treatment
levo-alpha-acetylmethadol
manual-guided treatments
matching hypothesis
methadone maintenance treatment
Minnesota model
motivational enhancement therapy
naltrexone
outpatient treatment
pharmacotherapy
psychotherapy
residential treatment
self-help groups
treatment compliance
treatment involvement
Twelve step facilitation therapy

Suggested Readings

Alcoholics Anonymous World Services. (1976). *Alcoholics Anonymous*, 3rd ed. New York: Author.

Fuller, R. K., and Hiller-Sturmhoffel, S. (1999). Alcoholism treatment in the United States. *Alcohol Research and Health* 23:69–77.

Miller, W. R., Zweben, A., DiClemente, C. C., and Rychtarik, R. G. (1999). *Motivational Enhancement Therapy Manual. A Clinical Research Guide for Therapists Treating Individuals with Alcohol Abuse and Dependence.* (NIH Publication No. 94–3723). Rockville, MD: National Institute on Alcohol Abuse and Alcoholism.

National Institute on Alcohol Abuse and Alcoholism (1995b). *Cognitive-Behavioral Coping Skills Therapy Manual. A Clinical Research Guide for Therapists Treating Individuals with Alcohol Abuse and Dependence.* (NIH Publication No. 94-3724.) Bethesda, MD: National Institute on Alcohol Abuse and Alcoholism.

National Institute on Alcohol Abuse and Alcoholism (1995c). *Twelve step Facilitation Therapy Manual. A Clinical Research Guide for Therapists Treating Individuals with Alcohol Abuse and Dependence.* (NIH Publication No. 94-3722.) Bethesda, MD: National Institute on Alcohol Abuse and Alcoholism.

National Institute on Drug Abuse (1999a). *Principles of Drug Addiction Treatment. A Research-Based Guide.* (NIH Publication No. 99-4180.) Bethesda, MD: National Institute on Drug Abuse.

CHAPTER THIRTEEN

Counseling Schools and Techniques

Chapter Outline

Learning Objectives

Upon completing study of this chapter you should be able to:

1. Discuss the main ideas of behavioral counseling.
2. Outline the features of client-centered counseling.
3. Identify the rationale behind cognitive counseling.
4. Describe the nature of existential counseling.
5. Characterize the approach of Gestalt counseling.
6. Discuss the concepts and strategies of psychodynamic counseling.
7. Describe the distinctive aspects of substance abuse-specific counseling.
8. List and discuss the three relationship-focused techniques.
9. Identify and explain the use of the three emotion-focused techniques.
10. Discuss the use of the four kinds of cognition-focused techniques.
11. Describe the four behavior-focused techniques.

This chapter addresses the basic concepts of counseling strategy and technique for entry-level students of chemical dependency. Here you will learn about the major schools of counseling and their treatment rationales, as well as the techniques used by counselors in treating chemically dependent clients. Although this chapter is written primarily for the novice, you will find the material of value regardless of your level of sophistication. It will be most valuable to you if chemical dependency counseling or addiction psychotherapy is a new interest of yours. Although the counseling approaches discussed here are used in treating many kinds of mental health problems, they can be modified to fit the particularity of the substance abusing client.

In previous chapters you learned the general principles of chemical dependency treatment and assessment. In this chapter we are going to get more specific, and you will learn something of the ins and outs of counseling—

of what actually goes on in a counseling session. This is a how-to chapter, although it also tries to say why counselors do what they do. The great romantic poet William Blake wrote, "The road of excess leads to the palace of wisdom." With chemical dependency, unfortunately, it more often leads to the cemetery. Your job is to direct as many as possible of those on the road of excess to the palace rather than to the other location. This chapter is about how to guide them there.

13–1   Schools of Counseling

Chemical-dependency counseling entails unique ways of helping people recover from chemical dependency, but it also draws from and builds upon already existing schools of counseling. Uniting assumptions about human behavior—both normal and abnormal—with prescriptions for treatment, a *school of counseling* is an organized conceptual system that guides our understanding of psychopathology and our therapeutic interventions. Although each of these traditions was originally applied to individual counseling, they are now also applied to couple, family, and group work as well.

Each major school is more than a set of techniques. In all schools counseling techniques are based on an understanding of human nature, a body of empirically derived knowledge, and a theory about how human beings learn, grow, and change. Given how complex people are, it is hardly surprising that the various schools do not see human beings in the same way. In this section you will learn about seven major schools of counseling and their distinctive therapeutic agendas. Table 13–1 summarizes the major schools and their objectives.

Over the last century a number of ways of going about counseling have been elaborated. They all help in treatment, and yet they all have limitations. Although the methods used by these schools all work, no single one works always and for everyone. Most chemical dependency counselors develop an *eclectic approach* to counseling, one that utilizes a variety of concepts and methods borrowed from

Table 13–1. Schools of counseling

School	Objectives
Behavioral	Help the client overcome faulty learning and learn effective coping skills
Client-centered	Use the therapeutic relationship to foster the client's personal growth
Cognitive	Change the client's irrational beliefs and maladaptive thinking
Existential	Aid the client's confrontation with facts of existence and spirituality
Gestalt	Help the client fully experience the here-and-now
Psychodynamic	Promote insight into the unconscious roots of the client's symptoms and personality
Substance abuse-Specific	Integrate multiple strategies to foster abstinence and prevent relapse

many schools. With experience, they evolve a style that suits their personalities, their training, their knowledge, their temperament, and their population. In all probability your own style will go on evolving as your knowledge and experience increase. As songwriter Bob Dylan put it, "He not busy being born is busy dying."

Behavioral Counseling

Behavioral counseling, or *behavior therapy*, is an approach that uses the principles of learning theory to help people change (Emmelkamp 1994). As you learned in Chapter 5, behaviorists believe that substance abuse, as well as other forms of psychopathology, is caused by faulty learning. They seek to correct the symptoms that result from faulty learning by means of classical and operant conditioning procedures.

The operant procedure of *reinforcement* is most characteristic of behavior therapy. Reinforcement can be employed to teach new skills and to improve upon existing skills. *Punishment*, another operant procedure, also has applications. In aversion therapy for example, alcoholism is treated by pairing a painful stimulus (the punisher) with drinking in a controlled setting. However, because of ethical and legal questions surrounding the use of punishment, reinforcement is the preferred operant strategy.

Behavioral counselors have been ingenious in applying the principles of classical condi-

tioning to healing mental and emotional illness. For example, the use of *flooding*, that is, deliberately intensifying anxiety until it extinguishes, can be effective in reducing fears. Flooding can even relieve compulsive behaviors fueled by fears if the client is not allowed to carry out the compulsive activity and so must experience the anxiety until its extinction.

Psychiatrist Joseph Wolpe (1969, 1995), a pioneering behavior therapist, developed a classical conditioning strategy called *systematic desensitization* to treat fears and phobias. Through a mechanism called reciprocal inhibition, the fear response is reduced when countered by relaxation exercises. The therapist and client construct a stimulus hierarchy, ranging from the least anxiety-provoking stimulus to a maximum anxiety-provoking stimulus. For example, in the case of fear of flying, the client would start with a picture of an airplane and work up to actually flying in a plane, imagining progressively more anxiety-provoking situations associated with flying. The client performs relaxation exercises during stimulus exposures until the fear is completely extinguished. Although substance abuse counselors are not likely to do formal systematic desensitization, they can adapt behavioral methods like relaxation training to fit the client's needs.

Ultimately, the goal of behavioral counseling is to reduce the client's maladaptive behavior patterns and to teach the client more effective coping skills. Later in this chapter you will learn about behavioral techniques that are suited to the chemically dependent client.

Client-Centered Counseling

The approach known as **client-centered counseling** emphasizes the role of the therapeutic relationship in providing a context in which the client can grow and heal. Also known as *nondirective counseling*, this approach is strongly associated with its originator, psychologist Carl Rogers. Rogers, who had studied to be a clergyman, was one of the founding fathers of modern clinical psychology. He brought nonmedical professionals into the field of therapy, and his research established the centrality of counselor traits to successful counseling (Rogers 1961, Rogers and Sanford 1985). As you already learned in Chapter 11, the traits—or perhaps the attitudinal stance—that make for counseling success are a nonjudgmental attitude, unconditional positive regard, genuineness, and the capacity for empathy. Research has demonstrated that Rogers was right: no matter what the counselor's theoretical orientation or school, those traits predict success (Greenberg et al. 1994).

Nondirective counseling is an outgrowth of Rogers's belief that the counselor's attitude in and of itself heals, and that human beings have an innate drive for health and for growth. The potential cure already lies within the client, and what the counselor must do is provide the right environment for the client's healing forces to manifest themselves. In a sense the client-centered philosophy is: "Provide the plants with sun, water and nutrients, and they will grow and flourish."

So the client-centered counselor does two basic things: stays out of the way by being nondirective, and waters the plants attitudinally by being who he or she is. But it is not quite so simple. The client-centered counselor also provides sunlight by reflecting the light—the emotional awareness—back to the client. As the client opens up in the safety of the counseling relationship and has feelings reflected back, his or her self-concept expands and is enriched. More and more of the self becomes available to the client and

the gap between the *ideal self* (what the client would like to be) and the *real self* (what the client thinks he or she is) narrows. Another way to say this is that client-centered counseling raises self-esteem while lowering unrealistic grandiose expectations.

Both the significance of the counselor–client relationship and the role of counselor attitudes are central to treating chemical dependency. Nevertheless, substance abuse counseling is not entirely a client-centered enterprise. Although this approach has obvious applicability to treating chemically dependent clients, we think even Rogers would acknowledge that his approach does not perfectly fit the situation of the substance-abusing client. Rogers worked mostly with what he called "normal neurotics," often in educational settings such as college counseling services. His research on the applicability of his approach to more seriously disturbed clients concluded that it wasn't particularly effective.

Rogers's contributions to our understanding of human nature and of how to facilitate growth are magnificent. Nevertheless, too many substance-abusing clients are in the process of self-destruction for a radically nondirective approach to make sense for them. However, where this approach becomes increasingly appropriate and useful is after the client achieves sobriety. The client-centered technique of *reflection* is an important element of counseling and will be examined in a later section of this chapter.

Cognitive Counseling

Cognitive models of psychopathology emphasize the role of *maladaptive cognition*—maladaptive beliefs and thinking—in mental health problems. Extending this view into treatment, **cognitive counseling** assumes that emotional and behavioral problems can be overcome by changing a person's irrational beliefs and thoughts. For example, a belief that "I am only a worthwhile person if I get straight *A*s," confuses a desirable academic goal with a condition for having self-esteem. It is an irrational belief that predisposes the believer to depression. An equally irrational belief held by many alcoholics is that "drinking helps my depression," which of course it does not. In fact, drinking magnifies depression, while the belief that it helps only magnifies the drinking.

Cognitive counseling is about changing ideas and the way people think by challenging their irrational beliefs and maladaptive attitudes. It is an active, engaging, anything-but-neutral approach to counseling. The most prominent figures associated with this school are psychologist Albert Ellis (1962, 1995) and psychiatrist Aaron Beck (Beck 1976; Beck and Weishaar 1995). Although their notions of therapy were not originally focused on chemical dependency, many of their cognitive principles can be extended to that problem (Beck et al. 1993).

Today, in fact, most substance abuse counseling is heavily weighted toward the cognitive side. Like the character in the Molière play who discovered that he had been speaking prose all his life, if you are a substance-abuse counselor you have probably been a cognitive counselor all along, as substance abuse counselors spend most of their time trying to correct their client's mistaken beliefs, irrational thoughts, and counterproductive attitudes. Even the Twelve step programs can be understood as cognitive group counseling. Look at the A.A./N.A. slogans and how they seek to change irrational beliefs and modify attitudes:

- Get out of the driver's seat.
- Addiction is the disease of more.
- KISS ("Keep it simple, stupid!").

In order for counseling to work, the cognitive counselor must sincerely believe that his or her perception of reality makes sense and that it is more rational than the client's. The obvious dangers here consist of being doctrinaire and of not examining your own presuppositions. Yet there is no doubt that the substance abuse counselor's commitment to recovery is more rational than the client's commitment to self-destructive behavior. The cognitive counselor relies on education and confrontation, or what is called disputing the client's irrational beliefs. However, cognitive counselors not only work on thoughts, but

also are equally aware that emotion is important. For that reason, Ellis called his approach *Rational-Emotive Therapy (RET)*.

Existential Counseling

The philosophy of *existentialism* explores man's confrontation with the ultimate facts of existence: life, death, meaning, freedom, responsibility. Grounded in this philosophy, **existential counseling** is a school that concentrates on ultimates, the basic, inescapable aspects of human existence (Valle et al. 1989). In this view, mental illness, including substance abuse, is an avoidance, an attempt to escape the ultimate realities. But of course they cannot be escaped, and the avoider suffers as a consequence. For example, a drug addict driven by his fear of death paradoxically endangers his life by his substance abuse.

In existential counseling, clients are obliged to address and come to terms with the ultimates in their own lives by pursuing answers to life's large questions:

- How do I live a meaningful life in the time I have to live?
- How can I take responsibility for my own life?
- How do I foster my strengths and accept my limitations?

The existential school has no particular set of techniques, and in general plays down the role of technique. Rather, what distinguishes existential counseling is an attitude and perspective marked by the counselor's genuineness and willingness to "swim at the deep end of the pool" in aiding the client's struggle with ultimates (May 1953, May and Yalom 1995).

The counselor must be open to his or her fear of death, difficulties in accepting that some things are not possible, and sense clearly that there can be no escape from responsibility for life's decisions. Additionally, counselors should be aware of their own fears that it is all meaningless, or as Shakespeare put it, "a tale told by an idiot full of sound and fury signifying nothing." Only then can the client become open to his or her parallel fears, share them, and begin to come to such terms with them as is possible.

In his book *Escape from Freedom*, the respected existential therapist Eric Fromm (1941) argues that psychological problems result from efforts to avoid personal freedom and responsibility. Knowing we are free and responsible beings is frightening. Anxiety, the philosopher Kierkegaard (1843) wrote, is the "dizziness of freedom." Although Fromm's view was not originally directed at chemical dependency, his notion fits it well. There is no more radical escape from freedom than addiction. The anxiety that comes with the renewed freedom of recovery and the realization that choice is not only possible but also inevitable can also endanger recovery.

Existential themes play a major role in substance abuse counseling. All of our clients have to come to terms with the ultimates of existence. The substance use has been a period of prolonged avoidance, but now in recovery that is no longer possible. The Twelve step programs know that and they provide meaning through participation in the community and helping others (Twelve-Step work), they also make taking responsibility tolerable by reducing guilt. This is yet another reason why counseling combined with Twelve-Step participation gives the best odds of recovery.

That brings us to the spiritual aspects of existential counseling. Spirituality has become an overused word that has lost meaning in much the same way "co-dependency" has. Spirituality has been used to indicate everything from going to a séance or wearing love beads to meditating and finding meaning in life. Everything from the most vapid, touchy-feely charlatanism to the most serious quest to transcend self and connect with the totality of things is now called "spiritual." This is unfortunate, but we are afraid that the word won't go away. What it denotes, at its best, is important to clients and is a vital area of human life that counselors must deal with.

Recovery does indeed entail coming to terms with the ultimates and the spiritual. And the counselor must be there for the client who is going through that quest without imposing his or her answers on the client. It is also well to remember that spirituality and religion are not the same. Not all clients are religious, but atheists, agnostics, Sunday Christians, sincere believers, and religious fanatics can all suffer substance abuse and need spiritual recovery. There is no particular belief system that is necessary to recovery. Accepting mortality, taking responsibility for one's life and one's choices, finding meaning or accepting meaninglessness, connecting with the community and the universe or accepting aloneness are more than can be achieved in the course of substance abuse treatment. Indeed, they are more than can often be achieved in the entire course of life. Nevertheless, substance abuse counselors can and should be there for the client as he or she starts on the new and wondrous yet perilous road, the road to coming to terms with existentialist ultimates—now experienced rather than anesthetized or repressed.

Close Up: Spirituality and the History of Substance abuse Counseling

Carl Jung, the Swiss psychiatrist, brought the notion of spirituality into the substance abuse field. The story is told in the A.A. literature of Roland H., a wealthy alcoholic American businessman, who went to Jung for analysis. He left Zurich apparently cured, but before long he was back, drunk as ever. Jung told him that he was hopeless and that he would either die or go mad. Roland begged Jung to relent and finally Jung relented and told Mr. H. that there was one hope—namely that he would have a "transvaluation of values," a phrase Jung borrowed from the existentialist philosopher Friedrich Nietzsche. A transvaluation of values is a radical change in one's state of being, a deep, strongly emotional realization that the path one is on is wrong and that the direction must be reversed. It is what was later called hitting bottom and surrender, concepts you learned about in Chapter 12.

Roland had such an experience and joined the *Oxford Movement*, also known as the *Moral Rearmament Movement*. It was a sort of upper-class revival movement, led by Frank Buchman (who was also something of a con man), that had a series of steps of spiritual growth. Roland remained sober and told many people in the Oxford Movement of his spiritual experiences, including Ebby Thacker, an alcoholic friend of Bill Wilson, the man who was to become the founder of A.A. Thacker joined the Oxford Movement and became sober also. He visited his drinking buddy, Bill Wilson, who was drunk as usual and in the last stages of alcoholism. Ebby told Bill his story and Wilson went off for detoxification. While in Town's Hospital, an expensive drying-out tank in New York City, Wilson had a peak or mystical experience such as Jung had told Roland was the only hope. He never drank again. Leaving the hospital, Wilson joined the Oxford Movement and started working with drunks. Not being one to follow for long, and critical of the Oxford Movement for its preachiness and its propensity to talk down to drinkers, Bill Wilson went his own way and founded A.A. after saving another drunk, Dr. Bob Smith, by "running his story," that is, sharing his experience of drinking and recovery. Ebby Thacker didn't make it; he relapsed and died of alcoholism in a state hospital.

Many years later, Bill Wilson wrote to Carl Jung and told him the story of Roland H. and the founding of A.A. Jung (1961) wrote back and in his letter punned in Latin that the cure for alcoholism was *Spiritum contra Spiritus* (the spiritual against the spirits). Jung's view was that alcoholism and drug addiction are mistaken spiritual quests—the quest being admirable, but the path deplorable. The only hope for cure is to redirect the spiritual quest. Without a genuine outlet for spiritual needs and aspirations recovery is not possible.

Gestalt Counseling

Frederick (Fritz) Perls, founder of Gestalt therapy, declared as his slogan: "Lose your mind and come to your senses." **Gestalt counseling** is an approach that endeavors to bring the client into fully experiencing the reality of the here-and-now (Yontef and Simkin 1989). It emphasizes moving the client "out of his head," out of the squirrel cage of obsession and rumination, and into immediate experience. Perls (1969) wrote that the goal of Gestalt counseling was for the client to become capable of fully and deeply experiencing joy, grief, anger, and orgasm.

Gestalt is a German word for "whole"—a complete and organized form. Perls borrowed the term from Gestalt perceptual theory, which views perception as an active process in which we organize our perceptions to achieve completed forms. Gestalt counselors help their clients complete the *gestalt* by getting closure and moving on and by working on unfinished business. They do that through intense, confrontational, here-and-now interaction between counselor and client. Gestalt counseling also applies the notion of closure to emotion. Gestalt counselors carefully observe and comment on the client's demeanor and body language, pointing out discrepancies between what the client is saying and he or she is expressing through his or her body language.

Gestalt counselors are very active, engaged, and reactive in treatment. They employ specialized methods like the "empty chair" intervention, in which clients address an imagined figure in an empty chair. The counselor may say, "I want you to pretend that your father is sitting in that chair and tell him how you felt when you were 12 and he came home drunk and pissed on the lawn in front of your friends." They also use role playing and psychodrama, techniques in which conflicts are reenacted. Because Gestalt counseling entails "opening" the client very emotionally it is important to get closure and to give the client an opportunity to process what has occurred in the session.

Ideas from the Gestalt tradition are of great value in substance abuse work, although the counselor must be cautious not to open up feelings prematurely. If the client can't handle the feelings that are elicited by Gestalt confrontation and role playing, it can be a setup for a slip, just as unprocessed feelings are. For that reason, the Gestalt approach is used more in inpatient settings than in outpatient treatment.

Psychodynamic Counseling

The oldest counseling tradition is the psychodynamic. "Psycho" comes from the Greek word *psyche*, meaning mind or soul, while "dynamic" refers to the contending forces struggling within the psyche. **Psychodynamic counseling** highlights the psychic conflicts within the client and attempts to help the client gain insight into the roots of those conflicts. Many schools of counseling recognize that human beings are conflicted. The contending forces within us pull in many directions. What makes the psychodynamic tradition unique is its belief that unconscious forces—aspects of ourselves of which we have no awareness—determine much of our lives. Sigmund Freud (1856–1939), who developed the psychodynamic approach, was himself afflicted with two substance dependencies—to cocaine (which he overcame) and to nicotine (which killed him). Author of a vast, complex body of work, his ideas evolved over half a century, during which he changed his mind about many things. Freud's beliefs, which form the core of the psychodynamic theory, include:

- The importance of childhood and infancy in shaping adult character and behavior
- The continuing living influence of the past on the present
- The unconsciously driven revival of old relationships in present relationships
- The power of unconscious thoughts, feelings, beliefs, and fantasies over our lives
- The continuity of disease and health
- The centrality of conflict—the war within—in human life and behavior
- The meaningfulness of dreams, slips of the tongue, and psychological symptoms

Conflict and Defense. As you learned in Chapter 6, Freud's psychodynamic view characterized psychic conflict in terms of the interactions between parts of the personality. In his *structural model*, Freud posited three agencies of personality, called the id, ego, and superego, as illustrated in Figure 13–1. Each agency struggles with the others for

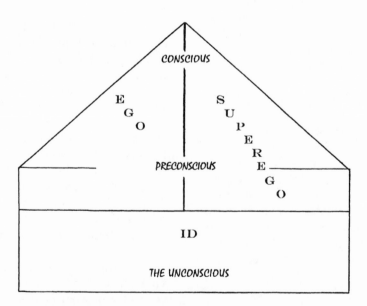

Like an iceberg whose greatest portion lies beneath the surface of the water, most mental activity occurs beneath the surface of conciousness, that is, at preconcious and unconcious levels.

Figure 13.1. Freud's structural model of the mind

dominance as well as with the external world. These intrapsychic conflicts generate anxiety and other emotional distress, which in turn spur the defense mechanisms into action.

Another significant contribution was Freud's elaboration of the mechanisms of psychic defense. The **defense mechanisms** are largely unconscious strategies that serve to lessen conflict and emotional distress. However, these defenses do not eradicate the conflicts, but merely postpone their resolution. Table 13–2 summarizes the major defense mechanisms. Among substance abusers, the predominance of denial, projection, and rationalization is so characteristic that these defenses are said to be *pathognomic*, that is, they define the disease (Hartocollis 1968, Wurmser 1978). A crucial task for psychodynamic counselors is to assist the client in recognizing the role of maladaptive defenses in order to replace them with more health-promoting coping. The work of confronting and interpretating maladaptive defenses while simultaneously trying to use as much as possible of the client's defensive style in the service of sobriety is the essence of substance abuse counseling. Psychologist John Wallace (1995) argues in favor of therapeutically implementing the early-recovery client's *preferred defense structure*:

> Once the denial and rationalization associated with drinking have been confronted and dealt with, the recovering alcoholic typically is faced with many very real and difficult life problems . . . It is precisely here that variants of denial and rationalization become important. Through direct tuition, we can help the alcoholic to the position that things will work out if he just will stay sober, that even though his life is complicated at the moment, at least he is sober, that sobriety is his number one priority, and so on and so forth. In other words, we as therapists are appealing to his preferred use of denial and rationalization to give him a toehold on abstinence. [pp. 27–28]

Resistance. Psychodynamic theory assumes that symptoms, such as substance abuse,

Table 13–2. Defense mechanisms

Defense Mechanism	Function
Denial	Refusing to admit to or accept facts and reality
Displacement	Finding substitute outlets or targets for feelings
Externalization	Acting out rather than experiencing feelings and conflicts
Identification with the aggressor	Identifying with an aggressive figure or model
Intellectualization	Treating emotional issues with an unemotional, intellectual attitude
Introjection	Experiencing dangerous aspects of the environment as part of the self
Isolation of affect	Separating thought and feeling to isolate feelings
Projection	Attributing to others aspects of the self
Projective identification	Inducing an unacceptable feeling of one's own in someone else
Rationalization	Finding weak reasons or excuses for behavior and feelings
Reaction formation	Turning feelings and urges into their opposites
Regression	Retreating to a lower developmental level to avoid adult tasks
Repression	Pushing distressing feelings and thoughts out of awareness
Splitting	Dividing the world and objects into all-good and all-bad categories
Turning against the self	Deflecting a feeling away from its intended target and turning it inward against the self

serve a purpose for the client. Alcohol abuse, for example, may temporarily quell feelings of guilt or fear. Consequently, one can see why clients often struggle against shedding their symptoms. Freud called this struggle against wellness **resistance**, and stressed the need for counselors to identify its signs for the client. Learning to deal with resistance—and there's always resistance—is a vital part of counseling.

Substance abusers love their substances and cling to them tenaciously. Clients are often unaware of how attached they are, how much they love their addictions, and how afraid they are to change. The counselor can help to make this conscious by saying such things as:

- "You love coke more than you love your family."
- "You're so loyal to your beloved—heroin—that your love may kill you."
- "No matter how horrible your life is, it's familiar and you're afraid to change."

Resistance also arises from *secondary gain*, what the illness or addiction does for the patient. Secondary gains range from the tangible—say, remaining eligible for a disability check—to such intangibles as being the center of family discussion or not having to take part in an aspect of parenting the children that the user wishes to avoid. It is important for the counselor to recognize and deal with the resistance flowing from the secondary gain the client is deriving from his or her substance use.

Transference and Countertransference. One of Freud's most important discoveries was **transference**, the unconscious reenactment of early relationships in present ones. This is, so to speak, something like making a new edition of an old book. Transference always involves distortion and projection and may include behavioral manipulation designed to induce behavior in the people in the present relationship that is similar to the behavior of people in the old relationship. Thus a child of an angry father who provokes anger in male authority figures, and then reacts to them as

if they were his father, is a clear illustration of a transference reaction utilizing this mechanism. In counseling, the transference—the projection of the client's experience with parents and siblings onto the counselor—is inevitable. But in counseling the situation is different than in life, because the counselor tries to be aware of the transference and to use it as a therapeutic tool.

In substance abuse counseling we note the transference and occasionally interpret it. For example, "You're angry with me for interfering with your pleasures just like your mother did," or "You're angry at me because I threaten your drinking." Commenting on the relationship and on what is going on between client and counselor is almost always helpful. In chemical dependency counseling, comments on the here-and-now counseling relationship are preferred to interpretations that relate the present to the past. Transference can be positive, when the counselor is warmly regarded by the client and early experiences of loving and being loved are revived—or negative, when the counselor is hated, envied, and devalued and early experiences of anger and hatred are revived.

In *countertransference* the counselor projects his past experience onto the client. There will be clients who you just can't work with because they remind you too closely of your Uncle Bob who beat his kids before he committed suicide. But generally speaking, countertransference is not disabling—rather it is the inevitable result of being human. The most important thing about countertransference is to be aware that it is always present to some degree, and to use that self-awareness to no let it interfere with the work. One of the best ways to do this is to increase your self awareness through your own counseling o psychotherapy and by discussing your coun tertransference feelings in supervision. To day countertransference also denotes th counselor's feelings in general, includin those induced by the client. Your feelings sadness, despair, futility, anger or joy durir the session are important data about what th client is experiencing and about what the cl ent is inducing in you.

Close Up: Resistance and the Stages of Change

The *stages-of-change* research has demonstrated that recovery is a prolonged, complex process and that change rarely happens in a sudden moment of illumination even though that may seem to be the case (Prochaska and DiClemente 1984). Rather, substance abusers are first in the *pre-contemplative stage* (that is, not even thinking about quitting); then in a *contemplative stage* (not ready to change but increasingly aware that substance abuse is causing problems); then in the *action stage* (where change actually takes place); and finally in the *maintenance stage* (working to hold onto their changes and improvements). At each stage counseling interventions should prepare clients to move ahead to the next stage and work to prevent regression. With addicts, for example, relapse is inevitable without effective maintenance-stage work. Keep in mind that therapeutic change is not necessarily a gradual step-by-step progress to health, but rather has a more cyclical, or revolving-door quality: one step forward, two steps back, one step forward, and so forth (Prochaska 1984).

A significant idea from the *stages-of-change model* is that different interventions are called for at different stages (Prochaska et al. 1992). Consequently, the counselor must be able to correctly assess the client's current stage in order to intervene appropriately. Because the expression of resistance varies at different stages, the counselor needs to intervene differently. Resistance is so strong in the pre-contemplative stage that the best the counselor can do is to plant some seeds—for example, suggest some advantages of sobriety and point out adverse consequences of substance use in the client's life. Ambivalence is strong even in the contemplative stage, and the counselor is best advised to not go head-to-head with the resistance. Rather, both sides of the ambivalence, the reasons for quitting and reasons for continuing, should be elicited, explored, and worked through. Resistance is still present in the action and maintenance stages, but now the counselor should confront the resistance more directly. As is also true with other therapeutic issues, the effective treatment of resistance does not just mean doing the right thing, but doing it at the right time.

Substance abuse-Specific Counseling

Despite their importance in the treatment of chemical dependency, none of the schools discussed so far are specifically concerned with substance abuse issues. In contrast to those schools, **substance abuse-specific (S-A-S) counseling** is an approach that focuses directly on the objective of helping clients to overcome dependency and achieve recovery. Unlike other schools of therapy, S-A-S counseling does not assume the chemical dependency is necessarily due to other problems that need to be corrected first, but rather emphasizes the substance abuse as *the* target problem. In addition, this approach is not grounded in one particular model of human nature or psychopathology, although it does lean more to the disease model of addiction than to any other particular theory. However, an important feature of this approach is its *theoretical integrationism*, that is, its tendency to use concepts and hypotheses from a variety of theoretical sources. As you learned in Chapter 5, the modern disease model takes a *biopsychosocial view*, characterizing chemical dependency in biological, psychological, and sociocultural terms (DuPont 1997, Levin 1995). While owing allegiance to no particular theory, S-A-S counseling is open to ideas from many schools. In this regard it is inclined toward a *transtheoretical view*, one which cuts across, or transcends, current theories (Prochaska 1984).

S-A-S counseling is not simply a ragtag collection of borrowed ideas thrown together from other schools. Instead it meaningfully integrates those ideas with its own knowledge base—the findings of addiction researchers—and with its own way of working with clients. A *three-stage model* of counseling is a core feature of this approach:

Stage 1: Confront the addiction and initiate abstinence.

Stage 2: Work on relapse-prevention skills.

Stage 3: Address the underlying psychological determinants of chemical dependency.

The implementation of this model calls into play many specific counseling techniques that will be discussed later in this chapter. For now, we will concentrate on two general concerns of S-A-S counseling: the eclectic approach and directive counseling.

The Eclectic Approach. Chemical dependency counselors usually take an **eclectic approach**—a strategy that utilizes ideas and techniques from a variety of schools. In psychotherapy circles this approach is often referred to as *technical eclecticism* (Lazarus & Beutler 1993). Like cognitive counseling, substance abuse-specific counseling emphasizes cognitive change. In addition it also uses the attitudinal components of client-centered counseling and borrows heavily from the psychodynamic and existential traditions. When appropriate, it adopts concepts from every tradition. An eclectic style, however, should not be just a grab bag of unrelated tricks. Rather it should be an integrated way of counseling in which the elements borrowed from diverse sources fit together in a harmonious way. Over time you will do more of what works for you and your clientele and less of what doesn't work for you and your clientele. In other words, your style will be shaped by your experience. Letting your experience shape your approach to counseling is both *pragmatic*—that is, what you choose to do will be determined by its "cash value"—and *rational*, in that it is determined by the requirements of the situation.

Despite its popularity, not all counselors take an eclectic approach. Some advocate and practice just one school of counseling. The authors of this book respect those counselors who find that a particular way of working is best for them. The practitioners of each of the schools do indeed help people. Nevertheless, we believe that in treating substance abusers a borrowing from each of the major counseling traditions, when integrated both with other borrowings and with techniques belonging to substance abuse counseling alone, gives the counselor the best chance at helping his or her clients.

Directive Counseling. Just as the director of a film is charged with responsibility to guide the action, substance abuse counselors take responsibility for guiding the course of treatment. **Directive counseling** is defined by the counselor's direction of the client, through offering instructions, giving information, and challenging maladaptive behavior. Although a directive strategy is central to S-A-S counseling, it also resonates with the approach of other schools, in particular behavioral and cognitive counseling.

Directive counseling is of the essence in treating substance abusers. You will find it necessary to direct your clients toward abstinence, sobriety, Twelve-Step participation, appropriate medical and psychopharmacological help, a healthier social system, and continuing involvement in treatment. Counselors give a good deal of guidance and advice, but of course that is not all they do. If all we had to do was to tell the client to straighten up, we would all be out of jobs in short order. But things don't work that way. Even though directive counseling is quite the opposite of a client-centered approach, giving direction is most effective when it takes place in the context of rapport, therapeutic alliance, and unconditional positive regard. The use of the directive approach is a necessary, if not sufficient, component of substance abuse-specific counseling. Without it few clients would achieve sobriety.

After reading the chapter to this point you might be considering choosing another profession. Yes, we have covered a lot, but you don't have to absorb it all at once. In fact, that is impossible. So view all that you have learned now as an introduction, and be consoled that these ideas will become more meaningful to you as you gain clinical experience.

Counseling Schools and Counseling Techniques

Each school of counseling offers a distinctive view of human beings and their behavior. Based on their views of psychopathology, schools have evolved general treatment *strategies* and specific treatment *techniques*. Treatment strategies are broad-based ways of going about counseling. Like movie scripts, they describe plots, characters, acts, and finales. Counseling techniques, however, are what provide the counselor with tools for implementing treatment strategies. They might be characterized as the particular lines in the script.

Most schools of counseling are distinguished by several techniques, and in fact certain techniques are common to different schools. Although each technique is unique in terms of its procedures, rationale, and tradition of use, some overlap is found. For example, the technique called "affect labeling" involves elements of two other techniques: interpretation and reflection. Nevertheless, it has a flavor and purpose all its own.

In counseling, the term *intervention* refers to the application of any technique. In substance abuse counseling, most practitioners find all of the techniques useful from time to time. Of course, that does not imply that you will necessarily use every technique with all your clients. With experience you will learn to customize your interventions according to the needs and style of the client. By the time you finish this chapter, you should have a pretty good book knowledge of the counseling process and the tools to use in a session. However, all of this won't be fully real to you until you get to apply what you learn in this chapter when you take your internship. Be sure to re-read this chapter when you finally get your hands on a real live breathing client. It is important to remember that technique in and of itself does not cure. Relationship does. Your use of technique—the tools of the trade—must be embedded in the context of a therapeutic relationship as a stance, a way of being of the kind you learned about in Chapter 11.

In the remaining parts of this chapter you will learn about the four main types of counseling techniques and the concepts on which they are based. Table 13–3 summarizes these techniques.

13–2 Relationship-Focused Techniques

The client–counselor relationship, or *therapeutic alliance*, is the primary interpersonal context in which counseling works, or fails to work. All counseling schools recognize that the effectiveness of interventions depends on the quality of that alliance. Thus, the first order of business for the counselor is to create a

Table 13–3. Four types of counseling techniques

Type of Technique	Specific Techniques
Relationship-focused	Active listening
	Establishing rapport
	Confrontation
Emotion-focused	Reflection
	Affect labeling
	Relaxation training
Cognition-focused	Education
	Interpretation
	Exploration
	Clarification
	Making drink/drug signals conscious
Behavior-focused	Direct guidance
	Modeling
	Reinforcement
	Assertiveness training

stable working relationship with the client. The formation of an effective therapeutic relationship is fostered by three techniques: establishing rapport, active listening, and confrontation.

Establishing Rapport

The first thing a counselor must do is establish rapport. Simply put, **establishing rapport** means to create a comfortable interpersonal bond between client and counselor. For the counselor, rapport entails a feeling of empathy and acceptance, for the client a feeling of trust and safety, and for both counselor and client a feeling of shared purpose. This bond is the core of the therapeutic activity. How is rapport achieved? Essentially, by being there to meet the client's needs rather than your own and by having something to offer the client, such as your knowledge and skill. If you are connecting with the client in a truly nonjudgmental fashion, rapport will come about by indirection.

There is no specific method or gimmick to establish rapport; rather, it flows from your *therapeutic attitude*—basically, from everything you do and are as a counselor. Of course there are clients (in some settings the majority of clients) whose life experience makes them suspicious, even paranoid, and who cannot readily connect with anyone, including a counselor. Additionally, substance abusers are commonly filled with shame and guilt, and are highly invested in protecting and defending their addictions. All of these factors make it difficult to establish rapport. In such cases all you can do is to maintain your therapeutic attitude and hope that your client stays long enough so that the two of you have a history of going through things together. That "going through things together" builds rapport so that the client is able to move from being "alone alone" to being "alone together." Aloneness is inherent in human life. We are all ultimately alone. But that aloneness can be shared. When there is rapport both client and counselor are alone together and that togetherness is curative in and of itself.

Active Listening

You have already become acquainted with active listening in Chapter 11. However, it is so important, so close to the core of all effective counseling, that we are going to emphasize it again here. **Active listening** means avidly taking in as much of the client's communication as is possible without straining or trying too hard, and conveying by attitude, body language, and appropriate reference to the client's words and nonverbal communications that you are attending in a very special nonjudgmental way to all that is happening in the session. Active listening is listening at many different levels for *manifest content*, the obvious information being consciously expressed, as well as *latent content*, the unspoken or hidden meaning unconsciously behind the words. Of course, no one can take it all in, and our description of active listening is intended as an ideal to strive for, not a standard for the counselor to literally reach.

Freud (1913) recommended that the therapist have an *evenly hovering attention*, that is, that the therapist or counselor not pay more attention to one thing than to another, and not have preconceived ideas about what is important or what is not. The idea is to let the order of importance emerge from the client's communication itself. Here too much theory, too self-consciously used, gets in the way. Theories guide our observation but they are themselves just generalizations from experience. Try not to let them screen the living reality of what is going on in the room. Of course, there is a place for *selective attention*, and we always make choices about what to respond to, based on what we consider relevant to the counseling task. Both evenly hovering attention and selective attention have their place in substance abuse counseling, and both have their place in active listening.

Active listening is, at bottom, attitudinal; it means attending and caring and being open to the client's feelings, thoughts, beliefs, struggles, pain and joy. Without it no counseling can occur.

Confrontation

Building an effective therapeutic relationship does not necessarily mean that you "play nice" all the time. Given the nature of chemical dependency, many clients will present you with denial, deception, avoidance, and antagonism. To sustain the counseling process you will need to use **confrontation**, the identification and challenging of the client's maladaptive attitudes and actions.

Depending on your temperament you may find that confrontation of a client feels hostile and unempathic, or you may regard it as a welcome opportunity to unleash your aggression thoughtlessly as if it were "in the client's interest." Confrontation as a psychological intervention is neither. There is nothing unempathic about confronting self-destructive behavior or a maladaptive defense such as denial. On the contrary, not to confront is the unempathic response. On the other hand, confrontation is not an opportunity to duke it out with a client. However, you do need a certain amount of assertiveness to confront. The counselor's motivation for confrontation should not be retaliation, humiliation, or expression of anger. Of course, clients will sometimes make you angry, and it is good to feel and be aware of that anger. Nevertheless, being angry and experiencing it is not the same as expressing it in inappropriate confrontation with the client. It is our experience that far more counselors, especially novices, inhibit themselves and do not confront, rather than confront to express their own frustration. If you find that you are pulling your punches (for that is what confrontation is to you, a "punch," if you never confront) then you should find out why. This is best done in supervision and/or personal counseling. Confrontation is essential to substance abuse counseling. Some confrontations challenge the substance abuse itself, some the client's denial, some the client's repudiated emotions, and some the client's unacceptable behavior. Consider the following examples of confrontation:

> Mr. Smith, being arrested for DWI (driving while intoxicated) for the fourth time can't possibly be the result of being stopped for a taillight being out. If you weren't drunk, all the mechanical defects in the world wouldn't get you arrested.
>
> Mary, when your father beat you with his belt until you had welts all over your body that wasn't strict discipline, it was child abuse.
>
> John, it's just not true that you don't want to smoke weed anymore. You dream about getting high every night.
>
> Sally, do you realize that your shouting, "Like hell I'm angry, you SOB" proves that you are angry?

Within the client–counselor relationship confrontation can serve the purpose of *limit setting*, that is, pointing out the client's transgression of boundaries or rules. Limit setting is an important part of substance abuse counseling because it informs the client of what is and is not acceptable. However, it does not necessarily involve confrontation, but can involve simple instruction and even humor as in the example of the counselor who said to the client: "If you commit suicide I will refuse to see you anymore." Novice counselors are often in doubt about when to confront their clients. If you sense that your client needs something—a feeling, a false belief, a behavior—brought to his or her attention, then confront. Try to use therapeutic tact, your sense of what the client can hear and can stand at a given time, in deciding if a necessary confrontation should take place now or later. If the resistance is too high and the client is unable to deal with the insight that confrontation would bring about, then store your observation away for future use. The client will give you many other chances to confront whatever the issue is. On the other hand, remember that confront you must. The timing of confrontation should be based on your clinical judgment of how helpful it will be for the client, not on your own trepidation or fear of the client's response. Do not expect your clients to thank you for confronting them—at least not right away. Instead be aware that your confrontations are quite likely to provoke clients' anger and resentment. Your response to and handling of those reactions entails the use of the emotion-focused techniques that are discussed in the following section.

13–3   Emotion-Focused Techniques

Counseling is a process charged with strong emotions. Like other types of clients, the substance-abusing client experiences very powerful and distressing emotions: anxiety, depression, guilt, and anger, to name a few. In addition, substance-abusing clients are more likely to feel coerced and threatened than other clients, because they often are in counseling not of their own free will but because they "got caught." Typically, your clients will have entered counseling because of pressures from the law, family members, the boss, and other external sources. In addition to their internal turmoil, chemically dependent clients all too often are embattled from without as well. Needless to say, the counselor's task is to aid the client in sorting through and resolving these many emotional issues. Reflection, affect labeling, and relaxation training are three important techniques that focus on the client's emotional needs.

Reflection

Reflection means providing feedback to the client about his or her feelings, thoughts, and behavior. In other words, the counselor is like a mirror that reflects back the client's expressions. In using reflection as an intervention, the counselor refrains from making directive statements, giving interpretations as to why the client said something or what it means, or judging the value of the client's expressions. Rather, the counselor acts as a mirror that distorts as little as possible. For example, as a client is talking about her struggle with her desire to "do a line" at the party Saturday night, the counselor reflects: "You felt deeply torn." Note that in reflecting the counselor doesn't comment on the client's putting herself in jeopardy by going to a party where cocaine was available. Nor does the counselor strategize with her about how to handle the situation, or confront her active craving for the drug, or do anything but reflect back the intense conflict the client has told the counselor she has experienced.

In substance abuse counseling we often reflect feelings and conflicts. This is highly useful to the client because it heightens awareness of the feeling or conflict. Nevertheless, the strictly hands-off aspect of reflection alone is sometimes untenable in substance abuse counseling. It is too nondirective when it is used as the dominant technique. Most often we first reflect, and then, if there is danger, comment on the danger or suggest an alternate behavior. In spite of this caveat, we are aware that reflection is an extremely powerful technique. While it may seem simple, doing it well is a true art form that requires considerable practice. When do you use reflection? It is best to use reflection when you must increase your client's awareness of feelings and to intensify the emotion. Sometimes reflection can seem too simple-minded; for example, the client says: "I'm really pissed off," and the counselor says: "You're enraged." Simple or foolish as it may seem, this reflection increases the client's awareness of his emotional state and may lead him to question it. If it serves a therapeutic purpose, don't hesitate to make "simple-minded" reflective interventions.

Affect Labeling

Affect labeling simply means highlighting the client's feelings by giving them a name. It is one of the most helpful things that substance abuse counselors do. Affect labeling is a form of interpretation, because it is an interpretation of what the client is feeling. That might sound tricky and even presumptuous, and in a way that's true. How can the counselor know more about what the client is feeling than the client? In some basic sense we are each alone in our experience and nobody can know what we are feeling better than we can. Our experience is our experience and no one else's. Yet there are factors that mitigate against this intuitive conclusion. Substance abuse muddies and confuses, so that clients literally don't know what they are feeling. Repression and suppression, conscious and unconscious "stuffing," makes feelings unavailable to immediate awareness. And then clients may not have labels for the inchoate feelings seething around within them—they cannot put words to what they are feeling affectively. Additionally, the client's early experience may have been so traumatic and/or deficient that they never learned to label feelings accurately in the first place. For all of these reasons, clients badly need counselors to give them names for what they are experiencing.

On the counselor's side, many factors, including his or her own experience, the client's presentation and body language, the counselor's understanding of what is going on within him- or herself during the session, and the counselor's empathy, make it surprisingly easy for counselors to accurately label affects. Of course, we make mistakes and sometimes even our most strongly felt intuitions about what the client is feeling are off-base. But that rarely happens if the counselor is attuned to the client, and when it does the client corrects us, so little or no damage is done. Don't be afraid to label feelings, or to stick to your guns if you think the client is blocking or repressing in his or her denial of your affective interpretation. Affect labeling really helps.

The technical word for not being able to put feelings into words is *alexithymia*. It is a good word to know. You will come across it in your reading and it characterizes a number of the more severe mental illnesses. There is an important theory about the development of affect that casts light on why affect labeling is so vital in substance abuse counseling. Krystal and Raskin (1976), who worked extensively with substance abusers, hypothesized that at the beginning of life infants and toddlers experience their feelings as global, massive, somatized (that is, experienced as bodily states), undifferentiated, overwhelming, and unverbalized. As children grow and mature their feelings become more fine-tuned, or as psychologists put it, differentiated; feelings are less one big ball of wax, more manageable, and de-somatized, (that is, experienced more in language and less as bodily states). They also come to have names so they can be verbalized.

This developmental sequence doesn't happen automatically, but requires interaction with loving caretakers. Mom or Dad says, "Honey, you're crying because you are sad/angry/hurt because your dolly broke." Thus, the child learns a name for a feeling. In highly dysfunctional families, like the ones many substance abusers grow up in, this process doesn't take place, and consequently the child is vulnerable to alexithymia. Such children are likely to experience feelings as bodily states, to be vulnerable to psychosomatic illness, to experience feelings as massive, undifferentiated, and overwhelming, and to be deficient in the ability to verbalize feelings.

To make matters worse, Krystal and Raskin hypothesize that trauma, including the trauma of substance abuse itself, causes *emotional regression*, which is characterized by de-differentiation, resomatization and deverbalization. The substance abuse counselor's job is to reverse this regression by giving names to feelings, and the more of this you do the better.

Relaxation Training

Substance abuse clients have few resources to induce relaxation besides substance use. Tension and anxiety are among the most common reasons cited by clients for their substance abuse, and for their relapses. **Relaxation training** is a general label for techniques that teach clients skills for reducing tension and anxiety. The objective of relaxation techniques is not just to provide momentary comfort for the client during the session, but more importantly to give the client a skill that with practice can be applied in any situation. Many variations on the theme of relaxation training have been employed, and here we examine four popular methods: (1) progressive muscle relaxation, (2) guided imagery, (3) meditation, and (4) hypnosis.

The most popular type of relaxation training is *progressive muscle relaxation* (PMR) training (Jacobson 1938). This technique entails systematic exercises to first increase muscle tension and then relax those muscles. You might begin with finger and hand exercises, and then progress through muscles in the arms, shoulders, neck, and so forth until all major muscle groups have been used. Typical instructions follow this example.

Feel the tension in your fingers. They are getting tenser and tenser. Feel how tight they are. Now let the tension go. You can feel the tension leaving your fingers. They are getting more and more relaxed. More and more relaxed. Feel the difference between the tension and relaxation in your fingers.

By the time the exercise is over the client is in a deep state of relaxation and after a time the client begins to use self-induced relaxation. Relaxation training can be conducted either in a group setting or in individual work.

Relaxation can also be induced through *guided imagery*, an exercise in which the client imagines calming events.

> Imagine yourself on a quiet beach on a glorious midsummer day. The sand is warming your back, and the heat of the sun melts away all the tension in your body. You lose yourself in listening to the gentle rhythm of the waves as they fall back and forth upon the beach. As you feel the soft air covering you like a warm blanket, you grow more and more relaxed.

The best image for inducing relaxation for a particular client is elicited by exploration before the guided imagery exercise begins. Obviously our example wouldn't work for a client who had been bitten by a shark. Guided imagery can be used for many purposes, including getting in contact with the unconscious. But in substance abuse counseling it is generally used as a relaxation technique. This is an area where you can let your creativity flow freely.

Meditation refers to a variety of practices ranging from Zen to Transcendental Meditation. Although originally conceived by Eastern religions as an exercise in spirituality, meditation is a versatile activity that can be used for strictly secular purposes like relaxation. At its core, meditation requires a few simple ingredients.

- Go to a quiet spot and sit or lie in a comfortable position.
- Find a mental focus such as a word or phrase (*mantra*), an image, or an external stimulus, and concentrate on it as fully as possible.
- Breathe in a rhythmic, comfortable pattern preferably using diaphragmatic breathing.

- Maintain mental focus on the thing you have chosen, and if you lose focus come back to it.

Naturally, meditation cannot cure chemical dependency, but it can be helpful to recovering persons. Researchers find that meditation has general benefits for mental health, and that it is an effective piece of stress management work.

Hypnosis is method that incorporates elements of other relaxation training techniques, like guided imagery and meditation, but applies them in a rather different manner. In contrast to other relaxation methods that clients can do by themselves, hypnosis relies on the hypnotist's careful use of suggestions to the client. Through the use of suggestions—as ideas or instructions—the hypnotist leads the client to therapeutic improvement. Be aware that hypnosis requires special training, and even though most counselors will not employ this technique, we mention it here for the sake of completeness. There are many methods that can induce a hypnotic state, but all move the client from ordinary consciousness to another state closer to that of daydreaming or reverie.

Hypnosis is used for several purposes: to put the client in contact with unconscious material, particularly with repressed traumatic memories; to help the client control behavioral excess like bad habits; and, of course, to relax the client. Our experience with hypnosis for behavioral excess (for example, smoking) is that it is a valuable adjunct, but not a cure in itself. For the client who sincerely wants to stop smoking, but is having trouble with impulse control, hypnosis will help, but not if the willingness and desire are absent.

13–4 Cognition-Focused Techniques

Changing the client's maladaptive cognitions—beliefs, attitudes, perceptions—and fostering the client's development of health-promoting ideas are two central concerns in counseling. Cognition-focused techniques aim to achieve those goals. These techniques include education, interpretation, exploration, clarification, and making drink/drug signals conscious.

Education

In some sense every counseling intervention is a kind of teaching, and every counseling technique an educational tool. Broadly defined, in counseling **education** refers to any intervention that facilitates the client's learning. Freud (1912) spoke of psychoanalysis, the grandfather of talk therapies, as "re-education," the purpose of which is to correct faulty learning or miseducation. The famous Greek philosopher Socrates taught that evil (dysfunction) was ignorance and that, "to know the good was to do the good." Accordingly, he derived a method, one we now call Socratic inquiry, in which the philosopher helps the pupil to discover the truth within. The Socratic teacher brought to conscious awareness what until then was latent in the pupil, and that awareness was held to be transforming.

Socrates' method remains a model for most of what modern counselors do. Its premise is simple: as nineteenth-century German thinkers put it, *Wissen macht Frei* (knowledge liberates). However, the Socratic method educates, in its root meaning of educing or drawing out, rather than teaching in a more didactic sense. When we speak of educational interventions in this book, we are talking not about the drawing-out function of all counseling, but rather about that component of counseling that is explicitly teaching—the conveying of information. You may say that nobody has ever gotten sober by listening to a lecture, and that is true. Emotional resistance, denial, physiological dependence, and a host of other factors mitigate against it. Nevertheless, being sane entails knowing how to be sane. Knowledge is a necessary, if not sufficient, condition of human transformation, as well as recovery. The great seventeenth-century philosopher Baruch Spinoza described the passion to understand and to know the truth, which integrates reason and affect into a mutative experience. Something mutative is that which brings about mutation—radical change. Spinoza also said that only an affect

could change an affect, pointing to the fact that emotion is always intrinsic to the understanding and insight that move human beings to a better place.

Substance abuse counselors educate in the narrow sense of imparting knowledge all the time. In fact, one distinctive quality of substance abuse counseling is the major role of *didactic intervention*, or teaching. You can't teach what you don't know; therefore mastery of the factual basis of substance abuse counseling, mastery of what scientists and addiction specialists have learned about what drugs do to the body, mind, and spirit, is absolutely vital if you're going to be an effective substance abuse counselor. Let us look at some examples of educational/didactic interventions.

> Mr. Smith, do you know that alcohol, although it may give you some temporary relief because it's an anesthetic, actually makes your depression worse? As we said yesterday, your drinking is really self-medication—you're trying to treat your depression. I think I can understand that. Your depression is so painful you'll do anything to get some relief. Unfortunately, this medicine you're using—martinis—is making you even more depressed. That's because alcohol depresses the central nervous system—your brain and spinal cord. The pharmacology is all wrong and it works against you. But there are medicines that do help depression and I want you to talk to our psychiatrist about them.

That example is a long intervention and it may be more than poor Mr. Smith can take in. In that case, start with the first sentence of this intervention and discuss it with Mr. Smith. There is plenty of time to complete Mr. Smith's education on depression. Give him bite-size pieces and then sum up and repeat. We need to be simple, clear, and redundant. Otherwise our clients have trouble taking in what we say, both because their brains are poisoned by their drug use and they aren't playing with a full deck, and because resistance and denial are defending the client against hearing more than he or she wants to hear.

> Ms. Brown you thought the police were looking in your window because you

freebased last night. Freebasing hits you a lot harder than snorting a line so you had lots of cocaine in your bloodstream. Cocaine raises the level of a chemical called dopamine in your brain. People who have the terrible mental illness called paranoid schizophrenia have too much dopamine working in certain parts of their brain. That's what happened to you. You got paranoid because your freebasing threw off the chemical balance in your brain. For a few hours your brain was working the same way a paranoid schizophrenic's does.

If Ms. Brown is in no shape to take all that in, the counselor could simply have said: "Ms. Brown, freebasing poisoned your brain and made you paranoid." A fuller explanation can wait for later. Mr. Post had an intensely paranoid episode on coke that was far worse than Ms. Brown's. He was terrified. When he "came down" he entered into a passionate discussion with the counselor in which he insisted the counselor validate his experience by agreeing that the FBI was after him. The counselor refused to be drawn into a futile debate. Instead he said:

> Mr. Post if the FBI really has you staked out and has wired your apartment, you'll have to give up coke or you'll be arrested and go to jail. But if the FBI isn't there, then your coke use is making you paranoid and crazy—so you will have to stop if you don't want to go out of your mind. So it doesn't matter what I think about the reality of the FBI being there. Either way, you will have to stop because if you keep using you're in deep trouble— you're either heading for jail or for the nuthouse.

Mr. Post actually did stop using cocaine, although unfortunately not other drugs.

As a counselor, the more you know the better you can educate. Therefore, your professional life should be one of continuous growth—new learning and integration of that new learning with what you already know. The ideal counselor, like Chaucer's clerk in the *Canterbury Tales*, will "gladly learn and gladly teach." Educational interventions are not only about specifics like the depressive effects of alcohol and the paranoia induced by cocaine

use. They are also about larger, more conceptual issues like the disease concept of addiction and the nature of the Twelve-Step programs. Most counselors subscribe to the disease model of addiction, as do the authors of this text. However, we are aware that there are cogent and powerful arguments against the disease model as an explanation of addiction, and that there are respected workers in the field who have concluded that the disease model is not the best explanation of addiction. It is helpful to recall that models are not realities, they are ways of understanding realities. With a phenomenon as complex as addiction, it may be the case that multiple models are needed, where one perspective best explains one thing and other perspectives other things.

Why, you might ask, do clients need to be taught any theory of addiction? The answer is that doing so strongly enhances their chances of recovery. Addiction is chaos; it is bewilderment; it is confusion; it is desperation; it is pain; it is the continuing experience of awful things happening for no apparent reason. Theories, like the disease model, make sense of that chaos. Suddenly the client has an explanation of why his or her life has gone downhill so precipitously. The model offers a cognitive structure that makes the irrational rational and reduces anxiety. Awareness of the disease model gratifies the desire to know and to understand, even as it provides fuel to power recovery. Share what you know and believe, but don't indoctrinate, bully, or insist that your client adopt your perspective. No particular belief is necessary for recovery, including belief in the disease model. Therefore be as convincing as you can, and then respect the client's conclusions.

Counselors also teach clients about the Twelve-Step programs. Every client should be exposed to the Twelve-Step movement and have a chance to be educated about it and to ask questions about it. Some clients will take other routes to recovery—Twelve-Step is just not for them—and their values should be respected. The majority of your clients will wind up in Twelve-Step programs. The combination of counseling and Twelve-Step participation during the first year of recovery certainly gives the client the very best chance to make it. There are clients who don't have the least interest in spiritual growth and the rest of the "Twelve-Step stuff"; they just want not to get high and to learn some tricks for handling drug signals and the like.

After all these qualifications, it must be said that teaching about Twelve-Step groups and their ideologies is a central part of substance abuse counseling. You must have knowledge of the Program, its history, its ideology, the steps themselves, the sponsor–sponsee relationship, and idiosyncrasies of local meetings. You will have ample opportunity to talk about all of these things as they come up naturally in the course of treatment. Consider the following examples of educational intervention about the Twelve-Steps:

Client: They said at the meeting I should have a sponsor. But I have you so why do I need a sponsor?

Counselor: The sponsor does different things than a counselor. You need both. I help you with professional knowledge while your sponsor helps you by sharing his experience. Your group is right, getting a sponsor would be helpful.

Client: "I'm having trouble with the third step—the one about turning our will and our lives over to God as we understand him. I'm a nonbeliever and I'm not comfortable with that.

Counselor: There are N.A. members with all sorts of beliefs and they are all able to benefit from participating in the program. If it makes you more comfortable, you can secularize the third step into "Let it happen," or "Go with the flow," or "Get out of your own way." The third step is about relaxing the need to control, to run the show, which no one can really do—it only sets you up for frustration. So try going more with the flow.

Another issue related to teaching the Twelve-Step approach has to do with abstinence. As you know, we espouse the position that abstinence is necessary for recovery from full-blown addiction (as opposed to problem drinking or drugging). Nevertheless, you are inevitably going to have to deal with clients who do not accept abstinence as a goal. In those cases, counselors need to make *least-harm interventions*. For example, not to tell an active intravenous drug user who has no intention of stopping about your city's needle-exchange program is not only cruel, it is criminal. Nor would we fail to tell a pregnant teenager who has no intention of giving up drinking and drugging long-term about the fetal alcohol syndrome, in the hope that she will at least remain abstinent until delivery. Such simple least-harm educational interventions save lives. The counselor should never put ideology above the client's needs. However, that does not mean that you have to go on treating clients who have no intention of stopping their use if you're working from an abstinence-model stance.

Interpretation

An interpretation is an explanation of why something happens; it offers reasons for the client's behavior, thoughts or feelings. The technique of interpretation is most characteristic of the psychodynamic school. In fact, classical (Freudian) psychoanalysis relies on it almost entirely. In contrast to psychoanalytic interpretations, which explain events in terms of developmental events and/or unconscious conflicts, interpretations offered by substance abuse counselors tend to relate client behaviors and experiences to the substance use itself.

Selectively and wisely used, interpretation is one of the most therapeutic of interventions. An accurate interpretation resonates. The client not only hears it, he or she feels it—and feels it deep down where it counts. Interpretation cures not only because of content (what the counselor actually says that enables insight), it also cures by giving the client the feeling of being understood. That strengthens rapport, feels supportive, and deepens the bond between client and counselor. And this is true even if the content of the interpretation is painful. We use interpretation to increase insight and to raise the client's self-awareness. To do that, the interpretation must not only be accurate, it must be timely. An interpretation given before the client is ready to hear it grates, strengthens the client's resistance, and generally backfires. Knowing when to interpret requires that intangible commodity called therapeutic tact. That comes with experience and the kind of sensitivity counselors develop as they work with clients. There is no cookbook recipe for knowing when—rather it is something you will develop as you gain experience, and also something you can get help with in your clinical supervision.

One danger in overusing interpretation is that the counseling can become too intellectual. Interpretations can also engender resentment over what feels to the client like being understood "from above," that is, condescendingly. It is generally better to let the client have an experience and to be in a feeling state before offering an interpretation. Affect first, then an understanding of the affect. When Freud and Joseph Breuer (1895) wrote the first book on psychodynamic psychotherapy, *Studies on Hysteria*, they concluded that their clients suffered from strangulated affect, or what we would call stuffed feelings. They recommended *abreaction*, or *catharsis*, a de-repression and expressive release of the strangulated affect, which they believed was associated with repressed traumatic memories. As they put it, clients suffered from reminiscences. Whatever it is called, release of repressed emotion plays a central part in all counseling, including substance abuse counseling.

As Freud gained experience, he concluded that catharsis was not enough; insight was also needed. Consequently, he shifted the emphasis of his therapeutic technique to interpretation. Modern substance abuse counselors often rely on catharsis for the expression of feelings, as well as interpretation to increase understanding and insight. So use interpretation when you want to deepen the client's self-understanding and you sense that the client is ready to hear what you have to say. If you can, make a connection with the substance abuse a part of your interpretation.

There is an interpretive aspect to all interventions, if only in their selectivity, that is, in the counselor's implied selection of one thing rather than another as being the most relevant

and important for the client to hear at that moment. Although you will do so sparingly, you will definitely interpret. If you think you see something that the client doesn't see and that seeing would help the client, don't hesitate to verbalize your insight.

There are two main types of interpretation: here-and-now, and then-and-there. The *here-and-now interpretation* makes some connection between current events. In contrast, *then-and-there interpretations* connect the present with the past and make the client aware that current feelings or behavior are being driven by a "blast from the past." In substance abuse counseling we use mainly here-and-now interpretations. Sometimes interpretation contains both here-and-now and there-and-then elements. Some common examples are found in transference interpretations that involve the relationship with the counselor. *Transference interpretations* can focus on the immediate interactions between client and counselor, or they can connect the client's reaction to the counselor to the client's past. All of this may sound fairly abstract. Some examples will make interpretation real.

- *Here-and-now interpretations:*
  "Mr. Adams, you're angry at your wife because she doesn't like you to get high, not because, as you say, she's a 'bitch.'"

  "Mr. Adams you're depressed because booze isn't working for you anymore."

  "You're enraged with me because I confronted you on missing meetings."

- *Then-and-there interpretations:*
  "You're enraged at me because my confrontation about you missing the meeting reminded you of your hated father's beatings when you disobeyed him."

  "You think that your relapsing will hurt and punish me the way your drinking affected your mother when you were a teenager."

The possibilities for interpretation are infinite, limited only by your creativity and by the client's needs. Deeper insight into yourself, gained through personal counseling or psychotherapy, will make you a better interpreter.

Exploration and Clarification

Exploration is a technique whereby counselors and clients search for and discover significant aspects of the client's mental life. The process of exploration helps people open up and learn more about themselves. Counselors sometimes explore by asking questions. For example, "What were you thinking before you walked into the liquor store?" Or they may explore by encouraging the client to do so. For example, by saying "Tell me more about that." If the imperative, "Tell me," feels too bossy, controlling or pressuring, then the counselor might say, "Can you tell me more about that?" Or, "How do you know that when your mother exposed herself she was stoned?"

Generally speaking, using *interrogatories* (questions) is the better approach, but sometimes you may want to put on a little pressure by using the imperative voice: "Tell me just what you mean by that remark." Exploration can be very open-ended: "Just say whatever comes to mind." Or it can be very focused: "When did you realize that the hook would pull out of the ceiling when you tried to hang yourself from it?" Exploration may be about the client's inner world: "Can you go deeper into your anxiety and tell me how your body feels when the anxiety wells up in you?" Or about the environment: "Is there a way to get home from work without passing the corner where you used to cop?"

Exploration is one of the most useful counseling techniques; you will use it often. But always use it with discretion. Exploration is called for when the client needs to learn more about self or situation, not when the counselor is curious for his or her own reasons. As with any intervention, in deciding whether or not to use that intervention, ask yourself, "What does the client need to learn or experience now?" If exploration facilitates that learning or experience then use it. If not, don't. Generally speaking, exploration opens things up. But in substance abuse counseling we also have to focus on keeping the client's attention on the substance use and its consequences. That means holding off on asking general and open-ended exploratory ques-

tions (for example, "What was your childhood like?") when they take the client away from the central problem—chemical dependency. Use them when you believe that the client needs more self-knowledge, or when it is important, to you as counselor, to know more about some aspect of the client's life or situation that is not easily brought forth by a direct question.

A **clarification** intervention is a counselor's request for more accurate, precise, unambiguous information. Clarification clears things up; it highlights and pinpoints, and also intensifies. A clarification is the counselor's equivalent of underlining. It puts the spotlight on whatever is being discussed:

> "Your comment that you only smoke 'because the crowd did, but that I didn't want to' confused me. Can you tell me what that means?"

In some instances as a counselor you will offer the client a clarification:

> "When you said your father only beat you when he was sober, were you saying that his drunkenness was better for you than his sobriety?"

Beginning counselors are often afraid to say "I don't understand that," or "I'm confused by what you said," or "I can't make much sense of that." They are afraid of looking stupid, of offending the client, or of hurting the client's feelings. Don't be afraid to ask for clarification or to offer it if that will facilitate the work you are doing at the moment. Substance abusers are prone to use confusion and ambiguity as defenses, as places to hide—particularly to hide their substance abuse. They are also not infrequently genuinely confused. Therefore, clarifying interventions, especially those requiring clarification by the client, are extremely useful.

Making Drink/Drug Signals Conscious

All substance abusers have triggers that provoke their drinking and drugging; these triggers are known as **drink/drug signals**.

Substance abuse counselors work hard to make clients aware of their triggers—the places, people, things, and feelings that set off substance use and relapse. This work involves a combination of exploration, education, and interpretation. Once the client is aware of the trigger, he or she is in less danger of acting on it. The danger is further reduced if the counselor can suggest or help the client to find an alternate coping mechanism, perhaps by rewarding herself with a milkshake instead of a double scotch for surviving the workday. Both the process of gaining awareness of triggers—for example, the end of the workday—and learning alternate responses to them are of the essence in optimizing the client's chances of maintaining recovery. This process is an essential part of relapse prevention, which will be further discussed in Chapter 14.

In conjunction with increasing the client's awareness of drink/drug signals, the behavior therapy technique of *cue exposure* can also be used. In cue exposure therapy, the client is systematically exposed to or presented with drink/drug signals under conditions in which drinking and drugging are not permitted. The rationale for this method is based on classical conditioning principles. The signals, for example, the sight of a whisky bottle, act as conditioned stimuli that provoke the urge or impulse to use the substance. When a person is exposed repeatedly to those stimuli while being prevented from actually using the substance, the urge gradually lessens. Ultimately, the association between the signal and substance use is weakened, and the client learns more control over the urge to use (O'Brien et al. 1990).

The cue exposure method might strike you as counterintuitive and even potentially dangerous. Ordinarily, chemical-dependence counselors urge their clients to avoid the people, places, and things that trigger substance consumption, and that advice is right on target. The key to successful use of cue exposure is to present the drink/drug cues under controlled circumstances such that there is no possibility of use, and to repeat the exposure until the conditioned urges are extinguished. You would certainly not advise your alcoholic client to go to the neighborhood watering hole

and hang out for a while as a cue exposure intervention! In fact cue exposure is most sensible later in recovery after the client has had a period of sustained abstinence and has acquired some degree of control and confidence.

13–5 Behavior-Focused Techniques

In this last section we consider the use of *behavior-focused techniques* whose purpose is mainly to help clients acquire new skills to enhance recovery. Although these techniques are most closely associated with the behavioral school, they are not the exclusive property of that tradition. Counselors working from a variety of perspectives can adapt these interventions to suit their clients' needs.

Direct Guidance

The straightforward offering of advice or instruction to guide your client's actions is what we mean by **direct guidance**, or simply, *direction*. Although some counselors, especially client-centered counselors, shy away from direct guidance, it is a necessary and inevitable component of substance abuse counseling. "Go to a (Twelve-Step) meeting tonight" is probably the most common direction in substance abuse counseling.

When someone is stepping in front of a speeding truck it is empathic to call out "Stop!" Substance abusers are forever stepping in front of speeding trucks. While it is true that we neither can nor should live our clients' lives for them, it is equally true that many of our clients (especially in early treatment) have poor judgment and impaired reality testing. They really need guidance and direction, and your judgment is better than that of someone suffering from the effects of prolonged substance abuse. You should not let false modesty or fear of being "bossy" inhibit you from giving appropriate direction and guidance. Keep in mind that direct guidance does not require the wisdom of Socrates. Simple advice, given with confidence and sincerity can make a big difference:

- "You need to stop running and stand still
- "This isn't the time to quit your job."

- "Go to the party late and leave early."
- "Stay away from George—he's trouble."

Direct guidance overlaps with limit-setting, which we discussed previously. Don't be afraid to be directive or to set limits on your client's behavior. Impaired, early-recovery clients need to have things clearly structured. Mere advice-giving may not feel like professional counseling work, and that may be a reason that you are reluctant to do it. However, your clients are not there to increase your sense of professional pride. They are there to get help. Likewise, if you are temperamentally inclined to be bossy or controlling, be aware of it and limit your use of directive interventions.

As clients become more stably sober and consolidate their recovery, use less and less directive technique. Keep in mind, though, that your clients are not going to get to that point if they step in front of those trucks. So make use of directives early and then back off. Needless to say, directives aren't always heeded and advice isn't always taken. The client's noncompliance can be very upsetting to the novice counselor, so remember that you cannot step aside from the truck for the client, you can only warn him or her that it is about to hit.

Modeling

Demonstrating how a behavior is performed is **modeling**. In counseling, modeling is usually not so much a deliberate, planned technique as something that just happens in the course of treatment. Clients observe and imitate their counselors whether or not their counselors know it or want it. Counselors need to be aware that they are models and exhibit behaviors that are good for their clients to emulate.

What is it that the counselor should be modeling? Tolerance, self-acceptance, openness, contact with feelings, sobriety in the sense of avoiding excess (for you may be a social drinker), honesty, empathy, and compassion for self and others head the list. It is especially important to model the exploration of powerful feelings and experiences.

You may be uncomfortable with this instant canonization—and if you are not, we are worried about you. Of course, you aren't all of these things consistently or reliably. Rather, they are ideals you and all counselors strive for. Nevertheless, you embody some characteristics and values that many clients don't have. Their identification with aspects of you and their internalization of you as a model can be extremely helpful to them. Don't go out of your way to disillusion your clients; they will find out your flaws soon enough.

In addition to this unselfconscious modeling by the counselor, there is the deliberate, consciously crafted use of modeling as a teaching device. This occurs, for example, when *role playing* is used to teach a specific behavior, such as communication. With a client whose communication skills are limited, you might role play a scenario in which you are the client asking his boss for a day off and giving a clear reason for the request. In less contrived but still quite deliberate modeling, you might use opportunities that arise in the course of the session. For instance, in modeling the expression of sorrow, the counselor displays that emotion by experiencing and expressing the feeling in the course of a session. Let's say that the client's disclosure of childhood abuse makes the counselor feel sad and the counselor shares the feeling by saying, "Listening to you I feel so sad, I'm almost crying." By modeling your feelings you can help your clients learn how to express their own.

Counselors model many things, from refusing a drink to setting limits for children. Clients are often unable to do particular things, and modeling is often the best technique for teaching them how. Do not be afraid to model if you sense that your client will learn from it.

Reinforcement

Based on principles from the behavioral school, **reinforcement** is a method by which positive consequences are used to strengthen a behavior. In everyday terms, reinforcement means rewarding good behavior. Reinforcement is a very directive technique. It means telling the client that some behaviors are desirable. The withholding of reinforcement also lets the client know that some behaviors are undesirable. Although the theory behind reinforcement is identified with the behavioral school, its practical application in counseling is flexible and versatile enough to transcend the boundaries of any single approach.

In theory, psychodynamic and client-centered counselors avoid the use of reinforcement. Instead they try to maintain an attitude of nonjudgmental, technical neutrality, meaning that the counselor deliberately does not take one side or another in dealing with the client's conflicts or struggles with the world. Generally, however, in substance abuse counseling we do not assume the attitude of technical neutrality. Here we have a definite goal. We want to lead the client toward recovery. We are advocates of sobriety, and are not at all neutral about that. That doesn't mean that there aren't times in substance abuse counseling when it isn't useful for the counselor to remain neutral. On the contrary, there are many such moments and situations. Nevertheless, we are advocates, not neutral observers.

How do we advocate sobriety? In many ways: by education, by direct guidance, by example, and certainly by selectively reinforcing desired behaviors. The most apparent way to reinforce is by giving *verbal approval* of your client's actions. You might remark, for instance:

- "I'm delighted you went to an A.A. meeting when you realized how upset you were."
- "Turning down that job after you realized that it was so stressful it might threaten your sobriety was a wise and mature decision."
- "Pouring all the liquor in the house down the drain was really a good move."

Reinforcement is also delivered in *nonverbal behavior* as well as in verbal approval. A smile, a lifted eyebrow, moving closer to or even touching the client, and other gestures and body language can convey potent reinforcing messages. Perhaps the most underrated reinforcement technique is simply paying attention. Just good listening and an indication of understanding—for example, a nod of your head—can reinforce the client's expression of some thought or feeling. Because nonverbal communications are more difficult to monitor—they often just slip out—it is especially important to become aware of the ways in which you nonverbally signal your approval or interest in your client's actions and remarks, as well as your disapproval and lack of interest.

Unless you are aware of the many reinforcing messages that you send, you might find that you are unwittingly reinforcing behavior that has no therapeutic value for the client. One example might be a male addict who has a long history of exciting drug-taking escapades, and who elicits intense interest from the counselor upon the telling and retelling of his tales. The reinforcement from the counselor's attention to those drug stories can strengthen the client's emotional involvement in the actions being recalled. Keep in mind that for many longtime addicts and alcoholics their drinking and drugging has been the primary source of reinforcement in their lives. Therapeutic use of reinforcement directs them away from chemical dependency and toward more health-promoting behaviors.

Sometimes reinforcements are tangible consequences, such as the granting of privileges—for example, TV time in an inpatient setting. But for the most part they are social, that is, carried in messages, both verbal and nonverbal, from other people. Don't underestimate their efficacy because they are merely words or gestures. If your client has established a therapeutic alliance with you, your approval is of the greatest significance. Your clients will not only look to you for signs of approbation, but will also be motivated to do what gains reinforcement for themselves. Don't be afraid to use the leverage you have to promote your clients' health.

A more structured kind of reinforcement technique is **shaping**, which means reinforcing approximations to a desired behavior. In everyday language, shaping means that the counselor gradually rewards the client's progress toward some goal or target. Shaping does not produce overnight change, but instead gradually moves the client toward the goal one step, often a very small step, at a time. The counselor continues to reinforce each step along the way until the client has mastered that step. Then reinforcement is applied to the next step on the path and so on until the goal is reached. Consider the following example:

> Your client, Mr. Smith, has frequent rages that get him in trouble at work. In the past he was frequently physically violent and this had led to substance use, among other difficulties. Mr. Smith has been working on anger management. He comes in and relates how he abstained from punching out an associate who irritated him by a trivial trespass on his feelings. Mr. Smith tells the counselor, "I really wanted to put out his lights, but I controlled myself and told him to go fuck himself." The counselor says, "I'm really proud of you, Mr. Smith." Now the counselor doesn't think blowing up and cursing someone out for a trivial offense is a desirable behavior, but he does think that it's an improvement over physical violence, so he reinforces it. This is shaping. Once Mr. Smith is securely beyond punching people's lights out, cursing will no longer be reinforced. Now tolerating minor offenses (real or imagined) will be reinforced, and so on until the goal of anger management has been reached.

Substance abuse counselors do a good deal of shaping, sometimes carefully planning and strategizing their course, and sometimes shaping more intuitively. Naturally, the primary target for shaping is abstinence from drugs and alcohol. However, many other behaviors in the chemically dependent client can be shaped to good effect, such as taking responsibility, participation in group sessions, coming on time for sessions, attending Twelve-Step meetings, and many more steps to recovery.

Assertiveness Training

Substance abusers are often rambunctious, surly, rageful and generally hard to be around, but they are rarely effectively assertive. **Assertiveness training** entails teaching effective self-expression and the skills required to stand up for one's rights. Assertiveness train-

ing incorporates several other techniques, including role playing, shaping, modeling, and homework assignments. Positive reinforcement by fellow group members and by counselors is generously disbursed. Assertiveness training is usually taught in a group, where the counselor and group members role play assertiveness, starting with easy situations and progressing to difficult ones. Angry, aggressive, blustering clients are deficient in assertiveness; that deficiency, after all, is one reason they are so angry and aggressive—they don't know how to get what they want. In addition, the quiet depressive type of substance abuser—the miserable mouse and human doormat—is just as lacking in assertiveness skills. Even clients who do not fit those extreme patterns can benefit from assertiveness training.

It is very important for the counselor who conducts assertiveness training to distinguish assertiveness from aggression, because ordinarily, your clients mistakenly suppose that they are the same. A major difference is that there is no hostility behind assertiveness. Assertiveness is motivated by a desire to speak your mind, be heard, and get your due. In contrast, anger, revenge, or a wish to harm motivates aggression. Where aggression involves antisocial self-expressions, assertiveness involves healthful and productive self-expression. Clients need to know that assertiveness covers both negative self-expressions, like "I don't appreciate your drinking when I'm around," and positive self-expressions such as "I really like it when you tell me you're proud of my sobriety." Ultimately, assertiveness training enables clients to be more honest and open with others, and with themselves.

Counselors also need to clarify the connection between unassertiveness and low self-esteem, so that the client understands the lack of assertiveness as both an emotional problem and a skill deficit. Assertiveness training concentrates on overcoming the skill deficit. First the counselor models, then the client role-plays, and finally the client is given homework so that he or she can try out new skills in the real world. Clients are instructed to report back on how they have done and they are reinforced (encouraged) and, if necessary, shaped. All of this can be done in individual counseling as well as in group. This is another place to be creative. Besides improving your role-playing skills by practice, try exploring areas where your clients are having difficulties with assertion and developing scenarios related to those situations.

Chapter Summary

13–1

The seven major schools of counseling are discussed along with their therapeutic rationales. To help people change, behavioral counseling applies learning principles from classical and operant conditioning, including reinforcement, punishment, flooding, and systematic desensitization. Client-centered counseling emphasizes the centrality of the therapeutic relationship, the therapist's attitudes, and the nondirective approach. In cognitive counseling psychological problems are overcome by changing irrational beliefs and teaching more rational, adaptive ideas. Existential counseling concentrates on the ultimates of existence and emphasizes the spiritual dimension of treatment. In Gestalt counseling the focus is on here-and-now experience, and the use of an active, confrontational style. Psychodynamic counseling helps clients gain insight into their conflicts by examining defense mechanisms and interpreting resistance and transference. In substance abuse-specific counseling the focus is on overcoming chemical dependency and achieving recovery, using an eclectic and directive approach.

13–2

Relationship-focused techniques aim to strenghten the therapeutic alliance between counselor and client on the assumption that counseling lives or dies on the basis of that relationship. Establishing rapport means to create a comfortable bond between the counselor and client through empathy, acceptance, trust, and a shared purpose. In active listen-

ing, the counselor attends nonjudgmentally to all the communications—verbal and non-verbal—of the client. Identifying and challenging clients' maladaptive attitudes and actions is the technique of confrontation which is used to inform, reveal denial, and set limits.

13–3

Emotion-focused techniques help clients identify, address, and resolve significant emotional issues. Reflection gives clients feedback about their feelings, thoughts, and behavior in order to heighten awareness in a nonjudgmental manner. The technique of affect labeling gives a name to clients' feelings as a way of helping clients acknowledge, recognize, and differentiate among affective states. Relaxation training involves the use of several methods to lessen tension and anxiety, including progressive muscle relaxation, guided imagery exercises, meditation, and hypnosis.

13–4

The objective of cognition-focused techniques is to change maladaptive cognitions: beliefs, attitudes, and perceptions. Educational interventions facilitate client learning; counselors use didactic methods when they provide information to clients, as well as by teaching, correcting, questioning, and lecturing. Interpretations are the counselor's explanations of reasons for the client's behavior, thoughts, or feelings; they include here-and-now, there-and-then, and transference interpretations. Counselors use exploration techniques when they search for aspects of their clients' mental life via active questioning. Clarification requests seek more detailed and accurate information from clients. Helping clients make their drink/drug signals conscious enables them to be more aware of triggering cues and to take some control.

13–5

A behavior-focused technique helps clients acquire new skills to aid recovery. Through direct guidance (direction), counselors give specific behavioral advice to clients to structure their entry into recovery. Counselors use modeling when they demonstrate how to perform a behavior to their clients, as in role-playing exercises. Reinforcement is a technique to strengthen behaviors by using positive consequences or rewards, as in shaping, a method for rewarding approximations to a desired behavior. Assertiveness training teaches clients self-expression and how to stick up for themselves.

Terms To Remember

active listening
affect labeling
assertiveness training
behavioral counseling
clarification
client-centered counseling
cognitive counseling
confrontation
defense mechanism
direct guidance
directive counseling
drink/drug signals
eclectic approach
education
establishing rapport
existential counseling
exploration
Gestalt counseling
interpretation
modeling
psychodynamic counseling
reflection
reinforcement
relaxation training
resistance
shaping
substance abuse-specific counseling
transference

Suggested Reading

Corsini, R. J., and Wedding, D. (1995). *Current Psychotherapies*, 5th ed. Itasca, IL: F. E. Peacock.

CHAPTER FOURTEEN

Understanding, Preventing, And Managing Relapse

Chapter Outline

Learning Objectives

Upon completing study of this chapter you should be able to:

1. Define and distinguish between relapse and lapse.
2. Differentiate between the three major conceptualizations of relapse.
3. Identify the main biological influences on relapse.
4. Describe the role of classical and operant conditioning mechanisms in relapse.
5. Discuss the impact of personality variables on relapse.
6. Outline the process of relapse from the cognitive-behavioral perspective.
7. Identify the important social factors in relapse.
8. Discuss the primary high-risk situations for relapse.
9. Indicate the techniques involved in teaching clients to cope with cravings.
10. Outline the means whereby clients can utilize social supports and develop healthy lifestyles.

14–1   Understanding Relapse

In a perfect world your clients' recovery from chemical dependency would progress steadily from day to day in a constantly ascending curve of improvement and health. However, in the real and less than perfect world in which we live, the road to lasting recovery is full of potholes, breakdowns, detours, and delays. Indeed it is a very rare client who will navigate the way to recovery without one or more serious setbacks. An essential part of your job as a chemical dependency counselor is to help your clients find their way through these setbacks and return to the road to recovery.

What Is Relapse?

True to its roots in the traditional disease model of addiction, relapse is a term borrowed from the field of medicine. In a medical sense, relapse means a return of symptoms after a period of remission. A cancer patient, for example, whose tumor disappears with chemotherapy is said to relapse when a new tumor appears. Medical relapses are relatively clearcut events. In chemical dependency, however, because the symptoms are expressed in so many areas—physiological, behavioral, emotional, and cognitive—relapse is not necessarily so easily defined. Ordinarily, in chemical-dependence parlance, **relapse** means that after a significant period of abstinence the person returns to a problematic level of substance use marked by substance-related impairment.

Researchers estimate that between 50 and 90 percent of chemically dependent patients relapse, and relapse is especially likely during the first year of recovery (Brownell et al. 1986, National Institute of Alcohol Abuse and Alcoholism 1996b). For example, in a recent large, nationwide alcoholism treatment study called *Project MATCH* (Project MATCH Research Group 1997) involving more than 1,700 clients, only 35 percent of patients in aftercare (post-hospitalization) treatment and 19 percent of those in outpatient treatment remained abstinent for one year.

Many experts point to the high relapse rate among chemically dependent clients as evidence that addictions are chronic relapsing illnesses, and for many clients this characterization is quite correct (Leshner 1997). Nevertheless, it is worth noting that not all clients who break their abstinence will exhibit complete relapse, and those who do relapse will not do so in exactly the same way. Despite consistently high relapse rates for abusers of all types of substances, many variations in the patterns of relapse occur. For some clients, relapse involves a discrete period of severe bingeing, for others a more extended period of heavy use, and for still others a degree of abuse and dependence that exceeds even their earlier pre-abstinence consumption (Leukefeld and Tims 1989, Miller 1996).

Given the variability in patterns of relapse, many debates have been sparked over how much post-abstinence substance use is problematic and how much impairment is needed to indicate a full-blown relapse (Miller 1996). For some counselors, particularly those steeped in a traditional disease model, even one drink or one instance of getting high may be considered a relapse. In contrast, others consider relapse to mean a resumption of substance use at the level found prior to abstinence. For practical purposes, most counselors distinguish between a **lapse** (or *slip*) as a single instance of substance use resumption, and a full-blown relapse with its more persistent consumption and harmful consequences. Of course a lapse can be the first step to a more serious relapse, but a lapse will not always lead to relapse.

The conventional view of lapses and relapses focuses on resumption of substance use, that is, the behavior of consuming drugs. Typically, overt drug use is the expression of a chain of psychological events leading up to the actual behavior. The preliminary emotional, cognitive, and experiential events that anticipate the actual substance use are called *psychological relapse*, while the substance consumption per se is called *drug relapse* (Khantzian et al. 1990). Perhaps the most familiar element of psychological relapse is what A.A. advocates label "stinking thinking," a pattern of thinking that increases risk of drinking. A common type of stinking thinking is feeling overconfident, as illustrated in the case of Roy:

Having completed a month-long inpatient treatment period, Roy was involved in an outpatient program where he attended weekly individual and group sessions as well as Alcoholic Anonymous meetings. After nearly five months of sobriety—his longest period of sobriety in fifteen years— Roy felt quite sure that he was well along in recovery. Acting against the recommendations of his counselors, fellow group members, and A.A. sponsor, Roy decided to go to his cousin's fortieth birthday party. Although he admitted that his cousin and many other people who were going to be at the party were heavy drinkers, he believed he was in enough control to avoid drinking. He was going to prove to himself and other people that he could handle it. But he didn't, and his poor judgment led to a relapse period of more than two months during which he drank every day, missed many days of work, and temporarily discontinued his treatment.

Conceptualizing Relapse

In order to facilitate recovery, chemical dependency counselors must assist their clients in understanding and responding to the dangers of relapse. As the field of chemical dependency counseling has matured, several models of relapse have appeared, each of which provides a different perspective on the meaning of relapse and its relevance for recovery. Here we consider three major conceptualizations of relapse: the all-or-none model, the process model, and the transtheoretical model.

Closely identified with the classic disease theory of alcoholism (Jellinek 1960), the **all-or-none model** views any violation of abstinence as an indication of relapse. By defining relapse as a return of any substance use symptoms, no clear distinction is made between a slip and relapse. Because the model allows for only two options, abstinence or addiction, it has also been labeled the *binary model* of relapse (Miller 1996). Assuming that chronic addiction is fueled by powerful biological and psychological vulnerabilities that result in the loss of control, the all-or-none model contends that even a single slip can, and in the course of time almost certainly will, trigger a full-blown relapse. Consequently, in this view total abstinence is the only path to recovery.

The traditional all-or-none (binary) model of relapse has played a significant role in the development of chemical-dependence counseling. However, today the classic all-or-none view is more a historical straw man than a widely accepted approach. At present this model is most closely affiliated with the Twelve step programs, but Twelve step advocates acknowledge that relapse is a common, albeit unwanted, part of the recovery process (Gorski 1989, Nowinski et al. 1995).

While chemical-dependence counselors assert that abstinence is the only goal for the addicted person, they also insist that relapse should not necessarily be seen as a complete failure of recovery. In fact relapse is part of recovery for most clients. As a result, the counselor's task is not easy: you will be required to encourage and support abstinence and also normalize relapse. To normalize relapse, however, does not mean to condone or approve it, nor does it mean to act as if you expect it (and by your expectation lead your client to expect it also). What is required is to frame the client's understanding of relapse in a realistic and therapeutic manner, so the client perceives the real danger of relapse and is focused on ways to avoid it as well as to cope with it if it occurs. It is important that the relapsed client views the event as a learning experience and takes from the lesson some knowledge that will further subsequent recovery. As you will learn in a later section of this chapter, the client's cognitive interpretation of his or her relapse is significant in determining the response to relapse and its consequences for long-term recovery.

A more contemporary view of relapse is the **process model**, which conceives of relapse as a multidetermined and extended series of events that can recur in the course of recovery (Brownell et al. 1986, Marlatt and Barrett 1994). The theoretical background of this model is found in the cognitive-behavioral perspective. According to the process model, lapses and relapses are normative events in recovery. Derived from clinical and empirical studies of relapse risk factors, this model is one facet of the broader cognitive-behavioral approach to relapse prevention and management whose specific features will be discussed in later sections of this chapter.

A key feature in the process model is the belief that relapse vulnerability is largely due to a lack of adequate coping responses to high-risk situations (for example, the people, places, and things associated with substance use). For those who lack good coping skills, a high-risk situation can initiate a cascade of behavioral and cognitive events that makes relapse more likely. The counselor's task, therefore, is to frame relapse prevention in terms of the development of effective coping. While your clients should be made aware of the high risk for relapse, they should be mindful that it is not inevitable and that they can acquire skills that lessen its likelihood.

In Chapter 3 you were introduced to the *stages-of-change* concept of recovery and its five stages of behavior change: (1) precontemplation, (2) contemplation, (3) preparation, (4) action, and (5) maintenance. The stages-of-change view is part of a **transtheoretical model** that conceives of relapse and recycling through the stages as integral parts of the course of recovery (DiClemente and Scott 1997). Recovery is not a straight shot from addiction to abstinence, but instead involves a circular and repetitive movement forward and back among the stages.

By framing lapse and relapse events within the stages-of-change guidelines, chemical dependency counselors can help their clients understand the place of those events in long-term improvement.

> Relapse experiences contribute information and feedback that can facilitate or hinder subsequent progression through the stages of change. Individuals may learn that certain goals are unrealistic, certain strategies are ineffective, or certain environments are not conducive to successful change. [DiClemente and Scott 1997, pp. 139–140]

Two distinctive advantages of the transtheoretical model are that it is stated in terms general enough to accommodate many different counseling interventions, and it is not tied to any specific theoretical system. Consequently, it serves as a kind of theoretical neutral ground for counselors with different perspectives, and offers a versatile and flexible model from which to approach recovery.

14–2 What Causes Relapse?

In previous chapters you have learned that the *biopsychosocial model* of addictions stresses their multidetermination by many biological, psychological, and social influences. Likewise, in understanding the causes of relapses among addicted individuals it is necessary to consider a multitude of contributing factors. To date, numerous theories of relapse have been constructed, some emphasizing psychological influences and others biological influences. While pointing to important elements in the relapse process, no single theory manages to explain everything about all relapses (Conners et al. 1996). Each theory, however, does offer helpful ideas from which the chemical dependency counselor can draw therapeutically beneficial insights.

Naturally, you would expect many individual differences in the forces behind different clients' relapses—after all, no two clients are exactly the same. Studies of recovering addicts seek to identify the critical variables in relapse; however, research on risk factors for relapse is a complicated matter. Researchers differ in terms of their theoretical perspectives and methodology, as well as in the kinds of addiction that they study. Despite the fact of individual differences, several general findings do emerge about **common relapse factors** that cut across different types of addictions (McKay 1999). They are:

- Negative affect: depression, anxiety, anger, and other unpleasant emotional states
- Increased cravings: desires or urges to drink or get high
- Cognitive factors: attitudes about oneself, expectations about drug effects, reduced commitment to abstinence
- Interpersonal problems: family conflicts, social pressure, relationship distress
- Lack of coping and effort: poor coping skills, deficient motivation, yielding to temptation

Of course these risk factors do not necessarily act independently of one another, but instead tend to converge, interact, and reverberate with one another in driving relapse. As a chemical dependency counselor, you need to maintain your attention to many aspects of your clients' behavior, attitudes, and circumstances in order to monitor the risk of relapse. In the following sections you will learn about the biological, psychological, and social influences that contribute to your clients' relapse risk.

Biological Influences on Relapse

In reading Chapter 6 you learned about the complex biology of addiction. Many neurological and biochemical processes contribute to the development of the addicted brain. These mechanisms of neuroadaptation involve the interplay among numerous brain regions and neurotransmitter systems and result in relatively enduring alterations of the addicted person's physical functioning. These neuroadaptive changes in the addicted brain are also involved in the relapse process (Leshner 1997).

Although many biochemical systems in the brain contribute to addiction and relapse, the dopamine system plays the central role. Persistent abuse of addictive substances leads to chronic dysregulation of the *mesolimbic dopamine system*, the part of the brain whose actions are essential in the experience of reward or reinforcement (Wise 1998). Ultimately, the consequence of prolonged substance abuse is **dopamine sensitization**, a chronic increase in the responsiveness of the dopamine neurons (Lyvers 1998). Because of their hypersensitized dopamine pathways, addicts are strongly prone to drug cravings. Cravings, of course, are powerful motives for relapse. Even after an extended period of abstinence, recovering addicts are vulnerable to cravings that can easily be induced by a variety of dopamine system primers, such as drugs, stress, and environmental cues (Robinson and Berridge 1993, Self and Nestler 1998).

Besides the neuroadaptive changes in their dopamine reward system, chemically depen-

dent people also show persistent dysregulation of their body's stress-response system. The stress-response system is called the *HPA axis* because it includes the hypothalamus (a brain structure) and two endocrine glands, the pituitary and adrenal glands. Like the dopamine reward system, the HPA stress system is also sensitized by chronic exposure to addictive substances. *HPA sensitization* makes the addict's stress system more responsive to stressors (stress cues), which in turn increases relapse risk (Kreek and Koob 1998). The sensitization of both dopamine and HPA systems places the recovering addict in a state of double jeopardy for relapse.

Despite some common biological ground, all addictive drugs do not work exactly the same way in the brain (see Chapter 2). The biology of relapse, therefore, is not always identical in each and every kind of addiction. A promising alcohol-specific model is presented in the **limbic kindling hypothesis**, which attributes relapse to alcohol cravings induced by hyperarousal in the limbic system (Adinoff et al. 1995). According to this hypothesis, a key factor is the overexcitation of the limbic system during withdrawal from alcohol that results in a condition of chronic hyperexcitability, or *kindling*, which induces cravings and increases the risk of relapse.

Despite the growing sophistication of our understanding of the biology of addiction and relapse, you should keep in mind that the aforementioned hypotheses are not firmly established or proven facts. As with all hypotheses, they are still under investigation and only time will tell how significant the mechanisms they proposed are for relapse. Undoubtedly biological processes matter in drug and alcohol relapse, but they are not the complete story, and in the following sections we examine a number of psychological contributors.

Learning Mechanisms and Relapse

Both classical conditioning and operant conditioning principles help us to understand the process of relapse. Classical conditioning models emphasize the learned associations between drug cues and drug-induced responses, while operant models focus on the availability of reinforcers in the environment.

Originally developed as a model of heroin relapse, the **conditioned withdrawal theory** states that over time drug cues come to be linked with withdrawal responses, and thus acquire the power to induce conditioned withdrawal that motivates a resumption of use (Wikler 1980). In this theory, the desire to alleviate the unpleasant feelings of conditioned withdrawal become the main incentive for relapse. Although conditioned withdrawal effects do occur in some addicts, experimental and clinical evidence indicates that relief of withdrawal effects is not usually the dominant influence on relapse (Lyvers 1998).

Drawing on biological evidence such as the dopamine sensitization phenomenon, the **priming theory** of relapse emphasizes the importance of learned associations between drug cues and conditioned craving responses. In the language of classical conditioning, both internal cues (for example, anxiety) and external cues (for example, drug paraphernalia) can act as conditioned stimuli that induce feelings of craving. Cravings serve as the motivational basis of subsequent drug use (Carroll and Comer 1996, Stewart et al. 1984). In contrast to the conditioned withdrawal theory, priming theory stresses the person's desire to pursue the pleasurable effects of the drug rather than to avoid the unpleasurable effects of withdrawal.

Principles of operant conditioning are the basis of the *behavioral theory of choice*, a view that explains relapse to drug use as a reaction to the actual or threatened loss of reward sources (Vuchinich and Tucker 1996). Focused mainly on alcoholism, this theory contends that recovering alcoholics can maintain their sobriety as long as they are able to experience the pleasures of reward sources other than drinking. Significant *life-health rewards* are contingent on intimate relationships, family interactions, and vocational activity, and when those rewards are disrupted or threatened the person may turn to alcohol as a quick and dependable source of reward. Relapse risk increases along with the severity of the disruption of life–health rewards.

Personality and Relapse Vulnerability

Although the concept of the addictive personality has not held up well to empirical testing, the belief that personality functioning, or malfunctioning, is central to addiction and relapse is today represented in two leading psychological perspectives: the psychodynamic perspective and the social learning perspective.

The modern psychodynamic perspective asserts that both addiction-proneness and relapse risk are related to **self-regulation vulnerability**, as reflected in problems in self-care, self-esteem, emotion, and relationships. Persistent problems in these areas indicate the *character disorder* behind the addiction. Early warning signs of impending relapse are often expressed as disruptions in self-regulation and may indicate the beginning of a psychological relapse that foreshadows the actual drug taking (Brehm and Khantzian 1997, Khantzian et al. 1990). The danger signs of relapse associated with self-regulation problems are summarized in Table 14–1.

A few good months into aftercare Ronnie began to look unkempt and agitated in group sessions. He denied using drugs and urine tests backed him up, but he was clearly slipping mentally into a danger zone. Besides his deteriorating personal appearance he was exhibiting extremely intense feelings of rage and resentment against his parents as well as a lot of shame and hopelessness. His recent decline started when his father informed him that he would have to move out and get his own place in six weeks because he and Ronnie's mother couldn't take the stress of living with him anymore. He had gone through detox and aftercare twice before and relapsed seriously both times while living in his parents' home. He saw their ultimatum as a sign that they had no faith in him at all and proof that he was a failure. He had been thinking more and more about getting high and was afraid he was going to slip again.

From the perspective of social-learning theory the key personality factor in recovery and relapse is *self-efficacy*, the belief in one's own capacity to control one's actions. Inasmuch as low self-efficacy can contribute to the

Table 14–1. Self-regulation areas and relapse danger signs

Self-Regulation	*Area Relapse Danger Signs*
Self-care	Client neglects personal hygiene
	Client engages in risky thrill-seeking
	Client puts self in dangerous settings
	Client stops health-promoting behaviors
Self-esteem	Client feels ashamed, depressed, useless
	Client makes self-deprecating statements
	Client sets self up to fail
	Client acts extremely egocentric
Emotions	Client shows extremely intense affect
	Client lacks tolerance for ambivalence
	Client acts very moody
	Client is oversensitive or undersensitive
Relationships	Client reports interpersonal conflicts
	Client shows erratic social interactions
	Client neglects friends and family
	Client becomes isolative and withdrawn

development of an addiction it can also make the difference between abstinence and a lapse, and between a lapse and relapse. Three kinds of self-efficacy are relevant to recovery and relapse:

- Resistive efficacy: belief in one's ability to resist urges, cravings, and temptations to use
- Recovery efficacy: belief in one's ability to cope with the demands of abstinence and a drug-free lifestyle
- Interpersonal efficacy: belief in one's ability to interact with others and handle interpersonal problems

When levels of these self-efficacies are high, recovery is maintained, but when they are low, relapse is likely (Bandura 1997).

Cognitive and Affective Factors in Relapse

The role of cognitive and affective factors in relapse is highlighted in the cognitive-behavioral model of Marlatt and his colleagues (Marlatt 1996, Marlatt and Barrett 1994, Marlatt and Gordon 1985). As you see in Figure 14–1, the model describes a sequence of cognitive-affective events linking relapse with **high-risk situations**, that is, circumstances in which the likelihood of relapse is heightened. The most common high-risk situations are

divided into two types, (1) intrapersonal, or (2) interpersonal, based on their main determinants, as shown in Table 14–2:

The client who finds himself in a high-risk situation without adequate coping skills to handle the situation experiences a lowering of self-efficacy and also an increase in positive beliefs about substance effects. For example, the recovering alcoholic client who is apprehensive about losing his job due to workplace cutbacks feels his control over his future (self-efficacy) is slipping and begins to think about how much a few drinks would help him calm down. If those events lead to actual substance use, that is, a lapse, the likelihood of a full-blown relapse increases. Relapse is especially likely when the lapse induces the client to experience the **abstinence violation effect** (AVE), a cognitive-affective process in which the client feels conflict and guilt over the lapse and also blames himself for it. In addition, the individual may believe that the lapse means he is doomed to continue using. The result of the abstinence violation effect is extreme demoralization, loss of motivation, and undermined commitment to abstinence, all of which may fuel a prolonged drug relapse. Cognitive-behavioral therapists are highly critical of Twelve step programs for propagating a mindset about addictions that increases the lapsing client's chance of experiencing the abstinence violation effect.

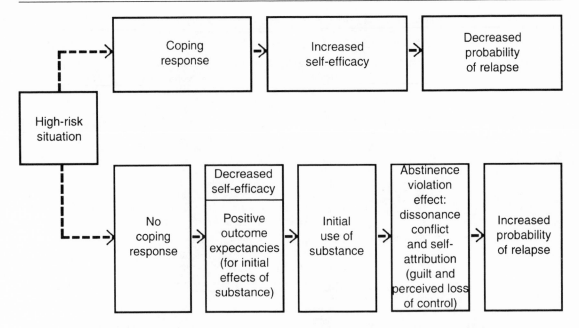

Figure 14–1. Marlatt's cognitive-behavioral model of the relapse process
Source: Marlatt and Barrett (from *American Psychiatric Press Textbook of Substance Abuse*, ed. M. Galanter and H. Kleber. Copyright © 1994 by American Psychiatric Press and used with permission.)

Because they can precipitate a chain of events culminating in relapse, high-risk situations and their management are an important focus of counseling. Although certain high-risk situations happen to clients for reasons beyond their control, many clients will find themselves in such situations as a result of their own conscious or unconscious choices. Sometimes *apparently irrelevant decisions* are outcomes of the client's habitual defensive style of denial and rationalization. For example, an alcoholic client who slips and has a few beers at a ballgame with his friends might blame his lapse on social pressure, but in fact his decision to go to the game with known drinkers might be his way of trying to prove that he's in control or just find an excuse to drink.

As you see in Table 14–2, most high-risk relapse situations involve unpleasant or negative feelings or events. However, positive emotional states are also potentially risky. Although this notion may seem counterintuitive, studies show that the likelihood of relapse increases when the recovering client feels good. Feeling good is a more potent risk factor for male clients than females (Stocker 1997), but for both genders it can create a mental climate in which poor decisions are made: "Everybody's having fun, so what harm can one drink do?" Given the recovering client's history of using substances to induce pleasurable affects, an experience of feeling good can be an emotional cue that primes cravings to use.

Table 14–2. High-risk situations for relapse

Intrapersonal Determinants	Interpersonal Determinants
Negative emotional states	Interpersonal conflicts
Negative physical states	Social pressure
Positive emotional states	Positive emotional states
Testing personal control	
Urges and temptations	

Social Factors in Relapse

Understanding relapse requires taking a look into the social context in which recovering clients function. Interpersonal relationships and interactions often trigger the process of relapse. In addition, the larger sociocultural milieu of the client can also enhance relapse risk.

One of the most commonly reported reasons for relapse is interpersonal conflict, especially family conflicts (McKay 1999). Although some clients will find it convenient to rationalize their relapse by blaming other people—spouses, parents, children—in many instances the conflicts are quite genuine and troublesome. People who have had long-standing chemical dependencies ordinarily have also had a great deal of interpersonal distress well before they began their recovery. Becoming abstinent does not magically erase the sources of that distress, but in fact will often bring these long-standing conflicts into clearer relief. For example, the alcoholic whose drinking had helped him ignore marital problems finds that they are unavoidable in recovery.

Spouses and other family members many times have unrealistic expectations about how abstinence should transform the chemically dependent person. Their frustrations about the person's absorption in recovery work, such as Twelve step meetings, group sessions, and other rehabilitation necessities, can easily be perceived as selfishness by family members who have long felt neglected.

Spouses' frustrations over the pace and demands of recovery work can spark exchanges of intense negative feeling and behavior. Research on recovering alcoholics, for example, finds that a spouse's expression of anger, threat, and coercive behavior is associated with a greater chance of relapse, shorter time to relapse, and more severe relapse (O'Farrell et al. 1998a).

As significant as family relationships might be, the social context in which relapse occurs extends far beyond the boundaries of the family. Many alcoholics and other drug addicts have developed lifestyles in which their economic well-being is in constant jeopardy, their

involvement with the criminal justice system is ongoing, and their job history is shaky at best (Johnson and Muffler 1997). These problems are especially exaggerated among long-time illicit substance abusers such as heroin addicts. The stresses of unemployment, poverty, discrimination, and inadequate housing that were present during the time of active addiction are not automatically resolved by abstinence, and consequently can become important in triggering relapse.

Chronic abusers of illicit drugs, such as crack and heroin, tend to become alienated from the mainstream world and to occupy a marginalized place in society. For a recovering client whose social world was organized around a drug subculture the loss of former social supports can be a significant threat, even though those supports fostered drug involvement. For a client whose friends are substance abusers, the detachment is likely to be a demoralizing and isolating experience. Commonly, clients feel that abstinence not only deprives them of the pleasure of getting high, but also of their friends and social life. In fact, such feelings of loss are quite valid, and must be addressed by the counselor.

14–3 Preventing Relapse

It's easy to stop smoking, I've done it hundreds of times.

—Mark Twain

Like Mark Twain, most substance abusers will tell you that it's easy to stop using, but very hard to stay clean. Maintaining abstinence and making progress in recovery is hard work. For many of your clients their history of substance use has produced deep habits of thought, feeling, and action that readily promote drinking and/or drugging with little effort or awareness. Recovery, in contrast, demands **mindfulness**, that is, concerted, sustained effort guided by conscious determination (Tiffany 1990). Consequently, mindfulness is a key to relapse prevention. In earlier chapters you learned about the many counseling strategies and techniques that can be applied in fostering your clients' recovery. In addition, however, you will need to employ other techniques that are more specific to relapse prevention and management. Although all schools of counseling emphasize relapse work, most of the research on its effectiveness comes from the cognitive-behavioral tradition. Overall, this research demonstrates that relapse-prevention methods are equally helpful across different substances, and as a rule reduce both the probability of relapse events and their severity (Carroll 1996).

In this section you will examine relapse-prevention strategies organized around four general themes: (1) identifying and dealing with high-risk situations, (2) coping with cravings, (3) utilizing social support systems; and (4) developing a healthy lifestyle (Daley and Marlatt 1997).

Identifying and Dealing with High-Risk Situations

The world that recovering clients inhabit is fraught with risk. Situations marked by unpleasant emotions, conflicts with other people, and social pressures are the most risky for your clients, especially those in early recovery (Marlatt and Barrett 1994). Designing a meaningful relapse-prevention plan requires that you become attuned to your clients' particular high-risk situations and can teach them the skills they need to handle those situations.

Monitoring Relapse Triggers. People with long-standing chemical dependency have learned strong associations between substance use and environmental stimuli—people, places, and things. As you might guess, the situations most consistently linked with past substance use are those that present the greatest risk for relapse. Depending on their individual drug-use histories, clients will have different drinking/drugging associations. By reviewing your client's history you will be able to develop a list

of his or her most significant risky situations. In Table 14–3 you will find a summary of some common substance-related people, places, and things to watch out for.

Strange as it might seem, many of your clients may be quite unclear about what constitutes a high-risk situation. People who are persistently and habitually substance impaired often fail to make the connection between their substance use and the particular circumstances and events of everyday life. In relapse-prevention counseling you will need to help the client recognize those connections and monitor the occurrence of risky situations. This recognition eliminates vulnerability by sudden ambush because with awareness the client knows when he is in danger and can do something about it.

Typically, high-risk situations are risky because of the negative feelings that occur within those situations or in their aftermath. Because relapse can result from a chain reaction of events that begins with feeling bad, clients must become more aware of their own emotions. Given the role drugs and alcohol have played in clients' self-medicating against negative emotion, those states are prime triggers for lapse and relapse. Certainly many negative emotions can contribute to relapse risk, but a helpful shorthand way to keep your client mindful of key feelings is to use the popular *H-A-L-T* acronym from the Twelve step tradition (Nowinski et al. 1995):

H – hungry
A – angry
L – lonely
T – tired

Knowing that feelings of hunger, anger, loneliness, and fatigue are common predictors of a slip, your clients can be on guard to be

Table 14–3. Monitoring people, places, and things

People	Places	Things
Drinking buddies	Bars, hangouts	Drugs and alcohol
Drug dealers	Liquor stores	Drug paraphernalia
Drug users	Parties	Extra cash
Family members	Home	TV

especially careful when they find themselves in those states.

Dealing with High-Risk Situations and Negative Emotions. When your clients learn to be more aware of potential relapse triggers, they have taken the first step is being able to deal with them. However, an essential second step is to learn coping skills that enable the client to effectively navigate through high-risk situations without a slip or relapse.

The simplest advice, although not necessarily the easiest to follow, is to avoid high-risk situations. In early recovery *avoidance strategies* are particularly important because clients do not yet possess sufficient confidence or ability to contend with strong temptations to use. Total avoidance of people, places, and things is difficult, if not impossible, for many clients whose lives have long been organized around drinking and/or drugging. Unless your advice to avoid high-risk situations is tempered by recommendations for alternative behaviors, your clients can easily feel resentful at being so limited in their choices. Alternatives, such as attendance at Twelve step meetings, provide a healthy substitute for drug-involved activity.

In addition to avoidance, *active coping strategies* are needed to aid clients in dealing with high-risk situations and negative emotions that will inevitably be experienced. A number of *stress management techniques* can be utilized to help client's manage their way through high-risk situations. Muscle relaxation skills, meditation, and guided imagery (see Chapter 13) are particularly beneficial. Interpersonal conflicts, too, can be actively addressed by methods like assertiveness training (see Chapter 13) and other *social problem-solving training*. Keep in mind that social skills that some counselors might take for granted are not necessarily part of your client's social repertoire. Some of the areas of social problem-solving that can be beneficial for recovering clients are:

- How to compromise with other people
- How to take the perspective of other people
- How to identify shared goals with other people

- How to communicate one's needs and feelings to other people
- How to cooperate in a common endeavor with other people

Cognitive skills are also key elements in active coping. You can help your client to identify and correct *cognitive distortions*, or errors in thinking, that might increase relapse risk. For example, if your client is prone to *catastrophizing*, that is, making a mountain out of a molehill, you can teach him or her to think more rationally about events and to judge things more realistically.

Client: I heard a rumor at work today that the company might be going out of business or downsizing staff. I don't know what will happen to me, but if I lose my job I'm dead. That'd be the worst thing that could happen right now.

Counselor: I agree that losing your job would be bad, but it wouldn't be the end of the world. There are a lot worse things that could happen, for example, you could lose a leg in a car wreck, or someone in your family could die suddenly. Don't you suppose that those things would be worse than losing your job?

Client: I guess so, but it would be terrible if I was out of work. I don't know what I'd do.

Counselor: Yeah, it'd be a setback, but let's talk about what would really happen if you lost your job and what your options might be.

A straightforward way of enhancing your client's cognitive control is to use *reminder cards*, index cards with simple self-instructions. When confronted with a high-risk situation or negative emotional state, the client can take out the reminder cards, as illustrated in Table 14–4, and

Table 14–4. Reminder cards

Card 1:	Stop, look, listen
Card 2:	Stay calm
Card 3:	Stay the course
Card 4:	Review events
Card 5:	Plan your next step
Card 6:	Ask for help

Source: Laws (1995).

read through their advice. Reminder cards serve two purposes: first, they distract the client from the high-risk situation or feeling; and second, they reorient the client to the task of recovery.

Another method for dealing with high-risk situations is **relapse rehearsal**, a cognitive-behavioral strategy entailing imagined confrontation and coping with those situations (Marlatt and Barrett 1994). Clients are instructed to imagine themselves in a high-risk situation and to experience whatever thoughts and emotions are triggered during the imagined event. In addition, clients imaginally rehearse coping skills that help them to handle the situation and get through it with success. Relapse rehearsal permits clients to anticipate and practice coping with real-life circumstances.

Coping with Cravings

Psychologically, the most compelling reason for lapses is craving. These urges to drink or get high can be very powerful and irresistible for some clients. Even after intiating complete abstinence, total *deactivation*, or elimination of cravings, takes a long time, ordinarily at least a year (National Institute on Drug Abuse 1993a). During that period of recovery clients are very vulnerable. For most, yielding to

cravings is the first step to a lapse and perhap even a full-blown relapse. Teaching clients t overcome their cravings is essential to relaps prevention.

Cue Extinction. The behavior modificatio technique of **cue extinction**, or *cue exposure*, i a procedure that reduces cravings by system atically exposing the client to drug cues or trig gers. Cue extinction has been successfully usec with a variety of clients, but is most commonly used in treating cocaine addicts (National In stitute on Drug Abuse 1993a,b, O'Brien et al 1990). Based on a classical conditioning mode of learning (see Chapter 5), this technique pro duces an extinction, or deconditioning of the association between drug-relevant stimul (cues or triggers) and conditioned cravings Tables 14–5 and 14–6 depict the basic element of conditioning and cue extinction.

To use cue extinction properly, the coun selor and client must monitor the client's trig gers, cravings, and responses to cravings. It is desirable for the client to keep a cravings diary or log in which cravings are recorded along with the times, places, and activities associated with them in daily life. The triggers used in cue-extinction sessions are drawn from the client's diary. Extinction sessions are re peated with a specific cue until the client no longer experiences craving in response to the

---

Table 14–5. Conditioning a craving response

Conditioned Response—Drugs

Stage 1

Stimulus	→	*Unconditioned Response*
Use drugs in environment with many stimuli	→	Get high

- After numerous repetitions, addicts become conditioned to stimuli such as holding a pipe.

Stage 2

Stimulus	→	*Conditioned Response*
Exposed to stimuli associated with using drugs	→	Craving

- After connection of the pipe and the anticipation of getting high are linked, the conditioned response has been established.

Source: National Institute on Drug Abuse (1993c).

Table 14–6. Cue extinction for conditioned craving

Cue Extinction—Drugs				
• Stage 1				
Pipe	→	Getting high		
• Stage 2				
Pipe	→	Craving	→	Getting high
• Stage 3				
Pipe	→	Craving	→	Not getting high
• Stage 4				
Pipe	→	No Craving	→	Not getting high

Source: National Institute on Drug Abuse (1993c).

cue. Cue-exposure clients need to distinguish between degrees of craving, that is, from mild-to-moderate and moderate-to-extreme, in order to differentiate between weak and powerful triggers and to assess their progress in cue extinction over time.

According to conditioning theory, each time a cue-induced craving occurs without leading to drug use the association between the cue and craving lessens, and eventually the cue will no longer provoke the craving. Theoretically, simply exposing the client to the cues under conditions where no drug use is possible should eradicate the cravings. Such *passive extinction*, however, appears to have limited benefit. When cue exposure is combined with active coping strategies the resulting extinction of craving is far more effective (Drummond et al. 1995).

Active Coping Skills in Cue Extinction.
Although passive cue exposure can lessen cravings, the use of active coping skills during cue exposure produces superior outcomes. These skills are excellent tools that your clients can rely on in high-risk settings where drug cues are present (National Institute on Drug Abuse 1993b).

One of the most helpful coping tools for cue extinction clients is *relaxation*. When a client experiences craving he is in a state of mental and physical arousal, and by using relaxation skills that arousal state can be relieved. Deep-breathing exercises, meditation, and muscle relaxation are good ways to counteract cravings. In addition to relaxation exercises, other alternative behaviors can be performed to break the chain that connects cravings with

drug use. Physical exercise activities such as lifting weights, jogging, and swimming are feasible alternatives to drugging. In fact just about any activity that delays the client from acting on the craving is beneficial.

Imagery skills in cue extinction are also important. Imagery is employed for two purposes: (1) to highlight the negative and positive consequences of using or not using drugs, and (2) to provide a sense of mastery over cravings. In using *negative/positive consequences imagery*, the client mentally envisions the negative consequences of acting on the drug craving. For example, the cocaine addict might imagine getting arrested and incarcerated, losing his job, or being separated from his wife as negative consequences of a slip. Additionally, imagining the positive consequences of resisting the craving is encouraged. Feeling proud of himself, saving money, and keeping his marriage together might be some positive consequences. The use of imagery emphasizes to the client that he does have a choice about whether or not to yield to the craving, and that his choices have important consequences.

In **mastery imagery**, the client is instructed to imagine himself as a strong, powerful person or force capable of controlling and defeating the craving. This technique is intended to bolster the client's self-efficacy in regard to craving control. By imagining himself successfully controlling the craving experience the client comes to anticipate that he will be able to do so when the real thing occurs.

One version of mastery imagery is called *urge surfing*; here the client imagines "riding" the craving like a surfer rides a wave until the wave disappears. The following paragraph describes an urge-surfing protocol for alcoholic clients:

> Urges are a lot like ocean waves. They are small when they start, grow in size, and then break up and dissipate. You can imagine yourself as a surfer who will ride the wave, staying on top of it until it crests, breaks, and turns into less powerful, foamy surf. The idea behind urge surfing is similar to the idea behind many martial arts. In judo, one overpowers an opponent by first going with the force of the attack. By joining with the opponent's force, one can take control of it and redirect it to one's advantage. [Kadden et al. 1995, p. 28]

Mastery-imagery techniques like urge surfing are based on cognitive-behavioral notions of relapse dynamics. It is worth noting, however, that this approach is antithetical to the beliefs of the Twelve step/disease model. Within that perspective this technique might send the client the wrong message, namely that the client has more power over urges than is really the case. Here we have a fundamental split between those who believe that admitting to powerlessness is the best path to recovery, and those who believe that teaching the client that he does indeed have power is the best route.

Close Up: Managing Your Relapsing Client

Given the statistics on relapse rates, you can be sure that most of your clients will experience relapse on their way to recovery. Therefore, you must set the table for successful relapse management long before relapse begins by establishing an open, honest, and supportive working relationship with your clients. The shame and sense of failure felt by relapsing clients can lead them to disengage from treatment rather than confess their relapse to a counselor. Obviously, you cannot help your client if he terminates counseling. What the relapsing client needs most is honest communication, the opportunity to reflect on events, and a recommitment to the pursuit

of recovery (National Institute on Drug Abuse 1993a).

In early recovery, counselors and clients need to devise a *relapse plan*, a sequence of concrete steps for the client to follow in the event of relapse. A recommended first step in a recovery plan is to ask for help from the counselor, sponsor, or fellow group members. Instructions about where to go for help, telephone numbers of contact people, emergency room addresses, and other specific pieces of advice are useful. Of critical importance is getting the client re-engaged in treatment as soon as possible. All available treatment resources—individual counseling, groups, and Twelve step meetings—can be brought to bear on helping the client reflect on the experience of relapse in order to use it to learn lessons that can further subsequent recovery. People who have relapsed and then returned to abstinence recognize the value of taking it seriously, learning from it, and returning to their prior recovery routine as quickly as possible.

For chemical dependency counselors, the management of client relapse also requires counselors to manage their own reactions to the relapse. Novice counselors sometimes mistakenly perceive a client's relapse as a sign of their own professional failure. Do not personalize the client's setback, but take it for what it is—an unfortunate but typical part of the long, hard process of recovery. But don't dismiss it as insignificant just because it is so commonplace. Instead, follow the same advice that you give your relapsing client: try to learn from the experience so that in the future you are better prepared to anticipate and perhaps even head off the problem.

Utilizing Social Supports

Having problems in dealing with other people is one of the most frequent reasons for relapse. Alcoholics and drug addicts tend to have severely limited interpersonal skills and their relationships with others are highlighted by conflict, manipulation, and self-centeredness.

In the interest of preventing your clients from relapsing, a considerable amount of work is needed to enhance their health-promoting bonds with other people. Two approaches to bolstering social supports involve *couples and family work* and *group work*.

Couples and Family Work. Both clinical experience and controlled research demonstrate the importance of couples and family work in relapse prevention (Kadden et al. 1995, Marlatt and Barrett 1994, O'Farrell et al. 1998b). During the course of their addictions your clients' relationships with their significant others—spouses, partners, children, and parents—generally have been dysfunctional. When disturbed relationships have become the norm, recovery often requires a reorganization of interpersonal habits and roles.

In relapse-prevention work, the counselor is well advised to incorporate couples and family sessions. These sessions allow the counselor to educate significant others about the nature of recovery and relapse, to enlist their help in monitoring and supporting the client's recovery, and to assist them in stabilizing their relationships. As you learned in Chapter 9, many complex issues in family life are linked with chemical dependency. Although you cannot expect to resolve all the interpersonal dilemmas that affect your clients, you can guide them and their loved ones in working together toward the main goal, namely, full recovery. At the same time you should be aware that a common outcome of recovery is divorce, and that many codependent marriages are too damaged to survive. The primary goal of couples counseling is relapse prevention, not necessarily saving the marriage.

After a two-month stint in rehab, Eddie returned home only to find the same family problems that were present before he left. Poor communication with his wife, money troubles, and difficulties raising the kids were the norm in his home life. Furthermore, Eddie's wife often betrayed her anger over his past drug use and felt abandoned by him during his treatment. Her expectation that Eddie would be fully recovered after his

discharge from the program was a lurking factor that would eventually lead to several lapses. Eddie's wife insisted they enter counseling before he had a full-blown relapse. This was a good sign.

Although she had a lot of firsthand experience living with a drug addict, Eddie's wife had many misconceptions about the nature of addiction and recovery. It was important for her to understand that although her husband was ultimately responsible for his actions, there were things she could do either to facilitate or hinder his recovery. With this in mind the couple began a course of communication training designed to focus on their specific problems, not his character, and to prevent disputes from escalating into major arguments. In addition they benefited from learning a behavior modification program that helped them improve their child-rearing skills and minimize fights over how to raise their children.

Group Work. Group work is an essential component of chemical dependency counseling. In relapse-prevention, group work has been shown to make a significant difference for recovering alcoholics and for heroin and cocaine addicts (Khantzian et al. 1992, National Institute on Drug Abuse 1993a, Nowinski et al. 1995).

With respect to relapse prevention, groups are important in serving several purposes for the recovering client.

1. They provide emotional support for the client.
2. They help to overcome the client's sense of isolation and shame.
3. They give corrective information, guidance, and challenges to the client.
4. They confront the client about regressive behavior.
5. They establish a network of people who have a common goal and who can act as resources for one another.
6. They monitor the progress and problems of the client.
7. They are an opportunity for the client to act in a non-egocentric fashion.
8. They are a forum for practicing social skills.

Beyond their significance in preventing relapse, groups act to re-engage clients in treatment after a slip or relapse. Since senior group members may have personal relapse stories, they can offer the relapsed client some insight into getting back on track.

Sally was in a relapse-prevention group of eight early-recovery cocaine addicts. She arrived at a session feeling and acting "antsy." Bob commented, "Sally, you look uptight." Sally stiffened and said defiantly, "Yeah, I'm bored." Kathy jumped in and said, "Boy, you've got a chip on your shoulder tonight. You have a hand on a line and it's halfway up your nose." Sally shot back "Drop dead. I'm just bored." The group jumped on boredom and how it's hard to deal with in recovery. Several members reported that boredom had been a trigger in their slips. Sensing that the group was focused on how painful boredom is and was romanticizing the excitement of a cocaine high, the counselor commented on Sally's observations and suggested that the group redirect their efforts to come up with nonchemical ways of dealing with boredom. She did this while maintaining a degree of empathy for their restlessness and ennui. The group shifted and worked well in developing coping strategies to deal with boredom. Sally was simply ignored. Agreeing with Kathy that Sally was in imminent danger, the counselor redirected the group's attention to her with fifteen minutes remaining in the session. Sally was both supported and confronted. By the end of group she jocularly said, "Well, if I can't do anything else, I can always masturbate." Everyone laughed, but Sally was now relaxed and aware of how close to a slip she had been. Larry remarked that he had never realized just how dangerous boredom was, and other group members nodded agreement. The counselor echoed this sentiment and thanked Sally for her honesty, noting how important it had been for the group to discuss boredom. Sam, a devoted Twelve step member, got in the last word by concluding that boredom is "just our disease talking to us and setting us up for a slip."

Developing a Healthy Lifestyle

Successful recovery is not simply stopping substance use. True success means a revolution in lifestyle. Because drinking and drug-ging were central concerns of the chemically dependent person's life, recovery can seem to be a kind of deprivation. It is common for clients to complain about all the things they are not able to do anymore. To reduce the chance of relapse, counselors need to orient their clients toward the development of health-promoting alternatives to drinking and getting high.

G. Alan Marlatt, a leading figure in relapse prevention work, advocates the development of **positive addictions**, pleasurable and healthful habits that can substitute for the client's prior destructive habits (Marlatt and Barrett 1994). Positive addictions are behaviors that satisfy the *adaptive wants*, or good desires, of the client and balance the many difficult "shoulds" of recovery. Some of the positive addictions that help are exercise regimens (like jogging or swimming), hobbies (like collecting or painting), and intellectual pursuits (like taking a class or reading).

Chapter Summary

14–1

Relapse is a return to problematic substance use after a period of abstinence, while lapse indicates a single instance of resumed use. Most recovering clients exhibit episodes of lapse and relapse. Relapse is conceptualized in three models. The all-or-none model is linked with the disease concept of addiction and views any resumption of use as a sign of relapse. The cognitive-behavioral process model sees lapses and relapses as normative events in a prolonged process of recovery. The transtheoretical model conceives of recovery and relapse in terms of the stages-of-change theory.

14–2

Relapse is a multidetermined event with biological, psychological, and social causes. Biological influences on relapse include drug-induced sensitization of the dopamine neurons and HPA axis, as well as hyperarousal (kindling) of the limbic system. Classical and operant conditioning learning mechanisms contribute to relapse potential via processes of conditioned withdrawal, craving priming, and habitual patterns of pleasure-seeking behavior. Personality vulnerabilities to relapse take the form of problems in self-regulation areas such as self-care, self-esteem, emotion, and relationships. Low self-efficacy is also a personality predictor of relapse. The cognitive-behavioral model of relapse emphasizes the cognitive and affective reactions to high-risk situations, as illustrated by abstinence violation effect. Social factors, especially family conflict, play a role in relapse.

14–3

Relapse prevention is a multifaceted approach to reducing the risk and severity of relapse. Clients need to identify and cope with high-risk situations. By learning to monitor relapse triggers (people, places, things), clients can anticipate risky settings and avoid them. Active coping strategies include stress-management techniques, social problem-solving, and cognitive skills, as embodied in the relapse rehearsal method. Cue extinction is a technique for lessening cravings through exposure to drug stimuli. Relaxation and imagery skills are also involved in cue-extinction work. To prevent relapse, clients should learn to utilize their social support systems through couples and family counseling as well as by group work. True recovery requires developing a healthy lifestyle replete with positive addictions.

Terms To Remember

abstinence violation effect
all-or-none model
common relapse factors
conditioned withdrawal theory
cue extinction
dopamine sensitization
high-risk situations
lapse
limbic kindling
positive addictions
process model
mastery imagery
relapse
relapse prevention
self-regulation vulnerability
transtheoretical model

Suggested Reading

Gorski, T. T. (1989). *The Relapse/Recovery Grid*. Center City, MN: Hazelden.
Marlatt, G. A., and Gordon, J. R. (1985). *Relapse Prevention: Maintenance Strategies in the Treatment of Addictive Behaviors*. New York: Guilford.
National Institute on Drug Abuse (1993c). *Cue Extinction: In-Service Training Curriculum*. Rockville, MD: National Institute on Drug Abuse.

Counseling Special Populations

Chapter Outline

Learning Objectives

Upon completing study of this chapter you should be able to:

1. Discuss the clinical features of alcoholism and drug abuse in women.
2. Present differences in the origins of alcoholism in women versus men.
3. List and explain special considerations in the treatment of chemical dependency in women.
4. Explain assessment treatment considerations in children and adolescents.
5. Discuss ageism and its relationship to chemical dependency in the elderly.
6. Discuss the role of racism in the development of chemical dependency in African Americans.

7. Describe the influence of machismo in the development and treatment of addiction with Hispanic/Latino Americans.
8. Explain the connection between sexual prejudice and chemical dependency in the gay, lesbian, and bisexual population.
9. Describe integrated chemical dependency treatment for mentally ill chemical abusers.
10. Define disability and discuss special treatment considerations with the disabled population.

Chemical dependency is an equal opportunity destroyer. People of all social classes, ethnic groups, ages, religious affiliations, and sexual orientations suffer from chemical dependency. So do people with special problems, such as the mentally ill and the physically and cognitively disabled. Although it is true that addiction is much the same for all its victims, there are differences in its causes, progression, and consequences depending on gender, age, minority status, and the presence of a coexisting disability. Because of these group differences, a number of additional treatment issues arise for the counselor who works with these special populations. Despite the many important distinctions among individuals in these groups, it is our belief that the most important factor in successfully counseling people from a variety of backgrounds is attitude. In your work as a counselor you would do well to be sensitive to ethnic differences, the effects of poverty, the impact of disability, and the effects of discrimination. If you are willing to learn about the experiences of being black, Hispanic, gay, of the opposite gender, of a different religion, or of a different socioeconomic and occupational background, you will be more successful with all types of clients (Strassner 2000).

Most of the empirical research with special populations addresses the problem of alcoholism. Regrettably, less is known about other forms of substance abuse in those populations. We will discuss substance abuse and its treatment in women, different age groups, racial and ethnic minorities, gays and lesbians, and other special populations such as the mentally and physically disabled. One important treat-ment issue with special populations concerns whether treatment for individuals in these groups should be heterogeneous or homogeneous. For example, should women be treated in all-female groups, or would participation in co-ed groups be more effective? The same question arises for members of other groups, such as homosexuals, young people, the elderly, and the disabled.

Twelve step programs address this dilemma rather well inasmuch as their general meetings are open to all and stress the universality of addictive experience. Their viewpoint is that addiction is the same relentless process of loss and regression regardless of who you are or where you came from. Yet they also have specialty meetings, which are sometimes gender specific, sometimes restricted to a particular sexual orientation, and sometimes designed for members of a particular profession. Such formats give the recovering person an opportunity to participate in both the universal and the particular aspects of recovery. They afford people the opportunity to be enriched by all of the variety of human experience, while at the same time offering members a chance to discuss issues unique to their situation and their background with people of similar background. When feasible, this model should be adapted to your professional work, in order to offer clients experiences that speak to their humanity and to their individuality.

In individual counseling, the analogous dilemma has to do with whether the counselor should be of the same ethnicity, sexual orientation, or race as the client. There is no clearcut answer to this, as some people work best with people of similar backgrounds and others perform more effectively with people who are quite unlike themselves. Considering that most counselors are white, middle-class individuals and that a large percentage of their patients are not, sensitivity to the values, languages, and perceptions of diverse populations is critical. This notion is reflected in the **cultural responsiveness hypothesis**, which proposes that effective treatment depends on the ability of the counselor to respond successfully to culturally relevant information and behavior in the patient (Sue et al. 1996). Studies of ethnically and racially diverse client groups support this notion. Special significance is attached to the matching of language and values between the counselor and client.

When client and counselor are too much alike, the danger is that they may both be blind to certain cultural problems that an outsider would readily spot. The advantage is a ready empathy and identification. In the real world, there are seldom opportunities to do very precise matching, especially in large metropolitan areas where people come from such diverse cultures that counseling agencies cannot possibly have a staff that represents all of those cultures. Therefore, we as counselors must do our best to cultivate our sensitivity to differences and to show a willingness to learn and be taught.

It is also important for us to note that substance abuse clients sometimes use their differences in the service of denial. They may say such things as, "You can't possibly understand me and why I get high because you're not gay." The counselor should not be taken in by such manipulations. Another common form of denial takes the form of "I can't possibly be alcoholic because I'm Jewish and Jews don't drink very much." Another manipulation is reflected in statements like "What do you mean I'm addicted to drugs? I'm a respectable professional." The best way to handle such forms of denial is to discuss them frankly and interpret to the client their defensive nature.

Generalizations drawn from the epidemiological literature should not get in the way of seeing substance abuse in a particular client. For example, there is a relatively low incidence of alcoholism in the elderly, in Jews, in people living in rural areas, and in the religious. Nevertheless, if you stay in this field long enough, you are going to meet an elderly, Orthodox Jewish woman from rural Wyoming who drinks two quarts of rotgut a day. One of the great advantages of practicing counseling is that it provides a free education. In the course of your work you will learn about all sorts of worlds that you had no previous knowledge of, and the only tuition is receptivity. Clients by and large are happy to teach us about their worlds. What we need to do is to let them know that we are

interested, that we care, and that we want to learn.

In this chapter you will learn about the issues that pertain to working with substance abusers belonging to several special populations. In no way do we pretend to cover every relevant issue or every conceivable special population. Rather, this chapter will serve to raise your consciousness about your work with a diverse client base.

15–1 Chemically Dependent Women

For many years clinicians and researchers in the field of chemical dependency focused their attention on drug and alcohol problems in men. Women, however, were a forgotten population. Recent years have seen a dramatic turnabout in this attitude. Today, a considerable amount of effort is devoted to understanding the unique dynamics of female addictions. Research is beginning to show gender differences in the biology of drug abuse, the causes and consequences of drug abuse, and prevention and treatment (National Institute on Drug Abuse 1999c). Alcoholism will be the principal focus of this section because the largest body of literature on any single special population concerns alcoholic women.

Alcoholism in Women

At one time alcoholism was considered an almost exclusively male disease; it is now known that this is certainly not the case. Nearly one-third of alcoholics are female, and this constitutes a very large number of pathological drinkers. It is also known that alcoholic women are more likely to suffer from depression than are alcoholic men (Kessler et al. 1994).

Female Alcoholic Types. Some researchers note significant differences between female and male alcoholism. Although "female alcoholism" is not an altogether unique form of alcoholism, there are a number of distinguishing features of female alcoholics. Women, for instance, are more likely than men to be *depressive secondary alcoholics*, that is, they suffer depression as a result of their alcoholism; in contrast, men are more likely to be *sociopathic secondary alcoholics*, or alcoholics who engage in antisocial behavior due to alcoholism (Winokur et al. 1971). Winokur was the first to make the distinction between *primary alcoholism* (addiction) and *secondary alcoholism*. In the former, substance use is the primary disorder and the psychiatric symptoms of depression, anxiety, and antisocial behavior are secondary to it, whereas secondary alcoholism (substance abuse) involves primary psychiatric symptoms, and the addiction is a consequence of a misguided attempt at self-medication. The two conditions Winokur thought most often lead to secondary alcoholism are depression and antisocial (sociopathic) personality disorder, the first being generally found in women and the second in men.

MacAndrew (MacAndrew and Geertsma [1963]) studied the personality profiles of alcoholics using the *Minnesota Multiphasic Personality Inventory* (see Chapter 3). He found two personality patterns: (1) an angry, rebellious, acting-out, externalizing, slightly manic type he called a primary alcoholic profile, and (2) a depressed, anxious, low-self-regarding pattern he called secondary alcoholism. Men tend to exhibit the first type, while women more often conform to the second. In other words, women are far more likely to be **MacAndrew secondary alcoholics** whose alcoholism is associated with depression and other forms of significant emotional distress. It is well to remember, however, that these studies describe statistical averages and that any particular chemically dependent man might be severally depressed, while any chemically dependent woman might be a sociopath.

Effects of Drinking in Women. Aside from their differing psychological characteristics, female alcoholics have consistently been found to suffer more somatic damage from lower doses of alcohol consumed for shorter periods of time than do men. There is no question that women suffer earlier and more severe physical, emotional, and social consequences of their drinking. They are particularly vulnerable to liver damage. In recent years, women have come to be diagnosed and treated for alcoholism much more frequently than in the past. Whether this means

that female alcoholism is becoming more common or that it is simply better detected is not clear. Young women are drinking more, and heavy drinking by women in their twenties is reported in the recent prevalence literature. Whether this will eventuate in an epidemic of female alcoholism remains to be seen.

Origins of Alcoholism in Women

Given the distinctive emotional features of alcoholic women, it should not surprise you that women develop alcoholism for reasons that often differ from those of men. In your work as a counselor, you will do well to be mindful of some of these common causal factors.

Compared to men, women are more likely to drink to alleviate intolerable feelings of worthlessness; that is, they suffer more than male alcoholics do from devastatingly low levels of self-esteem. In other words, for many female alcoholics drinking acts as self-medication for their depression. Blane (1968) thought that women drink to deal with feelings of inferiority and that men drink to deal with repressed dependency needs. The research data, although fragmentary, tends to support his contention. The relatively high incidence of depression in alcoholic women is compelling; the other findings are more questionable (Winokur et al. 1971). Women do appear to have more difficulty maintaining self-esteem in our society; it is not known, however, whether their struggle is commonly self-medicated with alcohol or whether such self-medication is an important factor in the etiology of female alcoholism.

Another view of the etiology of female alcoholism is described by the **sex-role conflict hypothesis**, which states that women drink to alleviate sex-role conflicts and to feel more feminine (Wilsnack 1973). Wilsnack's (1973, 1984) research uses the *Thematic Apperception Test* (see Chapter 3), a projective technique in which subjects are asked to make up stories in response to a picture on a stimulus card. Her findings demonstrated that the stories told by women who drank heavily in a simulated social situation dealt with "feminine" material and themes. These findings were interpreted as evidence that the women drank to feel more feminine, on the assumption that the stories were projections of their inner feelings. There is also some evidence that female alcoholics have above-average rates of gynecological problems, but it is not clear if this increases sex-role conflict, makes them feel less feminine, or is a causal factor in their alcoholism (Wilsnack 1991). Although some data seem to confirm the sex-role conflict hypothesis, the overall evidence is too fragmentary to permit any broad conclusions.

Women more often than men report a precipitating event, such as loss of a loved one or failure to conceive a child, as the cause of their alcoholism. Similarly, they are more likely to report traumatic childhoods. Whether these self-reports reflect real differences in the prevalence of stressful life events in the lives of alcoholic men and women is questionable. The gender difference might be an artifact of the greater social shame associated with alcoholism in women and their concomitant need to find a justifying reason for their drinking. In addition, self-reported differences in precipitating events might also result from men's greater reluctance to self-disclose. However, there are high rates of reported childhood incest (sexual abuse) in alcoholic women (Wilsnack and Beckman 1984).

> Samantha was a 35-year-old woman with a long history of alcohol and drug abuse. At the time of her entry into counseling, she had given up drugs and was drinking about a quart of cheap vodka every night after work. During assessment Samantha reported vague memories of being physically and sexually abused as a child by her father, her older sister, and her sister's teenage friends. By the time she entered junior high school, Samantha was doing alcohol and every drug she could get her hands on. It was clear that she was self-medicating to keep from feeling the painful emotions of her childhood abuse.

Issues in Counseling Alcoholic Women

Whether or not treatment of female alcoholism should be distinct from treatment of male alcoholism is a vexing question. Female alcoholics sometimes reject A.A., seeing it as a male-oriented ideology. In particular, these women object to such core A.A. experiences as the requirement for "surrender" and admitting they are "powerless" over alcohol. While the A.A. philosophy of surrender might be just the thing for male alcoholics, many women spend their lives in a state of powerlessness, and these women are not about to surrender the power they had fought so hard to acquire (Nancy Roberts, personal communication, March 1991). A recent issue of the *A.A. Grapevine* was largely devoted to letters for and against revising the "Big Book" of Alcoholics Anonymous (Alcoholics Anonymous World Services 1976), to remove sexist language and outlook.

Awareness of Depression during Treatment.

Because of the strong likelihood that female alcoholic clients are also comorbidly depressed, counselors need to pay close attention to depression symptomatology as well as to the drinking. Although the first order of business is helping your client achieve abstinence, the combination of alcoholism and depression can be quite debilitating and can have a particularly devastating impact on motivation. Feelings of hopelessness and helplessness are pervasive in the depressed alcoholic client, and engaging the client in treatment can be especially challenging. For female clients the experience of depression is strongly linked with their interpersonal relationships. A common chain of events proceeds as follows: interpersonal conflict or disturbances such as marital problems trigger feelings of depression, which in turn prompt more drinking.

Depression and Suicide.

Along with paying extra attention to depression and interpersonal disturbances in female alcoholic clients, counselors also should monitor suicidal urges and fantasies. Compared to men, women are less likely to commit suicide, but twice as likely to attempt it (National Institute of Mental Health 1998). Furthermore, the combination of alcoholism and severe depression is a very volatile mix as far as suicide risk is concerned. The most important predictor of suicide potential is a history of suicide attempts. In addition, counselors must be attuned to other danger signals for suicide potential, as outlined below.

- Self-reported suicidal ideas or fantasies
- Increase of self-damaging, risky behavior
- Intense feelings of hopelessness
- Uncharacteristic changes in behavioral routines
- Closure behavior, that is, finishing unfinished business such as paying off old debts

Because of the heightened risk of depression and suicide among alcoholic women, counselors will do well to consider additional clinical work on depression. Additionally, it is recommended that a severely depressed client be referred to a psychiatrist for medication evaluation.

Female Alcoholism and Child Abuse. Not only do female alcoholics exhibit an elevated risk of harming themselves, they are also more likely than the average woman to harm their children. Despite the stereotyped image of a child abuser being a man, the fact is that mothers are most likely to act abusively toward their children. The alcoholic mother is a high-risk candidate for child abuse for several reasons. *First*, she has close contact with the children and limited tolerance for the stress of parenting. *Second*, she is more easily frustrated because of alcohol-impaired coping abilities and frustration often leads to aggression. *Third*, alcohol leads to a disinhibition of emotional responses like anger, thereby making it easier for the woman to lose control and lash out at her children.

> After giving birth to her third child, Martha became severely depressed (postpartum depression) and began to drink heavily. One day, her infant daughter would not stop crying and so Martha began to drink. After more than two hours of the child's incessant crying, Martha bolted toward the baby, picked her up, and threw her out the fourth-floor window of her apartment. Fortunately, the baby survived, because her fall was broken by branches of a large tree limb. After months of legal wrangles, Martha was remanded into a dual-diagnosis treatment for her depression and alcoholism.

It is clear from Martha's case that many depressed, alcoholic women can benefit from parent skills training as well as working on recovery from alcoholism.

Other Addictions in Women

One of the few things we know with certainty about women chemical dependents other than alcoholics is that women constitute a majority of crack/cocaine users. We also know that, just as they do with alcoholism, women suffer more socially, physically, and emotionally from drug involvement than do males. The social stigma they endure is also much stronger than that of men. Problems of sexually transmitted diseases secondary to the prostitution used to support drug habits are also not uncommon. This may be further complicated by the presence of children, some of whom may have been born addicted to one drug or another.

Addiction to Tranquilizers. One of the more prevalent chemical dependency problems in women has long been addiction to tranquilizers. Many common tranquilizers or anxiolytic (antianxiety) medications like Valium are members of the benzodiazepine family, a highly addictive group of psychoactive drugs (see Chapter 2). In cases in which chemical dependency is brought about by a prescribed medication it is called an **iatrogenic addiction**, that is, one caused by the physician. Because women seeking such medications are typically suffering from one or more anxiety or stress disorders, they eventually develop a comorbid package of emotional and addiction symptoms. It is also relatively common to find female alcoholics who are cross-addicted to anxiolytic drugs.

Counselors working with anxiolytic-addicted clients must be ready to deal with the dramatic upsurge of anxiety symptoms that will occur when drug use is terminated. Given that feelings of anxiety are major emotional triggers for drug abuse in those clients, some clinical attention to anxiety-control strategies is essential.

Special Treatment for Addictions in Women. Compared to what has been done in the field of alcoholism, much less effort has been put into the study of drug abuse and addiction treatment for women. This relates to the question raised earlier in this chapter about whether women require special treatment because of their unique female issues, which may include poverty, sexual and physical abuse, sexually transmitted diseases, and raising children, to name a few. Drug use during pregnancy is a major problem unique to women. As shown in Figure 15–1, nearly 19 percent of women who give birth use alcohol during their pregnancy and another 5 percent use illicit drugs (National Institute on Drug Abuse 1995). Whereas a few studies show that adult male and female alcoholics do about as well when treated in the same program, there is much less agreement on this little-researched area in women.

What we do know is that, more so than men, women do best in treatment when they are involved in supportive interpersonal relationships. Both the number and quality of supportive relationships and the number of life stressors are strong predictors of treatment outcome. This means that you should consider couples and/or family therapy as an adjunct to addiction-specific treatment. With regard to levels of interpersonal support, women appear to need a continuing relationship with a counselor, community services support, and aftercare services (Substance Abuse and Mental Health Services Administration 1997).

Comprehensive Services. Many drug-addicted women require comprehensive services because they often have basic unmet needs in addition to the fact of their addiction (National Institute on Drug Abuse 1999b). A comprehensive treatment program for women should make provisions for:

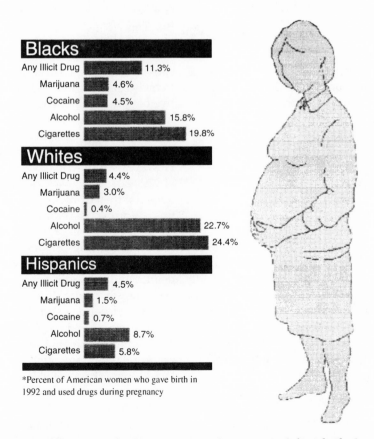

*Percent of American women who gave birth in 1992 and used drugs during pregnancy

Figure 15–1. Drug use during pregnancy* among racial and ethnic groups
Source: National Institute on Drug Abuse (1999c).

- Food, clothing, and shelter
- Transportation
- Job counseling and training
- Legal assistance
- Literary training and educational opportunities
- Parent training
- Family therapy
- Couples counseling
- Medical care
- Child care
- Social services
- Social support
- Psychological assessment and mental health care
- Assertiveness training
- Family-planning services

15–2   Special Age Groups

Although chemical dependency is usually considered a problem of young to middle adulthood, it can be found in all age groups from preadolescents to the elderly. In Chapter 5 you learned about the age-related issues involved in the development of substance abuse across the lifespan, and those developmental factors have important implications for counseling. Clinically, it should be obvious that adaptations in technique and approach must be made depending on the age of the client. In this section we will examine three special populations: children, adolescents, and the elderly.

Substance Abuse in Children

Unfortunately, it is not uncommon, particularly in the inner cities and major metropolitan areas, to encounter substance abuse in very young children. One of the authors has taught a class for many years that almost always has New York City school teachers in it, and he has repeatedly heard reports from elementary school teachers that children come to school high on one drug or another. We also know that babies are born addicted to crack, methadone, heroin, and other drugs. We know little about treating such children although it is obvious that active intervention must be made with the families if any change is to take place.

Chemical dependency in preadolescents is quite rare. When it does occur, however, the addicted child is more likely to have a severely dysfunctional family and other serious emotional and behavioral problems. All of these disadvantages certainly complicate the work of the counselor. Ordinarily, the treatment of such children is best left to counselors who have special training and expertise in childhood psychopathology, child therapy, and family therapy.

Substance Abuse in Adolescents

Diagnosing substance abuse in adolescents is problematic because the validity of *DSM-IV-TR* criteria in this population is questionable. One study (Kaczynski et al. [1999]) of nearly 400 male and female adolescents ages 13 to 19 revealed that 31 percent were "diagnostic orphans," meaning that even though they were regular drinkers and many were in alcohol treatment programs, they failed to meet *DSM-IV-TR* criteria for either alcohol abuse or dependency.

Nevertheless, while the data on adolescents show that problem drinking by youths is extremely common, that is not necessarily predictive of adult alcoholism. Although this manifestation of rebellious acting out can have serious consequences, as when kids drink and drive, it does not in itself mean very much. However, those who have a family history of alcoholism do increase their risk of adult alcoholism if they drink heavily as teenagers. For this reason, alcohol education can help prevent alcoholism in this population. On the other hand, diagnosing problem-drinking adolescents as having a "disease" tends not to be helpful and is mainly untrue. Certainly, however, some adolescents do develop full-blown alcohol addiction, and for those cases the disease model and corresponding treatment interventions—abstinence, Twelve step program, relapse prevention—are essential. Although teenage problem drinkers can be turned off by the disease model, counselors do well to educate them about the course of alcoholism. Surely, most problem drinkers do not end up as alcoholics, but most alcoholics did start out as problem drinkers, often during adolescence.

Controlled Drinking. Vaillant (1983) advocates teaching young people how to drink in a socially controlled and acceptable manner as the best prophylactic against problem drinking. Moderate drinking, rather than abstinence, is frequently the treatment goal with this population. Enormous controversy surrounds the moderate-drinking approach, particularly when any drinking by a minor is illegal. Counselors have to be very careful about encouraging minors to engage in illegal activity, whether that may be drinking or anything else. From an ethical and legal point of view the best course is to encourage abstinence by minors.

Adolescent Drug Abuse. Adolescents are also prime candidates for abusing drugs other than alcohol. The *National Household Survey on Drug Abuse* (National Clearinghouse for Alcohol and Drug Information 2000) reports that while only about 10 percent of 12- to 17-year-olds indicate recent illicit drug use, more than 15 percent of 16- to 17-year-olds and nearly 20 percent of 18-

to 20-year-olds do. In fact, as shown in Figure 15–2, illicit drug use is higher among late adolescents than in any other age group.

Adolescent Substance Abuse and Mental Disorders. Yifrah Kaminer (1994) makes several interesting observations on adolescent substance abuse. The first is that antisocial personality disorder as a comorbid condition is radically underdiagnosed in adolescent girls since we like to think of them as "sugar and spice and everything nice," when that may be anything but the truth. Correspondingly, depression among acting-out adolescent substance-using boys is also underdiagnosed because what the observer sees is the acting out and the antisocial behavior, while missing the depression. Kaminer notes that adolescent substance abusers who suffer from depression in addition to conduct disorder (a term for antisocial behavior in young people) have a much better prognosis. He postulates that the reason for this is that depression is so painful that it keeps the youngsters in treatment.

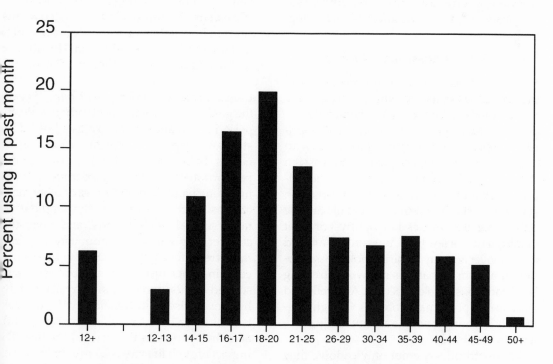

Figure 15–2. Past month use of any illicit drug by age, 1998
Source: Substance Abuse and Mental Health Services Administration (1999).

Types of Treatments.   It has long been noted that adolescents tend to do better in groups than in individual therapy. We do not disagree with this but nevertheless wish to emphasize that some youngsters do much better in individual counseling and should be given an opportunity to participate in such one-to-one work if they want it. The crucial problem for adolescents, substance-abusing or not, is conflict around autonomy and separation. When families are available and amenable to participation, family counseling is often the treatment of choice, but in our experience should not be the exclusive treatment. That is, the youngster who participates in family therapy should also be in either a group, or in individual treatment, or both.

It is particularly vital in treating young people that educational and vocational problems be addressed and that appropriate remediation be offered if necessary. Substance-abusing youngsters often dig themselves into such developmental holes that they totally despair and find it almost impossible to stay clean unless counseling can provide them with some sort of realistic map that depicts a route by which to return to social, academic, and occupational functioning.

Substance Abuse in the Elderly

For many novice counselors the most surprising finding about alcoholism and drug abuse in the elderly is that it exists; chemically dependent elderly people are a "hidden" population. Much of the surprise has to do with *ageism*, in which younger people often assign different quality-of-life standards to the elderly. Such attitudes are reflected in common statements like "Grandma's cocktails are the only thing that makes her happy" or "Let Grandpa have a few belts, he won't be around much longer anyway." The unspoken assumption of ageism is that it is not worth treating substance abuse in older people. Also reflected is the assumption that problems we fight vigorously in younger people are not really problems in the elderly.

These attitudes are not only callous, they are misconceptions. Most adults can and do

live independently. Furthermore, Grandma cocktails do not make her happy. She is probably self-medicating with alcohol and/ prescription drugs in order to salve the emotions that come with her problems. Old people who drink are likely to have had a problem drinking spouse, to have lost the spouse death, to have experienced depression, and have been injured in a fall. The reality is th substance abuse in the elderly takes an ev greater toll than it does in younger people. the baby boomers approach old age, it will increasingly difficult for elderly substan abuse to remain a hidden problem (Substan Abuse and Mental Health Services Admin tration 1998).

Prevalence.   There are no firm statistics garding the prevalence of chemical depe dency in the elderly because it often goes u detected and few studies have targeted th population. Nevertheless, it appears that it more common than you might imagine. F example some studies show that from 6 11 percent of elderly people admitted to h pitals exhibit signs of alcoholism, and pro lem drinking in nursing homes is as high 49 percent. The rate of alcohol-related adm sions to hospital emergency rooms is simi to rates for heart attacks (National Institute Alcohol Abuse and Alcoholism 1998a).

Causal Factors and Complications.   Hard the golden years for many elderly people, t period of advancing age brings a host of l stressors, especially chronic, disabling nesses. To be sure, the elderly consume a d proportionate amount of prescription dru including painkillers and a host of other me cations. Furthermore, elderly people oft take several medications and over-th counter preparations continuously, as part their treatment regimen. Sadly, these dr combinations often are not properly p scribed or monitored. Many physicians ha little expertise with the elderly. Insufficie income and a lack of social support frequen add their stress to the list of illnesses. T impact of such life stressors in turn can res in anxiety and depressive disorders for wh tranquilizers and antidepressants often are prescribed. The long-term use of pain killers, other medications, and psychotropic drugs represents a dangerous and possibly lethal situation in addition to the risk of addiction. Psychiatric symptoms increase the risk of alcohol abuse as well (Brennan and Moos 1997, National Institute on Drug Abuse 1996b).

Alcohol abuse is serious at any age, but it is especially dangerous in the elderly because of its health implications. Through its deleterious effects on every organ system, excessive alcohol consumption can exacerbate existing illnesses, create new ones, and increase the risk of injury. Also, excessive drinking causes cognitive and behavioral deficits that older people are less likely than younger people to recover from. The intellectual deficits seen in elderly alcoholics are caused by accelerated aging of the brain; geriatric alcoholics show more degeneration of brain tissue than age-matched nonalcoholics (National Institute on Alcohol Abuse and Alcoholism 1998a, Oscar-Berman et al. 1997, Pfefferbaum et al. 1997).

Most elderly alcoholics are survivors of a lifelong career of alcohol abuse, but some are newly recruited to the ranks of the alcoholism. Late-life stressors are powerful influences on late-life alcoholism. Many turn to drinking because of their inability to handle the losses of later life and the narcissistic blow inflicted by retirement.

> A retired woman librarian in her seventies developed late-onset alcoholism when she could not adjust to retirement. She was a classic "old maid," prim, proper, and rather supercilious. She responded to treatment, became sober, and joined A.A., where she met a hell-raising retired sailor who had been in more beds and in more ports than she had books in her library. They fell in love, married, and lived happily for eight years until he died of a heart attack. She is still sober and active in A.A.

When elderly people are physically sick, lonely, and depressed, they are likely to self-medicate with alcohol. Late-life alcohol abuse is not uncommon in some retirement communities as well, where social drinking is the norm (National Institute on Alcohol Abuse and Alcoholism 1998a).

Drug Abuse. It is rare to see an elderly person injecting heroin, smoking crack, or tripping on LSD. Instead, the majority abuse prescription drugs, particularly tranquilizers like the benzodiazepines. When these drugs are combined with alcohol the results can be absolutely disastrous. It is important to investigate the medical situation and the possible abuse of prescription drugs in all clients, but particularly in elderly clients. When working with elderly clients, counselors are well-advised to keep the lines of communication open with their clients' physicians and family members.

Treatment of Chemical Dependency in the Elderly. In treating substance abuse in elderly people you cannot assume that elders are simply older versions of younger people. As with any special population, treatment should be tailored to each person's individual needs. Hospitalization is more likely with the elderly because of the likelihood of concurrent medical conditions that require careful monitoring. It is recommended that all but the mildest cases of detoxification should take place in the hospital setting (Abrams and Alexopoulos 1991).

In all treatment settings, a wide variety of therapeutic approaches are used with elderly substance abusers. Brief interventions and motivational counseling are preferred. Because the person is likely to be ashamed of his or her problem, it is particularly important for the counselor to be nonconfrontational and supportive. The *FRAMES approach* discussed in Chapter 12 can be especially useful as a type of brief intervention (Substance Abuse and Mental Health Services Administration 1998).

Generally, elderly clients do not do well in Twelve step programs, although there are exceptions. There is some question, too, whether the strict abstinence required by such programs is necessary for the elderly. There is also some evidence that they seem to do better in peer groups with professional leadership, that is, in groups of older people with a professional leader. The focus on such groups is usually not exclusively on the substance abuse but very much on the problems of aging, of loss, of loneliness, and of dealing with diminution of their physical and mental capabilities (Atkinson 1995).

Group work is very important with the elderly, but family interventions are critical because family members may be enablers through their ignorance of substance abuse in older people. Outcome studies of individual psychotherapy are lacking. Nonetheless, if you do individual psychotherapy with the elderly, you will find it particularly challenging. It requires extreme sensitivity to the depth and extent of their losses (Abrams and Alexopoulos 1991).

The use of medications to promote abstinence has received very little research attention. Generally, medications like Antabuse and naltrexone are used infrequently. Medications are usually restricted to the antianxiety and antidepressant drugs prescribed to combat the psychiatric symptoms that often go along with chemical dependency in this population. Of course, antianxiety drugs must be prescribed cautiously or not at all because of their abuse potential (Abrams and Alexopoulos 1991, National Institute on Alcohol Abuse and Alcoholism 1998a).

15–3 Substance Abuse in Minority Groups

Substance abuse is found in all groups within our society, including minorities. This fact should not minimize these differences, as they apply to substance abuse treatment. On the contrary, the special circumstances in which minority group members find themselves have considerable relevance to the development and treatment of their drug and alcohol problems. Of particular importance for minorities are the intermingled issues of social stress, community environment, and discrimination.

Of course, there are numerous minority groups in American society so it is impossible to elucidate the uniqueness of each of them. Overall, not enough is known about chemical dependency in minority groups. Rather than attempt to cover substance abuse for every minority group, we will focus on those for which we have the most research and clinical information. In the following sections we consider the challenges for chemical dependency counselors working with members of selected racial or ethnic minority groups, and with gay, lesbian, and bisexual clients.

Substance Abuse in African Americans

African Americans are the most studied ethnic minority group in the United States. The data on African Americans show that black males have a lower rate of alcoholism and drug abuse than their white counterparts, and that African-American women generally show a lower prevalence of chemical dependency than black males (National Clearinghouse for Alcohol and Drug Information 1999a). Because many black women are the primary wage-earners in single-parent homes, they are far more likely than males to be abstinent. But black women, if they drink at all, are more likely to develop alcoholism than is true for white women. Consistent with Wilsnack's (1973) sex-role conflict hypothesis, it is possible that black women forced into traditionally male roles drink to feel more feminine.

Sociocultural Risk Factors. The vast majority of African Americans manage to avoid chemical dependency and lead productive lives, even under the worst of circumstances, while others succumb, depending partly on the sociocultural context in which drinking and drugging occur (Herd 1994). There is little doubt that alcoholism and illicit drug abuse among African Americans is associated with stressful loss; it is often a reaction to life circumstances characterized by traumatic social and psychological stress. Racism, whether actual or perceived, unemployment, economic disadvantage, and separation from families can lead to demoralization and feelings of hopelessness and helplessness (Clark et al. 1999, Johnson and Jennison 1994). Illicit drug abuse among African Americans, as in other minorities, tends to cluster in the lower socioeconomic portions of the population. Ghetto drugging is very similar in its dynamics to ghetto drinking, but it also has a strongly economic etiology insofar as drug dealing may seem to be the only available career route for impoverished adolescents.

The noted sociologist Emile Durkheim (1897) described a condition of **anomie**, or extreme social alienation, as the consequence of failure to integrate with and participate in the broader social community. For African Americans and other disenfranchised minorities, anomic drinking and drugging reflects the alienation and isolation of these groups from mainstream (that is, white middle-class) society. Alcoholism can serve as both a passive-aggressive expression of rage and as a means of anesthetizing that rage.

Medical Complications. Another significant counseling issue with African-American alcoholics is the greater prevalence of medical complications due to alcoholism in this group. This is especially true of cirrhosis of the liver (National Institute on Alcohol Abuse and Alcoholism 1994). Whether this difference is mainly due to genetic-biological factors or to economic and social factors is not known, but the differential rate is well established (Lex 1985). In all likelihood a number of contributing influences are to blame. In working with African-American males with advanced alcoholism, it is important to have them referred for a thorough medical evaluation.

Treatment Options. Notwithstanding obvious racial or ethnic differences between whites and blacks, there is no compelling evidence that African Americans fare any better or worse than whites in existing treatment programs. Variables that you might expect to be critical, such as type of treatment and especially patient–counselor congruence, do not seem to make a difference in treatment outcome. Community structure, environment, and pretreatment employment are more predictive of success than ethnicity (Substance Abuse and Mental Health Services Administration 1997).

Clinical experience tells a different story, however. The treatment of choice for disadvantaged African-American clients requires more than the usual substance abuse treat-

ments. It is important to provide hope through the offering of educational and occupational opportunities that give people a real reason to get clean. This approach is particularly true for the younger portion of this economically deprived population, but the same applies to older people as well.

The promotion of culturally accepted institutions is a critical adjunct to prevention and treatment of African-American substance abuse. For example, inner-city addiction treatment programs have created alliances with local churches to strengthen recovery through fellowship, mentorship, community activism, spiritual guidance, and drug-free alternatives. Chemical dependency counselors should familiarize themselves with the cultural institutions of African Americans and encourage ethnic identity through awareness of African-American history and tradition, identification with drug-free African-American friends, or participation in African-American cultural activities like *Kwanzaa*. Ethnic identification confers some protection and lessens drug use (National Institute on Drug Abuse 2000, Substance Abuse and Mental Health Services Administration 1997).

Substance Abuse in Hispanic/Latino Americans

Before embarking on a discussion of counseling issues that pertain to work with Hispanic/Latino clients, it is well worth noting that this is not a homogeneous population. The term Hispanic/Latino comprises Spanish-speaking populations from Puerto Rico, Mexico, Cuba, the Dominican Republic, Central and South America, and Spain. Indeed, any familiarity with these cultures will tell you that the differences among those groups can be even greater than their similarities. The danger of overgeneralizing is great; be cautious about lumping together or stereotyping individuals on the basis of their language and heritage. Hispanic/Latino clients groups are well aware and proud of their uniqueness. Their counselors should also make themselves aware.

Machismo. Hispanic/Latino males, who have high rates of alcoholism, are postulated to have a unique drinking pattern related to the cultural attitude of *machismo*. Heavy drinking for some Hispanic/Latino males is normative and an important part of their identification as men. To not be able to drink is a profound threat to self-esteem and to identity. This must be addressed by the counselor. Because Hispanic/Latino culture takes in an enormous range of customs and has enormous variation, this kind of machismo drinking is not true of all Hispanic/Latinos, but it is of many. The extent to which machismo attitudes directly contribute to alcoholism has not been clarified by research. Nevertheless, as they do in other ethnic groups, cultural traditions play an important role. For example, for many Hispanic/Latinos there appears to be greater cultural tolerance, that is, a culturally conditioned acceptance of alcohol use, among men than among women. Of course, most cultures are less restrictive of men's drinking, so the cultural tolerance among Hispanic groups is not necessarily distinctive.

Treatment Options. Like African Americans, Hispanic/Latino clients benefit from strengthening of ethnic identification and cultural ties, and utilization of available Hispanic/Latino community resources. The goals of chemical dependency counseling are furthered by encouraging family involvement. With strong traditions of family unity and interdependence, Hispanic/Latino clients are often more responsive to family-oriented interventions than are other groups. Motivating change requires the counselor to highlight the impact of alcoholism or other addictions on family members. Concern for the family's well-being can induce the client's desire to change. Hispanic women tend to drink very little and have traditionally been expected to be in the home while the men were out doing, among other things, drinking. As acculturation takes place these distinctions become blurred, and we will probably see more Hispanic women in our treatment programs as they become more Americanized.

Fortunately, there are many Spanish-speaking A.A. and N.A. groups, participation in which allows members to be sober without feeling that their masculinity is threatened. The presence of other recovering male Hispanics is enormously reassuring and bolsters self-esteem. One type of Hispanic/Latino A.A. group involves *terapia dura* (rough therapy). This approach adapts expressions of machismo values to produce more socially effective alternatives. The second type of group is a less confrontational version in which machismo is muted. Unfortunately, Hispanic/Latino A.A. groups make few provisions for women and gay/lesbian individuals (Hoffman 1994, Quinlan 1995). For the client who does not wish to go to a Twelve step program, the best advice is to discuss the very real threat that *not* drinking poses emotionally, psychologically, and in terms of identity for such clients.

Substance Abuse in Gays, Lesbians, and Bisexuals

There is a paucity of solid research regarding the nature, prevalence, and treatment of substance abuse in the gay, lesbian, and bisexual population. It is commonly believed that factors such as social stigma, denial, alienation, discrimination, and the cultural importance of bars place these individuals at higher risk of developing substance abuse problems (National Clearinghouse for Alcohol and Drug Information 1994).

Psychosocial Risk Factors. Many gays, lesbians, and bisexual individuals who have "come out" feel quite comfortable with their sexual orientation. Others, however, experience isolation and self-hatred stemming from conflicts around morality and religion as well as harassment and abuse. Despite the fact that modern diagnostic manuals, such as the *DSM-IV-TR* (see Chapter 4), do not classify homosexuality or lesbianism as a mental disorder, many among the general public consider it abnormal, disgusting, and even immoral. As you well know, victimization and incidents of gay-bashing are all too common.

Whereas many gay, lesbian, and bisexual people are well adjusted and do not have problems with drugs or alcohol, some turn to substances to cope with the anxiety, depression, and alienation that sometimes follow their sexual orientation. Compared to people in the general population, gay, lesbian, and bisexual people have an increased risk of depressive disorders, anxiety disorders, substance-related disorders, and suicide, and are more likely to have multiple disorders. Gay and lesbian hate-crime survivors have crime-related fears, a poor sense of mastery, and tend to attribute their personal setbacks to sexual prejudice. Gay, lesbian, and bisexual teenagers are prone to conduct disorder, prostitution, running away, and school difficulties. Thus, treatment efforts for this population must address substance abuse in the broader context of social stigma and risk of comorbid mental health problems (Fergusson et al. 1999, Garofalo et al. 1999, Herek et al. 1999).

Drug Preferences.   Counselors should also be aware that although gay, lesbian, and bisexual clients use all types of drugs, they are likely to prefer alcohol and methamphetamine (speed). Indeed, speed is becoming the drug most often mentioned by gay, lesbian, and bisexual clients seeking drug abuse treatment, and more than 50 percent of these people inject it (National Clearinghouse for Alcohol and Drug Information 1996c). Whether methamphetamine abuse comes before or after other substance abue, its ramifications for chemical dependency counselors must be addressed.

Treatment Options.   In treating gay, lesbian, and bisexual clients you should be cognizant that they are members of an often-persecuted minority and that they have many of the same problems that other minority members do. They demonstrate problems pertaining to self-esteem, identification with the aggressor, suppressed rage, and the possibility of acting out or anesthetizing all of those problems through the use of substances, rather than dealing with them.

In most urban areas there are gay and lesbian Twelve step meetings, so that the client may participate both in general A.A. or N.A. meetings and in meetings restricted to people of the same sexual orientation. We encourage gay and lesbian clients in Twelve step programs to attend both types of meetings. They provide different experiences, both of which are helpful.

The question of whether or not the counselor needs to be of the same sexual orientation as the client frequently comes up. Occasionally, a gay or lesbian client may strongly prefer to work with a counselor who shares that sexual orientation, but that is rarely the case. If the client is insistent, then the request should of course be honored, if at all possible. However, an exploration of the client's motivation is in order to evaluate whether the request serves a defensive purpose. In most instance sexual orientation is not a major issue once it is on the table and discussed openly.

Gay, lesbian, and bisexual clients frequently ask straight counselors what their feelings are about homosexuality, and the counselor should answer honestly. If the straight counselor regards homosexuality as sinful or psychopathological, it would not be advisable for such a counselor to treat homosexual clients. This is seldom a real problem but it does sometimes occur. For the most part, differences in sexual orientation do not seem to be disabling in substance abuse counseling. Gay and lesbian substance abuse counselors treat many straight clients and that does not seem to be a problem either.

15–4   Other Special Populations

In this final section we examine some of the concerns that pertain to chemical dependency counseling with individuals who have other severely handicapping conditions in addition to their substance problems. Here we focus on two groups: the mentally ill and the physically or cognitively disabled.

Mentally Ill Chemical Abusers

In Chapter 8 you learned about the relationship between chemical dependency and mental health problems, and your study of Chapter 12 taught you about attending to mental disorders in planning and implementing treatment. In this section we will address special concerns in this population.

Dual-Diagnosis Clients.   Individuals who have both a substance-related disorder and a severe mental disorder are referred to as

mentally ill chemical abusers (MICAs). People in this population are also sometimes known as *dual-diagnosis clients*. Notwithstanding chicken-and-egg dilemmas about which came first, the mental disorder or the substance-related disorder, it is clear that chemically dependent clients are likely to have co-existing psychiatric problems. Substance abuse may be either primary or secondary to a mental disorder, and you will encounter many MICAs in the course of your treatment efforts.

Prevalence. The prevalence rates of alcoholism in those suffering from major psychiatric illness have been estimated to range between 50 percent and 86 percent; comorbidity prevalence rates involving other types of substances vary depending on the precise mental disorder or drug abuse combination. In any event, comorbidity prevalence rates are alarmingly high (Kessler et al. 1994).

Causal Factors. Years of research and clinical experience have shown that it is difficult to discover separate causes for mental disorders and substance-related disorders. That being the case, you might imagine that the comorbidity for these conditions is even more difficult to estimate; any explanation is likely to be either inadequate or simplistic. Nevertheless, part of the reason for comorbidity is undoubtedly the unwise, poorly managed deinstitutionalization of psychiatric patients who lack the inner resources to cope with life on the outside. Deinstitutionalized mental patients often turn to alcohol and other drugs both as self-medication and as a prosthesis to provide for needs they cannot provide for themselves, such as self-esteem and inner calm. For most, however, drinking or drugging fail both as self-medication and prosthesis, and their condition worsens.

For cases in which substance abuse is primary, there is no doubt that chronic drinking and drugging creates a plethora of interpersonal, financial, and medical problems that can induce abnormal mental conditions. From this standpoint, mental illness is an unfortunate but understandable reaction to a life ruined by chemical dependency. For example, alcoholics with secondary comorbid depression are at

increased risk for psychosocial and interpersonal problems, treatment noncompliance, relapse, and attempted and completed suicid (Modesto-Lowe and Kranzler 1999).

Assessment of Comorbidity. Today, improvements in assessment and diagnosis permit the ready identification of mental illness in substance abusers. In the past, the failur to make dual diagnoses for many clients wa in part a result of a kind of professional blind ness among some counselors whose trainin led them to deny or minimize psychopathol ogy other than the chemical dependency. A though it is not without some merit, the atti tude that "It's the booze that does it, stupid, can cause a counselor to overlook or misinter pret signs of comorbid mental illness. How ever, the current focus on dual diagnosis nov allows us to speak of the anxiety disorders mood disorders, personality disorders, an other mental disorders that occur along witl alcoholism and substance abuse.

Treatment Issues. Common sense says tha whatever the causal vector, mentally il chemically abusing clients have no chance t recover unless both of their disorders are ad dressed in an integrated manner. The psychi atric disorder must be treated or else the cli ent will continue to use substances, an unless the client stops abusing substances i is unlikely that treatment of the mental ill ness will be successful. For that reason it i vital that the counselor work closely witl other mental health professionals who ar treating the psychiatric disorder, and that th counselor constantly reinforce the necessit of treating both disorders for recovery. Men tally ill clients have fewer resources to under take the journey to recovery than those with out psychiatric disability, and therefore the need a great deal of guidance, structure, re inforcement, and encouragement.

There are now Twelve step meetings ex plicitly for MICA clients, and if one is available the client's participation should be strongl urged. In addition there are other non-Twelve step programs being developed. Before the late 1980s, *parallel* or *sequential treatment* was the rule for dealing with comorbid conditions. Thi meant that the mental and substance-related conditions were either treated separately and simultaneouly, or separately in sequence. This approach rarely achieved a positive outcome for either condition. Since the late 1980s we have witnessed a trend toward **integrated treatment**, meaning that mental health and substance-related disorders are treated simultaneously (not sequentially) by the same person, team, or organization. This does not mean applying chemical dependency treatments for mental illness or using mental illness treatment strategies to break addiction. A successful integrated treatment program is a thoughtful, well-designed blend of various treatments intended to tackle both problems as facets of one all-encompassing difficulty (Mueser et al. 1997). Table 15–1 describes the important ingredients of an integrated treatment program.

Physically and Cognitively Disabled Substance Abusers

A **disability** is any disease, disorder, or injury, whether congenital or acquired, that significantly impairs an individual's ability to function in various areas of life. Using this definition, it is estimated that nearly 15 percent of the American population is disabled. Many of these people have struggled for years and have encountered barriers to employment, hurtful stereotyping, and inaccessibility to community services. In order to redress these obstacles, President George Bush signed into law the *Americans with Disabilities Act* (ADA) in 1990. The ADA prohibits discrimination on the basis of disability and guarantees full participation in American society (Substance Abuse and Mental Health Services Administration 1998).

Table 15–1. Common ingredients of integrated mental health and substance abuse treatment programs

Ingredient	Function
The same professionals provide mental health and substance abuse treatment	Coordinating mental health and substance abuse treatments; avoiding sending "mixed messages" or failing to treat relevant problems areas
Case management	Attending to the range of clinical housing social and other needs that may be affected by either substance abuse or mental health problems
Assertive outreach	Providing services directly in the community to engage patients, address pressing needs, and to follow-up and re-engage relapsing patients
Group interventions	Providing peer support, persuading patients to address substance use behavior, and promoting sharing of coping strategies for managing urges to use substances and for social situations
Education about substance abuse and mental illness	Informing patients about the nature of their psychiatric disorders and the effects of substance abuse to highlight negative effects of drugs and alcohol
Motivational techniques	Engaging patients in working toward substance use reduction and abstinence by identifying personally relevant goals that become a focus of treatment

Source: Mueser, et al. (1997).

Types of Disabilities. Disabilities are classified into four categories of impairment: (1) physical, (2) cognitive, (3) affective, and (4) sensory (see Table 15–2). *Physical disabilities* are those that cause impairment by disease, disorder, injury, or trauma. *Sensory disabilities*, like blindness or deafness, cause impairment by their effects on sensory organs. Disruptions of thinking, perception, communication, and spatial or temporal disorientation constitute *cognitive disabilities*. Finally, *affective disabilities* involve disruptions in the way emotions are processed or expressed. Using this classification, the ADA considers chemical dependency to be a disability in and of itself because of the serious functional limitations it carries (Substance Abuse and Mental Health Services Administration 1998).

Prevalence and Risk Factors. Compared to people in the general population, individuals with physical and cognitive disabilities are at increased risk to have a comorbid substance abuse disorder, but exact prevalence rates are unknown. What is clear is that, despite ADA legislation, many people with disabilities

Table 15–2. Types of disability

Category	Disability
Physical	Spina Bifida
	Spinal cord injury
	Amputation
	Diabetes
	Chronic fatigue syndrome
	Carpal tunnel
	Arthritis
Cognitive	Learning disability
	Traumatic brain injury
	AD/HD
Affective	Depression
	Bipolar disorder
	Schizophrenia
	Eating disorder
	Anxiety
	Post-traumatic stress disorder
Sensory	Blindness
	Deafness
	Visual impairment
	Hard of hearing

Source: National Clearinghouse for Alcohol and Drug Information (1999a).

remain stigmatized and shut out from the mainstream of society. Dealing with one disability is challenging enough, but physically or cognitively disabled substance abusers must cope with more than one disability. Physical, attitudinal, and communications barriers often limit the treatments that the disabled receive and so they are less likely than the nondisabled to enter or complete treatment.

Treatment Issues. The field of chemical dependency has matured to the point where growing experience with other special populations has challenged counselors to make treatment modifications to accommodate the disabled. We can now say that treatment effectiveness with the disabled has improved markedly. Indeed, this population has finally begun to receive the special treatment it deserves as witnessed by the *New York University Department of Rehabilitation Counseling*, which recently initiated a combined master's degree in rehabilitation and substance abuse counseling.

Successful substance abuse treatment for disabled clients requires the commitment of all levels of the treatment staff, including the system, organizational, and client counselor levels. Without such involvement change does not occur, because systemic and organizational inconsistencies or disarray will filter down to treatment personnel. When counselors do not receive the proper support from above, they become frustrated and cannot do their job effectively. Eventually, the client suffers the isolation that is at the core of addiction.

Perhaps even more so than with all special populations, clients with physical and/or cognitive disabilities require special accommodations. Recognizing the variety of disabilities and clients' attitudes about them means that treatment plans should be formulated on a case-by-case basis if at all possible (Substance Abuse and Mental Health Services Administration 1998).

The successful treatment of addicted clients with disabilities requires a *strengths-based approach*. This means that the treatment staff must evaluate the client's personal assets and weaknesses and help the client utilize those assets in recovery. This is no simple task, because the client's lack of awareness and *denial* are major obstacles to overcome. Besides the denial that is usually part and parcel of addiction, people with physical and/or cognitive disabilities also may be unwilling to accept their disability, especially if it has occurred recently. For many people, adjustment to a severe, life-changing disability is a lifelong process. Moreover, substance abusers with physical and/or cognitive disabilities may use their addiction as a form of bargaining in which excessive drug use is viewed as something that is allowed as a sort of compensation for the disability. In such cases, clients may self-medicate to quell painful emotions. Individuals with double denial (to the addiction and the disability) certainly will test your clinical skills. You may find it necessary to refer the client to a *Center for Independent Living* whose staff will help the client come to terms with his or her disability.

Another particularly poignant issue in treatment planning and implementation is *risk-avoidance* and *risk-taking*. For many disabled clients, personality factors or experience make risk avoidance a comfortable way to cope with the disability. Consequently, behaviors that will help the individual become more independent and drug-free may be difficult to introduce. For example, the individual may be reluctant to take a bus, go to a shopping mall, attend a Twelve step meeting, or trust an unfamiliar group member. Such avoidance will reinforce both the disability and the addiction and foster more isolation and low self-efficacy, the very factors that maintain the addiction (Substance Abuse and Mental Health Services Administration 1998).

In contrast, others will take excessive risks because of insufficient skills or poor judgment. Excessive risk-taking puts the client in no-win situations that lead to unpleasant outcomes and maintenance of the addiction, as illustrated in the following case excerpt.

Ralph was a 37-year-old with cerebral palsy, epilepsy, and alcoholism. A short time after entering outpatient treatment, he took a part-time job sweeping floors at a local pharmacy where he met a 22-year-old "normal" woman to whom he was attracted. Against the advice of his counselor, Ralph pursued the relationship, thinking that the attraction was mutual. It was apparent to Ralph's counselor that the woman was merely being nice to him. On the unfounded assumption that they would get married, Ralph decided to purchase an engagement ring. Shortly thereafter, he proposed and she turned him down. Devastated by the rejection, Ralph tried to return the ring to the jeweler, but discovered that the sale was final. Losing his money and suffering a major blow to his self-esteem, Ralph sank deeper into his alcoholism.

In conclusion, working with clients in any special population is challenging and rewarding work. As long as you are willing to be flexible and eager to learn you will find that your success with these individuals will enrich your experience as a chemical dependency counselor.

Summary

15–1

Nearly one-third of alcoholics are female. Women are more likely than men to be depressive secondary alcoholics; men are more likely to be sociopathic secondary alcoholics. Women are likely to be MacAndrew secondary alcoholics whose alcoholism is associated with emotional distress. Female alcoholics suffer more somatic damage from lower doses of alcohol consumed for shorter periods of time than do men. Another view of the etiology of female alcoholism is described by the sex-role conflict hypothesis, which states that women drink to alleviate sex-role conflicts and to feel more feminine. Women more often than men report a precipitating event, such as loss of a loved one or failure to conceive a child, or a traumatic childhood as the cause of their alcoholism. Women often reject A.A. because they object to A.A. core experiences such as "surrender" and admitting they are "powerless" over alcohol. Because of the strong likelihood that female alcoholic clients are also comorbidly depressed, counselors need to pay close attention to the depression symptomatology and suicide cues. Drug addiction in females parallels female alcoholism but the risk of prostitution and sexually transmitted diseases is greater. Women do best in treatment when they are involved in supportive interpersonal relationships. Family and couples therapy may be indicated in addition to community-services support, along with aftercare services that comprehensively meet women's unique needs.

15–2

Substance abuse is uncommon in preadolescents but fairly common in adolescents. In preadolescents it is often associated with severe family dysfunction and other serious emotional and behavioral problems. Ordinarily, the treatment of such children is best left to counselors who have special training and expertise in childhood psychopathology, child therapy, and family therapy. Diagnosing substance abuse in adolescents is problematic because tha validity of *DSM-IV-TR* criteria in this population is questionable. For adolescent problem-substance abusers, education can help in prevention. Vaillant advocates controlled drinking as the best prophylactic against problem drinking. Moderate drinking, rather than abstinence, is frequently the treatment goal with this population. Adolescents are also prime candidates for abusing drugs other than alcohol as evidenced by the National Household Survey on Drug Abuse and the Monitoring the Future Study. Antisocial personality disorder as a comorbid condition is radically underdiagnosed in adolescent girls, and depression among acting-out adolescent substance-using boys is also underdiagnosed. Adolescents tend to do better in groups than in individual therapy. Family counseling is often the treatment of choice when families are available and amenable to participation. Educational and vocational problems should also be addressed. Substance abuse in the elderly involving painkillers, alcohol, and prescription medications is not uncommon. A host of life stressors, especially chronic, disabling illnesses, are associated with abuse in the elderly. Treatment should be tailored to the person's individual needs and may involve hospitaliza-tion for concurrent medical conditions. Brief interventions and motivational counseling are preferred. It is particularly important for the counselor to be nonconfrontational and supportive. Group work is very important with the elderly, but family interventions are critical because family members may be enablers through their ignorance of substance abuse in older people.

15–3

Most African Americans avoid chemical dependency and lead productive lives, but others succumb, depending partly on the sociocultural context in which drinking and drugging occur. Alcoholism and illicit drug abuse among African Americans is associated with stressful loss, racism, unemployment, economic disadvantage, and separation from families, and can lead to demoralization and feelings of hopelessness and helplessness. Illicit drug abuse among African Americans clusters in the lower socioeconomic portions of the population. There is no compelling evidence that African Americans fare any better or worse than whites in existing treatment programs. Community structure, environment, and pretreatment employment are more predictive of success than ethnicity. The treatment of choice for disadvantaged African-American clients requires the provision of hope through the offering of educational and occupational opportunities. The promotion of culturally accepted institutions is a critical adjunct to prevention and treatment of African-American substance abuse. Hispanic/Latino males are postulated to have a unique drinking pattern related to the cultural attitude of machismo. Like African Americans, Hispanic/Latino clients benefit from strengthening of ethnic identification and cultural ties, and from utilization of available Hispanic/Latino community resources. The goals of chemical dependency counseling are furthered by encouraging family involvement and participation in Spanish-speaking A.A. and N.A. groups. Factors such as social stigma, hate crimes, denial, alienation, discrimination, and the cultural importance of bars place the gay, lesbian, and bisexual population at higher risk for developing

Counseling Special Populations

substance abuse problems. Many gay, lesbian, and bisexual people turn to substances to cope with the anxiety, depression, and alienation that sometimes accompany their sexual orientation. Counselors also should be aware that although gay, lesbian, and bisexual clients use all types of drugs, they are likely to prefer alcohol and methamphetamine. Treatment should address problems pertaining to self-esteem, identification with the aggressor, suppressed rage, and the possibility of acting out all of those problems or anesthetizing them through the use of substances, rather than dealing with them. In most urban areas there are gay and lesbian Twelve step meetings.

15–4

People with comorbid mental and drug-related disorders are called mentally ill chemical abusers. Improvements in assessment and diagnosis permit the ready identification of mental illness in substance abusers. Mentally ill chemically abusing clients have no chance to recover unless both of their disorders are addressed in an integrated manner. There are Twelve step meetings explicitly for MICA clients. Since the late 1980s we have witnessed a trend toward integrated treatment, meaning that mental health and substance-related disorders are treated simultaneously (not sequentially) by the same person, team, or organization. It is estimated that nearly 15 percent of the American population is disabled. Many of these people have struggled for years and have encountered barriers to employment, hurtful stereotyping, and inaccessibility to community services. Disabilities are classified into four categories of impairment: physical, cognitive, affective, and sensory. Many people with disabilities remain stigmatized and shut out from the mainstream of society, which can lead to substance abuse. Physical, attitudinal, and communications barriers often limit the treatments that the disabled receive, and so they are less likely than the nondisabled to enter or complete treatment. Treatment effectiveness with the disabled has improved markedly. Successful substance abuse treatment for disabled clients requires the commitment of all levels of the treatment staff, including the system, organizational, and client-counselor levels, in addition to special accommodations, a strengths-based approach, and assessment of risk-avoidance and risk-taking.

Terms to Remember

anomie
cultural responsiveness hypothesis
disability
iatrogenic addiction
MacAndrew secondary alcoholics
mentally ill chemical abusers
sex-role conflict hypothesis

Ethical And Legal Issues in Counseling

Chapter Outline

Learning Objectives

Upon completing study of this chapter you should be able to:

. Identify the twelve principles that constitute the ethical standards for alcoholism and drug abuse counselors.
. Discuss the four transdisciplinary foundations of chemical dependency counseling.
. List and describe the eight major dimensions of professional practice in chemical dependency counseling.
. Define and discuss the scope of confidentiality in counseling.
. Identify the most common exceptions to the nondisclosure rule.

6. Discuss the legal and ethical issues involved in the duty to protect.
7. Outline the ten basic principles that pertain to client rights.
8. Describe the meaning of malpractice and identify the main reasons for malpractice charges in counseling.
9. Define dual relationships and discuss the legal and ethical issues that are involved.

The development of chemical dependency counseling as an independent health profession has been marked by contributions from people with diverse backgrounds and training in many fields. As you learned in Chapter 1, the evolution of chemical dependency counseling has progressed through the integration of concepts and values from many disciplines. Today, as a consequence of its unique history, it is a *transdisciplinary field*. In regard to ethical and legal matters chemical dependency counselors often have proceeded with codes of behavior from their primary profession, such as medicine, social work, or psychology. An indication of the increasing maturity and independence of chemical dependency counseling is the adoption of a code of ethics by its main professional organization, the *National Association of Alcoholism and Drug Abuse Counselors* (1995). Table 16–1 summarizes the twelve fundamental ethical principles.

Like other health professionals, chemic dependency counselors perform their jobs a social climate that demands careful atte tion to ethical and legal standards of practi However, chemical dependency counselo work is more likely to entail ethical and gal dilemmas than the work of other heal professionals, for two reasons: (1) the illeg ity of drug use by clients; and (2) other crim nal involvements of drug- and alcoh abusing clients. In this chapter we intend address the main issues in law and ethics th affect chemical dependency counselors a their clientele.

Table 16–1. Ethical standards of alcoholism and drug abuse counselors

Principle	Specifications
1. Nondiscrimination	Do not discriminate against clients or professionals based on race, religion, age, gender, disability, national ancestry, sexual orientation, or economic conditions.
2. Responsibility	Use objectivity and integrity; maintain highest standards in providing services.
3. Competence	Recognize national standards of competency; recognize the need for ongoing education.
4. Legal and moral standards	Uphold legal and moral codes pertaining to professional conduct.
5. Public Statements	Respect limits of present knowledge in public statements concerning alcoholism and drug abuse.
6. Publication credits	Give credit to all who contribute to published material and the work on which publication is based.
7. Client welfare	Promote the protection of public health, safety, and welfare, and the best interests of the client.
8. Confidentiality	Protect client rights under confidentiality; do not disclose confidential information without appropriate consent.
9. Client Relationships	Safeguard the integrity of the counseling relationship, ensure client reasonable access to effective treatment, and provide clients with information about the professional relationship.
10. Interprofessional relationships	Treat colleagues with respect, courtesy, fairness, and good faith.
11. Remuneration	Set financial arrangements in accord with professional standards that safeguard the best interests of the client first.
12. Societal obligations	Engage legislative processes, educational institutions, and the general public to make possible opportunities and a choice of service for those impaired by alcoholism and drug abuse.

Source: National Association of Alcoholism and Drug Abuse Counselors (1995).

16–1 Chemical Dependency Counselor Competencies

All professions are distinguished by their members' unique talents and abilities, which provide the tools whereby professionals fulfill their occupational responsibilities. Perhaps the most fundamental ethic and legal obligation bearing on any professional is to proceed with an adequate degree of competence. Beginning in 1993 a national consortium of addiction treatment professionals instituted the Addiction Transfer Technology Center Program in order to establish basic standards of competency for addictions counselors. Over the next few years the collaboration of many addictions experts and professional organizations culminated in the publication of a set of guidelines to serve as a national standard. These guidelines define **counselor competencies** as the basic knowledge, skills, and attitudes needed for competent professional practice in the field (National Curriculum Committee of the Addiction Technology Transfer Center Program, 1995). Summarized in Table 16–2, these guidelines have been widely acknowledged as a suitable framework for chemical dependency counselor education and assessment.

Transdisciplinary Foundations

Regardless of their educational or professional background, chemical dependency counselors need a body of knowledge about addictions in order to be competent to practice in the field. As you see in Table 16–2, the four transdisciplinary foundations of counseling are understanding addiction, treatment knowledge, application to practice, and professional readiness.

The competent counselor is one who is knowledgeable about the many theories and models of chemical dependency as well as about the many other social, psychological, and physical problems associated with substance abuse. Counselors must recognize the complex context (e.g., social, economic, etc.) in which chemical dependency occurs and be mindful of both the risk and the protective factors that affect substance abusers. In addition, having an *understanding of addiction* means that the counselor is aware of the numerous effects that drugs have on the user and others, and recognizes that substance disorders can both mimic and coexist with other medical and mental disorders.

Treatment knowledge competency means that the counselor knows about the philosophies and practices of accepted and scientifically supported treatment and care models for substance-dependent persons. The counselor also must understand the importance of interdisciplinary approaches to treatment and the importance of research on treatment. Finally, treatment knowledge encompasses the recognition of family, social, and community resources in treatment and recovery.

A counselor demonstrates competence in regard to *application to practice* by understanding and applying principles of diagnosis and treatment suited to the specific needs and

Table 16–2. Addiction counseling competencies

Category	Competencies
Transdisciplinary Foundations	Understanding addiction Treatment knowledge Application to practice Professional readiness
Professional Practice	Clinical evaluation Treatment planning Referral Service coordination Counseling modalities (e.g., group work) Client, family, and community education Documentation Professional and ethical responsibilities

Source: National Curriculum Committee of the Addiction Technology Transfer Center Program (1995).

circumstances of the client. Counselors are obliged to know how to use a variety of treatment strategies to address the client's symptoms and status, and to be able to adapt treatment to the personal and cultural identity of the client. In addition, the counselor should be familiar with all available treatment options (for example, the medical treatment) and settings (for example, the therapeutic community).

Besides the areas of counselor knowledge described above, the attitudes of the counselor also matter a great deal in determining the level of *professional readiness*. For example, two kinds of essential attitudes are: (1) understanding the importance of cultural diversity and cultural needs in one's clientele; and (2) appreciating the importance of self-awareness, or insight into one's own conflicts and emotions. In addition the counselor must be aware of the significance of ethical conduct in his or her work and strive to improve professionally through ongoing supervision and education.

Professional Practice

Beyond the acquisition of the fundamental knowledge areas described in the previous section, chemical dependency counselors must also demonstrate competence in the performance of many specific job skills and responsibilities. As you see in Table 16–2, there are eight major dimensions of professional practice that must be mastered: (1) clinical evaluation, (2) treatment planning, (3) referral, (4) service coordination; (5) counseling methods, (6) education, (7) documentation, and (8) professional and ethical responsibilities.

In previous chapters you have learned the fundamentals of many clinical skills, but naturally, mastery of these skills takes considerable time and practice. Do not feel intimidated if you flounder at the start of your counseling career—everyone does at first. However, with increasing experience you should find yourself honing these skills more sharply year after year.

Clinical Evaluation.   Conducting a careful, systematic screening and assessment of your client is *clinical evaluation*. In Chapter 4 you learned about a variety of assessment methods that chemical dependency counselors and related professionals employ to evaluate their clients' status and needs. In the initial contact with a client, you are usually required to conduct a *screening*, that is, a determination of the best course of action to follow based on your evaluation of the client's current condition and available resources. Essential to client screening is data collection. You must know how to create a rapport with the client so that the client will be forthcoming with relevant information; including current and past substance use, other mental and physical health problems, consequences of substance abuse, history of prior treatment, and social and financial circumstances. In addition you will have to ascertain the client's readiness to change, consider available treatment options, and develop a specific plan of action for initiating treatment.

Another part of clinical evaluation is *assessment*, an ongoing process of gathering and interpreting information to guide treatment and judge client change. It is important to realize that assessment never ends, but continues for as long as your client is in treatment, and ideally even after treatment ends. Because so many aspects of the client's being are relevant to treatment, the counselor needs a good clinical eye—that is, sensitivity to many things, both the obvious and the subtle. Your competence at clinical evaluation requires ongoing assessment of numerous issues in the client's life beyond just drugging and drinking, such as job history, family status, interpersonal relationships, legal entanglements, spirituality, mental health, physical health, community involvements, education, and lifestyle. With ongoing assessment you will be able to judge the progress of treatment and the possible need for changes in the course of treatment.

Treatment Planning and Referral.   Professional competence in **treatment planning** involves the ability to determine treatment objectives and the best strategies to attain those objectives. Successful treatment planning depends on collaboration with the client and significant others in identifying client needs and assessing client readiness to engage in treatment. In planning your client's treatment you will be expected to specify both the desired objectives of treatment and the strategies necessary to achieve them. In addition you will often need to coordinate treatment efforts with community resources.

Many chemical dependency clients are multiply handicapped in terms of their social, medical, and financial status. Consequently, professional counselors must be able to help them utilize social and community resources via the **referral** process. Successful referral is based on the counselor's knowledge of client needs and available resources. Such knowledge depends on the counselor's ongoing contacts with civic and community groups as well as with other health professionals.

Service Coordination. As a professional chemical dependency counselor, you are obliged not only to oversee the clinical treatment of your clients but also to mediate between your clients and other service agencies and providers in a manner fitting client needs. In performing the task of **service coordination,** counselors take the role of case manager and client advocate in collaborating with other members of the treatment team and in acting as a go-between with community services.

The three major objectives in service coordination can be summarized as follows: (1) implement the treatment plan; (2) consult with significant others (for example, physicians, family members) to ensure the treatment plan is being followed; and (3) maintain ongoing assessment and adjust the treatment plan according to the client's progress and changing life circumstances.

Counseling and Education. Counseling skills are obviously a central part of professional competence in this field. In earlier chapters you have learned about the many schools and techniques of counseling that are available to you. Your success depends on an appreciation and understanding of the proper use of many therapeutic tools. Mastery of counseling techniques includes learning about different modalities such as individual counseling, group counseling, and family/couples counseling.

In addition to the use of therapeutic methods, the chemical dependency counselor often provides educational services to clients and their families as well as to the community at large. Consequently, professional competence also includes the ability to accurately present information about the nature of substance dependency, prevention, and recovery.

Documentation. Another area of professional competence is **documentation**, that is, keeping accurate records of assessement information, treatment plans, progress notes, and other client-related facts. Although it is not the most glamorous or enjoyable activity, proper documentation procedure is mandatory for clinical, ethical, and legal reasons. A concern that arises in regard to documentation is ensuring the privacy or confidentiality of client records. We will address confidentiality issues in more detail later in this chapter.

Professional and Ethical Responsibilities. The final area of professional competence to consider is the counselor's duty to adhere to the professional and ethical codes of his or her profession. Counselors are responsible for knowing these codes and for receiving supervision to ensure that they follow them appropriately. Beyond adherence to your professional code you must also stay abreast of federal and state laws that pertain to the treatment of clients so that you can act in accordance with those regulations. Remember that ignorance of the law is no excuse.

16-2   Confidentiality

One of the most fundamental ethical obligations of health professionals is to protect the privacy of information revealed to them by their clients. **Confidentiality** means that statements, actions, and communications of the client are kept private in the confines of the therapeutic relationship. As you can well imagine, confidentiality is essential to the client's trust in the counselor and to the maintenance of an effective counselor–client relationship. Not only is confidentiality a critical ethical issue, it is also the focus of a number of legal concerns.

The Scope of Confidentiality

Problems involving confidentiality are among the most frequently encountered ethical challenges for mental health professionals, including chemical dependency counselors. These problems can arise through intentional, legally required breaches of confidentiality, or through counselor carelessness, as in the following hypothetical case.

> During an intake interview the prospective client informs you that he has decided to seek treatment at your agency on the recommendation of a friend who is currently a member of one of your early recovery groups. The new client tells you that he was motivated to begin treatment because he has seen how much his friend has been helped. Meaning to encourage the interviewee about the wisdom of his decision, you mention that his friend has certainly made a lot of progress in the few months of his treatment and state that he has been completely abstinent since coming to the agency. You let the new client know that you believe he could do just as well if he were to start treatment as soon as possible.

So where did you go wrong? First, simply acknowledging to the interviewee that you know his friend is a client of the agency violates the regulations protecting confidentiality. On top of that, by divulging information about your client's progress you have compounded the infraction. Even well-intentioned violations of confidentiality are unacceptable, unethical, and illegal. The protection of confidentiality requires that you maintain the privacy not only of the client's status and communications, but also of any written, audiotaped, or videotaped records of treatment. Federal laws strictly protect the confidentiality of clients in drug and alcohol treatment. In fact the regulations regarding confidentiality for drug and alcohol clients are even more strict than those governing other kinds of mental health clients (Brooks 1997). Despite variations in state laws about confidentiality, in this matter federal laws take precedence over less-restrictive state regulations.

In accordance with federal law, the general **nondisclosure rule** for drug and alcohol clients means that disclosure of records or other personal information about them is prohibited. The nondisclosure rule covers not only the counselor but also other staff, both counseling and nonclinical. In addition, the nondisclosure rule forbids even identifying a person as a client in a drug or alcohol treatment facility. A good rule is to say nothing about any client even when you know that the person making an inquiry already knows that your client is in treatment. The best response is to inform the inquiring party that federal law prevents you from answering the question.

Besides its prohibition of direct, explicit breaches of client confidentiality, the nondisclosure rule also applies to indirect actions that cause confidentiality to be breached. In other words, it is not just what you do, but also what you do not do that can lead to a confidentiality violation. Consider, for example, the following situation:

> Don was a "freshman" counselor at a community agency that provided outpatient drug and alcohol counseling as well as a spectrum of other services, including adult literacy tutoring for community members. Instead of locking his files securely in the designated cabinet, he had gotten into the habit of leaving them in an unlocked desk drawer in the counseling office. Because other people also used the same office they could have easy access to those client files. A literacy tutor who happened upon the files while he was using the office recognized one of Don's clients as the son of a neighbor, and he later asked the agency director about how this client was doing in treatment. Don soon found himself looking for a position elsewhere.

The most obvious reason to preserve your clients' confidentiality is that it is in the clients' best interest to have private information safeguarded. Breaches of confidentiality can result in extreme embarrassment to your clients and can even jeopardize their jobs, safety, and families. Because of the illegality of many drugs, your clients might face criminal prosecution for information that you have revealed. Aside from protecting your clients from the adverse consequences of breaches of confidentiality, you will also be acting in your own self-interest. Clients can sue their counselors and the treatment facility for *malpractice* if a breach of confidentiality results in harm to the patient.

Private communications between patients and their therapists are often protected not only by ethical principles but also by law. Like conversations between attorney and their clients, information revealed in the context of therapy is sometimes considered **privileged communication**, meaning that the privacy of the information is legally protected when that information is at issue in litigation (Smith-Bell and Winslade 1994). Because of laws in all states regarding privileged communications, mental health professionals cannot be coerced into revealing information about their patients. However, the laws regarding privileged professions vary from state to state, and so it is important that you find out about the laws in the state where you practice.

Common Exceptions to Nondisclosure

Although privileged communications are legally protected at both state and federal levels, some exceptions to that privilege do exist. Under certain circumstances, mental health professionals are legally obliged to reveal information that they have obtained in their interactions with patients. The most common exceptions to the confidentiality and privileged communication laws (Brooks 1997, Corey et al. 1993) are found in the following circumstances.

- Valid written consent by a client to disclose information
- Legal commitment, involuntary hospitalization, and competence hearings
- Child abuse reported by a client
- Civil suits in which the client introduces the issue of his or her mental health
- Threats against the President of the United States
- Patient presenting imminent danger to self or others
- Medical emergency

A client had a heart attack in the counselor's office. When the police and emergency medical service people arrived they wanted to know the client's medical history. Since the client's medical emergency took precedence over confidentiality, the counselor told the police what he knew. What he did not know was that the client was using cocaine that very day, a relevant medical fact that was not obtained until the autopsy on the deceased client.

In general, it is good practice to inform your clients of the rules regarding confidentiality and the exceptions to confidentiality at the outset of therapy. Although many possible situations requiring disclosure of confidential client information can arise, the average counselor is most likely to encounter three such circumstances:

1. Disclosure authorized by client consent; for example, your client authorizes you to release his diagnosis and treatment plan to an insurance company;
2. Disclosure within the treatment agency or organization; for example, in your supervision work you discuss the details of your client's drugging with your supervisor; and
3. Disclosure due to court order; for example, your client is a probationer whose conditions of probation mandate that his treatment progress be reported to the probation officer

The most common reason chemical dependency counselors provide confidential information about their clients is that clients authorize them to do so. Various motives compel clients to give consent to release information about themselves. For some, the desire to have a spouse or parent apprised of treatment progress is the reason for consent. Often, however, drug- and alcohol-dependent clients are pressured into giving consent by the legal system, employers, and health insurance providers. Before you give any information about your client, even at the client's own request, you must be certain that you have obtained a valid written consent. A **consent form** is a document that authorizes the release of confidential information. The organization or format of consent forms can vary, but they should contain the components (Brooks 1997) set out here.

- Name of the person or agency making the disclosure
- Name of the person or agency receiving the disclosure
- Name of the client about whom disclosure is made
- Purpose of the disclosure
- Limits of the disclosure (e.g., diagnosis, treatment plan, treatment schedule, etc.)
- Statement regarding revocability of consent
- Expiration date of consent
- Signature of consenting client
- Date of consent

Form 16–1 sets out a sample version of a generic consent form.

The disclosure of client information is also permissible when the staff of the treatment agency or organization needs such information in order to administer or provide services to the client. In these situations, information about the client can be disclosed only to the extent that the information is directly relevant to the provision of treatment. The most usual reason for such intra-agency disclosure in-

volves supervision. As a counselor you will work under the supervision of more senior staff members, and in the course of receiving supervision you will necessarily have to reveal personal information about your clients.

In most cases disclosure with client consent is routine and unremarkable. An exception to the rule occurs when clients are criminal justice system referrals and their consent to release information is a mandated prerequisite to treatment. For example, a client whose conditions of probation require him to undergo counseling is obliged to give consent. In addition, such mandated clients often do not retain the right to revoke consent as long as they remain under court-appointed supervision. Counselors working with court-mandated clients find that it is necessary to clarify with the probation or parole officers the extent of the terms of consent. Most probation or parole officers are primarily interested in keeping abreast of information that pertains directly to the client's legal mandate to engage in treatment. The potential for difficulties is great, however, because clients may be involved in

Form 16–1. Sample consent form

XYZ Agency

I have been informed that under state law client records and communications between client and counselor are confidential and may not be disclosed by the counselor or agency to third parties except with client's written consent, by a court order, or if the counselor or agency deems that not disclosing information would result in a clear danger to me or others. I understand and accept the statement of confidentiality stated above.

I, _____, give my consent to _____
      Client Name   *Counselor/Agency*

to release to _____ the following
                                       Person/Organization

information: _____
_____.

This consent to release information is for the purpose of _____
_____.

I understand that I may terminate this consent at any time except if this consent has already been acted upon. Unless already revoked by me this consent will terminate on _____.
                                                           Termination Date

_____   _____

Client Signature   Date of Signature illegal activity, which violates the conditions of their probation or parole.

The Duty to Protect

As you learned in the previous section, communications between patients and counselors are ethically and legally protected, but there are limits to confidentiality. One controversial exception is found in cases in which a client informs a counselor about an intention to harm another person. Consider the following case:

> On October 27, 1969, Prosenjit Poddar went to the home of a young woman named Tatiana Tarasoff, whereupon he shot, stabbed, and killed her. Poddar, a graduate student at the University of California at Berkeley, had dated Tatiana the previous year, but after a few months she broke off their relationship. The following summer she left the country for several months, and Poddar, depressed about the breakup, sought help from a psychologist at the campus counseling center. Because he revealed his intention to obtain a gun, the psychologist reported Poddar to the campus police, urging that he be committed as dangerous. The police detained him only shortly and released him. A few days later he killed Tatiana. Because he was diagnosed with paranoid schizophrenia, he was not convicted of murder; instead he was convicted of voluntary manslaughter and sent to prison. The Tarasoff family successfully sued the University of California on the grounds that the psychologist should have warned Tatiana that she was in danger (Schwitzgebel and Schwitzgebel 1980).

In the 1976 case of *Tarasoff* v. *Regents of the University of California*, the California Supreme Court ruled in support of the **duty to protect**, which means that when a therapist knows or should know that a client presents a serious threat of violence to someone there is an obligation to take reasonable steps to protect the intended victim. In other words, a therapist should contact the police, inform the threatened person, or tell someone who can inform the threatened person. Although the duty to protect requires therapists to violate the confidentiality of their clients, it is widely

accepted that the duty to protect others from harm takes precedence over confidentiality (Appelbaum 1994).

In some jurisdictions the duty to protect also has been extended to property as well as persons. In the case of *Peck* v. *Counseling Service of Addison County*, for example, the Vermont Supreme Court ruled that a therapist is obliged to inform someone whose property has been threatened by a patient. The Peck case involved a man who told his therapist that he was going to burn down his father's barn because he was angry at him and wanted to get back at him.

In general the courts have not widely extended the duty to protect to property. However, the prospect of further extensions of the duty-to-protect principle is a matter of concern to mental health professionals. Suppose, for example, that you are treating a chemically dependent HIV-positive client who tells you about his intention to have unprotected sex with a specific person, thus placing that person at high risk for HIV infection. Do you have an obligation to warn the individual? If the therapist does not warn, is he or she liable in the event that the person actually becomes infected? For now, such questions have not been clarified by the courts, and consequently you must take care to learn about the laws that apply in the state in which you are employed, and seek legal advice from the attorney for your workplace (Appelbaum 1994, Brooks 1997).

Mental health professionals have had to adapt to Tarasoff and other duty-to-protect rulings. Most counselors routinely inform their new patients of their duty to protect and the reasons for it and discuss any concerns that the patient might have about confidentiality. Although the likelihood of your being involved in a Tarasoff-like situation is very low, planning against such an eventuality is a good idea.

> One of the authors (J. L.) treated a man who told him of his participation in a murder. This event was in the remote past and presented no danger to anyone in the present. The counselor was under no obligation to report the crime under the laws of his state, and the rule of confidentiality took precedence.

Another duty related to the legal requirement to protect others against the threat of harm by a client is the obligation to report child abuse. A counselor is legally bound to report incidents of known or suspected child abuse by a client, when in the counselor's judgment the child in question is in clear danger of harm. Counselors can report suspected child abuse anonymously and are protected legally against suits by clients. Federal and state laws both acknowledge that the protection of the welfare of children takes precedence over confidentiality. The mandate to report actual or suspected child abuse only applies to making the initial report to child welfare authorities, but does not require counselors to reveal any other confidential information or to provide any information about subsequent events.

16–3 The Rights of Clients

Like other health professionals, chemical dependency counselors do their work within a complex societal framework in which the principles of practice are entwined with those of individual rights. Because laws vary in different jurisdictions, counselors must ensure that they are up-to-date in their understanding of the legal issues that apply in regard to client rights in their locales. In this section we will examine the basic principles pertaining to client rights and several key issues regarding the protection of client welfare.

Client Rights: Basic Principles

Historically, the field of chemical dependency counseling has been fragmented because of the many different professions that have participated in the treatment of drug- and alcohol-dependent clients. In recent years, however, the pressures of managed care have prompted cooperation among the major health professions, leading to considerable progress in clarifying the basic principles of treatment. In recognition of their shared mission to provide quality care for their clients, health professionals have emphasized the importance of **client rights**, the moral entitlements that apply to the individual in treatment.

In 1997, the *American Psychological Association* (APA) released a statement of principles for the provision of mental health and substance abuse treatment (American Psychological Association 1997, Cantor 1999). These principles were the product of collaboration between the APA and many other health professions, representing more than one-half million professionals. The ten principles are summarized in the following section.

Principle 1: The Right to Know.   Individuals have the right to be provided with clear information about their treatment benefits, about the professional expertise of their treatment provider, and about any contractual limitations (for example, limits to treatment) affecting their care.

Principle 2: Confidentiality.   Individuals have the right to protection of the confidentiality of treatment information except in circumstances where laws and/or ethics require disclosure of that information.

Principle 3: Choice.   Individuals have the right to choose any duly licensed or certified professional for treatment services and the right to obtain any relevant information about the professional in making their choice.

Principle 4: Determination of Treatment. Individuals have the right to make decisions about their treatment in conjunction with a licensed/certified professional, and those decisions should not be made by a third-party payer.

Principle 5: Parity.   Individuals have the right to receive benefits for mental health and substance abuse treatment equal to those provided for medical illness.

Principle 6: Nondiscrimination.   Individuals should not be penalized when seeking health insurance simply because they have used mental health or substance abuse treatment benefits.

Principle 7: Benefit Usage.   Individuals are entitled to the full scope of their benefits as outlined in their plans.

Principle 8: Benefit Design: Individuals in mental health or substance abuse treatment are entitled to take advantage of whatever of their benefit plans offers the greatest coverage.

Principle 9: Treatment Review. Individuals have the right to be ensured that any review of their treatment shall involve duly licensed or certified professionals who have no financial interest in the decision.

Principle 10: Accountability. Individuals have the right to hold accountable any professional who causes them injury due to incompetence or negligence; accountability applies to both health-care providers and third parties whose decisions influence treatment.

Although the mental health professions have articulated the basic principles that should define the rights of clients, those principles are not necessarily codified in law, and when they are they are not always consistent from state to state. As we have already mentioned several times in this chapter, each counselor must make a determined effort to know the laws that apply in his or her state. Because laws regarding the practice of chemical dependency change with new legislative and court actions, you will have to keep abreast of such changes throughout your professional career.

Safeguarding Your Client's Welfare

The maxim, *"Do no harm,"* borrowed from the practice of medicine, expresses an obligation that applies to all health professions, including chemical dependency counseling. Most counselors strive to work according to the legal and ethical codes that apply in their chosen field. Some, however, fail to live up to those codes and in so doing jeopardize not only the welfare of their clients but also of their profession. In this section we consider some of the legal and ethical pitfalls that chemical dependency counselors need to avoid.

Malpractice Issues. An important concern of all health professionals is **malpractice**, a legal term that refers to a circumstance in which a professional has caused harm to the client or patient, either by action or inaction. In other words, malpractice can involve a harmful result due to something that the professional

did or failed to do. States vary in their malpractice laws, but generally those laws assume that the therapist has a responsibility to adhere to a standard of conduct and that when the responsibility is neglected it causes damage or loss to the patient (Reisner and Slobogin 1990).

In our litigious society malpractice lawsuits against health professionals are commonplace. Although most counselors will never be charged with malpractice, you will do well to be aware of the many reasons for possible suits. In earlier sections of this chapter we have discussed the issues most commonly involved in malpractice cases. Below we summarize a few of the more typical malpractice charges.

- Incompetence — Acting outside of one's area of expertise or training
- Lack of consent — Failure to obtain proper informed consent
- Negligence — Neglecting to act in the service of client needs
- Rights violation — Violating client rights, for example, confidentiality

Any counselor can be charged with malpractice by a client, whether or not the charge is warranted. Obviously, the best way to prevent such an occurrence is to act in accordance with the ethical and legal principles that govern your discipline. Beyond the obvious, however, it is also a good idea to keep excellent records about your clients and their treatment. In the unfortunate event of a malpractice suit, honest and accurate client records can be an invaluable asset to the counselor (Bissell and Royce 1994). In some cases it can be beneficial to keep not only good written records of treatment, but also audio- and/or videotaped records. Of course, many clients are reluctant to consent to tape recording every session, and consent is needed before so doing. Because of the potentially serious consequences due to *professional liability,* counselors do well to avail themselves of risk-management workshops and to make sure that they have insurance coverage, either through the workplace or privately.

Dual Relationships.   One of the stickiest and most complex concerns in counseling is the nature of the relationship between the counselor and the client. Ideally, the client–counselor relationship should be restricted to the confines of the clinical setting and by the therapeutic objectives for the client. However, in the real world of human relationships it is difficult for people to limit their bonds so strictly. Beyond their counseling relationship, clients and counselors can also be neighbors and co-workers, or members of the same church, synagogue, or social club. The potential for ethical and legal dilemmas is high in such **dual relationships**, where client and counselor have associations outside the therapeutic setting.

The most serious dual-relationship problem involves sexual interaction between client and counselor. All mental health professions expressly forbid practitioners to engage in sexual relationships with their patients. Those who ignore that prohibition are subject not only to ethics sanctions by their profession but also to civil suits and even criminal charges. Despite its potentially grave consequences, sexual misconduct by therapists is one of the most commonly investigated ethical breaches (American Psychological Association 1993).

The true extent of sexual misconduct on the part of mental health professionals will perhaps never be known. Obviously, only reported incidents are available for study, and presumably many go unreported. Studies of therapists indicate that the majority experience sexual feelings toward clients at least on some occasion (Pope and Tabachnick 1993). Of course sexual attractions between people can be perfectly normal and natural, but acting on them in the therapeutic relationship is not. Despite their sexual feelings, the vast majority of counselors and therapists do not engage in inappropriate sexual interactions with their clients. However, some do, but estimates of how many are of questionable accuracy. Clearly, therapists are reluctant to admit such misconduct, and so results of surveys are suspect. The reported estimates have shown wide variation, from less than one percent for both male and female therapists (Borys and Pope 1989) to around 10 percent

of male and 3 percent of female therapists (Hawkins et al. 1994).

Research on the effects of sexual misconduct is sketchy at best, but some findings shed light on the magnitude of its impact. The vast majority of clients who admit to having been sexually involved with their therapist report that the psychological effects have been negative (Pope and Bouhoutsos 1986). Needless to say, the process of therapy is irreparably damaged, often requiring the patient to terminate and start over elsewhere. For these clients, feelings of guilt, depression, low self-esteem and isolation are common, and some respond with symptoms resembling posttraumatic stress disorder (Pope and Bouhoutsos 1986; Williams 1992).

Sexual relationships are usually between a male therapist and a female client and are consistently viewed as having harmful effects on the client. Although therapists sometimes defend their actions by blaming the client for seducing them or inviting their overtures, the therapist alone is ethically and legally accountable for the consequences. Counselors should be aware that there are clients, fortunately very rare, who seek to entrap their counselors, or who make false accusations about sexual misconduct. Therefore, counselors should never put themselves in jeopardy; for example, never hold sessions late at night in an otherwise empty building. Some common sense goes a long way in this matter, as illustrated in the following case.

> Alice was more than gorgeous; she was ravishing. She had sought counseling for help in dealing with her alcoholic husband. Before long she became seductive, sometimes overtly, sometimes more covertly. The counselor alternately ignored this behavior, hoping that it would extinguish from lack of reinforcement, and pointed out its inappropriateness. Neither strategy had the slightest impact on the client's behavior.
>
> The counselor sensed the hostility behind her behavior and came to dread their sessions, feeling increasingly uncomfortable, a discomfort intensified by his attraction to her. She escalated her teasing when she reported: "Last night when my husband and I were making love and just as I came I almost blurted out your name. The whole

time I was thinking about you." The counselor knew enough about her history to recognize that Alice was sexualizing a desperate need for attention. Neither her alcoholic husband nor her alcoholic father paid the least attention to her unless they wanted something from her. Sex had been her only way of getting attention since she was 14. The counselor told her this; that is, he interpreted her behavior in a nonretaliatory way although he was angry and frustrated. This discussion eventuated in Alice's getting in contact with deep feelings of sadness, loss, and deprivation, leading her to question why she stayed with a man who did not care for her and who had no intention of stopping drinking.

Notice that if the counselor had either acted on his feelings and taken up her sexual offer, thereby trashing his ethical and legal obligations, or had retaliated by expressing his fury, not only would those ethical and legal canons have been violated, but a marvelous therapeutic opportunity would have been lost, and the client would not have received the help she sought. Further, irreparable damage would have been done, as the client was repeating a self-destructive pattern of setting herself up to be used by men with little interest in her except for their own pleasure or convenience.

Unlike other mental health professionals, chemical dependency counselors are sometimes in a unique position of being in recovery themselves. The pros and cons of recovering addicts and/or alcoholics acting as counselors have long been debated, and in general the recovering chemical dependency counselor has both advantages and disadvantages compared with others. One potential problem that can arise for recovering counselors is the occurrence of dual relationships that may exist because of the counselor's participation in Twelve step groups in which clients are also participants. Where possible, the counselor should avoid membership in a self-help fellowship that includes clients. In urban areas that have a multitude of different groups it is usually easy for the counselor to accomplish this goal. But in smaller communities, especially in rural areas that have perhaps only a single Alcoholics Anonymous group, it is not so easy. Although it is not

strictly unethical for a counselor to attend a program that his or her client also attends, the counselor must be very careful to establish clear boundaries. In no way should the counselor act as if the Twelve step program is an extension of the counseling work with the client (Alcoholics Anonymous World Services 1993).

Chapter Summary

16–1

Counselor competency encompasses four transdisciplinary foundations and eight dimensions of professional practice. The transdisciplinary foundations include understanding addictions, treatment knowledge competency, applications to practice, and professional readiness. Professional practice competency includes the skills of clinical evaluation, treatment planning and referral, service coordination, counseling, education, documentation, and professional and ethical responsibilities.

16–2

Confidentiality means that patient communications and actions are kept private. The nondisclosure rule prohibits the disclosure of patient records to third parties. Common exceptions to confidentiality and nondisclosure requirements include circumstances in which the client consents to disclosure, disclosure occurs within the treatment agency as part of client treatment, and court-ordered disclosure. The duty to protect is a legal issue that also provides for exceptions to nondisclosure. Counselors are also legally obliged to report suspected child abuse.

16–3

The ten basic principles behind the rights of clients are the right to know, confidentiality, determination of treatment, parity, nondiscrimination, benefit usage, benefit design, treatment review, and accountability. Malpractice means that a professional has caused harm to a client through action or inaction. Common reasons for charges of malpractice are incompetence, lack of consent, negligence, and rights violations. Dual relationships, especially sexual relationships, between client and counselor are problematic from an ethical and legal viewpoint.

Terms To Remember

client rights
confidentiality
consent form
counselor competencies
documentation
dual relationships
duty to protect
malpractice
nondisclosure rule
privileged communication
referral
service coordination
treatment planning

Suggested Reading

Bissell, L., and Royce, J. E. (1994). *Ethics for Addiction Professionals*, 2nd ed. Center City, MN: Hazelden.

References

Abadinsky, H. (1993). *Drug Abuse: An Introduction*, 2nd ed. Chicago: Nelson-Hall.

Abrams, D. B., and Niaura, R. S. (1987). Social learning theory. In *Psychological Theories of Drinking and Alcoholism*, ed. H. T. Blane and K. E. Leonard, pp. 131–178. New York: Guilford.

Abrams, R. C., and Alexopoulos, G. (1991). Geriatric addictions. In *Clinical Textbook of Addictive Disorders*, ed. R. J. Francis and S. I. Miller, pp. – . New York: Guilford.

Aceto, M. D., Scates, S. M., Lowe, J. A., and Martin, B. R. (1995). Cannabinoid precipitated withdrawal by a selective antagonist, SR14176A. *European Journal of Pharmacology* 282:R1–R2.

Ackerman, N. (1994). *The Psychodynamics of Family Life: Diagnosis and Treatment of Family Relationships*. Northvale, NJ: Jason Aronson.

Adinoff, B., O'Neill, H. K., and Ballenger, J. C. (1995). Alcohol withdrawal and limbic kindling. *American Journal on Addictions* 4:5–17.

Akers, R. L. (1992). *Drugs, Alcohol, and Society*. Belmont CA: Wadsworth.

Alcoholics Anonymous World Services. (1952). *Twelve Steps and Twelve Traditions*. New York: Author.

——— (1976). *Alcoholics Anonymous*, 3rd ed. New York: Author.

——— (1984). *'Pass it on': The story of Bill Wilson and How the A.A. Message Reached the World*. New York: Author.

——— (1993). *A.A. guidelines: For A.A. Members Employed in the Alcoholism Field*. New York: A.A. General Service Office.

Allen, J. P., Hauser, S. T., and Borman-Spurrell, E. (1996). Attachment theory as a framework for understanding sequelae of severe adolescent psychopathology: an 11-year follow up study. *Journal of Consulting and Clinical Psychology* 64:254–263.

Alterman, A. I., O'Brien, C. P., and McClellan, A. T. (1991). Differential therapeutics for substance abuse. In *Clinical Textbook of Addictive Disorders*, ed. R. J. Francis and S. I. Miller, pp. 369–390. New York: Guilford.

American Psychiatric Association (1987). *Diagnostic and Statistical Manual of Mental Disorders*, 3rd ed., revised. Washington, DC: Author.

——— (1994). *Diagnostic and Statistical Manual of Mental Disorders*, 4th ed. Text Revision Washington, DC: Author.

——— (1995a). Practice guideline for the treatment of patients with substance use disorders: alcohol, cocaine, opioids. *American Journal of Psychiatry* 152 (Suppl.):1–62.

——— (1995b). Practice guideline for psychiatric evaluation of adults. *American Journal of Psychiatry* 152 (Suppl):63–80.

American Psychological Association (1993). Report of the Ethics Committee 1991 and 1992. *American Psychologist* 48:811– 820.

——— (1997). Principles for the provision of mental health and substance abuse treatment services. Washington DC: Author.

Anastasi, A. (1988). *Psychological Testing*, 6th ed. New York: Macmillan.

Anawalt, P. R. (1997). Flopsy, Mopsy, and Tipsy. *Natural History*, April, pp. 24– 25.

Anthony, J. C. (1995). Comorbidity and vulnerability. In *Encyclopedia of Drugs and Alcohol*, vol. 1, ed. J. H. Jaffe, pp. 257–260. New York: Macmillan.

Appelbaum P. S. (1994). *Almost a Revolution: Mental Health Law and the Limits of Change*. New York: Oxford University Press.

Apte, M. V., Wilson, J. S., and Korsten, M. A. (1997). Alcohol-related pancreatic damage. In *Alcohol World Health and Research: Alcohol's Effect on Organ Function* 21(1):13–20.

Atkinson, R. (1995). Treatment programs for aging alcoholics. In *Alcohol and Aging*, ed. T. Beresford and E. Gromberg, pp. 186–210. New York: Oxford University Press.

Azar, B. (1996). What factors lead to child drug abuse? *APA Monitor*, October, p. 50.

Babor, T. F., Hoffman, M., DelBoca, F. K., et al. (1992). Types of alcoholics I: evidence for an empirically derived typology based on indicators of vulnerability and severity. *Archives of General Psychiatry* 49:599–608.

Bagasra, O. Kajdacsy-Balla, A., and Lischner, H. W. (1989). Effects of alcohol ingestion on in vitro susceptibility of peripheral blood mononuclear cells to infection with HIV and of selected T-cell functions. *Alcoholism: Clinical and Experimental Research* 13:636–643.

Ball, S. A., Carroll, K. M., Babor, T. F., and Rounsaville, B. J. (1995). Subtypes of cocaine abusers: support for a Type A–Type B distinction. *Journal of Consulting and Clinical Psychology* 63:115–124.

Ball, S. A., Carroll, K. M., and Rounsaville, B. J. (1994). Sensation-seeking, substance abuse, and psychopathology in treatment-seeking and community cocaine abusers. *Journal of Consulting and Clinical Psychology* 62:1053–1057.

Balster, R. (1995). Behavioral pharmacology of two novel substituted quinoxalinedione glutamate antagonists. *Behavioral Pharmacology* 6:577–589.

Bandura, A. (1977a). *Social Learning Theory.* Englewood Cliffs, NJ: Prentice Hall.

—— (1977b). Self-efficacy: toward a unifying theory of behavior change. *Psychological Review* 84:191–215.

—— (1982). Self-efficacy mechanisms in human agency. *American Psychologist* 37:122–147.

—— (1986). *Social Foundations of Thought and Action: A Social Cognitive Theory.* Englewood Cliffs, NJ: Prentice Hall.

—— (1997). *Self-Efficacy: The Exercise of Control.* San Francisco: W. H. Freeman.

Bandura, A., and Walters, R. H. (1963). *Social Learning and Personality Development.* New York: Holt, Rinehart and Winston.

Barber, J. P., Frank, A., Weiss, R. D., et al. (1996). Prevalence and correlates of personality disorder diagnoses among cocaine dependent outpatients. *Journal of Personality Disorders* 10:297–311.

Barlow, D. H., and Durand, V. M. (1995). *Abnormal Psychology: An Integrative Approach.* Pacific Grove, CA: Brooks/Cole.

Baron, M., Gruen, R., Ranier, J. D., et al. (1985). A family study of schizophrenic and normal control probands: implications for the spectrum concept of schizophrenia. *American Journal of Psychiatry* 142:447–455.

Bateson, G. (1971). The cybernetics of self: a theory of alcoholism. *Psychiatry* 34:1–18.

Bateson, G., Jackson, D. D., Haley, J., and Weakland, J. (1956). Towards a theory of schizophrenia. *Behavioral Science* 1:251–264.

Baumrind, D. (1987). A developmental perspective on adolescent risk-taking in contemporary America. In *Adolescent Social Behavior and Health,* ed. C. E. Erwin, pp. 93–125. San Francisco: Jossey-Bass.

Bean-Bayog, M. (1991). Alcoholics Anonymous. In *Clinical Manual of Chemical Dependence,* ed. D. A. Ciraulo and R. I. Schader, pp. 359–375. Washington, DC: American Psychiatric Press.

Beautrais, A. L., Joyce, P. R., Mulder, R. T., et al. (1996). Prevalence and comorbidity of mental disorders in persons making serious suicide attempts: a case-control study. *American Journal of Psychiatry* 153:1009–1014.

Beauvais, F. (1992). Volatile substance abuse: trends and patterns. In *Inhalant Abuse: A Volatile Research Agenda.* ed. C. Sharp, F. Beauvais, and R. Spence, NIDA Research Monograph 129, pp. 13–42. Rockville, MD: NIDA.

Beck, A. (1976). *Cognitive Therapy and Emotional Disorders.* New York: International Universities Press.

—— (1978). *Depression Inventory.* Philadelphia: Center for Cognitive Therapy.

Beck, A. T., and Weishaar, M. E. (1995). Cognitive therapy. In *Current Psychotherapies,* 5th ed, ed. R. J. Corsini and D. Wedding, pp. 229–261. Itasca, IL: F. E. Peacock.

Beck, A. T., Wright, F. D., Newman, C. F., and Liese, B. S. (1993). *Cognitive Therapy of Substance Abuse.* New York: Guilford.

Berg, R., Franzen, M., and Wedding, D. (1987). *Screening for Brain Impairment. A Manual for Mental Health Practice.* New York: Springer.

Berglas, S. (1987). Self-handicapping model. In *Psychological Theories of Drinking and Alcoholism,* ed. H. T. Blane and K. E. Leonard, pp. 305–345. New York: Guilford.

Berglund, M. (1984). Suicide in alcoholism. *Archives of General Psychiatry* 41:888–891.

Bernat, J. L. (1994). *The Neurological Complications of Alcohol and Alcoholism,* Unit 7, 2nd ed. Timonium, MD: Milner-Fenwick.

Bertalanffy, L. von (1968). *General Systems Theory: Foundation, Development and Applications.* New York: Braziller.

Bion, W. R. (1961). *Experiences in Groups.* New York: Basic Books.

Bissell, L. and Royce, J. E. (1994). *Ethics for Addiction Professionals,* 2nd ed. Center City, MN: Hazelden.

Blackson, T. C., Tarter, R. E., Martin, C. S., and Moss, H. B. (1994). Temperament mediates the effects of family history of substance abuse on externalizing and internalizing child behavior. *American Journal on Addictions* 3:58–66.

Blane, H. T. (1968). *The Personality of the Alcoholic: Guises of the Tendency.* New York: Harper and Row.

Blane, H. T., and Leonard, K. E., eds. (1987). *Psychological Theories of Drinking and Alcoholism.* New York: Guilford.

Bleuler, D. M. (1955). Familial and personal background of chronic alcoholics. In *Etiology of Chronic Alcoholism,* ed. O. Dretheim, pp. 110–166. Springfield, IL: Charles C Thomas.

Blot, W. J. (1992). Alcohol and cancer. *Cancer Research* (Supplement) 52:2119–2123.

Blum, E. (1966). Psychoanalytic views of alcoholism. *Quarterly Journal of Studies on Alcohol* 27:259–299.

Blum, K., Cull, J. C., Braverman, E. R., and Comings, D. E. (1996). Reward deficiency syndrome. *American Scientist* March–April, pp. 1–18.

Blume, S. B., and Lesieur, H. R. (1987). Pathological gambling in cocaine abusers. In *Cocaine: A Clinician's Manual*, ed. A. M. Washton and M. S. Gold, pp. 208–213. New York: Guilford.

Bode, C., and Bode, J. C. (1997). Alcohol's role in gastrointestinal tract disorders. In *Alcohol World Health and Research: Alcohol's Effect on Organ Function*, 21(1):76–83.

Bohn, M. J., and Meyer, R. E. (1994). Typologies of addiction. In *Textbook of Substance Abuse Treatment*, ed. M. Galanter and H. D. Kleber, pp. 11–24. Washington, DC: American Psychiatric Press.

Borys, D. S., and Pope, K. S. (1989). Dual relationships between therapist and client: a national study of psychologists, psychiatrists, and social workers. *Professional Psychology: Research and Practice* 20:283–293.

Bowen, M. (1974). Alcoholism as viewed through family systems theory and family psychotherapy. *Annals of the New York Academy of Sciences* 233:115–122.

—— (1978a). *Family Therapy in Clinical Practice.* New York: Jason Aronson.

—— (1978b). On the differentiation of self. In *Family Therapy in Clinical Practice*, pp. 467–528. New York: Jason Aronson.

Bowlby, J. (1988). *Parent–child Attachment and Healthy Human Development.* New York: Basic Books.

Bradshaw, J. (1988a). *The Family: A Revolutionary Way of Self-Discovery.* Deerfield Beach, FL: Health Communications.

—— (1988b). *Healing the Shame That Binds You.* Deerfield Beach, FL: Health Communications.

Brady, K. T., Dustan, L. R., Grice, D. E., et al. (1995). Personality disorder and assault history in substance-dependent individuals. *American Journal on Addictions* 4:306–12.

Brady, K. T., Grice, D. E., Dustan, L., and Randall, C. (1993). Gender differences in substance use disorders. *American Journal of Psychiatry* 150:1707–1711.

Brecht, M. L., Anglin, M. D., Woodward, J. A., and Bonnet, D. G. (1987). Conditioned factors of maturing out: personal responses and preaddiction sociopathy. *International Journal of Addictions* 22:55–69.

Brehm, N. M., and Khantzian, E. J. (1997). Psychodynamics. In *Substance Abuse: A Comprehensive Textbook.* 3rd ed., ed. J. H. Lowinson, P. Ruiz, R. B. Millman, and J. G. Langrod, pp. 90–100. Baltimore: Williams and Wilkins.

Brennan, P. L., and Moos, R. H. (1997). Life stressors, social resources, and late-life problem drinking. In *Addictive Behaviors. Readings on Etiology, Prevention, and Treatment*, ed. G. A. Marlatt and G. VandenBos, pp. 805–828. Washington, DC: American Psychological Association.

Breslau, N., Kilbey, M. M., and Andreski, P. (1993). Nicotine dependence and major depression: new evidence from a prospective investigation. *Archives of General Psychiatry* 50:31–35.

Brody, S. L., Slovis, C. M., and Wrenn, K. D. (1990). Cocaine-related medical problems: consecutive series of 233 patients. *American Journal of Medicine* 88:325–331.

Brook, J. S., Brook, D. W., Gordon, A. S., et al. (1990). The psychosocial etiology of adolescent drug use: a family interactional approach. *Genetic, Social and General Psychology Monographs* 116 (No. 2).

Brook, J. S., Cohen, P., Whiteman, M., and Gordon, A. S. (1992). Psychosocial risk factors in the transition from moderate to heavy use or abuse of drugs. In *Vulnerability to Drug Abuse*, ed. M. Glantz and R. Pickens, pp. 359–418. Washington, DC: American Psychological Association.

Brook, J. S., Whiteman, M., Cohen, P., and Shapiro, J. (1995). Longitudinally predicting late adolescent and young adult drug use: childhood and adolescent precursors. *Journal of the American Academy of Child and Adolescent Psychiatry* 34:1230–1238.

Brooks, M. K. (1997). Ethical and legal aspects of confidentiality. In *Substance Abuse: A Comprehensive Textbook*, 3rd ed., ed. J. H. Lowinson, P. Ruiz, R. B. Millman, and J. G. Langrod, pp. 884–899. Baltimore: Williams and Wilkins.

Brooner, R. K., Schmidt, C. W., Felch, L. J., and Bigelow, G. E. (1992). Antisocial behavior of intravenous drug abusers: implications for diagnosis of antisocial personality disorder. *American Journal of Psychiatry* 149:482–487.

Brooner, R. K., Schmidt, C. W., and Herbst, J. H. (1994). Personality trait characteristics of opioid abusers with and without comorbid personality disorders. In *Personality Disorders and the Five-Factor Model of Personality*, ed. P. T. Costa and T. A. Widiger, pp. 131–148. Washington DC: American Psychological Association.

Brown, S. A. (1993). Drug effect expectancies and addictive behavior change. *Experimental and Clinical Psychopharmacology* 1:55–67.

Brown, S. A., Inaba, R. K., Gillin, J. C., et al. (1995). Alcoholism and affective disorder: clinical course of depressive symptoms. *American Journal of Psychiatry* 152:45–52.

Brown, T. A., and Barlow, D. H. (1992). Comorbidity among anxiety disorders: implications for treatment and *DSM-IV-TR. Journal of Consulting and Clinical Psychology* 60:835–844.

Brownell, K. D., Marlatt, G. A., Lichtenstein, E., and Wilson, G. T. (1986). Understanding and preventing relapse. *American Psychologist* 41:765–782.

Bruce, M. L., Takeuchi, D. T., and Leaf, P. J. (1991). Poverty and psychiatric status: longitudinal evidence from the New Haven Epidemiologic Catchment Area Study. *Archives of General Psychiatry* 48:470–474.

Buchsbaum, D. (1994). Effectiveness of treatment in general medicine patients with drinking problems. *Alcohol Health and Research World* 18:140–145.

Bukstein, O., and Kaminer, Y. (1994). The nosology of adolescent substance abuse. *American Journal Addictions* 3:1–13.

Bureau of Justice Statistics (1992). *Drugs, Crime, and the Justice System.* A National Report from the Bureau of Justice Statistics: U.S. Department of Justice, Bureau of Justice Statistics, NCJ-133652, Washington, DC.

Bushman, B. J., and Cooper, H. M. (1990). Effects of alcohol on human aggression: an integrated review. *Psychological Bulletin* 107:341–354.

Butcher, J. N. (1989). *MMPI-2 Users Guide.* Minneapolis, MN: National Computer Systems.

Cadoret, R. J., Troughton, E., O'Gorman, T. W., and Heywood, E. (1986). An adoption study of genetic and environmental factors in drug abuse. *Archives of General Psychiatry* 43:1131–1136.

Cadoret, R. J., Yates, W. R., Troughton, E., et al. (1995). Adoption study demonstrating two genetic pathways to drug abuse. *Archives of General Psychiatry* 52:42–52.

Caine, S. B., Heinrichs, S. C., Coffin, V. L., and Koob, G. F. (1995). Effects of dopamine D-1 antagonist SCH233390 microinjected into the acumbens, amygdala, and striatum on cocaine self-administration in the rat. *Brain Research* 692:47–56.

Caine, S. B., and Koob, G. F. (1993). Modulation of cocaine self-administration in the rat through D-3 dopamine receptors. *Science* 260:1814–1816.

Cannon, W. (1932). *The Wisdom of the Body.* New York: Norton.

Cantor, D. W. (1999). Ensuring the future of professional psychology. *American Psychologist* 54:922–930.

Cappell, H., and Greeley, J. (1987). Alcohol and tension reduction: an update on research and theory. In *Psychological Theories of Drinking and Alcoholism,* ed. H. T. Blane and K. E. Leonard, pp. 15–54. New York: Guilford.

Carlen, P. L., and McAndrews, M. P. (1995). Complications: neurological. In *Encyclopedia of Drugs and Alcohol,* vol. 1, ed. J. H. Jaffe, pp. 300–305. New York: Macmillan.

Carlson, E. A., and Sroufe, L. A. (1995). Contribution of attachment theory to developmental psychopathology. In *Developmental Psychopathology: Vol. 1. Theory and Methods,* ed. D. Cicchetti and D. Cohen, pp. 581–617. New York: Wiley.

Carroll, K. M. (1996). Relapse prevention as psychosocial treatment: a review of controlle• clinical trials. *Experimental and Clinical Ps•chopharmacology* 4:46–54.

Carroll, M. E., and Comer, S. D. (1996). Anim• models of relapse. *Experimental and Clinical Ps•chopharmacology* 4:11–18.

Centers for Disease Control and Prevention (1997a• *AIDS: Basic Statistics.* Atlanta: Author.

——— (1997b). *Sexually Transmitted Diseases Su•veillance 1995.* Atlanta, GA: Author.

——— (1997c). *HIV/AIDS Surveillance Report 199•* Atlanta, GA: Author.

——— (1997d). *Questions and Answers About T•* Atlanta, GA: Author.

Chasnoff, I. J., Burns, W. J., Schnoll, S. H., an• Burns, K. A. (1985). Cocaine use in pregnancy *New England Journal of Medicine* 313:666–669.

Chassin, L., Curran, P. J., Hussong, A. M., an• Colder, C. R. (1996). The relation of parent al coholism to adolescent substance use: a longi tudinal follow up study. *Journal of Abnorma• Psychology* 105:70–80.

Chassin, L., Pillow, D. R., Curran, P. J., et al (1993). Relation of parental alcoholism to early adolescent substance use: a test of three mediating mechanisms. *Journal of Abnormal Psy chology* 102:3–19.

Cherpitel, C. J. (1997). Brief screening instruments for alcoholism. *Alcohol Health and Research World* 21:348–351 (NIH Publication No. 98–3466). Washington, DC: US Government Printing Office.

Chien, I., Gerard, D. L., Lee, R. S., and Rosenfeld, E. (1964). *The Road to H: Narcotics, Delinquency, and Social Policy.* New York: Basic Books.

Chin, J., and Lwanga, S. K. (1992). Estimation and projection of Adult AIDS cases: a simple epidemiological model. *Bulletin of the World Health Organization* 69:399–406.

Chitwood, D. D., McCoy, C. B., and Comerford, M. (1990). Risk behavior of intravenous drug users: implications of intervention. In *AIDS and Intravenous Drug Use: Future Directions for Community-Based Prevention Research,* ed. C. G. Leukefeld, R. J. Battjes, and Z. Amsel, pp. 120–133. National Institute on Drug Abuse Research Monograph 93 (Publication No. 94–3714). Washington, DC: US Government Printing Office.

Cho, A. K. (1990). Ice: a new dosage of an old drug. *Science* 259:631–634.

Ciarrocchi, J. W., Kirschner, N. M., and Falik, F. (1991). Personality dimensions of male pathological gamblers, alcoholics, and dually addicted gamblers. *Journal of Gambling Studies* 7:133–141.

Ciraulo, D. A., and Shader, R. I. (1991). *Clinical Manual of Chemical Dependence.* Washington, DC: American Psychiatric Press.

Clancy, J. (1964). Procrastination: a defense against sobriety. *Quarterly Journal of Studies on Alcohol* 22:511–520.

Clark, R., Anderson, N. B., Clark, V. R., and Williams, D. R. (1999). Racism as a stressor for African Americans. *American Psychologist* 54:805–816.

Clayton, R. R. (1992). Transitions in drug use: risk and protective factors. In *Vulnerability to Drug Abuse*, ed. M. Glantz and R. Pickens, pp. 15–52. Washington, DC: American Psychological Association.

Cloninger, C. R. (1983). Genetic and environmental factors in the development of alcoholism. *Journal of Psychiatric Treatment and Evaluation* 5:487–496.

——— (1987). Neurogenic adaptive mechanisms in alcoholism. *Science* 236:410–416.

Cloninger, R., Bohman, M., and Sigvardsson, S. (1981). Inheritance of substance abuse: cross-fostering analysis of adopted men. *Archives of General Psychiatry* 38:861–867.

Cloninger, R., Sigvardsson, S., and Bohman, M. (1988). Childhood personality predicts alcohol abuse in young adults. *Clinical and Experimental Research in Alcoholism* 12:494–505.

Cloninger, C. R., Svrakic, D. M., and Przybeck, T. R. (1993). A psychobiological model of temperament and character. *Archives of General Psychiatry* 50:975–990.

Cohen, J. D., and Servan-Schreiber, D. (1993). A theory of dopamine function and its role in cognitive deficits in schizophrenia. *Schizophrenia Bulletin* 19:87.

Cohen, S. (1981). *The Substance Abuse Problems.* New York: Haworth.

Collins, R. L. (1993). Drinking restraint and risk for alcohol abuse. *Experimental and Clinical Psychopharmacology* 1:44–54.

Cone E. J. (1997). New developments in biological measures of drug prevalence. In *The Validity of Self-Reported Drug Use: Improving the Accuracy of Survey Estimates*, ed. L. Harrison and A. Hughes, pp. 108–130, National Institute on Drug Abuse (NIDA Research Monograph 167). Rockville, MD: National Institutes of Health.

Cone, E. J., Hillsgrove, M. J., Jenkins, A. J., et al. (1994). Sweat testing for heroin, cocaine, and metabolites. *Journal of the Annals of Toxicology* 18:298–305.

Conger, J. J. (1956). Alcoholism: theory, problem, and challenge. II. Reinforcement theory and the dynamics of alcoholism. *Quarterly Journal of Studies on Alcohol* 13:296–305.

Conners, G. J., Maisto, S. A., and Donovan, D. M. (1996). Conceptualizations of relapse: a summary of psychological and psychobiological models. *Addiction* 91(Suppl):S5–S13.

Cook, B. L., and Winokur, G. (1995). Complications: mental disorders. In *Encyclopedia of Drugs and Alcohol*, vol. 1, ed. J. H. Jaffe, pp. 295–300. New York: Macmillan.

Cook, C. C. H., and Gurling, H. M. D. (1991). Genetic factors in alcoholism. In *The Molecular Pathology of Alcoholism*, ed. T. N. Palmer, pp. 181–210. New York: Oxford University Press

Cook, P. J. (1995). Social costs of alcohol and drug abuse, In *Encyclopedia of Drugs and Alcohol*, ed. J. H. Jaffe, vol. 1, pp. 993–997. New York: Macmillan.

Cook, R. F., Bernstein, A. D., and Andrews, C. M. (1997). Assessing drug use in the workplace: a comparison of self-report, urinalysis, and hair analysis. In *The Validity of Self-Reported Drug Use: Improving the Accuracy of Survey Estimates*, ed. L. Harrison and A. Hughes, pp. 247–272, National Institute on Drug Abuse (NIDA Research Monograph 167). Rockville, MD: National Institutes of Health.

Corey, G., Corey, M. S., and Callanan, P. (1993). *Issues and Ethics in the Helping Professions*, 3rd ed. Pacific Grove, CA: Brooks/Cole.

Cornelius, J. R., Salloum, I. M., Mezzich, J., et al. (1995). Disproportionate suicidality in patients with comorbid major depression and alcoholism. *American Journal of Psychiatry* 152:358–364.

Corsini, R. J., and Wedding, D. (1995). *Current Psychotherpies*, 5th ed. Itasca, IL: F. E. Peacock.

Cox, W. M. (1987). Personality theory and research. In *Psychological Theories of Drinking and Alcoholism*, ed. H. T. Blane and K. E. Leonard, pp. 55–89. New York: Guilford.

Criqui, M. H. (1986). Alcohol consumption, blood pressure, lipids, and cardiovascular mortality. *Alcoholism* 10:564–569.

Crits-Christoph, P., and Siqueland, L. (1996). Psychosocial treatment for drug abuse. *American Journal of Psychiatry* 53:749–756.

Croop, R. S., Faulkner, E. B., and Labriola, D. F. (1997). The safety profile of naltrexone in the treatment of alcoholism. results from a multicenter usage study. Archives of General Psychiatry 54:1130–1135.

Daghestani, A. N., and Schnoll, S. H. (1994). Phencyclidine. In *Textbook of Substance Abuse Treatment*, ed. M. Galanter and H. D. Kleber, pp. 149–156. Washington, DC: American Psychiatric Press.

Daley, D. C. and Marlatt, G. A. (1997). Relapse prevention. In *Substance Abuse: A comprehensive Textbook*, 3rd ed., ed. J. H. Lowinson, P. Ruiz, R. B. Millman, and J. G. Langrod, pp. 458–467. Baltimore: Williams and Wilkins.

Daras, M. (1996). Neurological complications of cocaine. In Neurotoxicity and Neuropathology Associated with Cocaine Abuse, ed. M. D. Majewska, pp. 43–65 (NIDA Research Monograph No. 163). Washington, DC: US Government Printing Office.

Daras, M., Tuchman, A. J., Koppel, B. S., et al. (1994). Neurovascular complications of cocaine. Acta Neurologica Scandinavica 90:124–129.

Davison, G. C., and Neale, J. M. (1994). *Abnormal Psychology*, 6th ed. New York: Wiley.

Deci, E. L., and Ryan, R. M. (1987). The support of autonomy and the control of behavior. *Journal of Personality and Social Psychology* 53:1024–1037.

DeLeon, G. (1994). Therapeutic communities. In *Textbook of Substance Abuse Treatment*, ed. M. Galanter and H. D. Kleber, pp. 391–414. Washington, DC: American Psychiatric Press.

Dennis, M. L. (1998). Integrating research and clinical assessment: measuring client and program needs and outcomes in a changing service environment. Issue paper, pp. 1–15. Rockville, MD: National Institute on Drug Abuse Center for Health Services Research.

Derogatis, L. R. (1994). SCL-90-R. *Administration, Scoring, and Procedures Manual*, 3rd ed. Minneapolis, MN: National Computer Systems.

DeRubeis, R. J., and Crits-Christoph, P. (1998). Empirically supported individual and group psychological treatments for adult mental disorders. *Journal of Consulting and Clinical Psychology* 66:37–52.

DeVane, W. A., Dysartz, F. A. III, Johnson, M. R., et al. (1988). Determination and characterization of a cannabinoid receptor in rat brain. *Molecular Pharmacology* 34:605–613.

Devor, E. (1994). A developmental-genetic model of alcoholism: implications for genetic research. *Journal of Consulting and Clinical Psychology* 62:1108–1115.

DiCicco, L., Unterberger, H., and Mack, J. E. (1978). Confronting denial: an alcoholism intervention strategy. *Psychiatric Annals* 8:596–606.

DiClemente, C. C., Bellino, L. E., and Neavins, T. M. (1999). Motivation for change and alcoholism treatment. *Alcohol Research and Health* 23:86–92.

DiClemente, C. C., Fairhurst, S. K., and Piotrowski, N. A. (1995). Self-efficacy and addictive behaviors. In *Self-Efficacy, Adaptation, and Adjustment: Theory, Research, and Application*, ed. J. E. Maddux, pp. 109–141. New York: Plenum.

DiClemente, C. C., and Scott, C. W. (1997). Stages of change: interactions with treatment compliance and involvement. In *Beyond the Therapeutic Alliance: Keeping the Drug-Dependent Individual in Treatment*. National Institute on Drug Abuse, Monograph 165. Rockville, MD: National Institute on Drug Abuse.

DiNardo, P. A., Brown, T. A., and Barlow, D. H. (1994). *Anxiety Disorders Interview Schedule for DSM-IV (ADIS-IV)*. Albany, NY: Graywind.

Donovan, J. M. (1986). An etiologic model of alcoholism. *American Journal of Psychiatry* 143:1–11.

Doyle-Pita, D. (1994). *Addictions Counseling: A Practical Guide to Counseling People with Chemical and Other Addictions*. New York: Crossroad.

Drug Enforcement Administration (1997a). *Crime, Violence, and Demographics*. DEA Briefing Book, U.S. Department of Justice. Arlington, VA: Author.

——— (1997b). *Federal Trafficking Penalties*. DE Publication: Drugs of Abuse. Arlington, V⁄ Author.

Drummond, D. C., Tiffany, S. T., Glautier, S., an⁄ Remington, R. (1995). *Addictive Behavior: C⁄ Exposure Theory and Practice*. New York: Wile⁄

Duncan, T. C., Duncan, S. C., and Hops, H. (1996 The role of parents and older siblings in predic⁄ ing adolescent substance use: Modeling deve⁄ opment via structural equation latent growt⁄ methodology. *Journal of Family Psycholog⁄* 10:158–172.

DuPont, R. L. (1984). *Getting Tough on Gatewa⁄ Drugs: A Guide for the Family*. Washington, D⁄ American Psychiatric Press.

——— (1997). *The Selfish Brain: Learning from A⁄ diction*. Washington, DC: American Psychiatr⁄ Press.

Dupont, R. L., and Saylor, K. E. (1991). Sedative hypnotics and benzodiazepines. In *Clinic⁄ Textbook of Addictive Disorders*, ed. R. J. France⁄ and S. I. Miller. New York: Guilford.

Durkheim, E. (1897). *Suicide*. New York: Fre⁄ Press, 1966.

Edwards, R. (1996). Drug use trends among el⁄ ementary school children. *News and Views*, 1 3. RMBSI, Inc., Spring.

Ellickson, P., Hays, R., and Bell, R. (1992). Steppin⁄ through the drug use sequence: longitudina⁄ scalogram analysis of initiation and regula⁄ use. *Journal of Consulting and Clinical Psycholog⁄* 101:441–451.

Ellinwood, E. H., and King, G. R. (1995). Cause⁄ of substance abuse: drug effects and biologica⁄ responses. In *Encyclopedia of Drugs and Alcoho⁄* vol. 1, ed. J. H. Jaffe, pp. 195–204. New York Macmillan.

Ellis, A. (1962). *Reason and Emotion in Psycho⁄ therapy*. New York: Lyle Stuart.

——— (1995). Rational emotive behavior therapy In *Current Psychotherapies*, 5th ed., ed. R. J Corsini and D. Wedding, pp. 162–196. Itasca⁄ IL: F. E. Peacock.

Ellis, D. A., Zucker, R. A., and Fitzgerald, H. E (1997). The role of family influences in develop⁄ ment and risk. In *Alcohol Health and Researc⁄ World* 21:218–226 (NIH Publication No. 98-3466). Washington, DC: US Government Print⁄ ing Office.

Emmelkamp, P. M. G. (1994). Behavior therapy with adults. In *Handbook of Psychotherapy an⁄ Behavior Change*, 4th ed., ed. A. E. Bergin and S. L. Garfield, pp. 379–427. New York⁄ Wiley.

Emrick, C. D. (1994). Alcoholics Anonymous and other 12-Step groups. In *Textbook of Substance Abuse Treatment*, ed. M. Galanter and H. D⁄ Kleber, pp. 351–358. Washington, DC: American Psychiatric Press.

Errico, A. L., Nixon, S. J., Parsons, O. A., and⁄ Tassey, J. (1997). Screening for neuropsychological impairment in alcoholics. In *Addictive Behaviors. Readings on Etiology, Prevention, and Treatment*, ed. G. A. Marlatt and G. R. VandenBos, pp. 309–322. Washington DC: American Psychological Association.

Ewing, J. A. (1984). Detecting alcoholism: the CAGE questionnaire. *Journal of the American Medical Association* 252:1905–1907.

Exner, J. E. (1986). *The Rorschach: A Comprehensive System*, vol. 1, 2nd ed. New York: Wiley.

Fackelmann, K. A. (1993). Marijuana and the brain. *Science* 143:88–94.

Fergusson, D. M., Horwood, L. J., and Beautrais, A. L. (1999). Is sexual orientation related to mental health problems and suicidality in young people? *Archives of General Psychiatry* 56:876–880.

Fils-Aime, M.-L., Eckardt, M. J., George, D. T., et al. (1996). Early-onset alcoholics have lower cerebrospinal fluid 5-hydroxyindoleacetic acid levels than late-onset alcoholics. *Archives of General Psychiatry* 53:211–216.

Finn, P. R., Kessler, D. N., and Hussong, A. M. (1994). Risk for alcoholism and classical conditioning to signals for punishment: Evidence for a weak behavioral inhibition system? *Journal of Abnormal Psychology* 103:293–301.

Finn, P. R., and Pihl, R. O. (1987). Men at high risk for alcoholism: the effect of alcohol on cardiovascular response to unavoidable shock. *Journal of Abnormal Psychology* 96:230–236.

Finn, P. R., Sharkansky, E. J., Viken, R., et al. (1997). Heterogeneity in the families of sons of alcoholics: the impact of familial vulnerability type on offspring characteristics. *Journal of Abnormal Psychology* 106:26–36.

Finney, J. W., Hahn, A. C., and Moors, R. H. (1996). The effectiveness of inpatient and outpatient treatment for alcohol abuse. *Addiction* 91:1773–1796.

First, M. B., Gibbon, M., Spitzer, R. L., and Williams, J. B. W. (1997a). *Structured Clinical Interview for DSM-IV Axis I Disorders: Clinical Version (SCDI-I)*. Washington, DC: American Psychiatric Press.

——— (1997b). *Structured Clinical Interview for DSM-IV Axis II Personality Disorders (SCDI-II)*. Washington, DC: American Psychiatric Press.

Fitzgerald, H. E., Zucker, R. A., and Yang, H.-Y. (1995). Developmental systems theory and alcoholism: analyzing patterns of variation in high risk families. *Psychology of Addictive Behaviors* 9:8–22.

Flaum, M., and Schultz, S. K. (1996). When does amphetamine-induced psychosis become schizophrenia? *American Journal of Psychiatry* 153:812–815.

Flewelling, R. L., Rachal, J. V., and Marsden, M. E. (1992). Socioeconomic and demographic correlates of drug and alcohol use. *Findings from the 1988 and 1990 National Household Sur-vey on Drug Abuse*. Rockville, MD: National Institute on Drug Abuse.

Fox, C. L. and Forbing, S. C. (1991). Overlapping symptoms of substance abuse and learning handicaps: implications for educators. *Journal of Learning Disabilities* 24:24–31.

Foy, A., March, S., and Drinkwater, V. (1988). Use of an objective clinical scale in the assessment and management of alcohol withdrawal in a large general hospital. *Alcoholism: Clinical and Experimental Research* 12:360–364.

Frances, R., Franklin, J., and Borg, L. (1994). Psychodynamics. In *American Psychiatric Press Textbook of Substance Abuse Treatment*, ed. M. Galanter and H. D. Kleber, pp. 239–251. Washington, DC: American Psychiatric Press.

Franceschi, S., Talamini, R., Barra, S., et al. (1990). Smoking and drinking in relation to cancers of the oral cavity, pharynx, larynx, and esophagus in northern Italy. *Cancer Research* 50:6502–6507.

Freud, S. (1912). Recommendations to physicians practicing psychoanalysis. *Standard Edition* 12:109–120.

——— (1913). On beginning the treatment. *Standard Edition* 12:121–144.

——— (1921). Group psychology and the analysis of the ego. *Standard Edition* 18:65–144.

Freud, S., and Breuer, J. (1895). Studies on hysteria. *Standard Edition* 2:1–318.

Freund, G., and Ballinger, W. E., Jr. (1988). Loss of cholinergic muscarinic receptors in the frontal cortex of alcohol abusers. *Alcoholism* 12:630–638.

Friedland, G. (1991). Natural history of HIV infection in gay men and intravenous drug users. In *Longitudinal Studies of HIV Infection in Intravenous Drug Users*, ed. P. Hartsock and S. G. Genser (NIDA Research Monograph 109, DHHS Publication No. [ADM] 91-1786). Washington, DC: US Government Printing Office.

Fromm, E. (1941). *Escape from Freedom*. New York: Rinehart.

Fuller, R. K., and Hiller-Sturmhoffel, S. (1999). Alcoholism treatment in the United States. *Alcohol Research and Health* 23:69–77.

Gabel, S., and Schindledecker R. (1993). Parental substance abuse and its relationship to severe aggression and antisocial behavior in youth. *American Journal on Addictions* 2:48–58.

Gabriel, K., Hofmann, C., Glavas, M., and Weinberg, J. (1998). The hormonal effects of alcohol use on the mother and fetus. *Alcohol Health and Research World* 22:170–177.

Galanter, M., Castaneda, R., and Franco, H. (1991). Group therapy and self-help groups. In *Clinical Textbook of Addictive Disorders*, ed. R. J. Frances and S. I. Miller, pp. 431–451. New York: Guilford.

Gallant, D. (1994). Alcohol. In *Textbook of Substance Abuse Treatment* ed. M. Galanter and H. D.

Kleber, pp. 67–90. Washington, DC: American Psychiatric Press.

Garofalo, R., Wolf, R. C., Wissow, L. S., and Goodman, E. (1999). Sexual orientation and risk of suicide attempts among a representative sample of youth. *Archives of Pediatric and Adolescent Medicine* 153:487–493.

Gawin, F. H. (1991). Cocaine addiction: psychology and neurophysiology. *Science* 251:1580–1586.

Gawin, F. H., Khalsa, M. E., and Ellinwood, Jr. (1994). Stimulants. In *Textbook of Substance Abuse Treatment*, ed. M. Galanter and H. D. Kleber, pp. 111–140. Washington, DC: American Psychiatric Press.

Gawin, F. H., and Kleber, H. D. (1986). Abstinence symptomatology and psychiatric diagnosis in cocaine abusers. *Archives of General Psychiatry* 43:107–113.

Gelernter, J., Goldman, D., and Risch, N. (1993). The A1 allele at the D2 dopamine receptor gene and alcoholism. *Journal of the American Medical Association* 269:1673–1677.

George, F. R., and Ritz, M. C. (1993). A psychopharmacology of motivation and reward related to substance abuse treatment. *Experimental and Clinical Psychopharmacology* 1:7–26.

Gerstein, D. R., Johnson, R. A., Harwood, H. J., et al. (1994). *Evaluating Recovery Services: The California Drug and Alcohol Treatment Assessment General Report.* Sacramento, CA: California Department of Alcohol and Drug Programs.

Gianoulakis, C., Krishnan, B., and Tharundayil, J. (1996). Enhanced sensitivity of pituitary ß-endorphins to ethanol in subjects at high risk of alcoholism. *Archives of General Psychiatry* 53:250–257.

Glantz, M. (1992). A developmental psychopathology model of drug abuse vulnerability. In *Vulnerability to Drug Abuse*, ed. M. Glantz and R. Pickens, pp. 389–418. Washington, DC: American Psychological Association.

Glantz, M., and Pickens, R. W., eds. (1992). Vulnerability to drug abuse: introduction and overview. In *Vulnerability to Drug Abuse*, pp. 1–14. Washington, DC: American Psychological Association.

Gold, M. S. (1997). Cocaine (and crack): clinical aspects. In *Substance Abuse: A Comprehensive Textbook*, 3rd ed., ed. J. H. Lowinson, P. Ruiz, R. B. Millman, and J. G. Langrod, pp. 181–189. Baltimore, MD: Williams and Wilkins.

Golden, C. J., Purisch, A. D., and Hammeke, T. A. (1985). *Luria-Nebraska Neuropsychological Test Battery: Forms I and II (manual).* Los Angeles, CA: Western Psychological Services.

Golden, S. J., Khantzian, E. J., and McAuliffe, W. E. (1994). Group therapy. In *Textbook of Substance Abuse Treatment*, ed. M. Galanter and H. D. Kleber, pp. 303–314. Washington, DC: American Psychiatric Press.

Goldman, M. S., Brown, S. A., and Christiansen, B. A. (1987). Expectancy theory: thinking about drinking. In *Psychological Theories of Drinking and Alcoholism*, ed. H. T. Blane and K. E. Leonard, pp. 181–226. New York: Guilford.

Goldman, M. S., Brown, S. A., Christiansen, B. A., and Smith, G. T. (1991). Alcoholism and memory: broadening the scope of alcohol-expectancy research. *Psychological Bulletin* 110:137–146.

Goodwin, D. W. (1988). *Is Alcoholism Hereditary?* New York: Ballantine.

——— (1989). Alcoholism. In *Comprehensive Textbook of Psychiatry*, ed. H. I. Kaplan and B. J. Sadock, 5th ed., pp. 612–620. Baltimore: Williams and Wilkins.

Goodwin, D. W., and Warnock, J. K. (1991). Alcoholism: a family disease. In Clinical Textbook of Addictive Disorders, ed. R. J. Frances and S. I. Miller, pp. 485–500. New York: Guilford.

Gorodetzky, C. W. (1977). Detection of drugs of abuse in biological fluids. In *Handbook of Experimental Pharmacology*, ed. G. V. R. Born, O. Eichler, A. Farah, et al., pp. 319–323. Berlin: Springer-Verlag.

Gorski, T. T. (1989). *The Relapse/Recovery Grid.* Center City, MN: Hazelden.

Graham, J. R. (1990). *MMPI-2: Assessing Personality and Psychopathology.* New York: Oxford University Press.

Greenberg, L. S., Elliott, R. K., and Lietaer, G. (1994). Research on experiential psychotherapies. In S. L. Garfield, *Handbook of Psychotherapy and Behavior Change*, 4th ed., ed. A. E. Bergin, pp. 509–539. New York: Wiley.

Greene, R. I. (1980). *The MMPI: An Interpretive Manual.* New York: Grune and Stratton.

Gusfield, J. R. (1996). Moral passage: the symbolic process in public designations of deviance. In *Social Deviance: Readings in Theory and Research*, 2nd ed., ed. H. N. Pontell, pp. 196–206. Upper Saddle River, NJ: Prentice Hall.

Guydish, J., Werdegar, D., Sorenson, J. L., et al. (1998). Drug abuse day treatment: a randomized clinical trial comparing day and residential treatment programs. *Journal of Consulting and Clinical Psychology* 66:280–289.

Haley, J. (1976). *Problem-Solving Therapy.* San Francisco: Jossey/Bass.

——— (1984). *Ordeal Therapy: Unusual Ways to Change Behavior.* San Francisco: Jossey-Bass.

——— (1990). *Strategies of Psychotherapy*, 2nd ed. Rockville, MD: Triangle Press.

Halikas, J. A., Crosby, R. D., Pearson, V. L., et al. (1994). Psychiatric comorbidity in treatment-seeking cocaine abusers. *American Journal on Addictions* 3:25–35.

Hamilton, L. W., and Timmons, C. R. (1990). *Principles of Behavioral Pharmacology.* Englewood Cliffs, NJ: Prentice Hall.

Harden, P. W., and Pihl, R. O. (1995). Cognitive function, cardiovascular reactivity, and behavior in boys at high risk for alcoholism. *Journal of Abnormal Psychology* 104:94–103.

Harrison, L., and Hughes, A. (1997). Introduction—the validity of self-reported drug use: improving the accuracy of survey estimates. In *The Validity of Self-Reported Drug Use: Improving the Accuracy of Survey Estimates*, ed. L. Harrison and A. Hughes, pp. 1–16, National Institute on Drug Abuse (NIDA Research Monograph 167). Rockville, MD: National Institutes of Health.

Hartocollis, P. (1968). A dynamic view of alcoholism: drinking in the service of denial. *Dynamic Psychiatry* 2:173–182.

Hathaway, S. R., and McKinley, J. C. (1940). A multiphasic personality schedule (Minnesota): I. construction of the schedule. *Journal of Abnormal Psychology* 146:249–254.

Hawkins, G. C., Vera, M. I., Barnard, G. W., and Herkov, M. J. (1994). Patient–therapist sexual involvement: a review of clinical and research data. *Bulletin of the American Academy of Psychiatry and Law* 22:109–126.

Hawkins, J. D., Catalano, R. F., and Miller, J. Y. (1992). Risk and protective factors for alcohol and other drug problems in adolescence and early adulthood: implications for substance abuse prevention. *Psychological Bulletin*, 112:64–105.

Hayashida, M. (1998). An overview of outpatient and inpatient detoxification. Alcohol Health and Research World 22:44–46.

Hayashida, M., Alterman, A. I., McLellan, A. T., et al. (1989). Comparative effectiveness and costs of inpatient and outpatient detoxification of patients with mild-to-moderate alcohol withdrawal syndrome. *New England Journal of Medicine*, 320:358–364.

Helzer, J. E. (1987). Epidemiology of alcoholism. *Journal of Consulting and Clinical Psychology* 55:284–292.

Helzer, J. E., Burnam, A., and McEvoy, L. T. (1991). Alcohol abuse and dependence. In *Psychiatric Disorders in America*, ed. L. N. Rogers and D. A. Regier. New York: Free Press.

Hemphill, J. F., Hart, S. D., and Hare, R. D. (1994). Psychopathy and substance use. *Journal of Personality Disorders* 8:169–180.

Henriksson, M. M., Aro, H. M., Marttunen, M. J., et al. (1993). Mental disorders and comorbidity in suicide. *American Journal of Psychiatry* 150:935–940.

Herd, D. (1994). Predicting problem drinking among Black and White men: results from a national survey. *Journal of Studies on Alcohol* 55:61–71.

Herek, G. M., Gillis, J. R., and Cogan, J. C. (1999). Psychological sequelae of hate-crime victimization among lesbian, gay, and bisexual adults. *Journal of Consulting and Clinical Psychology* 67:945–951.

Hesselbrock, V. M., Myer, R. E., and Hesselbrock, M. N. (1992). Psychopathological and addictive disorders: the specific case of antisocial personality disorder. In *Addictive States*, ed. C. P. O'Brien and J. H. Jaffe, pp. 179–191. New York: Raven.

Higuchi, S., Matsushita, S., Murayama, M., et al. (1995). Alcohol and aldehyde dehydrogenase polymorphisms and the risk for alcoholism. *American Journal of Psychiatry* 152:1219–1221.

Hoffman, A. (1971). LSD discoverer disputes "chance" factor in finding. *Psychiatric News* 6:23–26.

Hoffman, F. (1994). Cultural applications of Alcoholics Anonymous to serve Hispanic populations. *The International Journal of Addictions* 29:445–460.

Hoffman, J. P., Brittingham, A., and Larison, C. (1996). *Drug Use among U.S. Workers: Prevalence and Trends by Occupation and Industry Categories.* Rockville, MD: SAMHSA Office of Applied Studies.

Holmes, D. S. (1997). *Abnormal Psychology*, 3rd ed. New York: Longman.

Hser, Y. I., Anglin, M. D., and Powers, K. (1993). A 24-year follow-up of California narcotics addicts. *Archives of General Psychiatry* 50:577–584.

Hughs, J., Smith, T. W., Kosterlitz, H. W., et al. (1975). Identification of two related pentapeptides from the brain with potent opiate antagonist activity. *Nature* 258:577–579.

Huizinga, D., Loeber, R., and Thornberry, T. P. (1994). *Urban Delinquency and Substance Abuse: Initial Findings. Research Summary.* Washington, DC: Office of Juvenile Justice and Delinquency Prevention.

Humes, D. L., and Humphrey, L. L. (1994). A multimethod analysis of families with a polydrug-dependent daughter or normal adolescent daughter. *Journal of Abnormal Psychology* 103:676–685.

Humphreys, K. (1999). Professional interventions that facilitate 12-step self-help group involvement. *Alcohol Research and Health* 23:93–98.

Humphreys, K., and Rappaport, J. (1993). From the community mental health movement to the war on drugs. *American Psychologist* 48:892–901.

Hyman, S. E., and Nestler, E. J. (1996). Initiation and adaptation: a paradigm for understanding psychotropic drug action. *American Journal of Psychiatry* 153:151–162.

Inciardi, J. A. (1994). HIV/AIDS among male, heterosexual, noninjecting drug users who exchange crack for sex. In *The Context of HIV Risk Among Drug Users and Their Sexual Partners*, ed., R. J. Battjes, Z. Sloboda, and W. C. Grace, pp. 26–39. NIDA Research Monograph 143 (NIH Publication No. 94–3750). Washington, DC: US Government Printing Office.

Inciardi, J. A., and Pottieger, A. E. (1991). Kids, crack, and crime. *Journal of Drug Issues* 21:257–270.

Institute of Medicine (1990). *Broadening the Base of Treatment for Alcohol Problems.* Washington, DC: National Academy Press.

Isenhart, C. E., and Silversmith, D. J. (1997). MMPI-2 response styles: generalization to alcoholism assessment. In *Addictive Behaviors: Readings on Etiology, Prevention, and Treatment,* ed. G. A. Marlatt and G. R. VandenBos, pp. 340–354. Washington DC: American Psychological Association.

Ito, T. A., Miller, N., and Pollack, V. E. (1997). Alcohol and aggression: a Meta-analysis on the moderating effects of inhibitory cues, triggering events, and self-focused attention. In *Addictive Behaviors: Readings in Etiology, Prevention, and Treatment,* ed. G. A. Marlatt and G. R. VandenBos. Washington, DC: American Psychological Association.

Jacob, T., Krahn, G. L., and Leonard, K. (1991). Parent–child interactions in families with alcoholic fathers. *Journal of Consulting and Clinical Psychology* 59:176–181.

Jacobs, B. L. (1987). How hallucinogens work. *American Scientist* 75:386–392.

Jacobson, E. (1938). *Progressive Relaxation.* Chicago: University of Chicago Press.

Jaffe, J. H. (1989a). Drug dependence: opioids, nonnarcotics, nicotine (tobacco), and caffeine. In *Comprehensive Textbook of Psychiatry,* 5th ed., vol. 1, ed. H. I. Kaplan and B. J. Sadock, pp. 642–685. Baltimore, MD: Williams and Wilkins.

——— (1989b). Psychoactive substance use disorders. In *Comprehensive Textbook of Psychiatry,* 5th ed., vol. 1, ed. H. I. Kaplan and B. J. Sadock, pp. 642–686. Baltimore, MD: Williams and Wilkins.

——— (1995a). *Encyclopedia of Drugs and Alcohol,* vol. 1. New York: Macmillan.

——— (1995b). Alcohol: history of drinking. In *Encyclopedia of Drugs and Alcohol,* vol. 1, ed. J. H. Jaffe, pp. 70–78. New York: Macmillan.

——— (1995c). Prohibition of alcohol. In *Encyclopedia of Drugs and Alcohol,* vol. 2, ed. J. H. Jaffe, pp. 885–888. New York: Macmillan.

——— (1997). Opiates: clinical aspects. In *Substance Abuse: A Comprehensive Textbook,* 2nd ed. ed. J. H. Lowinson, P. Ruiz, R. B. Millman, and J. G. Langrod, pp. 158–166. Baltimore, MD: Williams and Wilkins.

Jaffe, J. H., and Meyer, R. E. (1995). Disease concept of alcoholism and drug abuse. In *Encyclopedia of Drugs and Alcohol,* vol. 1, ed. J. H. Jaffe, pp. 367–375. New York: Macmillan.

Janis, I. L., and Mann, L. (1977). *Decision-Making: A Psychological Analysis to Conflict, Choice, and Commitment.* New York: Free Press.

Jansen, R. E., Fitzgerald, H. E., Ham, H. P., and Zucker, R. A. (1995). Pathways into risk: temperament and behavior problems in three- to five-year-old sons of alcoholics. *Alcoholism: Clinical and Experimental Research* 19:501–509.

Jellinek, E. M. (1946). *Phases in the Drinking History of Alcoholics.* New Haven, CT: Hillhouse.

——— (1960). *The Disease Concept of Alcoholism.* Highland Park, NJ: Hillhouse.

Jessor, R. (1987). Problem-behavior theory, psychosocial development and adolescent problem drinking. *British Journal of Addictions* 82:331–342.

Jessor, R., Donovan, J. E., and Costa, F. M. (1991). *Beyond Adolescence: Problem Behavior and Young Adult Development.* New York: Cambridge University Press.

Jeste, D. V., Gladjso, J. A., Lindamer, L. A., and Lacro, J. (1996). Medical comorbidity in schizophrenia. *Schizophrenia Bulletin* 22:413–430.

Jimerson, D. C., Lesem, M. D., Kay, W. H., and Brewerton, T. D. (1992). Low serotonin and dopamine metabolite concentrations in cerebrospinal fluid from bulimic patients with frequent binge episodes. *Archives of General Psychiatry* 49:132–138.

Johnson, B. A., and Ait-Daoud, N. (1999). Medications to treat alcoholism. *Alcohol Research and Health* 23:99–106.

Johnson, B. D. and Muffler, J. (1997). Determinants and perpetuators of substance abuse: sociocultural. In *Substance Abuse: A Comprehensive Textbook,* 3rd ed., ed. J. H. Lowinson, P. Ruiz, R. B. Millman, and J. G. Langrod, pp. 107–117. Baltimore, MD: Williams and Wilkins.

Johnson, J. G., Hyler, S. E., Skodol, A. E., et al. (1995a). Personality disorder symptomatology associated with adolescent depression and substance abuse. *Journal of Personality Disorders* 9:318–329.

Johnson, J. G., Spitzer, R. L., Williams, J. B. W., et al. (1995b). Psychiatric comorbidity, health status, and functional impairment associated with alcohol abuse and dependence in primary care patients: findings of the PRIME MD-1000 Study. *Journal of Consulting and Clinical Psychology* 63:133–140.

Johnson, K. A., and Jennison, K. M. (1994). African-Americans: results of a national survey. *Journal of Alcohol and Drug Education* 39:1–24.

Johnston, L., Backman, J., and O'Malley, P. (1995). *Monitoring the Future Study.* Rockville, MD: National Institute on Drug Abuse.

Johnston, L. D., O'Malley, P. M., and Bachman, J. G. (1999). Drug trends in 1999 are mixed. *University of Michigan News and Information Services.* Ann Arbor, MI (online). Online at: www.monitoringthefuture.org; accessed 02-12-2000.

Jones, B. T., and McMahon, J. (1994). Negative alcohol expectancy predicts posttreatment abstinence survivorship: the whether, when, and why of relapse to a first drink. *Addiction* 89:1653–1665.

ıdd, P. H., and Ruff, R. M. (1993). Neuropsychological dysfunction in borderline personality disorder. *Journal of Personality Disorders* 7:275–284.

ıng, C. G. (1961). *C. G. Jung: Letters, vol. II, 1951–1961.* Princeton, NJ: Princeton University Press.

aczynski Pollock, N., and Martin, C. S. (1999). Diagnostic orphans: adolescents with alcohol symptoms who do not qualify for *DSM-IV* abuse or dependence diagnoses. *American Journal of Psychiatry* 156:897–901.

adden, R., Carroll, K., Donovan, D., et al. (1995). *National Institute on Alcohol Abuse and Alcoholism Project MATCH Monograph Series Volume 3: Cognitive-behavioral coping Skills Therapy Manual.* Rockville MD: National Institute on Alcohol Abuse and Alcoholism.

adden, R. M., Kranzler, H. R., and Rounsaville, B. J. (1995). Validity of the distinction between "substance-induced" and "independent" depression and anxiety disorders. *American Journal on Addictions* 4:107–117.

alat, J. W. (1992). *Biological Psychology*, 4th ed. Belmont, CA: Wadsworth.

—— (1998). *Biological Psychology*, 6th ed. Pacific Grove, CA: Wadsworth.

aminer, Y. (1991). Adolescent substance abuse. In *Clinical Textbook of Addictive Disorders*, ed. R. J. Francis and S. I. Miller, pp. 320–346. New York: Guilford.

——. (1994). Cocaine craving. *Journal of the American Academy of Child and Adolescent Psychiatry* 33:483–493.

aminer, Y., Bukstein, O., and Tarter, R. E. (1991). The Teen-Addiction Severity Index: rationale and reliability. *International Journal of Addictions* 26:219–226.

aminer, Y., Wagner, E., Plummer, B., and Seifer R. (1993). Validation of Teen Addiction Severity Index (T-ASI). preliminary findings. *American Journal on Addictions* 2:250–254.

andel, D. B. (1982). Epidemiological and psychosocial perspectives on adolescent drug use. *Journal of the American Academy of Child Psychiatry* 21:328–347.

—— (1984). Marijuana users in young adulthood. *Archives of General Psychiatry* 41:200–209.

—— (1996). The parental and peer contexts of adolescent deviance: an algebra of interpersonal influences. *Journal of Drug Issues* 26:289–315.

andel, D. B., and Davies, M. (1992). Progression to regular marijuana involvement: phenomenology and risk factors for near daily use. In *Vulnerability to Drug Abuse*, ed. M. Glantz and R. Pickens, pp. 211–254. Washington, DC: American Psychological Association.

andel, D. B., and Yamaguchi, K. (1993). From beer to crack: developmental patterns of drug involvement. *American Journal of Public Health* 83:851–855.

Kaplan, H. B. (1996). Empirical validation of the applicability of an integrative theory of deviant behavior to the study of drug use. *Journal of Drug Issues* 26:345–377.

Kaplan, H. B., and Johnson, R. J. (1992). Relationship between circumstances surrounding initial illicit drug use and escalation of drug use: moderating effects of gender and early adolescent experiences. In *Vulnerability to Drug Abuse*, ed. M. Glantz and R. Pickens, pp. 299–358. Washington, DC: American Psychological Association.

Karan, L. D., Haller, D. L., and Schnoll, S. H. (1991). Cocaine. In *Clinical Textbook of Addictive Disorders*, ed. R. J. Frances and S. I. Miller, pp. 121–145. New York: Guilford.

Karch, S. B. (1993). *The Pathology of Drug Abuse.* Boca Raton, FL: CRC Press.

Keefe, R. S. E. (1995). The contribution of neuropsychology to psychiatry. *American Journal of Psychiatry* 152:6–15.

Kendall, D. (1996). *Sociology in Our Times.* Belmont, MA: Wadsworth.

Kendler, K. S., Heath, A. C., Neale, M. C., et al. (1992). A population based twin study of alcoholism in women. *Journal of the American Medical Association* 268:1877–1882.

—— (1993). Alcoholism and major depression in women: a twin study of the causes of comorbidity. *Archives of General Psychiatry* 50:690–698.

Kendler, K. S., MacLean, C., Neale, M., et al. (1991). The genetic epidemiology of bulimia nervosa. *American Journal of Psychiatry* 148:1627–1637.

Kessler, R. C., Foster, C. L., Saunders, W. B., and Stang, P. E. (1995). Social consequences of psychiatric disorders, I: Educational attainment. *American Journal of Psychiatry* 152: 1026–1032.

Kessler, R. C., McGonagle, K. A., Zhao, S., et al. (1994). Lifetime and 12-month prevalence of *DSM-III-R* psychiatric diagnosis in the U.S. *Archives of General Psychiatry* 51:8–19.

Khantzian, E. J. (1985). The self-medication hypothesis of addictive disorders: focus on heroin and cocaine dependence. *American Journal of Psychiatry* 142:1259–1264.

Khantzian, E. J. (1995). Causes of substance abuse: Psychological (psychoanalytic) perspective. In *Encyclopedia of Drugs and Alcohol*, vol. 1, ed. J. H. Jaffe, pp. 211–216. New York: Macmillan.

Khantzian, E. J., Halliday, K. S., Golden, S., and McAuliffe, W. E. (1992). Modified group therapy for substance abusers: a psychodynamic approach to relapse prevention. *American Journal on Addictions* 1:67–76.

Khantzian, E. J., Halliday, K. S., and McAuliffe, W. E. (1990). *Addiction and the Vulnerable Self: Modified Dynamic Group Therapy for Substance Abusers.* New York: Guilford.

Kierkegaard, S. (1843). *Fear and Trembling and the Sickness Unto Death*, (trans. W. Lowrie.) Garden City, NY: Doubleday, 1954.

Kilbey, M. M. and Asghar, K. (1991). Preface. In *Methodological Issues in Controlled Studies on Effects of Prenatal Exposure to Drug Abuse*, ed. M. M. Kilbey and K. Asghar, pp. iii–iv, (NIDA Research Monograph 114, DHHS Publication No. ADM 91-1837). Washington, DC: US Government Printing Office.

Kiyaani, M. (1997). On the peyote road. *Natural History* March, pp. 48–49.

Klatsky, A. L. (1987). The cardiovascular effects of alcohol. *Alcohol and Alcoholism* 22(Supplement):117–124.

Kleber, H. D. (1994). Opioids: Detoxification. In *Textbook of Substance Abuse Treatment*, ed. M. Galanter and H. D. Kleber, pp. 191–208. Washington, DC: American Psychiatric Press.

Klygis, L. M., and Barch, D. H. (1992). The role of ethanol in esophageal carcinoma. In *Alcohol and Cancer*, ed. R. R. Watson, pp. 73–79. Boca Raton, FL: CRC Press.

Koester, S., Booth, R., and Wayne, W. (1990). The risk of transmission from sharing water, drug mixing containers, and cotton filters among intravenous drug users. *International Journal of Drug Policy* 1:28–30.

Kosofsky, B. E. (1991). The effect of cocaine on the developing human brain. In *Methodological Issues in Controlled Studies on Effects of Prenatal Exposure to Drug Abuse*, ed. M. M. Kilbey and K. Asghar, pp. 128–143. (NIDA Research Monograph 114, DHHS Publication No. ADM 91-1837). Washington, DC: US Government Printing Office.

Kosten, T. A., Ball, S. A., and Rounsaville, B. J. (1994). A sibling study of sensation seeking and opiate addiction. *The Journal of Nervous and Mental Disease* 182:284–289.

Kottler, J. A., and Brown, R. W. (1992). *Introduction to Therapeutic Counseling*, 2nd ed. Pacific Grove, CA: Brooks/Cole.

Kranzler, H. R., and Anton, R. F. (1994). Implications of recent neuropharmacological research for understanding the etiology and development of alcoholism. *Journal of Consulting and Clinical Psychology* 62:1116–1126.

Kreek, M. J. and Koob, G. F. (1998). Drug dependence: stress and dysregulation of brain reward pathways. *Drug and Alcohol Dependence* 51:23–47.

Krug, S. E. (1980). *Clinical Analysis Questionnaire Manual. Champaign*, IL: Institute for Personality and Ability Testing.

Krystal, H., and Raskin, H. A. (1976). *Drug Dependence: Aspects of Ego Function*. New York: Jason Aronson.

Kushner, M. G., Sher, K. J., and Beitman, B. D. (1990). The relation between alcohol problems and the anxiety disorders. *American Journal of Psychiatry* 147:685–695.

Kwapil, T. R. (1996). A longitudinal study of drug and alcohol use by psychosis-prone and impulsive-nonconforming individuals. *Journal of Abnormal Psychology* 105:114–123.

Lambert, M. L., and Bergin, A. E. (1994). The effectiveness of psychotherapy. In *Handbook of Psychotherapy and Behavior Change*, ed. A. E. Bergin and S. L. Garfield, pp. 143–189. New York: Wiley.

Lang, A. R. (1983). Addictive personality: A viable construct? In *Commonalities in Substance Abuse and Habitual Behavior*, ed. P. K. Levinson, D. R. Gerstein, and D. R. Maloff, pp. 132–149. Lexington, MA: Lexington Books.

Lavelle, T., Hammersby, R., and Forsyth, A. (1993). Is the "addictive personality" merely delinquency? *Addiction Research* 1:27–37.

Laws, D. R. (1995). A theory of relapse prevention. In *Theories of Behavior Therapy: Exploring Behavior Change*, ed. W. O'Donohue and L. Krasner, pp. 445–473. Washington DC: American Psychological Association.

Lawson, G. W., Ellis, D. C., and Rivers, P. C. (1984). *Essentials of Chemical Dependency Counseling*. Rockville, MD: Aspen.

Lazarus, A. A., and Beutler, L. E. (1993). On technical eclecticism. *Journal of Counseling and Development* 71:381–385.

Lazarus, R. S., and Folkman, S. (1984). *Stress, Appraisal, and Coping*. New York: Springer.

LeBon, G. (1895). *Psychologie des Foules* Paris: Alcan. [*The Crowd: A Study of the Popular Mind* trans. R. Meton. London: Unwin, 1920.]

Lechtenberg, R. (1982). *The Psychiatrist's Guide to Diseases of the Nervous System*. New York: Wiley.

Leigh, B. C., and Stall, R. (1993). Substance use and risky sexual behavior for exposure to HIV *American Psychologist* 48:1035–1045.

Leino, E. V. Ager, C. R., Fillmore, K. M., and Johnstone, B. M. (1995). Meta-analysis of multiple longitudinal studies from the collaborative alcohol-related longitudinal project. *American Journal on Addictions* 4:141–149.

Leon, R. L., Bowden, C. L., and Faber, R. A. (1989) Diagnosis and psychiatry. In *Comprehensive Textbook of Psychiatry*, ed. H. I. Kaplan and B. J Sadock, 5th ed., pp. 449–467. Baltimore: Williams and Wilkins.

Lerner, R. M., Villarruel, F. A., and Tubman, J. G (1994). Assumptions and features of longitudinal designs: implications for etiological linkages. In *The Development of Alcohol Problems Exploring the Biopsychosocial Matrix of Risk*, ed R. A. Zucker, G. Boyd, and J. Howard, pp. 399–425. Rockville, MD: National Institute on Alcohol Abuse and Alcoholism.

Les, B. (1985). Alcohol problems in special populations. In *The Diagnosis and Treatment of Alcoholism*, ed. J. H. Mendelson and N. K. Mello 2nd ed., pp. 89–188. New York: McGraw-Hill

Leshner, A. I. (1997). Addiction is a brain disease, and it matters. *Science* 278:45–47.

Leukefeld, C. G. and Tims, F. M. (1989). Relapse and recovery in drug abuse: research and practice. *International Journal of the Addictions* 24:189–201.

Levin, J. D. (1987). *Treatment of Alcoholism and Other Addictions: A Self-Psychology Approach.* Northvale, NJ: Jason Aronson.

——— (1990). *Alcoholism: A Bio-Psycho-Social Approach.* New York: Hemisphere.

——— (1995). *Introduction to Alcoholism Counseling: A Bio-Psychosocial Approach,* 2nd ed., Washington, DC: Taylor and Francis.

Levine, S. R., Brust, J. C. M., Futrell, N., et al. (1990). Cerebrovascular complications of the use of the "crack" form of alkaloid cocaine. *New England Journal of Medicine* 323:699–704.

Lewinsohn, P. M., Hops, H., Roberts, R. E., et al. (1993). Adolescent psychopathology: I. Prevalence and incidence of depression and other *DSM-III-R* disorders in high school students. *Journal of Abnormal Psychology* 102:133–144.

Lex, B. W. (1985). Alcohol problems in special populations. In *The Diagnosis and Treatment of Alcoholism,* 2nd ed., ed. J. H. Mendelson and N. K. Mello, pp. 89–187. New York: McGraw-Hill.

Lillie-Blanton, M., and Arria, A. (1995). Ethnicity and drugs. In *Encyclopedia of Drugs and Alcohol,* vol. 1, ed. J. H. Jaffe, pp. 471–474. New York: Macmillan.

Ling, W., Wesson, D. R., Charuvastra, C., and Klett, C. J. (1996). A controlled trial comparing buprenorphine and methadone maintenance in opioid dependence. *Archives of General Psychiatry* 53:401–407.

Linnoila, M., DeJong, J., and Virkkunen, M. (1989). Monoamines, glucose metabolism, and impulse control. *Psychopharmacology Bulletin* 25:404–406.

Linnoila, M., Virkkunen, M., Scheinen, M., et al. (1983). Low cerebrospinal fluid 5-hydroxyindolacetic acid concentration differentiates impulsive from nonimpulsive violent behavior. *Life Science* 33:2609–2614.

Linszen, D. H., Dingemans, P. M., and Lenior, M. E. (1994). Cannabis abuse and the course of recent-onset schizophrenic disorders. *Archives of General Psychiatry* 51:273–279.

Liskow, B., Samuelson, S., Powell, B., and Campbell, J. (1995). Co-occurrence of psychiatric disorders and alcoholism in untreated alcoholic patients in a VA medical walk-in (triage) clinic population. *American Journal on Addictions* 4:150–155.

Litt, M. D., Babor, T. F., DelBoca, F. K., et al. (1992). Types of alcoholics, II: Application of an empirically derived typology to treatment matching. *Archives of General Psychiatry* 49:609–614.

Liu, X., and Kaplan, H. B. (1996). Gender-related differences in circumstances surrounding initiation and escalation of alcohol and other substance use/abuse. *Deviant Behavior* 17:71–106.

Loeber, R. (1991). Questions and advances in the study of developmental pathways. In *Models and Integrations: Rochester Symposium on Developmental Psychopathology,* vol. 3, ed. D. Cicchetti and S. L. Toth, pp. 97–116. Rochester, NY: University of Rochester Press.

London, E. D., Cascella, N. G., Wong, D. F., et al. (1990). Cocaine-induced reduction of utilization in the human brain. *Archives of General Psychiatry* 47:567–574.

Longabaugh, R., and Morgenstern, J. (1999). Cognitive-behavioral coping skills therapy for alcohol dependence. *Alcohol Research and Health* 23:78–85.

Lyng, S. (1990). Edgework: a social psychological analysis of voluntary risk-taking. *American Journal of Sociology* 95:851–886.

Lynskey, M. T., and Fergusson, D. M. (1995). Childhood conduct problems, attention deficit behaviors, and adolescent alcohol, tobacco, and illicit drug use. *Journal of Abnormal Child Psychology* 23:281–302.

Lyvers, M. (1998). Drug addiction as a physical disease: the role of physical dependence and other chronic drug-induced neurophysiological changes in compulsive drug self-administration. *Experimental and Clinical Psychopharmacology* 6:107–125.

MacAndrew, C., and Geertsma, R. H. (1963). Analysis of responses of alcoholics to Scale 4 of the MMPI. *Quarterly Journal of Studies on Alcohol* 26:23–38.

Mackinnon, R. A., and Yudofsky, S. C. (1986). *The Psychiatric Evaluation in Clinical Practice.* Philadelphia: Lippincott.

Maddux, J. E. (1995). Self-efficacy theory: an introduction. In *Self-Efficacy, Adaptation, and Adjustment: Theory, Research, and Application,* ed. J. E. Maddux, pp. 3–33. New York: Plenum.

Magee, W. J., Eaton, W. W., Wittchen, H.-U., et al. (1996). Agoraphobia, simple phobia, and social phobia in the National Comorbidity Study. *Archives of General Psychiatry* 53:159–168.

Maher, J. J. (1997). Exploring alcohol's effects on liver function. *Alcohol World Health and Research* 21:5–12.

Main, M. (1996). Introduction to the special section on attachment and psychopathology:2. Overview of the field of attachment. *Journal of Consulting and Clinical Psychology* 64:237–243.

Majewska, M. D. (1996). Cocaine addiction as a neurological disorder: implications for treatment. In *Neurotoxicity and Neuropathology Associated with Cocaine Abuse,* ed. M. D. Majewska, pp. 1–26. (NIDA Research Monograph 163, NIH Publication No. 96-4019). Washington, DC: US Government Printing Office.

Malinowsky-Rummell, R., and Hansen, D. J. (1993). Long-term consequences of childhood physical abuse. *Psychological Bulletin* 114:68–79.

Manderscheid, R. W., Rae, D. S., Narrow, W. E., et al. (1993). Congruence of service utilization estimates from the epidemiologic catchment area project and other sources. *Archives of General Psychiatry* 50:108–114.

Manning, W. G. (1991). *The Costs of Poor Health Habits*. Cambridge, MA: Harvard University Press.

Markou, A., Weiss, F., Gold, L. H., et al. (1993). Animal models of drug craving. *Psychopharmacology* 112:163–182.

Marlatt, G. A. (1996). Taxonomy of high-risk situations for alcohol relapse: evolution and development of a cognitive-behavioral model. *Addiction* 91(Suppl):S37–S49.

Marlatt, G. A., Baer, J. S., Donovan, D. M., and Kivlahan, D. R. (1988). Addictive behaviors: etiology and treatment. *Annual Review of Psychology* 39:223–252.

Marlatt, G. A. and Barrett, K. (1994). Relapse prevention. In *American Psychiatric Press Textbook of Substance Abuse Treatment*, ed. M. Galanter and H. Kleber, pp. 285–299. Washington, DC: American Psychiatric Press.

Marlatt, G. A. and Gordon, J. R. (1985). *Relapse Prevention: Maintenance Strategies in the Treatment of Addictive Behaviors*. New York: Guilford.

Marlowe, D. B., Husband, S. D., Lamb, R. J., et al. (1995). Psychiatric comorbidity in cocaine dependence: diverging trends, Axis II spectrum, and gender differentials. *American Journal on Addictions* 4:70–81.

Martin, C. S., and Winters, K. C. (1998). Diagnosis and assessment of alcohol use disorders among adolescents. *Alcohol Health and Research World* 22:95–106. (NIH Publication No. 98-3466.) Washington, DC: US Government Printing Office.

Mason, B. J., Salvato, F. R., Williams, L. D., et al. (1999). A double-blind, placebo-controlled study of oral nalmefene for alcohol dependence. *Archives of General Psychiatry* 56:719–724.

May, R. (1953). *Man's Search for Himself*. New York: Norton.

May, R., and Yalom, I. (1995). Existential psychotherapy. In *Current Psychotherapies*, 5th ed., ed. R. J. Corsini and D. Wedding, pp. 262–292. Itasca, IL: F. E. Peacock.

McCrady, B. S. (1994). Alcoholics Anonymous and behavior therapy: Can habits be treated as diseases? Can diseases be treated as habits? *Journal of Consulting and Clinical Psychology* 62:1159–1166.

McCrady, B. S., and Langenbucher, J. W. (1996). Alcohol treatment and health care system reform. *Archives of General Psychiatry* 53:737–746.

McCrady, B. S., and Miller, W. R., eds. (1993). *Research on Alcoholics Anonymous. Opportunities and Alternatives*. New Brunswick, NJ: Rutgers Center for Alcohol Studies.

McDermott, P. A., Alterman, A. I., Brown, L., et al. (1997). Construct refinement and confirmation for the addiction severity index. In *Addictive Behaviors. Readings on Etiology, Prevention, and Treatment*, ed. G. A. Marlatt and G. R. VandenBos, pp. 323–339. Washington DC: American Psychological Association.

McDougall, W. (1920). *The Group Mind*. Cambridge, England: Cambridge University Press.

McGue, M. (1997). A behavioral-genetic perspective on children of alcoholics. In *Alcohol Health and Research World* 21:210–217 (NIH Publication No. 98-3466). Washington, DC: U.S. Government Printing Office.

McGue, M., Pickens, R. W., and Svikis, D. S. (1992). Sex and age effects on the inheritance of alcohol problems: a twin study. *Journal of Abnormal Psychology* 101:3–17.

McKay, J. R. (1999). Studies of factors in relapse to alcohol, drug and nicotine use: a critical review of methodologies and findings. *Journal of Studies on Alcohol* 60:566–576.

McLellan, A. T., Alterman, A. I., Metzger, D. S. et al. (1994). Similarity of outcome predictors across opiate, cocaine, and alcohol treatments: role of treatment services. *Journal of Consulting and Clinical Psychology* 62:1141–1158.

McLellan, A. T., Grissom, G. R., Zanis, D., et al. (1997). Prolem–service "matching" in addiction treatment. *Archives of General Psychiatry* 54:730–735.

McLellan, A. T., Kushner, H., Metzger, D., et al. (1992). The fifth edition of the *Addiction Severity Index*: historical critique and normative data. *Journal of Substance Abuse Treatment* 9:199–213.

McLellan, A. T., Luborsky, L., Woody, G. E., and O'Brien, C. P. (1980). An improved diagnostic evaluation instrument for substance abuse patients. *Journal of Nervous and Mental Disease* 168:26–33.

McLellan, A. T., Luborsky, L., Woody, G. E., et al. (1983). Predicting response to alcohol and drug abuse treatments: role of psychiatric severity. *Archives of General Psychiatry* 40:620–625.

Menninger, K. A. (1938). *Man Against Himself*. New York: Harcourt.

Mieczkowski, T., and Newel, R. (1997). Patterns of concordance between hair assays and urinalysis for cocaine: longitudinal analysis of probationers in Pinellas County. In *The Validity of Self-Reported Drug Use: Improving the Accuracy of Survey Estimates*, ed. L. Harrison and A. Hughes, pp. 161–199. National Institute on Drug Abuse (NIDA Research Monograph 167). Rockville, MD: National Institutes of Health.

Milby J. B., Hohmann, A. A., Gentile, et al. (1994). Methadone maintenance as a function of detoxification phobia. *American Journal of Psychiatry* 151:1031–1037.

Miller, A. C. (1981). *Drama of the Gifted Child*. New York: Basic Books.

Miller, M. L., Donnely, B., and Martz, R. M. (1997). The forensic application of testing hair for drugs of abuse. In *The Validity of Self-Reported Drug Use: Improving the Accuracy of Survey Estimates*, ed. L. Harrison and A. Hughes, pp. 146–160, National Institute on Drug Abuse (NIDA Research Monograph 167). Rockville, MD: National Institutes of Health.

Miller, W. R. (1985). Motivation for treatment: a review with special emphasis on alcoholism. *Psychological Bulletin* 98:84–107.

——— (1996). Form 90. A structured assessment interview for drinking and related behaviors. *National Institute on Alcohol Abuse and Alcoholism. Project Match Monograph Series. National Institute of Health Monograph Series* (NIH Publication No. 96-4004). Bethesda, MD:National Institute on Alcohol Abuse and Alcoholism.

Miller, W. R., Benfield, R. G., and Tonigan, J. S. (1993). Enhancing motivation for change in problem drinking: a controlled comparison of two therapist styles. *Journal of Consulting and Clinical Psychology* 61:455–461.

Miller, W. R., and Rollnick, S. (1991). *Motivational Interviewing: Preparing People to Change Addictive Behavior*. New York: Guilford.

Miller, W. R., and Tonigan, J. S. (1997). Assessing drinkers' motivation for change: the stages of change readiness and treatment eagerness scale (SOCRATES). In *Addictive Behaviors. Readings on Etiology, Prevention, and Treatment*, ed. G. A. Marlatt and G. R. VandenBos, pp. 355–369. Washington DC: American Psychological Association.

Miller, W. R., Zweben, A., DiClemente, C. C., and Rychtarik, R. G. (1999). *Motivational Enhancement Therapy Manual. A Clinical Research Guide for Therapists Treating Individuals with Alcohol Abuse and Dependence*. (NIH Publication No. 94-3723.) Rockville, MD: National Institute on Alcohol Abuse and Alcoholism.

Millman, R. B., and Beeder, A. B. (1994). Cannabis. In *Textbook of Substance Abuse Treatment*, ed. M. Galanter and H. D. Kleber, pp. 91–109. Washington, DC: American Psychiatric Press.

Millon, T. (1986). The MCMI and the *DSM-III*: further commentaries. *Journal of Personality Assessment* 50:205–207.

Minuchin, S. (1992). Constructing a therapeutic reality. In *Family Therapy of Drug and Alcohol Abuse*, 2nd ed., ed. E. Kaufman and P. Kaufmann, pp. 1–14. Boston: Allyn and Bacon.

Minuchin, S., Montalvo, B. L., Guerney, B. G., Jr., et al. (1967). *Families of the Slums: An Exploration of Their Structure and Treatment*. New York: Basic Books.

Mirin, S. M., and Weiss, R. D. (1991). Substance abuse and mental illness. In *Clinical Textbook of Addictive Disorders*, ed. R. J. Francis and S. I. Miller, pp. 271–298. New York: Guilford.

Mirin, S. M., Weiss, R. D., and Michael, J. (1988). Psychopathology in substance abusers: diagnosis and treatment. *American Journal of Drug and Alcohol Abuse* 14:139–157.

Modesto-Lowe, V., and Kranzler, H. R. (1999). Diagnosis and treatment of alcohol-dependent patients with comorbid psychiatric disorders. *Alcohol Research and Health* 23:144–149.

Mohler, H., and Okada, T. (1977). Benzodiazepine receptor: demonstration in the nervous system. *Science* 198:849–851.

Monitoring The Future. (1999). Drug trends in 1999 among American teens are mixed [Press Release]. December 17. Online at www.monitoringthefuture.org

Monohan, J. (1992). Mental disorder and violent behavior. *American Psychologist* 47:511–521.

Morgenstern, J., Langenbucher, J., Labouvie, E., and Miller, K. J. (1997). The comorbidity of alcoholism and personality disorders in a clinical population: prevalence rates and relation to alcohol typology variables. *Journal of Abnormal Psychology* 106:74–84.

Moss, H. B., and Tartar, R. E. (1993). Substance abuse, aggression, and violence. What are the connections? *American Journal on Addictions* 2:149–160.

Moss, H. B., Yao, J. K., and Panzak, G. L. (1990). Serotonergic responsivity and behavioral dimensions in antisocial personality disorder with substance abuse. *Biological Psychiatry* 28:325–338.

Mueser, K., Bellack, A., and Blanchard, J. (1992). Comorbidity of schizophrenia and substance abuse: implications for treatment. *Journal of Consulting and Clinical Psychology* 60:845–856.

Mueser, K. T., Drake, R. E., and Miles, K. M. (1997). The course and treatment of substance use disorder in persons with severe mental illness. In *Treatment of Drug-Dependent Individuals with Comorbid Mental Disorders*, ed. L. S. Onken, J. D. Blane, S. Genser, and A. M. Horton, Jr., pp. 86–109 National Institute on Drug Abuse (NIH Publication No. 97-4172). Washington, DC: U.S. Government Printing Office.

Mulford, H. A. (1977). Stages in the alcoholic process toward a cumulative nonsequential index. *Journal of the Study of Alcohol* 38:563–583.

Murdoch, D. D., Pihl, R. O., and Ross, D. (1988). The influence of dose, beverage type, and sex of interactor on female bar patrons' verbal aggression. *International Journal on Addictions* 23:953–966.

Murray, H. A. (1943). *Thematic Apperception Test Manual*. Cambridge, MA: Harvard University Press.

Murray, J. B. (1993). Review of research on pathological gambling. *Psychological Reports* 72:791–810.

Musto, D. F. (1996). Alcohol in American history. *Scientific American*, April, pp. 78–83.

Nace, E. P., and Isbell, P. G. (1991). Alcohol. In *Clinical Textbook of Addictive Disorders*, ed. R. J. Frances and S. I. Miller, pp. 43–68. New York: Guilford.

Narrow, W. E., Regier, D. A., Rae, D. S., et al. (1993). Use of services by persons with mental and addictive disorders. Findings from the National Institute of Mental Health epidemiologic catchment area program. *Archives of General Psychiatry* 50:95–107.

National Association of Alcoholism and Drug Abuse Counselors (1995). Ethical standards of alcoholism and drug abuse counselors. National Association of Alcoholism and Drug Abuse Counselors *Code of Ethics*. Online at www.naadac.org

National Clearinghouse for Alcohol and Drug Information (1994). *ATOD Resource Guide: Lesbians, Gay Men, and Bisexuals*. Rockville, MD: Center for Substance Abuse Prevention, Substance Abuse and Mental Health Services Administration.

—— (1996a). Student use of most drugs reaches highest level in nine years—more report getting "very high, bombed, or stoned." *NCADI Press Release*, September 25.

—— (1996b). *Scientific American: Deaths Due to Alcohol*. Rockville, MD: Author.

—— (1996c). Meth, men, myths: increased risk in the gay community. *Prevention Online*, vol. 6, May/June.

—— (1997). *Making the Case for Prevention. A Discussion Paper on Preventing Alcohol, Tobacco, and other Drug Problems*. Rockville, MD: Author.

—— (1998). *Substance Dependence and Treatment*. Online at www.health.org.

—— (1999a). *1998 Household Survey on Drug Abuse*. Rockville, MD: Substance Abuse and Mental Health Services Administration.

—— (1999b). *Children of Alcoholics: Important Facts*. Rockville, MD: Author.

—— (2000). Any illicit drug use. *Prevention Online*, January 12, p. 3.

National Council on Alcoholism. (1976). Definition of alcoholism. *Annals of Internal Medicine* 85:764.

National Curriculum Committee of the Addiction Technology Transfer Center Program. (1995). *Addiction Counseling Competencies* (Technical Assistance Publication No. 21). La Jolla, CA: Center for Substance Abuse Treatment.

National Institute of Mental Health. (1998). *Suicide Facts*. Bethesda, MD: Author.

National Institute on Alcohol Abuse and Alcoholism. (1990). *Alcohol and Health, Seventh Special Report to the U.S. Congress*. Rockville, MD: Author.

—— (1992). *Alcohol and AIDS* (Alcohol Alert No. 15 PH 311). Rockville, MD: Author.

—— (1993a). *Alcohol and the Liver* (Alcohol Alert No. 19 PH 329). Rockville, MD: Author.

—— (1993b). *Alcohol and Cancer* (Alcohol Alert No. 21 PH 345). Rockville, MD: Author.

—— (1994). *Alcohol and Minorities* (Alcohol Alert No. 23, PH347). January, pp. 1–4.

—— (1995a). *Assessing Alcohol Problems: A Guide for Clinicians and Researchers*. NIAAA treatment handbook series 4. (NIH Publication No. 95-3745.) Washington, DC: US Government Printing Office.

—— (1995b). *Cognitive-Behavioral Coping Skills Therapy Manual. A Clinical Research Guide for Therapists Treating Individuals with Alcohol Abuse and Dependence* (NIH Publication No. 94-3724). Bethesda, MD: Author.

—— (1995c). *Twelve-Step Facilitation Therapy Manual: A Clinical Research Guide for Therapists Treating Individuals with Alcohol Abuse and Dependence* (NIH Publication No. 94-3722.) Bethesda, MD: Author.

—— (1995d). *The Physician's Guide to Helping Patients with Alcohol Problems* (NIH Publication No. 95-3769). Washington, DC: US Government Printing Office.

—— (1996a). Preventing Alcohol Abuse and Related Problems *Alcohol Alert* NIAA No. 34, PH 370.

—— (1996b). NIAAA reports Project MATCH main findings. December 17. Rockville MD: Author.

—— (1998a). Alcohol and aging *Alcohol Alert* NIAA No. 40. Washington, DC: US Government Printing Office.

—— (1998b). *Alcohol Use Among Special Populations*. (Alcohol World: Health and Research No. 22). Washington, DC: US Government Printing Office.

National Institute on Drug Abuse (1990). *Alcohol and Health*. Rockville, MD: Author.

—— (1991). Estimating the cost of alcohol abuse. *Alcohol Alert No. 11*, PH 293. Rockville, MD: Author.

—— (1993a). *Recovery Training and Self-Help: Relapse Prevention and Aftercare for Drug Addicts*. Rockville MD: Author.

—— (1993b). *Cue Extinction: Handbook for Program Administrators*. Rockville MD: Author.

—— (1993c). *Cue Extinction: In-Service Training Curriculum*. Rockville MD: Author.

—— (1995). *Drug Use Among Racial/Ethnic Minorities*. NIH Publication No. 95-3888. Rockville, MD: Author.

—— (1996a). *Epidemiologic Trends in Drug Abuse: Highlights and Executive Summary*, vol. 1 (NIH Publication No. 96-4126). Washington, DC: US Government Printing Office.

—— (1996b). *Diagnosis and Treatment of Drug Abuse in Family Practice–Epidemiology*. Bethesda, MD: Author.

—— (1997a). Cocaine abuse. *NIDA Capsule*. Rockville, MD: Author.

—— (1997b). Common substances of abuse. *NIDA Capsule*. Rockville, MD: Author.

—— (1997c). Methamphetamine Abuse. *NIDA Capsule*. Rockville, MD: Author.

—— (1997d). MDMA (ecstasy) *NIDA Capsule*. Rockville, MD: Author.

—— (1997e). LSD (lysergic acid diethylamide). *NIDA Capsule*. Rockville, MD: Author.

—— (1997f). Phencyclidine (PCP). *NIDA Capsule*. Rockville, MD: Author.

—— (1997g). Marijuana update. NIDA Capsule. Rockville, MD: Author'

—— (1997h). Inhalant abuse update. *NIDA Research Report*. Rockville, MD: Author.

—— (1997i). Inhalants. *NIDA Capsule*. Rockville, MD: Author.

—— (1997j). Marijuana antagonist reveals THC dependence in rats. *NIDA Notes*. Rockville, MD: Author.

—— (1997k). *Treatment of Drug-Dependent Individuals with Comorbid Mental Disorders* (NIH Publication No. 97-4172). Bethesda, MD: Author.

—— (1999a). *Principles of Drug Addiction Treatment. A Research-Based Guide* (NIH Publication No. 99-4180). Bethesda, MD: Author.

—— (1999b). Matching drug abuse treatment services to patient needs boasts outcome effectiveness. *NIDA Notes* pp. 5–8. (NIH Publication No. 99-3478). Bethesda, MD: Author

—— (1999c). *Overview of Research on Women's Health and Gender Differences*. Bethesda, MD: Author.

—— (1999d). *Treatment Methods for Women*. Bethesda, MD: Author.

—— (2000). Ethnic identification and cultural ties may help prevent drug use. *NIDA Notes* 14(3). Bethesda, MD: Author.

National Institute on Drug Abuse Collaborative Cocaine Treatment Study Group. (1999). Psychosocial treatments for cocaine dependence. *Archives of General Psychiatry* 56:493–502.

Nevid, J. S., Rathus, S. A., and Greene, B. (1997). *Abnormal Psychology in a Changing World*, 3rd ed. Upper Saddle River, NJ: Prentice Hall.

Newcomb, M. D. (1992). Understanding the multidimensional nature of drug use and abuse: the role of consumption, risk factors, and protective factors. In *Vulnerability to Drug Abuse*, ed. M. Glantz and R. Pickens, pp. 255–298. Washington, DC: American Psychological Association.

—— (1995). Identifying high-risk youth: prevalence and patterns of adolescent drug abuse. In *Adolescent Drug Abuse: Clinical Assessment and Therapeutic Interventions*, ed. E. Rahdert and D. Czechowicz, pp. 7–37. (NIDA Research Monograph 156). Rockville, MD: National Institute on Drug Abuse.

Newcomb, M. D., and Bentler, P. M. (1989). Substance use and abuse among children and teenagers. *American Psychologist* 44:242–248.

Newlin, D. B. (1989). The skin flushing response: autonomic, self-report, and conditioned responses to repeated administration of alcohol in Asian men. *Journal of Abnormal Psychology* 98:421–425.

Newlin, D. B., and Thomson, J. B. (1990). Alcohol challenge with sons of alcoholics: a critical review and analysis. *Psychological Bulletin* 108, 383–402.

Noble, E. P., Berman, S. M., and Ozkaragoz, T. Z. (1994). Prolonged P300 latency in children with the D2 dopamine receptor A1 allele. *American Journal of Human Genetics* 54:658–668.

Noble, E. P., Blum, K., Khalsa, M. E., et al. (1993). Allelic association of the D2 receptor gene with cocaine dependence. *Drug and Alcohol Dependence* 83:271–285.

Noll, R. B., Zucker, R. A., and Fitzgerald, H. E. (1990). Identification of alcohol by smell among preschoolers: evidence for early socialization about drugs in the home. *Child Development* 61:1520–1527.

Nowinski, J., Baker, S., and Carroll, K. (1995). *NIAA Project MATCH Monograph Series*, Vol. 1: *Twelve Step Facilitation Therapy Manual*. Rockville MD: National Institute for Alcohol Abuse and Alcoholism.

Nurco, D. N., and Lerner, M. (1996). Vulnerability to narcotic addiction: family structure and functioning. *Journal of Drug Issues* 26:1007–1025.

Nye, C. L., Zucker, R. A., and Fitzgerald, H. E. (1995). Early intervention in the path to alcohol problems through conduct problems: treatment involvement and child behavior change. *Journal of Consulting and Clinical Psychology* 63:831–840.

O'Boyle, M. (1993). Personality disorder and multiple substance dependence. *Journal of Personality Disorders* 7:342–347.

O'Brien, C. P. (1997). Recent developments in the pharmacotherapy of substance abuse. In *Addictive Behaviors. Readings, Etiology, Prevention, and Treatment*, ed. G. A. Marlatt and G. R. VandenBos, pp. 646–667. Washington, DC: American Psychological Association.

O'Brien, C. P., Childress, A. R., McLellan, T., and Ehrman, R. (1990). Integrating systematic cue exposure with standard treatment in recovering drug dependent patients. *Addictive Behavior* 15:355–365.

O'Connor, J. (1978). *The Young Drinkers: A Cross National Study of Social and Cultural Influences*. London: Tavistock.

O'Donnell, J., Hawkins, J. D., and Abbott, R. D. (1995). Predicting serious delinquency and substance use among aggressive boys. *Journal of Clinical and Consulting Psychology* 63:529–537.

O'Donnell, W. E., De Soto, C. B., and Reynolds, D. McQ. (1984b). Sensitivity and specificity of the Neuropsychological Impairment Scale (NIS). *Journal of Clinical Psychology* 40:553–555.

O'Donnell, W. E., Reynolds, D. McQ., and De Soto, C. B. (1984a). Validity and reliability of the Neuropsychological Impairment Scale (NIS). *Journal of Clinical Psychology* 40:549–552.

Oetting, E. R., and Beauvais, F. (1986). Peer cluster theory: drugs and the adolescent. *Journal of Counseling and Development*, 65:17–22.

—— (1991). Orthogonal cultural identification theory: the cultural identification of minority adolescents. *International Journal of the Addictions* 25:655–685.

Oetting, E. R., Edwards, R. W., Kelly, K., and Beauvais, F. (1994). Risk and protective factors for drug use among rural American youth. In *NIDA Technical Review, Rural Substance Abuse: State of Knowledge and Issues*. Rockville, MD: National Institute on Drug Abuse.

O'Farrell, T. J. (1993). A behavioral marital therapy couples group program for alcoholics and their spouses. In *Treating Alcohol Problems: Marital and Family Interventions*, pp. 170– 209. New York: Guilford.

O'Farrell, T. J., Choquette, K. A., and Cutter, H. S. G. (1998a). Couples relapse prevention sessions after behavioral marital therapy for male alcoholics: outcomes during the three years after starting treatment. *Journal of Studies on Alcohol* 59:357–370.

O'Farrell, T. J., Hooley, J., Fals-Stewart, W., and Cutter, H. S. G. (1998b). Expressed emotion and relapse in alcoholic patients. *Journal of Consulting and Clinical Psychology* 66:744–752.

Office for Substance Abuse Prevention. (1990). *Communicating About Alcohol and Other Drugs* (OSAP Monograph No. 5). Rockville, MD: Author.

Oldham, J. M., Skodol, A. E., Kellman, H. D., et al. (1995). Comorbidity of Axis I and Axis II disorders. *American Journal of Psychiatry* 152:571–578.

Olsen, G. D., and Murphey, L. J. (1995). Effects of morphine and cocaine on breathing control in neonatal animals. In *Biological Mechanisms and Perinatal Exposure to Drugs*, ed. P. Thadani, pp. 22–39. (NIDA Research Monograph 158, NIH Publication No. 95-4024.) Washington, DC: US Government Printing Office.

O'Malley, S. S., Jaffe, A. J., Chang, G., et al. (1992). Naltrexone and coping skills therapy for alcohol dependence: a controlled study. *Archives of General Psychiatry* 49:281–283.

Orcutt, J. D. (1996). Deviance as a situated phenomenon: variation in the social interpretation of marijuana and alcohol use. In *Social Deviance: Readings in Theory and Research*, 2nd ed., ed., H. N. Pontell, pp. 215–222. Upper Saddle River, NJ: Prentice Hall.

Oscar-Berman, M. O., Shagrin, B., Evert, D. L., and Epstein, C. (1997). Impairments of brain and behavior: the neurological effects of alcohol. *Alcohol Health and Research World:* 21:65–75.

Pattison, E. M. (1986). Clinical approaches to the alcoholic patient. *Psychomatics* 27:762–770.

Peele, S. (1989). *Diseasing of America: Addiction Treatment Out of Control*. Boston: Houghton Mifflin.

Perez, J. F. (1985). *Counseling the Alcoholic*. Muncie, IN: Accelerated Development.

Perez-Reyes, M., and Jeffcoat, A. R. (1992). Ethanol/ cocaine interaction: cocaine and coathylene plasma concentrations and their relationship to subjective and cardiovascular effects. *Life Science* 51:553–563.

Perls, F. S. (1969). *Ego, Hunger and Aggression*. New York: Vintage.

Petraitis, J., Flay, B. R., and Miller, T. Q. (1995). Reviewing theories of adolescent substance use: organizing pieces in the puzzle. *Psychological Bulletin* 117:67–87.

Pfefferbaum, A., Rosenbloom, M., Crusan, K., and Jernigan, T. L. (1988). Brain CT changes in alcoholics: effects of age and alcohol consumption. *Alcoholism* 12:81–87.

Pfefferbaum, A., Sullivan, E. V., and Mathalon, D. H. (1997). Frontal lobe volume loss observed with magnetic resonance imaging in older chronic alcoholics. *Alcoholism: Clinical and Experimental Research* 21:521–529.

Pickens, R. W., Svikis, D. S., McGue, M., et al. (1991). Heterogeneity in the inheritance of alcoholism: a study of male and female twins. *Archives of General Psychiatry* 48:19–28.

Pihl, R. O., Peterson, J., and Finn, P. (1990). Inherited predisposition to alcoholism: characteristics of sons of male alcoholics. *Journal of Abnormal Psychology* 99:291–301.

Pihl, R. O., Smith, M., and Farrell, B. (1984). Alcohol and aggression in men: a comparison of brewed and distilled beverages. *Journal on the Study of Alcohol* 45:278–282.

Pincus, H. A., and Fine, T. (1992). The "anatomy" of research funding of mental illness and addictive disorders. *Archives of General Psychiatry* 49:573–579.

Pokorny, A. D., Kanas, T., and Overall, J. E. (1981). Order of appearance of alcoholic symptoms. *Alcohol Clinical and Experimental Research* 5:216–220.

Pokorny, A. D., Miller, B., and Kaplan, H. (1972). A shortened version of the Michigan Alcoholism Screening Test. *American Journal of Psychiatry* 129:342.

Polich, J., Pollock, V. E., and Bloom, F. E. (1994). Meta-analysis of P300 amplitude from males at risk for alcoholism. *Psychological Bulletin* 115:55–73.

Polkis, A., Maginn, D., and Barr, J. L. (1987). Tissue disposition of cocaine in man: a report of 5 fatal poisonings. *Forensic Science International* 33:83–88.

Pope, K. S., and Bouhoutsos, J. C. (1986). *Sexual Intimacy Between Therapists and Patients*. New York: Praeger.

Pope, K. S., and Tabachnick, B. G. (1993). Therapists' anger, hate, fear, and sexual feelings: national survey of therapists' responses, client characteristics, critical events, formal complaints, and training. *Professional Psychology: Research and Practice* 24:142–152.

Powell Davids, J. (1993). *Clinical Supervision in Alcohol and Drug Abuse Counseling: Principles, Models, Methods*. New York: Lexington.

Prochaska, J. O. (1984). *Systems of Psychotherapy: A Transtheoretical Analysis*. Chicago: Dorsey.

Prochaska, J. O., and DiClemente, C. C. (1982). Transtheoretical therapy: toward a more integrative model of change. *Psychotherapy: Theory, Research, and Practice* 19:276–288.

——— (1984). *The Transtheoretical Approach: Crossing the Traditional Boundaries of Therapy*. Homewood, IL: Dow-Jones/Irwin.

——— (1986). Toward a comprehensive model of change. In *Treating Addictive Behaviors: Process of Change*, ed. W. R. Miller and N. Heather, pp. 3–27. New York: Plenum.

Prochaska, J. O., DiClemente, C. C., and Norcross, J. C. (1992). In search of how people change: applications to addictive behaviors. *American Psychologist* 47:1102–1114.

Project MATCH Research Group. (1997). Matching alcoholism treatments to client heterogeneity: Project MATCH posttreatment drinking outcomes. *Journal of Studies on Alcohol* 58:7–29.

Quinlan, J. W. (1995). *CSAP Implementation Guide: Hispanic/Latino Natural Support Systems*. Rockville, MD: Center for Substance Abuse Prevention, Substance Abuse and Mental Health Services Administration.

Rahdert, E. (1991). Adolescent assessment/referral system manual. Department of Health and Human Services, Publication No. (ADM) 91-1735. Rockville, MD. National Institute on Drug Abuse.

Rahdert, E., and Czechowicz, D. (1995). Adolescent drug abuse: clinical assessment and therapeutic interventions (NIDA Research Monograph 156). Rockville, MD: National Institute on Drug Abuse.

Ramsey, D. S., and Woods, S. C. (1997). Biological consequences of drug administration: implications for acute and chronic tolerance. *Psychological Bulletin* 104:170–193.

Regier, D. A., Farmer, M. E., Rae, D. S., et al. (1990). Comorbidity of mental disorders with alcohol and other drug abuse: results from the epidemiological catchment area (ECA) study. *Journal of the American Medical Association* 264:2511–2518.

Regier, D. A., Narrow, W. E., Rae, D. S., et al. (1993). The defacto U.S. mental and addictive disorders service system: Epidemiologic Catchment Area prospective 1-year prevalence rates of disorders and services. *Archives of General Psychiatry* 50:85–94.

Reisner, R., and Slobogin, C. (1990). *Law and the Mental Health System*, 2nd ed. St. Paul, MN: West.

Reitan, R. M., and Wolfson, D. (1985). *The Halstead-Reitan Neuropsychological Test Battery: Theory and Clinical Application*. Tucson, AZ: Neuropsychologists Press.

Rice, D. P., Kelman, S., and Miller, L. S. (1991). The economic of alcohol abuse. *Alcohol, Health, and Research World* 15:307–316.

Rice, D. P., Kelman, S. Miller, L. S., and Dunmeyer, S. (1990). *The Economic Costs of Alcohol and Drug Abuse and Mental Illness:1985*. Rockville, MD: National Institute on Drug Abuse.

Rich, J. A., and Singer, D. E. (1991). Cocaine-related symptoms in patients presenting to an urban emergency department. *Annals of Emergency Medicine* 20:616–621.

Richards, H. J. (1993). *Therapy of the Substance Abuse Syndromes*. Northvale, NJ: Jason Aronson.

Robbins, S. J. (1995). Causes of substance abuse: learning. In *Encyclopedia of Drugs and Alcohol*, vol. 1., ed. J. H. Jaffe, pp. 206–211. New York: Macmillan.

Robinson, T. E., and Berridge, K. C. (1993). The neural basis of drug craving: an incentive-sensitization theory of addiction. *Brain Research Reviews* 18:247–291.

Rogers, C. (1961). *On Becoming a Person: A Therapist's View of Psychotherapy*. Boston: Houghton Mifflin.

Rogers, C. R., and Sanford, R. C. (1985). Client-centered psychotherapy. In *Comprehensive textbook of psychiatry*, vol. 2, ed. H. I. Kaplan and B. J. Sadock, pp. 1374–1388. Baltimore, MD: Williams and Wilkins.

Rorschach, H. (1942). *Psychodiagnostics: A Diagnostic Technique Based on Perception*, trans. P. Lemkau and B. Kronenberg. Berne: Huber.

Rosecan, J. S., and Spitz, H. I. (1987). Cocaine reconceptualized: historical overview. In *Cocaine Abuse: New Directions in Treatment and Research*, ed. H. I. Spitz and J. S. Rosecan, pp. 101–114. New York: Brunner/Mazel.

Rosenstein, D. S., and Horowitz, H. A. (1996). Adolescent attachment and psychopathology. *Journal of Consulting and Clinical Psychology* 64:244–253.

Rosenthal, R. J. (1992). Pathological gambling. *Psychiatric Annals* 22:72–78.

Ross, M. W., Wodak, A. G., Gold, J., and Miller, M. E. (1992). Differences across sexual orientation on HIV risk behaviors in injecting drug users. *AIDS Care* 4:139–148.

Rothenberger, R., Woelfel, M., Stoneburner, R., et al. (1987). Survival with acquired immune deficiency syndrome: experience with 5833 cases in New York City. *New England Journal of Medicine* 317:1297–1302.

Rounsaville, B. J., Kosten, T. R., Weissman, M. M., et al. (1991). Psychiatric disorders in relatives of probands with opiate addiction. *Archives of General Psychiatry* 48:33–42.

Roy, A., Adinoff, G., and Linnoila, M. (1988a). Acting out hostility in normal volunteers: negative correlation with levels of 5-HIAA in cerebrospinal fluid. *Psychiatry Research* 24:189–194.

Roy, A., Adinoff, B., Roehrich, L., et al. (1988b). Pathological gambling: a psychobiological study. *Archives of General Psychiatry* 45:369–373.

Royce, J. E., and Stratchley, D. (1996). *Alcoholism and Other Drug Problems*. New York: Free Press.

Russell, M. (1990). Prevalence of alcoholism among children of alcoholics. In *Children of Alcoholics: Critical Perspectives*, ed. M. Windle and J. Searles, pp. 9–38. New York: Guilford.

Russell, M., Martier, S. S., Sokol, R. J., et al. (1994). Screening for pregnancy risk-drinking. *Alcoholism: Clinical and Experimental Research* 18:1156–1161.

Rutter, M. (1987). Psychosocial resilience and protective mechanisms. *American Journal of Orthopsychiatry* 57:316–331.

Ryan, R. M., Plant, R. W., and O'Malley, S. (1995). Initial motivations for alcohol treatment: relations with patient characteristics, treatment involvement, and dropout. *Addictive Behaviors* 20:279–297.

Sadava, S. (1987). Interactional theory. In *Psychological Theories of Drinking and Alcoholism*, ed. H. T. Blane and K. E. Leonard. New York: Guilford.

Saitz, R. (1998). Introduction to alcohol withdrawal. *Alcohol Health and Research World* 22:5–12.

Sansone, R., Fine, M. A., and Nunn, J. L. (1994). A comparison of borderline personality symptomatology and self-destructive behavior in women with eating, substance abuse, and both eating and substance abuse disorders. *Journal of Personality Disorders* 8:219–228.

Satel, S. L., Kosten, T. R., Schuckit, M. A., and Fischman, M. W. (1993). Should protracted withdrawal from drugs be included in *DSM-IV*? *American Journal of Psychiatry* 150:695–704.

Satel, S. L., Krystal, J. H., Delgado, P. L., et al. (1995). Tryptophan depletion and attenuation of cue-induced craving for cocaine. *American Journal of Psychiatry* 152:778–783.

Satir, V. (1972). *People Making*. Palo Alto, CA: Science and Behavior Books.

Sayette, M. A. (1993). An appraisal–disruption model of alcohol's effects on stress responses in social drinkers. *Psychological Bulletin* 114:459–476.

Scalzo, F. M., and Burge, L. J. (1995). Cardiovascular effects of cocaine in infant and juvenile piglets. In *Biological Mechanisms and Perinatal Exposure to Drugs*, ed. P. Thadani, pp. 40–57. (NIDA Research Monograph 158, NIH Publi-

cation No. 95-4024). Washington, DC: US Government Printing Office.

Scharff, D. E. (1992). *Refinding the Object and Reclaiming the Self*. Northvale, NJ: Jason Aronson.

Scharff, D. E., and Scharff, J. S. (1991). *Object Relations Family Therapy*. Northvale, NJ: Jason Aronson.

Schottenfield, R. S. (1994). Assessment of the patient. In *Textbook of Substance Abuse Treatment*, ed. M. Galanter and H. D. Kleber, pp. 25–33. Washington, DC: American Psychiatric Press.

Schreiber, M. D. (1995). Fetal cerebral vascular effects of cocaine exposure. In *Biological Mechanisms and Perinatal Exposure to Drugs*, ed. P. Thadani, pp. 67–87 (NIDA Research Monograph 158, NIH Publication No. 95-4024). Washington, DC: US Government Printing Office.

Schuckit, M. (1994). Goals of treatment. In *Textbook of Substance Abuse Treatment*, ed. M Galanter and H. D. Kleber, pp. 3–10. Washington, DC: American Psychiatric Press.

Schuckit, M. A., and Hesselbrock, V. (1994). Alcohol dependence and anxiety disorders: What is the relationship? *American Journal of Psychiatry* 151:1723–1734.

Schuckit, M. A., and Smith, T. L. (1996). An 8-year follow-up of 450 sons of alcoholics and control subjects. *Archives of General Psychiatry* 53:202–210.

Schuckit, M. A., Smith, T. L., Anthenelli, R., and Irwin, M. (1993). Clinical course of alcoholism in 636 male inpatients. *American Journal of Psychiatry* 150:786–792.

Schutte, K. K., Moos, R. H., and Brennan, P. L. (1995). Depression and drinking behavior among women and men: a three-wave longitudinal study of older adults. *Journal of Consulting and Clinical Psychology* 63:810–822.

Schwitzgebel, R. L,. and Schwitzgebel, R. K. (1980). *Law and Psychological Practice*. New York: Wiley.

Searles, J. S. (1988). The role of genetics in the pathogenesis of alcoholism. *Journal of Abnormal Psychology* 97:153–167.

Secretary of Health and Human Services. (1990). *Seventh Special Report to the U.S. Congress on Alcohol and Health*. Rockville, MD: National Institute on Alcohol Abuse and Alcoholism.

Self, D. W., and Nestler, E. J. (1998). Relapse to drug-seeking: neural and molecular mechanisms. *Drug and Alcohol Dependence* 51:49–60.

Selzer, M. (1971). The Michigan alcoholism screening test: the quest for a new diagnostic instrument. *American Journal of Psychiatry* 127:1653–1658.

Senay, E. C. (1994). Opioids: methadone maintenance. In *Textbook of Substance Abuse Treatment*, ed. M. Galanter and H. D. Kleber, pp. 209–221. Washington, DC: American Psychiatric Press.

———— (1997). Diagnostic interview and mental status examination. In *Substance Abuse: A Comprehensive Textbook*, 3rd ed., ed. J. H. Lowinson, P. Ruiz, R. B. Millman, and J. C. Langrod, pp. 364–369. Baltimore, MD: Williams and Wilkins.

Serper, M. R., Alpert, M., Richardson, N. A., et al. (1995). Clinical effects of recent cocaine use on patients with acute schizophrenia. *American Journal of Psychiatry* 152:1464–1469.

Shaper, A. G., Phillips, A. N., Pocock, J., and Walker, M. (1987). Alcohol and ischemic heart disease in middle-aged British men. *British Journal of Medicine* 294:733–737.

Shedler, J., and Block, J. (1990). Adolescent drug use and psychological health: a longitudinal inquiry. *American Psychologist* 45:612–630.

Sher, K. J. (1987). Stress response dampening. In *Psychological Theories of Drinking and Alcoholism*, ed. H. T. Blane and K. E. Leonard, pp. 227–271. New York: Guilford.

Sher, K. J., and Trull, T. (1991). Personality and disinhibitory psychopathology: alcoholism and antisocial personality disorder. *Journal of Abnormal Psychology* 103:92–102.

Sher, K. J., Wood, M. D., Wood, P. K., and Raskin, G. (1996). Alcohol outcome expectancies and alcohol use: a latent variable cross-lagged panel study. *Journal of Abnormal Psychology* 105:561–574.

Siegel, A. J., Sholar, M. B., Mendelson, J. H., et al. (1999). Cocaine-induced erythrocytosis in von Willebrand factor. *Archives of Internal Medicine* 159:1925–1930.

Sigvardsson, S., Bohman, M., and Cloninger, R. (1996). Replication of the Stockholm Adoption Study of alcoholism. *Archives of General Psychiatry* 53:681–687.

Simpson, D. D., Joe, G. W., Fletcher, B. W., et al. (1999). A national evaluation of treatment outcomes for cocaine dependence. *Archives of General Psychiatry* 56:507–514.

Simpson, D. D., Joe, G. W., Wek, L., and Sells, S. B. (1986). Addiction careers: etiology, treatment, and 12-year follow-up procedures. *Journal of Drug Issues* 16:107–121.

Skinner, B. F. (1974). *About Behaviorism*. New York: Knopf.

Skinner, H. A. (1987). Drug Abuse Screening Test (DAST-20). In *Alcohol and Drug-Related Problems*, pp. 51–54. Toronto, Canada: Faculty of Medicine, University of Toronto.

Smith, D. E., and Wesson, D. R. (1994). Benzodiazepines and other sedative-hypnotics. In *Textbook of Substance Abuse Treatment*, ed. M. Galanter and H. D. Kleber, pp. 179–190. Washington, DC: American Psychiatric Press.

Smith, D. F. and Seymour, R. B. (1995). Complications: route of administration. *Encyclopedia of Drugs and Alcohol*, vol. 1, ed., J. H. Jaffe, pp. 309–313. New York: Macmillan.

Smith, G. T., Goldman, M. S., Greenbaum, P. E., and Christiansen, B. A. (1995). Expectancy for social facilitation from drinking: the divergent paths of high-expectancy and low-expectancy adolescents. *Journal of Abnormal Psychology*, 104:32–40.

Smith-Bell, M., and Winslade, W. J. (1994). Privacy, confidentiality, and privilege in the psychotherapeutic relationship. *American Journal of Orthopsychiatry* 64:180–193.

Solomon, R. L. (1977). An opponent process theory of acquired motivations: the affective dynamics of addictions. In *Psychopathology: Experimental Models*, ed. J. D. Maser and M. E. P. Seligman, pp. 41–50. San Francisco: W. H. Freeman.

Spitzer, R. L., and Endicott, J. (1978). *Schedule for Affective Disorders and Schizophrenia*. New York: New York Psychiatric Institute, Biometrics Research Division.

Squires, R., and Braestrup, C. (1977). Benzodiazepine receptors in rat brain. *Nature* 266:732–734.

Stacy, A. W., Newcomb, M. D., and Bentler, P. M. (1991). Cognitive motivation and drug use: a 9-year longitudinal study. *Journal of Abnormal Psychology* 100:502–515.

Stampfer, M. J., Colditz, G. A., Willet, W. C., et al. (1988). A prospective study of moderate alcohol consumption and the risk of coronary disease and stroke in women. *New England Journal of Medicine* 319:267–273.

Steele, C. M., and Josephs, R. A. (1990). Alcohol myopia: Its prized and dangerous effects. *American Psychologist* 45:921–933.

Stein, D. J., Hollander, E., and Leibowitz, M. R. (1993a). Neurobiology of impulsivity and the impulse control disorders. *Journal of Neuropsychiatry and Clinical Neurosciences* 5:9–17.

Stein, D. J., Hollander, E., and Skodol, A. E. (1993b). Anxiety disorders and personality disorders: a review. *Journal of Personality Disorders* 1:87–104.

Steinglass, P. (1994). Family therapy. In *Textbook of Substance Abuse Treatment*, ed. M. Galanter and H. D. Kleber, pp. 315–329. Washington, DC: American Psychiatric Press.

Steinglass, P., Bennett, L., Wolin, S., and Reiss, D. (1987). *The Alcoholic Family*. New York: Basic Books.

Stephens, R. C., and Alemagno, S. A. (1994). Injection and sexual risk behaviors of male heterosexual injecting drug users. In *The Context of HIV Risk among Drug Users and Their Sexual Partners*, ed., R. J. Battjes, Z. Sloboda, and W. C. Grace, pp. 9–25 (NIDA Research Monograph 143, NIH Publication No. 94-3750). Washington, DC: US Government Printing Office.

Stewart, J., deWit, H., and Eikelboom, R. (1984). The role of unconditioned and conditioned drug effects in the self-administration of opiates and stimulants. *Psychological Review* 91:251–268.

Stewart, S. H. (1996). Alcohol abuse in individuals exposed to trauma: a critical review. *Psychological Bulletin* 120:83–112.

Stinchfield, R., and Owen, P. (1998). Hazelden's model of treatment and its outcome. *Addictive Behaviors* 23:669–683.

Stinson, F. S., and DeBakey, S. F. (1992). Alcohol-related mortality in the United States, 1979–1988. *British Journal of Addiction* 87:777–783.

Stocker, S. (1997). Men and women in drug abuse treatment relapse at different rates and for different reasons. *NIDA Notes* vol. 13, p. 1.

Strain, E. C., Stitzer, M. L., Liebson, I. A., and Bigelow, G. E. (1994). Comparison of buprenorphine and methadone in the treatment of opioid dependence. *American Journal of Psychiatry* 151:1025–1030.

Strassner, L., ed. (2000). *Ethnic-Cultural Issues in Substance Abuse Treatment*. New York: Guilford.

Stritzke, W. G. K., Lang, A. R., and Patrick, C. J. (1996). Beyond stress and arousal: a reconceptualization of alcohol-emotion relations with reference to psychophysiological methods. *Psychological Bulletin* 120:376–395.

Substance Abuse and Mental Health Services Administration. (1988). *The Mandatory Guidelines for Federal Workplace Testing Programs*. Federal Register (53 FR 11970–11989). Rockville, MD: Department of Health and Human Services.

——— (1994). *The Mandatory Guidelines for Federal Workplace Testing Programs*. Federal Register (59 FR 29908–29931). Rockville, MD: Department of Health and Human Services.

——— (1995a). *Substance Abuse and Mental Health Statistics Sourcebook*. Rockville, MD: Substance Abuse and Mental Health Services Administration Office of Applied Statistics.

——— (1995b). Drug abuse warning network. May 1995. Rockville, MD: SAMHSA Office of Applied Studies.

——— (1996a). *National Household Survey on Drug Abuse: Population Estimates 1995*. Rockville, MD: Author.

——— (1996b). Historical estimates from the drug abuse warning network. 1978–1994 estimates of drug-related emergency department episodes. *Advance Report Number 16*, August 1996. Rockville, MD: Substance Abuse and Mental Health Services Administration Office of Applied Studies.

——— (1997). *Overview of Addiction Treatment Effectiveness* (DHHS Publication No. [SMA] 97-3133. Washington, DC: US Government Printing Office.

——— (1998). *Substance Abuse among Older Adults* (Treatment Improvement Protocol (TIP) Series 26). Washington, DC: US Government Printing Office.

——— (1999). *National Household Survey on Drug Abuse 1998*. Washington, DC: US Government Printing Office.

Sue, D. W., Ivey, A. Z., and Pedersen, P. B. (1996) *A Theory of Multicultural Counseling and Therapy*. Pacific Grove, CA: Brooks/Cole.

Sullivan, J. T. (1995). Medical and behavioral toxicity overview. In *Encyclopedia of Drugs and Alcohol*, vol. 1, ed. J. H. Jaffe, pp. 285–295. New York: Macmillan.

Sullivan, J. T., Sykora, K., Schneiderman, J., et al. (1989). Assessment of alcohol withdrawal: the revised Clinical Institute Withdrawal Assessment for Alcohol Scale (CIWA-Ar). *British Journal of Addiction* 84:1353–1357.

Susser, E., Miller, M., Valencia, E., et al. (1996) Injection drug use and risk of HIV transmission among homeless men with mental illness. *American Journal of Psychiatry* 153:794–798.

Svrakic, N. M., Svrakic, D. M., and Cloninger C. R. (1996). A general quantitative theory o personality development: fundamentals of a self-organizing psychobiological complex. *Development and Psychopathology* 8:247–272.

Swanson, J. and Holzer, C. (1991). Violence and the ECA data. *Hospital and Community Psychiatry* 42:79–80.

Swift, R. M. (1999). Drug therapy for alcohol dependence. *New England Journal of Medicine* 340:1482–1490.

Szabo, G. (1997). Alcohol's contribution to compromised immunity. *Alcohol World Health and Research* 21:30–41.

Szeto, H. H. (1991). Discussion: methodologica issues in controlled studies on effects of prenatal drugs. In *Methodological Issues in Controlled Studies on Effects of Prenatal Exposure t Drug Abuse*, ed., M. M. Kilbey and K. Asghar pp. 37–44. (NIDA Research Monograph 114 DHHS Publication No. [ADM] 91-1837) Washington, DC: US Government Printing Office.

Tai, B., Grudzinskas, C. V. Chiang, N., and Bridge P. (1997). Preface. In *Medication Development fo the Treatment of Cocaine Dependence: Issues i Clinical Efficacy Trials*, ed. B. Tai, N. Chiang, an P. Bridge, pp. 1–4 (NIDA Research Monograph 175, NIH Publication No. 98-41). Bethesda, ML National Institute on Drug Abuse.

Tarter, R. E., (1992). Prevention of Drug Abuse therapy and application. *American Journal o Addictions* 1:2–20.

Tarter, R. E., Blackson, T., Martin, C., et al. (1993 Characteristics and correlates of child disci pline practices in substance abuse and norma families. *American Journal on Addictions* 2:18–2!

Tarter, R. E., Jacob, T., and Laird, S. B. (1993 Learning and memory capacity in sons of al coholic men. *American Journal on Addiction* 2:219–224.

Tarter, R., Laird, S., and Moss, H. (1990). Neuropsychological and neurophysiological characteristics of children of alcoholics. In *Children of Alcoholics: A Critical Review of the Literature*, ed. M. Windle and J. Searles, pp. 87–112. New York: Guilford.

Tarter, R. E., Ott, P. J., and Mezzich, A. C. (1991). Psychometric assessment. In *Clinical Textbook of Addictive Disorders*, ed., R. J. Frances and S. I. Miller, pp. 237–267. New York: Guilford.

Tarter, R. E., and Vanyukov, M. M. (1994). Stepwise developmental model of alcoholism etiology. In *The Development of Alcohol Problems: Exploring the Biopsychosocial Matrix of Risk*, ed. R. A. Zucker, G. Boyd, and J. Howard, pp. 303–330. Rockville, MD: National Institute on Alcohol Abuse and Alcoholism.

Taylor, S. P., and Gammons, C. B. (1975). Effects of type and dose of alcohol on human physical aggression. *Journal of Personality and Social Psychology* 32:169–175.

Thevos, A. K., Brady, K. T., Grice, D., et al. (1993). A comparison of psychopathology in cocaine and alcohol dependence. *American Journal on Addictions* 2:279–286.

Thomson, H. H., and Dilts, S. L. (1991). Opioids. In *Clinical Textbook of Addictive Disorders*, ed. R. J. Frances and S. I. Miller, pp. 103–120. New York: Guilford.

Tiffany, S. T. (1990). A cognitive model of drug urges and drug-use behavior: role of automatic and nonautomatic processes. *Psychological Review* 97:147–168.

Trotter, W. (1916). *Instincts of the Herd in Peace and War*. London: T. Fisher Unwin.

Tsai, G., Gastfriend, D. R., and Coyle, J. T. (1995). The glutaminergic basis of human alcoholism. *American Journal of Psychiatry* 152:332–340.

Tsou, K., Patrick, S., and Walker, M. J. (1995). Physical withdrawal in rats tolerant to delta-9-tetrahydrocannabinol precipitated by a cannabinoid receptor antagonist. *European Journal of Pharmacology* 280:R13–R15.

Turnbull, J. E., and Gomberg, E. S. L. (1988). Impact of depressive symptomatology on alcohol problems in women. *Alcoholism: Clinical and Experimental Research* 12:374–381.

Uhl, G. R. (1995). Causes of substance abuse: genetic factors. In *Encyclopedia of Drugs and Alcohol*, vol. 1, ed. J. H. Jaffe, pp. 204–206. New York: Macmillan.

Ungeleider, J. T., and Pechnick, R. N. (1994). Hallucinogens. In *Textbook of Substance Abuse Treatment*, ed. M. Galanter and H. D. Kleber, pp. 141–147. Washington, DC: American Psychiatric Press.

Vaillant, G. E. (1973). A 20-year follow-up of New York addicts. *Archives of General Psychiatry* 29:237–241.

——— (1983). *The natural History of Alcoholism: Causes, Patterns and Paths to Recovery*. Cambridge, MA: Harvard University Press.

——— (1988). What can long-term follow-up teach us about relapse and prevention of relapse in drug addiction? *British Journal of Addictions* 83:1147–1157.

——— (1996). A long-term follow-up of male alcohol abuse. *Archives of General Psychiatry* 53:243–249.

Vaillant, G. E., and Milofsky, E. S. (1982). The etiology of alcoholism: a prospective viewpoint. *American Psychologist* 37:494–503.

Valle, R. S., King, M., and Halling, S. (1989). An introduction to existential-phenomenological thought in psychology. In *Existential-Phenomenological Perspectives in Psychology: Exploring the Breadth of Human Experience*, ed. R. S. Valle and S. Halling, pp. 3–16. New York: Plenum.

Verebey, K. G., and Buchan, B. J. (1997). Diagnostic Laboratory screening for drug abuse. In *Substance Abuse. A Comprehensive Textbook*, 3rd ed., ed. J. H. Lowinson, P. Ruiz, R. B. Millman, and J. C. Langrod, pp. 369–377. Baltimore: Williams and Wilkins.

Volavka, J., Czobor, P., Goodwin, D. W., et al. (1996). The electroencephalogram after alcohol administration in high-risk men and the development of alcohol use disorders 10 years later: preliminary findings. *Archives of General Psychiatry* 53:258–263.

Volkan, K. (1994). *Dancing Among the Maenads*, vol. 5: *The Psychology of Compulsive Drug Use*. San Francisco: Lang.

Volkow, N. D., Fowler, J. S., and Ding, Y.-S. (1996). Cardiotoxic properties of cocaine: studies with positron emission tomography. In *Neurotoxicity and Neuropathology Associated with Cocaine Abuse*, ed., M. D. Majewska, pp. 159–174. (NIDA Research Monograph, NIH Publication No. 96-4019.) Washington, DC: US Government Printing Office.

Volpicelli, J. R., Alterman, A. I., Hayasgida, M., and O'Brien, C. P. (1992). Naltrexone in the treatment of alcohol dependence. *Archives of General Psychiatry* 49:876–880.

von Knorring, A.-L., Bohman, M., and von Knorring, L. (1985a). Platelet MAO activity as a biological marker in subgroups of alcoholism. *Acta Psychiatric Scandinavica* 72:51–58.

von Knorring, L., Palm, V., and Anderson, H. E. (1985b). Relationship between treatment outcome and subtypes of alcoholism in men. *Journal of Studies on Alcohol* 46:388–391.

von Knorring, L., von Knorring, A.-L., Smigman, L., et al. (1987). Personality traits in subtypes of alcoholics. *Journal of Studies on Alcohol* 48:523–527.

Vuchinich, R. E., and Tucker, J. A. (1988). Contributions from behavioral theories of choice to an analysis of alcohol abuse. *Journal of Abnormal Psychology* 97:181–195.

——— (1996). Alcoholic relapse, life events, and behavioral theories of choice. *Experimental and Clinical Psychopharmacology* 4:19–28.

Wagner, E. F. (1993). Delay of gratification, coping with stress, and substance use in adolescence. *Experimental and Clinical Psychopharmacology* 1:27–43.

Wallace, J. (1995). Working with the preferred defense structure of alcoholics. In *Dynamics and Treatment of Alcoholism*, ed. J. Levin and R. Weiss, pp. 222–232. Northvale, NJ: Jason Aronson.

Watson, R. B. (1995). Immunologic complications. In *Encyclopedia of Drugs and Alcohol*, vol. 1, ed. J. H. Jaffe, pp. 269–274. New York: Macmillan.

Watzlawick, P. (1978). *The Language of Change.* New York: Basic Books.

Way, E. L. (1982). History of opiate use in the Orient and the United States. In *Opioids in Mental Illness: Theories, Clinical Observations, and Treatment Possibilities*, ed. K. Verebey, pp. 12–23. New York: New York Academy of Sciences.

Weber, L. R. (1995). *The Analysis of Social Problems.* Boston: Allyn and Bacon.

Wegschieder-Cruse, S. (1985). *Choice Making.* Deerfield Beach, FL: Health Communications.

Weiss, C. J., and Millman, R. B. (1991). Hallucinogens, phencyclidine, marijuana, inhalants. In *Clinical Textbook of Addictive Disorders*, ed. R. J. Frances, and S. I. Miller, pp. 146–170. New York: Guilford.

Weiss, R. D. (1994). Inpatient treatment. In *Textbook of Substance Abuse Treatment*, ed. M. Galanter and H. D. Kleber, pp. 359–368. Washington, DC: American Psychiatric Press.

Wenar, C. (1994). *Developmental Psychopathology: From Infancy through Adolescence*, 3rd ed. New York: McGraw-Hill.

Westermeyer, J. (1991). Historical and social context of psychoactive substance disorders. In *Clinical Textbook of Addictive Disorders*, ed. R. J. Francis and S. I. Miller, pp. 23–40. New York: Guilford.

Westermeyer, J., Tucker, P., and Nugent, S. (1995). Comorbid anxiety disorders among patients with substance abuse disorders. *American Journal on Addictions* 4:97–106.

Whitaker, C. A., and Bumberry, W. M. (1988). *Dancing with the Family: A Symbolic-Experiential Approach.* New York: Brunner/Mazel.

Wicks-Nelson, R., and Israel, A. C. (1997). *Behavior Disorders of Childhood*, 3rd ed. Upper Saddle River, NJ: Prentice Hall.

Wikler, A. (1980). *Opioid Dependence.* New York: Plenum.

Wilk, A. I., Jensen, N. M., and Havighurst, T. C. (1997). Meta-analysis of randomized control trials addressing brief interventions in heavy alcohol drinkers. *Journal of General Internal Medicine* 12:274–283.

Williams, M. H. (1992). Exploitation and inference: mapping the damage from therapist–patient sexual involvement. *American Psychologist* 47:412–421.

Wills, T. A., McNamara, G., Vaccaro, D., and Hirky, A. E. (1996). Escalated substance use: a longitudinal grouping analysis from early to middle adolescence. *Journal of Abnormal Psychology* 105:166–180.

Wilsnack, S. C. (1973). Sex role identity in female alcoholism. *Journal of Abnormal Psychology* 82:253–261.

——— (1984). Drinking, sexuality, and sexual dysfunction in women. In *Alcohol Problems in Women: Antecedents, Consequences, and Interventions*, ed. S. C. Wilsnack and L. J. Beckman, pp. 189–228. New York: Guilford Press.

——— (1991). Sexuality and women's drinking: findings from a U.S. national study. *Alcohol and Health Research World* 15:147–150.

Wilsnack, S. C. and Beckman, L. J. eds. (1984). *Alcohol Problems in Women: Antecedents, Consequences, and Interventions.* New York: Guilford.

Wilson, G. T. (1991). The addiction model of eating disorders: a critical analysis. *Advances in Behavior Research and Therapy* 13:27–72.

Winick, C. (1962). Maturing out of narcotic addiction. *Bulletin on Narcotics* 14:1–7.

Winokur, G., Coryell, W., Akiskal, H. S., et al. (1995). Alcoholism in manic-depressive (bipolar) illness: familial course, course of illness, and the primary-secondary distinction. *American Journal of Psychiatry* 152:365–372.

Winokur, G., Rimmer, J. and Reich, T. (1971). Alcoholism IV: Is there more than one type of alcoholism? *British Journal of Psychiatry* 18:525–531.

Wise, R. A. (1988). The neurobiology of craving: implications for the understanding and treatment of alcoholism. *Journal of Abnormal Psychology* 97:118–132.

——— (1998). Drug-activation of brain reward pathways. *Drug and Alcohol Dependence* 51:13–22.

Wise, R. A., and Rompre, P. P. (1989). Brain dopamine and reward. *Annual Review of Psychology* 40:191–225.

Wolfarth, T. D., van den Brink, W., Ormel, J., et al. (1993). The relatiohship between social dysfunctioning and psychopathology among primary care attenders. *British Journal of Psychiatry* 163:37–44.

Wolin, S. J., and Bennett, L. A. (1984). Family rituals. *Family Process* 23:401–420.

Wolin, S. J., Bennett, L. A., and Noonan, D. L. (1979). Family rituals and the reoccurrence of alcoholism over generations. *American Journal of Psychiatry* 136:589–593.

Wolpe, J. (1969). *The Practice of Behavior Therapy.* Oxford, England: Pergamon.

———— (1995). Reciprocal inhibition: major agent of behavior change. In *Theories of Behavior Therapy: Exploring Behavior Change*, ed. W. O'Donohue and L. Krasner, pp. 23–57. Washington, DC: American Psychological Association.

Wood, P. B., Cochran, J. K., Pfefferbaum, B., and Arneklev, B. J. (1995). Sensation-seeking and delinquent substance use: an extension of learning theory. *Journal of Drug Issues* 25:173–193.

Woody, G. E., Mercer, D., and Luborsky, L. (1994). Individual psychotherapy: other drugs. In *Textbook of Substance Abuse Treatment*, ed. M. Galanter and H. D. Kleber, pp. 275–284. Washington, DC: American Psychiatric Press.

Woody, G. E., Urschel, H. C. III, and Alterman, A. (1992). The many paths to drug dependence. In *Vulnerability to Drug Abuse*, ed. M. Glantz and R. Pickens, pp. 491–507. Washington, DC: American Psychological Association.

Wren, C. S. (1999). Hair testing by schools intensifies drug debate. *New York Times* June 14, p. A16.

Wulfert, E., and Greenway, D. E. (1996). A logical functional analysis of reinforcement-based disorders: alcoholism and pedophilia. *Journal of Consulting and Clinical Psychology* 64:1140–1151.

Wurmser, L. (1974). Psychoanalytic considerations of the etiology of compulsive drug use. *Journal of the American Psychoanalytic Association* 22:820–843.

———— (1978). *The Hidden Dimension: Psychodynamics in Compulsive Drug Use*. New York: Jason Aronson.

Yates, W. R., and Miller, W. H. (1993). Comparative validity of five alcoholism typologies. *American Journal on Addictions* 2:99–108.

Yontef, G. M., and Simkin, J. S. (1989). Gestalt therapy. In *Current psychotherapies*, 4th ed., ed. R. Corsini and D. Wedding, pp. 323–362. Itasca, IL: F. E. Peacock.

Zakhari, S. (1997). Alcohol and the cardiovascular system: molecular mechanisms for beneficial and harmful action. *Alcohol World Health and Research* 21:21–29.

Zucker, R. A. (1987). The four alcoholisms: a developmental account of etiologic process. In *Alcohol and Addictive Behaviors: Nebraska Symposium on Motivation*, ed. P. C. Rivers, pp. 27–83. Lincoln, NE: University of Nebraska Press.

———— (1994). Pathways to alcohol problems and alcoholism: a developmental account of the evidence for multiple alcoholisms and for contextual contributions to risk. In *The Development of Alcohol Problems: Exploring the Biopsychosocial Matrix of Risk*, ed. R. A. Zucker, G. M. Boyd, and J. Howard. NIAAA Research Monograph 26:255–289. Washington, DC: US Government Printing Office.

Zucker, R. A., Ellis, D. A., Bingham, C. R., and Fitzgerald, H. E. (1996a). The development of alcoholic subtypes: risk variations among alcoholic families during the early childhood years. *Alcohol Health and Research World*, 20:46–54.

Zucker, R. A., Ellis, D. A., and Fitzgerald, H. E. (1993). *Other evidence for at least two alcoholisms, II: the case for lifetime antisociality as a basis of differentiation*. Unpublished manuscript, Michigan State University, East Lansing, MI.

———— (1994). Developmental evidence for at least two alcoholisms, I: Biopsychosocial variation among pathways into symptomatic difficulty. *Annals of the New York Academy of Sciences* 708:134–146.

Zucker, R. A., Ellis, D. A., Fitzgerald, H. E., et al. (1996b). Other evidence for at least two alcoholisms II: life course variation in antisociality and heterogeneity of alcoholic outcome. *Development and Psychopathology* 8:831–848.

Zucker, R. A., Fitzgerald, H. E., and Moses, H. D. (1995a). Emergence of alcohol problems and the several alcoholisms: A developmental perspective on etiologic theory and life course trajectory. In *Manual of Developmental Psychopathology*, vol. 2, ed. D. Cichetti and D. Cohen, pp. 677–711. New York: Wiley.

Zucker, R. A., Kincaid, S., Fitzgerald, H. E., and Bingham, C. R. (1995b). Alcohol schema acquisition in preschoolers: differences between children of alcoholics and children of nonalcoholics. *Alcoholism: Clinical and Experimental Research* 19:1011–1017.

Zuckerman, B. (1991). Selected methodological issues in investigations of prenatal effects of cocaine: lessons from the past. In *Methodological Issues in Controlled Studies on Effects of Prenatal Exposure to Drug Abuse*, ed. M. M. Kilbey and K. Asghar, pp. 45–54 (NIDA Research Monograph 114, DHHS Publication No. [ADM] 91-1837). Washington, DC: US Government Printing Office.

Zuckerman, M. (1987). Biological connection between sensation seeking and drug abuse. In *Brain Reward Systems and Abuse*, ed. J. Engel and L. Oreland, pp. 165–173. New York: Raven.

Glossary

A

abatement. A period when substance use is stopped or significantly reduced.

abscess. An area of infection and inflammation characterized by redness, stinging, itching, swelling, and pus formation.

abstinence. A complete stop to substance use, for a significant time.

abstinence violation effect. A cognitive-affective relapse process due to conflict and guilt over a lapse.

acculturation effect. An increase drug and alcohol use in ethnic groups following immigration to the United States.

acquired immune deficiency syndrome. An incurable disorder caused by the human immunodeficiency virus, which destroys the immune system and renders the individual susceptible to deadly infections.

active listening. Avidly taking in client's communications and providing nonjudgmental attention.

Addiction Severity Index. A 155-item semi-structured interview that evaluates alcohol- and drug-related problem functioning.

addictive personality. Hypothetical common core of traits for alcoholic and drug-addicted individuals.

adjustment. A condition in which a person demonstrates successful coping.

affect labeling. Highlighting client's feelings by giving them a name.

aggression. A behavior that directs intentional harm at another person.

agonist. A drug that mimics or increases the effects of a particular neurotransmitter.

alcohol. A generic term for a class of molecules that result from the process of fermentation of sugar.

alcohol challenge. A research technique in which subjects are given a controlled dosage of alcohol and responses are measured.

Alcohol Use Disorders Identification Test. A test designed to identify problem drinkers in primary health-care settings.

alcoholic cardiomyopathy. Heart muscle damage caused by heavy drinking.

alcoholic cirrhosis. A disease of alcoholic persons marked by dead liver cells and scar tissue that choke off blood vessels and impair liver function.

alcoholic hepatitis. An inflammation of the liver identified by fever, jaundice, and abdominal pain.

Alcoholics Anonymous. A self-help organization for alcoholics, based on the Twelve-Step program; abbreviated as A.A.

alliance-for-abstinence. A counseling relationship focused on maintaining the client's abstinence.

all-or-none model. A view that any violation of abstinence is an indication of relapse.

amnesia. Memory impairment that interferes with learning and recall.

amphetamines. Laboratory-synthesized stimulants used to arouse the nervous system and increase energy.

anomie. Extreme social alienation.

Antabuse. A drug that inhibits the activity of an enzyme that breaks down alcohol.

antagonist. A drug that blocks a neurotransmitter's actions.

antisocial alcoholism. A type of alcoholism with an early onset of abuse, severe and persistent alcohol-related problems, and antisocial behavior.

antisocial personality disorder. Also called psychopathy; a personality disorder marked by disregard for and violation of others' rights.

anxiety disorder. A disorder characterized by anxiety symptoms that cause significant impairment in everyday functioning.

assertiveness training. Teaching effective self-expression and skills to allow people to stand up for their own rights.

attachment theory. A view that attributes social, emotional, and psychological functioning to interpersonal attachments formed in childhood.

avoidant personality disorder. A personality disorder marked by social inhibitions, feelings of inadequacy, and sensitivity to negative evaluation.

B

barbiturates. Sedative-hypnotic drugs that decrease central nervous system activity.

behavioral counseling. An approach that uses principles of learning theory to help people change.

behavioral disinhibition. A condition in which an individual shows impulsiveness, impaired judgment, and emotional unpredictability.

behavioral family therapy. An approach that changes maladaptive past learning, present contingencies, reward patterns, and attitudinal components of dysfunction.

behavioral theory of choice. A view that drug use motivation is shaped by constraints against drug use and availability of nondrug reinforcers.

behavioral view. A view that learning mechanisms determine acquisition of habits that promote chemical dependence.

benzodiazepines. Depressants that are the most often prescribed antianxiety drugs.

biological markers. Characteristics with known genetic locations and that are linked with chemical dependency.

biopsychosocial model. A developmental model that emphasizes the interplay of biological, psychological, and social variables in alcoholism.

biopsychosocial model of alcoholism. Zucker's typology, based on the interplay between biological, psychological, and social variables.

bipolar disorder. Also called manic-depression; a mood disorder marked by a combination of major depressive and manic episodes.

borderline personality disorder. A personality disorder marked by instability in relationships, self-image, and emotions.

boundaries. The behavioral and emotional divisions among family members.

brief motivational therapy. A treatment approach that uses straightforward advice and information about the adverse effects of alcohol abuse in order to motivate patients to reduce or stop their harmful behavior.

bulimia nervosa. An eating disorder marked by eating binges and compensatory purging.

C

CAGE. A four-question instrument used to identify individuals who currently experience or have ever suffered from alcohol dependence.

cancer. A group of diseases marked by cells that grow out of control and the formation of tumors.

cannabinoids. Drugs whose psychoactive ingredient is tetrahydrocannabinol (THC), including marijuana or hashish.

cardiac arrhythmia. The abnormal beating rhythm of the heart due to electrical conduction problems.

cardiovascular system. The heart and blood vessels that transport blood.

cerebral atrophy. Decreased brain weight; characterized by increased space between brain regions and enlarged ventricles.

Certified Alcoholism and Substance Abuse Counselor. Basic professional credential in chemical-dependency counseling.

chemical dependency counseling. A mental health specialty that provides therapy for drug and alcohol addicts.

clarification. An intervention to request or offer more accurate information.

classical conditioning. A form of learning in which a reflexive response is associated with a new stimulus by pairing it with another reflex-eliciting stimulus.

client-centered counseling. An approach that emphasizes the role of the therapeutic relationship in counseling.

client rights. The moral entitlements that apply to the individual in treatment.

clinical evaluation. A careful, systematic screening and assessment of the client.

Clinical Institute Withdrawal Assessment for Alcohol (CIWA-A). A questionnaire that evaluates the presence and severity of various withdrawal symptoms.

clinical interview An interview in which the client's drug-taking behavior and other aspects of cognitive, emotional, and behavioral functioning are determined by asking probing questions and evaluating the patient's responses.

cocaine. The psychoactive ingredient of coca leaves; a stimulant drug.

cocaine abstinence syndrome. A three- stage cocaine withdrawal syndrome characterized by crash, withdrawal, and extinction phases.

cognitive-behavioral coping skills therapy. A family of related treatments for alcoholism and other substance-related disorders that aims to improve the cognitive and behavioral skills necessary to change problem behaviors.

cognitive counseling. A school of counseling that assumes emotional and behavioral problems are overcome by changing irrational beliefs and thoughts.

common relapse factors. Relapse factors that cut across different types of addictions.

comorbidity. The presence of two or more disorders that exist simultaneously.

compensatory adaptations. Drug-induced changes in the structures and functions of neurons that compensate for drugs' effects on neurons.

conditioned incentive model. An explanation of chemical dependenc in terms of the combined influences of classical and operant conditioning.

conditioned withdrawal theory. A view that drug cues linked with withdrawal responses induce a resumption of use.

confidentiality. Keeping private all statements, actions, and communications of the client.

confirmation methods. Drug-testing methods that yield results with high specificity and sensitivity.

confrontation. Identification and challenging of the client's maladaptive attitudes and actions.

consent form. A document that authorizes the release of confidential information.

cost of illness. An approach that measures the cost to society in terms of expenditures for drug- and alcohol-related problems and the loss or diversion of productivity.

counselor competencies. The basic knowledge, skills, and attitudes needed for competent professional practice in the field.

counselors. Health professionals who provide advice, guidance, and/or therapy for various populations.

cue extinction. A procedure that reduces cravings by exposing clients to drug cues or triggers.

cultural responsiveness hypothesis. A theory that proposes that effective treatment depends on the ability of the counselor to respond successfully to culturally relevant information and behavior in the patient.

D

defense mechanisms. Largely unconscious strategies to lessen conflict and emotional distress.

delirium. A severe disruption of consciousness, with cognitive and perceptual disturbances.

delta alcoholism. A type of alcoholism described by Jellinek, characterized by physical dependence and few symptoms.

dementia. A condition with multiple cognitive deficits in memory, language, and executive functions.

dependency-conflict theory. The view that counterdependent people meet their dependency needs by the use of substances.

depressants. Psychoactive drugs that slow the activity of the nervous system resulting in a tranquilizing effect, sleepiness, and impairment of higher mental functions, vision, and movement.

detoxification. A process by which a chemically dependent individual is taken off the substance, either abruptly or gradually.

developmental context. Any variables that influence development across the life span.

developmental continuity. A sequence in which later events are a continuation or extension of earlier events.

developmental fixation. An unresolved developmental problem.

developmental model. A representation of a developmental sequence and relationships among variables in the sequence.

developmental path. A progression of behaviors, events, and circumstances, and their influences on the progression of development over time.

developmental perspective. A view that examines the patterns and causes of change across the life span.

developmental phases. Periods of evolution of chemical dependence, defined by transitions from nonuse to use (initiation phase), use to abuse (escalation phase), and abuse to dependence (addiction phase).

developmentally limited alcoholism. One of Zucker's types of alcoholism, associated with socially deviant behaviors and affiliation with the peer group.

Diagnostic and Statistical Manual of Mental Disorders-Fourth Edition (DSM-IV). The most widely used psychiatric classification system for mental disorders.

differentiation. The articulation and organization of separate parts.

direct guidance. Offering advice or instruction to guide client actions.

directive counseling. An approach characterized by directing clients, through instruction, information giving, and challenging.

disability. Any disease, disorder, or injury, whether congenital or acquired, which significantly impairs an individual's ability to function in various areas of life.

disease model. The belief that alcoholism and other drug addictions are diseases or biologically based disorders.

documentation. Keeping accurate records of assessment information, treatment plans, progress notes, and other client-related facts.

Drug Abuse Screening Test. A test that consists of twenty items about drug use and related problems to which the client answers "yes" or "no."

drug testing. Laboratory examination of biological specimens for psychoactive substances or their metabolic by-products.

dual relationships. A condition in which the client and counselor have associations outside the therapeutic setting.

duty to protect. The obligation, when a therapist knows or should know that a patient presents a serious threat of violence to someone, to take reasonable steps to protect the intended victim.

dysthymic disorder. A mood disorder marked by persistent depressed mood.

E

eclectic approach. A strategy that utilizes ideas and techniques from various schools of therapy.

education. A type of intervention that facilitates learning.

empathy. Understanding of another's emotional state.

Employee Assistance Programs. Workplace-based programs set up to refer chemically impaired employees for treatment.

epidemiology. The study of the distribution of disorders in the general population.

epileptic seizure. Disorganized brain electrical activity.

establishing rapport. The technique of creating a comfortable client–counselor bond.

ethology. The scientific study of animal behavior.

existential counseling. A school that concentrates on ultimates, the basic aspects of human existence.

expectancy theory. A perspective that attributes drug use to expectations about the consequences of taking drugs.

experiential family therapy. An approach that emphasizes the immediate here-and-now experience with the counselor as the means of change.

exploration. The technique of searching for and discovering aspects of a client's mental life.

external social cost. A model in which the cost of substance dependence to society is equal to the economic harm that it imposes on people other the the user.

F

familial aggregation. The clustering in families of drug and alcohol problems.

familial alcoholism. A type of alcoholism characterized by a prominent family history of drinking problems, early onset, and severe dependence.

fetal alcohol syndrome. A condition in children, caused by prenatal exposure to alcohol and identified by prenatal and postnatal growth retardation, cranial/facial defects, central nervous system dysfunctions, and organ malformations.

flashback. A type of recurrent perceptual disturbance following hallucinogen use; also called hallucinogen persisting perception disorder.

Form 90. A group of structured interview schedules designed to provide information about drinking and related variables.

G

gamma alcoholism. Jellinek's type of chronic progressive alcoholism, marked by high psychological vulnerability to dependence, loss of control, emotional and psychological impairment, and tolerance and withdrawal symptoms.

gateway drug. A drug that introduces users to illicit drugs and promotes use of other drugs.

gateway theory. The view that early use of alcohol, cigarettes, and marijuana increases risk for later use of hard drugs.

general systems theory. A conceptualization in which the whole system is seen as something greater than the sum of its parts.

generalized anxiety disorder. A disorder marked by worries over many events, restlessness, and free-floating anxiety.

genogram. A family history chart.

genuineness. The honest presentation of self by the counselor.

Gestalt counseling. An approach that brings clients into experiencing the here-and-now.

global assessment of functioning. A *DSM-IV* dimension based on individual's rated overall functioning ranging from 1 to 100.

H

halfway house. A transitional living facility that provides a supportive environment and rehabilitive services for clients who have completed inpatient or residential treatment, but who are not fully prepared to reenter the community.

hallucinogens. Drugs that produce hallucinations and other psychedelic experiences.

hashish. An extremely potent form of cannabis, derived from the resin of the hemp plant.

Hazelden model. An approach that includes paraprofessional peer counselors in treatment for alcoholism.

heritability. The degree to which heredity contributes to a condition, trait, or behavior.

heroin. Diacetylmorphine; an opioid compound derived from morphine.

high-risk group. A group that has abnormally high risk for chemical dependency.

high-risk situations. Circumstances in which the likelihood of relapse is heightened.

homeostasis. The tendency of a family to maintain stability or equilibrium.

hypertension. High blood pressure.

I

iatrogenic addiction. A type of addiction caused by a physician.

immune system. A set of structures and bodily mechanisms that identify and eliminate foreign substances.

impulse-control disorders. Conditions marked by the individual's inability to resist harmful impulses or temptations.

inhalants. A chemically diverse group of volatile drugs that produce short-lived psychoactive effects when inhaled.

inpatient hospitalization treatment. The provision of medical and often psychological services within a hospital or similarly licensed facility designed to treat chemical dependency.

intensive outpatient treatment. A period of nine to seventy hours of treatment per week in an outpatient setting.

intergenerational systems family therapy. An approach whose cornerstone is differentiation of the family system.

interpretation. An explanation of reasons for a client's behavior, thoughts, or feelings.

K

Korsakoff's psychosis. A memory disorder in which the individual forgets incidents of daily life shortly after they occur.

L

labeling theory. The view that deviance is a social status conferred upon individuals because of their unacceptable behavior.

lapse. A single instance of substance use resumption; also called a slip.

levo-alpha-acetylmethadol. A drug similar to methadone, but with a longer half-life.

limbic kindling hypothesis. A view that attributes alcohol relapse to hyperarousal in the limbic system.

longitudinal method. A research strategy that monitors or tracks individual development over a long period of time.

lysergic acid diethylamide. A hallucinogen manufactured from the ergot fungus; often called LSD.

M

MacAndrew secondary alcoholics. Persons whose alcoholism is associated with depression and other forms of significant emotional distress.

major depressive disorder. A mood disorder marked by one or more major depressive episodes with depressed mood, loss of interest, and other somatic, cognitive, and behavioral symptoms.

malpractice. A legal term that refers to a circumstance in which a professional has caused harm to the client or patient, either by action or inaction.

manual-guided treatments. The application of specific, structured treatment techniques in a time-limited fashion.

marijuana. A cannabinoid derived from the leaves and flowering tops of the *Cannabis sativa* plant.

mastery imagery. A method in which a client is instructed to imagine himself as controlling and defeating craving.

matching hypothesis. The idea that improved results can be attained if treatment is tailored to individual patient needs.

maturing-out hypothesis. The belief that positive maturational changes explain low rates of chemical dependence in adults.

mental disorder. A clinically significant pattern of behaviors, thoughts, and emotions in an individual that is associated with distress or impairment or an elevated risk of suffering, death, disability, or loss of freedom.

mental status examination. A semistructured interview technique to evaluate and record all aspects of mental, emotional, and behavioral functioning.

mentally ill chemical abusers. Individuals who have both a substance-related disorder and another severe mental disorder.

methadone. A morphine-like opioid used in the treatment of heroin addiction.

methadone maintenance treatment. An outpatient clinic program that involves the substitution of heroin with a medically safe, long-acting medication of known purity, potency, and dosage, combined with biopsychosical treatment services.

methamphetamine. Methedrine; an amphetamine drug with a very high potential for abuse.

3-4 methylenedioxymethamphetamine (MDMA). An amphetamine derivative with stimulant and hallucinogenic properties.

Michigan Alcoholism Screening Test. A twenty-five-item screening instrument used in clinical and nonclinical settings.

Minnesota model. A treatment model characterized by the use of the Twelve-Step philosophy of A.A. as the foundation for therapeutic change.

Minnesota Multiphasic Personality Inventory. A self-report inventory that consists of 550 statements to which the person responds "true" or "false".

modeling. A form of social learning based on imitation of observed behavior.

modeling technique. A demonstration by the therapist of how a behavior is performed.

mood disorders. Persistent, disabling disturbances in a person's general emotional state.

morphine. A psychoactive chemical extracted from opium.

morphinism. An addiction to morphine.

motivational enhancement therapy. A systematic intervention that applies the principles of motivational psychology to mobilize rapid, internally motivated change.

N

naltrexone. An opioid antagonist that blocks opioid receptors in the brain.

narcissistic personality disorder. A type of personality disorder marked by grandiosity, need for admiration, and lack of empathy.

negative-affect alcoholism. A late-onset type of alcoholism preceded by negative emotional states.

negative identity. A self-concept organized around rejection of social norms.

neuron. A nervous system cell specialized to receive and transmit information.

Neuropsychological Impairment Scale. A fifty-item self-report scale that assesses complaints indicative of brain damage.

neuropsychological testing. Procedures designed to detect and measure brain damage and cognitive disability.

neurotransmitters. Chemicals released into the synapses of nerves.

nondisclosure rule. A general rule that disclosure of records or other personal information about the client is legally prohibited.

O

object relations family therapy. A psychodynamic approach that relies heavily on transference interpretation.

operant conditioning. A type of learning by which behavior is shaped through reinforcement and punishment.

opioids. Narcotic analgesic drugs derived from opium and related compounds, and having similar effects.

outpatient treatment. Nonresidential chemical dependency treatments for individuals who are able to function in the context of their usual living arrangements.

overdose. The severe intoxicating or physical effects of taking too much of a drug, or too potent a drug.

Oxford Group. A self-help movement emphasizing taking stock of oneself, confession of defects, and atonement.

P

pancreatitis. A disease of the pancreas, manifested by severe abdominal pain, nausea, vomiting, fever, and tachycardia.

panic disorder. An anxiety disorder marked by recurring, unexpected panic (anxiety) attacks.

paranoid personality disorder. A type of personality disorder marked by persistent suspiciousness and distrust of others.

pathological gambling. An impulse-control disorder marked by a persistent, maladaptive gambling habit.

peer cluster theory. A view that sees peer influence in peer groups as the social framework for deviant behaviors.

peer-counseling movement. A treatment approach employing recovering alcoholics and addicts as counselors.

peptic ulcer. An open sore in the lining of the stomach.

personality disorders. Enduring and maladaptive patterns of traits producing significant impairment.

pharmacodynamics. The influence of cultural traditions, taboos, expectations, and attitudes about drug use on the effects of drugs.

pharmacological model. A view that attributes chemical-dependence vulnerability to drug consumption patterns and consequences.

pharmacotherapy. The therapeutic use of drugs to alter brain chemistry.

phencyclidine. An illegally manufactured hallucinogen first introduced as an anesthetic in humans.

phobia. An anxiety disorder marked by excessive fear and the tendency to avoid or escape the feared stimulus.

positive addictions. Pleasurable, healthful habits that substitute for prior destructive habits.

posttraumatic stress disorder. An anxiety disorder marked by anxiety symptoms, numbing, and reexperiencing of the trauma, following a traumatic event.

prevalence rate. The percentage of a population or group that has a particular disorder.

prevention. Educational efforts that inform potential drug abusers about the risks associated with drug use.

primary alcoholism. A type of alcoholism in which problem drinking comes before and is independent of other mental disorders.

primary/secondary disorder distinction. The characterization of comorbid disorders in terms of their order of onset.

priming theory. The view that learned associations between drug cues and conditioned craving causes relapse.

privileged communication. Information that is legally protected when that information is at issue in litigation.

problem-behavior theory. The view that drug use by adolescents is one dimension of a pattern of deviance proneness.

Problem Oriented Screening Instrument for Teenagers. A test consisting of 139 yes/no items that screen for problems in ten areas of functioning.

process model. The cognitive-behavioral view of relapse as a multidetermined and extended series of events.

prohibition. The legal ban on the distribution, possession, and use of specified drugs, and the application of criminal penalties to violators.

projective tests. Instruments that measure aspects of personality functioning by asking subjects to interpret ambiguous stimuli.

protective factors. Variables that reduce the likelihood of drug involvement.

psychiatrist. A medical doctor who specializes in the treatment of mental illness.

psychoactive drug. Any drug that influences emotions, perceptions, thoughts, motivation, and behavior.

psychodynamic counseling. A school of therapy that highlights psychic conflict and helps clients gain insight.

psychodynamic family therapy. An approach that aims at insight into the family's behavioral patterns and their unconscious processes.

psychodynamic view. A perspective that views abnormal behavior as a product of unconscious drives and emotions and the defenses against them.

psychological tests. Instruments designed to provide insight into mental, emotional, and behavioral functioning.

psychologists. Professionals with either a masters degree or a doctorate in psychology.

psychotherapy. A spectrum of psychological treatments that aim to change problematic thoughts, feelings, and behaviors that play a causal role in abnormal behaviors.

psychotic disorder. A severe condition marked by dramatic disruption of judgment, poor reality perception, and mental disorganization; also called psychosis.

Q

Quantity/Frequency Questions. An instrument consisting of three questions that screen for the presence of an alcohol-use problem and quickly gauge the amount of alcohol consumed.

R

recovery. The process of maintaining a drug- and alcohol-free lifestyle and of developing coping skills to maintain abstinence.

recovery skills. Coping and self-management strategies that promote abstinence and long-term recovery.

referral. A process used to help clients utilize social and community resources.

reflection. Providing feedback to the client about the client's feelings, thoughts, and behavior.

regulation. The legal control over the distribution, possession, and use of specified drugs.

reinforcement. Methods that use positive consequences to strengthen a behavior.

relapse. The resumption of substance use following a period of abstinence.

relapse prevention. A multifaceted counseling approach that reduces the likelihood and severity of relapse.

relapse rehearsal. A cognitive-behavioral strategy entailing imagined confrontations and training in coping with high-risk situations.

relaxation training. Techniques that teach skills for reducing tension and anxiety.

remission. The arrest of the disease process and the disappearance of symptoms.

residential treatment. Treatment programs that provide twenty-four-hour care and support for people who live on the premises of the program for extended periods of time.

resistance. The struggle against wellness.

retrospective research. A method of collecting information about the past from recollections and reports.

reward-deficiency syndrome. A genetically based predisposition to underactivity in the dopamine system, causing vulnerability to addiction.

risk factor. A variable that increases the likelihood of a developmental event or behavior.

role. A socially defined pattern of behavior that serves one or more specific functions within a social system.

Rorschach inkblot test. A projective test that consists of ten cards with a symmetrical inkblot on each.

S

scapegoating. The displacement of distress and conflict onto another family member.

schizophrenia. A psychotic condition marked by disturbances in thinking, perception, emotion, and behavior.

SCL-90. A ninety-item self-report inventory that reflects psychological symptom patterns across nine dimensions.

screening instruments. Brief, easily administered questionnaires designed to identify problem alcohol or drug users.

screening methods. Commercially available drug-testing methods that are inexpensive and easy to perform.

self-efficacy. Expectations about capability to perform a behavior.

self-help groups. Peer-led groups that provide mutual support and guidance to deal with chemical dependency.

self-medication hypothesis. The view that drug and alcohol use are motivated by desire to alleviate pain and suffering.

self-regulation vulnerability. Problems in self-care, self-esteem, emotion, and relationships.

self-report inventories. Paper-and-pencil questionnaires that ask people to report about aspects of their psychological functioning.

serotonin deficiency hypothesis. The theory that a heritable deficit in serotonin systems predisposes to alcoholism.

service coordination. The collaboration with other members of the treatment team, as well as acting as a go between with community services.

sex-role conflict hypothesis. The idea that women drink to alleviate sex-role conflicts and to feel more feminine.

shaping. A method of reinforcing approximations to a desired behavior.

social cognitive theory. A view that explains personality, motivation, and behavior in terms of self-regulating processes.

social desirability hypothesis. The notion that people are reluctant to disclose illicit drug use because of its negative social image.

social developmental model. The view that healthy adolescent development depends on the presence of prosocial adults, norms against drug use, school bonding, and academic achievement.

social learning theory. A view of learning that emphasizes the role of cognitions and person–environment interactions.

social strain theory. A theory that explains deviation in terms of inadequate opportunities to achieve socially approved goals.

social stress hypothesis. A theory that psychological disturbances result from a stressful social environment.

social worker. A health professional specializing either in psychotherapy or social service facilitation.

sponsor. In Twelve-Step programs, a mentor who guides newcomers in recovery.

Stages of Change Readiness and Treatment Eagerness Scale. A nineteen-item assessment instrument that roughly corresponds to the stages-of-change model.

stimulants. Drugs that arouse the nervous system, increase energy and alertness, and produce euphoria.

strategic family therapy. An approach defined by strategies, especially involving communications and instructions.

stress-response dampening theory. A view that assumes that the motive for alcohol use is to dampen the intensity of the stress response.

stroke. A condition caused by a ruptured blood vessel in the brain.

structural family therapy. An approach that seeks to elucidate and change the structure of the family system.

structured interview. A systematic method to gather significant current and historical information concerning drug use and related problems.

subjective well-being. The self-perception of psychological health.

substance abuse. A maladaptive or abnormal pattern of substance use as shown by significant negative consequences related to the repeated use of substances.

substance-abuse-specific counseling. An approach that focuses directly on overcoming chemical dependency and achieving recovery.

substance dependence. A substance-related disorder marked by at least three symptoms indicative of tolerance and withdrawal or a compulsive pattern of drug use.

substance-induced anxiety disorder. An anxiety disorder directly resulting from substance use.

substance-induced mental disorder. Mental disorder resulting directly from substance use.

substance-induced mood disorder. A mood disorder that results directly from substance use.

substance-induced psychotic disorder. A psychotic disorder resulting directly from substance use.

substance-related disorders. Mental disorders marked by abnormal behaviors related to the taking of a drug of abuse, the side effects of a medication, or to toxin exposure.

T

temperament. An individual's basic emotional and response tendencies that are driven by heredity.

temperament model. An approach that proposes four temperament dimensions representing heritable, emotion-based skills and habits.

tension-reduction theory. The view that people are motivated to drink alcohol because it reduces tension.

Thematic Apperception Test. A popular picture–story test consisting of nineteen black-and-white sketches and one blank card.

therapeutic attitude. The counselor's attitudes of compassionate neutrality, optimism, confidence, and realism.

therapeutic communities. Residential treatment programs run by and for recovering addicts.

therapeutic double-bind. A strategy of prescribing the symptom.

tolerance. The need for increased amounts of a drug to get the same effect, or a markedly lesser effect from taking the same amount of the drug.

toxic shame. Shame that comes from having been abused as a child or from growing up in an addictive home.

transference. The unconscious reenactment of early relationships in present ones.

transtheoretical model. A stages-of-change view that conceives of relapse as an integral part of recovery.

treatment compliance. Actions on the part of the client to follow the instructions and requirements of treatment.

treatment involvement. The situation that results when the person is engaged in the treatment process, subscribes to the treatment rationale, and has formulated goals consistent with the treatment philosophy.

treatment planning. Plans made to determine treatment objectives and the best strategies to attain those objectives.

tuberculosis. A bacterial disease of the lungs caused by *Myobacterium tuberculosis*.

TWEAK. A new five-item screening instrument consisting of two items from the CAGE, two from the MAST, and one new item.

Twelve-Step facilitation therapy. A brief, structured, outpatient treatment to encourage affiliation and involvement in Alcoholics Anonymous.

Twelve-Step model. An approach to counseling that emphasizes the disease concept, abstinence, and the Twelve Steps.

Type A alcoholism. Babor's less-severe form of alcoholism, marked by a later onset, less severe dependence, fewer childhood risk factors, and better overall functioning.

Type B alcoholism. Babor's more severe form of alcoholism, marked by childhood problems, family history of dependence, more severe dependence, poor overall functioning, and other substance abuse.

Type 1 alcoholism. Cloninger's type of alcoholism, which is less severe, found in men and women, has an early onset, and is shaped by environmental factors.

Type 2 alcoholism. Cloninger's male type of alcoholism, which is heritable and marked by an early onset, heavy drinking, and an inability to abstain.

U

unconditional positive regard. A respectful attitude of the counselor for the client.

V

vulnerability. A condition of susceptibility to drug involvement based on a balance of risk and protection.

W

Washingtonians. A nineteenth-century self-help group that dealt with alcoholism.

withdrawal. An unpleasant substance-specific behavioral change, with psychological and mental symptoms, caused by stopping or reducing heavy and prolonged drug use.

Index

About the Authors

Jerome D. Levin, Ph.D., is Director of the Alcoholism and Substance Abuse Counselor Training Program at the New School University in Manhattan, where he also serves both on the Humanities Department faculty, and as co-director of the joint masters program in psychology and substance abuse treatment. He is editor of the Library of Substance Abuse and Addiction Treatment book series, adjunct Associate Professor of Social Science at New York University, and Senior Fellow of the Wolfson Center for Public Affairs. Dr. Levin has authored eleven books dealing with subjects ranging from the history of ideas, including (*Theories of the Self*), to narcissism (*Slings and Arrows: Narcissistic Injury and Its Treatment*), to addiction (*Treatment of Alcoholism and Other Addictions, Couple and Family Therapy of Addiction, Recovery from Alcoholism, Primer of Treating Substance Abusers, and Therapeutic Strategies for Treating Addiction: From Slavery to Freedom*), to contemporary affairs (*The Clinton Syndrome*). He maintains a psychotherapy practice in Manhattan and Suffolk County, New York.

Joseph Culkin, Ph.D., is Professor of Psychology in the Department of Social Sciences of Queensborough Community College / The City University of New York. He earned his doctorate from the Graduate Faculty of Political and Social Sciences at the New School for Social Research. Dr. Culkin teaches a variety of classes, including introductory and abnormal psychology, disorders of childhood, and lifespan development. He has worked as a private practitioner with individuals and families, In addition, he has worked in outpatient individual and group therapy with substance-dependent clients in a community agency. Dr. Culkin has co-authored two textbooks with Dr. Richard Perrotto: *Exploring Abnormal Psychology* and *Fundamentals of Psychology: Applications for Life and Work.*

Richard S. Perrotto, Ph.D., is Professor of Psychology in the Department of Social Sciences at Queensborough Community College / The City University of New York, where he has taught since 1978. Dr. Perrotto teaches courses in general, abnormal, and physiological psychology, and personality. He received his doctorate in psychology from the University of Delaware in 1979. A New York State licensed psychologist with postdoctoral training in behavioral psychotherapy, Dr. Perrotto maintains a private practice in Queens, New York, where he has accrued extensive experience in the evaluation and treatment of a wide variety of client problems, including substance abuse and dependence. A member of the American Psychological Association since 1982, Dr. Perrotto has published scientific articles in physiological psychology and abnormal psychology and has co-authored, with Dr. Joseph Culkin, two textbooks: *Exploring Abnormal Psychology* and *Fundamentals of Psychology: Applications for Life and Work.*